PROMOTING PEACE THROUGH INTERNATIONAL LAW

Promoting Peace Through International Law

Edited by

CECILIA MARCELA BAILLIET

and

KJETIL MUJEZINOVIĆ LARSEN

OXFORD
UNIVERSITY PRESS

OXFORD
UNIVERSITY PRESS

Great Clarendon Street, Oxford, OX2 6DP,
United Kingdom

Oxford University Press is a department of the University of Oxford.
It furthers the University's objective of excellence in research, scholarship,
and education by publishing worldwide. Oxford is a registered trade mark of
Oxford University Press in the UK and in certain other countries

First Edition published in 2015

Published in the United States of America by Oxford University Press
198 Madison Avenue, New York, NY 10016, United States of America

British Library Cataloguing in Publication Data
Data available

Library of Congress Control Number: 2014954510

ISBN 978–0–19–872273–1

Printed and bound by
CPI Group (UK) Ltd, Croydon, CR0 4YY

Jacket images: Shutterstock/iStockphoto

For

Kyrre and Selma, the peaceful ones
C.M.B and K.M.L

Foreword

It gives me great pleasure and satisfaction to write the foreword to this book. As a former Secretary-General of the International Peace Research Association and former Director of the Norwegian Human Rights Institute, it is a great encouragement to take note of the advances here made in the analysis of the role that international law can play in promoting peace. It can possibly be moved from a vague vision to an operative directive principle if underpinned by rigorous analysis and drafting.

The contributions in this book reflect a mature balance between ideal visions and realistic assessments of the slow but nevertheless progressive evolution of the building blocks that can serve to promote peace by international law.

Thirty years ago, the UN General Assembly proclaimed in its resolution 39/11 (1984) that the peoples of our planet have a sacred right to peace. The Assembly claimed that the preservation of the right of peoples to peace and the promotion of its implementation constitute a fundamental obligation of each state. That proclamation generated considerable international discussion and some interesting scholarship, but the idea died out after a relatively short period, for both political and technical reasons. Leaving politics behind, the proposal fell because of a lack of analytical clarity. Agreement could not be reached on the contents of that right, on preconditions or strategies for its implementation, on the mechanisms to monitor its implementation, or on institutions to administer sanctions in cases of non-compliance.

The international political climate was at that time not conducive to a constructive discourse on the avenues to the consolidation of a just and generally acceptable peace in the world community.

Since then, however, much has changed. The Cold War is over, and the North–South divide is less acute than it was in the 1980s. Democratization has expanded and with it also improvements in human rights performance. While several serious setbacks have occurred, the climate for a more constructive discussion seems to have improved.

This might be one of the explanations why the United Nations Human Rights Council in 2009 renewed interest in the subject, and entrusted its Advisory Committee to prepare a draft declaration on the right of peoples to peace. The Advisory Committee did so, and presented its draft to the Human Rights Council in 2012. It led the Council to establish an open-ended working group to engage in wide-ranging consultations to further work on the Declaration. There is, however, considerable opposition to the project, mostly from developed countries. It is necessary to take that opposition into account because it shows that substantially more analytic and constructive work is required, also by scholars of international law and politics, before a declaration can get a content that can have a significant impact. The work on the Declaration is still ongoing in the Council at the time of writing and is likely to continue for some time.

A major factor behind the disagreements is the lack of clarity of the components of the elusive concept of peace, and on the institutional and procedural mechanisms that would have to be in place in order to pursue a realistic promotion of peace through international law. This is where this book can make a significant contribution to the international discourse on this important subject. Inspired by the work within the Human Rights Council, but also sceptical about the underlying analyses thus far made, the editors of this book hosted in 2013, an international conference in Oslo to engage in an interdisciplinary and in-depth study of the subject. The result is found in this volume.

The starting point for the preparation of the book was the agreement reached by the participants on the most important components of peace, thereby getting a better grasp of the elements of this otherwise very elusive and slippery concept of peace. A major reason why this book can be very useful for further work is therefore that it disentangles the different dimensions of the issues by its elaboration of the components of peace, which are set out in Chapter 1.

The overall framework of the book is the promotion of peace through international law, which is built on the fundamental purposes of the United Nations: To maintain international peace, promoting peaceful settlements of disputes and advancing international co-operation in solving international problems of an economic, social, cultural, or humanitarian character, and in promoting and encouraging respect for human rights and for fundamental freedoms for all.

A precondition for the maintenance of international peace is a serious commitment to peaceful settlement of disputes: Peaceful and constructive (i.e. cooperative) settlement of disputes is probably the most essential factor in sustaining peace both at the international and the national level, and it has been addressed in several chapters of this book. Adequate institutions for settlements of disputes and for constructive reconciliation of conflicting interests and values are essential, and several contributions herein provide indicators and recommendations on how this can be furthered.

Mechanisms for dispute settlement have been developed both within the United Nations, by regional organizations, and within specialized agencies including some outside the United Nations such as the World Trade Organization. It is an important factor in the promotion of peace through international law that many issues are functionally subdivided and are handled by bodies or institutions other than the main political bodies of the United Nations. Provided they are all guided by a commitment to the enhancement of peace both at the national and the international level, this functional subdivision in our increasingly interconnected world can be an important safeguard in the promotion of peace.

There is, however, a basic structural difficulty involved here. It is addressed, directly and indirectly, throughout the book: how can the two sides of state responsibility be reconciled? All states have, first and foremost, a responsibility towards their inhabitants—to meet their human rights, their interests, and their expectations. In democratic countries, these expectations are expressed through the elected bodies of the government and reinforced by the most influential part of the national society. On the other hand is each state's responsibility to the common goals of the international community as a whole. These are generally expressed in terms such as the right to development, the right to a clean and sustainable environment, and the right to peace. These have sometimes been called meta-rights, or solidarity rights. Personally I prefer to see them as directive principles that should guide states in their international relations, as an implementation of their obligations under the United Nations Charter.

Reconciliation between those two responsibilities can be difficult and sometimes prevent constructive and fair settlements of disputes. Inhabitants of powerful and materially developed states expect their governments to ensure a continuation of their privileged position, while inhabitants of less developed and less strong states expect their governments to demand concessions to improve their relative position.

Nevertheless there is a growing world-wide recognition that we all have some overarching common concerns and that fair and reasonable accommodations are necessary to meet those concerns. Those accommodations have to take place through different institutions serving processes of dispute settlement both at high political levels and in a multitude of functionally subdivided agencies and bodies.

Let me conclude with the hope that the readers of this book may feel inspired to become engaged in the process by reflecting on, criticizing, and improving the components of peace as set out in the introductory chapter of this book, and to get involved in the international discourse on how global peace and sustainable development can be further promoted.

Asbjørn Eide

Acknowledgements

The editors wish to express their gratitude and appreciation to the Norwegian Centre for Human Rights, to PluriCourts (Centre of Excellence for the Study of the Legitimate Roles of the Judiciary in the Global Order), and to the Department of Public and International Law, all at the Faculty of Law at the University of Oslo, for their financial and academic support of this project. We also thank the Norwegian Centre for Human Rights for supporting the creation of the course on 'The Right to Peace', which we hope will serve as a model for other law schools around the world. Our special gratitude goes to our research assistants Agnieszka Cybulska, Thale Espeli, and Linn Elise Gjems-Onstad, for their invaluable work in the editing of the book. Finally, we are very grateful to the team at OUP, especially Anthony Hinton and Merel Alstein, for the pleasant cooperation and for their efforts in realizing this project.

C.M.B. and K.M.L.

Oslo
June 2014

Contents

III. CIVIL SOCIETY PARTICIPATION IN THE PROMOTION AND SAFEGUARDING OF PEACE

IV. INSTITUTIONAL IMPLEMENTATION OF PEACE

Table of Judgments and Decisions

A. JUDGMENTS ON INTERNATIONAL AND NATIONAL COURTS

International

Arbitral Tribunal

European Court of Human Rights

International Court of Justice

International Criminal Court

International Tribunal of the Former Yugoslavia

International Tribunal for the Law of the Sea

Permanent Court of International Justice

World Trade Organization

Dispute Settlement

B. DECISIONS OF INTERGOVERNMENTAL AND OTHER ORGANIZATIONS

UN General Assembly

Human Rights Committee

Human Rights Council

Other UN documents

List of Abbreviations and Acronyms

AB	Appellate Body
ASEAN	Association of South East Asian Nations
ATT	Arms Trade Treaty
AU	African Union
BATNA	Best alternative to negotiated agreement
BRIC	Brazil, Russia, India, and China
BWC	Biological Weapons Convention
CADE	Convention Against Discrimination in Education
CAT	Convention Against Torture
CBDRRC	Common but differentiated responsibility and respective capabilities
CEDAW	Convention on the Elimination of All Forms of Discrimination Against Women
CEH	Commission for Historical Clarification
CERD	Committee on the Elimination of Racial Discrimination
CESCR	Convention on Economic Social and Cultural Rights
CITES	Convention on International Trade in Endangered Species of Wild Fauna and Flora
CONADEP	Comisión Nacional para la Desaparición de Personas
CRC	Convention on the Rights of the Child
CRPD	Convention on the Rights of Persons with Disabilities
CSCE	Conference on Security and Cooperation in Europe
CVR	Peruvian Truth and Reconciliation Commission
CWC	Chemical Weapons Convention
DRC	Democratic Republic of Congo
DSM	Dispute settlement mechanism
DSU	Dispute settlement understanding
ECHR	European Convention on Human Rights
ECOSOC	(UN) Economic and Social Council
ECP	Environmental Cooperation for Peace-building
EctHR	European Court of Human Rights
FAO	Food and Agriculture Organization
FPU	(Indian) Formed Police Unit
GATS	General Agreement on Trade in Services
GATT	General Agreement on Tariffs and Trade
GHG	Greenhouse gas/es
HRC	Human Rights Council
HRCAC	Human Rights Council Advisory Committee
IC	Internatonal court
ICC	International Criminal Court
ICCPR	International Covenant on Civil and Political Rights
ICERD	International Convention for the Elimination of All Forms of Discrimination
ICESCR	International Covenant on Economic, Social and Cultural Rights

IACtHR	Inter-American Court of Human Rights
ICISS	International Commission on Intervention and State Sovereignty
ICJ	International Court of Justice
ICRC	International Committee of the Red Cross
ICTR	International Criminal Tribunal for Rwanda
ICTY	International Criminal Tribunal for the former Yugoslavia
IDPs	Internally Displaced Peoples
IFAD	International Fund for Agricultural Development
IGWG	Inter-Agency Gender Working Group
IHFFC	International Humanitarian Fact-Finding Commission
IHL	International humanitarian law
IHRL	International human rights law
ILO	International Labour Organization
IMF	International Monetary Fund
IMTFE	International Military Tribunal for the Far East
IMTN	International Military Tribunal for Nuremberg
INEE	Inter-Agency Network for Education in Emergencies
IO	International organization
IOM	International Organization for Migration
IPCC	Intergovernmental Panel on Climate Change
IR	International relations
KFOR	Kosovo Force
LGBT	Lesbian, gay, bisexual, and transgender
MDGs	Millennium Development Goals
MINURSO	UN Mission for the Referendum in Western Sahara
MINUSMA	Multidimensional Integrated Stabilization Mission in Mali
MINUSTAH	Mission des Nations Unies Pour la Stabilisation en Haïti
MONUSCO	UNO Stabilization Mission in the Democratic Republic of the Congo
NGO	Non-governmental organization
NIEO	New International Economic Order
NZDF	New Zealand Defence Force
OAS	Organization of American States
OPCW	Organization for the Prohibition of Chemical Weapons
OSCE	Organization for Security and Cooperation in Europe
OTP/ICC	Office of the Prosecutor of the ICC
P5	Five permanent members [of the Security Council]
PEP	Peace Education Programme
PICJ	Professional Issues in Criminal Justice
PMSC	Private military and security company
PRIO	Peace Research Institute Oslo
R2P	Responsibility to protect
REDD-plus	Reducing emissions from deforestation and forest degradation in developing countries
REMHI	Catholic Church's Interdiocesan Project for the Recovery of Historical Memory
RTA	Regional trade agreement
RtD	Right to development
RtoP	Responsibility to protect
SAARC	South Asian Association for Regional Cooperation

SADC	South African Development Community
SC	Security Council
SERF	Social and Economic Rights Fulfilment Index
SSIHRL	Spanish Society for International Human Rights Law
TJ	Transitional justice
TRC	Truth and Reconciliation Commission
TRIMS	Trade-Related Investment Measures
TRIPS	Trade-Related Aspects of International Property Rights
TWAIL	Third World Approaches to International Law
UCDP	Uppsala Conflict Data Program
UDHR	Universal Declaration of Human Rights
UN	United Nations
UNAMA	UN Assistance Mission in Afghanistan
UNAMID	The African Union/UN Hybrid operation in Darfur
UNCLOS	UN Convention on the Law of the Sea
UNCTAD	UN Conference on Trade and Development
UNDIR	UN Institute for Disarmament Research
UNDOF	UN Disengagement Observer Force
UNEP	UN Environment Programme
UNESCO	UN Educational, Scientific, and Cultural Organization
UNFCCC	UN Framework Convention on Climate Change
UNFICYP	UN Peacekeeping Force in Cyprus
UNGA	UN General Assembly
UNHCR	United Nations High Commissioner for Refugees
UNICEF	United Nations Children's Fund
UNIFIL	UN Interim Force in Lebanon
UNISFA	UN Interim Security Force for Abyei
UNMIH	UN Mission in Haiti
UNMIK	UN Interim Administration Mission in Kosovo
UNMISS	UN Mission in South Sudan
UNMOGIP	UN Military Observer Group in India and Pakistan
UNO	United Nations Organization
UNOCI	UN Operation in Côte d'Ivoire
UNODA	UN Office of Disarmament Affairs
UNRWA	UN Relief and Works Agency
UNSC	UN Security Council
UNSCR	UN Security Council Resolution
UNTAC	UN Transitional Authority in Cambodia
UNTAET	UN Transitional Administration in East Timor
UNTSO	UN Truce Supervision Organization
VCLT	Vienna Convention on the Law of Treaties
WCED	World Council on Environment and Development
WGBU	German Advisory Council on Global Change
WHO	World Health Organization
WTO	World Trade Organization

Notes on the Contributors

ABOUT THE EDITORS

Cecilia Marcela Bailliet is Professor Dr Jur., Director of the Master's Program in Public International Law and Coordinator at the PluriCourts Centre for the Study of the Legitimacy of the International Judiciary at the University of Oslo, Norway. She has a doctoral degree in law from the University of Oslo and combined JD/MA (honours) degree from the George Washington University Law School and Elliott School of International Affairs. She researches and teaches within the linked fields of international public law, human rights, refugee law, and peace. Among her publications are: *Non-State Actors, Soft Law and Protective Regimes* (2012), *Cosmopolitan Justice and Its Discontents* (co-edited with Katja Franko Aas, 2011), and *Security: A Multidisciplinary Normative Approach* (2009).

Kjetil Mujezinović Larsen is Professor of Law (Ph.D.), Director of Research, and Deputy Director at the Norwegian Centre for Human Rights at the University of Oslo, where he does research and teaching in human rights law and international humanitarian law. He is the author of the book *The Human Rights Treaty Obligations of Peacekeepers* (2012) and co-editor of the anthology *Searching for a 'Principle of Humanity' in International Humanitarian Law* (2013). He is the Norwegian editor of the Nordic Journal of Law and Justice ('Retfærd'), member of the Editorial Board of the Forum for International Criminal and Humanitarian Law, and responsible for entries concerning the laws of war in the Norwegian encyclopedia *Store norske leksikon*.

ABOUT THE CONTRIBUTORS

Bård A. Andreassen (Dr Polit.) is Professor at the Norwegian Centre for Human Rights, Law Faculty, University of Oslo, and Visiting Professor at the National University of Vietnam. His research focuses on human rights in processes of democratic change in ethnically divided societies (East Africa), human-rights-based development, development assistance and human rights, international election monitoring, economic and social rights, and corporate social responsibility. He holds a Diploma of International and Comparative Law of Human Rights from the International Institute of Human Rights, Strasbourg. His most recent book (edited with Gordon Crawford) is *Human Rights. Power and Civic Action: Comparative analyses of Struggles for Rights in Developing Societies* (2013). He is Editor-in-Chief of the *Nordic Journal of Human Rights*.

Kjølv Egeland holds an M.Phil. in Peace and Conflict Studies and a BA in International Studies, both from the University of Oslo. He is currently pursuing a doctorate in International Relations at St Anne's College, University of Oxford. Egeland is also engaged as a policy adviser at the International Law and Policy Institute in Oslo, working primarily on arms-related issues. His research interests include civil war and social movements, non-state actors, and the philosophy of international law.

Ola Engdahl is Associate Professor of International Law (Ph.D.) at the Swedish National Defence College. His main areas of research and teaching are international humanitarian law, human rights law, and international law aspects on peace operations. He is the author of *Protection of Personnel in Peace Operations* (2007), and co-editor of *The Law as it Was and the Law as it Should Be* (2008), and has authored several articles on the law of peace operations. He has served as Legal Adviser in the SFOR operation in Bosnia-Herzegovina and as an adviser on international law at the Ministry of Foreign Affairs. He is currently involved in the writing of a Manual for the Swedish Armed Forces on International Humanitarian Law.

Ole Kristian Fauchald is Professor at the Faculty of Law, University of Oslo, and Research Professor at the Fridtjof Nansen Institute. He publishes and teaches in international trade law, international investment law, and national and international environmental law. He is coordinator with responsibility for investment law at PluriCourts—Centre for the Study of the Legitimate Roles of the Judiciary in the Global Order. He is editor of the *Yearbook of International Environmental Law*, the *Nordic Journal of Environmental Law*, and a treaty database (www.jus.uio.no/treaties). (Accessed 3 Nov 2014)

Jemima García-Godos, Dr Polit. in Human Geography, is Associate Professor in Human Geography and Director of the Bachelor Program in Development Studies at the Department of Sociology and Human Geography, University of Oslo. Her research focuses on issues of transitional justice, particularly on victim reparations, and state–society relations in conflict and post-conflict settings, particularly in Latin America. She has authored several articles on transitional justice and was guest editor for the Special Issue on Land Restitution in Transitional Justice at the *NJHR* in 2010. She co-edited *Transitional Justice and Peacebuilding on the Ground: Victims and Ex-combatants* (2013).

Cecilie Hellestveit has her Ph.D. from the University of Oslo with a dissertation on 'Conduct of Hostilities under the International Humanitarian Law of Non-international Armed Conflict' (2014). She has studied and worked in several countries, and she has considerable field experience, including fact-finding missions in the Middle East. She holds a Norwegian law degree (LLM), and she has studied international law, Islamic law, and conflict studies, with a particular emphasis on the Arab and Muslim worlds. She has worked at PRIO (Peace Research Institute, Oslo), and the Norwegian Centre for Human Rights. She participated in the Gulf Research Unit at the University of Oslo, with a particular focus on Saudi Arabia and Iraq.

Maja Janmyr (Ph.D.) is a researcher at the Faculty of Law, University of Bergen, working on issues related to the international laws of responsibility and international human rights law, refugee law, and international humanitarian law. Her doctoral dissertation addresses the United Nations High Commissioner for Refugees' international responsibility in relation to human rights violations in refugee camps ('Protecting Civilians in Refugee Camps: Unable and Unwilling States, UNHCR and International Responsibility', 2014). Her current work, pursued under the auspices of the project 'Migration to Norway: Flows and Regulations', focuses on the forced return of failed asylum seekers in the Norwegian context. She has been a visiting researcher at Makerere University (2009), the Swedish College of Defence (2011) and at the American University in Cairo (2014).

Kristoffer Lidén is Researcher at the Peace Research Institute Oslo (PRIO), working on topics of peace-building, security, and humanitarianism within the disciplines of philosophy and International Relations. His research on peace-building situates the ethics of international peace operations within broader debates on the political philosophy of peace and peacemaking. His publications on this topic include 'In Love with a Lie? On the Social and Political Preconditions for Global Peacebuilding Governance', *Peacebuilding*, 1/1; 'Peace, Self-Governance and International Engagement: From Neo-Colonial to Post-Colonial Peacebuilding', in Shahrbanou Tadjsbakhsh (ed.), *Rethinking the Liberal Peace: External Models and Local Alternatives* (2011), and 'Building Peace between Global and Local Politics: On the Cosmopolitical Ethics of Liberal Peacebuilding', *International Peacekeeping*, 16/5.

Gro Nystuen is Dr. Juris. and currently Senior Partner at ILPI (International Law and Policy Institute). She was with the Norwegian Ministry of Foreign Affairs from 1991 to 2005, with the University of Oslo from 2000 to 2003, and from 2005 to 2009. She has taken part in several diplomatic processes within peace, humanitarian law, disarmament, and human rights. She was Chair of the Council on Ethics for the Norwegian Government Pension Fund—Global from 2004 to 2012. She has published extensively on the above issues, as well as on international terrorism, corporate social responsibility, and *jus ad bellum*. She took part in the negotiations of the Arms Trade Treaty on behalf of the Norwegian MFA.

Simon O'Connor is a legal adviser specializing in international humanitarian law at the Norwegian Red Cross. He is a barrister and served as a legal officer in the British Army Legal Services in advisory, prosecutorial, and operational roles. He holds graduate research degrees from the Universities of Tromsø and St Andrews and lectures regularly for the Law Faculty at the University of Oslo on international law and the use of force. He is a former visiting fellow and current research associate at the Institute for Ethics Law and Armed Conflict at the University of Oxford. He has published across a range of topics including child recruitment and use in armed conflict, nuclear weapons, and corporate criminal liability for war crimes.

Kjersti Skarstad is a Ph.D. candidate at the Department of Political Science, University of Oslo. Her research is mainly focused on the relation between human rights and violent conflicts/peace, and on disability human rights. Skarstad is part of a research project on disability rights led by the Harvard Law School Project on Disability and the Socio-Economic rights program at the Norwegian Centre for Human Rights (NCHR). She has previously worked, *inter alia*, as a research assistant and consultant at NCHR and as an intern at the Permanent Delegation of Norway to the Council of Europe.

Maria Sommardahl is currently working as Project Manager for Mediation Support at the Norwegian Refugee Council. She previously held the directorship at the Nansen Center for Peace and Dialogue in Norway. She has also worked as Adviser in Humanitarian Law and Policy at the Norwegian Centre for Human Rights and as Coordinator for Human Rights Education at the Institute for Human Rights at Åbo Akademi University in Finland. She has a background in law from Åbo Akademi University and the University of Turku in Finland, UN Civil-Military Training from Bosnia and Herzegovina, and Advanced Training in Humanitarian Law and Policy from the Program on Humanitarian Policy and Conflict Research at Harvard University. She holds an MA in Peace and Reconciliation Studies from Coventry University, UK.

Vibeke Blaker Strand is Associate Professor of Law (Ph.D.) at the Norwegian Centre for Human Rights at the Faculty of Law, University of Oslo. She conducts research and teaching in non-discrimination and equality law, human rights law, welfare law, and legal method. She has written several articles within these fields and the book *Diskrimineringsvern* *og religionsutøvelse. Hvor langt rekker individvernet?* (*Non-discrimination and Religious Practice: The Scope of Rights Afforded to Individuals*, 2012). She is editor of the Law Faculty's own open access law journal, *Oslo Law Review*.

Henrik Syse is Senior Researcher at the Peace Research Institute Oslo (PRIO), Lecturer at Bjørknes College, and Chief Co-Editor of the *Journal of Military Ethics*. He has previously been, *inter alia*, Fulbright Fellow at Boston College, Norwegian Research Council Fellow at the University of Oslo, Post-Doc Fellow at the Ethics Program at the University of Oslo, and part-time Associate Professor at the Norwegian Defence University College. Among his publications are a monograph on just war in Norwegian (*Rettferdig krig*, 2003), *Ethics of War: Classic and Contemporary Readings* (co-edited with Gregory Reichberg and Endre Begby, 2006), *Natural Law, Religion, and Rights* (2007), and *Religion, War, and Ethics* (co-edited with Gregory Reichberg, 2014).

Azin Tadjdini is a Ph.D. research fellow at the Department of Public and International Law, University of Oslo, where she also teaches courses in constitutional law. She received a Master in Law from the University of Oslo (2009) and an LLM in International Legal Studies from Georgetown University (2011). She spent the academic year 2013/14 as a visiting doctoral researcher at New York School of Law. Her dissertation project is on constitutional de-secularization, constitutionalism and equal liberty, to be submitted by the second half of 2015. Previous work experience includes the Permanent Mission of Norway to the United Nations; the UN Office of Disarmament Affairs; and the Norwegian Directorate of Immigration. She publishes in law journals, blogs, and newspapers.

Christina Voigt is Professor at the Department of Public and International Law, University of Oslo, Norway. She is the author of *Sustainable Development as a Principle of International Law* (2009) and the edited volumes *Sustainable Development in International and National Law* (with H. C. Bugge, 2008) and *Rule of Law for Nature* (2013). Her teaching and research is in international environmental law and public international law. She works in particular on legal issues of climate change, sustainability, and the interface between environmental and trade law. Christina was awarded the IUCN Academy of Environmental Law Junior Scholarship Prize in 2009. Currently, she is the programme coordinator for environmental law at the Center of Excellence—PluriCourts—at the University of Oslo.

Cornelia Weiss is a colonel in the US Air Force Reserve Judge Advocate General Corps. She hold a Bachelor of Arts in Women's Studies from the University of Utah, a Master's degree from Chile's National Academy of Strategy and Policy Studies (ANEPE), and a Juris Doctor from Vanderbilt University School of Law. Her 1989 law school paper on the need for the US to ratify CEDAW (the Convention on the Elimination of All Forms of Discrimination against Women) won second prize in the American Bar Association Bruno Bitker international law writing competition. Most recently the US Air Force recognized her with the Keenan Award as the Air Force lawyer who has made the most notable contribution to the development of international law.

Pål Wrange (Ph.D., LL M) is Professor of Public International Law at Stockholm University and director of the Stockholm Centre for International Law and Justice, a former principal legal adviser at the Swedish Ministry for Foreign Affairs and a former political adviser to the European Union's Special Representative for the Great Lakes Region. Dr Wrange has published widely on international law (including on the use of force), and international relations and theory and has consulted on international criminal justice and peace-building. He has been a visiting scholar and fellow at Harvard Law School and European University Institute.

Gentian Zyberi is Associate Professor of International Law at the Norwegian Centre for Human Rights, University of Oslo. He has conducted research and teaching in international human rights, humanitarian law, international criminal law, and public international law at different universities in Norway, the Netherlands, the US, China, and Albania. From 2004 to 2012 he provided legal assistance to defence teams in the *Limaj* et al. and the *Haradinaj* et al. cases tried before the ICTY. Throughout 2009 he acted as legal adviser and coordinator of the Albanian legal team in the Kosovo case before the ICJ. His current research focuses on issues related to transitional justice, responsibility to protect, and the contribution of international courts to interpreting and developing international human rights and humanitarian law.

1

Introduction

Promoting Peace through International Law

Cecilia M. Bailliet and Kjetil Mujezinović Larsen

> He who wishes to approach the aim of world peace in a realistic way must tackle this problem quite soberly, as one of a slow and steady perfection of the international legal order.
>
> Hans Kelsen[1]

1. Introduction

Peace is an inherently elusive concept, varying in its definition and valuation according to historical epoch and contextual application within different cultures, institutions, civil society groups, and academic disciplines.[2] It is especially vague within the realm of international law. One of the most prominent and influential scholars in international law, Hersch Lauterpacht, famously stated in the wake of World War II that 'international law should be functionally oriented towards both the establishment of peace between nations and the protection of fundamental human rights'.[3] Yet, while the protection of human rights steadily gained support as a primary purpose of international law; international legal literature largely abandoned promoting the establishment of peace as an independent, overarching aim of international law.[4] The present book returns to the Lauterpachtian

[1] Hans Kelsen, *Peace Through Law* (Clark: The Lawbook Exchange 2008, repr. University of North Carolina Press 1944), p. ix.

[2] On the different meanings of peace, see Ian M. Harris, 'Peace Education Theory', *Journal of Peace Education* 1 (2004), 7.

[3] Hersch Lauterpacht, 'The Grotian Tradition in International Law', *British Yearbook of International Law* 23 (1946), 1, 51.

[4] The most significant text that sought to pursue law as the key to implementation of peace was Grenville Clark and Louis B. Sohn, *World Peace through World Law* (Cambridge: Harvard University Press 1958, 1960, 1966). See also Grenville Clark and Louis B. Sohn, *Introduction to World Peace Through World Law* (Cambridge: Harvard University Press, 1984). See also Kelsen, *Peace Through Law*. See also James T. Ranney, 'World Peace Through Law—Rethinking an Old Theory', *CADMUS Journal* 1 (2012), 125.

approach, as it enquires to what extent peace is promoted through existing international and national normative and institutional frameworks. This book places itself in the intersection between international law and peace studies. Whether the reader prefers to consider it as legally oriented peace research or as peace-oriented international legal research may vary—the important premise for the book is rather that it attempts to build a bridge between two disciplines that have a lot in common but that for a long time have been remarkably unconnected.

However, in order to discuss how international law promotes peace, this book needs to adopt a working definition of what is meant by peace. For this end, section 2 addresses various substantive components of the concept of peace. Section 3 describes the importance of peace in the UN Charter, before section 4 introduces the highly contentious concept of 'the right to peace'. The final section 5 provides an overview of the chapters in the book, while also pointing towards some issues relating to peace that are not addressed in the present volume.

2. Definition of the Components of Peace

Peace is a multifaceted concept that lacks clear definition and boundaries. Considerable scholarly attention within peace research has been devoted to attempting to illuminate its scope and content, but no universally accepted definition has emerged. However, for the purposes of the present book, it is useful to focus on two important components of peace.

The first component of peace is that of *negative peace*, which may be characterized as the absence of war or armed conflict. If there is no war, there is peace. In international law such a dichotomy can be traced all the way back to Hugo Grotius' fundamental distinction between 'the law of war' and 'the law of peace'. The negative peace approach focuses on the prevention of armed conflict; it advocates non-violent dispute resolution and condemns the unlawful use of force or violence. Traditionally, it has generally applied at the international level referring to interstate relations, but it is now increasingly directed also at intrastate armed conflict and violence.[5]

The majority of peace research has focused on this negative component of peace, more specifically on the prevention of war or violence.[6] Yet, even in relation to negative peace there is a significant range of approaches, which can be categorized according to their emphasis on pacifism. *Principled pacifism* is the absolute belief in non-aggression and non-violence with no exceptions permitted whatsoever. It is based on moral-religious or secular (deontological) values.[7] *Realistic*

[5] See Oliver Corten, *The Law Against War: The Prohibition on the Use of Force in Contemporary International Law* (Oxford: Hart, 2012).

[6] Nils Petter Gleditsch, Jonas Nordkvelle, and Håvard Strand, 'Peace Research—Just the Study of War', *Journal of Peace Research* 54 (forthcoming 2014).

[7] For an overview of pacifism see the Stanford Encyclopedia of Peace, http://plato.stanford.edu/entries/pacifism/ (accessed 4 Nov 2014).

pacifism, on the other hand, accepts exceptions, primarily those contained within the UN Charter, i.e. the use of force in self-defence in accordance with Article 51 or with an authorization from the UN Security Council under Chapter VII. Within realistic pacifism there are divided opinions regarding the possibility of other exceptions from the prohibition on the use of force, primarily regarding the legality and legitimacy of humanitarian intervention and the status of the emerging doctrine on the 'Responsibility to Protect' (R2P).[8] A third category, namely *contingent/conditional/selective pacifism*, evaluates *jus ad bellum* and/or *jus in bello* and/or *jus post bellum* in order to oppose particular armed conflicts, such as those involving weapons of mass destruction, or those that violate the UN Charter.[9] A fourth category, *prudential pacifism*, involves the pragmatic concern for the cost/waste of war; it is consequentialist in orientation and may have particular relevance in this time of economic/financial crisis that may limit military options from a fiscal perspective.[10]

The present book does not advocate principled pacifism, nor is it primarily concerned with selective or prudential pacifism. This book rests on the unequivocal premise that the UN Charter's system, i.e. the prohibition on the use of force in Article 2(4) with two explicit exceptions from that prohibition, is a fundamental element of international law that this book does not set out to revise. In terms of negative peace, the book applies instead a concept of realistic pacifism (as described above), meaning that the chapters within this book set out to explain how international law promotes a realistic peace.

The second component of peace is a broader conception, namely *positive peace*. While negative peace refers to the 'absence of' something (namely war and violence), positive peace refers to the 'presence of' something. As articulated by Galtung, positive peace calls for the presence of cooperation between people and states and the 'integration of human society'; incorporating social justice (equal opportunity/enjoyment of social contract/human dignity), respect for human rights, and the elimination of 'structural violence' which causes poverty, inequality, exclusion, death, or disability through inequitable distribution of resources addressing basic human needs (such as food, medicine, housing), or denial of equal protection when addressing domestic violence, hate crimes, etc.[11] It may apply to both intrastate and interstate relations. Galtung intended this concept to shift attention away from the East–West Cold War tension in

[8] See Kjell Anderson, 'The Universality of War: Jus ad bellum and the Right to Peace in Non-International Armed Conflicts', in *The Challenge of Human Rights: Past, Present and Future*, David Keane and Yvonne McDermott (eds.) (Cheltenham: Edward Elgar, 2012). See also the chapters by Pål Wrange and Ola Engdahl in the present volume.

[9] See Leonard Hammer, 'Selective Conscientious Objection and International Human Rights', *36 Israel Law Review* 36 (2002).

[10] As noted by Mary Ellen O'Connell: '(T)he next development will simply be toward using less expensive force-think drone attacks and Stuxnet worms'. 'Energized by War Fatigue', *ESIL Reflections* (2014), http://www.esil-sedi.eu/node/522 (accessed 4 Nov 2014).

[11] e.g. Johan Galtung, 'Violence, Peace, and Peace Research', *Journal of Peace Research* 6 (1969) 167–91. Structural violence refers to the phenomenon of social structures or social institutions inflicting harm upon people by preventing them from meeting their basic needs.

favour of addressing the North–South divide (although one may argue that we may be returning to a new variation of East–West friction).[12] Nevertheless, this perspective was criticized for being aligned with Neo-Marxism.[13] An apparent consequence was that international legal scholars largely shied away from peace studies, in part due to the fear of association with pro-communist or pro-Soviet sympathies, and in part on account of concern that the scope of positive peace was too broad, pursuing utopianism.[14] Thus, peace research returned to the negative orientation of preventing war and violence. To the extent it addressed cooperation, it focused on how it might reduce violence, thereby falling in line with liberal peace theory.[15] This theory emphasizes state consent to institutions and legal regimes that create rules intended to promote harmonized interests based on shared norms and principles; thereby limiting state sovereignty and resort to military power in the interest of establishing a peaceful international order through cooperation.[16] Liberalism emphasizes the recognition of individuals as primary actors in society; further it supports tolerance, diversity, equal opportunity, freedom, the rule of law, institutional reform, free elections, and free markets.[17]

This volume is not limited to a negative concept of peace. Instead, we adopt a broad definition of peace that includes a wide-ranging, positive dimension.[18] Although peace research commenced with the incentive to prevent nuclear war; at present one may argue that the looming, gradual cataclysm presented by climate change, a marked increase in inequality in the world, and the phenomenon of failing and failed states require a reorientation of academic focus.[19] There is also a juxtaposition of concern for the inequitable consequences of globalization with the increased attention on the situation and role of individuals, groups, and other non-state actors such as corporations.[20] Hence, peace may be situated within the micro level of home and family, centring on interpersonal relations and the requirements of human dignity as an element of peace; as well as at the macro

[12] Gleditsch et al. 'Peace Research'. [13] Gleditsch et al. 'Peace Research'.

[14] Edward Gordon, Book Review: 'From Erasmus to Tolstoy: The Peace Literature of Four Centuries; Jacob Ter Meulen's Bibliographies of the Peace Movement Before 1899', in *Harvard International Law Journal* 34 (1993), 641.

[15] See Michael Doyle, *Liberal Peace: Selected Essays* (New York: Routledge, 2011) and John MacMillan, *On Liberal Peace: Democracy, War and the International Order* (London: Tauris Academic Studies, 1998). See also the chapter by Kristoffer Lidén and Henrik Syse in the present volume.

[16] Gleditsch et al. 'Peace Research'. On liberalism in international relations, see Anne L. Herbert, 'Cooperation in International Relations: A Comparison of Keohane, Haas and Franck', *Berkeley Journal of International Law* 14 (1996), 222.

[17] For a critical view of liberal peace see Roger MacGinty, *International Peacebuilding and Local Resistance: Hybrid Forms of Peace* (New York: Palgrave, 2011), 26.

[18] On the hybridity of negative and positive peace, see Oliver Richmond, *A Post-Liberal Peace* (London: Routledge, 2011).

[19] See Rafael Domingo, *The New Global Law* (Cambridge: Cambridge University Press, 2011); A. A. Cancado Trindade, *International Law for Humankind, Towards a New Jus Gentium* (Leiden: Martinus Nijhoff, 2010).

[20] See Cecilia M. Bailliet, (ed.) *Non-State Actors, Soft Law and Protective Regimes* (Cambridge: Cambridge University Press, 2012).

level, exploring the aspiration of equality between states and peoples.[21] This book discusses how international law promotes the establishment and protection of relevant criteria pertaining to social justice, such as non-discrimination and equality. The chapters also address the *link* between negative and positive peace by discussing the normative and institutional frameworks addressing prevention of war and violence, the promotion of sustainable development, and the protection of human rights, underscoring the holistic purposes articulated in UN Charter, Article 1:

1. To maintain international peace and security, and to that end: to take effective collective measures for the prevention and removal of threats to the peace, and for the suppression of acts of aggression or other breaches of the peace, and to bring about by peaceful means, and in conformity with the principles of justice and international law, adjustment or settlement of international disputes or situations which might lead to a breach of the peace;
2. To develop friendly relations among nations based on respect for the principle of equal rights and self-determination of peoples, and to take other appropriate measures to strengthen universal peace;
3. To achieve international co-operation in solving international problems of an economic, social, cultural, or humanitarian character, and in promoting and encouraging respect for human rights and for fundamental freedoms for all without distinction as to race, sex, language, or religion; and
4. To be a centre for harmonizing the actions of nations in the attainment of these common ends.

Students of international law are very familiar with a holistic interpretation of negative and positive rights in the field of human rights law, and this book applies a similar framework for negative and positive elements in the concept of peace—we consider these elements as indivisible, interrelated, and interdependent.[22]

3. The Law of Peace According to the UN Charter

The modern emergence of the law of peace is derived from various instruments that articulate a notion of peace as relating to interstate relations as the formulations address the prohibition of unlawful use of force and promotion of the use of dispute settlement mechanisms to avoid breaches of the peace, *inter alia* the Briand-Kellogg Pact which condemned 'recourse to war for the solution of international controversies' (1928), the Hague Convention of 1899 which established the Permanent Court of Arbitration, the Hague Convention of 1907 which resulted in the Convention on the Pacific Settlement of International Disputes,

[21] On the micro level, see Karen Warren and Duane L. Cady, (eds.) *Bringing Peace Home: Feminism, Violence and Nature* (Bloomington: Indiana University Press, 1996); on the macro level, see Gerry Simpson, *Great Powers and Outlaw States Unequal Sovereigns in the International Legal Order* (Cambridge: Cambridge University Press, 2004).

[22] See Asbjørn Eide, 'Interdependence and Indivisibility of Human Rights', in *Human Rights in Education, Culture and Science: Legal Developments and Challenges*, Vladimir Volodin and Yvonne Donders (eds.) (Aldershot: Ashgate, 2007), 11–52.

and the Covenant of the League of Nations (1919). Foremost at present is the UN Charter; the preamble states that the peoples of the UN have determined:

- to practice tolerance and live together in peace with one another as good neighbours, and
- to unite our strength to maintain international peace and security, and
- to ensure, by the acceptance of principles and the institution of methods, that armed force shall not be used, save in the common interest, and
- to employ international machinery for the promotion of the economic and social advancement of all peoples

Taken together with Article 1(1), (2), and (3), it is noted that 'peace is more than the absence of war'.[23] Article 1 sets forth that the purpose of the UN is to maintain international peace and security, and to that end to take effective collective measures for the prevention and removal of threats to the peace, suppression or acts of aggression or other breaches of the peace, and to bring about by peaceful means ... settlement of international disputes or situations which might lead to a breach of the peace. Article 2(3) states that all members 'shall settle their international disputes by peaceful means in such a manner that international peace and security, and justice, are not endangered.'[24] Article 2(4) calls upon members to 'refrain in their international relations from the threat or use of force against the territorial integrity or political independence of any state, or in any other manner inconsistent with the Purposes of the United Nations'. The ICJ confirmed this to constitute a *jus cogens* norm.[25] Article 2(7) prohibits interference by the UN in domestic affairs: 'Nothing contained in the present Charter shall authorize the United Nations to intervene in matters which are essentially within the domestic jurisdiction of any state or shall require the Members to submit such matters to settlement under the present Charter; but this principle shall not prejudice the application of enforcement measures under Chapter VII.'

This has revealed to be contentious in practice as the UN Security Council has expanded its consideration of issues deemed to be 'threats to the peace' to include human rights, internal conflicts, terrorism, and other situations previously considered subject to national jurisdiction, thereby earning characterization as a World Legislature, calling upon states to freeze financial assets of individuals, block arms sales, etc.[26] However, Tsagourioas advocates recognition

[23] Wolfrum Rüdiger, 'Article 1', in *The Charter of the United Nations: A Commentary*, Bruno Simma, Daniel-Erasmus Khan, Georg Nolte, and Andreas Paulus (eds.) (Oxford: Oxford University Press, 3rd edn. 2012), 110.

[24] See also Chapter VI, Art. 33: 'The parties to any dispute, the continuance of which is likely to endanger the maintenance of international peace and security, shall, first of all, seek a solution by negotiation, enquiry, mediation, conciliation, arbitration, judicial settlement, resort to regional agencies or arrangements, or other peaceful means of their own choice.'

[25] *Military and Paramilitary Activities in and against Nicaragua (Nicaragua* v. *United States)* (Judgment) [1984] ICJ. (Henceforth *Nicaragua* v. *United States*)

[26] See Stefan Talmon, 'The Security Council as World Legislature', *American Journal of International Law* 99 (2005), 175; Eric Rosand, 'The Security Council as "Global Legislator": Ultra Vires or Ultra Innovative?', *Fordham International Law Journal* 28 (2004), 542; see also Ian Johnstone,

of Article 2(7) as a an expression of the principle of subsidiarity which has the potential to filter the 'manifestations of legislative power by the Security Council and member states with regard to the common goal of peace and security'.[27]

It is noteworthy that membership in the UN 'is open to all other peace-loving states which accept the obligations contained in the present Charter and, in the judgment of the Organization, are able and willing to carry out these obligations'.[28] It has been noted that the 'peace-loving' criterion 'refers both to their past and present conduct'.[29] This was originally interpreted to include states that had engaged in the war against the Axis powers or had a non-Fascist past and also interpreted to preclude states that had governments that had been supported by the Axis powers (Spain). Of interest, at the time of the San Francisco conference, 'peace-loving' was not to be defined by reference to the internal level of democracy, because this would constitute unlawful interference in internal affairs. Yet, over time, references to democracy were made by Western countries when discussing the applications of Central and Eastern European nations. Nevertheless, states are generally considered 'peace-loving' by reviewing their external, international behaviour: 'including compliance with UN resolutions, guaranteeing innocent passage in territorial waters, settling border disputes peacefully, and respecting the principle of non-intervention.'[30]

Yet, the UN Charter does not espouse a principled, absolutist version of pacifism.[31] It is a pragmatic document that reflects realistic pacifism as it recognizes

'Legislation and Adjudication in the UN Security Council: Bringing Down the Deliberative Deficit', *American Journal of International Law* 102 (2008) 275. By UNSC Res. 1267 (15 October 1999) UN Doc. S/RES/1267 (1999); UNSC Res. 1333 (19 December 2000) UN Doc. S/RES/1333(2000); UNSC Res. 1390 (28 January 2002) UN Doc. S/RES/1390(2002), as reiterated in UNSC Res. 1455 (17 January 2003) UN Doc. S/RES/1455 (2003); UNSC Res. 1526 (30 January 2004) UN Doc. S/RES/1526 (2004); UNSC Res. 1617 (29 July 2005) UN Doc. S/RES/1617 (2005); UNSC Res. 1735 (22 December 2006) UN Doc. S/RES/1735 (2006); UNSC Res. 1822 (30 June 2008) UN Doc. S/RES/1822 (2008); and UNSC Res. 1904 (17 December 2009) UN Doc. S/RES/1904 (2009), the Security Council has obliged all states to freeze without delay the funds and other financial assets or economic resources, including funds derived from property owned or controlled directly or indirectly; prevent the entry into or the transit through their territories; prevent the direct or indirect supply, sale, or transfer of arms and related material, including military and paramilitary equipment, technical advice, assistance or training related to military activities, with regard to the individuals, groups, undertakings, and entities placed on the Consolidated List.

[27] See Nicholas Tsagourias, 'Security Council Legislation, Article 2(7) of the UN Charter, and the Principle of Subsidiarity', *Leiden Journal of International Law* 24 (2011), 549–50 concluding. 'Article 2(7) was placed at the intersection of United Nations' and member states' jurisdictional authority and provides the context in which the powers of the United Nations meet those of its member states in the pursuit of the common goal of peace and security.' See also Maziar Jamnejad and Michael Wood, 'The Principle of Non-Intervention', *Leiden Journal of International Law* 22 (2009), 345. The ICJ recognized non-intervention as a customary law principle in *Nicaragua* v. *US*, para. 245.

[28] 1945 United Nations Charter, Art. 4(1).

[29] Ulrich Fastenrath, 'Article 4', in *The Charter of the United Nations: A Commentary*, Bruno Simma, Daniel-Erasmus Khan, Georg Nolte, and Andreas Paulus (eds.) (Oxford: Oxford University Press, 3rd edn. 2012), 348.

[30] Fastenrath, 'Article 4', 348.

[31] Hedley Bull characterizes peace to be a goal of the society of states, not universal and permanent peace, but rather 'the maintenance of peace in the sense of the absence of war among member states of international society as the normal condition of their relationship, to be breached only in special circumstances and according to principles that are generally accepted'. Hedley Bull, *The Anarchical Society* (New York: Columbia University Press, 4th edn. 1995), 17. Hence, it may be

the exceptions of individual and collective self-defence against an 'armed attack' and protection of others, in accordance with Article 51 and Chapter VII, Article 42, as an enforcement measure at the direction of the UN Security Council; it has also been interpreted to support humanitarian intervention and self-determination movements.[32] As pointed out by Mónica García-Salmones, 'The maxim of "peace through law" goes, structurally, hand in hand with the maxim of "war through law"'.[33] The exceptions, along with evolving notions such as the 'Responsibility to Protect' have resulted in divisions between the Western governments as opposed to Eastern and Southern governments which staunchly contest the legitimacy of these actions and call for strengthened respect for the principle of non-intervention. The fact that Africa has accepted humanitarian intervention within its constitutive act demonstrates a shift towards increased recognition of R2P theory, but the other regions remain sceptical.[34] Nevertheless, the struggle to uphold non-intervention as a fundamental principle of international law is emphasized within Latin America, Russia, and China.

4. The Debate within International Law on the 'Right to Peace'

To comprehend fully the role of peace in the context of international law, one must be aware of the historical controversies surrounding the question of whether there exists a *right to peace*. The UN Human Rights Council (as well as its predecessor, the UN Commission on Human Rights) has witnessed polarizing debates regarding a soft law initiative to articulate a right to peace. There is disagreement as to whether peace may constitute a right, juxtaposing the notion of a 'liberty right' (correlating with freedom) as opposed to a 'claim right' (correlating with the duty of another).[35] The scope of any such right is a topic of contention.

argued that the international community is torn between the notion that war is an institution of international society or that it is 'a pathological occurrence in international dealings, leading to utterly inhuman behavior'. See Antonio Cassese, Paola Gaeta, Laura Baig, Mary Fan, Christopher Gosnell, and Alex Whiting, *Cassese's International Criminal Law* (Oxford: Oxford University Press, 3rd edn. 2013), 63. It is notable that the realistic perspective appears to have ancient roots, as Fatiha Sahli and Abdelmalek El Ouazzani remark that 'For the Muslims, peace, in theory could not be permanent. It was limited in time and appears like a truce which could not exceed a period of ten years.' Fatiha Sahli and Abdelmalek El Ouazzani, 'Africa North of the Sahara and Arab Countries', in *The Oxford Handbook of The History of International Law*, Bardo Fassbender and Anne Peters (eds.) (Oxford: Oxford University Press, 2012), 402.

[32] See generally Oliver Corten, *The Law Against War: The Prohibition on the Use of Force in Contemporary International Law* (Oxford: Oxford University Press, 2012). See also *Nicaragua* v. *United States* case, in which the ICJ confirmed the right to self-defence as a rule of customary international law. See also Ben Kioko, 'The Right of Intervention under the African Union's Constitutive Act: From Non-interference to Non-intervention', *International Review of the Red Cross* 85 (2003), 807–26.

[33] Mónica García-Salmones, 'Walter Schucking and the pacifist traditions of international law', *European Journal of International Law* 22 (2011), 767.

[34] See Kioko, 'The Right of Intervention'.

[35] See Wesley Newcomb Hohfeld, *Fundamental Legal Conceptions as Applied in Judicial Reasoning: and Other Legal Essays* (Lenox, Mass.: HardPress, 2012).

Furthermore, there is a lack of clarity as to what extent the international community of states and non-state actors have obligations in relation to peace. There are significant divisions within policy and academia on this issue. There is a considerable amount of resistance among policymakers and academics to the notion of a 'right to peace'. In part this may be the legacy of the identification of peace as being aligned with communist ideology, or a fear of the potential of weakening the exceptions within the UN charter (self-defence and Chapter VII operations). This book seeks to diminish the aversion to the discussion of peace within legal forums and teaching institutions. We believe that legal studies have an important role to play in reorienting discussions and practice towards the direction of realizing inter- and intra-state peaceful objectives, without thereby advocating that there is a 'right' to peace.

In January 2013, the editors of this volume hosted a Nordic Expert Consultation on the Right to Peace at the University of Oslo.[36] Based on the consultation, we issued Recommendations on the Components of Peace, as we suggested that the term 'right to peace' may be replaced with 'components of peace'. This would be in keeping with the notion of peace as being a meta-right, a type of overarching entitlement where reference to related enforceable human rights are used to explain its scope (similar to other solidarity rights, such as the right to a clean environment and the right to development). We consider these recommendations to represent our conception of peace as promoted within this book, and therefore reiterate them here.

Components of Peace

1. States should promote the maintenance of peace by seeking to resolve their internal and international disputes in a non-violent manner and refraining from the threat or use of force against the territorial integrity or political independence of any state, in accordance with the UN Charter.
2. Structural violence is incompatible with peace. States should seek to eliminate inequality, exclusion, and poverty among and within states.

Preconditions for Peace

3. Peace is strengthened by the recognition that everyone is entitled to a social and international order in which they are able to enjoy human rights and fundamental freedoms without discrimination.
4. The illegal arms trade is a threat to peace and requires suppression in order to prevent the illegal use of force and violations of human rights and international humanitarian law. States should maintain strict and transparent control of the arms trade.
5. a. A safe, clean, and productive environment is conducive to peace and human security. States should preserve and protect the environment, based among others on the principle of sustainable and equitable use of natural resources, as well as other principles of international law.

[36] Cecilia M. Bailliet and Kjetil Mujezinović Larsen, 'Nordic Expert Consultation on the Right to Peace: Summary and Recommendations', *Nordic Journal of Human Rights* 31 (2013), 262–78.

b. States should consider the creation and promotion of peace zones and nuclear weapon free zones. The use of weapons that cause widespread and severe damage to the environment, in particular radioactive weapons and weapons of mass destruction, is contrary to international law. Such weapons must be urgently prohibited. States that utilize them have the obligation to prevent damage to the environment, and in case of unavoidable damage, to restore the previous condition of the environment.

Individual Participation in the Promotion and Safeguarding of Peace

6. Individuals, groups, institutions, transnational corporations, and non-governmental organizations have an important role to play and a responsibility in safeguarding peace. Everyone has the right, individually and in association with others, to promote and to strive for the realization of peace at the national and international levels. Individuals have the right to freely seek, obtain, receive, publish, or disseminate information to/from others on peace, human rights, and fundamental freedoms without censorship.
7. States should promote increased representation and participation of women at all decision-making levels in national, regional, and international institutions and mechanisms for the prevention, management, and resolution of conflict and peace processes.
8. a. Individuals have the right to conscientious objection and to be protected in the effective exercise of this right.
   b. Conscientious objectors and peace or human rights activists subject to well-founded fear of persecution on account of their actions or beliefs have the right to seek and to enjoy refugee status.

Protection of Victims of Breaches of Peace

9. All individuals share the same human dignity and have an equal right to protection. Nevertheless, there are certain groups in situations of specific vulnerability who deserve special protection from discrimination and effective remedies. Among them are children, victims of enforced disappearances or arbitrary detention, elderly persons, persons with disabilities, displaced persons, asylum seekers, migrants, refugees, indigenous peoples, and minorities.
10. Breaches of the peace result in displacement of individuals and groups. Persons shall have the right to seek and enjoy refugee status if they have fled their country or place of origin on account of a well-founded fear of persecution by State or non-State agents, on grounds of race, sex, religion, nationality, sexual orientation, membership in a particular social group, or political opinion; or because of a risk to life, security, or liberty on account of generalized violence, foreign aggression, internal conflict, massive violation of human rights, natural or human-made disasters, or other circumstances that seriously disturb public order.

Education on the Components of Peace

11. All individuals should receive education on human rights, fundamental freedoms, non-violent dispute resolution, and protection of the environment as components and preconditions of peace.

5. Overview and Delimitations

As explained above, this book seeks to bridge the gap between negative and positive peace research within the framework of international law. We discuss the relation between these two notions within the context of international legal regimes. We examine, inter alia, to what extent international and national normative instruments and institutions are oriented towards reducing violence. The normative frameworks that address the maintenance of peace and security are subject to dilemmas resulting from the emerging doctrine of the 'Responsibility to Protect', but they are also challenged by their mandates oriented towards the promotion and protection of social justice, human rights, and human dignity, etc. Hence, the contributions in this book are divided into four main parts.

Part 1 discusses the normative scope of peace and its exceptions. The chapters that are included here explain the background for the conception of peace in international law, and they address a number of fundamental normative expressions of peace in international law.

In Chapter 2, Kristoffer Lidén and Henrik Syse discuss the origins of a liberal, rights-based conception of peace in the political thought of Hobbes, Locke, and Kant. The chapter outlines how this conception plays out in contemporary perspectives on international law as a source of peace, with a view to the strands of realism, internationalism, and cosmopolitanism. It is demonstrated how the argument for widening the scope of peace in international law beyond the regulation of interstate warfare relates to a liberal cosmopolitan challenge to the Westphalian state system, as defended by internationalism. It also indicates why realists and internationalists would reject such a move and insist on subjecting concerns for peace to the principle of state sovereignty. The chapter does not provide a comprehensive overview of conceptions of peace in international law but focuses on a particular strand of political philosophy associated with 'the liberal peace'. Because this idea has been highly influential in the international politics of peace over the past decades, the argument serves as a vantage point for critical analysis of the presuppositions of contemporary legal debate on peace and conflict. While the argument could be misunderstood as implying that considerations on peace in international law should be limited to a liberal political outlook of a Western kind, the chapter invites responses from non-liberal and non-Western perspectives.

In Chapter 3, Cecilia M. Bailliet traces the evolution of the international law of peace from the notion of a 'right to peaceful coexistence' to the *de lege ferenda* initiative to recognize a 'human right to peace' within the UN Human Rights Council. The chapter seeks to explain why achieving universal normative clarity within international law remains a challenge and suggests that it might be beneficial to focus on institutions addressing the components and preconditions of peace.

Chapter 4, by Simon O'Connor and Cecilia M. Bailliet, addresses the character of the obligations in the UN Charter with respect to the maintenance of international peace and security as articulated in Articles 1(1), (2), and (3), and

Chapters VI and VIII. This contribution discusses the sequential nature of the Charter to emphasize the obligations, first and foremost, to resolve disputes peacefully and prevent escalation. The chapter presents the framework of UN Bodies, including the Security Council, General Assembly, and office of the Secretary-General and their practice in implementing these obligations. Additionally, it underscores the importance of recourse to these fora in pursuing negotiations between States and non-State actors. Finally, it delineates the role of regional mechanisms in enabling states to fulfil their primary duty of pacific settlement. It concludes by examining whether future implementation should be strengthened within existing UN and regional institutions addressing the pacific settlement of disputes.

In Chapter 5, Pål Wrange offers a critical, conceptual analysis of collective security, both in the current UN shape and as a general concept. The basic premise for the chapter is that even though collective security is a fundamental goal of the UN Charter, the collective security system is fraught with many political and practical problems. The chapter analyses a number of conceptual difficulties, but argues that these difficulties do not mean that collective security is impossible. The chapter asks whether collective security could be improved better to maintain international peace and security or if there is an inherent contradiction in the idea. The analysis is informed by critical traditions in international law and international relations.

In Chapter 6, Ola Engdahl discusses how peace, in its various connotations, may be achieved through the use of military force. Protection against grave violations of human rights may also require the use of military force, and the connection between international peace and security and the respect for human rights is evident in the practice of the UN Security Council. The concept of a 'Responsibility to Protect' has grown out of a need to protect against grave violations of human rights when the Security Council has not been able to respond. The ideas behind this concept may thus to some extent be described as emphasizing protection of human rights over the prohibition on the use of force—and the maintenance of peace between states. International law does not yet provide a right of states to intervene with military force in another state to protect against human rights violations without a mandate from the UNSC, and thus seems to value peace among states more highly than protection against human rights violations. This begs the question how respect for human rights contributes to the maintenance of peace and how peace contributes to the protection of human rights, and, in a longer perspective, whether one could exist without the other.

Part 2 continues to address five important preconditions of peace. While Part 1 also discusses both the negative and positive dimension of peace, the chapters in Part 2 are forced to address the links between positive and negative peace more directly. The issues that are covered—such as human rights, the environment, or development—are issues that are may be included in a positive conception of peace, but the authors also have to consider their impact on peace in the negative sense. The linkage between negative and positive peace is described as particularly complex in the chapter examining structural violence and the challenge of attaining development in countries undergoing violent conflict. The concept of human rights protection as a foundation of both negative and positive peace is thus explored. The section then turns to examining dispute resolution mechanisms within the context of reclamations for greater equity within world trade. In addition, the section explains the link between peace and other solidarity rights, such as the right to a clean environment and the pursuit of sustainable development. Finally, it discusses the regulation of the arms trade as a precondition for peace.

In Chapter 7, Kjersti Skarstad observes that a central premise and promise of human rights law is that the protection of human rights leads to more peaceful societies. Yet, in empirical conflict research, rights violations have for the most part not been seen as a relevant conflict risk factor. Also in the human rights literature it is unclear why and how violations possibly lead to a higher risk of violent civil conflicts. This chapter explains theoretically how human rights violations can potentially increase the risk of violent civil conflicts. It argues that human rights abuses serve as both conflict facilitators and conflict multipliers. It then demonstrates empirically that violations of basic economic and social rights and physical integrity rights increase the risk of civil war, while the effects of other civil and political rights are minor. The main implication of these results is that human rights policies and the enforcement of human rights law are well worth pursuing in order to reduce conflict risk.

In Chapter 8, Bård A. Andreassen addresses how the doctrine of 'structural violence' refers to violence where social structures, relations, and institutions threaten peoples' basic interests and needs. It is inherently related to social injustices and the failure to fulfil basic human rights The right to development discourse, as it developed in the late 1990s with reference to the UN Declaration on the Right to Development, provides a framework for analysing such structural violence from new perspectives that combine various types of rights in analysing social injustices, poverty, and 'failed development'. The chapter explores the argument that the main constraint on development may not be a poverty trap (i.e. that people living in poverty lack capacities and access to productive resources that can enable them to move out of poverty), but rather traps of violence that constrain development at both macro and micro levels. Lack of functioning legal structures and institutions for rights protection and public policies addressing poverty are important factors explaining the difficulties of escaping poverty.

In Chapter 9, Christina Voigt describes how the protection and preservation of the natural environment, integrity of ecological systems, and the survival of species are positive conditions for peace and human security. Given the interdependent and complex nature of the global environment, no state alone can effectively protect it. Rather, global cooperative efforts to reach significant concessions on states' sovereignty to exploit their natural resources are necessary in order to halt, reverse, and prevent environmental degradation. At the same time, environmental protection in order to be a foundation for peace should be aligned with eco-sensitive development needs as aptly expressed in the principle of sustainable development. International environmental law is the branch of international law that aims to translate these conditions in its design, institutions, and implementation. The author shows, however, that progress is slow, and that a shift in the quality of international laws is required: a shift that recognizes the fundamental importance of healthy ecological conditions. Such realization requires a new vision of international law and international relations, where a healthy environment is recognized as the foundation for peaceful human societies. This chapter gives an overview over the inter-linkages between environmental protection, sustainable development, and peace. It looks at the tools and means of international environmental law in this context and highlights the importance of multilateralism and global cooperation to address these issues. It further looks at the particular example of climate change and the multilateral efforts under the UN to establish a collaborative climate effort—based on global equity and sustainable development.

In Chapter 10, Ole Kristian Fauchald discusses the relationship between peace and trade. The chapter takes as its starting point a historical account of the relationship between trade and peace. Its focus is on the dispute settlement mechanism (DSM) of the WTO, which is initially considered in the light of the general link between the WTO Agreement and the level of conflict and tensions between and within states. The chapter finds that in cases concerning interstate conflicts or tensions, the DSM is likely to reduce them, and benefit smaller and weaker states. Conversely, where cases involve internal conflicts or tensions, the DSM is more likely to increase them, and benefit bigger and more powerful states. These conclusions are based on a study of cases registered with the DSM, as well as general assumptions regarding the regulatory and institutional framework of the WTO and regarding states' use of trade measures and the DSM.

In Chapter 11, Gro Nystuen and Kjølv Egeland evaluate the potential of the Arms Trade Treaty (ATT) to reduce violations of international humanitarian law and human rights law. The chapter assesses the process and outcome of the negotiations of the ATT, the first international instrument that makes an explicit link between arms export and its potential consequences in terms of violations of international humanitarian law and human rights law. The authors present the negotiation history of the ATT, comparing it to other recent treaty negotiations within humanitarian disarmament, and discuss the association between international law and peace studies. The main aim of the chapter is to present the ATT's provisions for regulating in which situations arms exports will be prohibited.

Part 3 is based on the editors' firm conviction that civil society plays an instrumental role in the pursuit and promotion of peace. This section underscores the significance of ensuring equal participation of racial/ethnic groups, refugees, and women in the promotion of peace; equality and non-discrimination are central principles in relation to peace, nevertheless there is great discrepancy between normative language and its actual implementation and enjoyment in practice.

In Chapter 12, Vibeke Blaker Strand discusses the relationship between human rights norms pertaining to equality and non-discrimination, and peace. The author argues that a society that is based on inequality and discrimination is not a society where people live peacefully together. It is not a society in peace. The term 'positive peace' rests on an understanding of peace that includes this broader picture, as it considers respect for human rights and social justice as components relevant to peace. Human rights norms on non-discrimination and equality can be seen as the twin of the notion of positive peace, the author argues, in that the aim behind these norms is not only to achieve formal equality, but substantive equality. The aim of the chapter is threefold. First, it explores the rich approach towards substantive equality that is embedded in international human rights conventions. This exploration involves both an individualistic approach towards substantive equality and a group-based approach. Secondly, it addresses some of the challenges that have been detected under the present international legal regime, and how the UN supervisory committees have responded to such challenges. The author argues that the path towards substantive equality is characterized by the UN supervisory committees' dynamic interpretation in order to strengthen and develop the protection against discrimination and inequality. Thirdly, the chapter draws links between the legal sphere and the political struggles that have been, and are being, fought in this field.

In Chapter 13, Maja Janmyr explores how refugeehood is intrinsically linked to various aspects of peace. First, as is evidenced by the definition of 'refugee', refugees may be seen as consequences of breaches of peace. Second, the grant of asylum is a peaceful and humanitarian act that should not be regarded as unfriendly by another state. Third, the linkage between refugees and (a lack of) peace is apparent in the reality in which refugee protection is deeply affected by greater security issues. Finally, the notion of peace is also relevant in discussions of durable solutions for refugees; repatriation, resettlement, and local integration all have the ultimate goal of allowing refugees to rebuild their lives in dignity and peace.

In Chapter 14, Cornelia Weiss analyses the state of inclusion of women as peacemakers, peacekeepers, and peacebuilders in law and practice. The chapter explores the status and effect of the Convention on the Elimination of All Forms of Discrimination Against Women and UN Security Council resolutions that address women peacemakers, peacekeepers, and peacebuilders. It investigates compliance measures and how they can be used. It addresses options to influence practice when the law does not. This chapter argues that the pursuit of peace is illusory without the inclusion of women.

Part 4 discusses the institutional implementation of peace, including 'peace through justice' institutions, such as international courts and truth commissions. What is the impact of dispute resolution mechanisms, in particular courts, on peace? What is the relationship between the pursuit of truth, justice, and accountability in the context of peace-building? The section also includes critical review of other institutional mechanisms including peacekeeping, fact-finding procedures, and returns to an examination of Kantian ideals within the context of constitutional forums. We consider whether there is a need to reform international and national institutions in order to improve the enforcement of protection standards relating to peace. The epilogue advocates peace education, characterized by UN Secretary-General as the road to peace.[37]

[37] Ban Ki-moon, 'International Day of Peace: Education for Peace', 21 September 2013, http://www.un.org/en/events/peaceday/2013/sgmessage.shtml (accessed 4 Nov 2014).

In Chapter 15, Kjetil Mujezinović Larsen discusses the notion of 'peace' in international peace operations with a mandate from the United Nations Security Council, and how international law promotes or prevents the achievement of such peace. The chapter shows that international peace operations generally pursue a 'liberal peace', and it shows how this general concept of peace is translated into concrete functions in particular operations. The chapter shows further that international law does little to promote peace through the creation of peace operations, since international law neither requires nor encourages such creation even though it is permitted. The chapter discusses further how international humanitarian law, international human rights law, and other regimes that regulate the conduct of personnel might contribute to the achievement of peace in peace operations.

In Chapter 16, Jemima García-Godos addresses national and international efforts of post-conflict reconstruction and reconciliation in societies emerging from armed conflict or authoritarian regimes. Such efforts place great emphasis on the need for accountability for past human rights violations. The assumption behind these efforts is that justice must be addressed if the goal is a stable, long-lasting peace. Based on a discussion of victims' rights and the links between justice and peace, this chapter argues that transitional justice is a constitutive element of positive peace because it contributes to rebuild relations of trust in post-conflict societies. The chapter addresses the main transitional justice mechanisms applied by countries seeking to establish some form of accountability for past violations: prosecutions, truth commissions, and victim reparations, providing examples from specific transitional justice experiences in Latin America.

In Chapter 17, Gentian Zyberi discusses the role and impact of international courts and tribunals in the promotion of peace. The author argues that maintenance and restoration of peace is an essential community interest, clearly embedded in both treaty and customary international law and pursued through different institutional mechanisms and procedures, including international courts and tribunals. Courts can play an important role in efforts aimed at maintaining or restoring interstate or intrastate peace, alongside existing non-judicial means and methods of settling disputes that could endanger international peace and security. By settling interstate disputes, advising international organizations, or investigating and prosecuting those most responsible for having committed mass atrocity crimes, these courts and tribunals can potentially create the necessary conditions for the normalization of relations between States or between affected parts of a society in a post-conflict situation. The chapter discusses the role and contribution of principal international courts and tribunals, which through their case law have developed and interpreted important aspects of the scope of relevant legal obligations incumbent upon states, international organizations, and individuals. Despite their potential and eventual contribution, past and recent history shows that the role of courts in maintaining or restoring peace remains limited. For that reason this chapter addresses not only possibilities, but also institutional and other limitations related to the activity of courts which affect their potential contribution to peace.

In Chapter 18, Cecilie Hellestveit discusses various types of international fact-finding mechanisms and assesses their role in the promotion of peace. This chapter relies on a stringent view of peace as a reflection of the absence of armed conflict. The author shows that international fact-finding mechanisms have gained ground as tools by which the international community responds to man-made emergencies that may threaten peace, but they give rise to a number of dilemmas. The chapter asks a number of crucial questions in this regard: 'Do international fact-finding mechanisms serve to bemoan violations of international law while concealing inadequacies in international law's ability to respond to armed conflict and serious human rights abuse? Or is fact-finding an increasingly decisive component in the architecture of the international law of peace and its ability to contain, alleviate and ease recovery from armed conflict, responding to the predicament of fact-finding as "a significant weapon in the armoury of world order"?'

In Chapter 19, Azin Tadjdini addresses the constitutional dimension of peace. The chapter begins with the Kantian theory on constitutions as a prerequisite for peace. Having established the significant role of constitutions in this regard, the chapter continues with an analysis of peace promoting and peace threatening features in contemporary and past constitutions. The author argues that if we agree that the aim of peace is respect for each and every human being we can more easily identify constitutional features that are detrimental to peace, as these features will not see each human being as an end in itself. The chapter considers particularly three features: comprehensive doctrines, constitutional inequality and weak protection of human rights, and the lack of control mechanisms for impositions by the state. It is argued that a human-centric rather than state- or sovereign-centric constitution will in this regard be a more effective peace-promoting constitution.

In an epilogue (Chapter 20), Maria Sommardahl advocates education for peace, characterized by the UN Secretary-General as 'the road to peace'. The chapter builds on the idea that education on the components of peace, which are discussed in the previous chapters, constitutes a pivotal part of the institutional implementation of peace. The chapter explores and suggests a tangible approach to education for peace and explains its importance for promoting peace. The chapter concentrates largely on different sources from the United Nations and international law that refers to the promotion of peace as to keep in mind the institutional mechanisms to foster peace.

Even with this range of chapters, it must be acknowledged that the book doesn't cover a number of other issues that are also relevant to the promotion of peace in either the negative or the positive sense. For example, the book does not analyse the law of peace agreements.[38] A more fundamental issue that is also omitted is the relationship between democracy and peace. It may be argued that a well-functioning democracy is a fundamental precondition for peace (taken together with economic interdependence and international cooperation to form

[38] For an analysis of peace agreements, see Christine Bell, *On the Law of Peace: Peace Agreements and the Law Pacificatoria* (Oxford: Oxford University Press, 2008) and Christine Bell, *Peace Agreements and Human Rights* (Oxford: Oxford University Press, 2000).

the Kantian triad), yet there is already an impressive amount of literature within the social sciences testing this principle.[39] Other issues omitted concern the international law of self-determination, secession, humanitarian law, disarmament, and the human rights of minorities and indigenous peoples. We selected papers in part based on topics raised at the Nordic Expert Consultation on the Right to Peace. We wish to emphasize to the reader that international law does not only promote peace through a topical and compartmentalized approach; it is international law as a *whole*, as a *system*, that promotes peace. The chapters in this book must be regarded as a representative exemplification of relevant areas of international law, without any claim on behalf of the editors that these are the only relevant areas of international law. Finally, the editors wish to offer this book as a call for a new consciousness to replace the dominant post-9/11 narrative of the 'War on Terror' within international law, instead seeking to revitalize the idea of promoting peace through international law.

[39] Examples of Democracy and Peace literature include Håvard Hegre, 'Democracy and Armed Conflict', *Journal of Peace Research* 51 (2014), 159–72, see also Margaret G. Hermann and Charles W. Kegley J., 'Democracies and Intervention: Is there a Danger Zone in the Democratic Peace?', *Journal of Peace Research* 38 (2001), 237; see also Christopher Layne, 'Kant or Cant: The Myth of the Democratic Peace' 19 (2) *International Security* 19 (1994), 5. On Trade and Peace, see Katherine Barbieri and Gerald Schneider, 'Globalization and Peace: Assessing New Directions in the Study of Trade and Conflict', *Journal of Peace Research* 36 (1999), 387, or Håvard Hegre, John R. Oneal, and Bruce Russett, 'Trade Does Promote Peace: New Simultaneous Estimates of the Reciprocal Effects of Trade and Conflict', *Journal of Peace Research* 47 (2010), 763.

PART I

THE NORMATIVE SCOPE OF PEACE AND ITS EXCEPTIONS

2

The Politics of Peace and Law

Realism, Internationalism, and the Cosmopolitan Challenge

*Kristoffer Lidén and Henrik Syse**

1. Introduction

After the radical setbacks of World Wars I and II, the institutionalization and expansion of international law through the United Nations and the radical decrease in the incidence of international war have allowed for increased optimism concerning the role of international law in promoting peace, in spite of setbacks at the time of writing.[1] This situation confronts us with the difficult choice of either bolstering this international peace by reinforcing the principle of state sovereignty, or using the peace as an opportunity for widening the scope of international law at the expense of national sovereignty. The latter alternative entails the redefinition of state sovereignty for the promotion of peace across state borders through multilateral collaboration. Which of the two alternatives better ensures the further spreading of peaceful relations between nations, groups, and individual human beings?

The answer to this choice—maybe it is even right to call it a dilemma—relies on our conception of the relationship between peace and international law in world politics. Two overarching conceptions have to a large extent framed debates on war and peace within modernity: international law as a *source* of peace, and international law as a *result* of peace. According to the former (*internationalist* and *cosmopolitan*) view(s), international law has the potential of limiting or even abolishing war by constraining the actions of states. According to the latter (*realist* or *instrumentalist*) view(s), the peace regulated by international law is merely political, reflecting a situation in which powerful countries see themselves better served by peace than war: as soon as this situation changes, international law will change

* Thanks to Claudio Corradetti and Reidar Maliks, as well as the editors and fellow authors, for helpful comments and suggestions.

[1] See the datasets in the PRIO Uppsala Conflict Data Program (UCDP) at http://www.prio.no/Data/Armed-Conflict/ (accessed 4 Nov 2014) for overviews of armed conflicts since World War II. By current 'setbacks' we have in mind the situations both between Russia and Ukraine and in the Middle East.

with it and war return. Realists therefore assume that if international law gets too restrictive in an attempt at bolstering the peace of a particular world order, it forces states that would be better served with a different order to rebel. According to this view, any attempt at restricting the sovereignty of states through international law is doomed to fail, or at least doomed to be very dangerous to the peace.

Albeit framed in terms of theory, this is where the contemporary debate on the interpretation and reformation of international law stands in practical terms, too. Within the UN and international law framework, the influence of internationalist and cosmopolitan views has been especially evident. Since the end of the Cold War, UN mandates have increasingly involved the promotion of peace within states through international collaboration in the name of international peace and security. This agenda is not confined to the case for 'humanitarian intervention', the establishment of the International Criminal Court, and the adoption of the 'Responsibility to Protect' by the UN. It is equally evident in related practices such as international peace operations in war-torn countries, international statebuilding efforts, and a radical expansion of humanitarian assistance. This development is reflected in propositions for redefining the concept of peace in international law as a *right* that pertains to individuals as well as states (see the discussion on this idea in Ch.1). Such a redefinition opens the way for new interpretations of existing law, potentially with wide-ranging implications.

In normative political theory, the idea of widening the scope of peace in international law beyond the laws of war and temporary peace treaties has a long history stemming back to Immanuel Kant's political writings and beyond.[2] Short of propositions for world government, contemporary reiterations span from proposals for obliging states to assist foreign peoples whose basic rights are violated (e.g. John Rawls's *The Law of Peoples* (1999)), to more revolutionary ideas of redefining the very premises of international law, as in David Held's work on 'cosmopolitan democracy'.[3]

These positions reflect frameworks of understanding that also figure in legal debate on more concrete issues of war and peace discussed throughout this book. Standard categories of international legal theory, such as legal positivism, natural law, formalism, and instrumentalism touch upon these frameworks. Yet, they are more immediately expressed in the positions of *realism, internationalism*, and *cosmopolitanism*.[4]

[2] Prominent examples are Dante Alighieri's idea of a world monarchy in *On Monarchy* (1309–13), Abbé de Saint-Pierre's notion of a world federation in *Project for Making Peace Perpetual in Europe* (1713), and Immanuel Kant's *Toward Perpetual Peace* (1795).

[3] John Rawls, *The Law of Peoples* (Cambridge: Harvard University Press, 1999), David Held, *Democracy and Global Order: From the Modern State to Cosmopolitan Governance* (Cambridge: Polity, 1995). For an overview, see Catherine Lu, 'World Government', in *The Stanford Encyclopedia of Philosophy*, Edward N. Zalta (ed.) (Autumn 2012). See also sect. III of Amanda Perreau-Saussine, 'Immanuel Kant on International Law', in *The Philosophy of International Law*, Samantha Besson and John Tasioulas (eds.) (Oxford: Oxford University Press, 2010).

[4] For an introduction to these positions, see Nigel Dower, *The Ethics of War and Peace* (Cambridge: Polity, 2009).

In this chapter we will explore some of the philosophical underpinnings of these views, with a special focus on what James Turner Johnson has called 'the quest for peace': those views that aspire to create the right preconditions for the cessation and absence of armed conflict.[5] We will do so in two steps. First, we will take one step back from these contemporary positions, investigating their philosophical origins in early modern political philosophy, specifically in the writings of Thomas Hobbes, John Locke, and Immanuel Kant. (The exposition of Kant's idea of perpetual peace is quite brief and limited, though, as Kant's views are presented and discussed in later chapters). We argue that the way in which these thinkers recast previous contributions to international law is essential to the understanding of how international law is currently practiced. Against this background, we turn in the second part to the question of how these ideas from early modern political thought are reflected in the three contemporary positions already noted—realism, internationalism, and cosmopolitanism—on the role of international law in promoting peace.

Our argument aims to show how an *individual-centred conception of rights*, as contrasted with a more collectivist conception of peace and order, has played a crucial role in what we might call the 'liberal philosophy of peace' within modernity. This has resulted in a justification of political authority and the sovereign state that focuses on the protection of the rights of its citizens. As long as the state or collective is conceived as vital in this regard, such a philosophical underpinning reinforces support for state sovereignty through international law. However, if one assumes that the power and potential of the state to protect peace, order, and rights are waning and that strengthened international collaboration is required for protecting the rights of individual citizens worldwide, an adjustment of the principles of international law follows as a logical consequence.

A comprehensive account of the philosophical origins of peace in international law would obviously include an emphasis on the centuries before and after the seventeenth and eighteenth, as well. By concentrating on this period, we nonetheless highlight the emergence of a way of thinking normatively about war and peace that has been highly formative, while often remaining in the shadows of other theoretical debates, such as the one between an internationalism inspired by Hugo Grotius on the one hand and legal positivism inspired by a certain reading of Thomas Hobbes on the other. Indeed, the chapter does not provide a comprehensive account of philosophical positions on peace in international affairs, which would for instance include Marxist, non-Western, and explicitly religious perspectives. Instead, it concentrates on influential strands of Western political thought with global repercussions, inviting contrasting perspectives from other philosophical traditions.

[5] James Turner Johnson, *The Quest for Peace* (Princeton: Princeton University Press, 1987).

2. The Logic of the Law: From the Reason of the State to the Reason of the Citizen

2.1 Peace or war?

Let us commence with a very simple, yet immensely complex question: Should law and politics aim to facilitate war or peace?

In philosophy, the question is, literally, ancient. It preoccupied several of the Greek philosophers, surfacing poignantly in the opening to Plato's longest dialogue, the *Laws*, where one dialogue partner, Critias, insists that good laws ought to be instituted with a view to fighting war. The Athenian Stranger, the most prominent dialogue partner of Critias, answers that the ultimate aim of the city's laws should be peace. It is indeed this Athenian Stranger who goes on to describe the laws he envisages as the best available to an actually existing city-state. Thus, we are made to understand that even the militaristic and austere laws presented to us are meant to live up to his ideal: *They are meant to serve peace, not war.* To wit, the Athenian Stranger conspicuously places courage lower than the other virtues, since the art of war must be subservient to the requirements of moderation, prudence, and justice—a critical stab at the notion that laws should serve war rather than peace.[6]

A consistent and unequivocal definition of political peace is arguably not offered to us in Plato or his student Aristotle, yet both contrast peace to the incessant competition and strife of war and thus portray it as a harmony befitting human beings. Hence, peace is not only the cessation of hostilities, but a kind of togetherness that finds its ultimate realization in the harmonious city-state or in harmonious relations between city-states. Presumably, and at its best, peace makes that highest of human activities, philosophy, possible, even if any city—even the most philosophical one—must be prepared for war and be able to fight war well.[7]

This idea that peace is the aim of laws specifically and politics more generally is found among several pre-modern thinkers, not least within early and medieval Christianity, the most famous and influential example being Augustine of Hippo in the early fifth century. For Augustine, peace is that which all human beings strive for—actually and ideally. The peace we can create between human beings in this world is a reflection of the eternal peace we long for as creatures of God.[8]

What we will emphasize here is a crucial turning point in early modern political philosophy, which weds this ancient and Christian ideal of peace as the

[6] See Gregory M. Reichberg, Henrik Syse, and Endre Begby (eds.), *The Ethics of War—Classic and Contemporary Readings* (Oxford: Blackwell, 2006), 18–30, with passages from Plato, *Laws* (most importantly 628c–e); see also Karl Trampedach, *Platon, die Akademie, und die zeitgenossische Politik* (Stuttgart: Frank Steiner, 1994), 172, 251.

[7] See passages from Aristotle's *Politics*, bk. VII, in Reichberg, Syse, and Begby (eds.), *The Ethics of War*, 41–4.

[8] See Reichberg, Syse, and Begby (eds.), *The Ethics of War*, 70–90.

highest goal with the emerging idea of the 'natural rights of man', the latter being closely related to—some would say almost synonymous with—what we today know as human rights. The notion of human beings as holders of rights is arguably quite old, manifesting itself in both Roman jurisprudence and medieval Canon Law. However, the idea that human beings are *born* with certain rights, and that these form the starting-point as well as the rationale of political society, rather than society being, politically speaking, primary, with individual rights coming thereafter, does not emerge fully until the seventeenth century. It is an idea that we find, for instance, in the argument of Hugo Grotius in *On the Laws of War and Peace* (1625), but which comes into full bloom in Thomas Hobbes and John Locke.[9]

For the purposes of this chapter and this book, it is exactly the nexus between *peace, law,* and *individual rights* that is of special interest. We believe it can serve as a fitting introduction to the idea of a legally regulated peace, based on an idea of the individual as both rights-holder and focal point of political justice. This analysis, focusing on Thomas Hobbes and John Locke, two of the most prominent and influential political philosophers of the seventeenth century, should help us clarify the philosophical groundwork for an idea that links ideas of rights and peace closely together.

2.2. Thomas Hobbes: a right to live in peace?

Thomas Hobbes is famous for his notion of a 'right of nature', and indeed for letting that idea serve as the most basic building block of what becomes known in the tradition of political thought as the 'social contract'.

For Hobbes, right of nature (*ius naturale*) means what modern legal scholars often call 'subjective right', meaning a right that someone *has*, as opposed to a system of right to which someone *belongs* (which we would then, in legal-philosophical terminology, call 'objective right'). Hobbes describes this subjective right thus:[10]

> The right of nature, which writers commonly call jus naturale, is the liberty each man hath to use his own power as he will himself for the preservation of his own nature; that is to say, of his own life; and consequently, of doing anything which, in his own judgement and reason, he shall conceive to be the aptest means thereunto.

He follows up with his famous definition of liberty:

> By liberty is understood, according to the proper signification of the word, the absence of external impediments; which impediments may oft take away part of a man's power to do what he would, but cannot hinder him from using the power left him according as his judgement and reason shall dictate to him.

[9] For relevant passages from Grotius, see Reichberg, Syse, and Begby (eds.), *The Ethics of War*, 387–92.

[10] The following passages from *Leviathan* can be found in Reichberg, Syse, and Begby (eds.), *The Ethics of War*, 446. The cited version has removed the capitalizations and emphases found in Hobbes's original text.

This leads Hobbes to his description of the laws of nature:

> A law of nature, lex naturalis, is a precept, or general rule, found out by reason, by which a man is forbidden to do that which is destructive of his life, or taketh away the means of preserving the same, and to omit that by which he thinketh it may be best preserved. … And because the condition of man … is a condition of war of every one against every one, in which case every one is governed by his own reason, and there is nothing he can make use of that may not be a help unto him in preserving his life against his enemies; it followeth that in such a condition every man has a right to every thing, even to one another's body. And therefore, as long as this natural right of every man to every thing endureth, there can be no security to any man, how strong or wise soever he be, of living out the time which nature ordinarily alloweth men to live. And consequently it is a precept, or general rule of reason: that every man ought to endeavour peace, as far as he has hope of obtaining it; and when he cannot obtain it, that he may seek and use all helps and advantages of war. The first branch of which rule containeth the first and fundamental law of nature, which is: to seek peace and follow it. The second, the sum of the right of nature, which is: by all means we can to defend ourselves.

In his own time and later, Hobbes exerted significant influence on other thinkers with this idea of the grounding of the state in essentially individual rights, although he, as is well known, reaches an authoritarian conclusion to his argument, namely, that each individual must *surrender* his right and donate the full plenitude of power to the sovereign. This subjection of the liberty of citizens to political power serves an ultimate goal, however, which is the peace and safety of the commonwealth *and of every person in it*. Indeed, and as one of the authors of this article has claimed elsewhere, Hobbes's laws of nature are essentially *rules of peace*, peace being the absence of war or imminent war, and thus a state where no one has to live in continual fear for his or her life. These rules are meant to protect the individual, not the state.[11]

The historical backdrop to Hobbes's political philosophy, as it was to the philosophy of so many legal, theological, and political thinkers of his time, was the extreme unrest and violence of civil war, stirred, in Hobbes's view, by seditious religious and political doctrines, which encouraged opposition to the commonwealth and its laws. The right of every person to defend his life and liberty is basic to all human beings, but it must be given up by each individual and handed over to the sovereign in order to create a state of peace.

What *is* peace, then? In Hobbes's philosophy, as already indicated, peace consists in personal safety, societal security, and the absence of war (not least evident in the first book of his earlier work *De Cive*). War is the continual strife or readiness for strife that is created by a host of human passions, pride and fear foremost among them. By coming together through a social contract, whereby the right of nature to defend oneself according to one's own will and perception is given up, the commonwealth is created and peace is secured.

[11] See Henrik Syse, *Natural Law, Religion, and Rights* (South Bend, Ind.: St Augustine's Press, 2007), ch. 5, with reference to, *inter alia*, Norberto Bobbio, *Thomas Hobbes and the Natural Law Tradition* (Chicago: University of Chicago Press, 1993).

It can be useful to note here that in Hobbes's contemporary, Baruch de Spinoza, peace is understood somewhat differently, namely, as a *virtue* which comes from the mind and which creates harmony both within a human being and between human beings (see ch. 5 of his *Political Treatise*).[12] Much of the structure of Spinoza's argument, though, is similar to Hobbes's: namely, the natural rights of individuals to liberty must be *coordinated* and to a certain extent given up in order to safeguard that which is the aim of the state and thus the aim of the multitude of individuals, namely, peace and harmony rather than war or strife. Thus, proper civil peace builds on the *right* of individuals, even if peace per se is a virtue as much as it is a right.

In the kind of natural-rights liberalism instituted by Hobbes (and to a certain extent paralleled by Spinoza), political authorization comes from the individual, by nature. The argument is that fear, aggression, pride, and competition make it impossible for individuals to utilize their natural authority in their capacity as individuals without thereby also facilitating and performing actions that are—especially upon accumulation—*not* conducive to peace and thus not in the self-interest of those self-same individuals. Therefore, laws must be instituted that check the destructive forces leading to conflict. These laws, the most important of which Hobbes terms laws of nature, help build lasting peace through coordination, concord, and authority. This authority, however, is no more or less than the practical workings of individual right arranged in a particular form of unison.

This leads us to our central claim: At the root of the modern natural-rights and social-contract tradition, so important to the development of modern liberalism and by extension liberal internationalism—and further liberal cosmopolitanism—lies the basic ambition to avoid war, and to use laws based on the right of the individual to create and maintain peace. Human beings have a right to live peacefully, safely, and securely, and it is only when peace, safety, and security are being threatened that they may rightly rebel and use violent force. Hence, individual right comes before the state, and the state's sanctity is based on the right of the individual to live in peace.

What we do *not* find in Hobbes is a conscious utilization of the same framework for the purposes of international law or international peace. As there exists no mechanism to erect a common sovereign between nations, according to Hobbes, a contract-based and rights-based peace is therefore elusive. However, Hobbes's immediate predecessor Grotius had envisaged rules of peace across borders, based on natural law and an accompanying idea of individual rights. Whether in Grotius's case the concept of natural law is *based on* individual rights in the same way as in Hobbes, is a matter of some contention. The precepts of natural law that inform his famous outline of laws of war and peace are arguably grounded just as much in an ideal of virtue and common humanity as in the natural rights of individuals—thus placing him closer to the medieval natural-law tradition, in spite of his well-known secularization of that tradition. Grotius is clear that individuals are holders of rights, which limit the power individuals can have over each other and the power a state can have over its people. The rules and limits applying to warfare, the pursuit

[12] Reichberg, Syse, and Begby (eds.), *The Ethics of War*, 451–3.

of peace, and other forms of conduct in the international sphere, however, come from a proper understanding of the laws of nature and the rightful limits to be placed upon human conduct due to moderation, prudence, and justice.[13]

Even so, Grotius also represents a part of the movement in modern political thought that links the rights of individuals to laws authorized and erected *to create peace*. It is thus the basic and natural right of the individual that (a) grounds the authority of the laws, and (b) binds the laws and its magistrates to function and act in a manner conducive to peace.

It is, of course, common to portray the difference between Hobbes on the one hand and Grotius and later thinkers such as Kant on the other as much more deep-seated than this, especially when it comes to International Relations theory, with Grotius and Kant representing precursors of liberal internationalism and Hobbes representing realism and an underlying positivism.[14] Their common root in a conception of peace linked to individual rights is then, however, overlooked. This particular amalgamation, of an individual right to live in peace on the one hand and an erection of authorities that are to secure that peace for the sake of individuals on the other, is quite radical and remarkable, and it is only our living at the receiving end of that tradition that dulls our realization of its radicalness. It arguably represents, in its philosophical roots, a clear contrast to a pure *raison d'état* realism. An analysis of John Locke and some strands of the eighteenth-century development of the social-contract tradition can help bring this out further.

2.3. John Locke: liberty in peace—or liberty over peace?

The reactions against Thomas Hobbes in his own time were many, swift, and fierce, both because of his seemingly authoritarian conclusion in arguing for the unmitigated power of the sovereign, and because of his radical description of man as originally free and under no law or morality except his own quest for peace and security.[15] Thus, Hobbes was in essence attacked from two opposite flanks: from those who found him too authoritarian, and those who found him too liberal and individualistic.

[13] The different views are represented by, among others, Perez Zagorin, who has argued strongly that Grotius's view is much more community- and natural law-based than that of Hobbes, and Andreas H. Aure who, building on Knud Haakonssen and others, has claimed that individual rights are at the heart of Grotius's doctrine; see Perez Zagorin, 'Hobbes without Grotius', *History of Political Thought* 21 (2000), 16–40; Andreas Harald Aure, 'Hugo Grotius—Individuelle rettigheter som naturrettens kjerne', in *Politisk filosofi—fra Platon til Hannah Arendt*, Jørgen Pedersen (ed.) (Oslo: Pax, 2013), 285–311; and Knud Haakonssen, *Natural Law and Moral Philosophy* (Cambridge: Cambridge University Press, 1996).

[14] Worth noting is not least Howard Williams's work on the relationship between Hobbes and Kant. In *Kant's Critique of Hobbes: Sovereignty and Cosmopolitanism* (Cardiff: University of Wales Press, 2013) he emphasizes the cosmopolitan character of Kant's philosophy and sees this as a criticism of the self-centredness and state-centric character of Hobbes's thought.

[15] For an interesting collection of reactions to Hobbes, see Samuel Mintz, *The Hunting of Leviathan: Seventeenth-Century Reactions to the Materialism and Moral Philosophy of Thomas Hobbes* (Cambridge: Cambridge University Press, 2010).

John Locke is often seen as answering many of the challenges of—and solving many of the problems in—Hobbes's philosophical construction, while sticking to Hobbes's conceptual basis: the rights of individuals. It is worth noting that Locke very rarely refers to the much-maligned Hobbes, and never debates with him directly. There are indeed many others whom he much more explicitly criticizes, among them, famously, the apologist for absolute monarchy Robert Filmer (who was, interestingly, one of Hobbes's main philosophical critics). Having said that, Hobbes and Locke together influence the way in which later philosophers of rights and peace—among them, Rousseau and Kant—would frame these very issues, and it is thus natural for our purposes to concentrate on Hobbes and Locke and the continuity between them. There is little doubt that Locke's discussion of war and peace, while constituting an implicit rebuttal of Hobbes, also in its way represents a continuation of Hobbes's teaching by stressing the role of civil society in fostering peace through a regulation of individual rights.

There seems, however, to be a crucial difference between the two.[16] By placing the emphasis on liberty rather than peace, Locke apparently departs from Hobbes's main aim of the state and of the law of nature, which was maintaining peace and avoiding war. In Locke, liberty appears to be placed above peace. Interestingly (one could almost say paradoxically), Locke does so by gainsaying the Hobbesian portrait of the state of nature as a state of war. Locke, like Hobbes, speaks of a state of nature—that is, the community of human beings before or outside of civil society and without a common sovereign, a popular hypothetical construct at the time (given practical credence by the discoveries of 'primitive' peoples in the Americas). However, unlike Hobbes, he holds the state of nature *not* to be equivalent to a state of war. Even in the state of nature, claims Locke, human beings will be able to understand and abide by certain basic laws of nature, such as the maintenance of peaceful relations and goodwill, by use of their reason. However, the general climate in the state of nature will be one of unpredictability and lack of security, since all must preserve their own freedom and safety as best they can. Thus, the instituting of a sovereign through a social contract represents a great improvement. The greatest problem of the state of nature is the lack of a commonly recognized arbiter: everyone must be his or her own judge and jury or, as Locke puts it, the executor of the law of nature, in cases of disagreement and conflict. Therefore, this mostly peaceful but unpredictable and conflict-prone situation is abandoned in favour of an organized, civil society in which the thing we all wish to protect, our liberty, is better safeguarded.

Hence, it seems that in Locke, as in much of modern liberalism, the social contract most essentially ensures liberty rather than peace per se. If liberty is not secured, men should 'appeal to heaven' (i.e. use armed force) rather than continue to live under tyranny. Thus, the right of self-defence in response to unlawful use

[16] See the excerpts from Locke's *Second Treatise of Government* in Reichberg, Syse, and Begby (eds.), *The Ethics of War*, 462–8.

of power by the political magistrate(s) is clear and absolute: citizens can defend themselves by means of force, if necessary.

It is worth noting, however, that for Locke, such a right of self-defence against governmental power is much preferable to the concentration of all power in one sovereign, since the need for using armed force will be much *reduced* once the rule of law actually guarantees individual liberty. By opening the door to armed rebellion, the chance of rebellion radically decreases, argues Locke. Whether this is primarily an argument about *peace* or *liberty* is thus a very real question. It seems that the protection of liberty leads to the predominance of peace.

Most important in our context is Locke's insistence that the basic right of nature is a right to be free from compulsion, and thus to enjoy life, liberty, and property *in peace*. This is a right that obtains also in the state of nature, hence, it also obtains between states, although Locke—like Hobbes—does not envisage a securing of this right through some kind of international federation. For Locke, it is not a question of liberty *or* peace, but rather an attempt at safeguarding both, since they are mutually reinforcing forces. The right to live in liberty is also a right to live in peace, because a regulated liberty removes the most basic reasons for resorting to violence.

No passage in Locke as clearly showcases this emphasis on freedom from compulsion and the right to enjoy one's life and property in peace, even in the state of nature, as his analysis of the rights of conquest and the difference between just and unjust wars in chapter 16 of the *Second Treatise of Government*. Here Locke forcefully argues against the view that the right of conquest in a just war is total and lasting, leading to the full submission of the conquered people and thus in essence a continued state of war between the two parties. For Locke, no such right exists, since the wives, children, and future generations even of the fighting forces and responsible individuals on the unjust side of a war *have the same right as all other human beings to enjoy their freedom and property without compulsion or invasion from external parties*. Thus, relations between human beings under law—even under the law of nature—are, ideally speaking, relations in peace, marked by the absence of physical compulsion or forceful appropriation of property. This is true as much between citizens of different commonwealths as between citizens of the same commonwealth.

Thus, we are really confronted with a *basic, individual right to peace* as much as a basic right to liberty—or, rather, we have the two seen as parallel basic rights. Over the centuries, this conception of peace has been integrated in liberal political thought to the extent that it is often taken for granted as the objective meaning of peace within states. As we will see, it also figures centrally in debates on international peace, challenging the state-centric outlook of realism and non-liberal strands of internationalism, to which we will return.

This 'liberal peace' of Locke is, admittedly, mainly what modern theorists would call a *negative* peace: an absence of physical force or compulsion beyond whatever is necessary for the defence of liberty and property. Underlying this conception of peaceful relations as an absence of unlawful physical force, however, is an ideal of the equality of what Locke calls the 'native right' of all human beings—that is, a birthright to be respected as an individual person without being subject to arbitrary, physical compulsion. This negative conception of the liberal peace is therefore intrinsically linked to positive conceptions of how these rights are to be attained, namely, through peaceful cooperation.

2.4. Towards Kant's perpetual peace

When, in the century following Hobbes and Locke, thinkers such as Montesquieu, Rousseau, and Kant build on the notion of rights and law from seventeenth-century liberalism, they maintain the link between the equal right to freedom on the one hand and a basic right to a secure and predictable peace on the other.

In all their internal diversity, these thinkers insist that states must *work together* to avoid the constant danger of warfare. Based on the idea that even a state of war does not hand to the one side in war an arbitrary right over all subjects on the other side—which holds true even in the case of total victory in a just war—they gradually develop the idea of a set of rules or an organization of states or peoples that can, based on principles of right, reduce the danger of mass bloodshed and oppression brought by warfare. Such an organizing principle or federation could in the long run make it possible for different nations or peoples to live in peace, based on mutual respect for each other's rights and integrity, not only as states, but also as individuals. Indeed, the important point, especially evident in Kant's plan for a lasting ('perpetual') peace, is the fact that these rights are not primarily sovereign or state's rights. The existence of such rights had in many ways been the main point of the Westphalian system and remains the cornerstone of modern internationalism. However, in the argument and line of thinking we are exploring here, they are to a much larger extent *human* rights that individuals hold qua individuals.

Kant proposes to limit warfare first by committing states to a set of criteria including non-intervention, disarmament, and the honouring of peace treaties. On the basis of such a 'negative peace', he prescribes the building of a more stable 'positive peace', consisting of three domains of public law—domestic, international, and cosmopolitan: First, states shall adopt a liberal (or in Kant's terminology, republican) constitution. This is relevant because he regards republics as being less inclined to resort to war, because the individuals in them will have a say—indeed, a right—in deciding matters of war and peace, which will make war less likely. Second, international law shall be based on a federation of free states. This is not a world republic to which the states subject their sovereignty, but a voluntary arrangement of mutual interest to sovereign states. Third, states shall commit themselves to 'universal hospitality', that is, to allow for people to move freely across state borders.[17] This is the cosmopolitan component of his

[17] Immanuel Kant, 'Toward Perpetual Peace', in *Immanuel Kant: Practical Philosophy,* Mary J. Gregor (ed.) (New York: Cambridge University Press, 1996 [1795]). See also Reichberg, Syse, and Begby (eds.), *The Ethics of War*, 518–41. For instructive discussions on the interpretation of Kant's proposition, see Perreau-Saussine, 'Immanuel Kant on International Law', Georg Cavallar, 'Kantian

proposal. As we shall see, cosmopolitans today would regard this as too timid a proposal for cosmopolitan law as it represents a very limited obligation of states towards the citizens of foreign countries.[18] Yet, in his times, such a preoccupation with the welfare of foreigners was associated with the kind of interventionism and occupation that sparked international war. Furthermore, his proposition is not supposed to solve all problems in one go, but to lay the basis for a historical process towards the goal of perpetual peace. (For further elaboration on Kant's proposition, see Ch. 19.)

Arguably, the core idea running from Hobbes through Kant, in spite of all the diversity between these individual thinkers and their ideas about practical politics, is the idea of individual rights based on the original freedom of the individual human being combined with the natural right and inborn wish to live in peace. Rather than subsuming the individual under the state, and building a system built squarely on state's rights, the foundation of the eighteenth-century Kantian version of liberalism, with roots in the seventeenth-century ideas of thinkers such as Hobbes and Locke, is the right of each individual to live in a state of ordered liberty, and to have this liberty secured through a predictable and stable peace. What divides the thinkers of this tradition is, therefore, not their basic conception of peace as an individual right but their understanding of what it takes to secure this right through the organization of domestic and international relations. In this respect, their prescriptions for international peace represent different propositions for the universalizing of the liberal peace.[19]

To sum up, seventeenth- and eighteenth-century liberalism can be said, at its very root, to formulate a concern for individual rights that leads to arrangements for the creation of long-term peace (or, at the very least, a lower likelihood of war). Hence, we find a philosophical groundwork for a connection between the individual on the one hand and international order on the other, based on an idea of the necessity and primacy of peace for the securing of human wellbeing and flourishing.

Perspectives on the Democratic Peace: Alternatives to Doyle', *Review of International Studies* 27 (2001), 229–48, and Howard Williams, *Kant and the End of War* (Basingstoke: Palgrave, 2012). See also Michael W. Doyle, *Ways of War and Peace: Realism, Liberalism and Socialism* (New York: W. W. Norton, 1997), 251.

[18] Jürgen Habermas, 'Kant's Idea of Perpetual Peace: At Two Hundred Years' Historical Remove', *The Inclusion of the Other: Studies in Political Theory* (Cambridge, Mass.: MIT, 1998), 180–1.

[19] Richard Tuck argues that Hobbes has his notion of the state of nature from theories about the relations between states. Furthermore, he argues that when Kant applies the notion of moral autonomy to individuals as a basic premise of his moral and political philosophy, he similarly adopts it from political debates on the autonomy of states. These observations take the opposite direction of 'the domestic analogy', in which the character of states and their interrelations is derived from the relations between individuals in a society. (Richard Tuck, *The Rights of War and Peace: Political Thought and the International Order from Grotius to Kant* (Oxford: Oxford University Press, 1999) at chs. 4, 7). While valuable, this observation does not gainsay the thesis that political authority within this tradition is justified from the bottom up (i.e. from individuals to the state) rather than the other way around.

3. Peace and International Law

The theoretical groundwork of modern liberalism from the seventeenth and eighteenth centuries still plays a role in informing our views about peace and rights today. However, the theorization itself has moved on and has, as stated in the introduction, seen three main positions emerging: realism, internationalism, and cosmopolitanism. Let us now look at the theoretical underpinnings of those views, bearing in mind that the dividing lines between them are not absolute.

3.1. Realism

Realists argue that the lack of a sovereign authority above the state leaves the relations between states as a state of nature, or anarchy, in which no laws abide.[20] As laws have no power or morality of their own, and no supreme legal authority exists on the international scene, the binding force of laws relies on the political power of the states upholding them.[21] The common claim underlying this wide-ranging and diverse tradition is this: Political entities such as the Greek city-state, the medieval kingdoms, and the modern state competed (or still compete) for survival in a perpetual struggle of all against all. An idealistic reliance on a harmony of interests among states or on the benevolence and promises of adversaries rather than on one's own power or that of one's alliance partners is seen as a path to self-demise.[22] On these premises, peace agreements and alliances between states are only military strategic manoeuvres in the struggle for survival, and cannot themselves transform the nature of these relations into a qualitatively more peaceful condition. International law will then only be a continuation of war by other means—the weapon of the stronger—upheld by powerful states as long as it serves their self-interest.[23] International peace, according to this view, does not rest on law or right(s) as such.

This does not mean that realists ignore the role of law in international affairs. Laws facilitate the rule of predominant powers as long as a particular balance of power allows for it. E. H. Carr observes how hegemonic states tend to bolster their position

[20] Prominent contributions to this view in legal theory include John Austin, *The Province of Jurisprudence Determined* (London: Weidenfeld & Nicolson, 1954 [1832]); Carl Schmitt, *The Nomos of the Earth in the International Law of the Jus Publicum Europaeum* (New York: Telos, 2003 [1950]). In international relations theory, realist classics include Hans J. Morgenthau, *Politics among Nations: The Struggle for Power and Peace* (4th edn. New York: Knopf, 1967 [1948]); Edward Hallett Carr, *The Twenty Years' Crisis 1919–1939: An Introduction to the Study of International Relations* (Houndmills: Palgrave, 2001 [1939]), ch. 16; Kenneth N. Waltz, *Man, the State and War: A Theoretical Analysis* (New York: Columbia University Press, 2001 [1959]); John J. Mearsheimer, *The Tragedy of Great Power Politics* (New York: Norton, 2001).

[21] While associated with the work of Hobbes, these presumptions draw on philosophical writings stretching back to Thucydides and Machiavelli, and are in various and internally diverging ways developed in the works of Hegel and Nietzsche amongst others. As we pointed out above, Hobbes arguably builds on more than a merely realistic/positivistic conception of power and power struggle, although it is true that he envisages no basis for a commonly regulated international peace.

[22] Carr, *The Twenty Years' Crisis*, ch. 5.

[23] Carr, *The Twenty Years Crisis*, 163.

by partly constraining their own power and partly favouring weaker parties through international law, often combined with appeals to universal moral principles.

Just as the ruling class in a community prays for domestic peace, which guarantees its own security and predominance, and denounces class war, which might threaten them, so international peace becomes a special vested interest of predominant Powers. In the past, Roman and British imperialism were commended to the world in the guise of the pax Romana and pax Britannica. Today, when no single Power is strong enough to dominate the world, and supremacy is vested in a group of nations, slogans like 'collective security' and 'resistance to aggression' serve the same purpose of proclaiming an identity of interest between the dominant group and the world as a whole in the maintenance of peace.[24]

In this view, the UN Charter reflects the interests of the prevailing Powers of WWII. When calls for further strengthening the liberal imprints of the Charter and lowering the threshold of non-intervention were made throughout the 1990s, it is interpreted as a reflection of the shifting balance of power after the Cold War. At the point where the US was left as the sole superpower, backed by NATO, it arguably lost the incentives for relying on international law and started challenging the authority of the UN with an alternative pax Americana.[25] This constitutes a very different story about the current momentum of international peace than the one professed by liberal internationalists and cosmopolitans.

One might wonder whether this realist outlook, in many ways influenced by Hobbes's understanding of the relationship between states, is at all compatible with the individual-centred conception of rights and peace that we find in the writings of early liberalism (including Hobbes!). It seems that the concern for individuals very easily drowns in the pursuit of state survival, and that the logical consequence for an individual-centred thinking is a rejection of the principle of state sovereignty altogether. Against the backdrop of civil war and sectarian strife, Hobbes, however, saw no other source of at least a relative peace for the citizens of states than uniting in support of a sovereign ruler, notably on the condition of getting security in return. This view was criticized by Rousseau, who recognized the radical impediments to individual peace caused by unmitigated war between Leviathans in perpetual conflict.[26] Yet, perhaps Hobbes was right in insisting on state sovereignty as the logical response to the conflicts of his times. As argued by Roland Paris in a different context, later liberal thinkers have tended to underestimate the reliance of political liberalization on the establishment of an effective state.[27] Hobbes would probably have feared that the universal ascription of liberty rights to citizens everywhere found in Lockean and Kantian liberalism might undermine the minimum of security for those selfsame citizens obtained through

[24] Carr, *The Twenty Years' Crisis*, 76, see also 78–9.

[25] See G. John Ikenberry, *Liberal Leviathan: The Origins, Crisis, and Transformation of the American World Order* (Princeton: Princeton University Press, 2011).

[26] Jean-Jacques Rousseau, *A Lasting Peace through the Federation of Europe and the State of War* (Gloucester, Mass. Dodo, 2009 [1756]).

[27] Roland Paris, *At War's End: Building Peace after Civil Conflict* (Cambridge: Cambridge University Press, 2004), ch. 2.

a reliance on the logic of state survival. Perhaps a parallel can be drawn to the way in which American politicians clung to a realist foreign policy throughout the Cold War in the name of liberal values. Faced with an existential threat, the security of the state was seen as a prerequisite for liberty.

The argument of Hobbes does not rule out the idea of states entering treaties conducive to the limitation of war. He might therefore have welcomed the UN as a desirable arrangement.[28] In the absence of a global Leviathan, he would nonetheless share in realist warnings against a one-sided reliance on the UN and other legal instruments in upholding or transforming the peace.

3.2. Internationalism

The quintessence of the internationalist position is the rejection of realist or 'instrumentalist' scepticism against the potential of law in promoting peace among nations.[29] Modern internationalism is associated with the work of Grotius and his followers, deriving international law from a set of universal principles pertaining to 'the morality of states'. Both Locke and Kant are associated with this tradition, as they arguably prescribe not the allegiance of citizens to the sovereignty of their state alone, but to the sovereignty of all states, as regulated by international law. Building on this basis, laws advancing peace through the regulation of the conduct of states are prescribed. As reflected in its reliance on just war doctrine, internationalism does not outlaw war altogether. War is seen as a necessary means to uphold state sovereignty and the international system, essentially through military self-defence or the collective sanctioning of outlaw states. War is, however, not the default relationship between states.[30] Here we clearly see echoes of Locke's position against a Hobbesian view of the nature of interstate relations.

In contemporary IR theory, the internationalist position finds empirical support among thinkers in the 'English school', with their emphasis on international politics as evolving within a 'society of states'. Hedley Bull, one of its central proponents, claims that anarchy among nations does not exclude the commitment by states to a common set of rules to their mutual advantage.[31] If states agree to a set of rules, like the Peace of Westphalia, violating these rules can be sanctioned by other countries without relying on a sovereign.[32] The most prominent current case for internationalism in IR is nonetheless represented by the 'democratic

[28] See Noel Malcolm's argument in *Aspects of Hobbes* (Oxford: Oxford University Press, 2002), 439–48.

[29] Hedley Bull, *The Anarchical Society: A Study of Order in World Politics* (London: Macmillan, 1977), 25. See also Dower, *Ethics of War and Peace*, 52–60.

[30] Bull, *The Anarchical Society*, 17–18.

[31] Bull, *The Anarchical Society*, 46–7. This rejection of the empirical premises of Hobbes's position is echoed in Charles R. Beitz, *Political Theory and International Relations* (Princeton: Princeton University Press, 1979), 35–50.

[32] This view finds support in rationalist, institutionalist, and constructivist strands of international relations theory. See Christian Reus-Smit, 'The Politics of International Law', in Christian Reus-Smit (ed.), *The Politics of International Law* (Cambridge: Cambridge University Press, 2004), 18–24.

peace thesis' of 'liberal internationalism', according to which the combination of democracy, trade, and international organization is seen as a recipe for peaceful relations among nations.[33] Here, it is primarily the domestic order of states rather than the relations between them that determines the international order. In its influential formulation by Michael Doyle, this idea is presented as a direct continuation of Kant's argument about perpetual peace.[34]

Internationalist positions such as that of 'democratic peace' do not insist that the 'morality of states' is always upheld. War, as already indicated, will still occur. Yet, while realists cite such violations as proof of the hollowness of the norms, internationalists regard the restoration of the norms in times of peace as proof to the contrary. It is not peace but war that is the exception that proves the rule on this account. Against this backdrop, the UN can be seen as a highly successful manifestation of the morality of states, returning from the horrors of WWII with a vengeance. The League of Nations does not then appear as the fiasco described by Carr, but as an invaluable though fallible step towards the eventual establishment of the UN. Combined with the individualist philosophy underlying the UN Universal Declaration of Human Rights, arguably the most important UN statement and document alongside the UN charter, we see how internationalism also picks up on the basic thrust of seventeenth-century rights theory, in holding a peaceful order to be at the service of—or at least intimately related to—the basic human rights of individuals. However, as we will see, it is another outlook that more fully sees itself as the heir of a philosophy centred on the rights of individuals rather than the rights of states.

3.3. The liberal cosmopolitan challenge

In spite of coming across as naively idealistic to realists, the internationalist outlook is challenged by liberal cosmopolitans for not being sufficiently ambitious in promoting peace and human rights. These critics draw their inspiration from the same basic idea of individual rights from which Locke and Kant derived their support for internationalism, and argue that international laws protecting the rights of states rather than individuals are inconsistent with this outlook.[35] Echoing his influential argument against unmitigated state sovereignty,[36] former UN Secretary-General Kofi Annan writes in his memoirs:

> For far too long, the UN had been considered the sole prerogative of states and their representatives. ... From my first days in office, I reminded the heads of state that the first

[33] Bruce M. Russett and John R. Oneal, *Triangulating Peace: Democracy, Interdependence, and International Organizations* (New York: Norton, 2001).

[34] Michael W. Doyle, 'Kant, Liberal Legacies, and Foreign Affairs, Part I', *Philosophy & Public Affairs* 12 (1983), 205–35.

[35] See Thomas Pogge, 'Cosmopolitanism and Sovereignty', *Ethics & International Affairs*, 103 (1992), 48–75; Simon Caney, *Justice Beyond Borders: A Global Political Theory* (Oxford: Oxford University Press, 2005); Toni Erskine, *Embedded Cosmopolitanism: Duties to Strangers and Enemies in a World of 'Dislocated Communities'* (Oxford: Oxford University Press, 2008).

[36] e.g. Kofi Annan, 'Two Concepts of Sovereignty', *The Economist* 352 (18 Sept. 1999), 49–50.

words of the UN Charter did not refer to them—indeed, they were written in the voice of 'We the Peoples.' ... Instead of leading an organisation dedicated to the governments of the world, I would put the individual at the center of everything we did. ... A United Nations for the twenty-first century would have to create new partnerships, respond to the needs of individuals, and stand for the principle that national sovereignty could never be used as a shield for genocide or gross violations of human rights. It would have to advance a much broader view of security that integrated peace, development, women's empowerment, and human rights if it were to address successfully the challenges of a global age.[37]

From an individual-centric cosmopolitan view, international war is only one among many threats to human peace to be addressed by international law. Other threats include civil war, genocide, violent state repression, and terrorism. If the definition of peace is expanded to include the absence of all forms of organized violence, then issues such as criminal violence (for instance related to drugs and trafficking), police violence, and targeted political killings should also be included. This engagement is reflected in calls for redefining international peace and security in the names of human security and a human right to peace.[38]

Such concerns are admittedly also central to a state-centric conception of international politics. The difference is, however, that the state-centric outlook would refer such concerns to the domestic jurisdiction of states. From an internationalist perspective, the threat to state sovereignty posed is more pertinent than other forms of organized violence because it threatens the very foundations of international order.

It is presupposed by the internationalist that: (1) bolstering the status quo is the best way to hinder the outbreak of massive international war, and (2) the costs of such war exceed the benefits of reforming the system in order to address other threats to individual peace.

Yet, as seen from the brutalities of the twentieth century, the international state system is not always conducive to or a source of peace, and no sensible internationalist would bet her life on the survival of the UN system even 20 years from now. Hence, while the cosmopolitan challenge is associated with concerns for non-conventional threats to peace, the strongest argument for the cosmopolitan position questions the first presupposition of the internationalist regarding international war. Turning his attention from the current unprecedented international peace to the potential horrors of the future, Thomas Pogge writes:

In the existing global order, interstate rivalries are settled ultimately through military competition, including the threat and use of military force. Moreover, within their own territories, national governments are free to do virtually anything they like. Such governments therefore have very powerful incentives and very broad opportunities to develop

[37] Kofi Annan, *Interventions: A Life in War and Peace* (London: Penguin, 2012), 12–13.

[38] Various aspects of this cosmopolitan agenda are discussed throughout the chapters of this book. See Ch. 1 for an account of the idea of a human right to peace and how it relates to a notion of 'positive peace'.

their military might. This is bound to lead to further proliferation of nuclear, biological, chemical and conventional weapons of mass destruction. And in a world in which dozens of competing governments control such weapons, the outbreak of devastating wars is only a matter of time.

One might object that this problem is currently being handled through international treaties, sanctions, and the threat of military reaction under a Chapter VII mandate. However, Pogge does not trust that the current international institutional set-up is capable of hindering the outbreak of future war between states, premised as it is on state sovereignty and the veto of the permanent members of the UN Security Council.

It is unlikely that national control over weapons of mass destruction can be abolished within the existing world order—through a disarmament program that relies upon the voluntary acceptance and compliance of each and every national government, for example. The continuation of this order would thus probably lead to more and more national governments gaining the capacity to trigger a major catastrophe, and possibly to attempts by some pre-eminently to disarm others. Nonproliferation and gradual abolition of weapons of mass destruction presuppose a substantial centralization of authority and power at the global level—in violation of the prevalent idea of state sovereignty.[39]

Here, Pogge takes a somewhat realist-oriented view in not trusting current international law as a reliable measure against future international war. Yet, instead of thereby prescribing 'realist' measures of national self-preservation or benevolent hegemony as sources of peace, he proposes how the international system could be altered in order to reduce the incentives and opportunities for states to resort to war while also making the system more just.

It is the centralization of political authority involved in such cosmopolitan solutions, involving a further distancing of sovereign authorities from their subjects and the likelihood of merely replacing international with civil war, which led Hobbes, Locke, and Kant to non-cosmopolitan conclusions in spite of such a centralized global authority being a possible—some would say obvious—response to the problem of war between states. Contemporary proponents of cosmopolitanism such as Pogge argue, however, that the current world order is of a different kind than the world known to Hobbes, Locke, Kant, and their contemporaries: It is (1) a kind in which the capacity of states to protect their peoples without relying on binding international collaboration is reduced, hence making cosmopolitan law more *desirable*, and (2) a kind in which states already are united through the UN and an extensive web of other international institutions, making a collective decision to commit to and uphold cosmopolitan law more *realistic*. This combination of global challenges and a global governance apparatus associated with 'globalization' is cited as an important argument against the internationalist account of world politics.[40]

[39] Thomas Pogge, *World Poverty and Human Rights* (Cambridge: Polity, 2002), 182. The quoted chapter is based on his 'Cosmopolitanism and Sovereignty'.

[40] David Held, *Democracy and the Global Order*, and *Cosmopolitanism: Ideals and Realities* (London: Polity, 2010); Ulrich Beck, *Power in the Global Age: A New Global Political Economy*

Most contemporary cosmopolitans do not reject the state system altogether, however, but argue in favour of making state sovereignty conditional on the protection of the human rights of their citizens and the promotion of peace and human rights abroad, especially through active support of international institutions dedicated to this purpose.[41] The 'Responsibility to Protect' doctrine exemplifies this *solidarist* approach, balancing between internationalism and full-blown cosmopolitanism.[42] While associated with a weakening of state sovereignty, solidarism entails efforts at *strengthening* sovereign state institutions through international support and interference in conflict-ridden countries as a means of protecting human rights. Advancing political liberalism within the realms of what we might call conditional state sovereignty, liberal solidarism may be seen as upgrading Kant's perpetual peace to a new world order.

Jürgen Habermas represents a stronger version of liberal cosmopolitanism, regarding liberal solidarism merely as a transitional phase towards a truly cosmopolitan legal order.[43] He agrees with Carl Schmitt, the realist, that the solidarist legalization of intervention is liable to abuse by powerful countries. Contrary to Schmitt, however, Habermas sees this as a reason for further limiting the sovereignty of states in international law. He argues that Kant was wrong when seeing state sovereignty as compatible with human rights: 'Because Kant regarded the bounds of national sovereignty as inviolable, he conceived of the cosmopolitan community as a federation of states, not of world citizens. This was inconsistent in that Kant derived every legal order, and not just that within the state, from the original rights that attaches to every person qua human being'.[44] Habermas sees the existence of the UN as proof of the possibility of transcending the state system, and contends that the UN is only consistent with universal human rights if it is considered a transitional arrangement towards a world federation guaranteeing the rights of individuals rather than states under cosmopolitan law.

Related to this, Pogge draws an instructive distinction between three forms of cosmopolitanism at stake. First, he distinguishes between *legal* and *moral* cosmopolitanism. Legal cosmopolitanism prescribes the subjection of all of humanity, including states and political entities, to a common legal authority protecting their common interest as world citizens. In its liberal form, this position is associated with a world republic for the universal and equal protection of the individual rights of all human beings, as defended by Habermas. *Moral* cosmopolitanism might entail legal cosmopolitanism, but is also compatible with other forms of global political organization (as in Kant's liberal internationalism) and with

(Cambridge: Polity, 2005); Ronald Tinnevelt, 'Federal World Government: The Road to Peace and Justice?', *Cooperation and Conflict* 47 (2012), 220–38.

[41] Barry Buzan, *From International to World Society? English School Theory and the Social Structure of Globalisation* (Cambridge: Cambridge University Press, 2004), ch. 5.

[42] Gareth Evans, *The Responsibility to Protect: Ending Mass Atrocity Crimes Once and for All* (Washington, DC: The Brookings Institution, 2008). See also Ch. 6 of this volume. On solidarism, see Buzan, *From International to World Society?*.

[43] Habermas, 'Kant's Idea of Perpetual Peace'.

[44] Habermas, 'Kant's Idea of Perpetual Peace', 180.

other forms of political engagement than the prescription of legal and political arrangements.[45]

Pogge then distinguishes between two kinds of moral cosmopolitanism: *interactional* and *institutional*. Interactional moral cosmopolitanism 'assigns direct responsibility for the fulfilment of human rights to other individual and collective agents' and applies 'directly to the conduct of persons and groups'.[46] This approach may oblige states or individuals to protect the human rights of foreigners. It recalls familiar ethical and legal debates on how to respond to particular cases of war and suffering through measures such as humanitarian assistance, development aid, or military intervention. In addition to immediate 'interactional' responses, such pressing problems often provoke considerations of how laws and institutions can be formed in order to facilitate conduct that would be more consistent with a cosmopolitan response.

This in turn brings us to the 'institutional' kind of moral cosmopolitanism, which is concerned with institutional schemes—'ground rules and practices that regulate human interactions':

> [T]he responsibility of persons is, then, indirect—a shared responsibility for the justice of any practices one helps to impose. One ought not to cooperate in the imposition of a coercive institutional order that avoidably leaves human rights unfulfilled without making reasonable efforts to aid its victims and to promote institutional reform.[47]

The interactional approach entails considerations on how to respond to problems that confront us in the current international system, be it genocide, civil war, or the proliferation of nuclear weapons. The debate on humanitarian intervention, peace operations, or 'humanitarian disarmament' is often framed in such terms. The institutional response, on the other hand, leads our attention to the role of institutions in allowing the problems to appear in the first place. To what extent, for instance, do the institutions regulating state sovereignty and international trade facilitate the modern dynamics of civil war? The way in which the International Criminal Court holds individuals accountable for war crimes across state borders can be seen as the facilitation of effective reactions to individual crimes. From an institutional perspective, the way in which it alters the incentive structures of political and military leaders previously protected by the sovereignty of their state is nonetheless far more important. This institutional approach is a continuation of the social contract approach of the liberal tradition at the global level, rejecting the paradigmatic distinction between domestic and international politics. It demands of us to ask not what is immediately realistic but what is just and worth striving for.

As we saw, Pogge concludes that extensive global institutional reform is required in order to make it more consistent with an institutionalist commitment to human rights. However, he does not thereby propose the full transfer of

[45] Pogge, *World Poverty and Human Rights*, 169–70.
[46] Pogge, *World Poverty and Human Rights*, 170.
[47] Pogge, *World Poverty and Human Rights*, 170.

sovereignty from the state to a centralized world state. In line with other proposals for 'cosmopolitan democracy', he rather recommends a dispersion of sovereignty above, across, and below the state level.[48] The regulation of war and peace is nonetheless reserved for a centralized global authority.

A transformation of this kind would require, it seems, a realist recognition of the role and power of states in the international system, rooting the transformation in a gradual (internationalist) appeal to the morality of states and their citizens rather than rooting it in revolutionary appeals to replace the current world order in one radical move. Legal cosmopolitanism is best perceived as a long-term perspective, suggesting a set of guiding principles for piecemeal legal reform—principles that, one would assume, will nevertheless be rejected by realists and internationalists alike.

4. Conclusion

When, within the field of international law, we debate issues such as disarmament, human rights, the responsibility to protect, humanitarian assistance, peacebuilding, and statebuilding, we cannot evade the fact that philosophical presuppositions do play a crucial, albeit often unstated, role in framing our arguments. There are many such underlying philosophical questions: Whether facilitating peace or war is the aim of law and politics; whether individuals have a basic right to live in peace, or a basic right to live in liberty, and whether such a right constitutes the foundation of the legitimacy of the state; whether international politics and international law are mainly interest- or norm-based; and whether we have obligations towards the citizens of other states. All of these are decisive issues that will determine the way in which we formulate law and the way in which we think about international morality. However, in largely relying on the separation of law from an idea of international ethics—and to a large extent also from politics and political philosophy—international law has been resistant to recognizing the way in which issues of peace, war, and interstate relations *depend on* politics and on assumptions from political philosophy and ethics. Instead, an internationalist idea of the state as legal subject has predominated in the legal debates on war and peace—debates in which realism has been seen as the enemy of true internationalism, and cosmopolitanism as its utopian cousin. In this chapter we have in effect argued that internationalism and international law cannot derive its political legitimacy merely from the rights of states qua states. We cannot avoid the underlying questions about the rights of individual citizens, including a possible basic human right to live in peace—a key concern in early liberalism, as we have seen. Whether states serve the function of safeguarding such a right, and whether

[48] Pogge, *World Poverty and Human Rights*, 178. For other proposals for cosmopolitan democracy, see Held, *Democracy and the Global Order*; Richard Falk, *On Humane Governance* (Cambridge: Polity, 1995); Andrew Linklater, *The Transformation of Political Community: Ethical Foundations of the Post-Westphalian Era* (Cambridge: Polity, 1998); Caney, *Justice Beyond Borders*.

it is totally unrealistic to imagine a system that circumvents the state in favour of an individual-based cosmopolitanism, are questions we will continue to debate. Indeed, those debates are also dependent on several philosophical disagreements we have not explicitly discussed here, but which are alive and well between the lines, such as the tension between liberty-oriented and community-oriented understandings of the needs and rights of the individual.

In all these debates, the conflicting views of realism, internationalism, and cosmopolitanism will continue to play their roles. However, only by keeping their philosophical underpinnings in mind will the roles be played well—and we would add: only then will it be clearer to us which view in the end deserves to carry the day.

3

Normative Foundation of the International Law of Peace

*Cecilia M. Bailliet**

> Law is valued for providing an alternative to the use of force in the ordering of human affairs. In this sense, all of international law is law of peace …
>
> Mary Ellen O'Connell[1]

It is often noted that the Law of War is replete with instruments, whereas the Law of Peace is perceived as lacking. In truth, there is wide range of instruments dating back to the Peace of Westphalia (1648) which ended the Thirty Years War in Europe and promoted the notion of *pax optima rerum.*[2] This chapter explores the evolution of the international law of peace from the notion of a 'right to peaceful coexistence' to the *de lege ferenda* initiative to recognize a 'human right to peace'. The chapter seeks to explain why achieving universal normative clarity within international law remains a challenge and suggests that it may be beneficial to focus on institutions addressing the components and preconditions of peace.

1. Peaceful Coexistence

The concept of 'peaceful coexistence' implies mutual toleration between states of their differences (ideological, cultural, political, etc.) and use of non-violent dispute resolution mechanisms. In terms of normative development, David

* This chapter is partly adapted from a prior article titled 'Untraditional Approaches to Law: Teaching the International Law of Peace', *Santa Clara Journal of International Law* 12 (2014), 1–27.

[1] Mary Ellen O'Connell, 'Peace and War', in *The Oxford Handbook of The History of International Law*, Bardo Fassbender and Anne Peters (eds.) (Oxford: Oxford University Press, 2012), 272.

[2] This regime established state sovereignty, the principle of non-intervention in domestic affairs, and the basis for self-determination. See also the Briand-Kellogg Pact, Treaty Between the United States and Other Powers Providing for the Renunciation of War as an Instrument of National Policy (Paris, 1928), which condemned 'recourse to war for the solution of international controversies'. It was ratified by 62 nations but failed due to a lack of enforcement mechanisms. See also the Covenant of the League of Nations (Paris, 29 April 1919).

Schleicher traces the concept of a 'natural right to peaceful coexistence' to the foundations of public international law theory:

> Although their classic formulations of the constitutive laws of the interstate system centered principally upon the establishment of well-ordered and effective states and the incremental regulation, rather than the prohibition, of war or the institutionalization of international relations, Grotius, Pufendorf, and Vattel, the intellectual forefathers of international law, offered succor to proponents of normative visions of a more peaceful world by making manifest the emerging opinio juris that as mankind had the *natural right to peaceful coexistence* the international system of states was therefore to be steered by a normative current contrary to antecedent notions of the absolute right of states to wage war, particularly of the aggressive or preemptive and thus 'unjust' varieties.[3]

These theorists considered the law of nations as forming part of the normative order determined by nature that would bind states irrespective of consent, but states would also share a common interest in pursuing peaceful coexistence.[4] The Westphalian system is credited for 'situating the domestic and the international in the same context by relating orderliness and safety within states to peace and security among states'.[5] Yet, the rise of positivism and primacy of sovereignty sidelined natural rights, including that of peaceful coexistence. Kant considered the coexistence of states to be complicated by the fact that, in contrast to Pufendorf, he believed the natural condition of human society was that of insecurity and war. He suggested that there was a need to establish lawful forms of government (republics) at the national level and also recognize and implement the international rule of law. Kant proposed the theory that states could choose to establish a world federation through treaty and renounce war as a means to enforce their rights in order to bring about perpetual world peace.[6] This presented the challenge of achieving and maintaining peaceful coexistence among states while at the same time upholding sovereignty rights, stymieing the League of Nations and creating legitimacy concerns for the United Nations.[7]

This issue reemerged within the context of decolonization after World War II and the establishment of new states in Asia and Africa that sought to consolidate their independence and sovereignty against aggression and interference in order to pursue development.[8] The Sino-Indian Agreement of 29 April 1954 (known as the

[3] See David Schleicher, 'Liberal International Law Theory and the United Nations Mission in Kosovo', *Tulane Journal of International and Comparative Law* 14 (2005), 179.

[4] See Charles Covell, *Kant and the Law of Peace: A Study in the Philosophy of International Law and International Relations* (Hampshire: Palgrave 1998), 139. See also Michael Doyle, 'Liberalism and World Politics', *American Political Science Review* 80 (1986), 1151–69.

[5] Theodore Christov, 'Liberal Internationalism Revisited: Grotius, Vattel, and the International Order of States', *The European Legacy* 10 (2005), 561.

[6] Christov, 'Liberal Internationalism Revisited', 2–3.

[7] See Jochen Rauber, 'The United Nations—A Kantian Dream Come True? Philosophical Perspectives on the Constitutional Legitimacy of the World Organization', *Hanse Law Review* 5 (2009), 49.

[8] Wen Jiabao, 'Carrying Forward the Five Principles of Peaceful Coexistence in the Promotion of Peace and Development', speech by the Premier of the State Council of the People's Republic of China, at a rally commemorating the 50th Anniversary of the Five Principles of Peaceful Coexistence, repr. in *Chinese Journal of International Law* 3 (2004), 363–4.

Pancha Shila) established five principles of peaceful coexistence that emphasize negative peace characteristics and place sovereignty at the centre:

1. Mutual respect for territorial integrity and sovereignty,
2. Non-aggression,
3. Non-interference in internal affairs,
4. Equality and Mutual Benefit, and
5. Peaceful Coexistence.

The following year, the Asian-African Conference led to the acceptance by over 20 countries of the five principles within the Bandung Declaration on Promotion of World Peace and Cooperation (1955). This instrument broadened the potential of peaceful coexistence to move beyond negative peace to positive peace, but because of the vast scope of its aspirations it may be characterized as resembling more a policy document than a legal instrument. The Bandung Declaration added respect for fundamental human rights, the purposes and principles of the Charter of the United Nations, and the right of each nation to defend itself singly or collectively in conformity with the Charter of the United Nations. It also called for abstention from the use of arrangements of collective defence to serve the particular interests of any of the big powers or exertion of pressure on other countries. In addition, it advocated settlement of disputes by peaceful means and respect for justice and international obligations.[9] Further, the Bandung resolutions called for economic development within Asia and Africa, the facilitation of cultural contacts, respect for self-determination of peoples, the end of colonialism and subjection of peoples, disarmament, and the elimination of nuclear weapons.[10]

The principles of peaceful coexistence were actually considered to be the main force behind the Non-Aligned Movement.[11] They were reiterated in many of South and South East Asia's regional instruments on international law, including the 1976 Treaty of Amity and Cooperation of Southeast Asia that laid the foundation for the Association of South East Asian Nations (ASEAN) and the 1985 Charter of the South Asian Association for Regional Cooperation (SAARC).[12] Peaceful

[9] Leon Lipson, 'Peaceful Coexistence', *Law & Contemporary Problems* 29 (1964), 871, 873.

[10] Quincy Wright, 'Asian Experience and International Law', *International Studies* 1 (1959), 71, 86.

[11] The Non-Aligned Movement was convened by the Prime Ministers of Burma, Ceylon, India, Indonesia and Pakistan and brought together leaders of 29 states, mostly former colonies, from the two continents of Africa and Asia, to discuss common concerns and to develop joint policies in international relations. Prime Ministers Nehru, Soekarno, and Nasser led the conference. Third World leaders discussed the need to resist pressure by the major powers, how to maintain independence, and how to oppose colonialism and neo-colonialism. Prabhakar Singh, 'From "Narcissistic" Positive International Law to "Universal" Natural International Law: The Dialectics of "Absentee Colonialism"', *African Journal of International and Comparative Law* 16 (2008), 56–82. See also K. R. Narayan, 'The 50th Anniversary of Panchsheel', *Chinese Journal of International Law* 3 (2004), 369. The entire cultural fabric of eastern civilizations rests upon the rules of administration and governance that denounce subjugation of kings by kings, or sovereign by sovereign.

[12] Diane A. Desierto, 'Postcolonial International Law Discourses on Regional Developments in South and Southeast Asia', *International Journal of Legal Information* 36 (2008), 387.

coexistence was also articulated and promoted by the Soviet Union as the call for respect, competition, and cooperation between different political systems (capitalist and communist). It was touted by Khrushchev as a means by which to thaw the Cold War and culminated with Gorbachev's characterization of it as forming the basis for addressing depletion of resources, ecological risks, nuclear weapons, and social issues in the developing world.[13] Although some American academics considered the 'law of peaceful coexistence' to be responsive to Soviet foreign policy needs, one may point out that American foreign policy has itself been maladroitly linked to Kantian Democratic Peace theory/Liberal Peace theory in justification of its interventions.[14]

[13] Peaceful coexistence was a general principle of the international communist movement. Explaining the Soviet perspective, Victor P. Karpov states: 'In short, coexistence on a reasonable basis presupposes the recognition of the existence of different social systems, the recognition of the right of every people to deal independently with all political and social problems of its own country, respect for the sovereignty of other nations, adherence to the principle of non-interference in internal affairs of other countries, and the settlement of all international issues by negotiation. Thus, the Soviet view of peaceful coexistence of countries with different social and political systems does not simply imply an absence of war or a state of temporary and unstable armistice. It provides for the maintenance of friendly economic and political relations and envisages the establishment and development of a variety of forms of peaceful international cooperation.' Victor P. Karpov, 'The Soviet Concept of Peaceful Coexistence and its Implications for International Law', *Law & Contemporary Problems* 29 (1964), 858, 860. See also Nikita Khrushchev, 'On Peaceful Coexistence', *Foreign Affairs* 38 (1959), 3. Bernard A. Ramundo adds that some formulations also include peaceful settlement of disputes, self-determination, disarmament, prohibition of propaganda for war, equality of the socialist and capitalist systems, the illegality of colonialism, the illegality of military blocs, the illegality of the arms race, and the requirement that the states of the two systems actively collaborate to eliminate all that interferes with peaceful coexistence. Bernard A. Ramundo, 'Czechoslovakia and the Law of Peaceful Coexistence: Legal Characterization in Soviet National Interest', *Stanford Law Review* 22 (1969–70), 963–6. However, the Soviet Union did not equate peaceful coexistence with pacifism. The Soviets took the view that all norms inconsistent with peaceful coexistence had no juridical force; the doctrine had to be carefully circumscribed to apply only to those states *outside* the Soviets' claimed sphere of influence. Within the Warsaw Pact, control of the member states was maintained under the appealing rubric of 'socialist internationalism'. This doctrine required that national interests, as determined by the member states, were subordinated to the more important international interests of the whole socialist community, as determined by the then-Soviet Union. Hence, counter-revolution support by 'imperial' states against the development of socialism within one country would be perceived as a threat against all socialism, and merit military intervention by the Soviet Union according to the Brezhnev Doctrine. See Colonel James P. Terry, USMC (Ret.), 'Moscow's Corruption of the Law of Armed Conflict: Important Lessons for the 21st Century', *Naval Law Review* 53 (2006), 73–210.

[14] See Alwyn V. Freeman, 'Some Aspects of Soviet Influence on International Law', *American Journal of International Law* 62 (1968), 710–22. See Robert J. Delahunty and John Yoo, 'Kant, Habermas and Democratic Peace', *Chicago Journal of International Law* 10 (2010), St Thomas Legal Studies Research Paper No. 10-01; UC Berkeley Public Law Research Paper No. 1544063. Available at SSRN: http://papers.ssrn.com/sol3/papers.cfm?abstract_id=1544063 (accessed 5 Nov 2014). See also Roger MacGinty, 'The Liberal Peace', *International Peacebuilding and Local Resistance: Hybrid Forms of Peace* (Hampshire: Palgrave 2011), 1–18. See also Isaak I. Dore, 'The U.S. Invasion of Grenada: Resurrection of the Johnson Doctrine', *Stanford Journal of International Law* 20 (1984), 173, discussing the Monroe, Johnson, and Reagan Doctrines which supported intervention within Latin America in the guise of upholding peace and democracy. See also Michael W. Doyle, *Liberal Peace: Selected Essays* (Oxford: Routledge 2012), 3, 18, discussing the concept of a separate peace among liberal states and intervention against non-liberal states: 'Even though liberal states have become involved in numerous wars with nonliberal states, constitutionally secure liberal states have yet to engage in war with one another ... A liberal zone of peace, a pacific union, has been maintained and has expanded despite numerous particular conflicts of economic and strategic interest.'

2. Peaceful Coexistence and the UN Declaration on Principles of International Law Concerning Friendly Relations and Cooperation among States

It is notable that the Five Principles of Peaceful Coexistence were taken up by the International Law Association which established a Committee on Juridical Aspects of Peaceful Coexistence in 1956.[15] This later led to the establishment of a UN General Assembly Special Committee on Friendly Relations and Cooperation among States in accordance with the UN Charter. This Committee sought to draft a code of general principles of international law (including the principles of respect for sovereignty, non-aggression, non-interference in internal affairs, and equality of states). This was completed in 1970 when the UN General Assembly adopted the Declaration on Principles of International Law Concerning Friendly Relations and Cooperation among States (Resolution 2625), now considered to constitute customary international law. This declaration is actually an important example of peacemaking as it was the direct achievement of cooperation between legal scholars from opposing systems, the Soviet and the US, who worked together in the committees. Ironically, Western international law textbooks tend to ignore the history behind the Declaration, and thus diminish the recognition of the impact of 'peaceful coexistence' within international law.

The preamble of the UN Declaration on Principles of International Law Concerning Friendly Relations and Cooperation Among States (1970) recalls that the peoples of the United Nations are determined to practice tolerance and live together in peace with one another as a good neighbours. It reiterates the principles that states shall refrain in their international relations from the threat or use of force against the territorial integrity or political independence of any state or in any other manner inconsistent with the purposes of the United Nations. Furthermore, it sets forth that states shall settle their international disputes by peaceful means in such a manner that international peace and security and justice are not endangered; that states shall not intervene in matters within the domestic jurisdiction of a state; and that states have a duty to cooperate with one another in accordance with the Charter.

Finally, it recognizes the principles of equal rights, self-determination of peoples, sovereign equality of states, and that states shall fulfil their obligations in good faith. What is important regarding the Declaration's emphasis of a right of self-determination of peoples is that it sets forth the requirement that governments should be representative of 'the whole people belonging to the territory without distinction as to race, creed or colour', hence where a regime is

[15] See Edward McWhinney, 'The Renewed Vitality of the International Law Principles of Peaceful Coexistence in the Post-Iraq Invasion Era: The 50th Anniversary of the China/India Pancha Shila Agreement of 1954', *Chinese Journal of International Law* 3 (2004), 379–83.

non-representative and repressive against an ethnic group, denying democratic equality, it may be argued that they would be entitled to seek autonomy according to the Declaration.[16]

3. Further Normative Offspring of Peaceful Coexistence: Disarmament and the Prohibition of Aggression

The Declaration on Friendly Relations was further complemented by specific treaties addressing non-proliferation, partial test bans, nuclear and general disarmament, and the exclusion of nuclear weapons from space, thereby establishing the international law of detente. The Declaration on the Strengthening of International Security (1970)[17] set forth important objectives that are idealistic. It calls for an effective system of universal collective security without military alliances, the elimination of nuclear weapons and other weapons of mass destruction, and a global strategy to reduce and eliminate as soon as possible the economic gap between developed and developing countries. On the elimination of nuclear weapons, the ICJ was unable to confirm their total prohibition, but noted that states are obliged to conduct good faith negotiations on nuclear disarmament.[18] 'Peaceful Coexistence' is also recognized as a principle within the 1974 UN Charter of Economic Rights and Duties of States, Article 1f, thereby linking this principle to international economic relations, development, and protection of the environment.[19]

The Declaration on Friendly Relations was also supplanted by the Declaration on the Definition of Aggression (1974).[20] Aggression is defined as 'the use of armed force by a State against the sovereignty, territorial integrity or political independence of another State, or in any other manner inconsistent with the Charter of the United Nations ...'[21] It is further noted that 'a war of aggression is a crime against

[16] See Solomon Dersso, 'The African Human Rights System and the Issue of Minorities in Africa', *African Journal of International and Comparative Law* 20 (2012), 42–69. See also Robert Howse and Ruti Teitel, 'Humanity Bounded and Unbounded: The Regulation of External Self-Determination under International Law', *Law & Ethics of Human Rights* 7 (2013), 155.

[17] UNGA Res. 2374 (XXV) (16 December 1970).

[18] See *Legality of the Threat or Use of Nuclear Weapons Case*, ICJ Advisory Opinion (1996).

[19] UN General Assembly, Charter of Economic Rights and Duties of States: resolution adopted by the General Assembly, 17 December 1984, A/RES/39/163.

[20] UNGA Res. 3314 (XXIX) (14 December 1974).

[21] Art. 1. Art. 3 sets forth a list of aggressive acts (it is noted that the list is not exhaustive and that the Security Council may identify other acts of aggression):

(a) The invasion or attack by the armed forces of a State of the territory of another State, or any military occupation, however temporary, resulting from such invasion or attack, or any annexation by the use of force of the territory of another State or part thereof;
(b) Bombardment by the armed forces of a State against the territory of another State or the use of any weapons by a State against the territory of another State;
(c) The blockade of the ports or coasts of a State by the armed forces of another State;
(d) An attack by the armed forces of a State on the land, sea or air forces, or marine and air fleets of another State;

international peace'.[22] However, it provides an exemption for self-determination and anticolonial struggles,[23] and the interpretation of aggression continues to be considered as being selective, rather than universal.[24]

In terms of individual accountability for aggression, the crime of aggression has been problematic since its inception after World War II when it was applied by the Allies against the Axis powers.[25] In terms of establishing individual criminal responsibility for aggression, the London Charter of the International Military Tribunal defined crimes against peace as '(i) Planning, preparation, initiation or waging of a war of aggression or a war in violation of international treaties, agreements or assurances; (ii) Participation in a common plan or conspiracy for the accomplishment of any of the acts mentioned under (i)'. At present aggression is recognized as a crime under the Rome Statute of the International Criminal Court, pursuant to the 2010 Review Conference of the Rome Statute held in Kampala, Uganda. It amended the Rome Statute to include a definition of the crime of aggression and a regime establishing how the Court will exercise its jurisdiction over this crime. Nevertheless, the Court lacks jurisdiction until 2017, and there is an opt-out clause (with an exception in the case of a referral by the UN Security Council) that will limit its jurisdiction. Troy Lavers concludes that 'it will most likely never result in an investigation or prosecution, at least as far as powerful states are concerned'.[26]

Another problem is that aggression is limited to interstate actions, so that attacks from non-state actors are excluded from this category. At present, the threat of terrorist acts and intrastate violence involving non-state actors appear to present a greater threat to peace than interstate violence and the use of force. Moreover, the issue of structural violence between and within states adds another dimension to the analysis.

(e) The use of armed forces of one State which are within the territory of another State with the agreement of the receiving State, in contravention of the conditions provided for in the agreement or any extension of their presence in such territory beyond the termination of the agreement;
(f) The action of a State in allowing its territory, which it has placed at the disposal of another State, to be used by that other State for perpetrating an act of aggression against a third State;
(g) The sending by or on behalf of a State of armed bands, groups, irregulars or mercenaries, which carry out acts of armed force against another State of such gravity as to amount to the acts listed above, or its substantial involvement therein.

[22] Art. 5.

[23] Art. 7: Nothing in this Definition, and in particular Article 3, could in any way prejudice the right to self-determination, freedom and independence, as derived from the Charter, of peoples forcibly deprived of that right and referred to in the Declaration on Principles of International Law concerning Friendly Relations and Cooperation among States in accordance with the Charter of the United Nations, particularly peoples under colonial and racist regimes or other forms of alien domination: nor the right of these peoples to struggle to that end and to seek and receive support, in accordance with the principles of the Charter and in conformity with the above-mentioned Declaration.

[24] Art. 7.

[25] See Kirsten Sellars, *'Crimes against Peace' and International Law* (Cambridge: Cambridge University Press, 2013).

[26] Troy Lavers, 'The New Crime of Aggression: A Triumph for Powerful States', *Journal of Conflict & Security Law* 18 (2013), 1–24 at 2.

4. Peaceful Coexistence within the UN Charter

The principles of peaceful coexistence actually form part of the UN Charter, as pointed out by Boutros Boutros-Ghali:[27]

1. Mutual respect for each other's territorial integrity and sovereignty, Art. 2(1);
2. Mutual Non-Aggression, Art. 2(4);
3. Non-Interference in each other's internal affairs, Art. 2(7);
4. Equality, Preamble.

Boutros-Ghali states that pessimists consider the five principles of peaceful coexistence are being marginalized in part due to increased violations of territorial integrity via preventive military actions, humanitarian intervention, use of unilateral sanctions, and intervention under the pretext of promoting democracy and free markets for the sake of world peace. In addition, there is concern for the escalation of the number of failed/failing states and the strengthening of an increasingly hegemonic and hierarchical world order. In contrast, he describes optimists as having faith in global civil society or, alternatively, the rise of coalitions of developing countries with China and India. There is continuous debate about the need to reform the UN and strengthen the UN military structure, including activating the UN Military Staffs Committee, institutionalizing UN peacekeeping forces, and strengthening UNCTAD in order to improve the organization's legitimacy and the possibility of implementation of the principles of peaceful coexistence. At the normative level, Boutros-Ghali suggests that optimists conclude that there is a need to emphasize toleration of difference in order to realize peaceful coexistence: 'There can be no coexistence without diversity. Thus the prerequisite to peaceful coexistence is cultural, economic, and political diversity among nations. The dynamic dimension of peaceful coexistence implies opposition to 'uniformisation' of the planet. Cultural and political diversity belongs to humanity's heritage. It must and it can be protected by implementing the principle of peaceful coexistence.'[28] Nevertheless, Edward Keene articulates the challenge of reconciling two different aims with the international system: 'The contemporary pattern of international order embodies two distinct normative principles: that the sovereign independence of states should be respected, so as to encourage toleration of political and cultural differences: and that their sovereignty should be divided, so as to facilitate the promotion of civilization.'[29] The irreconcilable position of sovereignty when pursuing both objectives remains a contentious issue within international policy and practice.

[27] Boutros Boutros-Ghali, 'The Five Principles', *Chinese Journal of International Law* 3 (2004), 373.

[28] Boutros-Ghali, 'The Five Principles', 377.

[29] Edward Keene, *Beyond the Anarchical Society* (Cambridge: Cambridge University Press 2002), 143–4.

5. Present Reference to Peaceful Coexistence

At present, the principles of peaceful coexistence ('He Ping Gong Chu' in Chinese) are described as forming one of the foundations of China's foreign policy and are taught as the basis of international law within its law schools. It is interpreted as emphasizing international cooperation, equality between states, non-intervention in internal affairs, respect for territorial integrity, and the right of sovereignty.[30] Former Premier of the PRC State Council, Wen Jiabao, explained the vision of the Five Principles as impacting international law and practice:

> The Five Principles of Peaceful Coexistence ... have made a monumental contribution to the maintenance of peace and stability in Asia and the world over ... First, they provide a set of right guidelines for the establishment and development of relations among countries with similar or different social systems. Second, they point out an effective way to peacefully address the issues left over by history between countries or other international disputes. Third, they give a strong protection to the interests of developing countries and serve the improvement and expansion of North–South relations. Fourth, they have an important philosophical basis for the establishment of a new international political and economic order that is just and rational.[31]

A scholar, Chen Tiqiang, defines the Principles as containing the following 'due diligence' type elements that would expand peaceful coexistence beyond negative to positive characteristics:

> According to this principle, a state should not only refrain from doing anything to break the peace, such as committing aggression and intervention, or threatening, bullying and controlling other states, but should also take positive measures to lessen the danger of war, to oppose war plots, to withdraw armed forces stationed abroad, to dismantle military bases abroad, to carry out real and not fictitious disarmament, to try pacific means for settling international disputes, to create conditions for the economic prosperity and balanced development of all countries, to give economic assistance to

[30] In 2010, FM spokesperson MA Zhaoxu identified the Five Principles of Peaceful Coexistence as the foundation for their foreign policy: 'China always pursues an independent foreign policy of peace and is committed to developing friendly cooperation with countries around the world on the basis of the Five Principles of Peaceful Co-existence. We always hold that countries, big or small, weak or strong, poor or rich, are equal members of the international community. China has never bullied other countries or intervened in their internal affairs. Nor will it allow other countries to meddle with China's internal affairs or undermine China's sovereignty and security.' Cited by Zhu Lijiang, 'Chinese Practice in Public International Law: 2010', *Chinese Journal of International Law* 10 (2011), 428. On 4 November 2002 the Governments of the Member States of ASEAN and the Government of the People's Republic of China signed a Declaration on the Conduct of Parties in the South China Sea that declared commitment to: '(T)he purposes and principles of the Charter of the United Nations, the 1982 UN Convention on the Law of the Sea, the Treaty of Amity and Cooperation in Southeast Asia, the Five Principles of Peaceful Coexistence, and other universally recognized principles of international law which shall serve as the basic norms governing state-to-state relations.' The declaration calls for peaceful dispute resolution.

[31] Speech by Wen Jiabao, 'Carrying Forward the Five Principles of Peaceful Coexistence in the Promotion of Peace and Development', delivered at a rally commemorating the 50th anniversary of The Five Principles of Peaceful Coexistence (28 June 2004).

developing countries, to eliminate racial discrimination, to develop international cultural exchanges, etc.[32]

Yet, in spite of the significant normative and policy offspring of 'peaceful coexistence', it received criticism from Third World Approaches to International Law (TWAIL) scholars, such as Antony Anghie, who argued that the principles of peaceful coexistence promote a traditional approach that gives greater emphasis to sovereignty than human rights and thus contrasts with the democratic sovereignty approach: 'The Bandung version of sovereignty is more aligned with a classical approach to international law whereby the internal character of a state is irrelevant and what matters is whether a state abides by its international obligations in its external relations with regard to other states.'[33] This critique was also supported by Antonio Cancado-Trindade who accused 'peaceful coexistence' of being oriented towards interstate affairs as opposed to intrastate issues which he considered to be more pressing when discussing the attainment of peace.[34] Of particular importance, the UN Charter links inter- and intrastate dimensions of peace, as Article 55 calls for recognition of economic and social welfare and protection of human rights as preconditions for peace. This promotes a positive orientation towards peace and has resulted in the founding of specialized agencies to pursue these goals, such as FAO, IFAD, UNESCO, WHO, ILO, and (more controversially) the World Bank and the IMF:

> With a view to the creation of conditions of stability and well-being which are necessary for peaceful and friendly relations among nations based on respect for the principle of equal rights and self-determination of peoples, the United Nations shall promote:
> a. higher standards of living, full employment, and conditions of economic and social progress and development;
> b. solutions of international economic, social, health, and related problems; and international cultural and educational cooperation; and
> c. universal respect for, and observance of, human rights and fundamental freedoms for all without distinction as to race, sex, language, or religion.

Thus, the Law of Peace within the UN is narrow in the sense that it pursues realistic peace which recognizes exceptions permitting the use of force, i.e. self-defence (Art. 51) or Chapter VII operations, but it is also expansive because it combines negative and positive dimensions and preconditions of peace both in its normative instruments and in its institutional implementation of peace. The comprehensive normative language includes elements of a broad conception of peaceful coexistence, including the prohibition of aggression, promotion of peaceful dispute

[32] Chen Tiqiang, 'The People's Republic of China and Public International Law', *Dalhousie Law Journal* 8 (1984), 3, 24. He notes that China pursues this not out of pacifism but because it needs a peaceful environment to build up its economy. Leon Lipson, 'Peaceful Coexistence', *Law and Contemporary Problems* 29 (1964), 871, 875.

[33] Antony Anghie, The Grotius Lecture, ASIL 2010: 'International Law in a Time of Change: Should International Law Lead or Follow?', *American University International Law Review* 26 (2011), 1315, 1333.

[34] Antonio Cancado Trindade, 'The Historical Recovery of the Human Person as a Subject of the Law of Nations', *Cambridge Journal of International and Comparative Law* 1 (2012), 14.

resolution mechanisms, respect of human rights, development, and correction of structural inequality among states. It is suggested that problems arise from the actual implementation of mandates by the institutions, resulting in criticism of selective application of the normative language, such as 'threats to peace' and 'aggression', and it is arguable that Keene's 'civilizing aim' of the UN has overshadowed the aspiration for 'toleration of differences', thereby rendering the foundation of peace fragile.[35]

The following section will discuss the conception of peace as a human right and competing notions of its status as a solidarity right or as a civil and political right.

6. Whether Peace May be Considered a Human Right

6.1. Peace as a solidarity right or a civil and political right?

When peace first emerged within the context of human rights, it was characterized as a solidarity right, like the right to a clean environment, the right to development, and the ownership of the common heritage of mankind (e.g. the ocean floor). The right to peace 'concerns not only an individual's right to live in peace, but the greater right of societies to enjoy a common peace'.[36] Carl Wellman cites Karel Vasak's advocacy of solidarity rights as:

> (N)ecessary in order to overcome the solitary autonomy of competing individuals to develop their full human potentiality through cooperative participation in the social life of the various communities to which they belong. Moreover, these new human rights are needed now more than ever before to respond to the rapidly emerging global interdependence. The problems confronting any contemporary society can no longer be met by even the most resolute action of any single state. Maintaining peace, protecting the environment, and encouraging a sustained and equitable development of all economies require cooperative action on the national and especially the international level.[37]

It is a right that can be guaranteed and requires holistic implementation by states and non-state actors, including individuals and groups within civil society. The UN General Assembly has adopted specific resolutions on peace that articulate the language of a 'right to peace'. The preamble of the UN General Assembly resolution 33/73 Declaration on the Preparation of Societies for Life in Peace (1978)

[35] Edward Keene, *Beyond the Anarchical Society* (Cambridge: Cambridge University Press, 2002), 143–4.

[36] R. Scott Appleby, 'Religion, Violence and the Right to Peace', in *Religion and Human Rights: An Introduction*, John Witte Jr. and M. Christian Green (eds.) (Oxford: Oxford University Press, 2012), 346, 347, noting that this is a group right and not merely the several rights of individual members of the group. See Michael Ignatieff, *Human Rights as Politics and Idolatry* (Princeton: Princeton University Press 2001), 18, cited by Appleby, 'Religion, Violence and the Right to Peace', n. 17.

[37] Carl Wellman, 'Solidarity, the Individual and Human Rights', *Human Rights Quarterly* 22 (2000), 639, 642. He cites Karel Vasek, 'Pour une troisième génération des droits de l'homme', in *Studies and Essays on International Humanitarian Law and Red Cross Principles*, Christophe Swinarski (ed.) (Dordrecht: Martinus Nijhoff, 1984), 837, 839.

reaffirms the right of individuals, states, and all humankind to life in peace. This is linked to non-discrimination in Art. 1:

> Every nation and every human being, regardless of race, conscience, language or sex, has the inherent right to life in peace. Respect for that right, as well as for other human rights, is in the common interest of all mankind and an indispensable condition of advancement of all nations, large and small, in all fields.

The UN General Assembly resolution 39/11 Declaration on the Right of Peoples to Peace (1984) identifies an obligation of states to fulfil the right, and also calls upon IOs for implementation:

> Recognizing that the maintenance of a peaceful life for peoples is the sacred duty of each State: 1) Solemnly proclaims that the peoples of our planet have a sacred right to peace; 2) Solemnly declares that the preservation of the right of peoples to peace and the promotion of its implementation constitute a fundamental obligation of each State; 3) Emphasizes that ensuring the exercise of the right of peoples to peace demands that the policies of States be directed towards the elimination of the threat of war, particularly nuclear war, the renunciation of the use of force in international relations and the settlement of international disputes by peaceful means on the basis of the Charter of the United Nations; 4) Appeals to all States and international organizations to do their utmost to assist in implementing the right of peoples to peace through the adoption of appropriate measures at both the national and international level.

These resolutions were affirmed by the General Assembly in resolutions A/RES/57/216 of 27 February 2003, A/RES/60/163 of 2 March 2006, and A/RES/63/189 of 18 March 2009, the General Assembly declared 'that the peoples of our planet have a sacred right to peace and that the preservation and promotion of peace constitutes a fundamental obligation of each State'. UNESCO issued a declaration in 1997 that calls upon IOs and individuals to promote and implement the right to peace.[38] Philip Alston concluded that the right to peace is both an individual and collective right and implies duties and obligations from individuals to collectivities, including states and the international community as a whole.[39] Those espousing classic Western perspectives on human rights as supporting individual agency and autonomy may be sceptical of recognizing this solidarity right precisely because of its communitarian orientation. In contrast, those supporting collective orientation towards rights, such as those having Asian, Latin American, and African perspectives, would be positive.[40]

It is arguable that the right to peace may be better characterized as a collective right or meta-right enabling the enjoyment of human rights (because the individual right might quickly become confused with tort, civil, and criminal law situations). Alternatively, perhaps peace should be recharacterized as a duty as opposed

[38] UNESCO Report by the Director-General on the Human Right to Peace, document 29 C/59 (1997). It defines peace as both a right and a duty, inherent in all human beings. It sets forth that states, IOs, and individuals should promote and implement the right to peace.

[39] Philip Alston, 'Peace as a Human Right', *Security Dialogue* 11 (1980), 319, 329.

[40] See H. Patrick Glenn, *Legal Traditions of the World* (Oxford: Oxford University Press, 2010), 354.

to a right.[41] It may be perceived as a type of solidarity-based value/principle that imposes legal duties on individuals and states to act in the wider social interest.[42] Alfred de Zayes noted, 'But peace is much more than just an enabling right: it is also an over-arching and an end right. It is alpha and omega, the starting point, the means and also the end of human endeavor.'[43] In contrast Mazrui considered peace to be derivative of the dignity and worth of the human person.[44]

Yet, scholars writing in the 1980s characterized the right to peace in part addressing the individual right of conscientious objection and the right of states not to be subjected to violations of *jus ad bellum* or *in bello*. Consider the perspective of Stephen P. Marks:

> It is the right of every individual to contribute to efforts for peace, including refusal to participate in the military effort, and the collective right of every state to benefit from the full respect by other states of the principles of non-use of force, of non-aggression, of peaceful settlement of disputes, of the Geneva Conventions and Additional Protocols and similar standards, as well as from the implementation of policies aimed at general and complete disarmament under effective international control.[45]

Richard Bilder offers a similar view, linking the right to freedom of expression:

> (It) must embrace at least the related rights of every individual: (1) to participate in the formation of policies of his or her government which relate to its use of violence; 2) to question such policies; 3) to speak freely, petition and peacefully organize with others to change such policies; and 4) if the individual is morally convinced that such policies are wrong, to refuse to participate in implementing them. This right must also imply a correlative duty on the part of every government to insure that its citizens not be called on to sacrifice their lives in aggressive, illegal or immoral wars or to be required to kill other people who are often innocent and fundamentally uninvolved.[46]

[41] Philip Alston, 'Peoples' Rights: Their Rise and Fall', in *Peoples' Rights*, Alston (ed.) (Oxford: Oxford University Press, 2001), 281, discussing the internet search result list which links to 'peace and quiet' when searching for 'peace'.

[42] Kate Cook, 'Solidarity as a Basis for Human Rights: Part One: Legal Principle or Mere Aspiration?', *European Human Rights Law Review* 5 (2012), 504–15.

[43] Alfred de Zayas, 'Peace as a Human Right: The Jus Cogens Prohibition of Aggression', in *Making Peoples Heard: Essays on Human Rights in Honor of Gudmundur Alfredsson*, Asbjørn Eide, Jakob Th. Möller, and Ineta Ziemele (eds.) (Brill 2011), 28, 37. He also states: 'In a world of weapons of mass destruction, it is imperative to strengthen the early warning and peaceful settlement mechanisms of the United Nations. Armed conflict must be prevented through a collective commitment to negotiation. The use of force must not be allowed, except as a last resort, when all avenues of peaceful settlement have been exhausted, and only conditioned on Security Council approval. For the sake of the survival of the human species, the right to peace must be protected not only by norms and tribunals but by education toward a culture of peace. Indeed, the recognition of peace as a human right requires more than just the prohibition of war. What is necessary is to create the conditions for peace. A world without extreme poverty, a world without profound injustices, is a world less likely to go to war than our present world is.' (42)

[44] Ali Mazrui, *Towards a Pax Africana* (London: Weidenfeld & Nicolson, 1967), 137, cited by Hedley Bull, *The Anarchical Society* (4th edn. New York: Columbia University Press, 2012), 93.

[45] Stephen P. Marks, 'Emerging Human Rights: A New Generation for the 1980's?' *Rutgers Law Review* 33 (1980–1), 435 at 446.

[46] Richard Bilder, 'The Individual and the Right to Peace: The Right to Conscientious Dissent', Address at the Third Armand Hammer Conference on Peace and Human Rights—Human Rights and Peace, held in Warsaw, Poland, 3–6 July 1980.

He suggests this template of the elements of the right to peace: (1) Individuals are to claim the right from their governments; governments shall not suppress or violate human rights (such as repressing dissent) in the name of peace; (2) all people have a right to participate in the decisions of their governments regarding war and peace; (3) to petition government, to assemble, and organize associations to work for peace; (4) to conscientious objection; (5) to the truth about government actions and decisions, free information and communication without censorship.[47] He concludes:

> The right to peace includes the right of every individual to freedom of speech, petition and association in opposition to policies of his or her own government which may lead to or which involve war, the right freely to receive and impart information relevant to the reaching of a judgment on such policies, and the right of conscientious objection.[48]

Hence, these positions placed the right to peace squarely within the realm of civil and political rights and retained an individual focus, countering the perspective that it is a third-generation solidarity right, thereby resulting in both normative confusion and politicization according to ideology to the present day.

6.2. Soft law from civil society: the UN Draft Declaration on the Right to Peace

Philip Alston remarked that by the 1990s the Right to Peace had been 'dropped like a stone' within the UN, due to its lack of clear meaning as a collective right, thereby failing 'to capture the global imagination' or strengthen peoples' rights.[49] However, in 2012, it re-emerged within the UN Human Rights Council due to the initiative of an NGO, the Spanish Society for International Human Rights Law (SSIHRL). Carlos Villán Durán, president of the SSIHRL, identified the aim of this society 'to translate the universal value of peace into the legal category of a human right'.[50] SSIHRL drafted various declarations on the right to peace and then pursued introduction of the human right to peace into the agenda of the UN, via the Human Rights Council and its Advisory Committee.[51] SSIHRL has produced various declarations on the Right to Peace, including the Bilbao Declaration (2010), the Luarca Declaration (2006), the Barcelona Declaration, and the Santiago Declaration (2010).[52] Durán alleges that these declarations: '(W)ere drafted in accordance with the legal technique of the international human rights instruments ... articulated normative proposals from the civil society to the official codification and progressive development of the human right to peace, formulated with the aim that one day the UN General Assembly would

[47] Bilder, 'The Individual and the Right to Peace', 388.
[48] Bilder, 'The Individual and the Right to Peace', 389.
[49] Philip Alston, *Peoples' Rights* (Oxford: Oxford University Press, 2005), 279, 281.
[50] Carlos Villán Durán,'Civil Society Organizations Contribution to the Universal Declaration on the Human Right to Peace', *International Journal on World Peace* XXVIII (2011), 59.
[51] Durán,'Civil Society Organizations Contribution', 60–1.
[52] http://www.aedidh.org/?q=node/659 (accessed 6 Nov 2014).

approve the Universal Declaration on the Right to Peace.'[53] These civil society declarations address the positive elements of peace, calling for the eradication of structural violence produced by economic and social inequalities, the satisfaction of basic human needs, the elimination of cultural violence, gender-related violence, family violence, non-discrimination, respect for human rights and fundamental freedoms, a new international economic order, sustainable development, and the protection of the environment. Duran claimed that 85 per cent of the language contained in the UN Draft Declaration on the Right to Peace came directly from the Santiago Declaration and that he was committed to ensuring that the remaining 15 per cent would be included.[54] Duran notes that the civil society engagement (over 500 NGOs) added over 40 issues to the right to peace document. This may well be a disconcerting development from the perspective of normative coherence and clarity and presents a possible downside of the expansion and engagement of fragmented transnational civil society actors. The UN Human Rights Council Advisory Committee on the Right to Peace first text of the Draft Declaration on the Right to Peace[55] set forth in Article 1 that individuals and peoples have a right to peace, and that this right is 'universal, indivisible, interdependent, and interrelated', thereby indicating allegiance to Eide's holistic conception of human rights which joins negative and positive rights together.[56] It called upon states to renounce the use or threat of force and use peaceful means to settle any dispute. Further, it calls upon states to promote respect for the principles within the UN Charter, human rights, the right to development, and the right of peoples to self-determination. Article 2 addressed positive peace dimensions related to Roosevelt's concept of Freedom from Fear and from Want, *inter alia* the right to live in peace and the elimination of structural violence.[57] The initial text included 14 provisions that are encompassing of negative and positive dimensions of peace, however the draft did not provide a concrete definition of peace,[58] instead it referred to Human Security, Disarmament, Peace Education and Training, Right to Conscientious Objection to Military Service, Private Military and Security Companies, Resistance and Opposition to Oppression, Peacekeeping, the Right to Development, Protection of the Environment, the Rights of Victims and Vulnerable Groups, and Refugees and

[53] Carlos Villán Durán, 'The Human Right to Peace: A Legislative Initiative from the Spanish Civil Society', *Spanish Yearbook of International Law* XV (2009), 151.

[54] Statement made at an open seminar on the right to peace at the University of Oslo, 30 January 2013: http://www.jus.uio.no/ior/english/research/events/conferences/2013/20130130-right-to-peace.html (accessed 6 Nov 2014). The Santiago Declaration is available: http://www.sgep.org/index.php?option=com_content&view=article&id=109:declaracion-de-santiago-sobre-o-dereito-humano-a-paz&catid=14:documentos&Itemid=54&lang=en, (accessed 6 Nov 2014).

[55] A/HRC/20/31 (16 April 2012), available at: http://www.ohchr.org/EN/HRBodies/HRC/RightPeace/Pages/WGDraftUNDeclarationontheRighttoPeace.aspx (accessed 6 Nov 2014).

[56] Asbjørn Eide, 'Interdependence and Indivisibility of Human Rights', in *Human Rights in Education, Science and Culture*, Yvonne Donders and Vladimir Volodin (eds.) (UNESCO and Aldershot: Ashgate, 2007).

[57] See http://www.americanrhetoric.com/speeches/fdrthefourfreedoms.htm (accessed 6 Nov 2014).

[58] http://ap.ohchr.org/documents/dpage_e.aspx?si=A/HRC/20/31 (accessed 6 Nov 2014).

Migrants. In terms of implementation, it proved equally vast in orientation, as Article 13 calls upon all actors, including states, IOs, corporations, and civil society, and also calls upon the UN Human Rights Council to establish a special monitoring procedure within the UN:

1. The preservation, promotion and implementation of the right to peace constitute a fundamental obligation of all States and of the United Nations as the most universal body harmonizing the concerted efforts of the nations to realize the purposes and principles proclaimed in the Charter of the United Nations.
2. States should cooperate in all necessary fields in order to achieve the realization of the right to peace, in particular by implementing their existing commitments to promote and provide increased resources to international cooperation for development.
3. The effective and practical realization of the right to peace demands activities and engagement beyond States and international organizations, requiring comprehensive, active contributions from civil society, in particular academia, the media and corporations, and the entire international community in general.
4. Every individual and every organ of society, keeping the present Declaration constantly in mind, shall strive to promote respect for the right to peace by progressive measures, national and international, to secure its universal and effective recognition and observance everywhere.
5. States should strengthen the effectiveness of the United Nations in its dual functions of preventing violations and protecting human rights and human dignity, including the right to peace. In particular, it is for the General Assembly, the Security Council, the Human Rights Council and other competent bodies to take effective measures to protect human rights from violations that may constitute a danger or threat to international peace and security.
6. The Human Rights Council is invited to set up a special procedure to monitor respect for and the implementation of the right to peace and to report to relevant United Nations bodies.

Of interest, Duran characterized the UN Human Rights Council as the institution that would be responsive 'to the demands of Southern States with regard to human rights'. This is because the African and Asian states are in the majority, there is no veto, and resolutions are adopted by majority.[59] The first draft became politicized within the Council and resulted in polarization, as it was promoted by Cuba and supported by developing countries, while developed countries either abstained or voted against it.

[59] Duran, 'The Human Right to Peace', 65.

7. *Opinio Juris* on the Right to Peace—State Views

The draft divided the UN Human Rights Council in the vote on the promotion of the right to peace in July 2012. The countries of the East and the South voted in favour.[60] In particular, both Russia and China recognized this as an important collective right.[61] This may also be interpreted as in line with the Asian tradition of valuing social harmony through social relations, supporting conciliation and negotiation over adjudication, and rejecting the use of force or intervention.[62]

The United States of America voted against the declaration. It explained its vote, noting that the declaration 'would cover many issues that are, at best, unrelated to the cause of peace, and at worst, divisive and detrimental to efforts to achieve peace … Efforts to move forward with a "right to peace" have always ended in endorsements for new concepts on controversial thematic issues, often unrelated to human rights. We do not agree with attempts to develop a collective "right to peace" or to position it as an "enabling right" that would in any way modify or stifle the exercise of existing human rights.'[63] The US stated that key concepts remained undefined or not sufficiently defined and it was filled with overly broad or vague formulations. It also objected to human rights being assigned to groups or peoples rather than individuals, refuting the communitarian perspective. Further, it duplicated other human rights instruments or mechanisms and addressed environment and security issues.

However, the European nations changed from voting against to abstaining.[64] The European nations explained their vote of abstention: 'We do not recognize that a "right to peace" exists in international law, whether as a collective or individual human right, or otherwise. Given the deep conceptual flaws of the alleged "right to peace" and the potentially undermining effect of a future declaration on human rights law … We will abstain.'[65] However, the Asian, African, and Latin American states proved sufficient in number to carry forward the initiative within the Human Rights Council.

[60] Angola, Bangladesh, Benin, Botswana, Burkina Faso, Cameroon, Chile, China, Congo, Costa Rica, Cuba, Djibouti, Ecuador, Guatemala, Indonesia, Jordan, Kuwait, Kyrgyzstan, Libya, Malaysia, Maldives, Mauritania, Mauritius, Mexico, Nigeria, Peru, Philippines, Qatar, Russian Federation, Saudi Arabia, Senegal, Thailand, Uganda, and Uruguay.

[61] http://www.unog.ch/80256EDD006B9C2E/(httpNewsByYear_en)/741DF607AF802BAAC1257A320053916E?OpenDocument (accessed 12 June 2014). Indeed it is notable that solidarity rights are likely to receive increased support in the Human Rights Council because of the voting patterns, whereas other initiatives oriented towards equality and freedom rights touted by the West, e.g. LBGT rights, failed within the Council due to the opposition of the other regions: http://www.awid.org/Library/The-United-Nations-Human-Rights-Council-s-Backwards-Step-on-LGBT-Rights (accessed 6 Nov 2014).

[62] See H. Patrick Glenn, *Legal Traditions of the World* (Oxford: Oxford University Press, 2010), 335–6.

[63] http://geneva.usmission.gov/2012/07/05/20538/ (accessed 6 Nov 2014).

[64] Austria, Belgium, Czech Republic, Hungary, India, Norway, Poland, Republic of Moldova, Romania, Spain, and Switzerland.

[65] http://www.unog.ch/80256EDD006B9C2E/(httpNewsByYear_en)/741DF607AF802BAAC1257A320053916E?OpenDocument (accessed 12 June 2014).

On 12 February 2013, there was a meeting of the Open-ended Inter-Governmental Working Group on a draft declaration on the right to peace which resulted in various critical commentaries. The EU noted that 'the European Union itself is a peace project' but reiterated that its concern for the lack of legal basis for the right to peace (either individual or collective), the impossibility of finding a common definition, and vagueness that would impede justiciability.[66] Instead it called for strengthening of the ICC and the Rome Statute to pursue accountability for crimes against humanity, war crimes, and genocide, thereby indicating a preference for peace through justice institutions.[67]

Canada noted that 'it makes many assertions to rights which have no basis in international law, including "the right to peace" itself as well as other aspirational concepts such as the right to live in a world free of weapons of mass destruction, the right to a comprehensive peace and human rights education, and the right to a safe, clean and peaceful environment'.[68] Canada also was critical of the right to resist and oppose oppressive colonial or foreign occupation or dictatorial domination.

Australia was concerned that the right to peace would ignore the fact that international law permits use of force in individual or collective self-defence or pursuant to Security Council authorization under Chapter VII.[69]

The US reiterated its position that there is no right to peace, and that the issues within the draft were being addressed by other forums, such as those concerned with disarmament, peacekeeping, and refugees, and there were other issues already under discussion at the Human Rights Council, such as the right to development and the environment, and some issues are more appropriate for domestic regulation, like private military and security companies (PMSCs).[70] It dismissed the characterization of objectives as rights, such as the elimination of obstacles to the realization of the right to development, the servicing of unjust or unsustainable foreign debt burden and their conditionalities, or the maintenance of an unfair international economic order.

Singapore objected to the right to human security and a right to demand from a government the effective observance of the norms of international law as lacking conceptual clarity. Moreover, it opposed the right to conscientious objection to military service as infringing on the sovereign state's right to defend and preserve itself.[71] Nevertheless, Singapore stated that the document should be 'directed towards the elimination of the threat of war and aggression, the

[66] Korea also objected on the grounds of vagueness. Statement of the Republic of Korea, IGWG.

[67] EU General Statement, Open-ended Intergovernmental Working Group on a United Nations Draft Declaration on the Right to Peace (hereinafter IGWG) (15 February 2013).

[68] Canadian Position, IGWG, first session (18–21 February 2013).

[69] Statement by Australia, IGWG. This was also supported by Sri Lanka and Iran.

[70] US Statement at the IGWG.

[71] Singapore Pointers for Geneva Mission Statement on the Draft Declaration on the Right to Peace at the IGWG.

renunciation of the use of force in international relations and the settlement of international disputes by peaceful means on the basis of the Charter of the United Nations'—indicating support for a narrow conception of peace in the negative sense.

Sri Lanka indicated concern that the development gap between the North and the South challenged the enjoyment of the right to peace, and advocated education. Yet, it considered the document to be overly broad and intrusive, while at the same time indicating concern that it excluded terrorism.[72] Algeria added that reference to a right to internal peace should include recognition of the principle of non-intervention in domestic affairs of states.[73] Iran failed to recognize links between discrimination against women or gender perspectives in peacekeeping and peace. On the other hand, both Syria and Iran considered the issue of private military and security companies, the right to development, and environment and peace education and training as very important issues in relation to peace.

The majority of states considered the document to be too long and called for a succinct, concise, focused, precise document. The NGOs each presented arguments in favour of their niche areas of concern, e.g. women's rights, migrant's rights, etc., thereby representing the vast diversity within civil society. This illuminated the issue of the dilemmas resulting from NGO engagement in human rights lawmaking at the international level. SSIHRL presents its initiative as lawmaking from below, giving voice to the interest of developing nations in articulation and recognition of norms addressing prohibition of the use of force and structural violence, but it is interpreted as too convoluted to constitute a viable legal initiative. The utopian normative language in the draft, which merges *lex lata* with *lex ferenda*, varies from the output pragmatic, positivistic legal cultures. Although SSIHRL claims to have a broad network with other civil society organizations, neither Amnesty International nor Human Rights Watch have engaged on this issue. It may be argued that the state of the normative language reflects their absence, as the draft may be viewed as a conglomerate of particular issues raised by specialized NGOs with niche interests. Further, NGOs may adopt broader social justice policy perspectives that sacrifice technical finesse in normative output. The Intergovernmental Working Group on a draft UN Declaration on the Right to Peace considered a new text of the Draft Declaration on the Right to Peace in its second session (30 June to 4 June 2014). This draft significantly reduced the issues addressed and shifted from defining peace as an enforceable right, to instead emphasizing the link between peace and human rights. It also identified different

[72] Statement by Sri Lanka at the the IGWG. This was supported by Algeria, Intervention by Algeria at the IGWG.

[73] Intervention of the Syrian Arab Republic and Statement by the Islamic Republic of Iran at the IGWG.

stakeholders as having the responsibility to take positive measures on peace through the promotion of human rights and development:

Article 1

Everyone is entitled to the promotion, protection and respect for all human rights and fundamental freedoms, in particular the right to life, in a context in which all human rights, peace and development are fully implemented.

Article 2

States should enhance the principles of freedom from fear and want, equality and nondiscrimination and justice and rule of law as a means to build peace within societies. In this regard, States should undertake measures to bring about, maintain and enhance conditions of peace, particularly to benefit people in need of situations of humanitarian crises.

Article 3

States, the United Nations including its specialized agencies, as well as other interested international, regional, national and local organizations and civil society, should adopt all possible actions with the purpose of implementing, strengthening and elaborating this Declaration, including the establishment and enhancement of national institutions and related infrastructures.

Article 4

The provisions included in this Declaration shall be interpreted in light of the Charter of the United Nations, the Universal Declaration of Human Rights and other relevant international instruments ratified by countries

Hence, the second draft attempted to reach consensus by refraining from defining peace, instead pointing towards implementation of human rights and development as the means by which to attain peace. This draft remains subject to discussion within the Working Group through the end of January 2015.

8. Conclusion: Towards Implementation of Peace

At present the international community remains divided as to whether it is necessary or possible to establish a universal definition of peace and a correlative right to peace under international law; there is a lack of consensus needed to recognize a right to peace. Because the scope of a 'right to peace' remains vague, it is not clear which institutions would have primary responsibility nor whether states would be willing to devote greater resources towards support of the implementation of peace across all the institutional levels—international, regional, and national.

We are reminded that the UN Charter, Article 55 articulates the full enjoyment of human rights by all people as the prerequisite for peace among nations, and hence it is perhaps more appropriate to achieve peace through the pursuit of implementation of human rights rather than articulating a human 'right to peace'. Indeed this is recognized in the second text of the draft Declaration on the Right to Peace. Indeed this is recognized in the second text of the draft Declaration on the Right to Peace. Normative development appears to point towards the identification of peace as a meta-right, value, or obligation, instead of justiciable right per se, as articulated in the Introduction of the book.[74] The term 'peaceful coexistence' continues to resonate in the East, but as this has been more centred on negative peace, there is arguably a need to strengthen positive peace. Both the UN and regional instruments support a combination of negative and positive forms of peace.

Discussion of the law of peace invariably requires a focus on institutionsthe international community regards peace to be an important common value for humanity; the problems arise from defining the scope of the content of peace in a way that is specific enough to enable it to be implemented by institutions for positive preconditions for peace. Should we reform the UN Security Council, strengthen the ICJ, increase reliance on the regional institutions, or create peace ministries at the national level?[75] There is concern that the UN Security Council exhibits tensions within its mandates for both 'peace' and 'security', rendering peace subsidiary to security as pointed out by Hedley Bull.[76] Similarly, a caveat is necessary that national ministries of peace are sometimes created to address post-conflict nation-building and thus may be also linked to security interests such as counter-terrorism, thereby bringing to mind George Orwell's Ministry of Peace that pursued 'Perpetual War' in *1984*. It may be preferable to advocate strengthening positive peace objectives, including remedying structural violence as the primary means by which to attain negative peace.

Yet, the prospects for international institutional reform may be bleak. David Kennedy warns that even if the Security Council were to be reformed 'to reflect the great powers of the twenty-first, rather than the twentieth, century . . . it would be scarcely more effective as a guarantor of international peace and security'.[77] He grimly concludes:

> Globally, the permanent transition toward a universal legal order of equal sovereigns sustains one after another project of hegemony. As a result, rather than a toolkit of policy solutions which might be adopted in the global public interest, it would be more

[74] See Cecilia M. Bailliet and Kjetil Mujezinović Larsen, 'Nordic Expert Consultation on the Right to Peace: Summary and Recommendations', *Nordic Journal of Human Rights* 31 (2013), 262–78.

[75] See John J. Mearsheimer, 'The False Promise of International Institutions', *International Security* 19 (1994/5), 47, 49.

[76] See Bull, *The Anarchical Society*, 18.

[77] David Kennedy, 'Law and the Political Economy of the World', *Leiden Journal of International Law* 26 (2013), 36.

> accurate to see international law as a continuation of the politics of war and economic struggle … When international lawyers say that compliance with international law legitimates, whether on the battlefield or off, they mean that grinding poverty, terrible inequality, environmental destruction, and the premeditated destruction and death of war have become acceptable. It would be more accurate to count the vernaculars of legitimacy and the cramped channels of public order entrenched by international law among the root causes for the difficulties facing the world.[78]

This is a very different scenario than the World Peace through World Law perspective which highlights law as the mode by which to establish universal peace. This movement supported the creation of the International Court of Justice and arbitration tribunals, including the Permanent Court of Arbitration. In 1958, Louis B. Sohn and Grenville Clark proposed to revise the UN Charter in their book, *World Peace Through World Law*, citing President Eisenhower's concern for the rise of the military-industrial complex and his conviction that 'There can be no peace without law.'[79] They explained that this implied effective world law that would forbid violence as a means of dealing with international disputes. They suggested empowering the UN General Assembly as having the primary responsibility to address peace, assigning votes based on member nations' populations, removing veto from a reformed UN Security Council (to be called Executive Council), complete disarmament, and the creation of a World Police Force. Further, they advocated the creation of a world machinery to mitigate disparity in world economy and the protection of the environment and the ocean as being the common heritage of mankind.

James T. Ranney has sought to revive this vision with some amendments. He does not consider the establishment of a global legislature as necessary. Instead, he underscores the vast breadth of international instruments and institutions (including tribunals for dispute resolution), highlighting the WTO and Law of the Sea regimes. He calls for strengthened global economic regulations, improved human rights enforcement (in particular promoting gender equality), and pursuit of global rule of law by expanding the ICC, giving the ICJ compulsory jurisdiction, and the creation of an international equity tribunal. He is also in favour of the establishment of an international police force and arms reduction.

I suggest that perhaps there is need to re-examine conciliation as a mechanism that should be operationalized in a more preventive manner. Indeed, in 1960 Sohn and Clark called for conciliation/equity in these cases:[80]

1. Division of Korea and Vietnam;
2. Formosa (Taiwan), Quemoy and Matsu;
3. The Kashmir problem;

[78] Kennedy, 'Law and the Political Economy of the World', 37.

[79] Grenville Clark and Louis B. Sohn, *World Peace Through World Law* (Cambridge, Mass.: Harvard University Press, 1958), p. xi.

[80] Grenville Clark and Louis B. Sohn, *World Peace Through World Law: Two Alternative Plans* (Cambridge, Mass.: Harvard University Press 1960), 103.

4. The question of assured access to the oil of the Middle East;
5. The problem of international control of vital passages between seas and oceans, such as the Turkish Straits, Suez, and Panama;
6. The problem of fair apportionment of the waters of various international rivers;
7. The question of a less controversial regime for Berlin;
8. The division of Germany;
9. The problem of the repression in certain parts of Africa of non-white majorities by white minorities;[81]
10. Israeli–Arab hostility (considering issues including the resettlement of Arab refugees, the use of water from the Jordan River, access to the Gulf of Aquaba, Israel's right of transit through the Suez Canal, and the boundary disputes between Israel and its neighbours).

Some of these situations have been resolved and some remain ongoing. Malanczuk does not place much faith in conciliation in practice, noting: 'It seems that in the seventy years of the modern history of conciliation, less than twenty cases have been heard, rather more than the number of inquiry cases, but still not an overwhelming number if one considers the hundreds of treaties providing for conciliation.'[82] He bemoans the failure of conciliation in the former Yugoslavia, adding 'One has to accept that in international affairs, problems cannot be solved because the positions of the parties are simply irreconcilable.'[83] This conclusion appears too pessimistic and neglects the fact that in the same period it is arguable that there appears to have been both an overreliance on the use of force and an explosion in the use of international courts.[84] The former has brought a legitimacy crisis to the UN.[85] The latter is considered more appropriate to address situations after violations (given the length of time of proceedings and reparative and punishment functions) and yet some, such as ICTY, are criticized for not achieving reconciliation among constituents. It is suggested that it may be beneficial to reconsider preventive dispute resolution mechanisms in the interest of pursuing peace.

[81] At the time Clark and Sohn characterized this as falling under domestic jurisdiction (not endangering world peace), yet Clark later became a supporter of the civil rights movement.

[82] Peter Melanczuk, *Akehurst's Modern Introduction to International Law* (7th edn. New York: Routledge, 1997), 280.

[83] Melanczuk, *Akehurst's Modern Introduction to International Law*, 281.

[84] See Cesare Romano, Karen Alter, and Yuval Shany (eds.), *The Oxford Handbook of International Adjudication* (Oxford: Oxford University Press, 2014) for an overview of the vast scope of international tribunals.

[85] See A. J. Bellamy, 'Responsibility to Protect or Trojan Horse? The Crisis in Darfur and Humanitarian Intervention after Iraq', *Ethics & International Affairs* 19 (2005), 31–54.

4

The Good Faith Obligation to Maintain International Peace and Security and the Pacific Settlement of Disputes

Simon O'Connor and Cecilia M. Bailliet

Si vis pacem, para pactum! If you want peace, agree to keep the peace.[1]

As to peace—We are sure that our concord will win an enduring peace.[2]

1. Introduction

Malcolm Shaw sets forth that 'It is fair to say that international law has always considered its fundamental purpose to be the maintenance of peace'.[3] This suggests that the architecture of international law in its myriad forms must be directed towards that goal. The manner in which members of the United Nations are to settle their international disputes encompasses a variety of institutions and fora; from the ad hoc international arbitrations through the establishment of the Permanent Court of International Justice and the Permanent Court of Arbitration[4] (bodies founded following the Hague Peace Conference of 1899[5] and its 1907

[1] Robert Erskine Ely, *Proceedings of the National Arbitration and Peace Congress*, 14–17 April 1907 (New York: National Arbitration and Peace Congress), 333.

[2] The Tehran Conference, Declaration of the Three Powers, 1 December 1943.

[3] Malcolm Shaw, *International Law* (4th edn. Cambridge: Cambridge University Press, 2005), 717.

[4] See http://www.pca-cpa.org/showpage.asp?pag_id=363 (accessed 7 Nov 2014). The PCA was established by the first convention adopted at the 1899 (and 1907) Peace Conferences; The Convention on the Pacific Settlement of Disputes, see http://www.pca-cpa.org/showpage.asp?pag_id=1187 (accessed 7 Nov 2014). Whilst initially established as an arbitral tribunal for disputes between states (now hosting, as an intergovernmental organization, 115 member states) it has evolved into a practice of dispute resolution combining states, state entities, intergovernmental organization, and private parties, and a review of pending and past proceedings connote its continuing and arguably growing relevance, see http://www.pca-cpa.org/showpage.asp?pag_id=1029 (accessed 7 Nov 2014).

[5] As to the significance of that date for dispute settlement see James Crawford, 'Continuity and Discontinuity in Dispute Settlement', *Journal of International Dispute Settlement* 1 (2010), 3–24 at 9.

successor), to the establishment of the International Court of Justice and other tribunals.

Whilst the epigram to Michael Howard's *The Invention of Peace* cites the observation of Sir Henry Maine, in his *International Law*, that 'War appears to be as old as mankind, but peace is a modern invention',[6] the idea that international disputes ought to be settled by peaceful means can find certainly older precedent. Vattel dedicates a chapter in his celebrated *Les Droit des Gens* to 'The Manner of Settling Disputes Between Nations'. In this chapter Vattel's considers 'Nations are bound by natural law, which recommends peace concord and charity, to try the most peaceful methods of terminating their disputes' and provides four examples of the most peaceful means for terminating their disputes: Amicable adjustment; Compromise; Mediation; and Arbitration.[7] As a matter of natural law it might be suggest that Vattel's view is that the obligation extends only so far as 'trying', rather than a positive duty to conclude disputes peacefully. However, in what follows we will illustrate that the force of international law might be said to suggest otherwise.

This chapter will address what is the character of the obligations in the Charter with respect to those references to the maintenance of international peace and security and whether future implementation should be strengthened within existing institutions addressing the pacific settlement of disputes.

The chapter is divided into two principal parts. First, it will address the character of the obligation. And what we mean by 'character' is how should we understand, as a matter of law, the scope and extent of the obligation(s) to maintain or not endanger international peace and security. To do this we will consider the content of those references referred to already, in short that states are to settle disputes peacefully. We set forth that there exists a requirement to undertake meaningful negotiations to that end and to do so in good faith. On that last point, however, we will ask what is the significance of the promises states make to each in to, in effect, maintain the peace. Secondly, it will look at avenues open to states to meet that obligation, both within UN bodies and offices and through regional mechanisms.

Some might consider it inopportune, or even naive, we want to attempt in this chapter to consider Article 2(3) and the obligations of maintenance, as distinct from and in isolation from Article 2(4). However our intention in doing so is to avoid the risk of overemphasizing a direct correlation between the maintenance of peace through the absence of war or to have to address the causes for the oft-argued recourse to force in the pursuit of peace: *si vis pacem para bellum*.

[6] Henry S. Maine, *International Law* (London: John Murray, 1890), 8.

[7] Emmerich de Vattel, *The Law of Nations or the Principles of Natural Law Applied to the Conduct and to the Affairs of Nations and of Sovereigns*, trans. Charles G. Fenwick (Washington: Carnegie Institution of Washington, 1916), iii. 223.

2. Maintenance and Not Endangering

The UN Charter, Article 1(1) sets forth that the purpose of the UN is:

> To maintain international peace and security, and to that end: to take effective collective measures for the prevention and removal of threats to the peace, and for the suppression of acts of aggression or other breaches of the peace, and to bring about by peaceful means, and in conformity with the principles of justice and international law, adjustment or settlement of international disputes or situations which might lead to a breach of the peace.

Further, Article 2(3), places primary responsibility for the pacific settlement of disputes upon its members: 'All Members shall settle their international disputes by peaceful means in such a manner that international peace and security, and justice, are not endangered.'[8]

Both these references indicate a preventive approach and suggest the continuity, rather than the interruption, of peace. Their emphasis lies not in resorting to force to establish peace, but in preserving and perpetuating the peace one has. The obligation is thus first and foremost to maintain peace through the resolution of disputes peacefully.[9]

In any textbook on international law, one is bound to find a chapter that addresses the pacific settlement of disputes, and affirmations of the responsibility to settle disputes peacefully are legion.[10] There are, however, perhaps two principal UN documents—prior to a judicial declaration of the customary law status of such a rule—namely General Assembly Declarations 2625 (XXV) and 37/10 annexing the Declaration of International Law concerning Friendly Relations and Co-operation among States in accordance with the Charter of the United Nations,[11] and the Manila Declaration on the Peaceful Settlement of Disputes[12] respectively, that should be considered.

Though some twelve years apart, the Declarations naturally have a considerable amount of synergy, and in the context of the topic under discussion the following observations they made are worth recalling.

On *Friendly Relations*:

> States shall accordingly seek early and just settlement of their international disputes by negotiation, inquiry, mediation, conciliation, arbitration, judicial settlement, resort to regional agencies or arrangements or other peaceful means of their choice. In seeking

[8] For a concise introduction to the law of the Charter, see Robert Kolb, *An Introduction to the Law of the United Nations* (Oxford: Hart, 2010).

[9] This remark is not tautological. It is consistent with the sequence of the Charter.

[10] See Shaw, *International Law*; Vaughan Lowe, *International Law* (Oxford: Oxford University Press, 2007), 104; James Crawford, *Brownlie's Principles of Public International Law* (8th edn. Oxford: Oxford University Press, 2012), 718; Peter Malanczuk, *Akehurst's Modern Introduction to International Law* (7th edn. London: Routledge, 1997).

[11] UNGA Res. 2625 (24 October 1970), UN Doc. A/RES/25/2625.

[12] UNGA Res. 37/10 (15 November 1982), UN Doc. A/RES/37/590.

such a settlement the parties shall agree upon such peaceful means as may be appropriate to the circumstances and nature of the dispute.

The parties to a dispute have the duty, in the event of failure to reach a solution by any one of the above peaceful means, to continue to seek a settlement of the dispute by other peaceful means agreed upon by them.

On *Peaceful Settlement:*

Every State shall settle its international disputes exclusively by peaceful means in such a manner that international peace and security, and justice, are not endangered.

International disputes shall be settled on the basis of the sovereign equality of States and in accordance with the principle of free choice of means in conformity with obligations under the Charter of the United Nations and with the principles of justice and international law. Recourse to, or acceptance of, a settlement procedure freely agreed to by States with regard to existing or future disputes to which they are parties shall not be regarded as incompatible with the sovereign equality of States.

In 1984, when delivering its judgment in the *Military and Paramilitary Activities* case, the ICJ affirmed that 'the principle that the parties to any dispute, particularly any dispute the continuation of which is likely to endanger the maintenance of international peace and security, should seek a solution by peaceful means ... has ... the status of customary law'[13] and it is a 'principle [of] customary law that prescribes the peaceful settlement of international disputes'.[14]

Whilst adamant in its view, given its repetition in successive paragraphs of its judgment, the Court did not elaborate on the basis for its conclusion of the principle's customary status.[15] Whilst perhaps excusable, the significance that could be drawn is to suggest that the two remarks perhaps offer a slight discontinuity. The first states that parties are to *seek* a peaceful solution, the latter that it is a prescription of international law to settle international disputes peacefully.[16] Now it might be thought mere semantics to suggest distinction that a state should seek to resolve disputes peacefully, or that a state should resolve disputes peacefully. The demand of the latter though is arguably greater, though a prevailing view might well be to suggest that the extent of the legal obligation does not go so far as to demand peaceful resolution. (In other words, states are not always bound to resolve disputes by peaceful means.)

[13] *Military and Paramilitary Activities in and against Nicaragua (Nicaragua* v. *United States of America),* (Merits) [1986] ICJ Rep 1986, 14, para. 290. (Henceforth *Nicaragua* v. *United States.*)

[14] *Nicaragua* v. *United States*, para. 291.

[15] The paragraphs concern more the so-called Contadoro process (or negotiations) that the Courts had analysed in its earlier preliminary judgment on jurisdiction and admissibility, *Nicaragua* v. *United States* (Jurisdiction and Admissibility), ICJ Rep 1984, para. 392.

[16] Though there are again challenges that some contend are present in relation to the distinction between disputes and conflicts, it is generally accepted that the definition of disputes provided by the PICJ in *The Mavrommatis Palestine Concessions* (*Greece* v. *United Kingdom*), PICJ Rep Series A, No. 2 (1924), 11: 'a disagreement over a point of law or fact, a conflict of legal views or of interests between two persons'. This has been defined by Shaw as 'authoritative' (p. 719), though see also the demarcation by Lowe on disputes and conflicts.

This conclusion would seem to be consistent, in part with the commentary Tomuschat offers to Article 2(3).[17] In his remarks, Tomuschat considers what he terms 'the substance of the obligation' and addresses both its effect and what conduct the obligation entails. He is unequivocal that the principle of peaceful settlement is a legal obligation, relying on the imperative tense of 'shall' and the French and Spanish translated equivalents. It is no mere recommendatory provision. What then does it demand? For Tomuschat 'It should be noted that Art. 2(3), obliges states to strive for the resolution of a dispute existing between them only to the best of their abilities. There is no obligation to reach a specific result.' There exists only an obligation of conduct.[18] However, that conduct is, at the very least, to negotiate. Furthermore, Tomuschat notes that the text of Art. 33(1) states that 'parties are subject to a legally binding obligation to seek a peaceful solution'.[19] He explains that this requires best efforts, in particular in pursuing negotiations; however, parties may diverge on choice of procedure, as one party may wish to seek a judgment by a court while the other may prefer negotiations.[20] It is considered a basic principle that parties to a dispute retain the primary responsibility for settling the dispute, also in relation to engagement by UN or regional institutions.

3. The Obligation to Negotiate

Negotiation is the pursuit of direct dialogue between parties to a dispute. Parties have the duty to make genuine and reasonable efforts to reach a solution in good faith, thereby requiring goodwill, flexibility, and mutual understanding. States favour negotiation because they retain control of the process without having to cede to a third party. Parties may choose to make the settlement legally binding by drawing up a treaty, or instead they may opt for a non-binding exchange of notes. Negotiations may be pursued concurrently with resort to other dispute resolution mechanisms, such as the ICJ, the Security Council, or the General Assembly. The question of the characteristics of what would constitute the meaning of negotiations or the obligation to negotiate (that is a peaceful

[17] Christian Tomuschat, 'Article 2(3)', in *The Charter of the United Nations: A Commentary*, Bruno Simma, Herman Mosler, Andreas Paulus, Eleni Chaitidou, and Maurizio Giuliano (eds.) (Oxford: Oxford University Press, 2012), 181–99.

[18] Tomuschat, 'Article 2(3)', 190. That the obligation does not demand resolution Tomuschat contends, rests on the principle of sovereign equality. Consider, however, the Charter language compared to Art. 1 of the Hague Convention on the Peaceful Settlement of Disputes, 'with a view to obviating, as far as possible, recourse to force in the relations between States, the Signatory Powers agree to use their best efforts to insure the pacific settlements of international differences'.

[19] Christian Tomuschat, 'Chapter VI Pacific Settlement of Disputes', in Simma et al. *Charter of the United Nations*, 1074. He points out that the English text uses the word 'shall' and the French version employs the expression 'doivent'.

[20] Tomuschat, 'Chapter VI Pacific Settlement of Disputes', citing *Pulp Mills on the River Uruguay (Argentina* v. *Uruguay)*, (Judgment) [2010] ICJ Rep 2010, 14, para. 150, and *Application of the International Convention on the Elimination of All Forms of Racial Discrimination (Georgia* v. *Russian Federation)*, (Judgment) [2011] ICJ Rep 2011, 70, para. 158.

means of dispute resolution) has been dealt with on numerous occasions by the International Court of Justice and its predecessors. A helpful summary of that analysis has, relatively recently, been provided by the Court in its judgment in the *Application of Interim Accord of 13 September 1995*. These proceedings, following the break-up of the Socialist Republic of Yugoslavia, concerned application for membership of the United Nations of the 'former Yugoslav Republic of Macedonia'. The Court surmises thus:

'that the meaning of negotiations for the purposes of dispute settlement, or the obligation to negotiate, has been clarified through the jurisprudence of the Court and that of its predecessor, as well as arbitral awards. As the Permanent Court of International Justice already stated in 1931 in the case concerning *Railway Traffic between Lithuania and Poland*, the obligation to negotiate is first of all 'not only to enter into negotiations, but also to pursue them as far as possible, with a view to concluding agreements'. No doubt this does not imply 'an obligation to reach an agreement' or that lengthy negotiations must be pursued of necessity. However, States must conduct themselves so that the 'negotiations are meaningful'. This requirement is not satisfied, for example, where either of the parties 'insists upon its own position without contemplating any modification of it' or where they obstruct negotiations, for example, by interrupting communications or causing delays in an unjustified manner or disregarding the procedures agreed upon. Negotiations with a view to reaching an agreement also imply that the parties should pay reasonable regard to the interests of the other. As for the proof required for finding of the existence of bad faith (a circumstance which would justify either Party in claiming to be discharged from performance), 'something more must appear than the failure of particular negotiations'. It could be provided by circumstantial evidence but should be supported 'not by disputable inferences but by clear and convincing evidence which compels such a conclusion.'[21]

4. Good Faith and Promises

That states should seek the peaceful settlement of disputes and that an obligation to negotiate is incumbent upon them is, for the effective functioning of an international peaceful order, undeniable. Underlying such, as it equally underlies the meeting of obligations under the Charter as a treaty, is the principle of good faith, and we suggest associated with that are the promises uttered on which acts in good faith rely.

The idea of good faith (bona fides) has along with much else in jurisprudence a significant historical pedigree,[22] but it remains seminal to any functioning international system of rules. Indeed as the ICJ observed in one of its most recent

[21] *Application of Interim Accord of 13 September 1995 (the former Yugoslav Republic of Macedonia* v. *Greece)* (Judgment) [2011] ICJ Rep 2011, 664, para. 132, citations omitted.

[22] See John F. O'Connor, *Good Faith in International Law* (Aldershot: Dartmouth, 1991) for a historical review, though with significant emphasis in the Roman-Christian and Classicist traditions of international law.

decisions: 'Once a State has made a commitment concerning its conduct, its good faith in complying with that commitment is to be presumed.'[23]

Good faith is arguably omnipotent and pervades the essence of any negotiated system of rules, domestic or international. It might often be said to be one of the fundamental principles of international law.[24] Article 2(2) makes explicit the requirement to fulfil obligations assumed under the Charter in good faith. In the context of the purpose and principles of the UN, it is perhaps worth recalling that the obligations contained in Article 2 are directed towards positive steps to seek peaceful settlement of disputes and to *refrain* from the use of force.[25]

A sceptic of such an affirmative statement might suggest it is a rebuttable presumption. Indeed, amongst international law scholars there may be many who would easily ascribe to Henkin's adage, 'It is probably the case that *almost all nations observe almost all principles of international law and almost all of their obligations almost all of the time.*'[26]

However even in a realist's view there has to be considerable merit in the principle of good faith and the keeping of promises.

It seems generally accepted that the notion of good faith is imbued with certain underlying assumptions that inform the reliance that is placed upon it: the ideas of fairness and honesty are often cited. If someone is predictably fair and honest one will generally rely on the offers they make; they create legitimate expectations.

In the *Nuclear Tests* case, the ICJ was asked to order the cessation by France of atmospheric testing of nuclear weapons in the Pacific. France's declaration on the cessation of testing was the source, ultimately, of the Court decision that the case should not proceed. The case is considered by some to be a watershed, not in terms of its ultimate decision but with regard to the 'bindingness of unilateral assurances, ie promises in international law'[27] and, as Thomas Franck has concluded, '[t]he principle of good faith, the Court explained, can confer a binding character

[23] *Questions Relating to the Seizure and Detention of Certain Documents and Data (Timor-Leste* v. *Australia)* (Request for the Indication of Provisional Measures) General List No. 156 [2014] ICJ 1, para. 44.

[24] See Georg Schwarzenberger and E. D. Brown, *A Manual of International Law* (6th edn. Milton: Professional Books, 1976), 118; Steven Reinhold, *'Good Faith in International Law', Bonn Research Papers on Public International Law* 2/2013 (23 May 2013); O'Connor, *Good Faith in International Law*, 120; Hugh Thirlway, *The Law and Procedure of the International Court of Justice Fifty Years of Jurisprudence* (Oxford: Oxford University Press 2013); Marion Panizzon, *Good Faith in the Jurisprudence of the WTO* (Oxford: Hart, 2006), 11–47.

[25] There is a line of argument that might suggests that there is therefore no obligation in the Charter to use force. Art. 51 merely recognizes the inherent right to self-defence, thus entitling, but not obliging the use offorce. Similarly it is open to the Security Council to authorize the use of force under Art. 42 ('it may take'): it does not oblige them to do so. There might be an argument that states are obliged under Art. 43 to make forces available, but the essence of the observation here is the good faith duty towards the obligations under the Charter—peaceful settlement and avoidance of the use of force.

[26] Louis Henkin, *How Nations Behave* (New York: Columbia University Press, 1979) (italics in original).

[27] Christian Eckart, *Promises of States under International Law* (Oxford: Hart, 2012).

on universal declarations'.[28] Good faith and promises are topics with a rich vein of thought, both philosophically and jurisprudentially, that is perhaps more overlooked than it should be. Phillip Allott, for one, sees promise as the basis of law, and draws a distinction between *express* and *tacit* promising.[29] Christian Eckart has perhaps produced the only current monograph explicitly on the topic,[30] but that is not to say the issue has not been thought about judicially.

In those same proceedings Judge De Castro, in his dissenting opinion, offered what seems to be at least a way in which the Court could address the value and merit of promises in the context of the *Nuclear Tests* case:

> Even so, it must be added that the Court, as a judicial organ, must first and foremost have regard to the legal worth of the French authorities' statements. Upon the Court there falls the task of interpreting their meaning and verifying their purpose. They can be viewed as the announcement of a programme, of an intention with regard to the future, their purpose being to enlighten all those who may be interested in the method which the French authorities propose to follow where nuclear tests are concerned. They can also be viewed as simple promises to conduct no more nuclear tests in the atmosphere. Finally, they can be considered as promises giving rise to a genuine legal obligation.

De Castro continued by, albeit with some qualification, that it is possible to discern a 'promise envisaged as a source of legal obligations'. He continues

> For a promise to be legally binding on a State, it is necessary that the authorities from which it emanates should be competent so to bind the State (a question of internal constitutional law and international law) and that they should manifest the intention and will to bind the State (a question of interpretation).

De Castro does seem to recognize that if a liability is acknowledged and reliance is placed upon a consequent promise to discharge that liability, it can give rise to a legal (beyond merely moral) obligation to keep one's promise.[31] Whilst there are of course a significant number of other decisions that have addressed the topic,[32] Eckart cites three premises as the legal basis for promises that bind: presumed consent; state sovereignty and the intention to be bound; and good faith and reliance.[33]

Notwithstanding the constraints and capacity to withdraw that de Castro contends,[34] promising must remain a morally and legally significant act. One might suggest that if it's not, it's not a promise. Promising is elemental to unilateral

[28] Thomas M. Franck, *Fairness in International Law and Institutions* (Oxford: Clarendon, 1995), 52; see also T. M. Franck 'Word Made Law: The Decision of the ICJ in the Nuclear Tests Cases', *American Journal of International Law* 69 (1975), 612–20.

[29] Phillip Allot, *Eumonia: New Order for a New World* (Oxford: Oxford University Press, 1991).

[30] Eckart, *Promises of States under International Law*, 27.

[31] *Nuclear Tests Case (New Zealand* v. *France)* (Judgment) [1974] ICJ Rep 1974, 253, Dissenting Opinion of Judge de Castro, 374. Arguably not subject to mere presumption, the promise must be 'clearly manifested', and whilst not directly requiring reciprocity there should be acknowledgement of that promise and De Castro contends it to be revocable in the absence of acceptance.

[32] Eckart, *Promises of States under International Law*, 83–174, cites at least ten decisions from the ICJ.

[33] Eckart, *Promises of States under International Law*, 194–201.

[34] In *Promises of States under International Law*, 251–75, Eckart uses the term 'revocability'.

statements, the conclusion of treaties, and the application of good faith to both. Either independently or as an essential precursor, promises invoke the reliance and expectations on which international stability depends. Their normative significance should not be understated.

Parties to disputes who are also members of the UN are expected to make good faith efforts to resolve issues peacefully, and where they have exhausted pacific means unsuccessfully, they may turn to the UN, regional institutions, or other third parties for support. These institutions facilitate various forms of pacific settlement of disputes: Mediation is the process whereby a third party facilitates communication between parties and may make proposals for settlement. The mediator is active as he or she receives information from the parties and offers solutions. The term 'good offices' is used when a neutral party is sent to persuade parties to negotiate, thereby serving as a channel of communication. Conciliation requires parties to submit pleadings to the third party who may conduct an investigation, submit a report, and issue a non-binding decision that parties may choose whether or not to adopt.[35] Should parties wish to pursue a more formal process, they may select arbitration, which issues binding awards.

5. Pacific Settlement of Disputes within the UN

The UN Charter identifies the following entities as having the mandate to promote the pacific settlement of disputes: the Secretary-General, the Security Council, the General Assembly, and regional organizations. In addition, Art. 36(3) of the Charter sets forth that disputes should be referred to the ICJ; this is discussed separately by Zyberi in Chapter 17.[36]

5.1. UN Secretary-General

The Secretary-General may 'bring to the attention of the Security Council any matter that in his opinion may threaten international peace and security' and in turn the Security Council will coordinate with the Secretary-General to facilitate peace between parties.[37] The UN Secretary-General carries a 'good offices' and mediation function which seeks to prevent and resolve disputes between states and other parties to conflicts, at times employing special envoys, representatives, or coordinators (such as the Special Coordinator for the Middle East Peace Process) as well as a Mediation Support Unit within the UN Department of Political Affairs, thereby promoting peace.[38]

[35] See UNGA Res. 50/50 (11 December 1995) UN Doc. A/RES/50/50.

[36] Nsongurua J. Udombana, 'The Right to a Peaceful World Order', in *International Human Rights Law: Six Decades after the UDHR and Beyond*, Mashood A. Baderin and Manisuli Ssenyonjo (eds.) (Aldershot: Ashgate 2010), 137.

[37] Charter of the United Nations (signed 26 June 1945, entered into force 24 October 1945), Art. 99.

[38] See UN Charter, Art. 98.

In 2012, the Secretary-General submitted a report on mediation pursuant to General Assembly resolution 65/283. The report identified eight trends in respect of conflict and mediation.[39] Those trends included an increase in the number of conflicts and in complexity in terms of actors and objectives. It also noted that 'there remains a considerable number of low-intensity conflicts that could escalate into violence'. On the issue of mediation, the report recognized a shifting role of mediation in light of continuing developments in legal and normative frameworks, and noted perhaps unsurprisingly, the need for local ownership and engagement in mediation, with a particular emphasis on inclusivity. As the report confirmed 'Mediation is not the exclusive occupation of envoys and does not end with the signing of a peace agreement'. In the period between the Secretary General report in enhancing mediation (S/2009/189) and the 2012 report, it listed the following situations where parties to conflicts and disputes have sought United Nations-led or supported mediation, facilitation and good offices efforts: Afghanistan, Bangladesh, Côte d'Ivoire, Cyprus, Ecuador, Equatorial Guinea-Gabon, Fiji, Georgia, the Great Lakes region, Guinea, Guyana-Venezuela, Iraq, Honduras, Kenya, the Korean Peninsula, Kyrgyzstan, Lebanon, Libya, Madagascar, Malawi, Maldives, the Middle East (Israel-Palestine), Myanmar, Nepal, Panama, Peru, Solomon Islands, Sri Lanka, Sudan (Darfur), Sudan-South Sudan, Syrian Arab Republic, Thailand, Tunisia, Western Sahara and Yemen.

In a similar vein and pursuant to a request from the Security Council in 2011 the Secretary General submitted his report entitled Preventive Diplomacy: Delivering Results.[40] The report sought to focus, by its own admission on diplomatic activity aimed at mitigating or preventing conflict and look at methods available to such ends. This short report outlined a number of actors, instruments, and methodologies that could be employed, and gave particular emphasis to partnership and the significant role for regional institutions to meet these goals. On 22 September 2011 the President of the Security Council welcomed the report reaffirming the Security Council's primary responsibility for the maintenance of international peace and security, reiterating positively many of the conclusions in the report.[41]

The UN also has a Peacebuilding Commission which pursues a range of measures targeted to reduce the risk of conflict relapse by strengthening national capacity at all levels for conflict management, and lays the foundations for sustainable

[39] Report by Secretary-General, 'Strengthening the Role of Mediation in the Peaceful Settlement of Disputes, Conflict Prevention and Resolution', 25 June 2012, UN Doc. A/66/811, including an annexe on Guidance for Effective Mediation. The Guidance lists eight Key Mediation Fundamentals (though the guidance does not purport to offer exclusive or exhaustive lists). They are: preparedness; consent; impartiality; inclusivity; national ownership; international law and normative frameworks; coherence, coordination and complimentarity of the mediation effort; quality peace agreements.

[40] Report by Secretary-General, 'Preventive Diplomacy: Delivering Results', 26 August 2011, UN Doc. S/2011/552, http://www.un.org/wcm/webdav/site/undpa/shared/undpa/pdf/SG%20Report%20on%20Preventive%20Diplomacy.pdf (accessed 24 June 2014).

[41] UN Security Council, 'Statement by the President of the Security Council', 22 September 2011, UN Doc. S/PRST/2011/18, http://www.peacemaker.un.org/sites/peacemaker.un.org/files/SC_PRST201118%20%28english%29.pdf (accessed 24 June 2014).

peace and development.[42] It provides support for basic safety and security, including action on landmines, protection of civilians, disarmament, demobilization and reintegration, strengthening the rule of law, and initiation of security sector reform. It also buttresses political processes, including electoral processes, and promotes inclusive dialogue and reconciliation. Further, it grounds the provision of basic services, such as water and sanitation, health and primary education, and safe and sustainable return of refugees and internally displaced people. It seeks to restore core government functions, particularly basic public administration and public finance. Finally, it claims to underpin economic revitalization, including job creation, particularly for youth and demobilized former combatants. It has been active in Burundi, Sierra Leone, Guinea Bissau, Central African Republic, and Liberia. The Commission is buttressed by UN Peacebuilding Support Offices (which administer the UN Peacebuilding Fund), and UN Peacekeeping Operations.

5.2. UN Security Council

The UN Charter may be conceived as an instrument that seeks to expand the pursuit of peace beyond interstate relations. It confers primary responsibility for maintaining peace and security on the UN Security Council through settlement of interstate disputes via Chapter VI investigation, negotiation, mediation, referral to the ICJ, resort to regional agencies, or sanctions and ultimately use of force via Chapter VII.[43]

A comprehensive record of decisions of the Security Council concerning the pacific settlement of disputes can be found in its Repertoire.[44] Pursuant to Chapter VI of the Charter, the Security Council calls upon parties to settle disputes

[42] See: http://www.un.org/en/peacebuilding/ (accessed 24 June 2014). Accessed 7 Nov 2014. See also UN General Assembly, 'In Larger Freedom: Towards Development, Security and Human Rights for All', Report of the Secretary-General: addendum: Peacebuilding Commission: explanatory note by the Secretary-General, 23 May 2005, UN Doc. A/59/2005/Add.2, http://www.refworld.org/docid/4a54bbfb0.html (accessed 7 Nov 2014).

[43] See UN Charter, Art. 24(1). 'In order to ensure prompt and effective action by the United Nations, its Members confer on the Security Council primary responsibility for the maintenance of international peace and security, and agree that in carrying out its duties under this responsibility the Security Council acts on their behalf.'

Art. 33: '1. The parties to any dispute, the continuance of which is likely to endanger the maintenance of international peace and security, shall, first of all, seek a solution by negotiation, enquiry, mediation, conciliation, arbitration, judicial settlement, resort to regional agencies or arrangements, or other peaceful means of their own choice. 2. The Security Council shall, when it deems necessary, call upon the parties to settle their dispute by such means. According to Articles 36–38 of the UN Charter, the UN Security-Council may pursue settlement of inter-state disputes via mediation and may dictate the terms of settlement in the interest of maintenance of peace and security. In accordance with, Article 52 of the Charter, the Security Council should encourage the peaceful settlement of local disputes through regional organizations and may refer such disputes to them.' However, the Security Council also applies binding measures, including the applications of sanctions, e.g. travel bans, freezing of assets, and targeted arms embargos, as well as the use of force, against non-state actors, including terrorists and armed groups.

[44] See http://www.un.org/en/sc/repertoire/settlements.shtml. (Accessed 7 Nov 2014). There exists also a similar repertory for the UN Organs, see http://www.un.org/law/repertory/ (accessed 7 Nov 2014).

by peaceful means, endorses peace agreements concluded by parties to a conflict, or recommends settlement procedures, such as bilateral or multilateral negotiations, mediation, or conciliation by the Secretary-General, or referral to regional institutions. The resolutions issued under Chapter VI are considered-non-coercive and are not legally binding upon parties (with the exception of investigations). The Security Council has issued recommendations to states and non-state actors, calling for negotiations and peaceful solutions in conflict situations, *inter alia*: Afghanistan, Angola, Burundi, Cambodia, Chad, Côte d'Ivoire, Congo, Cyprus, El Salvador, Eritrea-Ethiopia, East Timor, the Falklands/Malvinas, Greece–Turkey, Georgia, the Great Lakes region, Guinea-Bissau, Iraq–Iran, Iraq–Kuwait, Lebanon, Libya, Liberia, the occupied Arab territories, Rwanda, Sierra Leone, Somalia, Sudan, Tajikistan, Yemen, and the former Yugoslavia.

In terms of scope, the Security Council has an advantage over the ICJ, as the latter cannot permit non-state actors to appear as parties to a case before it. Yet, the Security Council is a political body that has the primary interest of keeping the peace and not judging the legal issues of a dispute. Of concern, Tomuschat concludes that 'All observers agree that the SC has achieved only modest results in implementing Art. 33(2) and more generally within the entire framework of Chapter VI. Apparently, the institutional pressures exerted upon the parties to a dispute in accordance with Chapter VI are somewhat lacking in persuasive impact.'[45] There appears to be a need to strengthen the actual implementation of Chapter VI in order to reinvigorate the pursuit of peace in practice. Rather than be viewed as peripheral mechanisms, they should be given foremost attention by the international community.

Further dilemmas arise from the unrestrained use of veto by the permanent members within the Security Council. Indeed, as far back as 1949, the UN General Assembly issued Resolution 290 IV on the Essential of Peace which called upon the Permanent Members of the Security Council 'to broaden progressively their cooperation and to exercise restraint in the use of the veto in order to make the Security Council a more effective instrument for maintaining peace'.[46]

5.3. UN General Assembly

The General Assembly is considered a complement to the UN Security Council, as it is empowered to discuss any question or matter relating to the maintenance of international peace and security that is brought before it by a state or by the Security Council and may make recommendations to the state or states concerned

[45] Tomuschat, 'Chapter VI Pacific Settlement of Disputes', 1085. On 21 August 2014 the Security Council adopted Resolution 2171 on the maintenance of international peace and security—Conflict prevention (S/RES/2171)—in which it reaffirmed 'its commitment to the settlement of disputes by peaceful means and the promotion of necessary preventive action in response to disputes or situations, the continuance of which is likely to endanger the maintenance of peace and security'.

[46] Moreover, it considered disregard for UN Charter principles by states to be 'primarily responsible for the continuance of international tension'.

or to the Security Council or both.[47] It can 'recommend measures for the peaceful adjustment of any other situation, regardless of origin, which it deems likely to impair the general welfare or friendly relations among nations'.[48] Hence, the UN General Assembly shares responsibility for mediation.[49]

Where the Security Council, because of lack of unanimity of the permanent members, fails to exercise its primary responsibility for the maintenance of international peace and security, the General Assembly shall seize itself of the matter. Ten emergency special sessions have been convened: on the 1956 war between Israel and Egypt and the British-French attack on the Suez Canal zone to the Israeli occupation of Palestinian territory (adjourned in 2006 after having started in 1997).[50] The General Assembly lacks the enforcement powers of the Security Council, nonetheless, its issuance of recommendations in certain situations, such as the call to China desist from aggression in Korea and the appeal to Britain and France at the time of Suez have been considered 'politically expensive to resist'.[51] Yet, Tomuschat offers the critique that 'As a quasi-parliamentary body, the GA is ill-suited to become involved in an effective manner in disputes between two States. The SC, whose fifteen members can meet behind closed doors, is a much more appropriate body for this kind of mediation.'[52]

However, at the substantive level, the General Assembly has adopted specific resolutions on peace that articulate the language of a 'right to peace'. The preamble of the UN General Assembly resolution 33/73 Declaration on the Preparation of Societies for Life in Peace (1978) reaffirms the right of individuals, States and all mankind to life in peace. This is linked to non-discrimination in Art. 1:

> Every nation and every human being, regardless of race, conscience, language or sex, has the inherent right to life in peace. Respect for that right, as well as for other human rights, is in the common interest of all mankind and an indispensable condition of advancement of all nations, large and small, in all fields.

The UN General Assembly resolution 39/11 Declaration on the Right of Peoples to Peace (1984) identifies an obligation of states to fulfil the right, and also calls upon IOs for implementation:

> Recognizing that the maintenance of a peaceful life for peoples is the sacred duty of each State: 1) Solemnly proclaims that the peoples of our planet have a sacred right to

[47] UN Charter, Art. 11. [48] UN Charter, Art. 14.

[49] The Manila Declaration on the Peaceful Settlement of International Disputes was adopted by consensus on 15 November 1982 (annexe to UN Doc. A/RES/37/10), it reaffirmed the Charter Principle that all states shall settle their disputes by peaceful means and listed, *inter alia*, negotiation, mediation, and good offices as means of peaceful settlement. It highlighted the role of the General Assembly in this field. In July 2011, the General Assembly also adopted by consensus a resolution entitled 'Strengthening the Role of Mediation in the Peaceful Settlement of Disputes, Conflict Prevention and Resolution' (UN Doc. A/RES/65/283), which recognized the increased use of mediation.

[50] See UNGA Res. 377 A (V) (3 November 1950); Christian Tomuschat, 'Uniting for Peace' (United Nations Audiovisual Library of International Law, 2008), http://legal.un.org/avl/pdf/ha/ufp/ufp_e.pdf (accessed 24 June 2014).

[51] Evan Luard, *Conflict and Peace in the Modern International System* (New York: State University of New York Press, 1988), 216.

[52] Christian Tomuschat, 'Chapter VI: Pacific Settlement of Disputes', in *The Charter of the United Nations*, Simma et al. (eds.) 1072.

peace; 2) Solemnly declares that the preservation of the right of peoples to peace and the promotion of its implementation constitute a fundamental obligation of each State; 3) Emphasizes that ensuring the exercise of the right of peoples to peace demands that the policies of States be directed towards the elimination of the threat of war, particularly nuclear war, the renunciation of the use of force in international relations and the settlement of international disputes by peaceful means on the basis of the Charter of the United Nations; 4) Appeals to all States and international organizations to do their utmost to assist in implementing the right of peoples to peace through the adoption of appropriate measures at both the national and international level.

These resolutions were affirmed by the General Assembly in resolutions A/RES/57/216 of 27 February 2003, A/RES/60/163 of 2 March 2006, and A/RES/63/189 of 18 March 2009, the General Assembly declared 'that the peoples of our planet have a sacred right to peace and that the preservation and promotion of peace constitutes a fundamental obligation of each State'. The General Assembly considers the settlement of international disputes by peaceful means to be an intrinsic aspect of the right to peace.

6. Pacific Settlement of Disputes: Regional Instruments and Institutions

One of the central areas of debate regarding implementation of peace is whether increased regionalism promotes or inhibits peace.[53] The UN Charter, Article 52 underscores the role of regional institutions in the pacific settlement of disputes:

1. Nothing in the present Charter precludes the existence of regional arrangements or agencies for dealing with such matters relating to the maintenance of international peace and security as are appropriate for regional action provided that such arrangements or agencies and their activities are consistent with the Purposes and Principles of the United Nations.
2. The Members of the United Nations entering into such arrangements or constituting such agencies shall make every effort to achieve pacific settlement of local disputes through such regional arrangements or by such regional agencies before referring them to the Security Council.
3. The Security Council shall encourage the development of pacific settlement of local disputes through such regional arrangements or by such regional agencies either on the initiative of the states concerned or by reference from the Security Council.

This section provides a brief overview of the regional normative and institutional frameworks relating to peace, all of which cooperate with UN peacemaking institutions to promote the pacific settlement of disputes.

[53] See Charles Covell, *Kant and the Law of Peace: A Study in the Philosophy of International Law and International Relations* (New York: Palgrave 1998), 15.

6.1. Europe and the Organization for Security and Cooperation in Europe

The constitutive instruments of the regional institutions reiterate the identification of peace as an aim and underscore the components of peace. Within Europe the Treaty of Lisbon, Article 2, sets forth that 'the Union's aim is to promote peace, its values and the well-being of its peoples'. The 1957 European Convention for the Peaceful Settlement of Disputes sets forth in the preamble that the members of the Council of Europe confirm that 'the pursuit of peace based upon justice is vital for the preservation of human society and civilization' and thus agree to submit legal disputes to the ICJ, arbitration, or conciliation.

In 2012 the EU received the Nobel Peace Prize for advancing the causes of peace, reconciliation, democracy, and human rights in Europe. The Norwegian Nobel Committee said its decision was based on the stabilizing role the EU has played in transforming most of Europe from a continent of war to a continent of peace.[54] Indeed, the law of peace is in large part rooted in the European experience of regional integration. Interstate disputes and disputes regarding EU organs may be referred to the Court of Justice.

The EU also pursues Peace-building Partnerships, which envisage building the capacities of relevant organizations in pre-crisis situations to develop early-warning systems, provide mediation and reconciliation services, and to address intercommunity tensions. It also deals with measures for improving post-conflict and post-disaster recovery.[55] One of the most important aspects of the EU's peacebuilding programmes is that they address situations in other regions, such as Africa, Latin America, and Asia, thereby disproving concerns that regionalism would weaken the aspiration of pursuit of world peace.

Similarly, the Organization for Security and Cooperation in Europe (OSCE) pursues conflict prevention and resolution through mediation, such as in Nagorno-Karabakh, Transdniestria, and Georgia.[56] Nevertheless the formal procedures for settlement of bilateral disputes have not been utilized. At the normative level, the Conference on Security and Cooperation in Europe Final Act (Helsinki 1975) reaffirms the objective of promoting better relations among themselves and ensuring conditions in which their people can live in true and lasting peace free from any threat to or attempt against their security.[57] The CSCE included a Declaration on Principles Guiding Relations between participating states that set

[54] See 'Nobel Peace Prize 2012 Awarded to European Union, One Year On', EU, http://europa.eu/about-eu/basic-information/eu-nobel/ (accessed 24 June 2014).

[55] See 'The EU's Peace-building Partnership', European Union External Action, http://eeas.europa.eu/ifs/pbp_en.htm (accessed 24 June 2014); See also Steven Blockmans, Jan Wouters, and Tom Ruys (eds.), *The European Union and Peacebuilding Policy and Legal Aspects* (The Hague: T.M.C. Asser, 2010).

[56] See 'Conflict Prevention and Resolution', OSCE, http://www.osce.org/what/conflict-prevention (accessed 7 Nov 2014).

[57] See also the 1991 Valletta Report of the CSCE Meeting of Experts on Peaceful Settlement of Disputes, OSCE (8 February 1991), http://www.osce.org/secretariat/30115?download=true (accessed 7 Nov 2014).

forth sovereign equality and respect for the rights inherent in sovereignty, refrainment from the threat or use of force, inviolability of frontiers, territorial integrity of states, peaceful settlement of disputes, non-intervention in internal affairs, and cooperation among states. It called for use of negotiation, inquiry, mediation, conciliation, arbitration, and judicial settlement. However, it also included respect for human rights and underscored equality and self-determination of peoples. Although the Soviets suggested that the principle of non-intervention preceded respect for human rights, this instrument actually fomented strong social movements which open doors for political reforms and human rights protection.[58] Hence in practice, the Final Act's implementation merged negative and positive dimensions of peace.

6.2. The Americas

At the inter-American level, the preamble of the OAS Charter declares peace to be one of incentives for regional integration. Chapters I and II set forth that the purpose and principles of the organization is to 'achieve an order of peace and justice', to 'strengthen [the] peace and security of the continent', and 'to ensure the pacific settlement of disputes that may arise among the Member States'. It condemns wars of aggression and provides for common action on the part of those States in the event of aggression. Further, it underscores the duty of non-intervention and calls for use of peaceful procedures in international controversies between American states. Of interest, it seeks to limit conventional weapons in order to promote development, identifies social justice and social security as the bases of lasting peace, and requires that 'the education of peoples should be directed toward justice, freedom, and peace'.

Hence, the OAS Charter also pursues both negative and positive conceptions of peace. Chapter V of the OAS Charter sets forth that 'International disputes between Member States shall be submitted to the peaceful procedures set forth in this Charter.'[59] These are identified as peaceful procedures: direct negotiation, good offices, mediation, investigation and conciliation, judicial settlement, arbitration, and those procedures that the parties to the dispute may especially agree upon at any time.[60] Should a dispute be unresolved through the usual diplomatic channels, the parties shall agree on some other peaceful procedure that will enable them to reach a solution.[61] Similarly, the American Treaty on Pacific Settlement, the 'Pact of Bogota' (30 April 1948) states that the parties 'agree to refrain from the threat or the use of force, or from any other means of coercion for the settlement of their controversies, and to have recourse at all times to pacific procedures'. They will settle international controversies by regional procedures before referring them to the Security Council of the United Nations, utilizing negotiation, good offices, mediation, investigation, conciliation, or the ICJ. Compulsory

[58] See Daniel C. Thomas, *The Helsinki Effect: International Norms, Human Rights, and the Demise of Communism* (Princeton, NJ: Princeton University Press, 2001).

[59] Charter of the Organization of American States (OAS Charter) (entered into force 13 December 1951), Art. 24.

[60] OAS Charter, Art. 25.

[61] OAS Charter, Art. 26.

jurisdiction is recognized *ipso facto* for contentious cases between members, as is the option of seeking advisory opinions.

The OAS has a Peace Fund that supports the use of conflict resolution mechanisms contemplated under the OAS Charter, including direct negotiation, good offices, mediation, investigation, conciliation, confidence-building measures, judicial settlement, and arbitration. It has had peace missions addressing demobilization, disarmament, and peace-building and provided good-offices dispute resolution services for Nicaragua, Suriname, Haiti, Guatemala, Honduras, Belize, Guatemala, Venezuela, El Salvador, Ecuador, Costa Rica, and Colombia. The Fund supports the Inter-American Peace Forum which is used to strengthen the General Secretariat's knowledge and expertise in dispute settlement, as well as to support the development of programmes aimed at promoting a culture of peace. At present, Latin America's enjoyment of peace is marred by increased violence, impunity, and 'unrule' of law within Central America on account of the actions of narcotraffickers and related criminal groups.

6.3. Africa

Within Africa, the Constitutive Act of the African Union, Art. 3, states that one of the objectives of the Union is to promote peace, security, and stability on the continent. Article 4 sets forth that the principles of the AU include reference to negative peace in various manifestations, including peaceful resolution of conflicts, prohibition of the use of force or threat to use force among member states of the Union, non-interference in internal affairs, and, most interestingly, 'Peaceful co-existence of Member States and their right to live in peace and security.'

However Article 4 also recognizes an exception to peace in the form of humanitarian intervention and intervention to restore peace and security: 'The right of the Union to intervene in a Member State pursuant to a decision of the Assembly in respect of grave circumstances, namely war crimes, genocide and crimes against humanity' and 'the right of Member States to request intervention from the Union in order to restore peace and security'. This language creates a tension in relation to defining the scope of peace within the region, as it espouses realistic pacifism with recognition of exceptions. It may appear curious that the grounds for humanitarian intervention are tied to classic categories, and do not include situations that may be of concern within Africa, such as natural disasters, famine, etc.

The AU has a Non-Aggression and Common Defence Pact (2009) which has a preamble setting forth the aspiration of attaining regional peace pursuant to common 'respect for the principles of peaceful co-existence, non-aggression, non-interference in the internal affairs of Member States, mutual respect for individual sovereignty and territorial integrity of each State.' Article 2 describes the objectives of this Pact as rooted in the pursuit of peace:

(i) to promote cooperation among the Member States in the areas of non-aggression and common defence,

(ii) to promote peaceful co-existence in Africa,
(iii) to prevent conflicts of inter-State or intra-State nature, and
(iv) to ensure that disputes are resolved by peaceful means

Article 3 calls upon state parties to resolve 'any differences by peaceful means, in order to avoid endangering peace and security; to refrain from the use of force or threat to use force in their relations with each other and in any manner whatsoever, incompatible with the United Nations Charter. Article 15 sets forth that state parties involved in any dispute shall first seek a solution by negotiation, inquiry, mediation, conciliation, arbitration, judicial settlement, or resort to regional and continental mechanisms or arrangements, or other peaceful means. Consequently, no consideration whatsoever, be it political, economic, military, religious or racial shall justify aggression.' Further, states are to 'undertake to develop and strengthen the friendly and peaceful relations'. It further calls for the establishment of an African Peace Academy to develop an African peace doctrine.

In contrast to the OAS Treaty, which calls upon States to use regional mechanisms before turning to the UN Security Council, the AU Pact Article 17 recognizes the primary responsibility of the United Nations Security Council for the maintenance of international peace and security. Nonetheless, the AU has a Peace and Security Council which pursues *Pax Africana*, seeking itself to maintain peace.[62] It has objectives that address negative peace concerns: to promote peace, security and stability in Africa, anticipate and prevent conflicts, and where conflicts have occurred, undertake peacemaking and peace-building functions for the resolution of these conflicts.

It also has the positive peace aims of promoting and implementing peace-building and post-conflict reconstruction activities to consolidate peace and prevent the resurgence of violence; promoting and encouraging democratic practices, good governance, and the rule of law; and protecting human rights and fundamental freedoms. It has field missions in Somalia, Western Sahara, and the Central African Republic. Nevertheless, Dersso points out contradictions among the Peace and Security Council members: 'Not all of the current members of the PSC respect constitutional governance, the rule of law and human rights ... Similarly, not all current members of the PSC contribute to the promotion of peace and security, or possess the capacity to assume substantive responsibilities for regional and continental peacemaking and conflict resolution efforts.'[63] The AU has cooperated with other institutions, such as the EU, OIC (see further), and the Commonwealth (which itself provides Good Offices for Peace) in the pursuit of peace-building. The Council also has responsibility to coordinate and harmonize continental efforts in the prevention and combating of international terrorism in all its aspects and develop a common defence policy for the Union. This creates a dilemma in which the same institution that has a mandate for peace

[62] See Solomon A. Dersso, *Annual Review of the African Union Peace and Security Council 2013/2014* (Pretoria: Institute for Security Studies, 2014), 1.
[63] Dersso, *Annual Review*, 48.

also has a mandate for counter-terrorism, thereby leaving room for conflicts of aims and objectives in practice.

It is particularly notable that the African system has actually recognized the concept of a right to peace held by peoples. The African Charter on Human and Peoples Rights, Art. 23(1), sets forth: 'All peoples shall have the right to national and international peace and security.' This has been confirmed in a case by the African Commission in which it held that Burundi, Rwanda, and Uganda had violated the right to peace by occupying parts of Congo.[64]

The African system may also be considered to be very progressive from the normative perspective because the African Protocol on the Rights of Women adopts a gender policy in terms of peace participation rights and calls for the establishment of preconditions for peace through reduction of military expenditure in favour of development.[65] The Protocol also recognizes the importance of peace education in Art. 4(2), linking the pursuit of peace to intergenerational and cultural exchange.

6.4. Organization of Islamic Cooperation

The Organization of Islamic Cooperation also pursues peacekeeping, peacebuilding, and peacemaking initiatives. It has a Peace, Security, and Mediation Unit which provides culturally sensitive mediation/preventive diplomacy. It is active in some of the most contentious situations in the world, including Syria, the Occupied Palestinian Territory, Afghanistan, Somalia, Sudan, the Sahel, the Horn of Africa, Mali, Myanmar, Darfur, Guinea, Kashmir, and Yemen. It supported an Arab Peace Initiative promoted by the League of Arab States in 2002 which sought to bring peace between Israel and Palestine.[66] Like the African Peace and Security Council and the UN Security Council, it also addresses terrorism and extremism and must confront serious conflict and post-conflict situation within its region.

The regional institutions and normative instruments support recognition of the scope of the law of peace to address both negative and positive peace dimensions and promote the pacific settlement of disputes. Yet the regional mechanisms of pacific settlement of disputes seem to lack visibility, authority, and support for staffing and funding to increase the scope and impact of their endeavours.

[64] African Commission on Human and People's Rights, Communication 227/1999, *Democratic Republic of Congo/Burundi, Rwanda, Uganda*, Twentieth Activity Report, EX.CL/279(IX), Annexe IV Communications, pp. 111ff.

[65] Art. 10 establishes that: 1. Women have the right to a peaceful existence and the right to participate in the promotion and maintenance of peace. 2. States Parties shall take all appropriate measures to ensure the increased participation of women: a) in programmes of education for peace and a culture of peace; b) in the structures and processes for conflict prevention, management and resolution at local, national, regional, continental, and international levels. 3. States Parties shall take the necessary measures to reduce military expenditure significantly in favour of spending on social development in general, and the promotion of women in particular.

[66] The League of Arab States also promotes good offices, mediation, conciliation, and arbitration.

7. Conclusion

We earlier remarked on the notion of preventive diplomacy; the UN Charter is clearly written in a manner that intends a preventive approach in order to safeguard peace.

The aim of this chapter has been to illustrate the character of obligations that states have to maintain peace between (and within) themselves through pacific settlement of disputes. We sought to underscore the importance of faithful adherence to the provisions of the Charter. It is not without significance that one should pay heed to their sequence, i.e. the obligations in articles 1(1) and 2(3) preceding the obligation to refrain from using force in article 2(4), and the mechanisms in Chapter VI preceding those resorted to under Chapter VII. The foundation of the Charter rests on the recourse to pacific settlement. If that foundation is not shored up, through effective institutions, then the edifice of international order and its architecture can hardly be expected to endure.

If the current application of the framework for pacific settlement of disputes has been limited in the post-9/11 epoch, then we suggest that states must significantly enhance the strength of negotiation and mediation institutions at the international, regional, and national levels.[67] These entities require proper funding, competent staffing, increased authority, and strengthened visibility in order to move from the periphery of international law to the centre pursuant to the obligation to maintain and uphold the international law of peace.

[67] Winston Churchill is reported to have believed 'it was only the countries whose interests were directly affected by a dispute [that] could be expected to apply themselves with sufficient vigour to secure a settlement', quoted in Nigel D. White, *Democracy Goes to War: British Military Deployments under International Law* (Oxford: Oxford University Press, 2009), 63.

5

Protecting Which Peace for Whom against What? A Conceptual Analysis of Collective Security

*Pål Wrange**

1. Introduction

The UN Charter (the world constitution, if there is one) leaves no one in doubt about its pre-eminent goal: 'We the peoples of the United Nations, [are] determined to save succeeding generations from the scourge of war'; and it was to safeguard peace that the system of collective security was created, with the most powerful organ—the Security Council—at its helm. And yet, ever since its inception, the collective security system has been fraught with political and practical problems.

These problems can all be associated with unavoidable conceptual contradictions and it is, in fact, very difficult to imagine a truly effective collective security system. These conceptual difficulties—which I will analyse further—do not necessarily mean that collective security is impossible—practice sometimes demonstrates that the existing one can produce good. However, they mean that both the architecture of the system and its application in concrete cases will suffer from tragic dilemmas, in which any solution will entail costs.

What is collective security? Serious attempts to define it contain some common elements: (1) all states of the system should renounce the use of force; (2) all states must cooperate in meeting an armed attack (no neutrality, no unilateral actions); (3) the potential aggressor may be a member of the collective security system; and (4) collective action is mandatory. The core is security for all states

* I would like to thank the other contributors to the book, in particular Cecilia M. Bailliet, Ola Engdahl, and Kjetil Mujezinović Larsen, for comments on a draft version, as well as Martti Koskenniemi for comments on an earlier piece with the same theme. Remaining mistakes and obscurities are mine. As mentioned, an earlier text on this topic was published in Swedish in 1995 as 'Kollektiv säkerhet' (Collective Security), in *Tandlös eller tiger—sju uppsatser om FN*, Per Ahlin (ed.) (Stockholm: Juristförlaget, 1995), 147–89. While the essence of the argument has remained, the current text is considerably shorter, reorganized, updated, and partly revised, and it also builds on my intervening years of practice.

by all states, where 'all' includes not only all states that may be protected but also all states that might pose a threat. It is the latter aspect that distinguishes the collective security from the alliance, which is a union of some states against other states.[1]

Collective security is only one of several possible ways to safeguard peace and security. Historical examples include:

- The loose and shifting balance of power that existed in Europe during the 1700s. It was not linked to any prohibition of the use of force, and its main protagonists were the great powers.
- The Concert of Europe which managed the continent during the 1800s. Unlike collective security, only great powers had full 'membership'.
- The system of fixed alliances, which was cemented in the run-up to the First World War, and which prevailed (in a different shape) during the Cold War. In distinction to collective security, the alliance is focused on threats from non-members. There is also usually a substantial requirement for membership, such as shared values or interests.[2]
- The League of Nations' collective security arrangements with pre-determined criteria for sanctions—in distinction to the UN regime, which is managed by a small group of great powers.

Any proposal for a security arrangement must consider the following questions[3]:

1. Who should be protected—states or some other form of entity?
2. Where does the threat come from—states or other sources?
3. Security from what kinds of threats—war, economic threats, environmental disasters, or other threats?

At least until the turn of the millennium, these three questions have usually been answered 'international (interstate) military security'.

In addition, there are a number of other questions about how international security should be organized, which—unlike the first three questions—have been given different answers in different security arrangements.

4. To what extent are members required to renounce the unilateral use of force?

[1] See Werner Conze, 'Sicherheit, Schutz', in *Geschichtliche Grundbegriffe*, O. Brunner, W. Conze, and R. Koselleck (eds.) (1979), iv. 831, 861; Bruno Simma (ed.), *The Charter of the United Nations: A Commentary* (Oxford: Oxford University Press, 1994), 51; Rudolf L. Bindschedler, 'Grundfragen der kollektiven Sicherheit', in *Rechtsfragen der internationalen Organisation: Festschrift für Hans Wehberg zu seinem 70. Geburtstag*, Walter Schätzel and Hans-Jürgen Schlochauer (eds.) (1956), 67–8.

[2] The word 'interest' is used in this article to mean 'conception of interest'. Interests are not inherent or natural but contingent and constructed, partly based on legal concepts and institutions.

[3] Other writers have made similar lists of issues. See Andrew Hurrell, 'Collective Security and International Order Revisited', *International Relations* 11 (1992), 37, 39; Lynn H. Miller, 'The Idea and the Reality of Collective Security', *Global Governance* 5 (1999), 303.

5. What action is required of members in order to protect security (peaceful sanctions, military action, etc.)?
6. Who is within the system—all states or only some?—and what are the conditions for membership?
7. Who has the authority to make the decisions?

As will be explained, it is easy to see that the concrete collective security system set up through the Charter (I) has protected states (II) against the external threats from other states (III) in the form of military aggression; that (IV) it has been linked to a ban on the use of force and (V) has required that states participate in peaceful sanctions; (VI) that it has aimed to include all states without imposing substantive requirements for membership; and (VII) that decisions are to be taken by the Security Council.[4] It is also well known that this specific version of collective security has not been static, but has adapted, as will be discussed further.

For the better part of the post-war era, most of the argument turned on whether the current system corresponded to the real-life requirements, and this debate focused primarily on problems IV–VII.[5] Today, however, the first three questions are also being asked. It is no longer self-evident that states shall be protected ('inter-*national*') against external threats ('*inter*-national') which are military.

This chapter will provide an analysis and critique of the collective security system, both in the current UN shape and as a general concept. It will ask whether collective security could be improved better to maintain international peace and security or if there is an inherent contradiction in the idea. As will become evident, the analysis is informed by critical traditions in international law and international relations, but it also grows out of my practical experience as a legal adviser at the Swedish Ministry for Foreign Affairs. I believe that many other international lawyers involved in collective security affairs will recognize the conundrums that I identify.

I will start with questions IV–VII, proceed to questions I–III, and then add a few yet more fundamental problems at the end. For reasons of space, the discussion will be fairly abstract with few examples, assuming that the reader has some general familiarity with recent political history, including the practice of the Security Council.

Before I proceed to the analysis, two conceptual issues need to be sorted out. First: since the topic of this chapter is collective security, I will often refer to

[4] See also Martti Koskenniemi, 'The Place of Law in Collective Security', *Michigan Journal of International Law* 17 (1996), 455, 456, and Hurrell, 'Collective Security and International Order Revisited', 41, who finds that the existence of the veto meant that the UN system was not one of pure collective security.

[5] Mumulla Venkat Naidu, *Collective Security and The United Nations: A Definition of the UN Security System* (London: Macmillan 1974), 20–7; see also Inis Claude Jr., *Swords Into Plowshares: The Problems and Progress of International Organization* (4th edn. New York: Random House, 1971), 250–61; Adam Roberts and Benedict Kingsbury, 'Introduction: The UN's Role in International Society since 1945', in *United Nations, Divided World*, Adam Roberts and Benedict Kingsbury (eds.) (2nd edn. Oxford: Clarendon, 1993), 1, 30–1.

security rather than peace. However, in this context, what applies to threats to security generally also applies to threats to peace. The relation between peace and security is a difficult one. I will use the UN Charter as my starting point. As noted by Avril McDonald and Hanna Brollowski, almost all references to peace and security in the Charter are conjunctive, and the relation between the two is not explained.[6] As will be developed in section 2.8, I take it that the concepts are distinct but interrelated. Peace is the absence of war, while security is the absence of threats to important acquired values. The chapter fully recognizes the many potential conceptions of security, and by implication that suggests that the concept of peace is equally malleable.[7] Unless otherwise specified, however, it is assumed that the focus is on negative peace. I believe that there are good analytical reasons to keep the concept of peace distinct from other goods that are covered by the broader concept of positive peace. At the same time I fully acknowledge that this analytical clarity has a political cost, since it essentially means that 'peace'—a universally valued concept with great rhetorical value—entails status quo and therefore appears to justify conditions that for most people involve inequality and violations of human rights (cf. Section 2.9).

And now to the second issue: international law. As Nigel White explains, 'in collective security matters the law is not determinative, at least in a formalist sense'.[8] However, international law is still the framework for collective security in the UN, and probably in any conceivable collective security system. But law is as full of contradictions as is politics, and these contradictions can be translated into the opposition between universalism and particularism or between on the one hand the international community—with international law and collective security—and on the other hand sovereignty and national interest.[9]

International law is based on states as its basic units,[10] and the sovereign state is the medium through which international cooperation is carried out. International law and the UN are thus dependent on the sovereign states, and it is the sovereign states that provide the legitimacy of the UN and of international law. Conversely, states receive their legitimacy from international law. International law recognizes and protects sovereignty, and allows each state to develop according to its ability and desire. But this freedom cannot go too far, because then one state can threaten another state, or individuals. In other words, through international law,

[6] Avril McDonald and Hanna Brollowski, 'Security', in *Max Planck Encyclopedia of Public International Law*, Rüdiger Wolfrum (ed.) (2011), para. 3, http://opil.ouplaw.com/view/10.1093/law:epil/9780199231690/law-9780199231690-e399?rskey=HqScej&result=1&prd=EPIL (accessed 22 June 2014).

[7] For a useful table comparing various conceptions of peace and security, see Masatsugu Matsuo, 'Concept of Peace in Peace Studies: A Short Historical Sketch' (2007), paper published at http://home.hiroshima-u.ac.jp/~heiwa/Pub/E20/conceptofpeace.pdf, 23 (accessed 8 Nov 2014).

[8] Nigel D. White, 'On the Brink of Lawlessness: The State of Collective Security Law', *Indiana International and Comparative Law Review* 13 (2002), 237, 241.

[9] This is not to say that that is a fundamental contradiction which is the source of other contradictions. Contradictions can be traced, or translated, to other contradictions in a number of different ways.

[10] For a history of the concept of sovereignty, see *inter alia* Jens Bartelson, *A Genealogy of Sovereignty* (Cambridge: Cambridge University Press, 1995).

states provide a certain universalism—rules that apply to all—while international law, through states, ensures a good amount of pluralism—each state can develop as it wishes within the limits of the law. The problem is, of course, that these two positions are incompatible.[11] In every instance, in every situation where collective security is on the agenda, the question is whether it is the international community's values and interests or those of the individual state that should prevail. Thus if collective security becomes too collective, it will threaten the liberal pluralism that it is to protect and that is the basis of this law. On the other hand, pluralism, drawn to its limits, means that the international rule of law ceases, and with it the defence of sovereignty. One cannot have full pluralism and universalism (see Sections 2.1–2.4). One can have a little of both, but then it becomes impossible to determine when the one or the other should prevail. This contradictory nature of international law is replicated across the board for every single legal issue. That does not mean that international legal arguments cannot be resolved, but it does mean that what prevails—what is 'the better argument'—is not determined by logic but by other factors, by what is accepted in the discourse.

I will now proceed to discuss the various dimensions of collective security.

2. Dimensions of Collective Security

2.1. To what extent are members required to renounce the unilateral use of force?

The first question concerns the obligation to renounce the use of force. Domestic legal systems use violence to enforce the laws and seek to exclude unauthorized violence in order to create a state monopoly on the legitimate use of violence. In international law the situation is much more fragile. Over the centuries, different ways to overcome this problem have been chosen; the most radical one was perhaps the nineteenth-century view that the initiation of war simply lay outside international law, while current collective security requires states not only to refrain from force but also to suppress force from others.[12]

Article 2(4) of the Charter provides that '[a]ll Members shall refrain in their international relations from the threat or use of force against the territorial integrity or political independence of any state, or in any other manner inconsistent with the Purposes of the United Nations.' As every international lawyer knows, this brief provision is full of problems, but so would any alternative regulation be. The first difficulty is the definition of force. As we will discuss (Section 2.7), it is no longer clear that military force is the only threat, and 'force' is not a neutral

[11] Pluralism is good, but not too much, because then basic universal values will be threatened—and without some universal values there cannot be common law or society—while too much universalism will threaten pluralism.

[12] Says Andrew Hurrell: 'The model of collective security assumes that there can be a clear consensus as to what precisely the unlawful use of force means and what constitutes an unlawful act of aggression,' 'Collective Security and International Order Revisited', 42.

concept. Different states have different perceptions of what is legitimate, as well as different resources and opportunities to use different types of force, and different perceptions of what might threaten them (see Section 2.7).[13] Every definition of (prohibited) force therefore entails a redistribution of military might and hence of political power.[14]

The main problem under this item, however, is this: any prohibition requires one exception, namely the permission not to observe the prohibition against an actor who is violating it.[15] Certainly, one could in principle imagine a total ban that does not allow self-defence, but not even domestic legal systems in well-ordered states are that radical. Article 51 of the Charter states that '[n]o provision of this Charter shall impair the inherent right of individual or collective self-defence if an armed attack occurs against a Member of the United Nations, until the Security Council has taken measures necessary to maintain international peace and security.' On the one hand, if the meaning of the right of self-defence would be freely determined by each state, then the prohibition of force would implode. And this also goes for the right of self-defence, because without the prohibition of force there can be no legitimate self-defence, just plain violence.[16] On the other hand, if there would be no right of self-defence, that is, if the prohibition of force would be absolute, then states would have renounced their most basic right—the right to self-preservation. This would mean the loss of their security, and thus potentially also of their sovereignty.

Article 51 tries to cure this with an impossible compromise. Self-defence may take place, but only until the Security Council 'has taken measures necessary'. However, it is unclear who will decide what measures are necessary, that is, determine the boundary between sovereign self-preservation and collective security. The problem goes deeper than the particular drafting in San Francisco in 1945, because, as we shall see in Sections 2.2 and 2.4, there is no way to guarantee that the collective really will come to a victim state's defence.

[13] Third-world lawyers have long argued that economic coercion can be as devastating as military force. See Simma, *The Charter of the United Nations*, 112–13. This view seems to correspond to the idea that peaceful sanctions can force a state to succumb (which has happened on a number of occasions, most lately with regard to Iran and the issue of enrichment of uranium).

[14] If one form of force is prohibited, that means that a state that has the capability to use such force loses access to that instrument. Even for a state with little concern for international law, illegality has a political price. See Julius Stone, *Conflict Through Consensus: United Nations Approaches to Aggression* (Baltimore: Johns Hopkins University Press, 1977), 155–6. For a revisionist view of the prohibition on the use of force, ses Belatchev Asrat, *Prohibition of Force Under the UN Charter: A Study of Article 2(4)* (Uppsala: Iustus, 1992), 64, and my review 'Law, Force and Contingency: Notes on a Bold Monograph on Article 2(4) and the Problems of Finding a Proper Basis for International Legal Reasoning', *Nordic Journal of International Law* 61 (1992), 83–99.

[15] This idea is also expressed in Art. 60 of the Vienna Convention on the Law of Treaties and in Art. 22 of the Draft Articles on State Responsibility.

[16] The right to self-defence is meaningless without the ban. Self-defence is an exception to the ban and it is the ban that justifies and legitimizes the resort to force in self-defence. Cf. also David J. Scheffer, 'Commentary on Collective Security', in *Law and Force in the New International Order*, L. F. Damrosch and David J. Scheffer (eds.) (Boulder: Westview, 1991), 100, 102. See also Helmut Freudenschuss, 'Between Unilateralism and Collective Security: Authorizations of the Use of Force by the UN Security Council', *European Journal of International Law* 5 (1994), 492, 528.

2.2. What collective action is required of members to protect security?

The second question concerns the obligation to participate in sanctions and other collective measures.

Under Article 41, the Council may introduce peaceful measures, and Article 42 provides for the *ultima ratio*, force. For the latter purpose, member states were supposed to conclude agreements to make troops available to the UN according to Article 43. No such agreement exists, however. Therefore, all military enforcement measures actually implemented—such as Korea in 1950, Iraq–Kuwait in 1991, Libya in 2011, Afghanistan through ISAF from 2001—have been carried out not through binding decisions but with the 'authorization' of actions that the participating states had already offered to perform—in coalitions of the willing, under regional arrangements or as troop contributors to UN missions, like the recent intervention brigade in the Democratic Republic of the Congo (Resolution 2098). Hence, the Council does not have the power to direct states to participate. This has rightly been considered a failure, but it could not have been an unexpected one, since it follows from an insoluble contradiction.

On the one hand, if the duty to perform military sanctions would be total (i.e. if the Council's power to use force would not be subjected to voluntary agreements), any war could become World War III.[17] If needed, all states have to participate in military operations against an aggressor. Hans Morgenthau explains that '[b]y the very logic of its assumptions, the diplomacy of collective security must aim at transforming all local conflicts into world conflicts.'[18] So, a fully implemented collective security means that any war risks becoming total in every sense of the word, that is, the total loss of international peace and security, and therefore the negation of all that the UN wants to achieve. If peace is indivisible, each threat must be countered by each state as if it was itself under threat,[19] and then security must be collective.[20]

[17] Even the obligation to participate in peaceful sanctions may be dangerous, since a belligerent may feel tempted to take action against a state that supports one side in a conflict. See Hidemi Suganami, *The Domestic Analogy* (Cambridge: Cambridge University Press, 1990), 173–4. Pearl Harbour was the result of such calculations.

[18] Hans J. Morgenthau, *Politics Among the Nations* (3rd edn. New York: Knopf, 1961), 418. Cf. also Claude, *Swords Into Plowshares*, 252, and Carl Schmitt, *Der Nomos der Erde im Völkerrecht des Jus Publicum Europaeum* (Berlin: Duncker & Humblot, 1950), 219, which probably influenced Morgenthau; see Alfons Söllner, 'German Conservatism in America: Morgenthau's Political Realism', *Telos* 72 (1987), 161.

[19] Daniel S. Cheever and H. Field Haviland Jr., *Organizing for Peace: International Organization in World Affairs* (Houghton Mifflin, 1954), 828. See also Morgenthau, *Politics Among the Nations*, 412–13.

[20] Naidu, *Collective Security and The United Nations*, 15; R. B. J. Walker, *Inside/Outside: International Relations as Political Theory* (Cambridge: Cambridge University Press, 1993), 139. As Manfred Lachs noted, 'international peace and security' in Art. 1(1) should read 'international peace and international security', meaning that security is indivisible. Manfred Lachs in *La Charte des Nations Unis*, Jean-Pierre Cot and Alain Pellet (eds.) (2nd edn. Paris: Economica, 1991), 32.

On the other hand, if collective military action needs the consent of each participating state,[21] there is no reason to assume that a state will undertake such an assignment unless that is in its interest.[22] Morgenthau explains:

Collective security expects the policies of the individual nation to be inspired by the ideals of mutual assistance and a spirit of self-sacrifice which will not shrink even from the supreme sacrifice of war should it be required by that ideal. ... The fact of the matter is that states have conflicting interests which prevent their acting in harmony.[23]

As will be readily appreciated, collective security erodes if each state puts its own security first.[24] The working assumption of collective security was that this conflict would never come to a head, because the threat of collective action rarely or never would have to be implemented.[25] However, since deterrence is so terrible even for states that must contribute to the deterrent, it will be less credible, as the situation in Syria shows all too clearly.[26]

So, on the one hand, fully implemented collective security—including an obligation to participate in military measures—potentially means the total loss of peace for each state. On the other hand, since states individually cherish their peace, collective security can only be implemented when it happens to coincide with the interests of militarily able states. In Section 2.4, we shall see if a balance can be achieved through the rules on decision-making.

[21] In the context of the Korean war, the verb 'recommend' was used (UNSC RES 83), but it had the same effect.

[22] Michael Walzer points out that '[t]he same solidarity that makes noninvolvement at home morally questionable may well make it obligatory in the international arena: this group of men and women must save one another's lives first.' Michael Walzer, *Just and Unjust Wars* (New York: Basic Books, 1977), 237. Cf. also Hurrell, 'Collective Security and International Order Revisited', 48.

[23] Morgenthau, *Politics Among the Nations*, 417.

[24] As Anne Orford points out, 'John Bolton, the US Representative to the UN, spelt out in a letter to Members that "the Charter has never been interpreted as creating a legal obligation for Security Council members to support enforcement action in various cases involving serious breaches of international peace" and accordingly "a determination as to what particular measures to adopt in specific cases cannot be predetermined in the abstract but should remain a decision within the purview of the Security Council".' Anne Orford, *International Authority and the Responsibility to Protect* (Cambridge: Cambridge University Press, 2011), 1, 24. Of course, what Bolton wanted to safeguard was the US right to exercise the veto.

[25] Maurice Bourquin, *L'État Souverain et l'Organisation Internationale* (New York: Manhattan, 1959), 83. As noted by Gleason and Shaihitdinov, 'States that are at the forefront of efforts to combat terrorism and extremism are apt to be punished by becoming the targets of choice for terrorists and extremists. States that renege on a commitment to the goals of an anti-terrorist collective security organization are apt to be rewarded with fewer suicide bombings, fewer terrorist attacks, and fewer reasons to put themselves in harm's way.' Gregory Gleason and Marat E. Shaihutdinov, 'Collective Security and Non-State Actors in Eurasia', *International Studies Perspectives* 6 (2005), 274–8 at 278.

[26] Even if it had been the case that the Security Council could agree on military action in Syria, no state would be willing to undertake the mission.

2.3. Who is within the system—all, or some?—and what are the conditions for membership?

As implied, a collective security system must be global, because any war can affect any state and because all states must be involved to ensure that measures are effective.[27] It is in fact this requirement that distinguishes collective security from alliances. It is quite clear that the UN, unlike the League of Nations, has been a huge success in this respect.[28] Nevertheless, even this presents an insoluble problem.

The conditions for UN membership are not very demanding. They do not concern matters of substance (e.g. environmental or economic policy, domestic constitution, etc.). The only condition, under Article 4, is that members are 'peace-loving'.[29] What peace it is that they love is not clear. Many people believe that in order for global collective security to function, there must emerge a kind of international awareness, a global '*anima societas*', or, for instance, a common belief in democracy,[30] as has been suggested by proponents of a democratic caucus in the UN, a concert of democracies, and similar ideas.[31] Alternatively, as a minimum, it must be assumed that everyone believes that security really is international, that is, that the security of all is in the interests of all,[32] which in turn requires that all states have at least some shared interests.[33] But states differ by the very fact

[27] Bindschedler, 'Grundfragen der kollektiven Sicherheit', 75.

[28] The only significant country that voluntarily remained outside the UN for long is Switzerland (which became a member in 2002). By contrast, of the seven major powers during the interwar period (France, Germany, Great Britain, Italy, Japan, Soviet Union, the USA), only two were members of the League of Nations throughout its existence.

[29] Generally, order has been the privileged value (see Section 2.9). What has been relevant in international politics has been how a state has behaved in relation to other states, not how it has acted internally. (In international law terms, one could say that it has about the delineation of jurisdiction, not about how it should be exercised.) The conditions do not even concern the ability to contribute to collective security. What may Andorra or Palau do to maintain international peace and security?

[30] George Schwarzenberger, *The League of Nations and World Order: A Treatise on the Principle of Universality in the Theory and Practice of the League of Nations* (London: Constable, 1936), 44. See also Wilhelm G. Grewe, *Epochen der Völkerrechtsgeschichte* (2nd edn. Baden-Baden: Nomos, 1988), 762. Cf. also Michael Howard, 'The Historical Development of the UN's Role in International Society', in Roberts and Kingsbury (eds.), *United Nations, Divided World*, 64–5; Kenneth J. Twitchett, *The Evolving United Nations: A Prospect for Peace?* (London: Europa, 1971), 182; H. G. Nicholas, *The United Nations as a Political Institution* (3rd edn. London: Oxford University Press, 1967), 25; Freudenschuss, 'Between Unilateralism and Collective Security', 530; Quincy Wright, 'Collective Security in the Light of the Korean Experience', *Proceedings of the American Society of International Law* (1951), 179.

[31] See G. John Ikenberry and Anne-Marie Slaughter, 'Forging a World of Liberty under Law: U.S. National Security in the 21st Century' (Final Paper of the Princeton Project on National Security, 2006), 25–6, http://www.princeton.edu/~ppns/report/FinalReport.pdf (accessed 8 Nov 2014). This is an idea that took off in the 1990s, building on the notion of a democratic or liberal peace, often proceeding from Immanuel Kant's Perpetual Peace from 1795. For a recent expression of that idea, see Robert J. Delahunty and John Yoo, 'Kant, Habermas and Democratic Peace', *Chinese Journal of International Law* 10 (2009), 437.

[32] Manfred Lachs reads 'international peace and security' in Art. 1(1) of the Charter to mean that security is inidivisible. Manfred Lachs in Cot and Pellet (eds.), *La Charte des Nations Unis*, 32.

[33] Cf. also Alexander Wendt, 'Anarchy is What States Make of It', *International Organization* 46 (1992), 391. For a discussion on the two different liberalisms involved here (Charter liberalism and liberal anti-pluralism), see Gerry Simpson, 'Two Liberalisms', *European Journal of International Law* 12 (2001), 537.

that they have different interests, for otherwise there would be no justification for the protection of the multitude of sovereign states. This does not mean that all collective security cooperation is impossible—reality shows the opposite—but such cooperation tends to be thinner, the more different states are, and the more concepts like security and peace are stretched to cover ever more aspects of human life (see Section 2.7). Universality and local communities of interests (pluralism) appear to conflict with each other.

Hence, if one on the one hand endorses pluralism and retains low requirements for membership, it is in the nature of things that many members often will not be sufficiently interested in going to war for the sake of another, even if they have a general interest in upholding the system as such.[34] If one on the other hand would make an effort to deepen cooperation by setting higher standards for membership, this would result in equally large problems. If only states that share essential values would be involved, then the number of members would diminish, and collective security would lapse. Either it would be an alliance without any legitimacy to intervene against others,[35] or it would only protect against attacks from within the diminished system, thus creating only partial security.[36]

2.4. Who has the authority to make the decisions?

We have already noted that the two main duties of the members of the UN are to refrain from force and to participate in collective sanctions. The latter obligation implies two other issues: the determination of when the collective security machinery is activated (*casus foederis*) and the decision on which coercive measures to take. There are two possible methods for determining these duties: they are defined in advance for each state to apply on its own responsibility and then left to the individual state to apply, or it is left to a certain body to make the determination.[37] The first option was chosen in the Covenant of the League of Nations, the second in the Charter.

[34] As Gleason and Shaihutdinov observe, 'when the common aim is merely stability and maintenance of the status quo, coalitions have a tendency to become debating societies rather than security structures. Not all members benefit equally from the status quo. When grand coalitions achieve their ends they soon turn into coalitions of everybody against nobody.' Gleason and Shaihutdinov, 'Collective Security and Non-State Actors in Eurasia', 278.

[35] For sure, international legal rules may in principle allow alliances of that nature, but that would not be a collective security system but a hegemonic or some other system.

[36] Some regional organizations have traits of collective security, such as the OAS and the OSCE. Cf. Simma, *The Charter of the United Nations*, 694ff.; Naidu, *Collective Security and The United Nations*, 16.

[37] These two traits can also be combined, through an agency that makes decisions based on predetermined rules that specify the conditions for a particular decision. Art. 16(1) of the Covenant specified, *inter alia*, the conditions under which the Council would recommend the deployment of military forces, but it did not state how these forces would be constituted. In this discussion I will only bring up the two situations in pure form; combinations of the two do not, however, mean that the problems are eliminated, only that they are accumulated. At any rate, the point is, as explained by Koskenniemi, that '[n]o system of rule-application is "automatic" as envisioned by the academic distinction between collective security and balance of power.' Koskenniemi, 'The Place of Law in Collective Security', 457.

The League concept—predetermined rules, to be applied by each state individually[38]—leaves one with the problem of defining with sufficient precision what is prohibited force, as well as the need to determine in advance when sanctions are to be deployed, and to ensure that all states actually take part in these sanctions (see Sections 2.1 and 2.2). One can try to solve this problem by drafting more detailed rules, but it is very unlikely that one can reach a consensus on such duties other than in very general terms (see the introduction). Alternatively (in fact more realistically), the determination is deferred to the states, and then it can be assumed that they will interpret their duties in different ways because they have different perceptions of what constitutes a threat (see Section 2.6) and varying interests in intervening against threats (Section 2.2).

The second option is to refer this determination to a political body which decides ad hoc at its discretion.[39] After the League's failure, it was felt that a central and more flexible decision-making function was needed, and the Security Council was entrusted with a role similar to that of the Concert of Europe (with the difference that it is explicitly stated in Article 24 that the Council acts on behalf of all UN members).[40] The Council has been criticized both for acting arbitrarily (Libya) and for not acting (Syria). Could it be otherwise?[41]

Do the Council's decisions constitute legal sanctions or political police action? If the Security Council's action is in response to an unlawful act of force, then that suggests that it is a punitive sanction,[42] while it could be described as a police action if the objective is to get someone to change behaviour, rather than to punish.[43]

[38] See Arts. 10, 11, and 16 of the Covenant. According to an interpretative decision of the Assembly from 1921, it was ultimately up to each state to determine that unilaterally.

[39] Miller is sceptical: 'Nothing could be clearer, first, than that states today have no effective obligation to respond automatically to an act of aggression. An "automatic" response assumes the existence of a governmental authority capable of commanding it. Collective security has been given some of the appearance of governmental authority without its substance in the formal provisions of such bodies as the Security Council, which persists in behaving as an intergovernmental forum—since that is what it was created to be—rather than a world government.' Miller, 'The Idea and the Reality of Collective Security', 324. As will be explained, I believe that the problems go deeper than that.

[40] Under Art. 24, '[m]embers confer on the Security Council primary responsibility for the maintenance of international peace and security.'

[41] Claude, *Swords Into Plowshares*, 277, does not believe so.

[42] Bindschedler, 'Grundfragen der kollektiven Sicherheit', 70. Cf. Hans Kelsen, *Collective Security and International Law*, International Law Studies 49 (Newport, RI: Naval War College, 1957), 37. The use of the term 'crime' for state acts has always been controversial. See I. F. Dekker, 'Criminal Responsibility and the Gulf War of 1980–1988: The Crime of Aggression', in *The Gulf War of 1980–1988: The Iran–Iraq War in International Legal Perspective*, Ige F. Dekker and Harry H. G. Post (eds.) (Dordrecht: Martinus Nijhoff, 1992), 249; A. J. J. Hoogh, 'The Relationship between Jus Cogens, Obligations Erga Omnes and International Crimes', *Austrian Journal of Public International Law* 42 (1991), 183; Bruno Simma, 'International Crimes: Injury and Countermeasures: Comments on Part 2 of the ILC Work on State Responsibility', in *International Crimes of State: A Critical Analysis of the ILC's Draft Article 19 on State Responsibility*, Joseph Weiler, Antonio Cassese, and Mauro Spinedi (eds.) (Berlin: De Gruyter, 1989), 283.

[43] Cf. 'If general support for the use of sanctions as an effective instrument is to be maintained, care should be taken to avoid giving the impression that the purpose of imposing sanctions is punishment rather than the modification of political behaviour,' Boutros Boutros-Ghali, *An Agenda for Peace* (2nd edn. New York: United Nations, 1995), 25.

Out of the situations mentioned in Article 39, the first two clearly constitute violations of international law, which may suggests that the Council's reaction is a 'punishment', while the third ('threat against the peace') is unclear. However, the Security Council does not need to identify an attacker, and it can intervene when no unlawful act has taken place and even against a state other than the responsible one.[44] At any rate, both political and legal decision-making is problematic.

If the Security Council were to be reduced to an agency that only implements detailed legal provisions, that would diminish security for potential victims. Legal rules may make justice more predictable, but such certainty is purchased at the price of rigidity, which in fact degenerates into insecurity. In order to make the sanctions regime predictable, it must be specified which threats it must act against, and how. But since threats to international peace and security can take an infinite number of forms (see below, sections 2.7 & 2.8) threats cannot be predicted, and therefore, the potential victim can never know if the attack (military, economic, etc.) will be covered by the hypothetical inflexible rules or not.[45]

However, the alternative *modus decidendi*—political decision-making—also leaves potential victims as well as target states in uncertainty, since political decisions by nature are flexible and hence difficult to predict. One may ask whether it is legitimate to intervene, if there has not been a breach of a predetermined rule.[46]

[44] Bindschedler, 'Grundfragen der kollektiven Sicherheit', 70. See also Freudenschuss, 'Between Unilateralism and Collective Security, 530; Leland M. Goodrich, *The United Nations in a Changing World* (New York: Columbia University Press, 1974), 129. See also, for a comparative perspective on the League, Hans Wehberg, *Die Aechtung des Krieges* (Berlin: Franz Vahlen, 1930), 140. Tom Franck commented: 'In the simple world of the Charter, when fighting breaks out the Council must ultimately decide who started it and then order the community of states to act collectively to punish the initiator. The real world, however, rarely corresponds to this rather Old Testament-like expectation. Instead, the U.N. has found it all but impossible to fix responsibility for initiating a conflict, since, to do so, would require a sorting out of causes and effects as perceived through the lenses of incompatible ideologies.' Thomas M. Franck, *Nation Against Nation: What Happened to the U.N. Dream and What the U.S. Can Do About It* (New York: Oxford University Press, 1985), 169.

[45] The same could be said about the deterrent effect: 'Who decides when to react and how? Who pays for reaction or the costs of preparation? Who will command the collective force or decide on the objectives of common action and when they have been attained? If everything depends on the particular facts and circumstances, the rule-governed character of the procedure will disappear and, with it, the system's deterrent force.' Koskenniemi, 'The Place of Law in Collective Security', 464. The difficulties in agreeing on a definition of aggression—one of the key words in Art. 39 of the Charter—are well known. Julius Stone, *Aggression and World Order* (Berkeley: University of California Press, 1958); Bert V. A. Röling, *The 1974 U.N. Definition of Aggression*, in *The Legal Regulation of the Use of Force*, Antonio Cassese (ed.) (Leiden: Nijhoff, 1986), 413. As Bindschedler notes, in contrast to the often routine character of domestic legal issues, international legal disputes are often singular and involve important state interests. Bindschedler, 'Grundfragen der kollektiven Sicherheit', 79. See also Francis Harry Hinsley, *Power and the Pursuit of Peace: Theory and Practice in the History of Relations between States* (Cambridge: Cambridge University Press, 1967), 322, on the practice of the League, and Robert Redslob, *Théorie de la Société des Nations* (Paris: Rousseau, 1927), 55, specifically on the practice concerning Art. 11 of the Covenant.

[46] Bindschedler, 'Grundfragen der kollektiven Sicherheit', 70.

So, set rules may provide a signpost for the guilty, while flexibility can degenerate into capriciousness.

Even more importantly, it seems unlikely that major powers could agree without interest.[47] Collective security as a concert requires that the conductors of the concert (great powers) either do not have any vested interests at all (or at least no interests that are more important than the global interest of maintaining order), or that they have common interests.[48] If the first option were true, they would probably not be great powers, since great powers always have interests. And if they do not have any interests, how should one convince them to put their troops in harm's way? It was precisely their ability to put power behind the words that justified the special position of the permanent five.[49] If, however, the second alternative is at hand, that is, that the major powers really have common interests, this probably means that they want to preserve the status quo because new competitors have appeared. In that case the arrangement turns into a de facto alliance against the revisionists.[50] Or it means that the great powers impose their values on other members, of which many accused the Security Council under US leadership during the 1990s.[51] Hence, great powers cannot act both as major powers and as disinterested decision-makers in the international community's name, as the twin examples of Libya and Syria show.[52]

The paradoxes and contradictions referred to are very relevant for any collective security system, including the one created through the UN Charter, and they have all been debated throughout the existence of the organization. Today, however, even the formerly uncontested assumption that collective security in essence is about international military security is being challenged.

[47] It has been proposed that the five permanent members would agree to restrict the use of the veto. See letter of 22 November 2012 from Hans Corell to the members of the Security Council, 'Security Council Reform and the Rule of Law', http://www.havc.se/res/SelectedMaterial/20121122textoflettertopr.pdf (accessed 23 June 2014). See also, on the proposals from the Palme Commission, Franck, *Nation Against Nation*, 182.

[48] That does not necessarily relate to each specific situation. However, it is necessary that the general interest in upholding order and the security system must by stronger than parochial interests. Boutros Boutros-Ghali appeared to be sceptical: 'Power brings special responsibilities, and temptations. The powerful must resist the dual but opposite calls of unilateralism and isolationism if the United Nations is to succeed.' Boutros-Ghali, *An Agenda for Peace*, §80.

[49] Cf. also Hurrell, 'Collective Security and International Order Revisited'. The monopoly of the five permanent members (the P5) has been challenged for a long time, not least by Germany and Japan, and this has grown even more with the rise of BRIC, three of whom are not represented on the Council. Another variant of the first option is the possibility that the values concerned by the threats to security are not essential, and this in turn means that the (international military) security that the concert will maintain is no longer the vital one (see Section 2.2).

[50] One could also say that the great use of the veto actually suggests that the collective security system is still relevant, and it also means that the P5 has not evolved into an alliance against new challengers. Cf. already Bourquin, *L'État Souverain*, 90. Bourquin was one of the earliest users of the concept of collective security in the mid 1930s.

[51] Cf. Simma, *The Charter of the United Nations*, 22.

[52] Similarly Miller, 'The Idea and the Reality of Collective Security', 324.

2.5. Who should be protected?

What is it that is to be protected[53]—the state or something else? The traditional answer is 'the state',[54] but in order to protect the state, one needs to know what is the essence of the state, or in other words which values are to be protected[55]—the power of the government, the administrative apparatus, the government's control over the territory, or perhaps society or individuals? Different states have different perceptions of what is the state's essence. Some find that the territory is most important while for others the people are equally or more important, thus justifying violations of foreign borders to protect nationals abroad (US interventions in Grenada, 1983, and Panama, 1989, and the Russian intervention in Ukraine, 2014). It is hence not very surprising that the meaning of terms such as 'territorial integrity' and 'political independence' (Article 2(4)) have been much discussed for many years. Any universal definition of the object of protection entails a homogenization, that is, the opposite of the pluralism that international law also wants to accomplish.[56]

During the last couple of decades much criticism has been levelled at the very idea that only states should be protected.[57] We have seen terms such as 'societal security',[58] 'human security', and 'security of the planet'. In fact, a large number of UN peace operations have been launched in situations where groups of people rather than states have been threatened, such as Africans in Rhodesia (UNSC Resolutions 221, 232, etc.) and South Africa (Resolution 418), the Kurds in Iraq (Resolution 688), civilians in the former Yugoslavia (Resolutions 836, etc.), in the Democratic Republic of the Congo (Resolutions 1925, etc.), and in Sudan (Resolutions 1769, etc.). Some even believe that a state that threatens the population that it purports to represent can no longer count on respect for its sovereignty, and that such a government cannot be a recognized agent of the country.[59] There has been much discussion about whether the principles of non-intervention and sovereignty should yield to humanitarian concerns, and the Security Council has embraced the doctrine of a responsibility to protect

[53] See R. B. J. Walker, *Inside/Outside: International Relations as Political Theory* (Cambridge: Cambridge University Press, 1993), 140. See also David A Baldwin, 'The Concept of Security', *Review of International Studies* 23 (1997), 312.

[54] Gerd Oberleitne, 'Human Security: A Challenge to International Law?', *Global Governance* 11 (2005), 189.

[55] Cf. Baldwin, 'The Concept of Security'.

[56] Another complexity is that even if there is pluralism between states, the varying wishes and interests of states will in reality only be the wishes and interests of the local elites, generally upper-class males. Cf. Anne Orford, 'The Politics of Collective Security', *Michigan Journal of International Law* 17 (1995), 373, 408.

[57] Cf. Ole Waever, Barry Buzan, Morten Kelstrup, and Pierre Lemaitre, *Identity, Migration and the New Security Agenda in Europe* (London: Pinter, 1993), 57.

[58] *Our Global Neighborhood: The Report of the Commission on Global Governance* (Oxford: Oxford University Press, 1995), 80–4, 132, and 338.

[59] In international law, perhaps the clearest example of such conditionality is provided by the Friendly Relations Declaration, UNGA Res. 2625 (XXV) which, under the principle of self-determination, protects 'the territorial integrity or political unity' of a state that is 'possessed of a government representing the whole people belonging to the territory without distinction as to race, creed or colour'.

(Resolution 1973). Some would go even further and claim that states could intervene to protect civilians without a decision in the Council.[60] All this suggests that that which is inside the state—foremost the people—may have priority over the state.

However, this means that the basis for the international multi-state system is eroded, since it is difficult to justify the multitude of sovereigns unless they are respected tools for the security and the representation of their respective peoples, with their different needs and wishes.[61]

If an intervention is not based on the consent of the state, what are the alternatives? Does the 'international community' or some self-appointed representative thereof have the legitimate authority to intervene in the internal affairs of a state?[62] Such a right of intervention cannot be generalized, because then sovereignty disappears, and with it international law. What about civil society? Civil society, or groups in civil society, are not parties to the international legal order, and do not have rights and correlating legal claims for intervention. If others intervene against a state under an alleged right to protection of a non-state actor, that means that the intervening agent is undermining the basis of the international legal order, that is, the sovereign state. Of course, in a concrete humanitarian catastrophe, one will find authority wherever possible in order to stop the suffering, but in the follow-up to a humanitarian intervention the necessity of legitimacy will again become evident.

Hence, it is equally difficult to justify a focus on the protection of states and a focus on the protection of the peoples (or any other value inside the state); *in extremis* both approaches will undermine the international order of independent states, and the balancing between the two is a matter of judgement (at best), not of logic.

2.6. Where does the threat come from, states or other sources?

The next question is where the threat is coming from—from other states, from violent domestic forces, or perhaps from a completely different place.[63] The UN Charter has focused explicitly on interstate threats,[64] but out of the 32 ongoing armed conflicts in 2012, only one was interstate (international).[65] As the

[60] See the website of the International Coalition for the Responsibility to Protect, http://www.responsibilitytoprotect.org/, (accessed 8 Nov 2014).

[61] Of course things are not that simple. States may be tools for the private interests of local elites. However, the state community as such assumes that states can generally base their legitimacy on being representative and different; that Swedish interests are other than those of Denmark, France, or Suriname. Otherwise there is nothing that distinguishes Sweden from General Motors, except that the latter has a much greater turnover.

[62] Orford, *International Authority and the Responsibility to Protect*.

[63] Cf. Erskine Childers, 'Introduction', in *Challenges to the United Nations: Building a Safer World*, E. Childers (ed.) (New York: St Martin's Press, 1995), 1.

[64] Cot and Pellet (eds.), *La Charte des Nations Unis*, 32 (written by Manfred Lachs).

[65] UCDP/PRIO Armed Conflict Dataset v.4-2013, 1946–2012, http://www.pcr.uu.se/research/ucdp/datasets/ucdp_prio_armed_conflict_dataset/ (accessed 8 Nov 2014). This was a fact long before the end of the Cold War: 'Tendencies toward ethnic fragmentation have characterized world politics since the 1960s and have long been evident to observers who were not preoccupied by Cold War issues.' Ted Robert Gurr, 'Peoples Against States: Ethnopolitical Conflict and the Changing World System', *International Studies Quarterly* 38 (1994), 355–6.

former collaborator of Dag Hammarskjöld and UN veteran, Brian Urquhart, writes, this poses some fundamental questions about the UN's basic mission.[66] Thus it seems clear that the Charter concept in this respect no longer quite matches post-Cold War demands. A large number of UN actions have been undertaken in situations where a state was threatened by internal forces, such as the DRC, Bosnia, Sierra Leone, and Angola,[67] and the UN has even subjected groups and individuals to sanctions, such as the Republika Srpska, General Aidid in Somalia (Resolution 837), and al-Qaeda and other terrorist groups in recent years.

The problem is this: On the one hand, the more conservative view—that collective security applies only to threats from other states—is deeply problematic. First of all it would mean that the collective security system is oblivious to the fact that it is often the state that is the threat against its population (see Section 2.6).[68] More importantly for the discussion in this section, under this (outdated) view, assistance to the state against non-state actors would not be supported by collective security, and that means that one denies a state the assistance that it desires, and thus jeopardizes its sovereignty.[69]

On the other hand, if the United Nations intervenes against a non-state actor—as it frequently does these days—it does so via some form of acquiescence from the government, which represents a party to the UN Charter. However, if the UN finds it necessary to intervene, it is an indirect acknowledgement that the state has failed. But if the state has failed, then the government can no longer legitimize an intervention![70] (Certainly, the government will probably be 'recognized' even if it loses control over a part of the territory, but this continued recognition can only be explained by a qualifying, pragmatic doctrine, not by the basic legitimizing notion of territorial control or—alternatively—popular support.) If one would argue instead that the international community can intervene directly against non-state actors without a legitimization from the

[66] Brian Urquhart, 'The UN and International Security after the Cold War', in Roberts and Kingsbury (eds.), *United Nations, Divided World*, 87. Cf. also John F. Murphy, *The Nations and the Control of International Violence* (Manchester: Manchester University Press, 1983), 169.

[67] Out of the five peace-keeping missions existing in 1988, four were deployed in conflicts between states. Out of the eleven post-1988 operations in existence in 2012, all but two are in situations of internal conflict, and the remaining two are ambiguous. (MINURSO is deployed in a conflict between a state and an armed group from an occupied non-self-governing territory and UNISFA is deployed in a conflict which arose in the aftermath of the civil conflict in Sudan, after the independence of South Sudan.)

[68] See Orford, 'The Politics of Collective Security', 395.

[69] International law has been rather ambivalent on the question of unilateral intervention in civil war. A common view is that it is permitted to intervene on the government's side, at least before an open conflict has erupted. This is justified because the government has sovereign power to request assistance. When the opposition has gained strength and effectively challenges the government in a military way, however, many commentators believe that support for any side would constitute illegal intervention. Yet another view is that intervention is legal on the 'democratic' side, at least if that side also happens to be the government.

[70] The government receives its legitimacy through effective control over its territory or, alternatively, through popular support, and both the effective control and the popular support are often called into question in a civil war.

government, then that would mean that the UN has power directly over individuals and groups, without recourse to the state. After all, such non-state actors are not parties to the UN Charter, and have not accepted the authority of the Security Council. But, as we found in the previous section, such a direct power, without mediation of the state, would take us far from the intergovernmental paradigm that the UN is built upon.[71]

2.7. Safe from what? War, economic threats, or environmental disasters?

The third basic question is whether it is military threats that are most relevant. In 1945, the drafters of the Charter assumed that economic and other non-military threats, etc., are only indirect, that is, they could contribute to the weakening of a government and thereby expose it to the more decisive military threat. However, as the Security Council found in its first high-level meeting in 1992, '[t]he non-military sources of instability in the economic, social, humanitarian and ecological fields have become threats to peace and security.'[72] Since then, there have been many thematic debates in the Council on issues such as HIV/AIDS, climate change, and pandemics and in 2005, world leaders acknowledged a 'whole range of' 'multifaceted and interconnected challenges and threats'.[73] The broad understanding of security has been for a long time a 'commonplace' in international politics and diplomacy.[74]

Many of these threats, of course, come from sources without political ambitions or from 'acts of God'.[75] But there are also non-military threats from actors who have found that war is less useful as 'politics by other means'; the price in terms of human and material destruction is too high even for the winner,[76] and the international legal and political denunciation of violence has also made it more difficult to gain legitimacy for changes brought about by force. Instead,

[71] This problem may seem academic, since, for example, everyone agreed that it was necessary to intervene e.g. in Rwanda in 1994 and Libya in 2011, but the question of legitimacy had very real effects in both cases.

[72] Statement by the President of the Security Council, S/25696, 30 April 1993. Both the Secretary-General and the General Assembly recognize non-military threats. See Boutros-Ghali, *An Agenda for Peace*, §§5, 12, and 13. See also *An Agenda for Peace: Preventive Diplomacy, Peacemaking and Peace-keeping*, report of the UN Secretary-General, 17.6.1992, UN doc. A/47/277-S/24111.

[73] 2005 World Summit Outcome, UNGA Res. 60/1 (24 October 2005), paras. 6 and 69. Cf. also the preceding report from the UN Secretary-General: '78. The threats to peace and security in the twenty-first century include not just international war and conflict but civil violence, organized crime, terrorism and weapons of mass destruction. They also include poverty, deadly infectious disease and environmental degradation since these can have equally catastrophic consequences. All of these threats can cause death or lessen life chances on a large scale. All of them can undermine States as the basic unit of the international system.' 'In Larger Freedom: Towards Development, Security and Human Rights for All', UN Doc/59/2005, 24–5.

[74] Koskenniemi, 'The Place of Law in Collective Security', 468.

[75] See Hurrell, 'Collective Security and International Order Revisited'.

[76] See Francis Harry Hinsley, *The Fall and Rise of the Modern International System* (Canberra: Department of International Relations, Australian National University, 1981), 23. John J. Weltman, *World Politics and the Evolution of War* (Baltimore: Johns Hopkins University Press, 1995), 109.

for example, politically motivated disinvestment (sometimes as sanctions) and organized crime may threaten central government functions such as fiscal policies and law and order, etc.[77]

The development 'towards a more far-reaching and extensive collective security system' has been welcomed by many.[78] However, there are many problems here, too. First these threats often emanate from entities that are not states, and thus cannot be made directly accountable under international law (see Section 2.6, infra). And if you take international action against them, that implicitly acknowledges that they (criminal cartels, currency speculators, etc.) are equally important to (sometimes even more important than) states.

But there is also something about the threat itself that is deeply problematic. On the one hand, since everything can be subject to government control—it is difficult to imagine an area of human activity that is not regulated by government somewhere—any type of activity can constitute an interference in some state's internal affairs.[79] Not even positive acts, such as development assistance, trade, and cultural exchanges, escape this characteristic.[80] For some countries, it has been important not to receive help (as formerly Burma and Albania), and many have been afraid of the dissemination of foreign culture and information.[81] Furthermore, each interchange brings possibilities for pressure, for it is no coincidence that sanctions under Article 41 of the UN Charter include the interruption of economic and other relations. Hence, if one were to adopt a narrow definition of 'threat' that covers only military threats, that means lack of respect for the right of each state to determine what it is that threatens it. And the determination of the threat is tied to the determination of the state's tasks and functions, i.e., the form of government, which is the essence of sovereignty. On the other hand, if one were to accept a broad definition of 'threat'—that anything can constitute a threat to an important state function—then a state's legitimate pressure or perhaps even customary relations with another State may turn into potentially unlawful interference, and this means that all international relations constitute potential threats. And how can there be an international system without international relations? Another consequence of the wider concept of security—politically unappealing to many—is that security organs—domestic and international—are

[77] For instance, the peaceful constitutional changes in Eastern Europe 1989–91 were as dramatic as those that took place after the two world wars. These changes were to a large extent due to the malfunctioning of the domestic economic and political systems, but also of a conscious US policy to exhaust Soviet resources.

[78] Hurrell, 'Collective Security and International Order Revisited', 54.

[79] Baldwin, 'The Concept of Security', 17.

[80] For a similar argument, see Koskenniemi, 'The Place of Law in Collective Security', 469.

[81] Cf. the discussions on a New World Information and Communication Order during the 1970s. See Inger Österdahl, *Freedom of Information in Question* (Uppsala: Iustus, 1993); David Fischer, *Prior Consent to Satellite Broadcasting* (Leiden: Nijhoff, 1989). Contemporary echoes of these ideas are abundant regarding the Internet, which is subject to varying degrees of government control in countries such as China and Iran.

given broader jurisdiction, which potentially undermines the usual decision-making procedures.[82]

Thus, we can conclude that none of the three basic questions—who must be protected? against whom? and from what?—can have any conclusive answers. We have also noted that the complex problems are interconnected within a web of paradoxes. A couple of even more fundamental questions will now be considered.

2.8. Peace or security?

The first purpose of the United Nations is the maintenance of international peace and security. If one defines peace as the 'absence of war' and security as 'the absence of a threat to the state's existence or other important acquired values',[83] they can conflict, as has been noted in Section 2.2. In the practice of the Security Council, the maintenance—or reestablishment—of peace has always been more important than the maintenance of security, for the simple reason that there is usually not political momentum for the 15 members to agree to take action unless serious violence is underway. While the Council has discussed a broad range of threats—some of them only in abstract terms—it has generally been war and other forms of violence that has provided the *casus foederis*. At the domestic level, by contrast, states have generally been more concerned with security, for the equally simple reason that at any given moment most states are not involved in war. Nevertheless, at both levels, the problematic relation between the two concepts is always a factor. While the discussion in this section focuses on peace and security in narrow terms, the same argument could be made for broader conceptions of those concepts, although the discussion would then be more complex.

In general terms, the problem is, on the one hand, that if one cherishes peace, then aggression should be met with as little resistance as possible. For the collective security system, the corresponding choice is to localize (contain) conflicts as much as possible; the less there is of self-defence (cf. Section 2.2) and collective security, and the fewer who fight, the more there is peace.[84] However, if

[82] See Hitoshi Nasu, 'The Expanded Conception of Security and International Law: Challenges to the UN Collective Security System', *Amsterdam Law Forum* 3 (2011), 22–3.

[83] Cf. Baldwin: 'The point of departure is Wolfers' characterization of security as "the absence of threats to acquired values". Wolfers' phraseology will be reformulated as "a low probability of damage to acquired values".' David A. Baldwin, 'The Concept of Security', *Review of International Studies* 23 (1997), 312.

[84] See Hurrell, 'Collective Security and International Order Revisited', 46. As Nathaniel Berman has pointed out, there is a contradiction between alliance and containment or limitation ('localization') that cuts the other way. Nathaniel Berman, 'Between "Alliance" and "Localization": Nationalism and the New Oscillationism', *New York University Journal of International Law and Politics* 26 (1994), 449, 468–75, and 490. Limitation does not necessarily mean abstention or inaction. In fact, says Berman, one can think of much of the international community's quite active role in the former Yugoslavia—peacekeepers in Bosnia, Croatia, and Macedonia, bomb raids, aerial patrols, naval blockades, assistance to refugees, etc.—just as an active attempt to limit the conflict. These measures constitute a way to ensure international peace at the price of Bosnian national security, and a way to ensure international security at the price of peace in Bosnia.

one makes peace the short-term priority, it means that peace in the long term is compromised because then there is little willingness to resist an ambitious aggressor.

On the other hand, if it is security that is most valued, it may be the case that a war must be waged in order to promote security by pre-empting a potential threat.[85] Peace in the short term may need to be given up to maintain security in the long term. This is what the Bush Jr. regime believed when it invaded Iraq in 2003, under its doctrine of preventive ('pre-emptive') self-defence. While this may have forestalled (quite unlikely) attacks against US allies in the region, it came at the price of endemic insecurity in Iraq, as well as increased terrorism in the region.[86] But even if the US pre-invasion planning had been less reckless in this concrete case, the principle problem remains: the 'short term' must be extended indefinitely, because new threats will always appear on the horizon and not even the most vigilant security policy can guarantee security.[87] Moreover, any war could be universalized (see Section 2.2), and then each state risks being drawn into any war, which means the evaporation of security. In order to prevent new acts of terrorism, in the early years of this millennium a number of countries were persuaded (or cajoled) into sending troops to Afghanistan and Iraq, which not only put their troops in harm's way but also exposed them to revenge attacks from al-Qaida and affiliated groups.

2.9. Order or justice?

The last general issue that I will raise is whether to prioritize order or substantive justice. I here take 'order' to mean a combination of security and peace.[88]

Classical 'just war' doctrines allowed war as a means of attaining justice. Now it is war itself that is 'the supreme offence' and the UN Charter's regulation of violence is completely neutral: it does not address the reasons behind the use of force (unless it is a response to other uses of force). As noted by Miller, '[t]he sole legal wrong it assumes—aggression between states ... is only one of other behaviors one would expect to find restricted by a social contract.'[89]

[85] Innumerable wars were fought for this purpose during the age of the balance of power. See Vilho Harle, 'From Superpower Deterrence to European Balance-of-Power Politics', in *Challenges and Responses in European Security*, Vilho Harle (ed.) (Tampere: TAPRI Yearbook, 1986), 24, 26.

[86] See the comment by Gleason and Shaihitdinov cited earlier. Cf. also Hurrell: 'A second aspect of this problem arises out of the fact that the very policies designed to reinforce and further order at the level of the legal and political frameworks of the state system might at the same time be likely to undermine that order which is based on an accommodation of the social, religious, economic and political forces operating within and across the societies of the region.' Hurrell, 'Collective Security and International Order Revisited', 52.

[87] Another way of expressing this paradoxical relation is to say that '[t]o be unprepared for conflict is to invite aggression. To prepare for conflict is to inspire fear in an opponent that in turn invites aggression.' Gleason and Shaihutdinov, 'Collective Security and Non-State Actors in Eurasia', 277.

[88] To juxtapose two potentially contradictory concepts to create a third one is, of course, problematic but it is actually standard procedure in international law (and in many other discourses). Think of 'sustainable development', for instance.

[89] Miller, 'The Idea and the Reality of Collective Security', 325.

As implied in Section 2.4, collective security was meant to be a means only to uphold international peace and security, not to suppress violations of international law in general.[90]

However, as many observers have noted, the Security Council has pushed its mandate and has intervened in situations that fundamentally involved the gross abuses and violations of human rights (from Rhodesia to the former Yugoslavia, Sierra Leone and the DRC) or other violations of international law. Moreover, although the Council justified these interventions with the fact that the situations threatened international order and security, it seems as if many of the measures introduced actually were meant to promote human rights, that is, to force the affected parties to comply with their obligations.[91]

Every system of justice requires that order prevails, because otherwise justice cannot be upheld.[92] But if justice is to be safeguarded, there must be a consensus on what it is, otherwise order will be threatened by those who do not accept the prevailing conception of justice.[93] However, it seems impossible to reach consensus; as discussed in Section 2.4, consensus on the fundamental plane can be purchased only at the price of lack of concreteness, that is, that the controversy is postponed until the application.[94] Is justice about political rights, social justice, freedom of enterprise, or nationalistic aspirations?

If one by contrast gives priority to order over justice, then this regime loses its *raison d'être*. As Johan Galtung reminds us, the narrow concept of peace serves the interests of those who want status quo.[95] There is overwhelming evidence that people who perceive the existing order as unjust would rather rise up at the risk of death than live under the yoke.[96] Order and justice can only connect if the status quo is just, but there will always be different views on what is just.

[90] Claude, *Swords Into Plowshares*, 249. Further, cf. Koskenniemi, 'The Place of Law in Collective Security', 474.

[91] Cf. Brian Urquhart, 'The UN and International Security after the Cold War', in Roberts and Kingsbury, *United Nations, Divided World*, 81, 82; Martti Koskenniemi, 'Kollektiv säkerhet, internationell rätt och grunden för den internationella ordningen', in *Den eviga freden? Perspektiv på den nya världsordningen*, Per Ahlin and Pål Wrange (eds.) (Stockholm: Juristförlaget JF, 1992), 76–86; Katinka Svanberg-Torpman, 'The Security Council as a Law Enforcer and Legislator', in *Peace and Security: Current Challenges in International Law*, Diana Amnéus and Katinka Svanberg (eds.) (Lund: Studentlitteratur AB, 2004), 85–144.

[92] Hedley Bull, *The Anarchical Society: A Study of Order in World Politics* (New York: Columbia University Press, 1977), 86.

[93] See Bull, *The Anarchical Society*, 89 and 95. Cf. Julius Stone, *Conflict Through Consensus: United Nations Approaches to Aggression* (Baltimore: Johns Hopkins University Press, 1977), 157.

[94] Whoever doubts this proposition is encouraged to read carefully the Friendly Relations Declaration, resolution 2625 (XXV), an exemplary masterpiece in transforming disagreement in substance into agreement on paper.

[95] Johan Galtung, 'Social Cosmology and the Concept of Peace', *Journal of Peace Research* 18 (1981),183, 194.

[96] A strong belief in the justice of a particular cause might strengthen belligerent passions. (See Hayward R. Alker, Thomas J. Biersteker, and Takashi Inoguchi, 'From Imperial Power Balancing to People's Wars: Searching for Order in the Twentieth Century', in *International/Intertextual Relations*, James Der Derian and Michael J. Shapiro (eds.) (New York: Lexington, 1989), 135, 150–1; Carl Schmitt, *Theorie des Partisanen: Zwischenbemerkungen zu den Begriff des Politischen* (Berlin: Duncker & Humblot, 1963). Cf. also Suganami, *The Domestic Analogy*, 173.

More fundamentally, 'order' is not a neutral term but a contested concept. There are different views of the contents of the existing order. There is no order 'as such', but what constitutes the order must be determined within an analytical framework—for instance, law.

As with all of the conundrums above, the balance between order and justice can be set out in legal regulation. However, the law can never fulfil what is the core of its promise: fairness *and* predictability. Predictability means that like cases should be treated alike. But there are no two identical cases. In order to achieve predictability, every legal rule considers just a few selected circumstances. Most of the universe of causes behind every human action is thus excluded from the legal process. However, this also often means that the law cannot take into account the underlying reasons for an action, reasons that might put a seemingly unlawful act in different light: therefore it will be impossible to achieve justice. Consequently, judges sometimes have to go outside the legal text, but then of course with less predictability as a result. The general and predetermined law therefore collapses into either uncertainty or injustice.

3. Final Words

We have examined collective security from one perspective after another, and found that every question has been answered with an insoluble dilemma.[97] In some instances, the UN collective security system did not take a position for one or the other option, and oscillated between them. In other cases, the UN decided for one option, but then necessarily at the expense of the values that the other conception would protect.

The analysis could have been carried out in an infinite number of other ways with other intersections of problems than the ones that I happened to find most pertinent.[98] The conclusion is nevertheless unequivocal: collective security is inherently paradoxical.

Of course, collective security is not impossible just because total collective security is beyond reach. The UN can prevent and even end wars, making life more bearable for many people, despite the theoretical problems that I have indicated. And that is the best one can expect. As Inis Claude points out, no system can cope with a 'maximalist' analysis.[99] International law, as well as other legitimating discourses, has been good at using various tricks[100] to cover up these contradictions in order to make the system work.

[97] It is not only the case that each principle has a counter-principle. Every principle also contains its own contradiction. To speak in geometrical terms: it is not only the case that there are no parallel lines, there are no straight lines.

[98] Cf. Danid Kennedy, *International Legal Structures* (Baden-Baden: Nomos, 1986).

[99] Claude, *Swords Into Plowshares*, 283.

[100] See Martti Koskenniemi, 'The Normative Force of Habit: International Custom and Social Theory', *Finnish Yearbook of International Law* 1 (1990), 77.

It could even be said that although collective security is a vague concept, its merit is this very vagueness. This is because vagueness does not mean that anything goes. Though neither the concept of collective security nor the provisions of Chapters V, VI, and VII determine outcomes, they condition them. International security politics would have been different without the Security Council and without the Charter. As Miller notes, the Charter marks a concern with *jus ad bellum*, it advances the idea of a universal obligation to oppose aggression, and there is a general sense that a 'community response' is necessary against 'substantial outbursts of violence'.[101]

But the malleability of the collective security frame has enabled these notions to be stretched in new directions. The contradictions in the regulation of the use of force have facilitated some uses of force that one condones and some that one doesn't; the disconnect between Article 42 and Article 43 has summoned a new practice of authorizations that sometimes unites the collective need for action for universal values with national liberty to refrain from participation; Article 4 has been pushed into almost meaninglessness, thus allowing the organization to increase its universal legitimacy, but at the cost of many instances of inaction; the Security Council has maintained its political room of manoeuvre, but also built up a repertoire of best practices, precedents, and expectations that can be invoked against it; while the original benefactors of the system were states who were to be protected against international military threats, the plasticity of the expression 'threats against the peace' has allowed the Council to intervene against threats barely contemplated by the drafters of the Charter and even invoke a responsibility to protect that could have been imagined by only the most radical dreamers in 1945; while the Council has generally prioritized peace before security when the two have been contradictory goals, it has nevertheless become much more active in preventing threats from materializing; while the Council was not conceived as an instrument of justice, it has sometimes seized the conceptual contradictions in order to further justice, at least in some forms.

So, the fact that collective security contains paradoxes also means that there is space. For most or all of the nine questions asked earlier, some answers have suggested themselves despite the fact that the paradoxical nature of the problems makes another answer at least as plausible, in principle. But it is not always chance or power that determines if the one or the other answer is given. It may also (at best) be based on facts, analysis, and opinion informed by morality. The very fact that the paradox does not determine the decision means that there is room for our most important faculty—judgement.

There is nothing in the collective security or the UN Charter that necessarily leads to peace and security. But it is possible to utilize the procedures, rules, and doctrines that it contains and to exploit the contingencies for good. At any rate, there are no plausible alternatives on the horizon.

[101] Miller, 'The Idea and the Reality of Collective Security', 325–6.

6

Protection of Human Rights and the Maintenance of International Peace and Security

Necessary Precondition or a Clash of Interests?

Ola Engdahl

1. Introduction

The purpose of this chapter is to evaluate the relationship between the concept of Responsibility to Protect (R2P) and the proposed right to peace as expressed in the Draft Declaration of the Human Rights Council (HRC). Focus is on the relation between the maintenance of international peace and security and the protection of human rights which also can be described as the relation between positive and negative peace.

There is an established link between respect for human rights and the existence of peace. This is made clear, for example, in the Universal Declaration of Human Rights,[1] International Covenant on Civil and Political Rights,[2] the UN Charter,[3] and the Friendly Relations Declaration.[4] In the General Assembly resolution

[1] The opening text of the Universal Declaration of Human Rights reads: 'Whereas recognition of the inherent dignity and of the equal and inalienable rights of all members of the human family is the foundation of freedom, justice and peace in the world,' Preamble, Universal Declaration of Human Rights, 1948.

[2] 'Considering that, in accordance with the principles proclaimed in the Charter of the United Nations, recognition of the inherent dignity and of the equal and inalienable rights of all members of the human family is the foundation of freedom, justice and peace in the world,' Preamble, International Covenant on Civil and Political Rights, 1966.

[3] 'To develop friendly relations among nations based on respect for the principle of equal rights and self-determination of peoples, and to take other appropriate measures to strengthen universal peace;' Art. 1(2) United Nations Charter, 1945.

[4] '*Bearing in mind* the importance of maintaining and strengthening international peace founded upon freedom, equality, justice and respect for fundamental human rights and of developing friendly relations among nations irrespective of their political, economic and social systems or the levels of their development,' General Assembly Resolution, Preamble Declaration on Principles of International Law concerning Friendly Relations and Cooperation among States in accordance with the Charter of the United Nations, UN Doc. A/RES/25/2625 (1970).

on Promotion of peace as a vital requirement for the full enjoyment of all human rights by all, this link is established further.[5] The relation between peace and protection of human rights is also shown in the practice of the UN Security Council (SC), which has repeatedly determined that gross violations of human rights may be regarded as a threat to international peace and security. The SC, moreover, regularly includes in the mandates of peace operations based upon Chapter VII of the Charter the task of protecting civilians against threats of violence and attacks on their human rights.[6]

From the work of the Human Rights Council it is clear that the proposed right to peace is not only understood in its negative sense, the absence of war, but includes a strong element of positive peace, enabling individuals and populations to enjoy fully their human rights. This approach includes the use of force as a means of stopping grave human rights violations, also at the international level. There is thus a contradictory element in the right to peace. On the one hand, the need to enable the enjoyment of human rights by the individual might lead to a breach of the peace among states, while on the other hand concern for preserving international peace and security might have the effect of grave human rights violations being committed unhindered.

This tension is also illustrated by the R2P concept and the debate on humanitarian intervention. The idea of a right to intervene for the purpose of saving people from cruel rulers has long traditions and has its basis in the *just war* doctrine. The terminology has changed, but the underlying ideas are largely the same. The NATO-led intervention in Kosovo in 1999 brought the question of humanitarian intervention to the fore. In the following year the International Commission on Intervention and State Sovereignty (ICISS) was established and in 2001 it presented its influential report on R2P.[7] However, this development has not yet had an effect on the prohibition on the use of force and when the SC is blocked from taking any decision on military action, as in Syria, international law as it currently stands does not permit the coercive use of force to protect against grave human rights violations.

There is thus a clear connection between the proposed right to peace and R2P.[8] The Draft Declaration on the Right to Peace includes references to R2P and the proposed right to peace is thus broader than R2P. While the support of states for the notion of the R2P is evidenced by the World Summit Outcome Document of 2005 there is, however, considerable disagreement among states for developing a right to peace.[9] It is safe to say that the work and acceptance of a responsibility

[5] General Assembly Resolution, 'Promotion of peace as a vital requirement for the full enjoyment of all human rights by all', UN Doc. A/RES/60/163 (2005).

[6] 'Protecting Civilians in the Context of UN Peacekeeping Operations, Successes, Setbacks and Remaining Challenges', United Nations (2009).

[7] *The Responsibility to Protect, Report of the International Commission on Intervention and State Sovereignty* (2001) (ICISS Report).

[8] See Report of the Human Rights Council Advisory Committee on the right of peoples to peace, Human Rights Council (16 April 2012) UN Doc. A/HRC/20/31.

[9] Approximately one-third of the voting states have rejected the work on a right to peace during the last three resolutions. See UN Doc. A/HRC/RES/8/9 (18 June 2008); UN Doc. A/HRC/RES/11/4 17 (June 2009); and UN Doc. A/HRC/RES/14/3 (23 June 2010).

to protect has developed further than the work on a right to peace. Both aim to tie together established norms from different legal frameworks to create a more effective protection for individuals and populations. But since neither has yet developed into legal norms of their own they will in this chapter be described as concepts or ideas.[10] This is not to say that the right to peace and R2P have reached a similar standing, but rather to note that neither has developed into legal norms.[11]

2. International Peace and Security

The main purpose of the UN Charter is to maintain international peace and security. The SC has a special responsibility in this regard under Chapter VII of the Charter. All states are furthermore prevented from using force in international relations in accordance with Article 2(4) of the Charter, which states: 'All Members shall refrain in their international relations from the threat or use of force against the territorial integrity or political independence of any state, or in any other manner inconsistent with the Purposes of the United Nations.'[12] There are only two established exceptions to this rule. States may, individually or collectively, exercise their inherent right of self-defence against armed attacks. In return for prohibition on the use of force and the limited right of self-defence, the UN Charter vests the SC with great powers. When the Council finds that a situation constitutes a threat to international peace and security it may decide on appropriate measures, up to and including the use of force, in order to maintain or restore peace and security.[13] The SC is a political body and any decision to intervene in a conflict depends on the fact that none of the five permanent members votes against such a proposition. Thus a weakness of the current system is that political considerations may prevent an intervention in situations where it could have averted large-scale human right violations.

Another possibility open for the use of force is to retrieve the consent of the state in question. Strictly speaking, this is not an exception to the rule on the prohibition on the use of force as it would be premised on the conditions by the inviting state. This is, for instance, common in peace operations, where states in the absolute majority of such operations invite forces to assist the government. Sovereign states are permitted to invite the assistance of other states, including their military forces. From a legal point of view it is necessary that the invitation comes from the recognized representatives of the state concerned. In a conflict with armed groups on its territory the state may thus invite other states to help it in the particular conflict. No similar right exists for rebel groups. Or, to be more

[10] See Lyal S. Sunga, 'The Human Rights Council', in *An Institutional Approach to the Responsibility to Protect*, Gentian Zyberi (ed.) (Cambridge: Cambridge University Press, 2013), 157.

[11] Bellamy, for instance, refers to R2P as a concept in the period between the ICISS introduction of R2P until the World Summit in 2005 when world leaders accepted and also altered R2P. He asserts that R2P thereafter matured into a principle. Alex J. Bellamy, *Responsibility to Protect* (Cambridge: Polity, 2009), 7.

[12] Art. 2(4) of the UN Charter.

[13] Arts. 39, 41, and 42 of the UN Charter.

correct, if such groups were to invite other states to assist against government forces this would represent a breach of the principle of non-intervention for states to intervene on the basis of such an invitation.[14]

3. Responsibility to Protect

Norms protecting the individual are found in established legal frameworks such as human rights law, international humanitarian law, refugee law, and, indirectly, international criminal law. These frameworks share a humanitarian perspective, providing safeguards and protection for individuals and populations against atrocities. The principle duty bearers are states in relation to individuals and populations within their jurisdictions. Some acts are of such a grave nature that they would meet the stipulated crimes of genocide, war crimes, or crimes against humanity. The *erga omnes* nature of these crimes means that the international community as a whole has an interest in their prevention and punishment.[15] When states, in whose jurisdictions such crimes are committed, are not able or willing to stop their commission the question arises as to what the international community, through states and international organizations, is legally permitted to do.

3.1. Evolution of the concept

When the ICISS started its work in the aftermath of the 1999 NATO-led intervention in Kosovo it found that the notion of intervention became an obstacle in the discussion on protecting peoples in need. Instead, the Commission's position was to shift the debate from the notion of a 'right to intervene' to that of a 'responsibility to protect'.[16] The heart of the debate would thus center on a duty to protect peoples from gross human rights violations. Second, a responsibility to protect acknowledged that the primary responsibility to protect people from such violations rested with the state concerned. It is only when such a state was unable or unwilling to fulfil its responsibilities that it would become the responsibility of

[14] In the words of the ICJ in the Nicaragua case, the principle of non-intervention would 'certainly lose its effectiveness as a principle of law if intervention were to be justified by a mere request for assistance made by an opposition group in another State. ... Indeed, it is difficult to see what would remain of the principle of non-intervention in international law if intervention, which is already allowable at the request of the government of a State, were also to be allowed at the request of the opposition. This would permit any State to intervene at any moment in the internal affairs of another State, whether at the request of the government or at the request of its opposition.' *Military and Paramilitary Activities in and against Nicaragua (Nicaragua* v. *United States of America).* (Merits) ICJ Rep 1986, 14 para. 246.

[15] See the ICJ in the Barcelona Traction case where it confirmed that obligations *erga omnes* derive, 'for example, in contemporary international law, from the outlawing of acts of aggression, and of genocide, as also from the principles and rules concerning the basic rights of the human person, including protection from slavery and racial discrimination'. *Barcelona Traction, Light & Power Company, Limited (Belgium* v. *Spain) Second Phase* (Judgment) [1970] ICJ Rep. 3, para. 34.

[16] ICISS Report, para. 2.28-9.

the international community to act in its place. Third, a responsibility to protect would include more than a responsibility to react—that is, a 'responsibility to prevent' and a 'responsibility to rebuild'.[17]

The ICISS Report suggests, as part of a larger concept, that there should be a right (*lex ferenda*) for states and international organizations to take military action when the SC is incapable of taking a decision in relation to a particular situation, in accordance with a set of decided conditions. This controversial part of the Report has gained insufficient support among states and the customary development that could have taken off after the Kosovo intervention has ceased. That became particularly clear after the World Summit in 2005 where the leaders of the world did not support such a development.[18] However, the authorization by the SC to intervene in Libya for the purpose of protecting civilians was clearly influenced by the R2P concept, though the decision to intervene was well within the powers of the Council and in this respect could not factor in as a development or change in international law. Inaction by the Council in relation to Syria has again revived the question of a third exception to the prohibition on the use of force. After the use of chemical weapons, both the UK and the US declared its intention to intervene in the conflict in Syria.[19] The UK explicitly referred to the doctrine of humanitarian intervention.[20]

The idea of R2P was incorporated in the work of the UN. In 2003 the Secretary-General formed the High-level Panel on Threats, Challenges and Change which issued its report in 2004, entitled 'A More Secure World: Our Shared Responsibility'.[21] The conclusion by the High-level Panel was supported by the Secretary-General in his Report 'In Larger Freedom', which also addressed the heads of states in the coming World Summit in 2005.[22] The result of the meeting between the heads of states and governments in 2005 is presented in the World Summit Outcome Document.[23] In two articles the question of the responsibility to protect was addressed:

138. Each individual State has the responsibility to protect its populations from genocide, war crimes, ethnic cleansing and crimes against humanity. This responsibility entails the prevention of such crimes, including their incitement, through appropriate and necessary means. We accept that responsibility and will act in accordance with it.

[17] ICISS Report, para. 2.29.

[18] 2005 World Summit Outcome, UNGA Res. 60/1 (24 October 2005) UN Doc. A/60/L.1.

[19] The motion by the Government was, however, rejected by the Parliament, BBC, 'Syria Crisis: Cameron loses Commons vote on Syria action', 30 August 2013 http://www.bbc.co.uk/news/uk-politics-23892783 (accessed 9 Nov 2014).

[20] UK Government, Prime Minister's Office, 10 Downing Street, 'Guidance: Chemical Weapon use by Syrian Regime: UK Government Legal Position', 29 August 2013, https://www.gov.uk/government/publications/chemical-weapon-use-by-syrian-regime-uk-government-legal-position/chemical-weapon-use-by-syrian-regime-uk-government-legal-position-html-version (accessed 9 Nov 2014).

[21] The Secretary-General's High-level Panel Reports on Threats Challenges and Change. 'A More Secure World: Our Shared Responsibility', 2 December 2004, UN Doc. A/59/565.

[22] Report of the Secretary-General, 'In Larger Freedom: Towards Development, Security and Human Rights for All', 26 May 2005, UN Doc. A/59/2005, para. 135.

[23] 2005 World Summit Outcome, UNGA Res. 60/1.

The international community should, as appropriate, encourage and help States to exercise this responsibility and support the United Nations in establishing an early warning capability.
139. The international community, through the United Nations, also has the responsibility to use appropriate diplomatic, humanitarian and other peaceful means, in accordance with Chapters VI and VIII of the Charter, to help protect populations from genocide, war crimes, ethnic cleansing and crimes against humanity. In this context, we are prepared to take collective action, in a timely and decisive manner, through the SC, in accordance with the Charter, including Chapter VII, on a case-by-case basis and in cooperation with relevant regional organizations as appropriate, should peaceful means be inadequate and national authorities manifestly fail to protect their populations from genocide, war crimes, ethnic cleansing and crimes against humanity.[24]

When the heads of states had the opportunity of addressing the concept of R2P it became clear that the idea that other actors would be able to take coercive measures, for humanitarian purposes, was rejected. References to 'collective action', the SC, and 'in accordance with the UN Charter', would not seem to leave any room for an additional exception to the prohibition on the use of force.[25] It should also be noted that the threshold for military intervention has been raised from states being 'unable or unwilling' to fulfil their responsibilities to protect (ICISS Report), to the point where 'national authorities manifestly fail to protect their populations from genocide, war crimes, ethnic cleansing and crimes against humanity'.[26]

The World Summit Outcome Document became very influential on the development of the R2P concept within the UN system. In January 2009 a report by the UN Secretary-General was issued entitled, 'Implementing the Responsibility to Protect'.[27] Based on the outcome of the World Summit the Secretary-General proposed a conceptual understanding of R2P resting on three pillars.

(a) Pillar one is the enduring responsibility of the State to protect its populations, whether nationals or not, from genocide, war crimes, ethnic cleansing and crimes against humanity, and from their incitement. …
(b) Pillar two is the commitment of the international community to assist States in meeting those obligations. It seeks to draw on the cooperation of Member States, regional and subregional arrangements, civil society and the private sector, as well as on the institutional strengths and comparative advantages of the United Nations system. …
(c) Pillar three is the responsibility of Member States to respond collectively in a timely and decisive manner when a State is manifestly failing to provide such protection.

[24] 2005 World Summit Outcome, UNGA Res. 60/1, Arts. 138 and 139.

[25] Stahn finds, however, that the Outcome Document does not exclude completely the possibility of unilateral responses. Carsten Stahn, 'Responsibility to Protect: Political Rhetoric or Emerging Legal Norm?', *American Journal of International Law* 101 (2007), 99–120 at 109.

[26] Diana Amnéus, 'Responsibility to Protect by Military Means—Emerging Norms on Humanitarian Intervention?', *Global Society* 26 (2008), 269.

[27] Report of the Secretary-General, 'Implementing the Responsibility to Protect', 12 January 2009, UN Doc. A/63/677.

In September the General Assembly adopted its first resolution on the responsibility to protect.[28] It took note of the report by the Secretary-General and decided to continue the work on R2P. The Secretary-General has since issued four more reports on particular aspects of R2P,[29] which all have been debated within the General Assembly.[30] There is not sequence between the three pillars and they are all of equal importance. However, the concept emphasizes the obligations of states in relation to their populations and responsibility of the international community to assist states in meeting their obligations and to be able to respond collectively if needed. There is also a growing realization that R2P does not primarily concern the choice between doing nothing or military intervention.[31] The focus is rather on early warning systems, diplomatic solutions aimed at prevention of conflict.[32] However, when such measures fail, a situation requiring military action may occur.

The R2P concept has evolved into a recognized political concept rooted in international law. The implementation of R2P after the World Summit has been described in terms of 'three pillars—four crimes'.[33] The crimes from which individuals should be protected are genocide, war crimes, ethnic cleansing, and crimes against humanity, commonly referred to as mass atrocity crimes.[34] The R2P concept clearly identifies a duty of states to protect its populations from these crimes. This is a positive duty where failing to do so may lead to responsibility under international law. The duty to protect populations from these crimes stems from existing legal norms and the concept of R2P does not add legal obligations on the part of states.[35] Against this background, and given the broad range of duties tied together through the R2P concept, it may not even be possible to refer to R2P as an emerging legal norm. Rather, the question

[28] UNGA Res. 63/308 'The Responsibility to Protect' (7 October 2009) UN Doc. A/RES/63/308.

[29] Report of the Secretary-General, 'Early Warning, Assessment and the Responsibility to Protect', 14 July 2010, UN Doc. A/64/864; Report of the Secretary-General, 'The Role of Regional and Sub-regional Arrangements in Implementing the Responsibility to Protect', 27 June 2011, UN Doc. A/65/877–S/2011/393; Report of the Secretary-General, 'Responsibility to Protect: Timely and Decisive Response', 25 July 2012, UN Doc. A/66/874–S/2012/578, and Report of the Secretary-General, 'Responsibility to Protect: State Responsibility and Prevention', 9 July 2013, UN Doc. A/67/929–S/2013/399.

[30] For an overview of the debates and dialogues of the General Assembly, see http://responsibilitytoprotect.org/index.php/about-rtop#sg_report (accessed 22 June 2014).

[31] Bellamy, *Responsibility to Protect*, 199.

[32] Report of the Secretary-General, 'Implementing the Responsibility to Protect', 12 January 2009, UN Doc. A/63/677.

[33] Diana Amnéus, 'The Coining and Evolution of Responsibility to Protect: the Protection Responsibilities of the State', in Zyberi (ed.), *An Institutional Approach to the Responsibility to Protect*, 12.

[34] It should be noted that ethnic cleansing as such is not an international crime in its own right but could constitute an act of genocide, war crime, or crime against humanity. Notwithstanding that it is not a criminal act, ethnic cleansing would no doubt violate norms of human rights law and international humanitarian law.

[35] According to the Secretary-General, the responsibility to protect is 'consistent with existing obligations under international human rights, humanitarian and refugee law, which are binding on all States.' Report of the Secretary-General, 'Responsibility to Protect: State Responsibility and Prevention', 9 July 2013, UN Doc. A/67/929–S/2013/399, para. 6.

should be asked whether the development in this respect has modified existing international norms.[36]

3.2 R2P and *jus ad bellum*

It is only in situations where a state manifestly fails to provide such protection that a responsibility to act falls on the international community. In extreme situations where non-consensual force is required to halt atrocities, the right authority to decide on such use of force is the SC. However, as yet there is no duty on the part of the Council to act and non-action by the SC would not result in responsibility under international law. It should also be emphasized that the Council can only *authorize* military action. Since the UN has no forces of its own any military intervention is ultimately dependent on the will of member states to contribute personnel and equipment to any operation.

The R2P concept was no doubt of great importance in the decision by the SC to intervene in Libya in 2011. However, comparison with Syria shows that it is not powerful enough to convince the SC to take action in all situations of similar character.[37] The situation in Syria from 2011 to the present day has once again brought the question of protecting against human rights violations and the maintenance of international peace and security to the fore. The SC, due to the veto, has not been able to decide on the use of military action, or any other coercive measures, to halt the continuing killing.[38] The US has hesitated to become involved and the international community at large has officially condemned the Syrian regime only for committing transgressions of human rights law and international humanitarian law against the civilian population. The situation radically changed when it became clear that chemical weapons had been used in the war.[39]

The US had previously declared that use of chemical weapons was the red line which when crossed would trigger US military action.[40] The US rhetoric was centred on the fact that the use of chemical weapons was a clear violation of the prohibition on the use of such weapons in war, and furthermore contravened the principle of distinction. From the US perspective it was necessary to act against

[36] Mehrdad Payandeh, 'With Great Power Comes Great Responsibility? The Concept of the Responsibility to Protect within the Process of International Law Making', *Yale Journal of International Law* 35 (2010), 469.

[37] Terry D. Gill, 'The Security Council', in Zyberi (ed.), *An Institutional Approach to the Responsibility to Protect* (Cambridge: Cambridge University Press, 2013), 107–8.

[38] UN News Centre, 'Syria: Ban voices deep regret after Security Council fails to agree on resolution', 4 February 2012, http://www.un.org/apps/news/story.asp?NewsID=41144#.U5Ges3Y4VaQ (accessed 9 Nov 2014).

[39] See Note by Secretary-General, 'United Nations Mission to Investigate Allegations of the Use of Chemical Weapons in the Syrian Arab Republic: Report on the Alleged Use of Chemical Weapons in the Ghouta Area of Damascus on 21 August 2013', http://www.un.org/disarmament/content/slideshow/Secretary_General_Report_of_CW_Investigation.pdf (accessed 9 Nov 2014).

[40] Lindsay Boerma, 'Obama "I have not made a decision" on Syria military strike', CBS News, 29 August 2013, http://www.cbsnews.com/news/obama-i-have-not-made-a-decision-on-syria-military-strike/ (accessed 9 Nov 2014).

such use and to send a clear message that the use of chemical weapons could never be accepted.[41]

The UK Prime Minister supported an intervention but the proposition was rejected by Parliament.[42] The UK government presented its position on the legal basis for intervention following an attack of chemical weapons in Syria.[43] It declared that the use of chemical weapons was a serious crime under international law and constituted both a war crime and a crime against humanity. Contrary to the US position, the legal basis for an intervention was humanitarian. The aim was not to punish the Syrian regime for the use of chemical weapons but rather 'to relieve human suffering by deterring or disrupting the further use of chemical weapons'.[44] In view of the fact that the SC was blocked, the UK argued that it was permitted to use force to alleviate human suffering by deterring the further use of chemical weapons under the doctrine of humanitarian intervention, provided that three conditions were met:

(i) there is convincing evidence, generally accepted by the international community as a whole, of extreme humanitarian distress on a large scale, requiring immediate and urgent relief;
(ii) it must be objectively clear that there is no practicable alternative to the use of force if lives are to be saved; and
(iii) the proposed use of force must be necessary and proportionate to the aim of relief of humanitarian need and must be strictly limited in time and scope to this aim (i.e. the minimum necessary to achieve that end and for no other purpose).[45]

The UK found that the first two conditions were clearly met and that accordingly 'as an exceptional measure on grounds of overwhelming humanitarian necessity' it was entitled under international law 'to strike specific targets with the aim of deterring and disrupting further such attacks'. The force required would be 'necessary and proportionate'. Under these circumstances an 'intervention would be directed exclusively to averting a humanitarian catastrophe, and the minimum judged necessary for that purpose'.[46]

The UK has relied on this argumentation also in relation to the protecting the Kurds in Northern Iraq in 1991; maintaining the No Fly Zones in Northern and

[41] It became increasingly clear that the reasons behind the planned attack were of punitive character and would in legal terms constitute an armed reprisal, which is clearly prohibited under international law. Kathleen Hennessey and Christi Parsons, 'Obama to address a skeptical nation Tuesday on Syria', *Los Angeles Times*, 6 September 2013, http://www.latimes.com/world/worldnow/la-fg-wn-obama-syria-20130906,0,6749160.story#axzz2nYLHxp70 (accessed 9 Nov 2014).

[42] Nicholas Watt and Nick Hopkins, 'Cameron forced to rule out British attack on Syria after MPs reject motion', *The Guardian*, 29 August 2013, http://www.theguardian.com/world/2013/aug/29/cameron-british-attack-syria-mps (accessed 9 Nov 2014).

[43] UK Government, Prime Minister's Office, 10 Downing Street, 'Guidance: Chemical Weapon use by Syrian Regime: UK Government Legal Position', 29 August 2013, https://www.gov.uk/government/publications/chemical-weapon-use-by-syrian-regime-uk-government-legal-position/chemical-weapon-use-by-syrian-regime-uk-government-legal-position-html-version (accessed 9 Nov 2014).

[44] UK Govt., PM's Office, 'Guidance: Chemical Weapon use by Syrian Regime'.

[45] UK Govt., PM's Office, 'Guidance: Chemical Weapon use by Syrian Regime'.

[46] UK Govt., PM's Office, 'Guidance: Chemical Weapon use by Syrian Regime'.

Southern Iraq from 1991; and the use of force against the Federal Republic of Yugoslavia in relation to Kosovo in 1999.[47] The UK position, that it is permitted to take coercive action under a doctrine of humanitarian intervention when certain conditions are met, is a minority view and does not reflect *lex lata* on the prohibition on the use of force in international relations as expressed in Article 2(4) of the UN Charter. It raises, however, the important question on proper reaction by the international community when in the extreme case the SC is prevented to act due to the exercise of the veto, and other options have failed. A situation powerfully described by the then UN Secretary-General Kofi Annan: 'If humanitarian intervention is indeed an unacceptable assault on sovereignty, how should we respond to a Rwanda, to a Srebrenica, to gross and systematic violations of human rights?'[48]

An interesting development in this respect is the right of the African Union (AU) to intervene in the territories of its member states in situations of mass atrocity crimes.[49] The Constitutive Act of the AU provides a right for the Union 'to intervene in a Member State pursuant to a decision of the Assembly in respect of grave circumstances, namely: war crimes, genocide and crimes against humanity'.[50] The right to intervene by the AU is thus clearly influenced by the R2P concept. The legal basis, however, is a treaty-based consent of the member states. As noted already, military intervention based on consent is permitted under international law.[51] The link between the ideas behind a responsibility to protect and a right to peace is particularly noticeable in the African context. According to the African Charter on Human and Peoples Rights, 'All peoples shall have the right to national and international peace and security.'[52] The African Charter is so far the only treaty where 'peace' is expressed as a human right. The reference to national and international peace indicates a right of negative peace (absence of war of both an international and non-international character) as well as positive peace on the national level (protection of human rights).

The right to positive peace, the ability of individuals and populations to enjoy fully their human rights, is strengthened by the right of the AU to intervene to halt atrocity crimes—even without a mandate of the SC. On this regional

[47] See Further supplementary written evidence from the Rt. Hon. Hugh Robertson MP, Minister of State, Foreign and Commonwealth Office: 'Humanitarian Intervention and the Responsibility to Protect', 3 (14 January 2014), http://justsecurity.org/wp-content/uploads/2014/01/Letter-from-UK-Foreign-Commonwealth-Office-to-the-House-of-Commons-Foreign-Affairs-Committee-on-Humanitarian-Intervention-and-the-Responsibility-to-Protect.pdf (accessed 9 Nov 2014).

[48] Kofi A. Annan, *We the Peoples: The Role of the United Nations in the 21st Century*, (New York: United Nations, 2000) (Millenium Report), 48. A *lex ferenda* perspective on the possibility to intervene without mandate from the Security Council is discussed in Section 5.

[49] See Dan Kuwali, 'Protect Responsibly: The African Union's Implementation of Article 4(h) Intervention', in *Yearbook of International Humanitarian Law* 11 (2008), 51.

[50] Constitutive Act of the African Union, 1 July 2000, 2158 UNTS 3.

[51] That invitation of foreign military forces as such is permitted under international law is evidenced by the following definition of aggression: 'The use of armed forces of one State which are within the territory of another State with the agreement of the receiving State, in contravention of the conditions provided for in the agreement or any extension of their presence in such territory beyond the termination of the agreement.' UNGA Res. 3314 (XXIX), Article 3(e) Definition of Aggression.

[52] African Charter on Human and Peoples Rights (1981), Art. 23.

level there thus seems to be a potential for strengthening the aspects of positive peace over negative peace (on the international level), or explained in different terms: a potential of strengthening the protection of human rights over the interest of maintaining international peace and security. However, a prior treaty-based consent would not suffice, according to this author, if the consent is revoked at the time of the intervention. Such prior treaty-based consent 'cannot waive the right of the receiving state to withdraw the consent'.[53] In a situation where an AU member state, in contravention of its treaty obligations under the Constitutive Act, would object to a military intervention, the combined legal authority of Articles 2(4) and 103 of the UN Charter would prevent the AU from depending on the prior treaty-based consent.[54] In this perspective a prior consent of this nature would not carry the legal weight it indicates.[55]

4. Peace as a Human Right

The idea of a right to peace as a human right has been on the agenda of the Human Rights Council for some years, partly initiated by the *Luarca* Declaration of 2006, drafted by the Spanish Society for International Human Rights Law,[56] and in 2010 by an expert workshop convened by the High Commissioner of Human Rights.[57] In 2011 the Human Rights Council Advisory Committee issued a progress report on the right of peoples to peace,[58] and in April 2012 the Committee presented a Draft Declaration on the right of peoples to peace.[59] The topic has proved controversial and a number of states have voted against the resolutions of the Human Rights Council on the work on such a right.[60] However, among states commenting on this work

[53] Gustaf Lind, *The Revival of Chapter VIII of the UN Charter: Regional Organisations and Collective Security* (Stockholm: Stockholms Universitet, 2004), 165.

[54] See Rudolf Bernhardt, 'Article 103', in *The Charter of the United Nations: A Commentary*, ed. Bruno Simma et al. (2nd edn. New York: Oxford University Press, 2002), ii. 1297; Amnéus, 'Responsibility to Protect by Military Means', 418–21.

[55] However, see Ademola Abass, *Regional Organisations and the Development of Collective Security: Beyond Chapter VIII of the UN Charter* (Oxford: Hart, 2004), 204.

[56] The Luarca Declaration on the Human Right to Peace, 30 October 2006, http://www.concernedhistorians.org/content_files/file/TO/271.pdf (accessed 22 June 2014).

[57] HRC Res. 8/9, 'Promotion on the Right of Peoples to Peace' (18 June 2008), and HRC Res. 11/4, 'Promotion and Protection of All Human Rights, Civil, Political, Economic, Social and Cultural Rights, including the Right to Development' (30 April 2009); Report of the Office of the High Commissioner on the outcome of the expert workshop on the right of peoples to peace (17 March 2010) UN Doc. A/HRC/14/38, paras. 9–10. See also UNGA Res. 53/243, 57/216, 60/163, and 63/189.

[58] Progress report of the Human Rights Council Advisory Committee on the right of peoples to peace (1 April 2011) UN Doc. A/HRC/17/39.

[59] Report of the Human Rights Council Advisory Committee on the right of peoples to peace (16 April 2012) UN Doc. A/HRC/20/31.

[60] Progress report of the Human Rights Council Advisory Committee on the right of peoples to peace (1 April 2011) UN Doc. A/HRC/17/39. See also Promotion on the right of peoples to peace (18 June 2008) UN Doc.A/HRC/RES/8/9; Promotion on the right of peoples to peace (17 June 2009) UN Doc. A/HRC/RES/11/4, and Promotion on the right of peoples to peace (23 June 2010) UN Doc. A/HRC/RES/14/3. See also the chapter by Cecilia Bailliet in this book.

there has been a general agreement that human rights, peace, and development are interdependent and mutually reinforcing. It has also been noted that the concept of the right to peace is not new but recognized in soft law instruments.[61] Delegations opposed to the work on a declaration on a right to peace stated that there was no stand-alone right to peace under international law and held that peace was not a human right in and of itself. Rather it was a goal, which was best realized by the implementation of existing human rights.[62]

In the 2010 expert workshop on the right of peoples to peace, convened by the High Commissioner of Human Rights, one expert noted 'that the expansion and increasing complexity of international law had led to a greater need for overarching principles to sustain the unity of the system as a whole'.[63] She found that the right to peace had not yet developed into a human right within the context of human rights law, but 'the distinct linkages which were being forged between human rights law and peace and security and disarmament needed further analysis and might be useful in situating and further understanding an emerging right to peace'.[64]

Another expert observed that a right to peace should not be regarded as a collective right but 'peace was also a personal right, prior to and indispensable to other rights'.[65] He found that 'peace must be seen as an enabling right that empowered individuals to enjoy civil, political, economic, social and cultural rights'.[66] In that respect one could not view a right to peace as being merely an absence of war but rather it 'must be understood and implemented in a holistic manner through, among other things, respect for civil and political rights, and must include a focus on the obligations that peace imposed both on States and individuals'.[67]

So far the right to peace has not been clearly defined, but there seem to be an understanding that such a right includes both negative and positive aspects. The negative aspect (absence of war) lacks a clear definition and the precise threshold between peace and war is difficult to identify in all situations. The existence of armed conflict, however, is decisive on the application of international humanitarian law and would probably also designate the threshold between peace and war under a right to peace. In the *Tadic* case the ICTY was faced with the question of defining an armed conflict. According to the Court,

> an armed conflict exists whenever there is a resort to armed force between States or protracted armed violence between governmental authorities and organized armed groups

[61] Such as UNGA Res. 39/11, 'Declaration on the Right of Peoples to Peace' (12 November 1984); HRC, Report of the Open-ended Inter-Governmental Working Group on the Draft United Nations Declaration on the Right to Peace (26 April 2013), UN Doc. A/HRC/WG.13/1/2, para. 20.

[62] HRC, Report of the Open-ended Inter-Governmental Working Group, UN Doc. A/HRC/WG.13/1/2, para. 21.

[63] Report of the Office of the High Commissioner on the outcome of the expert workshop on the right of peoples to peace (17 March 2010) UN Doc. A/HRC/14/38, para. 9

[64] Report of the Office of the High Commissioner, UN Doc. A/HRC/14/38, para. 14.

[65] Report of the Office of the High Commissioner, UN Doc. A/HRC/14/38, para. 15.

[66] Report of the Office of the High Commissioner, UN Doc. A/HRC/14/38, para. 15.

[67] Report of the Office of the High Commissioner, UN Doc. A/HRC/14/38, para. 15.

or between such groups within a state. International humanitarian law applies from the initiation of such armed conflicts and extends beyond the cessation of hostilities until a general conclusion of peace is reached; or, in the case of internal conflicts, a peaceful settlement is achieved.[68]

The negative aspect of a right to peace thus needs to consider both the existence of international armed conflict and non-international armed conflict. While human rights law continues to apply during armed conflict, it is the existence of an armed conflict that signifies the non-existence of peace.[69] Though the application of the international humanitarian law is linked to the negative aspect of peace, it is noteworthy that the International Committee of the Red Cross and the Red Crescent Movement both support the notion of positive peace. In the Preamble of their Statutes it is declared that the Movement promotes a lasting peace, which is defined as 'not simply the absence of war, but is a dynamic process of cooperation among all States and peoples, cooperation founded on respect for freedom, independence, national sovereignty, equality, human rights, as well as on a fair and equitable distribution of resources to meet the needs of peoples'.[70] Hence even the guardians of international humanitarian law do not define peace as merely the absence of war but rather as a process of cooperation that includes respect for both national sovereignty and human rights.

The balance struck between negative peace and positive peace resembles the equilibrium sought between sovereignty and human rights that characterizes discussion on R2P.[71] The next section examines the Draft Declaration on the Right to Peace, primarily the paragraph referring to a responsibility to protect. The balance between positive peace and negative peace will be at the centre of the analysis.

5. The Draft Declaration of 2012

The proposed right to peace is broad and contains a number of sections pertaining to peace, such as disarmament, peacekeeping, and education. One section refers

[68] *Prosecutor* v. *Tadic* (Appeal on Jurisdiction) ICTY-95- IT-94-1-AR72 (2 October 1995), para. 70. The existence of non-international armed conflicts has been further identified in later judgments.

[69] In this respect it should also be noted that legal protection stemming from both international humanitarian law and human rights law may be of a stronger character during an armed conflict than during the crises leading up to it. It has been recognized that cases of internal upheaval where states might derogate from their human rights obligations may provide less protection compared with the factual more violent situations of an armed conflict in which the laws of war apply. See the work on Fundamental Standards of Humanity, e.g. Report of the Secretary-General, Fundamental Standards of Humanity (3 March 2006) UN Doc. E/CN./4/2006/87.

[70] ICRC, Statutes of the International Red Cross and Red Crescent Movement, adopted in Geneva in 1986, amended in 1995 and 2006, http://www.icrc.org/eng/assets/files/other/statutes-en-a5.pdf (accessed 22 June 2014).

[71] See Antonio Cassese, 'Ex iniuria ius oritur: Are We Moving towards International Legitimation of Forcible Humanitarian Countermeasures in the World Community?', *European Journal of International Law* 10 (1999), 27.

to human security and encompasses language similar to that of R2P.[72] The right to peace, however, lacks a coherent definition. The Advisory Committee suggested a focused approach and argued 'that peace should be conceived as both the absence of organized violence within a country or between countries and the comprehensive and effective protection of human rights, gender equality and social justice, economic well-being and free and widespread expression of different cultural values, without discrimination or restraints'.[73] This approach encompasses absence of armed conflict of both international and non-international character, as well the positive aspects of protection of human rights—all of importance in relation to R2P aspects. However, the deference to negative peace on the international level permeates much of the Draft Declaration. In its Preamble, the Human Rights Council states:

> *Reaffirming also* that the principal aim of the United Nations is the maintenance of international peace and security, . . .
>
> *Recalling further* that all Members shall refrain in their international relations from the threat or use of force against the territorial integrity or political independence of any State or in any other manner inconsistent with the purposes of the United Nations,
>
> *Convinced* that the prohibition of the use of force is the primary international prerequisite for the material well-being, development and progress of countries, and for the full implementation of the human rights and fundamental freedoms proclaimed by the United Nations,
>
> *Expressing* the will of all peoples that the use of force must be eradicated from the world, including through full nuclear disarmament, without delay.[74]

The overriding prerequisite for peoples to live in peace seems, according to the Preamble, to be linked to non-use of force between states. From a general perspective the use of force could certainly be regarded as the antithesis to peace. The fact that this Preamble gives the impression of almost a pacifist view is problematic, since it does not seem to recognize that the full enjoyment of human rights may sometimes require the use of force to stop grave abuses being committed against such rights. The reference to the principal aim of the UN includes the right of the Council to authorize military interventions for the protection of human rights. This could have been acknowledged in more precise terms in the Preamble.

The notion of positive peace is expressed most prominently in Article 2 on Human Security. Paragraph 1 reads:

> Everyone has the right to human security, which includes freedom from fear and from want, all constituting elements of positive peace, and also includes freedom of thought, conscience, opinion, expression, belief and religion, in conformity with international

[72] The HRC in fact has on a number of occasions adopted resolutions on the notion of R2P and is thus well suited for approaching that particular question and its relation to a purported right to peace.

[73] Progress report of the Human Rights Council Advisory Committee on the right of peoples to peace (1 April 2011) UN Doc. A/HRC/17/39 (2011) paras. 16–17.

[74] Report of the Human Rights Council Advisory Committee on the right of peoples to peace (16 April 2012) UN Doc. A/HRC/20/31 (16 April 2012) Preamble.

human rights law. Freedom from want implies the enjoyment of the right to sustainable development and of economic, social and cultural rights. The right to peace is related to all human rights, including civil, political, economical, social and cultural rights.[75]

The enjoyment of human rights requires that states take positive steps to create conditions for their fulfilment. The linkage between a right to peace and human security, however, has been criticized by states that have pointed out that the concept of human security lacks a universal definition and that the General Assembly is currently discussing the idea.[76] The work of the Special Adviser on Human Security was also referred to in this respect.[77]

The responsibility to protect is not explicitly mentioned in the Draft Declaration but it is clearly referred to in paragraph 3 of Article 2:

> Everyone has the right to be protected from genocide, war crimes, the use of force in violation of international law, and crimes against humanity. If States are unable to prevent these crimes from occurring within their jurisdiction, they should call on Member States and the United Nations to fulfil that responsibility, in keeping with the Charter of the United Nations and international law.[78]

While the paragraph is clearly influenced by the R2P concept there are some important differences.[79] Paragraph 3 is drafted as a right for individuals and not as a duty of states. Everyone is entitled to protection from genocide, war crimes, and crimes against humanity, which corresponds with the duties of states. However, the reference to 'use of force in violation of international law' indicates an obligation of a different nature. The exact meaning of 'use of force in violation of international law' is difficult to ascertain in this respect. It indicates protection against the use of force in violation of Article 2(4) of the UN Charter, which would mean any illegal use of force by another *state*. The fact that a previous version instead referred to 'wars of aggression' strengthens this impression.[80] However, the following sentence of the paragraph refers to all these acts as *crimes*. Not all illegal uses of force would be regarded as crimes under international law because individual criminal responsibility cannot always be assigned. Use of

[75] Report of the HRCAC, UN Doc. A/HRC/20/31, Art. 2.

[76] Report of the Open-ended Inter-Governmental Working Group on the Draft United Nations Declaration on the Right to Peace (26 April 2013) UN Doc. A/HRC/WG.13/1/2, para. 42.

[77] Report of the Open-ended Inter-Governmental Working Group, UN Doc. A/HRC/WG.13/1/2, para. 43.

[78] Report of the HRCAC, UN Doc. A/HRC/20/31, Art. 3. The reference to 'jurisdictions' instead of 'borders' is interesting as the term 'jurisdiction' in the jurisprudence of the human rights courts has generally been interpreted to mean effective control over territory or individuals. That may have the effect of widening the area over which states have responsibilities to individuals if they exercise necessary control over territory outside their borders. In a similar way the territory over which the state exercises control may decrease if, due to heavy fighting, it is not able to control the whole of its territory.

[79] The earlier version of this paragraph, in the Advisory Committee's Progress Report of 2011, a footnote referred to paragraphs 138 and 139 of the World Summit Outcome Document dealing with the responsibility to protect.

[80] Progress report of the Human Rights Council Advisory Committee on the right of peoples to peace (1 April 2011) UN Doc. A/HRC/17/39, para. 34.

force in violation of international law is not a crime in itself but could fall into any of the other categories of crimes (genocide, war crimes, or crimes against humanity). Use of force in violation of international law could also constitute a crime of aggression. In 1973 the UN General Assembly adopted a definition of aggression where it considered it to be 'the most serious and dangerous form of the illegal use of force'.[81] States that are parties to the International Criminal Court, moreover, have agreed on a definition, largely founded on the 1973 definition, of the crime of aggression to be included in the Rome statute. The new crime of aggression is in part defined as an act 'which, by its character, gravity and scale, constitutes a manifest violation of the Charter of the United Nations'.[82] War of aggression is prohibited for states whereas the crime of aggression is an act entailing individual criminal responsibility. There is no doubt, from the perspective of the responsibility of states, that 'aggression' denotes the most serious violation of the prohibition on the use of force in international law. The move from 'wars of aggression' to 'use of force in violation of international law' indicates a much broader approach encompassing all acts in violation of the prohibition on the use of force (from the perspective of individual responsibility it is, however, only the act of aggression that is criminalized). Or, in terms of a right to peace, an approach biased towards negative peace over positive peace, for example, a limited non-consensual military intervention, without a mandate from the SC, to halt the ensuing genocide in Rwanda would probably not have been characterized as an aggression but rather an illegal but legitimate use of force.

The next part of the paragraph strengthens the impression of a traditional sovereignty-oriented approach, biased towards negative peace of an international character, based upon a subjective criterion placing the decision to intervene exclusively in the hands of the state.[83] This stands in contrast to the R2P concept, which entails a subsidiary responsibility of the international community to take appropriate action if the state manifestly fails in its protection—or, in the ICISS version, the state is unable or unwilling to protect. The right to peace paragraph transmits the signal that the international community should only intervene if (1) states are unable (but not unwilling) to provide protection and (2) the state itself calls for assistance. The current draft would seem to focus chiefly on the negative right to peace, in relation to wars of an international character, while the absence of non-international wars and the positive part of the right to peace (understood in this context as the right to be protected from mass atrocity crimes) comes second. Given that the right to peace and R2P rest on similar values there would be added worth if the right to peace in the 'R2P-part' were to include a similar language, including an objective criterion triggering the subsidiary responsibility of the international community, thus strengthening development in this respect.

81 UNGA Res. 3314 (XXIX), Art. 3(e) Definition of Aggression.

82 Resolution RC/Res.6* The Crime of Aggression, 11 June 2010, http://www.icc-cpi.int/icc-docs/asp_docs/Resolutions/RC-Res.6-ENG.pdf (accessed 22 June 2014).

83 On 'traditional sovereignty', see Bellamy, *Responsibility to Protect*, 15–18.

An alternative text could be: 'Everyone has the right to be protected from genocide, war crimes, ethnic cleansing and crimes against humanity. If States are manifestly failing to provide such protection the United Nations and its Member States should take appropriate action to protect against such crimes, in keeping with the Charter of the United Nations and international law.' This text emphasizes the responsibility of the state in whose jurisdiction any crimes are committed and it is only in situations where such a state manifestly fails to protect the population that responsibility is transferred to international level. The reference to the UN Charter makes it clear that under the current state of international law any coercive intervention requires a decision by the SC. However, it makes room for a progressive interpretation of the Charter should a right to intervene without a decision of the Council in the future take form.

Taken together with the Preamble of the Draft Declaration it becomes clear that the negative peace at international level (between states), which is ultimately a traditional sovereignty-driven approach, has so far strongly influenced the work of the Advisory Committee. This is also in many respects a reflection of a *lex lata* interpretation of *jus ad bellum*. However, the situation in Syria has once again pushed the question of humanitarian intervention to the fore and both the UK and the US have argued, in different ways, for a right to intervene. A potential development of *jus ad bellum* in that direction could result in a third exception to the prohibition on the use of force—and thereby for breaching the peace at international level—but could at the same time create conditions for a positive peace which otherwise would not exist. Section 6 will briefly discuss the balance of these interests in a *lex ferenda* setting including both the concept of R2P and a right to peace.

6. Should the Balance between International Peace and Security and Protection of Human Rights be Shifted?

In situations of mass atrocity crimes where the SC is blocked there will inevitably be a question of whether states or international organizations could intervene without a mandate from the Council. The balance in the extreme cases between, on the one hand, the sovereignty of states and the interests of international peace and security, and on the other the protection of human rights and the security of the individual, invite a discussion beyond *lex lata*. The balance of similar interests has in fact long traditions following attempts to regulate the use of force in international relations. It can be traced back to early Christian thinking where the idea of *just war* was developed in reaction to the notion of pacifism.[84] It also found its antecedents in the natural law. Prominent legal authorities such as Grotius argued for a right to intervene in other states under a *just war* doctrine. The arguments were indeed of a similar type in aiming to protect individuals against rulers who

[84] Alex J. Bellamy, *Just Wars, From Cicero to Iraq* (Cambridge: Polity, 2006), 20–9.

mistreated their subjects contrary to the law of nature.[85] The increasing development of positive law put further strains on recourse to the use of force with the founding of the UN Charter as the pinnacle of the prohibition on the use of force in international relations, with only two established exceptions.

A *lex ferenda* discussion would need to consider whether international law indeed strikes the right balance between these fundamental interests.[86] The risks associated with a military intervention might prompt a situation where intervention worsens matters and a discussion concerning a balance between these interests must therefore address criteria surrounding such a right to enable it to be effective. Such criteria may benefit from the ICISS report but the main question, then and now, is that of right authority. It seems to be established that a fairly limited military intervention could have prevented much of the genocide in Rwanda.[87] If a future situation of a similar nature develops, where the SC is blocked or otherwise fails to act, this would certainly revive the discussion on humanitarian intervention. This does not mean that there is a military solution to all circumstances where atrocity crimes are committed and the SC is helpless due to the veto. The discussion here concerns whether it should be an option at all. *When* a military intervention could be used would be up to the criteria surrounding such a right—bearing in mind the constant risk of abuse.

From a non-legal perspective it may be difficult to claim the sacred value of state sovereignty and the maintenance of international peace and security over protection against genocide, war crimes, and crimes against humanity. Indeed, would not an international system be designed to protect individuals against precisely these types of abhorrent acts?[88] In this respect Tesón has made a powerful philosophical argument in defence of humanitarian intervention. Based on the conviction that the justification for the existence of states is ultimately the protection of the human rights of their citizens, a government that engages in massive human rights violations loses its legitimacy both internally and externally. In these situations other states are, under certain conditions, permitted to use force to protect the victims.[89]

What possible arguments could then be advanced in order to claim that the crimes of genocide, crimes against humanity, or war crimes should not be prevented with the use of force (when the SC is blocked) when all other means

[85] Alexander Orakhelashvili, 'Natural Law and Justice', in *Max Planck Encyclopedia of Public International Law,* August 2007, para. 38, http://opil.ouplaw.com/view/10.1093/law:epil/9780199231690/law-9780199231690-e730?rskey=JR75OP&result=1&prd=EPIL (accfessed 22 June 2014).

[86] According to Chesterman, the current normative system does not prevent interventions taking place, the reason is rather that '[i]nterventions do not take place because states do not want them to take place'. Simon Chesterman, *Just War or Just Peace? Humanitarian Intervention and International Law* (New York: Oxford University Press, 2001), 231.

[87] Carnegie Corporation of New York, *Final Report With Executive Summary: Preventing Deadly Conflict* (1997). Major General Romeo Dallaire stated that with a force of 5,000 trained troops and an appropriate mandate he could have prevented thousands of deaths, 51 n.1.

[88] Nicholas Wheeler, *Saving Strangers* (New York: Oxford University Press, 2000), 28.

[89] Fernando R. Tesón, *Humanitarian Intervention: An Inquiry into Law and Morality* (3rd edn. New York: Transnational, 2005), 16.

have proved futile? Arguments claiming the importance of international borders over the need to protect against mass atrocity crimes seem based on a conviction that preservation of the current system is an overriding value. From a utilitarian point of view it might be possible to argue that the preservation of the current balance has prevented another world war and that idly standing by while genocide is committed is better than intervening without a mandate from the SC, thereby risking a greater war with even more casualties. Such argument could possibly be of importance if there was a real risk of an armed conflict developing that would pit the major states against one another. If that is not the case, such an argument could hardly carry greater weight than the need to halt an ongoing genocide.[90]

An oft-repeated argument is the risk of abuse if states were to intervene for humanitarian purposes without a mandate from the SC. New avenues for the use of force would by definition erode the prohibition on the use of force in international relations. The risk of abuse is perhaps the strongest argument for limiting the right to use force in situations permitted under current international law. From a realpolitik point of view this is certainly the case, since states when they have had the opportunity, have not been willing to include a third exception. However, even if there is a risk for abuse this argument does not really address the status of genuine humanitarian interventions where the intervening states act in accordance with a narrowly drafted exception for the only purpose of halting human rights violations.[91] Chesterman has in this respect warned against a third exception as it would probably lead to more interventions undertaken for purposes other than purely humanitarian. Rather, it is better to keep the current prohibition on the use of force, even for interventions on humanitarian grounds, but in the extreme situation the international community may tolerate such a transgression of the law.[92]

Illegal but legitimate was also a common opinion on the NATO intervention in Kosovo in 1999. According to this argument the current system would be preserved but depending on the particular situation the intervening states would not suffer condemnation due to the legitimate purpose of the intervention.[93] However, even if this were to be true for a limited period, it is questionable whether such a solution would not inevitably lead to a change of *jus ad bellum*. States might try to stop this evolution by claiming the illegality of such an intervention, but such arguments would have a hollow ring if the states at the same time acknowledged the legitimate purpose of the interventions in specific situations.[94]

While the values of human rights protection and the maintenance of international peace and security in the short-term perspective could be seen as being in opposition, that is not necessarily so in the longer perspective. We have in the

[90] Tesón, *Humanitarian Intervention*, 124–8. [91] Tesón, *Humanitarian Intervention*, 112.

[92] Chesterman, *Just War or Just Peace?*, 231.

[93] Thomas Franck and Nigel Rodley, 'After Bangladesh: The Law of Humanitarian Intervention by Military Force', in *American Journal of International Law* 67 (1973), 290.

[94] Cassesse, 'Ex iniuria ius oritur'.

SC practice seen ample evidence that grave violations of human rights, even within a state, have been regarded as threats to international peace and security (Libya). The connection between massive human rights violations in a similar situation (Syria) would certainly also constitute a threat to international peace and security—even though the Permanent Five are not, due to the veto, able to conclude that. The actual link between human rights violations and international peace and security has been established repeatedly by the SC and international instruments. The fact that the Council is not able to declare that a particular situation constitutes a threat to international peace does not in reality mean that this link is not established, but rather is dependent on the political reality of the Council. The established link between prevention of massive human rights abuses and the maintenance of international peace and security in the long-term perspective is in fact a further argument for shifting the balance between human rights protection and peace among states towards human rights protection in the short-term perspective. Sustainable peace depends on the protection of human rights—and most certainly on the prevention of genocide, war crimes, and crimes against humanity. However, the maintenance of international peace is also rooted in realpolitik in the short perspective and military interventions outside the realm of the SC may certainly lead to greater risks of international conflict between powerful states. However, this situation must be balanced against both the independent value of protecting against massive human rights violations and the effect that such transgressions have on the maintenance of international peace and security.

In view of the progressive work of the HRC on a right to peace, it is indeed interesting to note the traditional sovereignty-oriented approach permeating the Draft Declaration on such a right. Instead of supporting the work on R2P and the 'three pillars—four crimes' approach, it appears to emphasize the prohibition of the use of force between states and the principle of non-intervention. The proposed right to peace, moreover, is biased towards the absence of war of an international character.[95] The absence of war of a non-international character (as in Syria) would not seem to carry the same weight. The focus of protection against international armed conflicts should also be viewed against the fact that today most armed conflicts are of a non-international character and the right to peace should include this perspective to a greater extent. A right to peace would naturally need to develop within the confines of international law and its current state does not permit non-consensual military operations without a mandate from the UNSC or for the purpose of self-defence. The discussion on Syria has proved that the idea of humanitarian intervention is not dead, that it still might be necessary, and may gain further support by states if situations of a similar nature were to recur. It is, however, beyond doubt that the SC has the legal

[95] It is perhaps telling that the states of Cuba, Venezuela, Pakistan, China, Egypt, and Nicaragua, who questioned the need of a Special Adviser on Responsibility to Protect (and to some extent the concept as such), are all in favour of developing a right to peace. See UN Press Release GA/AB/3832 and e.g. A/HRC/RES/8/9, A/HRC/RES/11/4, and A/HRC/RES/23/16.

option to authorize an intervention when it finds that the circumstances in question constitute a threat to international peace and security. A right to peace would need to acknowledge the powers of the Council in more express terms and not least the political concept of R2P, which might have an effect on the decision-making of the Council. Even if it is believed by proponents of a human right to peace that military interventions should be prevented as far as possible, the work on such a right must further acknowledge that military interventions can have a profound impact on stopping atrocity crimes—in situations where all other options have failed.

7. Conclusions

The debate for and against military intervention for the purpose of protecting against mass atrocity crimes, fuelled by the recent operation in Libya and the lack of military action in Syria, seems to have moved into yet a new arena. It is difficult to move away completely from the impression that the development of a right to peace in some respects is used as a tool for limiting current practice of military intervention by the SC and the discussion of a potential right for states and organizations to intervene to halt mass atrocities in circumstances where the Council is blocked. The proposed right to peace is formulated within the confines of current international law. The focus on the prohibition on the use of force in international relations gives the impression that the most important aspect of a right to peace is the absence of war of an international character. Absence of non-international armed conflicts, by far the most common form of war, and the positive aspect of a right to peace, that of being protected from mass atrocity crimes, seems to come second to the absence of international armed conflicts. It is suggested here that the work on a right to peace could adopt more of the language of R2P and strengthen the idea of three pillars and four crimes. The future work on a right to peace should acknowledge the basic similarities with R2P and instead of moving away from that concept should recognize the common ground and opportunity to strengthen both concepts. The right to peace and the responsibility to protect both acknowledge the crucial connection between protection of human rights and the absence of war. Current language on the right to peace introduces new conditions that are at odds with the R2P concept. It would of course be beneficial to both international peace and security and the protection of human rights if such concepts as a 'right to peace', 'responsibility to protect', and 'human security' could all adopt a similar language in relation to the common ground between them. There thus seems to be an opportunity for strengthening the crucial link between peace and security and the protection of human rights—both in the long- and short-term perspectives.

PART II

PRECONDITIONS OF PEACE

7

Human Rights Violations and Conflict Risk: A Theoretical and Empirical Assessment

*Kjersti Skarstad**

1. Introduction

A central premise and promise of human rights law is that the protection of human rights leads to more peaceful societies. From the very beginning of the movement, part of the justification for human rights has been their perceived ability to promote both domestic and international peace.[1] As evident from, for example, the UN Charter Article 55 and the preamble of the Universal Declaration of Human Rights (UDHR) in particular, the protection of human rights is seen as a necessary condition for creating peace and stability. The interdependency between human rights and peace has also been reiterated more recently in, for example, Security Council resolution 1674 and in the Draft Declaration on the Right to Peace.

Preamble paragraph 1 of UDHR states that the recognition of the 'inherent dignity and of the equal and inalienable rights of all members of the human family is the foundation of freedom, justice and peace in the world'.[2] Fulfilment of human rights is thus seen as a necessary condition for peace in both the positive and negative sense. Paragraph 3 of the preamble, makes the link between peace and violent conflicts even more explicit stating that 'it is essential, if man is not to be compelled to have recourse, as a last resort, to rebellion against tyranny and oppression, that human rights should be protected by the rule of law'.[3]

* The author thanks Håvard Strand for reading and commenting on an earlier version of the chapter.

[1] David P. Forsythe, *Human Rights and Peace: International and National Dimensions* (Lincoln: University of Nebraska Press, 1993); James W. Nickel, *Making Sense of Human Rights* (2nd edn. Malden: Blackwell,, 2007); Henry J. Steiner, Philip Alston, and Ryan Goodman, *International Human Rights in Context: Law, Politics, Morals: Text and Materials* (3rd edn. New York: Oxford University Press, 2007); Mary Ann Glendon, *A World Made New: Eleanor Roosevelt and the Universal Declaration of Human Rights* (New York: Random House Digital, 2002).

[2] Universal Declaration of Human Rights, 1948, Preamble, para. 1.

[3] UDHR 1948, Preamble, para. 3.

Here the understanding is that human rights violations may directly motivate persons to initiate (violent) rebellions. Despite the strong assumptions of the effect of human rights in human rights law, human rights literature is unclear as to why and how violations possibly lead to a higher risk of violent civil conflicts.

In contrast to the message of human rights law, rights violations have for the most part not been seen as a relevant conflict risk factor in empirical conflict research. The main trend within conflict research has instead been a focus on economic 'business' explanations as to why violent conflicts occur. A central argument within the conflict literature is that grievances or repression do not increase the risk of violent conflicts since they are so common. Yet, empirical research putting the assumptions of human rights law to the test is conspicuous by its absence.

The gap between human rights scholars and conflict researchers is problematic for several reasons. Bridging the gap between human rights law and scholarship on the one hand and empirical conflict research on the other will add to our understanding of the mechanisms that might lead to civil wars. Only a good understanding of such mechanisms will help us to create effective legal remedies and peace-building policies that prevent outbreaks of violence.

In this chapter I investigate whether human rights violations increase the risk of domestic violent conflict onsets between the government and a rebel group. Hence, the focus is on peace in a negative sense (the outbreak of direct violence). I set out a theoretical explanation for how human rights violations can potentially increase the risk of violent civil conflicts by connecting the conceptual division between structural and triggering factors within peace and conflict research with the conceptual division of positive and negative aspects of rights within human rights law. I argue that factors relating to positive aspects of rights are potential *facilitators* of conflict while factors relating to negative aspects of rights violations can be conflict *multipliers*.

I present the results from an empirical test of the relationship between violations and conflict onsets. The results show that violations of basic economic and social rights and physical integrity rights increase the risk of civil war, while the effect of other civil and political rights are minor. The implication of this result is that human rights policies and enforcement of human rights law are well worth pursuing in order to reduce conflict risk, and that more attention should be given to the protection of economic and social rights.

As one aim of the chapter is to bridge the gap between empirical conflict research on the one hand and human rights literature on the other, I start with an assessment of previous empirical literature in the field. These findings are informative for the construction of a realistic theory in the second part of the chapter and the interpretation of the empirical results presented in the third part.

2. The State of Current Empirical Conflict Literature

Empirical research on the causes of war can roughly be divided into research that applies either greed- or grievance-based explanations for civil wars.[4] Greed relates to atypical circumstances that generate profitable opportunities while relative deprivation relates to largely felt injustices and discrimination. In contrast to the assumption of human rights law, the dominant view for around the last 15 years in conflict research has been that greed rather than grievances increases the risk of civil war. In one of the most cited articles in civil war research Collier and Hoeffler state that '[t]he grievances that motivate rebels may be substantially disconnected from the large scale social concerns of inequality [and] political rights.'[5] A highly influential study by Fearon and Laitin argues that state capacity (or state weakness) explains civil wars.[6] Mueller rejects grievance-based explanations of violent conflicts outright by stating that rebel groups now consist of criminals and thugs.[7]

Lately, the grievance-based perspective has gained more momentum within the empirical conflict literature. In contrast to previous grievance-based literature that operationalized grievances as total inequality levels within a society (vertical inequality), new grievance research focuses on inequalities between pre-existing ethno-linguistic groups (horizontal inequality).[8] One of the central claims of the new grievance-based theories of horizontal inequalities is that since civil wars are group conflicts, grievances must be measured and understood at the group level. This research does not focus solely on economic differencse, but also on social, political, and cultural differences such as access to education and political representation. Despite the obvious links to human rights, human rights are rarely explicitly mentioned.

[4] This is not a sharp divide and it is common that research incorporates elements from both the greed and grievance perspectives.

[5] Paul Collier and Anke Hoeffler, 'Greed and Grievance in Civil War', *Oxford Economic papers* 56 (2004), 589. In a later study they conclude that rebellion will occur when it is feasible and that motivation, which can be based on either greed or grievance, is indeterminate. Paul Collier, Anke Hoeffler, and Dominic Rohner, 'Beyond Greed and Grievance: Feasibility and Civil War', *Oxford Economic Papers* 61 (2009).

[6] James D. Fearon and David D. Laitin, 'Ethnicity, Insurgency, and Civil War', *American Political Science Review* 97 (2003), 75–90.

[7] John Mueller, 'War Has Almost Ceased to Exist: An Assessment', *Political Science Quarterly* 124 (2009), 297–321.

[8] See Lars-Erik Cederman, Kristian Skrede Gleditsch, and Halvard Buhaug, *Inequality, Grievances, and Civil War* (New York: Cambridge University Press, 2013); Lars-Erik Cederman, Nils B. Weidmann, and Kristian Skrede Gleditsch, 'Horizontal Inequalities and Ethnonationalist Civil War: A Global Comparison', *American Political Science Review* 105 (2011), 478–95; Frances Stewart, 'Horizontal Inequalities: A Neglected Dimension of Development', *Working Paper 81* (2002); Frances Stewart, 'Crisis Prevention: Tackling Horizontal Inequalities', *Oxford Development Studies* 28 (2000), 245–62; Gudrun Østby, 'Inequality and Political Violence: A Review of the Literature', *International Area Studies Review* 16 (2013), 206–31, and Gudrun Østby, 'Polarization, Horizontal Inequalities and Violent Civil Conflict', *Journal of Peace Research* 45 (2008), 143–62.

There has, however, been some explicit research on the effect of human rights violations in terms of violent civil conflicts. This research has mainly focused on how violations of physical integrity rights can contribute to conflict escalation.[9] Rost, for example, find a strong relationship between state repression and the risk of civil wars, particularly in concert with state weakness.[10] Mebane and Poast also find a relationship between torture and an increased risk of internal armed conflict, but do not investigate whether the result could be due to the lack of control of other factors.[11] In contrast, Jakobsen and de Soysa find that state repression has no independent effect on conflict, and that it might in fact reduce the risk of conflict in fractionalized societies.[12] Thoms and Ron show that armed conflicts tend to occur in poor, underdeveloped, and repressive countries.[13]

2.1. Problems with existing empirical literature

While there have been a few notable studies on the effects of human rights violations and while there are obvious parallels to human rights explanations within the 'grievance camp' of conflict research, mainstream conflict research does not take the premises of human rights law seriously.

First, according to human rights law, human rights are per definition *individual* rights. Accordingly, a human-rights-based explanation of violent civil conflicts must take the individual as the central unit of observation.[14] In contrast, grievance research has (ethno-linguistic) groups or class differences as their starting point. They state that grievances (which might also impart human rights violations) are not relevant unless they hit pre-existing (ethno-linguistic) groups. The central conflict mechanism that leads to violence and anger is that groups compare themselves to others that are in a better or worse situation than they are. It follows from the individual focus of human rights that another conflict mechanism might be more relevant: rather than comparing themselves to others, persons compare themselves to an absolute ideal—that of human rights.[15]

[9] See Sabine C. Carey, 'The Dynamic Relationship between Protest and Repression', *Political Research Quarterly* 59 (2006), 1–11; Christian Davenport, 'State Repression and Political Order', *Annual Review of Political Science* 10 (2007), 1–23; Christian Davenport, 'State Repression and the Tyrannical Peace', *Journal of Peace Research*, 44 (2007), 485–504; Ronald A. Francisco, 'The Dictator's Dilemma', in *Repression and Mobilization*, Christian Davenport, Hank Johnston, and Carol Mueller (eds.) (University of Minnesota Press, 2005), 58–85.

[10] Nicolas Rost, Gerald Schneider, and Johannes Kleibl, 'A Global Risk Assessment Model for Civil Wars', *Social Science Research* 38 (2009), 921–33.

[11] Walter R. Mebane and Paul Poast, 'Causal Inference without Ignorability: Identification with Nonrandom Assignment and Missing Treatment Data', *Political Analysis* 21 (2013), 233–51.

[12] Tor G. Jakobsen and Indra De Soysa, 'Give Me Liberty, or Give Me Death! State Repression, Ethnic Grievance and Civil War, 1981–2004', *Civil Wars* 11 (2009), 137–57.

[13] Oskar N. T. Thoms and James Ron, 'Do Human Rights Violations Cause Internal Conflict?', *Human Rights Quarterly* 29 (2007), 674–705.

[14] Kjersti Skarstad and Håvard Strand, 'Do Human Rights Violations Increase the Risk of Civil War?' (forthcoming 2015).

[15] Skarstad and Strand, 'Do Human Rights Violations Increase the Risk of Civil War?'.

A second problem is the way that human rights violations have been operationalized. The empirical research that has been conducted has mostly focused on the respect notion or the negative aspects of physical integrity rights. If the effects of economic and social rights have been investigated one has looked at the positive aspects of those rights. A larger problem with economic and social rights is, however, that researchers have struggled to separate the concept of general social and economic conditions with the concept of human rights. In particular, rights have not been operationalized according to the maximum available resources imperative of the International Convention on Economic Social and Cultural Rights (CESCR) article 2.

The third problem relates to methodology. While Thoms and Ron find that armed conflicts tend to occur in poor, underdeveloped, and repressive countries, this does not prove that it was human rights violations that led to the conflict and not the other way around.[16] In order to look at effects we must look at the level of human rights violations well ahead of time before the conflict onset is measured.

Fourthly, and informing all the other problems, is the lack of an explicit human rights peace and conflict theory. This can partly explain why there has been so little empirical testing. From the human rights literature it is not clear which rights or which aspects of rights might increase conflict risk. It is also uncertain why and how violations possibly lead to a higher risk of violent civil conflicts. In the next section I seek to provide such a theoretical explanation within the framework of positive and negative aspects of rights.

3. Theoretical Framework: Human Rights Violations as Conflict Multipliers and Conflict Facilitators

In human rights law the understanding of human rights and the corresponding state duties have evolved into incorporating both negative and positive aspects of rights. While state duties originally were mostly negative, in the sense that the responsibility of the state was mainly to avoid direct infringement upon the rights of citizens, state authorities are now also responsible for actively protecting citizens from both direct and indirect violence committed by state or non-state actors. They are also responsible for promoting and fulfilling human rights, and for putting an end to discriminatory structures within society. This framework of state duties is called the UN *respect* (avoid violating), *protect* (hinder violations from third-parties), *fulfil* (aid and promote) framework.[17] All rights have these corresponding duties.

When explaining violent conflict onsets it is useful to separate structural or contextual factors from triggering factors. Structures within a society are relatively

[16] Oskar N. T. Thoms and James Ron, 'Do Human Rights Violations Cause Internal Conflict?'.

[17] Asbjørn Eide, Catarina Krause, and Allan Rosas, *Economic, Social and Cultural Rights: A Textbook* (Boston: Martinus Nijhoff, 2001).

stable and change slowly, while a civil war onset happens quickly. Whether an event can trigger a conflict outbreak is highly context-specific. While structural factors are the dry wood, triggering factors are the matches that light the fire. This conceptual division within peace and conflict research can be aligned with the conceptual division of positive and negative aspects of rights within human rights law.

While violations of the positive aspects of rights (fulfilling rights) can constitute a structural-contextual factor increasing conflict risk, violations of negative aspects of rights (respecting rights) can be a trigger factor. Hence, the respect and the fulfilment aspects of rights play different roles in terms of increasing conflict risk. Neither event-based nor structure-based violations are sufficient in themselves in terms of explaining why a civil war occurs.

Factors relating to positive aspects of rights violations (structural and widespread societal injustices) are thus potential *facilitators* of violent conflict, meaning that they create an environment in which civil wars are more likely to occur. Factors relating to the negative aspects of rights violations (direct actor-based violations) can be conflict *multipliers*. How do the different aspects of human rights violations increase conflict risk?

3.1. Conflict facilitators

Rebels can have greed-based, grievance-based motivations for fighting, or a combination of both. Because a minimum protection of human rights is necessary for living a decent life, grave human rights violations might be one of the reasons that directly motivate people to take up arms and form rebel groups. The *campesinos*[18] in El Salvador, who had long been repressed by the government and landowners, for example, participated in the El Salvadorian rebellion first and foremost because of moral and affective reasons.[19] The Lord's Resistance Army (LRA) under the leadership of Joseph Kony is a prominent example of the contrary.

Rebel leaders and rebel group members can have different types of motivation for fighting. In terms of conflict facilitation it is also highly important to be aware of the fact that civilians' perceptions of the government and the human rights situation in the country are highly relevant. A government that cannot provide security for its inhabitants takes the risk that citizens will look for alternatives to the status quo. If the government enhances a system where citizens are restrained from fulfilling basic rights, rebel groups can be regarded as the only feasible alternative for protection. Poor persons can be more easily recruited if the rebel groups provide them with nutrition and an income.[20]

Also, structural violence or systemic repression leads to hostility, minimal social capital, and lack of trust. Widespread violations of core human rights are likely to lead to a lack of support for the government and responsible authorities. In terms

[18] Persons involved in agricultural activity.

[19] Elisabeth Jean Wood, *Insurgent Collective Action and Civil War in El Salvador* (New York: Cambridge University Press, 2003).

[20] Skarstad and Strand, 'Do Human Rights Violations Increase the Risk of Civil War?'.

of counter-insurgency, human rights violations can lead to a lack of trustworthy information for the abusive government. Because people do not trust the government they might not cooperate with police investigators. Human rights violations thus make it more difficult for governments to fight and deter terrorists or rebel groups.[21] In sum, it is easier for a rebel group to thrive and grow in a society with many human rights violations than in a society where human rights are generally fulfilled. The lack of fulfilment of human rights thus increases the risk of violent conflict in at least two ways: it makes the recruitment process for rebel leaders easier, and it reduces the ability of governments to fight rebel groups.

In other words, human rights violations increase the risk of violent conflicts regardless of the motivation of rebel group leaders. This means that human rights explanations need not be in opposition to the greed perspective of civil war. Human rights violations could make it more likely that both greed-motivated and rights-motivated rebel groups and resistance movements are established.

It is easier for citizens to place the responsibility on the government when it has failed to respect a human right than if it has failed to fulfil rights, as the question of attribution in the latter case is often more blurred, particularly in less-developed states. However, when dissatisfaction occurs and becomes activated in structurally unjust societies, and the government does not show any willingness to change the system even though it has the capacity to do so, the government can quickly become the target of dissatisfaction.[22]

It is important to note that an alternative explanation for why conflict occurs in countries where human rights violations are systemic is that the state is often weak, and accordingly the government might not have the capacity to implement rights or fight rebel groups.[23] Separating the effect of state capacity from human rights violations is inherently difficult, as the two are likely to influence one another.

3.2. Conflict multipliers

When human rights work as conflict multipliers, human rights violations directly motivate persons to protest. One or a few events in isolation are not relevant, but rights abuses can become highly relevant as a triggering factor if it interacts with an underlying conflict or structural injustices. Event-based violations can also increase the risk of conflict in themselves if they become widespread.

The violent conflict onset in Romania in 1989 exemplifies that an event-based human rights violation can serve as a conflict multiplier. When the government attempted to evict a pastor because of his criticism of the regime, it sparked massive uprisings.[24] The immediate event that triggered the onset of the Arab spring

[21] Skarstad and Strand, 'Do Human Rights Violations Increase the Risk of Civil War?'.

[22] J. Goodwin, 'State-Centered Approaches to Social Revolution: Strength and Limitations of a Theoretical Tradition', in *Theorizing Revolutions*, John Foran (ed.) (London: Routledge, 1997), 9–36, as referred to by Cederman, Gleditsch, and Buhaug, *Inequality, Grievances, and Civil War*, 49–50.

[23] Neil A. Englehart, 'State Capacity, State Failure, and Human Rights', *Journal of Peace Research* 46 (2009), 163–80.

[24] Forsythe, *Human Rights and Peace.*

was a grocery vendor setting himself on fire in response to what he perceived as discriminatory treatment. One of the sparks of the Syrian civil war was the arrest and mistreatment of more than 15 children that had painted anti-government graffiti on a school wall.[25] In all these cases, structural human rights violations and underlying dissatisfaction prevailed. Human rights violations were therefore both a triggering and a potential facilitating factor.

If event-based or direct human rights violations are grave and widespread they need not trigger violent conflicts only if they happen in an already structurally unjust society. The use of indiscriminate violence and hence violations of physical integrity rights can quickly change the nature of a dispute fundamentally. If widespread violence is applied it forces people to take sides in a conflict. Indiscriminate violence (violations of physical integrity rights) helps overcome collective action problems not only because it serves as a strong individual motivational factor for revenge, but also because it usually hits not completely random individuals, but individuals that have something in common.

The civil war in Aceh, Indonesia (active in parts from around 1976 to 2005) happened in an area more affluent than other regions. The rebel group Gerakan Aceh Merdeka (GAM) was motivated by concerns other than human rights violations and the civil war can be explained quite well by the greed model.[26] Yet, it is the massive and brutal human rights violations, applied by the government as a counter-insurgency tactic and affecting the whole population in Aceh, that explain the dramatic increase in active support of the rebel group.

3.3. Which rights are relevant?

Human rights are a multifaceted and comprehensive concept. Having stated that both the 'respect' and 'fulfil' notions of rights are relevant in terms of increasing conflict risk, are all rights equally relevant?

Even though all rights may be important in order for a person to live a life in dignity, and although they are connected, it is unlikely that all types of human rights violations are equally important in terms of increasing conflict risk. In particular, what is regarded as morally correct varies between (and within) countries and perceptions of what is considered morally correct also vary over time. How, then, can one say something in general about the effect of human rights on conflict risk?

Lately, there has been increased scholarly attention concerning legal mobilization or the mobilization potential of human rights law.[27] This view sees

[25] Joe Sterling, 'Daraa: The Spark That Lit the Syrian Flame', *CNN*, 1 March 2012, http://edition.cnn.com/2012/03/01/world/meast/syria-crisis-beginnings/ (accessed 23 June 2014).

[26] Michael L. Ross, 'Resources and Rebellion in Aceh, Indonesia', *Paper Prepared for the Yale-World Bank Project on 'The Economics of Political Violence'* (2003).

[27] See Beth A. Simmons, *Mobilizing for Human Rights: International Law in Domestic Politics* (New York: Cambridge University Press, 2009); Thomas Risse-Kappen, Stephen C. Ropp, and Kathryn Sikkink, *The Power of Human Rights: International Norms and Domestic Change* (New York: Cambridge University Press, 1999); Samuel Moyn, 'Do Human Rights Treaties Make Enough of a Difference?', *The Cambridge Companion to Human Rights Law* (2012), 329.

international human rights law and domestic codification of such law as important civil society mobilization tools against repression. However, awareness of human rights law is not needed in order to protest. While human rights law might also be an important mobilization tool, it is first and foremost social mobilization that has led to human rights law.

Human rights law is the result of political processes led by the aim of codifying some universal moral rules applicable to all. The International Bill of Human Rights can be viewed as the international community's best attempt to codify such moral values. Hence, it would be wrong to view human rights law as perfectly matching local interests and the values of local identities. Rather, human rights law should be seen to tap into the universal need for dignity and equality that all human beings have. This knowledge has consequences for how we operationalize human rights in empirical conflict research. Rather than measuring the law in detail, we should measure the core concepts of the rights believed to be particularly relevant when it comes to conflicts on a global scale.

As mentioned, the perceptions of the content of the governments' duties and the extent to whether human rights violations are viewed as illegitimate, not only in the eyes of the victim but also by the general public, vary with time and space. However, the need for human beings to live decent lives with access to a minimal amount of welfare, security, and liberty is not context-specific but universal.

Shue argues that physical integrity rights (protection against murder and assaults) and subsistence rights (adequate food and water, clothing, shelter, and minimal preventive public healthcare) constitute basic rights.[28] They are basic rights in the sense that it is impossible to fulfil other rights without protecting these two categories. Protection of these rights is indeed undisputedly central for the quality of life for people worldwide. As such, violations of these rights should be particularly relevant for increasing the conflict risk.

Following the logic of the theory of basic rights, democratic rights (such as the rights to vote, rights of assembly, and the freedom of speech) first and foremost become relevant in terms of conflict when physical and/or subsistence rights are violated. If governments violate physical and/or subsistence rights and the situation is not perceived to improve, democratic rights are called upon mainly because they represent a solution to the governance problem. This does not mean that there are no individuals willing to risk their lives for democratic rights even though other rights are fulfilled. Nor does it mean that a lack of a democratic system does not contribute to a lack of positive peace. However, few persons are actively involved in politics, and factors that affect the everyday lives of people are likely to be more relevant in terms of increasing conflict risk. I view the effect of democratic rights to be mainly conditional on other physical and subsistence rights violations.

[28] Henry Shue, *Basic Rights. Subsistence, Affluence, and U.S Foreign Policy* (Princeton, NJ: Princeton University Press, 1996).

4. Empirical Analyses: Do Human Rights Violations Increase the Risk of Violent Civil Conflicts?

Based on the theory presented, three central hypotheses have emerged:

1. Human rights violations increase the risk of violent civil conflicts.
2. Not all human rights are equally important in terms of increasing conflict risk; physical integrity rights and economic and social rights have a stronger effect.
3. Both the failure to fulfil rights (or avoidance of structural violence) and event-based violations increase conflict risk.

In addition, I began this chapter with the claim that in contrast to what contemporary grievance-based conflict theories argue:

4. Human rights violations represent an independent conflict mechanism and need not be targeted towards an existing ethnic group in order to be relevant.

Next I present the research design and the empirical results from Skarstad and Strand regarding these hypotheses, but I discuss the results in the light of the theory presented in this chapter.[29] Skarstad and Strand present, to my knowledge, the first study that tests the effect of both civil and political rights (including physical integrity rights) and economic and social rights using longitudinal regression techniques.

4.1. Research design

Skarstad and Strand apply a quantitative study in order to investigate the hypotheses. Quantitative analyses do not suffer (at least not as much) from case selection bias as qualitative research, and are better suited for generating universally generalizable results.[30] As we wanted to say something about the *effect* human rights violations have in terms of conflict risk, we applied longitudinal data, meaning that we had data that spanned many years. This put us in a better position in terms of investigating whether the cause predates the effect. The available data allowed us to investigate the years 1977 to 2008 for around 143 countries. That gave us around 3,800 observations, which is a good number when we want to derive reliable general conclusions.

We used regression analyses in order to answer our hypotheses. When applied correctly, regression analyses establish what the relationship is between the output (dependent variable)—in our case whether there is an onset of civil

[29] Skarstad and Strand, 'Do Human Rights Violations Increase the Risk of Civil War?'.

[30] Gary King, Robert O. Keohane, and Sidney Verba, *Designing Social Inquiry: Scientific Inference in Qualitative Research* (Princeton, NJ; Princeton University Press, 1994).

war or not—and the explanatory factors (independent variables)—in our case human rights.

There are however, serious methodological challenges to establishing cause and effect.[31] Most seriously, we know that civil war leads to human rights violations, as well as to economic downturns and instability. These factors are also used as some of the main explanatory causes of civil war. To circumvent the problem of endogeneity we looked at the level of human rights violations three years before the conflict onset was measured. As we know that countries that have had civil wars are more likely to experience civil war again, we included a modelation of the time passed since the last conflict for each country in the analyses. Another factor that might distort our result is the fact that (as seen, for example, during the the Arab Spring) a violent conflict in one country might affect the onset of a violent conflict in another country. We controlled for this by including a variable that measures the number of violent conflicts in neighbouring countries.

4.1.1. Operationalizations

The dependent variable is violent civil conflicts. The variable is from the UCDP/PRIO Armed Conflict Dataset,[32] and is defined as a contested incompatibility that concerns government and/or territory where the use of armed force between two parties, of which at least one is the government of a state, results in 25 battle-related deaths. The low threshold of battle deaths is a major advantage in terms of reducing endogenity problems. In addition, all cases where less than two calendar years of peace have been observed prior to the start of a new conflict were excluded.

The human rights variables measure implementation of human rights policies (as they are conceptualized in the International Bill of Rights) in practice. A major challenge for all quantitative studies on human rights is the lack of data. Due to the lack of availability of global time series human rights data it is not possible to investigate all the aspects and corresponding duties of all rights. The data available restrict one to only the fulfilment aspect of economic and social rights and the respect aspect of physical integrity rights. Hence the effect of economic and social rights will be particularly important in terms of establishing whether human rights violations facilitate violent conflicts, and the effect of physical integrity rights will be particularly important in terms of establishing whether human rights violations work as conflict multipliers.

The Political Terror Scale (PTS) is used in order to measure physical integrity rights. The scale measures the level of extrajudicial killing, torture, or similar physical abuse, disappearances, and political imprisonment, carried out by the

[31] From a philosophical point of view, causality can indeed never be proved.

[32] Nils Petter Gleditsch et al. 'Armed Conflict 1946-2001: A New Dataset', *Journal of Peace Research* 39 (2002), 615–37; Lotta Themnér and Peter Wallensteen, 'Armed Conflicts, 1946–2011', *Journal of Peace Research* 49 (2012), 565–75.

government or its agents as documented by Amnesty International and US State Department reports.[33]

The Social and Economic Rights Fulfilment Index (SERF) is used for measuring economic and social rights. SERF is an index of a large number of related data sources documenting the rights of food, education, health, housing, and decent work.[34] In accordance with article 2 of the CESCR, the index measures the protection of rights relative to the country's economic capacity by adopting an 'achievement possibility frontier'.

Data on civil and political rights are from the Freedom House. The political rights dimension of the variable is based on the subcategories of electoral process, political pluralism and participation, and functioning of government. The civil rights dimension is based on the four subcategories of freedom of expression and belief, associational and organizational rights, rule of law, and personal autonomy and individual rights.[35]

As previous studies have identified economic underdevelopment (measured as a low GDP), regime type, regime transitions, ethnic groups, previous conflicts, and natural resource dependency as the most important factors increasing the risk of civil war, these variables are, of course, controlled for.

4.2. Results

We found support for all four hypotheses. All of the findings were statistically significant, meaning that the variations in the estimates are too small to be the probable artefact of a random process in which human rights violations and armed conflict are unrelated.[36] Hence, violations of physical integrity rights and economic and social rights do increase the risk of violent civil conflicts. Violations of civil and political rights have almost no effect and were only weakly significant in one of the models where we used another operationalization than SERF on economic and social rights. Also, violations do not need to be targeted against existing ethnic groups in order to increase the risk.[37]

The effects of human rights violations are not large, but still strong and substantially important. A change from the best physical integrity rights situation to the worst, measured by the PTS, leads to a yearly increase in the probability of conflict of 4.0 percentage points (see Fig. 7.1). This represents an increase of almost 34 percentage points over a ten-year period. For economic and social

[33] Reed M. Wood and Mark Gibney, 'The Political Terror Scale (PTS): A Re-Introduction and a Comparison to CIRI', *Human Rights Quarterly* 32 (2010), 367–400.

[34] Susan Randolph, Sakiko Fukuda-Parr, and Terra Lawson-Remer, 'Economic and Social Rights Fulfillment Index: Country Scores and Rankings', *Journal of Human Rights* 9 (2010), 230–61.

[35] Freedom House, 'Methodology Summary', http://www.freedomhouse.org/sites/default/files/Methodology%20Summary,%20FIW%202012.pdf (accessed 3 March 2012).

[36] Skarstad and Strand, 'Do Human Rights Violations Increase the Risk of Civil War?'.

[37] We tested this by investigating whether the effects of human rights violations were washed out when we controlled for the political relevance of ethnic groups. Human rights violations increase the risk of conflict even when ethnicity is irrelevant.

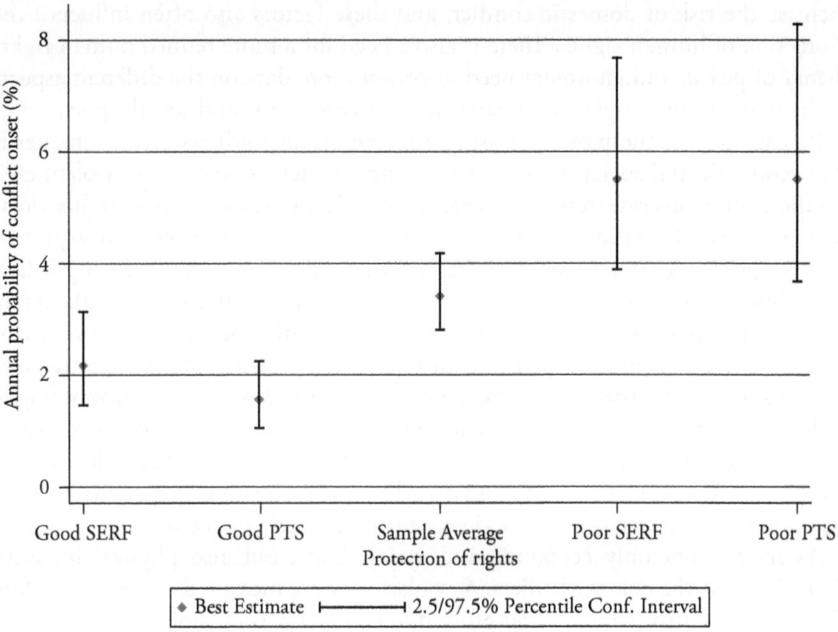

Figure 7.1 The effect of human rights on conflict onsets

rights (measured by the SERF index) a change from the 5th to the 95th percentile results in a yearly increase of 3.2 percentage points (see Fig. 7.1). This corresponds to an increase of about 27 percentage points over a ten-year period.

4.3. Implications

The results show that violations of human rights are part of the very complex mechanisms that increase the risk of violent civil conflicts. The results clearly give empirical support to the claim that protecting human rights is one of the preconditions for peace. This should have several important implications for law and policy-making and further research on the field. Evidently, if a change of policy can reduce the risk of violent conflict by more than 20 percentage points for a ten-year period, then that change must surely be worthwhile to pursue.[38]

Conflict researchers need to start to take the effects that human rights violations might have on the risk on violent civil conflicts seriously if we are to come closer to a better understanding of why such conflicts occur. Human rights researchers need to take seriously that human rights is only one part of the explanation and that attention should also be paid to the factors conflict research have found to increase risk. Poverty, lack of state control and capacity, and lack of resources

[38] Skarstad and Strand, 'Do Human Rights Violations Increase the Risk of Civil War?'.

increase the risk of domestic conflict, and these factors also often influence the protection of human rights. There is also a need for a more refined human rights theory of peace, and an urgent need to collect more data on the different aspects of the many human rights, and particularly on economic and social rights.

Perhaps one of the most surprising and important findings of this chapter is that economic and social rights violations clearly increase the risk of violent civil conflicts. Previous research has not taken the effect of these types of rights violations seriously. Fulfilling economic and social rights is an important aspect of positive peace. A government's effort in terms of, for example, reducing infant mortality rates does not directly affect conflict risk, but that does not make it any less relevant when we want to explain how violent conflict occurs. Widespread violations of human rights create the conditions where violent civil conflicts are more likely to occur. In other words, the failure to fulfil rights makes a society fragile and less robust against the threat of armed conflicts. As structural-contextual and event-based violence are likely to intervene, it would be inadequate to address only event-based direct violence. We must go beyond addressing symptoms and ask why and when actor-based direct violence is more likely to occur.

As shown, not only economic and social rights, but also physical integrity rights increase the risk of conflicts. As violations were measured three years before the conflict onset we are on safer ground to claim that such violations are important conflict-risk factors in themselves—they are not just an artefact of a violent conflict that is escalating. Other civil and political rights were not found to be that relevant. This is an interesting finding as arguments about the peaceful effect of democratic rights are often heard in the popular press. Development aid is also often targeted on the premises that the recipient country protects formalistic democratic rights. Based on the results, development agencies and human rights activists should have a more holistic approach to rights. Governments should be careful concerning implementing only democratic rights while disregarding physical integrity and economic and social rights that seem to be more related to conflict onsets. As others have argued, democratic institutions must be supported by the protection of human rights, which of course, also includes the equal rights of minorities.[39]

What is the role of human rights law in all this? Law enforcing bodies have a very important role in protecting individual human rights. As human rights violations represent an independent conflict mechanism and need not be targeted against ethnic groups in order to have an effect, the long-term solution should be targeted efforts towards protecting equal individual rights. Political trade-offs between different interest groups in the society (as is often the way conflicts are solved today) are not suitable long-term solutions unless there is equal protection of everyone's individual rights.

The results also expose a limitation of international human rights law as it is today. Human rights law is first and foremost meant to be enforced domestically,

[39] Kjersti Skarstad, 'Do Human Rights Violations Increase the Risk of Civil War?', Master Thesis, University of Oslo (2012), 68–9.

but it is difficult to see how some individual countries can grapple with particularly the challenges of economic and social rights violations on their own. Weak state structures and the enforcement capacity of some countries also make it difficult for them to protect human rights. A comprehensive framework in terms of preventing violent conflicts is needed, and international efforts in terms of working on poverty reduction and equal protection and access to basic rights are important. Such efforts are not only good for peace-building in the negative but also in the positive sense. Obviously, protection of human rights is an invaluable good in itself.

5. Conclusion

In this chapter I have investigated a central premise of human rights law, namely that violations of human rights will increase the risk of violent conflicts. Despite the strong assumptions of the peace inducing effects of human rights there have been few empirical investigations on its actual effects so far. I have put forward a theory of how human rights violations might increase the risk of violent civil conflict onsets between the government and at least one rebel group by building on both human rights and conflict research literature. A central point of the chapter has been to show that human rights violations work both as conflict facilitators, in the sense that they create the conditions where conflicts are more likely to occur; and conflict multipliers, in the sense that they can escalate and aggravate underlying disputes. My claims have been supported by the use of longitudinal regression analyses. Violations of basic economic and social and physical integrity rights increase the risk of civil war, while the effects of other civil and political rights are minor. The main implication of these results is that human rights policies and the enforcement of human rights law are worth pursuing in order to reduce conflict risk and to promote peace.

8

Traps of Violence

A Human Rights Analysis of Relationships between Peace and Development

Bård A. Andreassen

1. Introduction

Below the foundation stone of the International Labour Organization's building at Sécheron on the shores of Lake Geneva lies a document with a short text: 'Si vis pacem, cole justitiam' ('If you desire peace, cultivate justice'). The stone was laid down on 21 October 1923 (four years after the establishment of the ILO as part of the Treaty of Versailles in 1919), and 46 years later, in 1969, the ILO received the Nobel Peace Prize as a reward for its work in improving peace among classes and pursuing justice for workers. The Treaty of Versailles also gave birth to the League of Nations and stated, 'the League ... has for its object the establishment of universal peace, and such a peace can be established only if it is based upon social justice'.

In hindsight, the Treaty of Versailles is not best known for its lasting contribution to the creation of the conditions for international peace. On the contrary, the Treaty was a major source of reference for the political breakdown and tragedies of European politics in the 1920s and 1930s leading to a world in flames from 1939 to 1945. But the 'si vis pacem, cole justitiam' dictum remained a normative and social argument, inspiring developmentalists and peacebuilders for generations, right up to the present.

This chapter takes a critical view of this widely supported dictum, which suggests that social justice and development are preconditions for peace. While the purpose is to ask about the links between development failure (indicated by high prevalence of poverty) and violent conflict, that is, the absence of peace, the validity of this normative dictum will be examined and criticized, with reference to empirical studies. Is it rather that peace (the absence of violence) is a major prerequisite for development?

Yes, it is. Contrary to much of existing literature, the chapter argues that although poverty traps, that is, that people living in poverty lack economic capacities and access to productive resources that enable them to move out of poverty, represent important constraints on development, poverty often emanates from and is caused by *traps of violence.* Traps of violence are linked to weak institutions, clientelist politics, and governance structures that give scope for 'calculated violence of neglect, that is the deliberate failure of government and state officials to carry out their duties in order to benefit from the ensuing disorder and distress'.[1] This illustrates that so-called greed causes of violence are different from grievance causes. We shall address both these explanatory strategies; the chapter explores the relationship between these and other approaches and examines evidence and data on how multiple forms of violence prevent people from escaping poverty. In short, how does violence distort development?

Studies of development/justice and violence/peace that address socio-economic and political-institutional conditions aim to explain or understand the likelihood of achieving sustainable peace. Positive and sustainable peace requires more than cessation of war; it requires removal of structural impediments (or 'structural violence') to peace, that is, political, economic, and institutional structures that prevent genuine peace from being secured. In this chapter, I argue that before structural and institutional impediments can be corrected, violence needs to be ended and its causes handled, in other words, 'Si vis pacem, cole justitiam' should be replaced or at least complemented with the reverse dictum: 'Si vis justum, cole pacem'.

After this introduction, Section 2 addresses the normative foundation of the debate. I seek to establish normative linkages between peace and development from a human rights perspective. Section 3 discusses the concept of structural violence, and relationships between violent conflict, peace, and development. Section 4 examines in empirical detail traps of violence as obstacles to development. Section 5 addresses changing patterns of violence and discusses how new forms of violence trap development, and Section 6 explores institutional responses to violence in a development perspective. The concluding section returns to the initial question on how violence undermines development, and the structural foundations for lasting peace.

2. Normative Foundations of the Rights to Peace and Development Nexus

Peace and development are frequently referred to in human rights law. A basic reference is the Universal Declaration of Human Rights (UDHR), which states in the Preamble 'recognition of the inherent dignity and of the equal and inalienable rights of all members of the human family is the foundation of freedom, justice and peace in the world'. According to Article 28, a just and fair international order is a precondition for development: '(e)veryone is entitled to a social and international order in which the rights and freedoms set

[1] Patrick Chabal, *Africa: The Politics of Suffering and Smiling* (New York: Zed Books, 2009), 153.

forth in this Declaration can be fully realized.' The oft-ignored Article 30 of the Declaration says that '(n)othing in this Declaration may be interpreted as implying for any State, group or person any right to engage in any activity or to perform any act aimed at the destruction of any of the rights and freedoms set forth herein.'

With reference to Article 30, we may argue that organized violence in local or international contexts irrevocably entails 'engagement' that implies 'destruction' of the rights of the Declaration. The links to peace, defined at a minimum as the absence of violence and war, are immediately clear. If war is defined as large-scale organized violence between combatants it no doubt threatens a large number of rights of the UDHR such as the rights to life, health, education, food, employment, free movement, and fundamental civil and political rights.[2] In the tradition of Henry Shue, war and large-scale violence represent 'standard threats' to basic human rights and values.[3]

A number of other human rights documents suggest normative links between peace and development. For instance, the Preamble of the Declaration on the Right to Development claims, 'international peace and security are essential elements for the realization of the right to development'. The Declaration states that the possible peace dividend resulting from disarmament should be used for 'comprehensive development', in particular in developing countries (Article 7). But even if these are normatively fine statements, they do not give evidence of empirical and causal linkages between peace and development.

In the same normative tradition, the proposed UN Draft Declaration on the Right to Peace (the Draft) proposes normative claims on peace and justice.[4] Article 9 of the Draft states that all people 'have the right to the elimination of obstacles to the realization of the right to development, such as the servicing of unjust and unsustainable foreign debt burdens and their conditionalities or the maintenance of an unfair international economic order that generates poverty and social exclusion' (Article 9). Again, this normative statement assumes that there is a positive relationship between peace and development. In fact, the Draft entails a positive notion of peace that emphasizes that peace rests on fair and just social and economic conditions. It reverberates the 'Si vis pacem, cole justitiam' dictum.

This being the case, a declaration on the right to peace will necessarily be operationalized in light of knowledge and analyses of the social, economic, and political conditions for sustainable peace. What conditions are at stake, and does the right to development provide a framework for addressing social justice issues and societal obstacles ('structural violence') to peace?

[2] On the definition of war, see Øyvind Østerud, *Hva er krig?* (Oslo: Universitetsforlaget, 2009), 9.

[3] Henry Schue, *Basic Rights: Subsistence, Affluence and US Foreign Policy* (Princeton, NJ: Princeton University Press), 29ff.

[4] HRC, Report of the Human Rights Council Advisory Committee on the right of peoples to peace (16 April 2012) UN Doc. A/HRC/20/31.

3. Structural Violence, Violent Conflict, and Development

Structural violence entered the vocabulary of peace research with an article authored by Johan Galtung in 1969.[5] Galtung addresses how social structures, institutions, and mechanisms may prevent people from escaping poverty, or, as Galtung expressed it, meeting their 'basic needs'. The denial of rights because of the nature of social structures, cultural traditions and customs, and the way social institutions function, represents obstacles to meeting people's needs. The lack of income due to high levels of unemployment, landlessness, or lack of health and sanitation systems, represents *violations* in the tradition of the 'structural violence' literature. In more recent scholarship, other terms are used to bring out similar arguments, and poverty analysis talk about 'poverty traps' speaks to the same phenomena: social constraints on people's choices represent obstacles that prevent people from moving out of poverty that result from institutional discriminatory practices and policies neglecting the needs of people living in poverty.

Hence, the structural violence notion addresses issues of social injustice, and unequal distribution of resources and wealth, that is, 'violence that is "built into" structures, institutions, ideologies and histories'.[6] Implicitly, these are societal threats to development, and under certain conditions, to peace. Article 2(7)_ of the Draft encompasses this assumption: 'Mechanisms should be developed and strengthened to eliminate inequality, exclusion and poverty, as they generate *structural violence*, which is incompatible with peace' (emphasis added).

Turning to one of the most severe forms of poverty, permanent or 'chronic' poverty, the Chronic Poverty Report (2008–9) identified five poverty traps, or development failures that represent structures and institutional practices that cause poverty.[7] The first trap is insecurity in broad terms, encompassing both insecure environments (crime) and lack of resources and assets to cope with development 'shocks and stresses'. A second poverty trap is the lack of effective citizenship. People in deep-seated poverty lack effective social or political representation of their interests and access to justice. Third, chronic poverty has a spatial dimension—it disproportionally affects people living in remote areas with vulnerable or scarce living resources. They also suffer comparatively more than others from natural calamities and climate change problems. Or, they may live in urban centres with poor access to institutions securing basic needs such as health, sanitation, and other socio-economic conditions for living worthwhile lives.

[5] Johan Galtung, 'Violence, Peace, and Peace Research', *Journal of Peace Research* 6 (1969). For a recent discussion of the concept of 'structural violence', see the Special Issue revisiting Galtung's concept in *New Political Science* 34 (2012).

[6] Andrew Dilts, 'Revisiting Johan Galtung's Concept of Structural Violence', *New Political Science* 34 (2012), 191.

[7] Chronic poverty is defined as poverty that people suffer over an extended period of time. It may last for the whole life and may be 'inherited' from one generation to the next. Cf. Chronic Poverty Research Centre, *Chronic Poverty Report* (2008–9), 'Escaping Poverty Traps', 3.

Social discrimination is a fourth poverty trap where people experience social and other forms of marginalization; they are trapped in social relations of power, class, caste, and patronage which constrain their economic and social capabilities. And finally, people living in poverty lack work opportunities, and access to income. At best they get poorly-paid casual, day-to-day work without the possibility of increasing their assets, or giving their children education and opportunities to break out of out of the vicious circles of poverty.

An important reason why these poverty traps, or development failures, can be described as structural violence is that in today's world there are resources and knowledge about how to tackle and eradicate chronic poverty by reforms of national and international policies, and institutional transformations. Policies and institutions are not unchangeable; they are social constructs and relations, and hence, possible to alter. The language of structural violence does not primarily imply legal or physical violence, or breaches of law: It is violence in the sense of social constraints on people's capabilities and functioning.[8]

Research on chronic and other forms of poverty has recognized that violent conflict is an obstacle to development, yet, more analytic focus is needed to address this issue from a rights perspective and to analyse empirically how insecurity, violence, and unpeaceful environments distort development. According to the Chronic Poverty Report (2008–9), 19 out the 32 countries classified as chronically poor had experienced major violent conflicts since 1970.[9] Just as poverty can be a cause of war, wealth and commerce can start war as experienced by chronically poor countries, for instance in a situation of violent competition over natural resources. The protracted violence in Congo is a case in point; the high rate of violence and conflict in Nigeria is another.[10] The major challenge in such contexts is to deal with the powerful interests that are manufacturing and using violence—warlords, local and political elites, urban criminal gangs—in their pursuit of wealth and power. The negative effects of violent conflict on people's risk structures are huge and obstruct economic and productive activities; it also undermines the 'social contract' of loyalty based on rights and obligations and hence, social cohesion.[11]

A 'social contract' relies on political structures and institutions that can sustain the contract through law, and commitment by people and authorities to law and good governance. Lack of proper legislation and governance practices represent political poverty traps, and the problem is increased by failure to introduce economic policies that address poverty. Banik argues that political elites have an interest in keeping poverty at a certain level in order to benefit politically from

[8] Amartya Sen, *Development as Freedom* (New York: Oxford University Press, 1999).

[9] Chronic Poverty Report (2008–9), 88.

[10] For insights and references to the wars and ongoing violence in Congo, see 'DR Congo: Conflict Profile', Insight on Conflict (last updated August 2011), http://www.insightonconflict.org/conflicts/dr-congo/conflict-profile (accessed 5 March 2014). For a recent update on violence in Nigeria, see Iain Overton, 'The Violent Road: Violence in Nigeria', 9 May 2014, http://aoav.org.uk/2014/the-violent-road-nigeria-findings/ (accessed 24 June 2014).

[11] Chronic Poverty Report (2008–9), 93.

handouts in run-ups to national elections. Elites have a survival interest in the status quo in order to present themselves as 'saviours' of the poor in returning elections.[12] Corruption and inadequate institutional reforms of the judicial sector is another political poverty trap. Political elites are often resistant to reform and people living in poverty are weakly organized, if organized at all, and with little power to alter the status quo.

The structural violence argument is not just concerned with domestic sources and causes of violent conflict. Poor countries also experience external sources of violence, so-called external chocks. The structural violence literature emerged in the midst of the Cold War, in the late 1960s and early 1970s when many of the contemporary poor states came out of colonial bondage (most of them in the early 1960s), with high levels of violence and conflict potentials caused by colonial rule. The rivalry of the West and the East for continued post-colonial dominance and control added to this violence potential. A widespread governance response to this international situation was the growth of the neo-patrimonial state, which was not designed to mitigate conflict among groups with potential conflict escalation, but rather governed and managed conflicts by co-option, nepotism, or repression. Disorder became a political instrument.[13]

This implies that the nature of the state is essential for the right to peace. The neo-patrimonial state is personal, informal, and partisan. This is the typical character of African states, but it is its main features can also be observed elsewhere. Chabal and Daloz remark that 'all African states share a generalized system of patrimonialism and an acute degree of apparent disorder, as evidenced by a high level of governmental and administrative inefficiency, a lack of institutionalization, a general disregard for the formal political and economic sectors, and a universal resort to personal(ized) and vertical solutions to societal problems'.[14] In context of our analysis, these patrimonial structures of governance and decision-making are structural obstacles to development.

These features of governance become particularly relevant in reducing violence potential by domestic and local disarmament. In neo-patrimonial states, the balance of state power rests with alliances between national leaders and local clients in charge of networks based on patronage through kin structures, ethnicity, or other forms of parochial groups, for instance, death squads in Colombia and Maoists (Nexalites) in several parts of India. Hence, loyalty is either time-bound by temporary alliances and links of patronage or non-existent as in the cases of Colombia and India. Local groups do not risk disarming because of the uncertain future of their alliance opportunities. In another case, that of Kenya, the existence of local and traditional warfare caused by ethnically defined disputes about elections results in the Presidential elections in December 2007 led to political violence and high levels of instability. The displacement of people escalated and

[12] Dan Banik, *Poverty and Elusive Development* (Oslo: Universitetsforlaget, 2010), ch. 4.

[13] On the concept of patrimonialism and the hybrid neo-patrimonial state model, see Patrick Chabal and Jean-Pascal Daloz, *Africa Works. Disorder as Political Instrument* (Oxford: James Currey, 1999), 9.

[14] Chabal and Daloz, *Africa Works*, p. xix.

deepened. In Kenya, a case I will return to in more detail, governance structures were not robust enough to handle a serious internal shock.

Structural approaches to human rights studies have been relatively rare. Most human rights analyses and issues have revolved around predominantly legal prevention of individual human rights violations, and state obligations to respect, protect, and fulfil human rights. There are two exceptions to this: one is the radical critique of human rights, stemming from the early 1980s, which argued that the main cause of human rights violations was the suppressive capitalist mode of production and colonial domination. This position reflected a radical relativist view of human rights.[15] The second exception was the demand for a declaration or treaty on a right to development. It emerged as part of the discourse on a New International Economic Order (NIEO) in the 1970s. The latter is of interest to our discussion.

The quest for a human right to development is often attributed to the Senegalese Judge Keba M'Baye, who in the late 1960s and early 1970s argued that development and a just international order should be seen as a human right. In 1977 the then UN Human Rights Commission requested a study on 'The international dimensions of the right to development as a human rights in relation with other human rights based on international cooperation, including the right to peace, taking into account the requirement of the New International Economic Order and the fundamental human needs'.[16]

The demand for a resolution was highly controversial and politicized, as was the subsequent adoption of it. While the argument behind it was typically structuralist, that individual human rights are impossible to achieve without a just international economic order, most Western states argued that this right would serve as an excuse for violations of individual rights; it would confuse the international human rights agenda, and the right itself was legally ambiguous and not justiciable, hence impractical. It was a concealed attempt to commit richer states to pay the bill for development in 'underdeveloped' states.

It is interesting to note that the Declaration on the Right to Development (RtD) adopted in October 1986 was far more complex in its nature: Arguably it trespassed upon the structuralist approach and established the right as a composite of already recognized individual human rights.[17] In this interpretation the right to development manifests itself through the respect, protection, and fulfilment of all human rights enshrined in the two main UN human rights treaties, that is the Covenant on Economic, Social and Cultural Rights and the Covenant on Civil and Political Rights. The RtD is a right to a process where these other rights are being implemented. In that sense it is a kind of quasi-procedural right, and a statement about social and economic conditions for a comprehensive human rights

[15] Cf. Adamantia Pollis and Peter Schwab (eds.), *Human Rights: Cultural and Ideological Perspectives* (Westport, Conn.: Praeger, 1979).

[16] UN Commission on Human Rights, Resolution 4 (XXXIII), 21 February 1977.

[17] Arjun Sengupta, 'The Human Right to Development', in *Development as a Human Right: Legal, Political and Economic Dimensions*, Bård A. Andreassen and Stephen Marks (eds.) (2nd edn. Antwerp: Intersentia, 2010).

agenda. The late Independent Expert on the RtD, the Indian Economist Arjun Sengupta, described the right as a *vector* where the violation of rights referred to in the two Covenants also effect a violation of the RtD. At the same time, the Declaration does not just speak to the need for adequate social and economic conditions (reflecting indeed Article 28 of the UDHR), it also pinpoints the individual as the main benefactor and participant in the processes of fulfilling human rights. It has an actor perspective of social agency, as complementary to the structural focus on contextual conditions. The RtD combines a demand for social justice, and implicitly, a demand for reforming and transforming structures and institutions that prevent the fulfilment of economic, social, and cultural rights. It requires that governance institutions respect the rule of law and political rights and freedoms enshrined in the UN Covenant on Civil and Political Rights. These rights require that public institutions operate in accordance with human rights norms and principles, including those of accountability and transparency. Human rights, in other words, are norms guiding the operation of public institutions and governance structures, yet as the Declaration on the Right to Development claims, implementation of human rights rests on conditions of peace and security, escaping traps of violence and war.

This brings us to the violence trap argument, which suggests an empirical direction where lack of peace (violence) is a main cause of failed development. In the next section we pursue this argument in more detail by reviewing recent empirical studies from different contexts that can help to give insight about, rather than firmly establish the argument discussed above.

4. The Traps of Violence: Experiences and Evidence

Cox, North, and Weingast argue that traps of violence undergird most of the economic poverty traps that much of the literature has focused on.[18] They claim that violent conflict is endemic and highly common in the developing world, including in the richer developing countries.[19] At the state level they find that among half the poorest countries in the world the median number of years for a violent regime change is seven, and twelve and a half years among the richest developing countries.[20] In the richest decile of countries, the medium is 60 years. Rich countries are successful in implementing measures and mechanisms that are preventive of violent conflict, which poor countries fail to do. They refer to this failure as the *violence trap*, and find it to be correlated with lack of appropriate incentives to avoid conflict, or, in their language, the cost of domestic conflict for ruling elites is too low. Hence, the 'costs' of violent domestic conflict for conflict entrepreneurs

[18] Gary W. Cox, Douglass C. North, and Barry R. Weingast, 'The Violence Trap: A Political-Economic Approach to the Problems of Development' (1 September 2013), Social Science Research Network, http://papers.ssrn.com/sol3/papers.cfm?abstract_id=2370622 (accessed 9 Nov 2014).

[19] Cox, North, and Weingast, 'The Violence Trap', 2.

[20] Cox, North, and Weingast, 'The Violence Trap', 3.

need to be 'raised', and the ability to access arms held by domestic elites reduced.[21] The most important way of increasing the costs of domestic political violence is to develop a differentiated economy with high degree of sectorial specialization; domestic economic investors will only be willing to invest if adequate political and security reforms to protect the investments are in place. Arguing from a political economy perspective, they hold that political and security development cannot be separated from economic development.[22] The violence trap undergirds much of the economic traps that poor countries experience.

One important field for measuring causal effects of violent conflict on development and poverty is to use Millennium Development Goals (MDGs) as dependent variables. In a recent study Gates, Nygård, Hegre, and Strand use regression analysis to measure direct and indirect effects of violence on MDGs. The MDGs have gained status as very useful indicators of development, including poverty reduction (the first and most important of the goals).[23] The seven other goals, and the many sub-targets and indicators developed to measure them, provide a robust framework for statistical analysis.

Gates et al. analysed five MDGs: ending poverty and hunger (1); universal education (2); child mortality (4); maternal mortality (5); and environmental sustainability (7). They distinguish between indirect and direct effects of conflict on development, where indirect effects seem to be much more severe than direct. The most immediate effect of violent conflict is the internal and involuntary displacement of people, and this displacement exposes people to new risk factors that significantly undermine their immediate living conditions, including income generation, accommodation, and sanitation. It also seriously affects their access to food, to safe water, and to health infrastructure and facilities.[24] In camps with internally displaced people (IDPs) diseases spread easily and often with fatal results, for instance by the spread of diarrhoea, and usually leads to higher mortality rates than does open war.[25]

Violent conflict also distorts development by destroying transportation infrastructure (among other things preventing local markets from operating), and constrains effective use of funds allocated to the health and education sectors. Civil wars tend to spill over into neighbouring countries, either by the spread of violence or by producing refugee populations, which disrupts economic life, reduces growth, and puts pressure on social infrastructures.[26] Overall, Gates and his colleagues find that 'A medium-sized conflict with 2500 battle deaths is estimated to increase undernourishment by an additional 3.3%, reduce life expectancy by about 1 year, increase infant mortality by 10%, and deprive an additional 1.8% of the population from access to potable water.'[27]

[21] Cox, North, and Weingast, 'The Violence Trap', 3.

[22] Cox, North, and Weingast, 'The Violence Trap', 4.

[23] Scott, Håvard Hegre, Håvard Mokleiv Nygård, and Håvard Strand, 'Development Consequences of Armed Conflict', *World Development* 40 (2012), 1713.

[24] Gates et al., 'Development Consequences of Armed Conflict', 1715.

[25] Gates et al., 'Development Consequences of Armed Conflict', 1715.

[26] Gates et al., 'Development Consequences of Armed Conflict', 1716.

[27] Gates et al., 'Development Consequences of Armed Conflict', 1713.

Supported by other research, they conclude that several studies 'confirm the popular perception that conflicts exacerbate poverty and hunger'.[28] Quoting Messer and Cohen with reference to data on Africa, they argue 'conflict causes food insecurity'.[29] Messer and Cohen also document that in Africa alone, between the mid-1960s and 2000, violent civil conflict cost the continent around US$120 billion in lost agricultural production, and hence, lack of development.[30]

Civil war, in other words, has structural effects on economies and hence on development. Collier argues that this happens through five mechanisms: destruction of resources, disruption of social order, diversion of public expenditure, lack of domestic saving for investment, and the shifting of values and assets out of the country.[31]

In a similar vein, Brozka and Croll argue 'it seems unlikely that the MDGs can be reached unless issues of security and conflict are brought into the diagnosis of the obstacles hindering their attainment'.[32] They recognize that security and peace were indeed referred to in the Millennium Declaration adopted by the UN General Assembly in September 2000, just as poverty and governance issues were addressed. But conflict resolution (just as governance issues) was never established as a development goal, and remained on the outside of debates and practices.[33] According to Brozca and Croll there remains a need for a concrete program to leveraging conflict prevention, post-conflict peace-building and for transferring resources from military processes and institutions to enhance security.[34]

This indicates that even if relationships between violent conflict and development have long been recognized, there has not been much effort to develop policies and programmes at international or national levels that would make this a central policy concern. Interestingly, this has been recognized by the Report of the High Level Panel of Eminent Persons on the Post 1015 Development Agenda, which concludes that one in five transformative shifts in a post-2015 agenda should be the recognition of 'peace and good governance as core elements of well-being, not an optional extra'.[35] And in the twelve 'illustrative' post-2015 goals discussed in the Annexe to the report, Goal 11, 'ensure stable and peaceful societies', explicitly states 'without peace, there can be no development'.[36] This is clearly a positive move, but needs further translation into goals, objectives, and measures in order to become practical and operational.

[28] Gates et al., 'Development Consequences of Armed Conflict', 1715.

[29] Ellen Messer and Marc Cohen, 'Breaking the Links between Conflict and Hunger in Africa', *2020 Africa Conference Brief 10* (International Food Policy Research Institute, 2004), 3.

[30] Messer and Cohen, 'Breaking the Links'.

[31] P. Collier, 'On the Economic Consequences of Civil War', *Oxford Economic Papers* 5 (1999).

[32] Michael Brzoska and Peter Croll, 'Investing in Development: An Investment in Security', United Nations Institute for Disarmament Research (UNIDIR) (Geneva 2005), 12.

[33] Interestingly, Nepal established 'Governance and human rights' as a 'national' MDG (the '9th MDG').

[34] Brzoska and Croll, 'Investing in Development', 12.

[35] The Report of the High Level Panel of Eminent Persons on the Post-2015 Development Agenda, *A New Global Partnership: Eradicate Poverty and Transform Economies Through Sustainable Development* (New York: United Nations Publications, 2013), 9.

[36] Report of the High Level Panel of Eminent Persons, 52.

As indicated in the introductory section, there have been different assumptions about causality in the links between conflict/violence and development/poverty. A prevailing view in donor circles has been that grievance among the poor causes conflict, and therefore poverty reduction has conflict-preventive effects (so-called grievance theory). On the other hand, more recent, especially development economic studies have emphasized that it is greed by economic actors and elites in order to capture resources and wealth that spur and cause conflict (greed theory). A third position is the so-called 'cost of conflict' perspective that holds that conflicts arise when the cost of engaging in it is low, and possible benefits high. While the main purpose of this chapter is to explore the violence trap statement, we also recognize that the causal arrows can point in either direction, and the analytical task is always to acknowledge that the particular direction they point relies on contextual situation and time.

In a study of the relationship between war and chronic poverty, Goodhand emphasizes that the understanding of the causal linkages is important because it often has policy implications.[37] He goes on, however, to argue and demonstrate empirically that it is increasingly accepted that violent conflict is a driver of chronic poverty, and that the reverse relationship—chronic poverty causes conflict—is much more contentious. Long-term conflict is a *maintainer* of chronic poverty. He stresses that the choice of the grievance or greed hypothesis as a good explanation depends on situational context and the type of existing poverty. He emphasizes, moreover, that even if there is not enough evidence to conclude that transient poverty, that is, people moving in and out of poverty due to social, political, and economic factors, will trigger violent conflict based on grievances, the chronically poor are generally less likely to engage in violent conflict.[38]

In addressing the structural relations between violent conflict and poverty, it is important to look at possible interlinkages of different perspectives. In the post-election violence in Kenya in early 2008 in the immediate aftermath of the presidential and parliamentary elections on 29 December 2007, the national and local political leaders' 'greed' for power, was intertwined with 'grievance'-led claims about land-grabbing by local farmers on the ground. The uncertainty surrounding the post-election counting and tallying process gave scope for local violence where politicians would incite the people living in poverty to attack their leaders' opponents in 'exchange' for access to a piece of land. This indeed suggests that the relationship between violence and development is complex and structured by local conditions.

Goodhand points out that an accountable, legitimate, and strong state is the best guarantor against 'deadly', violent conflict, and the chronic poverty it generates.[39] As a consequence, over the last decade the international donor community has 'invested' funding in good governance programmes to ensure a peaceful

[37] Jonathan Goodhand, 'Enduring Disorder and Persistent Poverty. A Review of the Linkages Between War and Chronic Poverty', *World Development* 31 (2003).

[38] Goodhand, 'Enduring Disorder and Persistent Poverty', 640.

[39] Goodhand, 'Enduring Disorder and Persistent Poverty', 641.

equilibrium. However, much of these 'investments' have failed due to poor understanding of the internal structures and processes that produce bad governance on the ground. In other words, the analysis of the political structures and dynamics that produce direct as well as structure-based violence have not been adequately captured and understood. The greed of leaders has to be understood in order to handle grievance among the poor. If greed is not tackled (in this case in the form of governance structures, elite capture, and clientelism) it is likely to increase perceptions of grievance and 'raise the prospects of violent conflict'.[40] In fragile states, with high levels of violence, the structural challenge is exactly the lack of an accountable and strong (in terms of legitimate and effective) state.

Understanding the nature of the state, in other words, is important for assessing how violence obstructs development. The challenges on the ground may be significant, not least when states that have gone through civil war or high levels of violence are faced with serious development challenges. Liberia is a case in point. After the signing of the Comprehensive Peace Agreement ending the civil war in 2003, the regime of Ellen Johnson Sirleaf's United Party entered on a process of reconstruction through a reform programme based on four pillars: security, economic recovery, governance and rule of law, and infrastructure and basic services. Yet, several years into the programme, which made quite some progress, McCandless observed that the reform process was hampered by rising lawlessness and inadequate security sector capacity. The fragile political and security environment made scope for former combatants, deactivated soldiers, 'disgruntled youth', and others to take economic advantage illegally by exploiting unsecured natural resources, which was detrimental to economic reconstruction.[41] The weakness of the state made it possible for 'political spoilers' to challenge the government's efforts at reconciliation and reconstruction.

Continued insecurity and the failure to disarm conflict entrepreneurs obstruct development and impede the social construction of positive peace in post-conflict situations. In short, peace-building must be integral parts of anti-poverty policies and incentives for continued conflict eradicated.[42]

5. Changing Patterns of Violence and Structural Bases for Peace

Over the last three decades the nature of large-scale violence has changed. Interstate wars are today rare, and the number of civil wars has declined significantly since 1990.[43] While interstate war declined after World War II, civil wars

[40] Goodhand, 'Enduring Disorder and Persistent Poverty', 641.

[41] Erin McCandless, 'Lessons from Liberia. Integrated Approaches to Peace Building in Transitional Settings'. *ISS Paper* 161 (April 2008).

[42] Hazel Jean L Malapit, Tina S. Clemente, and Cristina Yunzal, 'Does Violent Conflict make Chronic Poverty More Likely? The Mindanao Experience', *The Philippine Review of Economics* XL (2003).

[43] World Bank, *World Development Report 2011: Conflict, Security and Development* (2011), 51.

with more than 1,000 battle deaths per year increased during the Cold War, and peaked around 1990 with 21 active major civil wars in 1991–2. By 2002, civil wars with more than 1,000 battle deaths had fallen to less than 10.[44]

This section discusses some changing patterns of violence in order to examine the changing nature of violence as a trap of development. From a development perspective, it extends empirical arguments for the 'positive peace' focus of the Draft: peace is more than absence of war. Although large-scale organized violence today takes new forms it still has significant impact on development. The 'new' violence includes 'local violence involving militias or between ethnic groups, gang violence, local resources-related violence and violence linked to trafficking'.[45] Violence related to trafficking concerns in particular drug trafficking, not least the violence of the drug cartels in Latin America, and increasingly in Africa. It also entails global ideological violence, for example various types of national and international terrorism.

Hence, we observe new forms of socially significant organized crime occurring in repeated cycles of civil conflict.[46] Some types of violence, for instance vigilante or gang hostility, are related to other types, for instance election violence, which manifests itself as ethnic conflict, but have different layers of 'justification' and motivation. Many new and fragile democracies experience returning cycles of violence where violence is used during political contests and campaigning. Kenya, for instance, experienced serious ethno-political violence in three out of five national elections from 1992 to 2013 after multi-party democracy had been reintroduced in 1991. Drug-related violence has become almost endemic in certain parts of Latin America and Africa, and interlinks poor and affluent countries. And as usual, it is the urban poor 'foot-soldiers' that suffer the most: 'Drugs provide the money that enables organised criminals to corrupt and manipulate even the most powerful societies—to the ultimate detriment of the urban poor, who provide most of the criminals' foot-soldiers and who find themselves trapped in environments traumatized by criminal violence.'[47] The drug trafficking represents new structures of violence that trap people in poverty, that is, people who see this as their opportunity to improve their living standards, but in spite of their efforts end up as 'victims' of the violence they are part of themselves; they experience new types of structurally embedded traps of violence.

As noted, modern forms of organized violence occur in repeated cycles; civil wars tend to recur, election-related violence follows election cycles, and every civil war that broke out after 2003 has been a resumption of previous civil wars.[48] This is a new phenomenon that is significantly different from civil wars in the 1960s where 57 per cent of domestic conflicts were the first conflict, and conflicts occurred in newly independent states in the wake of decolonization.[49]

[44] World Bank, *World Development Report 2011*, 52.
[45] World Bank, *World Development Report 2011*, 53.
[46] World Bank, *World Development Report 2011*, 53.
[47] World Bank, *World Development Report 2011*, 57.
[48] World Bank, *World Development Report 2011*, 57.
[49] World Bank, *World Development Report 2011*, 57.

But the fact of fewer civil wars has not ended high levels of violence: the pattern has just changed with continued and in many cases increased negative impact on development.

For instance, several Central American countries (Guatemala, Honduras, etc.) are now experiencing more violence from organized and criminal violence than they did during their civil wars in the 1980s and 1990s. The development impact is immense in terms of human suffering, trauma, and loss of social cohesion and trust in society, that is, the social infrastructure that makes a society thrive. There are immediate effects on the population in terms of loss of life, increasing levels of disability, displacement of people, and economic losses due to increasing levels of instability and insecurity. In a seven-country survey Bøås, Tiltnes, and Flatø report on the human costs of violence in Congo, Côte d'Ivoire, Sierra Leone, Gaza, West Bank, and Colombia, which provide good illustrations on how violence affects development.[50] In brief, '(p)eople in conflict-affected areas experience displacement, loss of contact, imprisonment, and humiliation, which affect entire families, disrupting life and destroying social capital. In Gaza a third of respondents reported that someone in their immediate family had been displaced in the last three years. In the West Bank, a third had experienced someone being imprisoned. In Sierra Leone, 35 per cent of the respondents reported that they lost contact with a member of their immediate family in the last three years.'[51]

Not surprisingly, vulnerable groups are most affected by violence, as they do not have the means or resources to escape situations of conflict; they are stuck in the social context, and trapped by the surrounding violence. This observation is evident at aggregate, national levels. Calculation of poverty data indicates that countries that experienced major violence in the period from 1981 to 2005 suffered from poverty levels that were continuously widening during the period and ended up 21 per cent higher in 2005.[52] Even in countries with low-scale violence, people are being displaced for long periods, some even, as with the Palestinians in the Middle East, permanently. Internally displaced persons usually have little opportunity to live worthwhile lives, and suffer disproportionately from poverty and other development failures. Once people suffer from displacement, the way back to their homes is very long and may lead to new conflicts when they return only to find their properties occupied or looted. Violence and development are nested in long-lasting circles of unresolved conflicts. Under such conditions, restoring economic growth rates is difficult. A recent study indicates that recovering to original growth rates takes about 14 years after peace has been restored in situations of civil war.[53]

Important reasons for such slow recovery is the hesitation of domestic and international investors to return and interruption of trade relations following

[50] Morten Bøås, Åge Tiltnes, and Hedda Flatø, 'Comparing the Cases, Background Paper for the World Development Report 2011', *Fafo-paper 2011:15* (2011).

[51] World Bank, *World Development Report 2011*, 56.

[52] World Bank, *World Development Report 2011*, 60.

[53] Anke Hoeffler, Sarah von Billerbeck, and Syeda S. Iljaz, 'Post-conflict Recovery and Peace Building', Background Paper for the World Development Report, 2011 (Washington, 2010).

from violence and armed conflict, which can last for decades before confidence and economic relations are restored. Such factors are structural obstacles to development with roots in high levels of conflict and violence. A social mechanism with significant effects on conflict and violence (though not always easy to measure) is diminishing social trust within society and between citizens and the state; violence corrupts the 'social contract' as referred to already. In addition, violence and conflict have serious regional effects where a conflict spreads to neighbouring countries and makes a whole region less attractive to foreign investments.

According to the economic argument referred to, violence becomes more likely if the costs of engaging in violence are low. What is considered 'costs' varies in social situations and among agents. Warlords have their own calculus; the rank and file has another. Over the years, the international community has tried to increase the cost of violence for some types of human rights violations. For instance, the risk of being prosecuted by the International Criminal Court represents an 'increase in the costs' of engaging in serious international crimes. Based on his own experiences from the civil war in the then Islamic Republic of Sudan, John Garang, the leader of the Sudan People's Liberation Movement, commented '(u)nder these circumstances the marginal costs of rebellion in the South became very small, zero, or negative; that is, in the South it pays to rebel.'[54]

A positive peace approach requires careful analyses of the structures and functioning of governance institutions and politics. It indeed matters whether governance institutions are able to respond to conflicts effectively and with legitimacy, and if they are able to prevent conflicts from venturing into vicious circles of violence.

Turning now to institutional responses to violence, the next section addresses some means and practices of resolving such cycles of violent conflict, primarily at national level. The argument here is that breaking vicious circles of violence first and foremost requires domestic political and institutional transformations. Yet, in the midst of conflict it is often a serious challenge to implement institutional reforms. Increasingly international intervention and support have been part of this transformative agenda, and have attempted to address the structural governance and institutional obstacles to handling conflicts and enhancing positive peace.

6. Institutional Responses to Structural Violence and Building Positive Peace

In the standard definition, structural violence is a form of violence where features of the social structure and economic, political, and cultural institutions harm people because they prevent them from living worthwhile lives

[54] Paul Collier and Nicholas Sambani (eds.), *Understanding Civil War: Evidence and Analysis*, i. *Africa* (Washington, DC: The World Bank, 2005), 193.

and having their basic needs met. Galtung was referring to structural violence as social injustice; hence for him, building positive peace was the removal of social injustices.[55] But there is more to the concept of positive peace that needs elaboration. Social justice is social in the sense that it manifests itself in the daily and social lives of people. People living in unjust relationships and conditions do not have jobs or adequate income; children are not able to get appropriate education because parents are not able to pay school fees; their voices are not heard in public; preventable diseases are not avoided; sanitation systems are not developed; and people living with disabilities do not get social support and assistance.

These 'social imperfections' or ills, however, do not exist in a vacuum; they are socially constructed, and result from the use or misuse of power, and the functioning of institutions and legislation that were supposed to correct them. Institutional functioning is a complex issue, but it is a political issue and related to politics, policy-making, and the relationships (and struggles) among political elites. Policy-making and the use of public resources take place within institutions. In short, social justice issues are addressed, or not addressed, by institutions. Structural violence, therefore, is related to governance and institutional performance, and building positive peace entails reforming and transforming the way institutions work. Countries with high levels of violence, and weak institutional legitimacy, often lack governance and institutional capacity to resolve serious and violent conflicts. Let us consider an example in some detail.

The post-election violence in Kenya in early 2008 illustrates how vicious circles of open violence embedded in social structures (and hence, 'structural violence') may be addressed through institutional transformation, and political settlements through elite pacts. This required building new institutions and a power-sharing, inclusive coalition government. The crisis in Kenya erupted in January 2008 immediately after the incumbent president Mwai Kibaki had been declared the winner of the presidential elections held on 29 December 2007. Supported by international observers, the opponent candidate Raila Odinga and his party, the Orange Democratic Movement, contested the results and alleged that the results were being manipulated. Extensive, spontaneous, and orchestrated violence occurred when angry 'wananchi'[56] attacked their opponents in several areas of the country. It was later established that violence in the Rift Valley had been supported by prominent political leaders, and encouraged by the use of local radio stations and text message communication.[57]

The humanitarian, political, and social crisis lasted for more than two months (January to mid-March), 1,333 people were killed (most by the use of machetes and other traditional tools and weapons), and about 600,000 people were internally

[55] Galtung, 'Violence, Peace, and Peace Research', 183.

[56] Kiswahili for 'common man'.

[57] In 2010 the International Criminal Court (ICC) opened up a case against two political leaders, Uhuru Kenyatta and William Ruto, and a journalist, Joshua arap Sang, who allegedly supported and initiated violence in the Rift Valley. See *Situation in the Republic of Kenya* (Pre-trial Chamber II) ICC No. 1/09 (31 March 2009).

displaced.[58] Violence was to a large extent ethno-political, with attacks on the Kikuyu tribe of Mwai Kibaki by supporters of Odinga's supporters from the Luo and Kalenjin tribes, while counter-attacks and revenge violence was conducted by Kikuyu youth. Indeed, some of the violence was social unrest and rioting, where poor, unemployed youth attacked and looted shopkeepers and others with wealth, notably in the Kibera slum in Nairobi and in the town of Kisumu.

The crisis soon triggered international involvement as the two antagonists were not able to resolve a crisis of escalating violence. The president of neighbouring Uganda, Yoweri Museweni, attempted to reconcile tension, and the African Union (AU) sent former president of Ghana, John Kufuor, as an official mediator. Having had limited success, Kufuor was soon replaced by former UN Secretary-General, Kofi Annan, as a representative of the group of Eminent Persons of the African Union. Annan succeeded in mediating an agenda for peace talks in late January, and finally succeeded in brokering a power-sharing agreement by the end of February. The agreement, known as at the National Accord and Reconciliation Act, established a coalition government between the two contending parties where Kibaki would retain the position as President and Odinga would receive a new post as Prime Minister. The office of a Prime Minister represented a key institutional response to the crisis.

This coalition was not ideal from anyone's perspective, but ended the violence, and represented a political resolution to the conflict. It also represented the invention of new institutions, that is, the coalition government and a power-sharing executive branch with the post of Prime Minister. An Act on the coalition government passed by the Parliament endorsed and made this institutional transformation legal. The deal also entailed an agreement to conclude a comprehensive constitutional reform process, which had gone on for more than fifteen years, but had stalled after a 'no' referendum vote in 2005. Other transformative governance and institutional issues included land reforms, political reforms, and talks about the distribution of wealth between regions and ethnic groups. These issues, land distribution and ethnic animosities, had remained major social and political cleavages in Kenyan politics since the 1960s. As part of the political settlement, a bill amending the constitution was adopted. The process also produced agreements to establish several commissions of inquiry, including the Independent Review Commission on the Elections, the Commission of Inquiry on Post-election Violence, a National Ethnic and Race Relations Commission, and the Truth, Justice, and Reconciliation Commission. These commissions of inquiry were aimed at reconciliation and building trust and confidence in the post-election process. Although the implementation of the power-sharing agreement was marred by controversies and conflicts of interpretation, it led to social calm and finally brought violence to an end. The interpretation and practising of the power-sharing (which was the nucleus of the agreement) included the

[58] See Bård A. Andreassen, Tiberius Barasa, Thomas Kibua, and Arne Tostensen, '"I Acted Under a Lot of Pressure", The Disputed 2007 Kenyan General Elections in Context', *NORDEM Report* 7/2008 (Oslo: Norwegian Centre for Human Rights, 2008).

establishment of the largest Cabinet in Kenya's history, with 40 ministries and 40 deputy ministries (picked from a Parliament with 210 members). According to Kibaki's party, the PNU, a large government was necessary in order to make it properly inclusive.

The Kenyan experience captures different dimensions of the challenges of breaking the cycles of violence and producing virtuous cycles of peaceful management of conflict in times of crisis and instability. A major factor of this process was to restore a minimum of trust among the political contenders of the conflict, a sufficient level of trust in the institutions that the peace process produced, and to restore some level of confidence among elites, between ethnic communities, and between citizens and elites. In fact the big and expanded 'unity' coalition government was an elite pact that in spite of its size was needed in order to be 'inclusive enough'.

The Kenyan case also illustrates other insights of institutional and political analysis of relationships between institutions and violence. Kenyan institutions of governance were too weak to manage the disputed result of the 2007 elections. The Electoral Commission's speedy and premature announcement of the final election results before controversies had been settled was a case in point. The endorsement of this announcement by the Chief Justice, who swore in the president, was another failed institutional performance in the midst of a serious political crisis, and immediately triggered an outbreak of violence. This made it clear how vulnerable the Kenyan society and institutions were to 'internal stress'.

The Kenyan case brings attention to the interlinkages of legitimacy and violence. An important issue in institutional analyses of how societies can move from violence to resilience and peace is whether confidence can be restored through transforming institutions, including the country's constitution. The immediate task of institutional transformation, or the invention of new institutions, is to restore legitimacy to the governance institutions. The lack of legitimate and effective institutions represents a particularly important type of structural deficiency, or 'violence' in Galtung's terminology. Governance institutions, moreover, garner legitimacy by being accountable as well as effective, or effective *enough*: institutions need to make citizens and elites confident, and accept norms of good governance and rule of law, and refrain from violence. This establishes an important link between structural violence and institutional deficiency on the one hand, and open violence on the other. The former triggers the second, and as the Kenyan case makes evident, failed governance and deficient legal institutions are manifestations of 'structural violence'.

The elite pact that was entered into in Kenya also pinpoints another important mechanism that limited and helped to stop violence. Pacts among elites are hard to establish and while mediation or negotiations go on, violence continues to escalate. In fact, political contenders may see the benefit of violent upheavals during negotiations. Building positive peace is an elusive process with contradictions and obstacles.

The human factor, and leadership, are also critical in negotiating peace and an end to violence. In Kenya it was certainly a positive factor that the two main contenders (Kibaki and Odinga) knew each other well, and had been political allies in the ruling National Rainbow Coalition from 2002 to 2005 with Kibaki as President. They knew each other's attitudes, personalities, and intentions. Pacts have a personal dimension that is important in building trust, and the human factor may become particularly important when institutions are weak. For more than a month much of Annan's efforts consisted in keeping a dialogue going and facilitating communication, building confidence, and identifying common goals. In order to address issues of structural obstacles to reconciliation the establishment of a truth and reconciliation commission was important in the early phases of the process, and among the issues it was supposed to address was a review of the ethnic differences and conflicts, identified as underlying, structural causes of the violence.[59]

In other words, transforming institutions and introducing policies that address structural violence is essential in building positive peace. Still these are demanding tasks, particularly in the usually low- and middle-income countries where structural violence is most acute. The World Bank suggests three key reasons why it is difficult to transform institutions in such societies:[60] first, to achieve an agreement of change is difficult because elites do not trust each other, and people generally do not trust state institutions. Second, agreements can easily be broken because of the uncertainty that they entail in the short term, and because of reactions from groups who lose power and benefit. Institutional change and transformation inevitably imply altering power relations. And third, a country going through institutional transformation may face a security threat that disturbs the process of change.

In response to these challenges of institutional transformation for positive peace, the World Development Report 2011 suggests a framework well worth exploring further, normatively and politically.[61] In order to achieve institutional resilience in a gradual process towards stable developing environments, three fundamental obstacles need to be managed: confidence and trust in institutions and social relations (collective action) need to be restored; priority and resources must be provided to institutions that contribute to citizens' security, justice, and job creation; external 'stresses' (economic and security) need to be governed; and tailor-made external support solicited. This framework is interesting, but not a blueprint. It needs to be adapted to different circumstances and contexts but provides a framework for further analysis and research. One major advantage is that it combines attention to the role of social and political actors in conflict resolution as well as to institutional and structural obstacles to positive peace, for example, what has been referred to in this chapter as 'structural violence'.

[59] In hindsight, too little institutional learning and reform has resulted from these reports. They helped to calm the situation in a transitional process, but their lasting positive impact on politics and institutions is far from clear-cut.

[60] World Bank, *World Development Report 2011*, 99ff.

[61] World Bank, *World Development Report 2011*.

7. Conclusion

Drafting a human right to peace requires reflection on the conditions for and obstacles to peace, and to view peace as a social process. Obstacles are certainly complex, but involve social, political, and institutional dimensions, sometimes referred to as structural violence, although other terminology (social injustice, poverty) captures the same phenomena. This chapter began by referring to a dictum saying that if you want peace, seek justice. It has argued, however, that injustices (and failure to comply with the principle of the right to development as a human right) are often trapped in vicious circles of violence. Violence traps development. This empirical observation seems to be equally valid with changing patterns of violence. There is no easy path out of this quagmire. Yet, the chapter has argued the importance of addressing the issue of violence from governance and institutional perspectives. It has approached institutional deficiencies and political factors as major structural obstacles to the cessation of violence, and hence untangled violence traps that hinder development. It has suggested, moreover, that untangling traps of violence requires institutional and political resolutions primarily in local and national contexts. The right to peace can only advance if governance practices and institutions are properly transformed and restructured.

9

Environmentally Sustainable Development and Peace

The Role of International Law

Christina Voigt

Peace, development, and environmental protection are interdependent and indivisible.[1]

The environment is a crucial aspect of the right to peace...An area of particular relevance is climate change.[2]

1. Introduction

A safe, clean, and productive environment is conducive to peace and human security while environmental stress is both a cause and an effect of political tension and military conflict. The protection and preservation of the natural environment, integrity of ecological systems, and the survival of species are positive conditions for peace.

Yet, the connections between environmental issues and conflict are many and complex. Environmental factors themselves are rarely, if ever, the sole cause of violence. But natural resources and other environmental factors are linked to violent conflict in a variety of ways often obscured by more visible issues, such as ethnic tension and power politics. Conflicts can arise from the marginalization of sectors of the population and from ensuing violence. This occurs when political processes are unable to handle the effects of environmental stress resulting, for example, from floods, erosion, and desertification. Nations have often fought to assert or resist control over raw materials, energy supplies, land, river basins, sea passages, and other key environmental resources. Such conflicts are likely to increase as these resources become scarcer, the human population becomes larger, environmental stress increases, and competition for resources increases. 'Environmental stress can thus be an

[1] Rio Declaration on Environment and Development, Rio de Janeiro, 1992, Principle 25.

[2] HRC, 'Progress Report on the Right of Peoples to Peace', 22 December 2010, UN Doc. A/HRC/AC/6/CRP.3, para. 38.

important part of the web of causality associated with a conflict and can in some cases be catalytic. Poverty, injustice, environmental degradation, and conflict interact in complex and potent ways. But the underlying causes often include the deterioration of the natural resource base and its capacity to support the population.'[3] Conflicts may arise not only because of political and military threats to national sovereignty; they may derive also from environmental degradation and the pre-emption of development options.

The global environmental commons cannot be managed from any national centre: The nation-state is insufficient to deal with global and accumulating threats to shared ecosystems, to the biosphere, or to the atmosphere. States should therefore cooperate to preserve and protect the environment as a *common interest* through international law, based on the principle of sustainable and equitable use of natural resources, as well as other principles of international law. Threats to environmental security can only be dealt with by states' cooperative management and multilateral procedures and mechanisms.[4]

The sheer number of existing laws, principles, case law, regulations, standards and so on that address environmental protection already constitute a vast and complicated apparatus of international legal norms. Yet, environmental degradation and with it political stress and conflict continue to rise despite such norm density. Existing environmental law is seemingly quite inadequate to solve the problem. But the solution lies not in *more* laws. What is urgently required is a more general realization that, in the conditions of the contemporary global situation, a truly *sustainable* international society must be built. What we need therefore is a shift in the *quality* of international laws, a shift that recognizes the fundamental importance of healthy ecological conditions. In this context, Mikhail Gorbachev noted that 'The root causes of the crises we are witnessing rest on outmoded theoretical concepts, values and institutions. Time has come for change, not incremental fixes.'[5] Such realization needs in fact a new vision of international law and international relations—a vision whereby a healthy environment is recognized as the foundation for peaceful human societies. After all, this is not just a question of ameliorating the tensions of human civilization but of survival.

This chapter seeks to explore ways in which law of sustainable development can contribute to the maintenance of peace in the sense of diminishing potential for conflict. Environmental sustainability and healthy ecosystems should be considered a condition for building peace and environmental protection and cooperation a factor in peacemaking. As a peacemaking tool, the environment offers some useful—perhaps even unique—qualities that lend themselves to building peace and transforming conflict: environmental challenges ignore political boundaries, require a long-term perspective, encourage

[3] 'Our Common Future', Report of the World Commission on Environment and Development (1987), http://www.un-documents.net/ocf-11.htm#I (accessed 10 Nov 2014).

[4] WCED, 'Our Common Future'.

[5] Green Cross, 'Green Cross Turns 20: The World at a Crossroads, Let's make the right choices for the future', http://www.gcint.org/green-cross-20-years (accessed 10 Nov 2014).

local and non-governmental participation, and extend community building beyond polarizing economic linkages. Where cooperation does take root, it may help to enhance trust, establish cooperative habits, create shared regional identities around shared resources, and establish mutually recognized rights and expectations. In this context, the present and potential role of public international law will be assessed. In particular, the international climate regime as an international agreement that purports sustainable resource use, conservation of ecosystems, sustainable management of commodities and cooperation in the management of a shared resource will be analysed for its potential to 'contribute to peace'.[6]

2. The Challenges of Resource Scarcity and Abundance

The complex relationship between peace and access to exploitable natural resources, whether they are abundant or scarce, is the subject of a large body of literature. Views on these issues differ and the discussion is contentious. In the following, only a brief overview of the various perspectives will be given.

2.1. Peace and resource scarcity

For many years there has been warning that 'Renewable resource scarcities of the next 50 years will probably occur with a speed, complexity and magnitude unprecedented in history ... We have come to understand that scarcities of renewable resources often produce insidious and cumulative social effects, such as population displacement and economic disruption. These events can, in turn, lead to clashes between ethnic groups as well as to civil strife and insurgency.'[7] Despite this warning, some contend that resource scarcity per se does not suffice to bring about conflict. Conflict may occur when scarcity interacts with severe discrimination and the mobilization of rebel armies.[8]

One controversial example is the question of fresh water resources. The disputes over water rights represent one of the principal causes of real or potential conflict in many different parts of the world. There are some who say that the great war of the next century could arise from a struggle for the control of fresh water, a resource increasingly under pressure from demographic expansion and economic

[6] For this reason, this chapter will not deal with the protection of the environment during armed conflict. For further references on this topic see *Nordic Journal of International Law* 82 (2013), in particular the contribution by Dieter Fleck, 'The Protection of the Environment in Armed Conflict: Legal Obligations in the Absence of Specific Rules', 7–20. See also Onita Das, *Environmental Protection, Security and Armed Conflict: A Sustainable Development Perspective* (Cheltenham: Edward Elgar, 2013).

[7] Thomas F. Homer-Dixon, 'Environmental Scarcity and Global Security', *Foreign Policy Association* 300 (1993), 38–9.

[8] Günter Baechler, *Violence through Environmental Discrimination* (Dordrecht: Kluwer Academic, 1999).

activities.[9] Others argue that resource scarcity leads to more cooperation and therefore less conflict.[10]

Experiences of cooperation and sustainable development in the area of management of supply and consumption of fresh water have led to the creation of mechanisms that aid users to define the norms for allocation, use, and transfer of water rights in a democratic process. In practice, this democratic process of resource allocation replaced previously existing conflict.[11] Matz-Lueck argues that 'At the local level, the gun has been replaced by meetings between neighbours or committees who must learn to share a watershed. On a macro level, international accords and committees can serve as substitutes for wars.'[12]

While resource scarcity can (but does not necessarily) lead in some cases to a situation of cooperation and diminished potential for conflict, it is difficult—and may in fact be dangerous—to generalize this position for all types of conflict over scarce natural resources.

2.2. Peace and resource abundance ('resource curse')

Natural resources pay for wars. Access to abundant natural resources is the fuel for many rebel armies. Unless rebel forces are financed from outside the country, they must generate income by operating business activities alongside their military operations. Rebel groups often hold their bases in rural areas and thus depend on the exploitation of primary commodities with high economic rents. Such 'conflict-commodities' often include ivory[13], timber[14], gemstones, and minerals.

Moreover, dependence upon the existence and exploitability of natural resources is much higher in developing countries than in the 'industrialized world' and mismanagement, loss of access, and pollution may have grave socio-economic consequences. For many developing countries natural resources are the only valuable assets that safeguard the livelihoods of their peoples and offer opportunities for bilateral or international trade.

Yet, natural resources are rarely the sole cause of conflict. Religion, ethnicity, ideology, poor governance, and corruption are equally important factors. The linkages between resource wealth and conflict are complicated and

[9] Laurence Boisson de Chazournes, Christina Leb, and Mara Tignino (eds.), *International Law and Freshwater: The Multiple Challenges* (Cheltenham: Edward Elgar, 2013).

[10] Nils Petter Gleditsch and Ole Magnus Theisen, 'Resources, the Environment and Conflict', in *Handbook of Security Studies*, M. D. Cavelty and V. Mauer (eds.) (Oxford: Routledge, 2010), 221–31.

[11] Nele Matz-Lueck, 'The Benefits of Positivism: The ILC's Contribution to the Peaceful Sharing of Transboundary Groundwater', in *Source Peace through International Law: The Role of the International Law Commission: A Colloquium at the Occasion of its Sixtieth Anniversary*, Georg Nolte (ed.) (Dordrecht: Springer, 2009), 129.

[12] Matz-Lueck, 'The Benefits of Positivism', 129.

[13] See ivory fuelling conflict in the democratic republic of Congo: Jeffrey Gettleman, 'Elephants Dying in Epic Frenzy as Ivory Fuels Wars and Profits', *New York Times*, 3 September 2012, http://www.nytimes.com/2012/09/04/world/africa/africas-elephants-are-being-slaughtered-in-poaching-frenzy.html?pagewanted=all&_r=0 (accessed 10 Nov 2014).

[14] See Wil de Jong, Deanna Donovan, and Ken-ichi Abe (eds.), *Extreme Conflict and Tropical Forests* (Dordrecht: Springer, 2007).

'for every resource-rich country that has suffered from violent conflict, two or three have avoided it'. However, where resource wealth exists, unsustainable exploitation can often underpin and lengthen those conflicts that do arise from other causes. And conflicts themselves can often increase the rate of natural resource extraction. The challenge therefore is to devise ways to break these links and ensure that natural resources can be exploited without stimulating or funding conflict.

One example is the link between wildlife poachers, traffickers, and armed conflict in some regions of Africa. According to the WWF, over 20,000 elephants are killed each year for their ivory tusks, many of them in central African conflict zones. Rebel groups use the illegal ivory trade as a source to generate finances or otherwise to benefit from such trade.

The UN has been warning that ivory has become a major source of finance for armed groups and has led to the depletion of elephants in Central Africa. According to a UN experts' report S/2014/42 on the Democratic Republic of the Congo dated 23 January 2014, the slaughter of elephants in the Democratic Republic of the Congo 'is one of the most tragic consequences of years of war and poor governance. Driven by growing demand in Asia and increases in prices, poaching by armed groups and criminal networks has decimated elephant populations throughout eastern Democratic Republic of the Congo.'

In a novel move, the United Nations Security Council adopted two Resolutions, 2134 (2014) and 2136 (2014) on 28 January and 30 January 2014 respectively, on UN sanctions targeting armed rebel groups in the Central African Republic and the Democratic Republic of the Congo financed by the illegal exploitation of natural resources, including poaching and illicit wildlife trade.[15] Individuals or entities involved will be subject to travel bans and asset freezes. With these resolutions, the Council de facto designated wildlife poaching and trafficking as threats to peace.

The new Security Council resolutions are certainly a prolongation and extension of previous practice of the Security Council on a positive concept of peace by recognizing wildlife poaching and trafficking as threats to peace. While the Council's motivation is anthropocentric (and not for the purpose of protecting animals from slaughter), a development towards a more holistic concept of peace has been set in motion. Peters states in this context: 'In the long run, however, an ecocentric approach to peace and security seems more appropriate to guarantee a sustainable peace for all living beings on earth. ... It is hoped that taking into account not only human security, but also the integrity of nature, the survival of species and the well-being of animals will be an increasingly relevant factor in global law and politics on peace and security.'[16]

[15] CITES, 'UN sanctions on armed groups financed by poaching and illicit wildlife trade in the Central African Republic and the Democratic Republic of the Congo', http://www.cites.org/eng/news/sundry/2014/20140203_un_sanctions.php (accessed 10 Nov 2014).

[16] Anne Peters, 'Novel practice of the Security Council: Wildlife poaching and trafficking as a threat to the peace', EJIL: Talk!, 12 Febuary 2014, http://www.ejiltalk.org/novel-practice-of-the-security-council-wildlife-poaching-and-trafficking-as-a-threat-to-the-peace/ (accessed 10 Nov 2014).

Another particular example are 'conflict diamonds'. In a number of African countries, for example, Sierra Leone, the Democratic Republic of Congo, Angola, Liberia, and Ivory Coast, diamonds are mined often by using forced child labour under horrendous labour standards. Moreover, these diamonds fuel armed conflicts in these regions, the activities of warlords and rebel movements aimed at overthrowing legitimate governments, and the illicit traffic in and proliferation of arms, especially small arms and light weapons. Diamonds are the 'currency of choice' for smugglers: they are portable, virtually untraceable, and universally valuable.

The extraction of and trade with conflict diamonds or 'blood diamonds' results in devastating impacts on the peace, safety, and security of people in affected countries and systematic and gross human rights violations.[17]

At the same time, high-value natural resources have the potential to promote and consolidate peace. In many post-conflict countries, revenues from resources such as oil, minerals, natural gas, gemstones, and timber are an integral part of the national economy. Lujala and Rustad note, 'When peace comes, the revenues from high value natural resources—when managed well—can help finance reconstruction and other vital peace-related needs. When mismanaged, however, resource revenues can undermine both economic performance and the quality of governance, and thereby increase the risk of violence.'[18]

The double-sided nature of valuable resources is exemplified in the 'blood diamond' example cited. Social outrage and strong critique (mostly of western NGOs) of the diamond trade involving blood diamonds led to a global debate on this issue which resulted in UN General Assembly Resolution 55/56(2000) calling on the international community to give urgent consideration to devising effective and pragmatic measures to address this problem. This resolution started the Kimberley process, a certification scheme where each shipment of rough diamonds is to be accompanied by a government-verified certificate that indicates the origin of each stone. This scheme is monitored by a working group, comprised of government, industry, and NGOs. Under the scheme, the trade between Kimberley members is restricted to certified non-conflict diamonds only.[19]

In Sierra Leone, together with the Kimberley Process Certification Scheme, the Diamond Area Community Development Fund aims to return revenues to communities and ensure that they have a say in their own development. One of the goals of the fund is to support local participation in decision-making about

[17] Jan Erik Wetzel, 'Targeted Economic Measures to Curb Armed Conflict? The Kimberley Process on the Trade in "Conflict Diamonds"', in *International Law and Armed Conflict, Challenges in the 21st Century*, Noëlle Quénivet and Shilam Shah-Davis (eds.) (The Hague: T.M.C. Asser, 2012), 161ff. See also Kazumi Kawamoto, 'Diamonds in War, Diamonds for Peace: Diamond Sector Management and Kimberlite Mining in Sierra Leone', in *High-Value Natural Resources and Post-Conflict Peacebuilding*, Pavivi Lujala and Siri Aaa Rustad (eds.) (Oxford: Routledge, 2012), 121ff.

[18] Päivi Lujala and Siri Aas Rustad, 'High-Value Resources: A Blessing or Curse?', in eid. (eds.), *High-Value Natural Resources and Post-Conflict Peacebuilding*, 3ff. Also Paul Collier and Anke Hoeffler, 'High-Value Natural Resources, Development, and Conflict: Channels of Causation', in Lujala and Rustad (eds.), *High-Value Natural Resources*, 293ff.

[19] For more information see: http://www.kimberleyprocess.com/ (accessed 10 Nov 2014).

natural resources and development, and to thereby address the grievances of mining communities. These are essential means for preserving peace.[20]

In many cases, fuelling conflicts through access to rich natural resources is being made possible through unrestricted international trade. One of the main avenues therefore for stopping trade in conflict-prone commodities and for promoting the peaceful and sustainable management of high-value natural resources is through international trade law and investment law, dealing, for example with conditions for banning 'conflict-commodities', targeted economic sanctions, reducing investment opportunities in conflict-prone natural resources, etc.[21] Even if this remains outside the scope of this chapter, it is important in this context to point to the important role of the WTO and other trade agreements: in order to promote peace, these regimes need to help building markets for sustainable, conflict-free goods—and restrict markets for the opposite.[22]

2.3. Peace and (global) environmental change

More recently, the 'resource abundance' and 'scarcity' paradigms have been joined by one stressing global environmental change as a driver of social unrest. So noted, for example, the UN High-level Panel on Threats, Challenges and Change, that environmental degradation per se is a threat to security.[23]

Global change discourses stress the idea that growth is bounded by limits. But in this case the limits are not scarce resources and commodities, but rather the disruption of global-scale environmental services and ecological functions

[20] Kawamoto, 'Diamonds in War, Diamonds for Peace', 131–2.

[21] The concern of WTO incompatibility with this scheme was addressed by the adoption of a waiver for conflict diamonds under Art. IX:3 Marrakesh Agreement Establishing the WTO—an example that targeted economic measures under international law (i.e. WTO law) can contribute to peace. For further discussion see the chapter by Ole Kristian Fauchald in this volume. See also Joost Pauwelyn, 'WTO Compassion or Superiority Complex?: What to Make of the WTO Waiver for "Conflict Diamonds"', *Michigan Journal of International Law* 24 (2003), 1177–207.

[22] Duncan Brack, 'Building Markets for Conflict-free Goods', in *Trade, Aid and Security, An Agenda for Peace and Development*, Oli Brown, Mark Halle, Sonia Peña Moreno, and Sebastian Winkler (eds.) (Oxford: Earthscan, 2007), 92ff.

[23] Report of the High-level Panel on Threats, Challenges and Change, 'A More Secure World: Our Shared Responsibility' (United Nations, 2004), http://www.un.org/en/peacebuilding/pdf/historical/hlp_more_secure_world.pdf (accessed 16 June 2014): '22. ... Disease and poverty ... are connected to environmental degradation; climate change exacerbates the occurrence of such infectious disease as malaria and dengue fever. Environmental stress, caused by large populations and shortages of land and other natural resources, can contribute to civil violence. ... 53. Environmental degradation has enhanced the destructive potential of natural disasters and in some cases hastened their occurrence. The dramatic increase in major disasters witnessed in the last 50 years provides worrying evidence of this trend. More than two billion people were affected by such disasters in the last decade, and in the same period the economic toll surpassed that of the previous four decades combined. If climate change produces more acute flooding, heat waves, droughts and storms, this pace may accelerate. 54. Rarely are environmental concerns factored into security, development or humanitarian strategies. Nor is there coherence in environmental protection efforts at the global level. Most attempts to create governance structures to tackle the problems of global environmental degradation have not effectively addressed climate change, deforestation and desertification. Regional and global multilateral treaties on the environment are undermined by inadequate implementation and enforcement by the Member States.'

that support life on earth. These services include climate regulation, water filtration and purification, nutrient cycling, atmospheric screening of ultraviolet radiation, and preservation of biological diversity. Scientists have just begun to understand the interconnections among land, oceans, atmosphere, and biosphere and have come to see the environment as a single, interconnected, living system. Accordingly, different conceptions about the link between environmental protection, the prevention of pollution and ecological degradation on the one hand and peace on the other developed.[24]

A narrower, traditional discourse looks at the link between environmental degradation and large-scale violence by aiming to adapt traditional military and intelligence tools to counter these threats.[25]

A broader conceptualization of the 'environmental foundation(s) of peace' leaves the use of force and military means aside. In this way, peace can be thought of as a continuum ranging from the absence of violent conflict to the inconceivability of violent conflict.[26] Conca, a prominent scholar in the field of international relations and environmental peace-building, has challenged dominant constructions of environmental scarcity, ecologically induced violence, and state failure by stressing the cooperative potential rather than violent inevitabilities, social transformation rather than social control, and peace rather than militarization. In essence, rather than seeking to pinpoint the environmental triggers of conflict, he is seeking to pinpoint the cooperative triggers of peace that shared environmental problems might make available.[27]

Such broader conception is referred to by some as 'ecological security', which 'means a much more fundamental rethinking of what we mean by security in a tightly couples world system. … One implication of this view is the need to shift social (and economic) resources away from traditional military means of defense (and attack) and toward preventive economic and social measures.'[28] In other words, the means of ensuring peace is through increased environmental protection through cooperation.

A definition of peace (and development) must therefore necessarily take into consideration aspects of environmental protection and sound environmental management. This involves typical transboundary issues, for example pollution of rivers or transboundary air pollution, as well as global threats to the biosphere and the atmosphere, such as climate change and the loss of biological diversity. All these problems may have significant consequences for states and their populations. Transboundary or global environmental risks also have in common that

[24] Ken Conca, 'The Case for Environmental Peacemaking', in *Environmental Peacemaking*, Ken Conca and Geoffrey D. Dabelko (eds.) (Baltimore: Johns Hopkins University Press, 2002), 1ff.; and Ken Conca and Geoffrey D. Dabelko, 'The Problems and Possibilities of Environmental Peacemaking', *Environmental Peacemaking*, 220ff.

[25] John Deutsch, former director of the US Central Intelligence Agency, speech to the Los Angeles World Affairs Council, Los Angeles, 25 July 1996.

[26] See Cecilia Bailliet and Kjetil M. Larsen, 'Introduction' to this volume.

[27] Bailliet and Larsen, 'Introduction'.

[28] Conca, 'The Case for Environmental Peacemaking', 2.

they can only effectively be addressed if states cooperate on a bilateral, regional, or global level. Co-operation is essential to the sustainable, wise, and equitable use of resources and for preserving their base for present and future generations. This helps ultimately to avoid the outbreak of internal and transboundary unrest, hostilities, and conflict.

3. Sustainable Development and Peace

Development depends crucially upon peace—and peace depends upon development. But not all kinds of development are equally conducive to peace. Economic, social, and ecological development are increasingly interdependent—and development in order to last and to be just must be based on all three 'pillars'. This idea is aptly captured in the concept of sustainable development.

Examples of current global trends which present formidable challenges to the achievement of both peace and sustainability include the problem of population growth above the carrying capacity of the known natural resource base and the predominant technology; mounting pressure on diminishing quantities of fresh water and topsoil; disputed jurisdiction over territorial areas containing strategic resources; the added impacts of climatic change to already vulnerable people and social groups; the destabilizing impact of widespread poverty and increasing social inequality; and a rising flow of migrants fleeing war, famine, natural hazards, and other vestiges of political, social, and economic breakdown.[29]

It is thus ever more urgent that the nexus between development and environmental protection in the context of sustainable development must be strengthened if peace is to be maintained or achieved. The nexus between sustainable development, environmental protection, and peace was aptly recognized in Article 25 of the 1992 Rio Declaration on Environment and Development, which states: 'Peace, development, and environmental protection are interdependent and indivisible.'[30]

Sustainable development has been defined as 'development that meets the needs of the present, without compromising future generations to meet their own needs'.[31] Its normative content is defined by the reconciliation of present and future economic, social, and environmental interests within the limits set by certain essential ecological functions.[32] Sustainable development also implies that ecological functions exist that are indispensable for a durable and equitable human society. Natural ecosystems provide the critical basis for all human societies. For a long time the fact has remained uncontested that societies derive a wide array of important life-support and economic benefits from the ecosystems

[29] Brack, *Trade, Aid and Security*, 4ff.

[30] Report of the United Nations Conference on Environment and Development, 'Rio Declaration on Environment and Development' (12 August 1992), UN Doc. A/CONF.151/26 (Vol. I), principle 25.

[31] WCED, 'Our Common Future'.

[32] Christina Voigt, *Sustainable Development as a Principle of International Law—Resolving Conflicts between Climate Measures and WTO Law* (Leiden: Martinus Nijhoff, 2009).

in which they exist.[33] In recent years an understanding across various disciplines has crystallized that human development, security, peace—humanity per se—depends on healthy ecological functions and conditions. Sustainable development requires nations to set out and implement concrete goals that submit all other activities to the protection of those essential natural conditions on which human societies depend.

This was something the World Commission called for and it is essential still. 'At a minimum', the Commission stated, 'sustainable development must not endanger the natural systems that support life on Earth', adding that there were objective limits to what nature could bear.[34] Yet, the 2012 Global Environmental Outlook 5 provided proof of the deterioration of a large number of essential ecosystem services and cautioned that 'if humanity does not urgently change its ways, several critical thresholds may be exceeded, beyond which abrupt and generally irreversible changes to the life-support functions of the planet could occur.'[35]

Sustainable development with the purpose of securing peace demands that economic and social development are pursued while ultimate ecological thresholds are respected. These thresholds define the ecological constraints for human activities and development, without which development cannot be sustainable.

These ecological limits—or planetary boundaries—are not unknown. There is a wealth of scientific data and knowledge.[36] These limits, defined on a planetary scale, need to be broken down to state level as obligations under international law and further defined at sub-state levels, such as regional, municipal, local, city, village, even individual levels. Science already has the answers. What is missing, however, is the willingness of states and sub-state actors to act accordingly. The current condition of the environment is not caused by failure or accident. It is wanted.

When designing new and interpreting existing international law, ecological limits to development have to be recognized, and these limits defined and included in the legal framework by clear, comprehensive, implementable, and reviewable rules concerning, for example, air, soil, biodiversity, and water quality standards.

Sustainable development as a guiding concept for international law does not and cannot (necessarily and under all circumstances) mean giving equal weight to all (economic, social) concerns. Sustainable development is eventually about making compromises. But these compromises have to be sustainable

[33] An ecosystem is a dynamic complex of plant, animal, and micro-organism communities and the non-living environment interacting as a functional unit.

[34] WCED, 'Our Common Future', 44–5.

[35] 'World Remains on Unsustainable Track Despite Hundreds of Internationally Agreed Goals and Objectives', UNEP New Centre, 6 June 2012, http://www.unep.org/newscentre/default.aspx?DocumentID=2688&ArticleID=9158 (accessed 10 Nov 2014).

[36] See Millennium Ecosystem Assessment, 'Living Beyond Our Means: Natural Assets and Human Well-Being' (March 2005), available at: http://www.maweb.org/en/index.aspx (accessed 10 Nov 2014); J. Rockström et al., 'Planetary Boundaries: Exploring the Safe Operating Space for Humanity', *Ecology and Society* 14 (2009), 32.

and—even more crucially—the *sum* of the compromises has to be sustainable. Because it will be the *sum* of all measures that gives an indication of their sustainability.

By constituting these essential ecological conditions as a *de minimis* requirement of sustainable development, the concept inhabits a non-derogable ecological core. At this core lie the 'unchanging and universal laws of nature' with which human activities need to be brought into and kept in harmony.[37] This core must be used as a point of departure and a '*principled priority*' guide on how otherwise widely divergent priorities relate to each other. Thus, when integrating the components of sustainable development, priority must be given to protecting fundamental, natural life-supporting systems in principle and in practice. This aspect of sustainable development is the most fundamental—the one without which the concept becomes indeterminate and eventually meaningless.

There has developed over the three decades an understanding and increasing appreciation that environmental degradation undermines peace. It is also ever clearer that the nexus between development and environmental protection in the context of sustainable development must be strengthened if peace is to be maintained or achieved.

'Exploitation of the Earth's resources', Judge Weeramantry noted,

> without regard to the future and the destruction of the environment are among the principal contemporary causes of global tension. Herein lie the seeds of future conflicts and sustainable development is an insurance against those conflicts and possibly wars of the future. ... True peace is impossible without justice. A principal element of justice is economic justice. Economic justice is impossible without sustainable development. Sustainable development is thus an important prerequisite of peace. If peace is an indispensable object of international law, sustainable development is indispensable to the attainment by international law of its most important goal.[38]

The relationship between peace and sustainable development is thus one of mutual dependence: unsustainable development drives conflict, while conflict makes sustainable development impossible.[39] It is in this understanding that the World Commission on Environment and Development summarized clearly in its final report 'Our Common Future', 'Certain aspects of the issues of peace and security bear directly upon the concept of sustainable development. Indeed, they are central to it.'[40]

[37] This is what the WCED noted early on: 'Human laws must be reformulated to keep human activities in harmony with the unchanging and universal laws of nature.' WCED, 'Our Common Future', 330.

[38] Christopher Weeramantry, *Universalising International Law* (Leiden: Martinus Nijhoff, 2004), 446. See also Christopher Weeramantry and John Burroughs, *International Law and Peace: A Peace Lesson,* A web-based part of Hague Appeal for Peace, Peace Lessons from Around the World, http://lcnp.org/global/Law_and_Peace.pdf (accessed 10 Nov 2014).

[39] Onita Das, *Environmental Protection, Security and Armed Conflict, A Sustainable Development Perspective* (Cheltenham: Edward Elgar, 2013).

[40] WCED, 'Our Common Future', 290.

4. International Environmental Law and Peaceful Cooperation

Law is a governing instrument for the international community of states. It is an approach to overcome anarchy and chaos—both on the national and international level. International law's main purpose was—and is—to achieve peace between states in an attempt to tame their absolute sovereignty which includes the use of force as an inherent component.

The collective pressure that states currently put on natural resources and ecological systems is starting to exceed—and partly already exceeding—ecological thresholds.[41] This development raises inconvenient questions as to the sustainability of the current economic and political model pursued by most states. It has become clear that significant political and legal interventions are necessary to realign development with the limits set by those thresholds.

Modern international law has to deal with a far wider variety of challenges than those deriving exclusively from forcible intervention in the affairs of other states. Various pressures of a modern, globalized world are forcing the international community of states (as the 'legislators' of international law) to think anew and recognize a more collectively oriented international legal system; socially oriented in the sense of recognizing international actors in their capacity to act in concert for the 'common good of all'. Global environmental threats, such as ozone depletion, global climate change, loss of biodiversity, and advancing desertification damage not only individual states, but the world at large. Pollution knows no national boundaries, nor does the problem of a changing global climate. The impact of climate change on the stability of the global community is expected to be dire. The challenges facing international law to construct equitable and cooperative global responses to shared problems are already tangible.[42]

Principles are abounding in international environmental law that aim to protect and preserve both common and states' environmental interests based on equity and fairness. These include, for example, the prohibition of significant environmental harm to the territory of other states or of areas beyond national jurisdiction,[43] the principle of sustainable development,[44] the principle of common but

[41] See OECD, 'OECD Environmental Outlook to 2050: The Consequences of Inaction' (March 2012), http://www.oecd.org/environment/indicators-modelling-outlooks/oecdenvironmentaloutlookto2050 theconsequencesofinaction.htm (accessed 10 Nov 2014); UNEP, Global Environmental Outlook 5, http://www.unep.org/geo/geo5.asp (accessed 10 Nov 2014); Millennium Ecosystem Assessment 2005, and Rockström et al., 'Planetary Boundaries', 32.

[42] See X. Wang, 'Sustainable International Climate Change Law: A Future Legal Research Agenda', in *Sustainable Development Law: Principles, Practices and Prospects*, Marie-Claire Cordonier Segger and Ashfaq Khalfan (eds.) (New York: Oxford University Press, 2004), 353–4.

[43] 'Report of the United Nations Conference on the Human Environment' (Stockholm Declaration), Stockholm (5–16 June 1972), UN Doc. A/CONF.48/14/Rev.1, principle 21; Rio Declaration, principle 2. The ICJ in its *Advisory Opinion in the Legality of the Threat or Use of Nuclear Weapons*, stated: 'The existence of the general obligation of States to ensure that activities within their jurisdiction and control respect the environment of other States or of areas beyond national control is now part of the corpus of international law relating to the environment.' (1995) ICJ reports 347.

[44] Voigt, *Sustainable Development as a Principle of International Law.*

differentiated responsibility and respective capabilities, the principle of common heritage of mankind,[45] the precautionary principle that deals with decision-making in the face of scientific uncertainty as well as the principle that indicates that the costs of pollution should be borne by the person, state, or company responsible for causing the pollution.[46]

Moreover, issues of universal importance such as conservation of biological diversity, mitigation of dangerous anthropogenic climate change, and transboundary movement of hazardous substances are nowadays subject to a large number of multilateral environmental agreements. Their own institutions, reporting requirements, exchange of information, and regular meetings of the parties enhance cooperation. Those states who collaborate to draft common plans for the management of natural resources, a joint framework based on substantive obligation and finance obligations in accordance with the principle of common but differentiated responsibility and respective capabilities, who rely on the procedures in place to address non-compliance and disputes should they arise, have all taken necessary safeguards to prevent and peacefully settle conflicts.[47] It is for these reasons that the United Nations Environment Programme (UNEP) is engaged in environmental cooperation for peace-building (ECP); noting on their website: 'UNEP aims to use environmental cooperation to transform the risks of conflict over resources into opportunities for stability and peacebuilding in war-torn or fragile societies.'[48]

The cooperation needed, in particular to tackle the climate change challenge, is, in Judge Weeramantry's words, 'not merely passive cooperation, but rather active cooperation. If we are to save our global inheritance, we must do so actively. We need, for this purpose, to be willing to surrender some part of sovereignty to the rest of the world, accepting common guidance by the global community.'[49] In this globalized and interdependent world, the recognition has therefore grown that states need to cooperate—to actively engage with each other—to stand a chance of addressing global challenges of an unprecedented nature.

For enhancing international laws potentially conducive to peace, legal regimes are necessary that support sustainable resource management, a high degree of environmental and human rights protection, and the building of markets for sustainable, conflict-free goods—and trestriction of markets for those that are not. Sustainable development requires a transformation in the way in which economic development is pursued. It requires first and foremost, that economic activities be guided by ecological boundaries. Its central premise is that human activity must

[45] P. Taylor, 'Common Heritage of Mankind Principle', in *Berkshire Encyclopaedia of Sustainability*, iii. *The Law and Politics of Sustainability*, Klaus Bosselmann, Daniel Fogel, and J. B. Ruhl (eds.) (Great Barrington: Berkshire, 2011), 64–9.

[46] See Sumudu A. Attapattu, *Emerging Principles of International Environmental Law* (Leiden: Martinus Nijhoff, 2006); Nicolas de Sadeleer, *Environmental Principles: From Political Slogans to Legal Rules* (New York: Oxford University Press, 2005).

[47] Matz-Lueck, 'The Benefits of Positivism', 137.

[48] 'Disaster and Conflicts', UNEP, http://www.unep.org/disastersandconflicts/Introduction/ECP/tabid/105948/Default.aspx (accessed 16 June 2014).

[49] Segger and Khalfan, *Sustainable Development Law*, p. xi.

not exceed the carrying capacity of planetary ecosystems. This premise needs to be reflected in the law.

5. Climate Change and Peaceful Cooperation for Sustainable Development: The Example of the UN Climate Change Regime

Can cooperation with the purpose of sustainable development render violent conflict less likely?[50] Much more research might be necessary to give a conclusive answer to this question. We will nevertheless attempt to sketch out one area of international law where a relationship between cooperation and mutual dependence is emerging: the international regime for addressing climate change.

From the outset we can state that not just cooperation per se is important as a factor for peace. Depending on the resource or environmental issue at stake, the form and content of cooperation might differ. The closer and more 'interdependent' the cooperation between states is, the greater might be the potential for positive side effects from that cooperation that can create positive synergies for peace.

5.1. Means of cooperation

Cooperation between states flows from the principle of 'good-neighbourliness' as included in Article 74 of the UN Charter. Together with the prohibition of significant transboundary harm—based on the maxim *sic utere tuo at alienum non laedas*—good neighbourliness in environmental matters has led to the development and application of rules promoting international environmental cooperation.[51] The principle of environmental cooperation is reflected in principle 24 of the Stockholm Declaration as a general political commitment and in principle 27 of the Rio Declaration stating that 'States and people shall co-operate in good faith and in a spirit of partnership in the fulfilment of the principles embodied in this Declaration and in further development of international law in the field of sustainable development.' Since then, the principle is reflected in many treaties and is supported by state practice.[52]

The principle of environmental cooperation is affirmed in virtually all international environmental agreements.[53] The general obligation to cooperate has been translated into more specific techniques to ensure the sharing of information and participation in decision-making. Exchange of information, notification,

[50] Segger and Khalfan, *Sustainable Development Law*, 9.

[51] Philippe Sands and Jacqueline Peel, *Principles of International Environmental Law* (3rd edn. Cambridge: Cambridge University Press, 2012), 203.

[52] Sands and Peel, *Principles of International Environmental Law*, 203.

[53] See 1982 United Nations Convention on the Law of the Sea (UNCLOS), Arts. 123 and 197; 1991 Alpine Convention, Art. 2(1); 1985 Vienna Convention on the Protection of the Ozone Layer, Art. 2(2); 1992 Convention on Biological Diversity, Art. 5.

consultation, and other forms of cooperation are examples of the implementation of the obligation of environmental cooperation. More specific cooperation commitments include rules on transboundary environmental impact assessments,[54] rules that ensure that neighbouring states or states importing hazardous substances receive all necessary information through required information exchange, consultation, and notification, and that there is the option to ban such imports,[55] and also rules on the provision of emergency information, and the transboundary enforcement of environmental standards.

State practice on environmental cooperation is further reflected in the decisions and awards of international courts and tribunals, including, for example, the *Lac Lanoux* case,[56] the *MOX plant* case,[57] the *Gabcikovo-Nagymaros project* case, and the *Pulp Mills* case.[58]

In international environmental law, cooperation is thus a central principle in order to prevent disputes, to provide timely notification of plans to carry out or permit activities that may entail transboundary or international interference or environmental harm, or a significant risk thereof, and to engage in good faith consultations to arrive at a fair and equitable resolution of the situation.

5.2. Cooperation in the international climate regime

5.2.1. Climate change and conflict

A very opportune example of international cooperation is the UN climate regime. Mitigation of and adaptation to climate change are very urgent issues, which if not tackled might have severe security implications.[59]

Without resolute counteraction, the effects of climate change are likely to exceed many societies' adaptive capacities to internal or external stresses within the coming decades. If not halted, the likelihood sharply increases that climate change will draw ever deeper lines of division and conflict in international relations as well as in national affairs. It has the potential to trigger numerous conflicts between and within countries over the distribution of resources (especially water and land), over the management of migration, or over compensation payments between the countries mainly responsible for climate change and those countries most affected by its destructive effects.[60]

[54] Convention on Environmental Impact Assessment in a Transboundary Context (Espoo, 1991).

[55] See the advanced informed agreement procedure in Art. 6 of the Cartagena Protocol on Biosafety to the Convention on Biological Diversity (Montreal, 2000).

[56] *Lac Lanoux arbitration (France* v. *Spain)* (1957) 24 ILR 101.

[57] *The MOX Plant case (Ireland* v. *United Kingdom)* (Interim Measure) (2002) 41 ILM 405.

[58] *Gabcikovo-Nagymaros (Hungary* v. *Slovakia)* [1999] ICJ Reports 7; *Pulp Mills on the River Uruguay (Argentina* v. *Uruguay)* (Judgment) [2010] ICJ Rep 2010 p. 14.

[59] Christina Voigt, 'Security in a "Warming World": Competences of the UN Security Council for Preventing Dangerous Climate Change', in *Security: A Multidisciplinary Normative Approach*, Cecilia M. Bailliet (ed.) (Leiden: Brill, 2009), 291–312.

[60] German Advisory Council on Global Change (WGBU), *World in Transition: Climate Change as a Security Risk* (London: Earthscan, 2007), 23.

If, by 2020, political efforts to limit temperature increases to 2°C have failed, the international community must prepare itself to deal with climate-related conflicts. If this temperature threshold is crossed, the likelihood of conflicts increases significantly. Such conflicts include disputes over resources (based on reduction of arable land, widespread shortage of freshwater, diminishing food and fish stocks, increased flooding and prolonged droughts) and over loss of territory, border clashes,[61] situations of fragility and increasing instability in weak or failing states, and tensions over energy supply.[62] The Intergovernmental Panel on Climate Change (IPCC) warns in its most recent report that climate change over the twenty-first century will have a significant impact on forms of migration that compromise human security. For example, it indirectly increases the risks from violent conflict in the form of civil war, inter-group violence, and violent protests by exacerbating well-established drivers of these conflicts such as poverty and economic shocks. A warming climate will place the world under enormous strain, forcing mass migration, especially in Asia, and thereby increasing the risk of violent conflict.[63]

Small island states and other places highly vulnerable to sea-level rise face major challenges to their territorial integrity. Some 'transboundary' impacts of climate change, such as changes in sea ice, shared water resources, and migration of fish stocks have the potential to increase rivalry among states.[64]

The High-level Panel on Threats, Challenges, and Change noted climate change as one of the global threats to security. The panel stated,

> In order to address problems of climate change modern economies need to reduce their dependence on hydrocarbons and should undertake a special effort to devise climate-friendly development strategies. Member States should place special attention on the development of low-carbon energy sources, including natural gas renewable power and nuclear power, and should place special emphasis on the development of low-greenhouse-gas technologies … States should provide incentives for the further development of renewable energy sources and begin to phase out environmentally harmful subsidies, especially for fossil fuel use and development.[65]

[61] In this context, the High Representative and the European Commission to the European Council note: 'Scientists project major changes to the landmass during this century. Receding coastlines and submergence of large areas could result in loss of territory, including entire countries such as small island states. More disputes over land and maritime borders and other territorial rights are likely. There might be a need to revisit existing rules of international law, particularly the Law of the Sea, as regards the resolution of territorial and border disputes. A further dimension of competition for energy resources lies in potential conflict over resources in Polar Regions which will become exploitable as a consequence of global warming. Desertification could trigger a vicious circle of degradation, migration and conflicts over territory and borders that threatens the political stability of countries and regions.' 'Climate Change and International Security', Paper from the High Representative and the European Commission to the European Council, S113/08 (14 March 2007), 4.

[62] 'Climate Change and International Security', 2–5.

[63] See Tom Bawden, 'Official prophecy of doom: Global warming will cause widespread conflict, displace millions of people and devastate the global economy', *The Independent*, 18 March 2014, http://www.independent.co.uk/environment/climate-change/official-prophecy-of-doom-global-warming-will-cause-widespread-conflict-displace-millions-of-people-and-devastate-the-global-economy-9198171.html (accessed 16 June 2014). A draft of the final version of the IPCC report was leaked to the magazine.

[64] Bawden, 'Official prophecy of doom'.

[65] Report of the High-level Panel on Threats, Challenges and Change, 'A More Secure World', 99.

However, there remains a certain degree of uncertainty as to the exact impacts of climate change on the local levels. The simple fact is that nobody really knows with any degree of precision what climate change will mean for human population movement and distribution.[66] This is unsurprising; the science of climate change is complicated. In addition, the interconnections between environmental conditions, societies with widely differing resources and varied capacities to adapt to external shocks, and the resulting conflict potential add a high degree of complexity. In the absence of absolute scientific certainty about the social and political impacts of climate change, the phenomenon is best viewed as a threat multiplier which exacerbates existing trends, tensions, and instability. In any event, preventing dangerous climate change means reducing the likelihood of climate-related individual and international security threats. Therefore, a pro-active climate protection policy must be in place with the aim of significantly reducing greenhouse gas emissions in order to keep global warming as close to the 2°C limit as possible. At the same time, strategies for adaptation to unavoidable climate change must be intensified and oriented towards the type of climate impact scenario that can be expected. The greater the delay in commencing efforts to mitigate climate change and to adapt to its impacts, the more expensive such efforts will become. Development that leads to missed opportunities to protect the climate will entail far higher costs—including instability and conflicts—than a reference scenario in which compliance with the 2°C target is achieved.[67]

5.2.2. Climate change and development cooperation

At its core, climate change regime is in reality a 'development regime': the effective reduction of greenhouse gas emissions requires transformative changes of (all) economies. This is only possible if development plans are aligned with the scientific limits set to remain within global temperature increases of 2°C. Greenhouse gas emissions come from all economic sectors. Whole sectors, whole economies need to be transformed to become low-carbon intensive or even carbon-neutral. The climate change regime will significantly define the development path of all its member states.

However, not all states have contributed equally to the problem of the increasing greenhouse gas concentrations in the atmosphere, nor do they possess the same means and capacities to address the reduction of greenhouse gas emissions or to adapt to the effects of climate change. While some states may have contributed minimally to the problem, they may become more seriously affected than others. For that reason it is imperative to cooperate across the board on finding a fair and effective way of burden-sharing and differentiating between states' obligations

[66] Report of the High-level Panel on Threats, Challenges and Change, 'A More Secure World', 99.

[67] The National Archives, HM Treasury, 'Stern Review on the Economics of Climate Change', 2006, http://webarchive.nationalarchives.gov.uk/20130129110402/ http://www.hm-treasury.gov.uk/stern_review_report.htm (accessed 16 June 2014).

and entitlements.[68] It is for this reason that the UN Framework Convention calls for the 'widest possible cooperation by all countries and their participation in an effective and appropriate international response, in accordance with their common but differentiated responsibilities and respective capabilities and their social and economic conditions'.[69]

5.2.3. The issue of global equity

The design of an equitable international climate response poses a paramount challenge to the traditional structure of public international law, which is based on the sovereign *equality* of states. States are supposed to be treated equally: as a starting point the same rights and duties apply to all. There is, however, growing understanding that in order to achieve equal treatment of states, their differences must be taken into account. Differentiation and positive discrimination (e.g. through affirmative action) is necessary in order to treat states that are different on an equal basis.

An equitable approach to the climate challenge is often understood as an approach based on the principle of common but differentiated responsibility and respective capabilities (CBDRRC) as mentioned in Article 3 UNFCCC, which says that 'parties should act to protect the climate system on the basis of equity and in accordance with their common but differentiated responsibilities and respective capabilities'.

This principle has so far mainly been used by major developing countries as an argument for demanding from developed countries an acknowledgement of their historic contributions to the increased concentration of greenhouse gases in the atmosphere and to act responsibly by taking the lead in climate mitigation and finance.[70] The other side of this argument is that developing countries—having historically contributed marginally to the current concentrations—should not be required to take on mandatory commitments to reduce their GHG emissions. Accordingly, differentiation has so far been along the dividing line of 'developed' and 'developing' states and according to historical contributions of developed countries to environmental degradation, as well as the capability of developed countries to engage in cost-intensive environmental mitigation action. These factors (criteria) have led to substantively stronger obligations of developed countries, with developing countries having milder or no obligations as well as entitlements to significant financial transfers and the contribution ofof capacity, technology, and know-how from developed countries. Based on these criteria, 'positive discrimination' in favour of developing countries has led to highly

[68] See Geir Ulfstein and Christina Voigt, 'Rethinking the Legal Form and Architecture of a New Climate Agreement', in *Toward a New Climate Agreement: Conflict, Resolution and Governance*, Todd L. Cherry, Jon Hovi, and David M. McEvoy (eds.) (London: Routledge, 2014), 183–98.

[69] United Nations Framework Convention on Climate Change (UNFCCC), UN 1992, preamble, item 6., See also Art. 3, para. 1; Art. 4 paras. 2(a) and 7.

[70] UNFCCC, Arts. 3, 4.2, and 4.7.

asymmetric environmental obligations coupled with mechanisms for capacity building and the transfer of financial resources and technology as well as compliance assistance.

However, the world today is characterized by disparities in resources and capabilities in different ways than applied 30 years ago. The antagonistic dividing line between developed and developing countries is becoming increasingly blurred. Each of the two groups, if they can be identified at all,[71] is no longer homogenous but marked by stark internal differences. In addition, the international landscape undergoes changes and fluctuations. Any attempt at categorization might be insufficient to capture such dynamism. Some developing countries that were marginally contributing to the climate challenge in 1992, count nowadays among the top global polluters. For that reason there need to be more differentiation[72] and differentiation should be flexible and dynamic and only granted on a temporary basis.

The question is thus how to reflect the different 'situations' of states and their dynamic development in the new agreement. The change in the world between 1992 and 2014 and beyond tells us that such differentiation cannot be static; it must be based on dynamic and flexible parameters that allow the structure of the agreement to evolve as the world evolves. Such a solution can be found only through negotiations and cooperation.

While so far, only one particular interpretation of the CBDRRC principle (i.e. differentiation based on historic contributions) has dominated the climate negotiations, the time has come for more countries to put forward their (evolved) understanding of that principle. A number of countries have recently come forward with their understanding that the CBDRRC principle is reflective of certain dynamism in the climate regime as it is not set in stone, but evolves over time. In the ongoing climate negotiations, many Parties therefore observed 'that the principles [of the Convention] are not rigid, and should be applied in a dynamic and evolving manner taking into account national circumstances, changing economic realities and levels of development.'[73] 'Principles ... need to be forward-looking and take into account what the world might look like in 2020.'[74] Some Parties stated also that the application of the Convention 'should be adapted in order to improve its vitality and relevance in the modern world and in order to enable it to become a modern instrument to address climate change. It was pointed out that

[71] According to the United Nations Statistics Division, 'There is no established convention for the designation of "developed" and "developing" countries or areas in the United Nations system.' See 'Composition of macro geographical (continental) regions, geographical sub-regions, and selected economic and other groupings', UNSD (n.C), revised 31 October 2013, http://unstats.un.org/unsd/methods/m49/m49regin.htm#ftnc (accessed 16 June 2014).

[72] See also Joost Pauwelyn, 'The End of Differential Treatment for Developing Countries? Lessons from the Trade and Climate Regimes', *RECIEL* 22 (2013), 29–41, who argues for more differentiation and further subdivisions.

[73] 'Summary of the Roundtable under Workstream 1, ADP1, part 2, Doha, Qatar, November–December 2012', Ad Hoc Working Group on the Durban Platform for Enhanced Action, Note by the Co-Chairs (7 February 2013), 3, http://unfccc.int/resource/docs/2012/adp1/eng/6infsum.pdf (accessed 10 Nov 2014).

[74] 'Summary of the Roundtable under Workstream 1', 3.

the Convention has evolved, and will continue to evolve over time, and thus the manner in which the principles apply also needs to evolve.'[75]

Yet, finding reliable but flexible and dynamic criteria or means to defining various (groups of) 'equals', and allocating rights and responsibilities accordingly, is a task where countries need to talk to each other and to cooperate, and such cooperation, for as long as it lasts, may prevent them from engaging in rivalry against each other.

5.2.4. Cooperation and the example of REDD+

One particular area where the climate negotiations have advanced significantly is the protection of forests in developing countries for the purpose of reducing emissions from deforestation and forest degradation. Tropical timber has for a long time been a commodity on which income-poor countries depended, but which also has fuelled countless conflicts.

No global agreement protects tropical forests or regulates forestry and the timber trade. In the absence of an international agreement, the inclusion of policy approaches and positive incentives on issues relating to reducing emissions from deforestation and forest degradation in developing countries (REDD+)[76] in the UNFCCC regime is a significant step forward.

Under the UNFCCC, REDD+ has the purpose of simultaneously addressing the interlinked issues of sustainable resource exploitation of timber, reducing emissions from deforestation and forest degradation (i.e. slowing, halting and reversing forest cover and carbon loss), generating financial flows from developed countries to developing countries that implement REDD-policies, and building sustainable governance frameworks through participatory requirements for all affected stakeholders, in particular indigenous peoples and local communities.[77] REDD-activities in developing countries shall be implemented in the context of sustainable development and be reducing poverty, while responding to climate change. Moreover, REDD-activities shall be undertaken in the context of transparent and effective national forest governance structures and shall respect the knowledge and rights of indigenous peoples and members of local communities.[78] These (and other) elements of REDD+ are referred to as 'safeguards'. It is also important to note, that only such REDD-activities will be financially rewarded, where the forest-owning country provides the most recent summary of information on how all the safeguards have been addressed and respected before it can receive results-based payments.[79]

[75] 'Summary of the Roundtable under Workstream 1', 3.

[76] See 'Report of the Conference of the Parties on its thirteenth session, held in Bali from 3 to 15 December 2007', Framework Convention on Climate Change, 14 March 2008, FCCC/CP/2007/6/Add.1, Decision 1/CP.13 Bali Action Plan, which also includes the role of conservation, sustainable management of forests, and enhancement of forest carbon stocks in developing countries in the scope of REDD+.

[77] See Decision 1/CP.16, paras. 71 and 72 and Annex I.

[78] Decision 1/CP.16, Annex I, 2 (c).

[79] Decision 9/CP.19 Work programme on results-based finance to progress the full implementation of the activities referred to in decision 1/CP.16, paragraph 70, para. 4.

The international framework has be designed with great care, taking into account the power imbalances in the forest sector, unsecured tenure, commercial drivers of deforestation, and conflicts over access to forests and their use and exploitation. If implemented accordingly, REDD+ has a great potential to strengthen the rights of marginalized groups, such as forest-dependent dwellers and indigenous groups. Further, it has the potential to channel financial resources and development support to needy parts of the population.

However, REDD+ strategies are challenging in their complex nature. For this reason, it is important to design and implement REDD policies very carefully. A recent study stated:

> Forest resource based conflict is one of the issues of great concern in the recent days. People everywhere compete for forest resources they need to survive as they are highly dependent on these resources. Forest is now not limited into the boundary of a country, rather it is now become a matter of international concern because of its role play as climate change mitigation and adaptation. Therefore conflict in forest resource management is not a matter of national, but also become a matter of international community. Timely response of the voices of forest dependent communities is vital to minimize any future risk.'[80]

A number of studies point to important implications with regards to REDD+ implementation and conflict management that can be useful for policymakers and practitioners involved in REDD+ strategy designs, as well as other areas of forest management involving outsiders and communities.[81] If implemented carefully and in accordance with the international framework and guidance, REDD+ activities can help to reduce the potential for conflicts and to provide resources for basic needs and create necessary social and economic infrastructures. REDD+ requires good governance, respect for the rule of law and basic human rights, and effective as well as participatory and uncorrupted governance structures.

Having countries cooperating and negotiating the international legal framework for the sustainable management of their forest resources might be one important way to stabilize peaceful situations.

[80] Such conflicts could involve: Conflict between community forests and free bounded labour, forest land encroachment, boundary conflicts, conflict among the communities' members who collect forest products from the state-owned forest, state–community conflict; see Dharam Raj Uprety, Harisharan Luintel, and Kamal Bhandari, *REDD+ and Conflict: A Case Study of the REDD+ Projects in Nepal* (The Centre for People and Forest, July 2011), http://www.forestaction.org/app/webroot/js/tinymce/editor/plugins/filemanager/files/REDD-conflict_Report%20 Dharam.pdf (accessed 28 January 2014). The authors noted: 'There could be several issues which could be potential risk factors to the forest dependent communities such as elite capture on benefits, potential loss of access to forest land, and lack of a system to take voices of poor in decision making,' 26.

[81] Toral Patel et al., 'Predicting Future Conflict under REDD+ Implementation', *Forests* 4 (10 May 2013), 343–63.

6. Conclusions

Environmental cooperation can help build peace.[82] Environmental cooperation does not—per se—cause peace, but there are useful catalytic roles for environmental law cooperation and in peacemaking—moving along the 'peace continuum'—ranging from the absence of violent conflict to the unimaginability of violent conflict. Specific forms of cooperation are designed to build the habit of cooperation, transform interstate bargaining dynamics, and deepen peaceful trans-societal linkages conducive to peaceful cooperation.[83]

Not all environmental cooperation is conducive to peace: the type of cooperation is important. Sustainability remains an important part of the foundation for a lasting peace, therefore environmental cooperation that facilitates more aggressive resource exploitation or continued patterns of unsustainable resource use is problematic. Short-term profits generated by unsustainable resource use may extrapolate political tensions—and may lead to even stronger conflicts in the longer run. Rather, cooperation needs to aim at sustainable resource management and the protection of life-saving ecological functions. The example of the international climate regime and the particular aspect of REDD+ shows the potential and possibilities of aligning environmental protection and development.

International environmental agreements that are based on sustainable development and equitable allocation of costs and benefits, where environmental commitments are aligned with financial and technology transfer entitlement of those countries that do not dispose of sufficient capacities themselves, may help increase acceptance for such policies among a greater circle of countries.

What is needed, however, is a clear strategy for eco-sensitive sustainable development law in the context of law for peace. An in-depth look at the different ways in which sustainable development can aid in the process of peace construction, however, is still needed.

Sustainable development, if achieved, contributes decisively to the dissipation, if not the elimination, of several of the primary causes of conflict. If a sustainable development strategy and law has been successful in terms of the reduction of poverty, the levelling of social inequalities, and the optimum allocation of scarce resources, all while respecting ecological boundaries that are set by life-sustaining ecological functions, then certainly many of the situations that exacerbate conflict between different groups, communities, and nationalities will be avoided. Improving the conditions for environmental and social justice in particular is fundamental to the promotion of peace in a variety of contexts throughout the world.

[82] For empirical evidence see Ken Conca and Geoffrey D. Dabelko (eds.), *Environmental Peacemaking* (Baltimore: Johns Hopkins University Press, 2002).

[83] Conca and Dabelko (eds.), 'The Problems and Possibilities of Environmental Peacemaking', 230.

The role of sustainable development is crucial in devising strategies for peace. As Conca aptly noted: 'Creating trust, reciprocity, transparency, cooperative knowledge, shared gains, and habits of cooperation among such entities might simply yield more than just the plundering of resources.'[84] Only if the state is an instrument of genuinely sustainable development, rooted in environmental and social justice, will improving and stabilizing interstate dynamics be likely to transform situations of insecurity. International law can help to nudge states towards a more sustainable, more peaceful future.

[84] Conca and Dabelko (eds.), *Environmental Peacemaking*, 11.

10

World Peace through World Trade? The Role of Dispute Settlement in the WTO

Ole Kristian Fauchald

Many wars have been waged over trade and commercial interests. Slowly, the world is inching towards a peaceful settlement of such issues. The dispute settlement mechanism of the WTO is not only an efficient avenue for Members in solving trade disputes, it is also a significant achievement in the global impetus towards peace and prosperity.

Julio Lacarte-Muró and Petina Gappah[1]

'High policy disputes' [are] to be prevented and settled through political negotiations.

Ernst-Ulrich Petersmann[2]

1. Introduction

The relationship between trade and peace is among the oldest and most fundamental topics of human societies.[3] The traditional political wisdom among Western liberalists has been that trade promotes peace and that peace promotes trade; therefore international agreements that facilitate international trade also promote and are the result of peaceful coexistence among states.[4] However, this

[1] Julio Lacarte-Muró and Petina Gappah, 'Developing Countries and the WTO Legal and Dispute Settlement System: A View from the Bench', *Journal of International Economic Law* 3 (2000), 401.

[2] Ernst-Ulrich Petersmann, 'Justice as Conflict Resolution: Proliferation, Fragmentation, and Decentralization of Dispute Settlement in International Trade', *University of Pennsylvania Journal of International Law* 27 (2006), 344.

[3] Antonio F. Perez, 'Traditional Paradigms for the Causes of War Applied to the International Trading System: Nation-State Institutions in a World of Market States', *Studies in Transnational Legal Policy* 37 (2005), 178.

[4] See Tomer Broude, 'Between Pax Mercatoria and Pax Europea: How Trade Dispute Procedures Serve the EC's Regional Hegemony', *Studies in Transnational Legal Policy* 37 (2005), 48: 'the proposition that increased international trade and economic interdependence promotes peaceful international relations—has pervaded liberal thinking for centuries, and is one of the fundamentals of Kantian peace theory'. See also Katherine Barbieri, *The Liberal Illusion: Does Trade Promote Peace?* (Ann Arbor: University of Michigan Press, 2002); Håvard Hegre, John R. Oneal, and Bruce

wisdom has been questioned from the viewpoints of both theoretical perspectives and empirical research.[5]

This chapter will focus on one aspect of this broader topic; whether and how the dispute settlement mechanism (DSM) of the WTO relates to peace. Among legal scholars, the dispute settlement regime has been hailed as being among the most successful and innovative aspect of the WTO Agreement. Its success is measured in terms of the number of cases, the extent of compliance with decisions, and its ability to bring important trade issues from the realm of contested politics to the realm of law.[6] It is thus of particular interest to look more closely at how this element of the WTO relates to peace.

Trade disputes adjudicated under GATT 1947 and the WTO have never involved states that were at war. Indeed, according to article XXI of GATT, article XIVbis of GATS and article 73 of the TRIPS Agreement:

> Nothing in this Agreement shall be construed ... (b) to prevent any contracting party from taking any action which it considers necessary for the protection of its essential security interests ... (iii) taken in time of war or other emergency in international relations; or (c) to prevent any contracting party from taking any action in pursuance of its obligations under the United Nations Charter for the maintenance of international peace and security.[7]

Hence, international trade commitments are generally suspended in times of armed conflict.[8] Moreover, unilateral trade sanctions adopted in situations of

Russett, 'Trade Does Promote Peace: New Simultaneous Estimates of the Reciprocal Effects of Trade and Conflict', *Journal of Peace Research* 47 (2010), 763–74; Mónika García-Salmones, 'Walther Schücking and the Pacifist Traditions of International Law', *European Journal of International Law* 22 (2011), 773–4, and Koen Stapelbroek, 'The Rights of Neutral Trade and its Forgotten History', *COLLeGIUM: Studies across Disciplines in the Humanities and Social Sciences* 10 (2011), 4, 7.

[5] Theoretical perspectives: e.g. E. van de Haar, 'The Liberal Divide over Trade, Peace and War', *International Relations* 24 (2010), 135–46. Empirical perspectives: on the effects of trade flows on peace prospects: Quan Li and R. Reuveny, 'Does Trade Prevent or Promote Interstate Conflict Initiation?', *Journal of Peace Research* 48 (2011), 437–53. For a combination, see Barbieri, *The Liberal Illusion*, and Padideh Ala'i, Tomer Broude, and Colin Picker (eds.), 'Trade as Guarantor of Peace, Liberty and Security? Critical, Empirical and Historical Perspectives', *Studies in Transnational Legal Policy* 37 (Washington, DC: ASIL, 2005).

[6] See John H. Jackson, 'Reflections on the Trade & Peace Relationship', *Studies in Transnational Legal Policy* 37 (2005), 29, and Petersmann, 'Justice as Conflict Resolution', 276.

[7] In GATS and TRIPS the term 'Member' replaces 'contracting parties'. See also Art. XXIII:1 of the Agreement on Government Procurement: 'Nothing in this Agreement shall be construed to prevent any Party from taking any action or not disclosing any information which it considers necessary for the protection of its essential security interests relating to the procurement of arms, ammunition or war materials, or to procurement indispensable for national security or for national defence purposes.' See Krista Nadakavukaren Schefer, *Social Regulation in the WTO: Trade Policy and International Legal Development* (Cheltenham: Edward Elgar, 2010), 123–6, and Hannes L. Schloemann and Stefan Ohlhoff, '"Constitutionalization" and Dispute Settlement in the WTO: National Security as an Issue of Competence', *American Journal of International Law* 93 (1999), 424.

[8] Even if the freedom to take trade measures in emergency situations has not been explicitly regulated in the WTO Agreement or most of the agreements in its Annexe 1A, we may assume that similar exceptions apply. The General Interpretative Note to Annexe 1A of the WTO Agreement states: 'In the event of conflict between a provision of the General Agreement on Tariffs and Trade 1994 and a provision of another agreement in Annex 1A to the Agreement Establishing the World Trade Organization ... the provision of the other agreement shall prevail to the extent of the conflict.'

'emergency in international relations' have gained in significance partly as a consequence of the outlawing of the unilateral use of force in Article 2(4) of the UN Charter.[9] Against this background, this chapter will not study the role of the DSM in times of armed conflict. It will focus on prevention of armed conflicts both between and within countries, and study whether and how the DSM affects the level and character of conflicts and tensions between and within states.

While the interstate dimension of peace (with a focus on what in this book is referred to as 'negative peace') has been the main focus of studies of the general relationship between trade and peace, this chapter will mostly focus on 'positive peace'. The 'negative peace' analyses are related to effects of the DSM on the risk of armed conflict between and within countries. The relationship between trade and negative peace can be explored in terms of trade as a trigger of war (e.g. where a state is denied access to essential raw materials), trade as fuelling war (e.g. where insurgents trade narcotics in order to fund military activities), or as a precondition for war (e.g. trade in arms and related technologies to states that do not have weapons production capacity). Among these three fundamental aspects of the relationship between trade and negative peace, due to the exceptions discussed above, the WTO Agreement would be relevant to the first only. The DSM's relationship to 'negative peace' will thus essentially be explored by looking at whether and how it might reduce the risk of armed conflict.

The 'positive peace' analyses are related to the effects that the DSM may have on the level of 'structural violence', as related to social justice and satisfaction of human needs, within or among states. As will be explored in the following, disputes brought to the WTO may have significant links to domestic policy, and disputes are frequently brought on behalf of strong interest groups. For example, the results of disputes may play an important role in politically controversial cases as leverage for domestic policy reform. Trade disputes may also in the long run improve transparency and good governance within and among disputing states.

The first part of this chapter will explore some main elements of the relationship between trade and peace in order to contextualize more specific issues (Section 2). Thereafter follows a discussion of the general challenge of balancing the quest for a legitimate and effective DSM against the call for promoting its relevance to peace (Section 3). The underlying issue is that promoting the mechanism's relevance to peace would inherently mean that it would be allowed to play an important part in resolving politically sensitive disputes. Section 4 will proceed to

Hence, an argument can be made that the agreements in Annex 1A apply in times of armed conflict if they do not explicitly state otherwise. Art. 3 of the TRIMS Agreement states otherwise: 'All exceptions under GATT 1994 shall apply, as appropriate, to the provisions of this Agreement.' Similar provisions have been left out of the WTO Agreement and the other agreements of Annexe 1A. On the other hand, it can be argued that the provisions of GATT, GATS, and the TRIPS Agreement are reflecting general rules of international law, as contained in chapter V on 'circumstances precluding wrongfulness' of the International Law Commission's Draft Articles on Responsibility of States for Internationally Wrongful Acts. Moreover, it does not make good sense to apply the specific and technical agreements of Annex 1A in times of war while the more general obligations under GATT, GATS, the TRIPS Agreement, and the TRIMS Agreement are suspended.

[9] See Schefer, *Social Regulation in the WTO*, 27.

study how the DSM has been used in cases related to peace, as well as how it has dealt with broader issues that have or might be perceived to have a link to peace.

2. The Context

While the nineteenth century was marked by significant liberalization of international trade, such liberalization was often based on military or economic domination, which resulted in a number of 'unequal treaties', and on bilateral treaties.[10] It can be argued that such a basis for trade liberalization is likely to contribute to a range of problems, such as discrimination among trading partners, strengthening of the position of powerful actors, disempowerment of weak actors, increased inequality and social injustice within and among states, and increased opportunities for corrupt practices. It can thus be argued that the characteristics of international trade agreements were one factor contributing to World War I. But it is clear that other trade-related factors were also at play, including the effects of increased international trade on 'social relations among land, labour, and capital, disrupting relations that had become embedded in social hierarchies and in political power.'[11]

In the period between the two World Wars, there were significant initiatives to establish multilateral trade agreements. The most important of these, the International Convention for the Abolition of Import and Export Prohibitions and Restrictions, was endorsed by the League of Nations in 1927, but failed to enter into force.[12] One of the most significant contributions of the International Convention would have been to reduce the occurrence of discriminatory practices among states.[13] It can be argued that the failure of multilateral agreements to facilitate trade in this period was among the factors contributing to World War II.[14]

We may thus hypothesize that the establishment of a global agreement to facilitate international trade would contribute significantly to peaceful relations among states after World War II. GATT has been essential in controlling the proliferation and design of regional and bilateral treaties, and has established an elaborate system for consideration and recognition of such agreements on the basis of article XXIV of GATT (and subsequently article V of GATS). Many authors

[10] See Baron Boris Nolde, 'Droit et technique des traités de commerce', *Receuil des cours: Académie de droit international* (Paris: Librairie Hachette, 1924), iii. 291–462.

[11] Michael W. Doyle, *Liberal Peace. Selected Essays* (New York: Routledge, 2012), 169.

[12] See League of Nations Treaty Series, Vol. XCVII (1929–30), 391–432, and Wallace McClure, 'National Economic Independence in the Light of the International Economic Conference', *American Journal of International Law* 21 (1927), 668–84. Concerning the International Convention Relating to the Simplification of Customs Formalities of 1923, see John Howard Jackson, *World Trade and the Law of GATT: A Legal Analysis of the General Agreement on Tariffs and Trade* (Indianapolis: Bobbs–Merrill, 1969), 440–1.

[13] See Richard Carlton Snyder, *The Most-Favored-Nation Clause: An Analysis with Particular Reference to Recent Treaty Practice and Tariffs* (New York: King's Crown, 1948).

[14] For a general discussion of state interests as related to bilateralism and multilateralism, see Schefer, *Social Regulation in the WTO*, 12–17.

have warned against undermining GATT and the WTO through regional and bilateral trade agreements, and some have also suggested that such developments will 'aggravate tensions between nations instead of securing peace'.[15] But bilateral and regional trade agreements may also promote peaceful relations among states, as exemplified by the award of the Nobel Peace Prize to the European Union in 2012. Of particular interest to this article is the relationship between dispute settlement under such regional and bilateral agreements and the DSM of the WTO. This issue will be further explored in Section 3.

The Havana Charter (1948), which was to establish the International Trade Organization and a potentially effective system for dispute settlement after World War II, mentioned contribution to 'peaceful and friendly relations among nations' among its core objectives.[16] The broad range of issues regulated in the Havana Charter, including promotion of peaceful interstate relations and the general welfare and employment within states, was not included in the provisional and narrowly framed GATT (1947).[17] Nevertheless, GATT and its eight subsequent negotiation rounds (including the Uruguay Round that established the WTO) have been perceived as effective in promoting peaceful coexistence among states by preventing the kind of economic developments that preceded World War II.[18]

Against this background, one would expect the WTO Agreement to address peace-related issues explicitly and implicitly. Peace is not explicitly mentioned among the objectives of the WTO Agreement or any of its annexed agreements.[19] However, objectives that are closely related to the concept of 'positive peace' are mentioned in the preamble of the WTO Agreement, in particular 'raising standards of living', 'ensuring full employment', 'sustainable development', 'protect and preserve the environment', 'ensure that developing countries, and especially the least developed among them, secure a share in the growth in international trade commensurate with the needs of their economic development', and 'elimination of discriminatory treatment in international trade relations'.

When considering the role of the DSM in promoting peace, it is essential first to assess the extent to which the rules to be applied are conducive to peace. Only a very general overview of relevant aspects of the rules can be provided here. First, we may consider the extent to which peace-related issues fall within the *scope* of

[15] Ala'i et al., 'Trade as Guarantor of Peace, Liberty and Security?', p. ix. See also Petersmann, 'Justice as Conflict Resolution', 278.

[16] Charter of the International Trade Organization, UN Conference on Trade and Employment, UN Doc. E/Conf. 2/78 (1948) (Havana Charter).

[17] See The Protocol of Provisional Application of the General Agreement on Tariffs and Trade, 30 October 1947.

[18] J. A. Lacarte, 'The Role of the Bretton Woods Institutions in Securing the Peace', *Studies in Transnational Legal Policy* 37 (2005), 3–4. See also Fiona Macmillan, 'The Emergence of the World Trade Organization. Another Triumph of Corporate Capitalism?', in *Events: The Force of International Law*, Fleur Johns, Richard Joyce, and Sundhya Pahuja (eds.) (New York: Routledge, 2011), 203: 'might we … argue that at a more general level, during each turbulent post-switch phase … the international community turns to international (economic) law making, perhaps as an alternative to war making, in order to manage conflict?'

[19] See Colin B. Picker, 'Trade and Security: Empiricism, Change, Emotion & Relevancy', *Studies in Transnational Legal Policy* 37 (2005), 199–200.

the rules of the WTO Agreement. A recurring issue of controversy in policy and legal discussions of GATT and the WTO has been the extent to which the rules and institutions should take into account other issues than those strictly related to trade, such as labour rights, environmental protection, human rights, and social injustice. Such issues have been discussed in detail in the voluminous literature on the general exceptions of GATT Article XX and GATS Article XIV. One argument frequently made has been that international trade law must focus on liberalization of international trade and that other concerns must be dealt with by rules and institutions that are established for such purposes. The main counter-argument is that the rules liberalizing trade are so closely related to other areas of policy and law that they must be closely integrated. While it may in general seem that both arguments are recognized as strong and valid and that the main differences among practitioners, scholars, and stakeholders concern the extent of integration of other areas with the WTO Agreement, the failure to launch the 'Millennium Round' of trade negotiations at the Seattle Ministerial Meeting in 1999[20] and the subsequent lengthy negotiations of the 'Doha Development Round' launched in 2001, demonstrate the controversies related to the scope of the WTO.[21]

Secondly, the content of the rules of the WTO have been subject to significant criticism. As demonstrated by the controversies surrounding multilateral trade negotiations under the WTO, there is widespread dissatisfaction among developing countries concerning the content of the rules and developed countries' implementation of their commitments.[22] It has been argued that 'the WTO is mandating that States adopt policies that harm certain people, and does nothing to ensure recompense for those who are harmed.'[23] One way of regarding the relationship between trade and peace is that trade agreements have replaced military intervention as a means to ensure access to goods, in particular raw materials, and export markets.[24] It has also been argued that the WTO Agreement places significant restraints on states' opportunities to pursue domestic policy objectives.[25]

[20] See Klaus Günter Deutsch and Bernhard Speyer (eds.), *The World Trade Organization Millennium Round: Freer Trade in the Twenty-First Century* (New York: Routledge, 2002).

[21] See Rorden Wilkinson and James Scott (eds.), *Trade, Poverty, Development: Getting Beyond the WTO's Doha Deadlock* (New York: Routledge, 2013), which has a particular focus on African countries. Some major but limited results of the Doha Round were achieved at the Bali Ministerial Meeting in 2013, see WTO Ministerial Conference Declaration, 7 December 2013, WT/MIN(13)/DEC.

[22] See Wilkinson and Scott, *Trade, Poverty, Development*, Sarah Joseph, *Blame it on the WTO? A Human Rights Critique* (Oxford: Oxford University Press, 2011), chs. 5–7. A number of authors emphasize the imbalance in favour of developed countries, see Debra P. Steger, 'Lessons from History: Trade and Peace', *Studies in Transnational Legal Policy* 3 (2005), 14, and Macmillan, 'The Emergence of the World Trade Organization', 193.

[23] See Joseph, *Blame it on the WTO?*, 291.

[24] This perspective can be illustrated by the 'rare earth' cases against China, which were triggered by Chinese export restrictions, see cases DS394, 395, 398, 431, 432, and 433. See also Stephen Schlesinger and Stephen Kinzer, *Bitter Fruit: The Story of the American Coup in Guatemala* (Harvard: Harvard University Press, 1999). It can be argued that rules ensuring non-discriminatory access to raw materials, essential products, services, and technologies are important in the context of negative peace.

[25] See Joseph, *Blame it on the WTO?*, ch. 4, and Geert van Calster and Denise Prévost, *Research Handbook on Environment, Health and the WTO* (Cheltenham: Edward Elgar 2013).

This is closely related to the increasing importance of WTO rules concerning countries' internal measures as a consequence of abolition border measures and reduction of tariffs. Hence, effective enforcement with the help of the DSM may accentuate the imbalances and inequities of the existing WTO rules.

One issue of particular interest for the purpose of this chapter is the extent to which the content of WTO rules is open-ended and thus defers clarification to subsequent decision-making procedures, including the DSM. The character of WTO rules varies from very detailed and technical rules to obligations phrased in very broad terms, such as the prohibitions against non-discrimination in Articles I and III of GATT and Articles II and XVII of GATS, the prohibition against technical regulations creating unnecessary obstacles to international trade in Article 2.2 of the TBT Agreement, and the obligation to base technical regulations and standards on international standards set out in Articles 2.4 and 4 as well as Annex 3 of the TBT Agreement. Given that the possibility of adopting interpretations under Article IX of the WTO Agreement has been used only in exceptional circumstances and that the possibility of not adopting panel and Appellate Body (AB) reports is very limited (Articles 16.4 and 17.14 of the Dispute Settlement Understanding—DSU), specification of the broadly phrased provisions is essentially left to panels and the AB.

3. Balancing Effectiveness and Peace-Related Functions

One main challenge when arguing that the DSM should serve peace-related functions is that such functions may undermine the effectiveness of the DSM in the long term. The underlying rationale for such a claim is that peace-related functions involve the handling of politically sensitive cases, and that making legally binding decisions in such cases would be likely to undermine the legal functions of the DSM. One reason is that the DSM could gradually be perceived as a political rather than an adjudicative body.[26] Moreover, the DSM could increasingly be accused of lack of neutrality and objectivity; in addition to going beyond its mandate. It can also be argued that politically sensitive cases are particularly resource-demanding and could lead to retaliatory use of the DSM.[27] Thus, they may divert resources from the core adjudicative functions of the DSM.

[26] See Broude, 'Between Pax Mercatoria and Pax Europea', 49: 'The main theoretical argument I present here is that for trade dispute settlement mechanisms to contribute to Pax Mercatoria workings, they must be of an effective, judicialized nature, rather than of a political/diplomatic one.' See also pp. 51–2 where 'preventing or reducing issue linkage to unrelated political disagreements between parties' and 'keeping the management of the trade dispute contained in a more rule-oriented, institutional context' are mentioned as main ways in which 'judicialized dispute settlement' promotes peaceful settlement of disputes.

[27] See the discussion raised by Australia in the WTO Dispute Settlement Body (DSB), 'Minutes of Meeting', 4 March 2013, WTO Doc. WT/DSB/M/327, para. 11.1. As to resource concerns, see WTO Doc. WT/DSB/M/334, 2 October 2013, para. 4.2.

As has been discussed at length in the literature, the effectiveness of dispute settlement through panels evolved gradually under GATT 1947.[28] The legal basis was contained in Articles XXII and XXIII which do not include institutional elements beyond references to the Contracting Parties. This chapter will not re-examine this development, but instead focus on the functions of the DSM under the WTO Agreement. Despite the claim that the adoption of the DSU represented a paradigmatic shift,[29] there is no clear-cut distinction between GATT 1947 and the WTO in this context. This is because the DSM follows up the panel procedure and jurisprudence of GATT 1947.

The fact that the parties to GATT 1947 were willing to reverse the rule on consensus for the adoption of panel and AB reports (Articles 16.4 and 17.14 of the DSU) and to strengthen enforcement procedures (Articles 21 and 22 of the DSU) demonstrates the extent to which panels under GATT 1947 had managed to build trust among the states. It also shows the frustrations that states were feeling regarding the political vulnerability of the panel procedure. The main safeguards were the possibility of appealing panel reports and the reservation that the '[r]ecommendations and rulings of the DSB cannot add to or diminish the rights and obligations provided in the covered agreements' (Article 3.2 of the DSU).

There are multiple factors by which to measure the effectiveness of the DSM: for example the extent to which it is resorted to (including by different groups of member states and related to different subject matters); its ability to provide decisions in a timely manner according to proceedings that are perceived as fair; the extent and quality of third-party participation; and the extent of timely compliance with rulings. The effectiveness of the DSM needs to be considered in the light of other mechanisms established to resolve trade concerns among WTO members, that is, numerous obligations to notify trade measures, committee discussions of trade measures, the Trade Policy Review Mechanism, and consultations, good offices, conciliation, and mediation (Articles 4 and 5 of the DSU). The DSM is important as a means of increasing members' willingness to resolve differences through these less confrontational mechanisms. In this sense, the DSM can be regarded as the best alternative to negotiated agreement ('BATNA'). In general, the perception seems to be that the DSM has a high degree of effectiveness.[30]

When considering the peace-related functions of the DSM it is useful to distinguish general systemic functions from individual instances of dispute resolution. As to the former, it has been discussed how the DSM affects the power relationship between states. One argument is that a well-functioning regime to resolve disputes

[28] For a thorough analysis, see Robert E. Hudec, *Enforcing International Trade Law: The Evolution of the Modern GATT Legal System* (Salem, NH: Butterworth Legal, 1993).

[29] Joseph H. H. Weiler, 'The Rule of Lawyers and the Ethos of Diplomats: Reflections on Internal and External Legitimacy of WTO Dispute Settlement', in *Efficiency, Equity, and Legitimacy: The Multilateral Trading System at the Millennium*, Roger B. Porter, Pierre Sauvé, Arvind Subramanian, and Americo Beviglia Zampetti (eds.) (Washington, DC: Brookings Institution, 2001), 341.

[30] See Jennifer Hillman, 'An Emerging International Rule of Law? The WTO Dispute Settlement System's Role in its Evolution', *Ottawa Law Review* 42:2 (2010–11), 269, and Steger, 'Lessons from History', 14.

serves to empower economically weak or small states, and to control the acts of economically strong or big states. The main rationale is that resolution of differences based on application of pre-established rules through a neutral third party is preferable to resolution of differences based on power relations. This rationale is dependent on the DSM being 'well-functioning', in particular that it provides similar opportunities regardless of power relationships, and that the rules to be applied strike a fair balance between the states. Several initiatives have been taken to level the playing field among parties to disputes.[31] However, significant concerns remain regarding imbalances in the actual use of the DSM. At the one end of the scale, the US and the EU are positioned as the dominant users. At the other end are the least developed countries, only one of which has used the DSM once.[32] As to geographical distribution, the absence of African countries is remarkable.[33] Similar patterns emerge when we look at participation in disputes as third parties, but developing countries, except African, have been more actively involved through this mechanism.[34] These imbalances indicate that the DSM has hardly had any relevance for least developed countries and African countries. The statistics also show that the DSM has been significant for some fast-growing economies (Brazil, China, and India), Asian countries, and Latin American countries.[35]

Secondly, the design of the DSM is arguably well suited to deal with politically sensitive disputes. One important element is the involvement of third parties. Third parties frequently participate both during the consultation phase (Article 4.11 of the DSU) and the subsequent panel and AB proceedings (Articles 10 and 17.4 of the DSU). The opportunity for other states to be involved increases transparency and means that agreements between and arguments of the parties to the dispute are likely to be scrutinized and criticized by others.[36] Another element is the

[31] There are several mechanisms that aim to strengthen the positions of disadvantaged states, including Arts. 8.10, 12.10, 12.11, 21.2, 21.7, 21.8, 24, and 27.2 of the DSU, and there is assistance from the WTO Secretariat and the Advisory Centre on WTO Law. The latter is open to all WTO members and countries in the process of acceding to the WTO. Least developed countries need not be members of the Centre in order to benefit from its services. The Centre has 11 developed country members and 31 developing country members.

[32] According to Kara Leitner and Simon Lester, 'WTO Dispute Settlement 1995–2013—A Statistical Analysis', *Journal of International Economic Law* 17 (2014), 193, the US and the EU have been complainants in 39% and respondents in 42% of the cases. The only least developed country to use the DSM was Bangladesh as complainant in DS306.

[33] Joan Apecu Laker, *African Participation at the World Trade Organization: Legal and Institutional Aspects, 1995–2010* (Leiden: Martinus Nijhoff, 2014), ch. 6 and annex XIV.

[34] Henrik Horn, Louise Johannesson, and Petros C. Mavroidis, 'The WTO Dispute Settlement System 1995–2010: Some Descriptive Statistics', *Journal of World Trade* 45 (2011), 1116–17: least developed countries participated only 13 times as third parties in panel proceedings (1%), while developing countries except for Brazil, China, and India participated 417 times (34%). African countries had used the opportunity to act as third parties only 35 times (3%).

[35] For more details, in particular regarding dispute settlement and power relationships, see Jonas Tallberg and James McCall Smith, 'Dispute Settlement in World Politics: States, Supranational Prosecutors, and Compliance', *European Journal of International Relations* 20 (2014), 127–31.

[36] Marc L. Busch and Eric Reinhardt, 'Three's a Crowd: Third Parties and WTO Dispute Settlement', *World Politics* 58 (2006), 448, have pointed out that 'when third parties join a dispute, they lower the prospects for early settlement and increase the likelihood that a case will go to a ruling'. This seems to correspond well with the arguments made here. They also find that '[a]mong

difference in composition of panels and the AB. While panellists are essentially selected from among diplomats who are familiar with negotiations and the views of states,[37] AB members must have 'demonstrated expertise in law' and many of them have had thorough knowledge of public international law.[38] This reflects a general division of labour between panels and the AB; panels have the final say regarding facts and the AB is the authority on interpretation and application of the agreements.[39] Taken together with the consultation phase, which is to some extent overseen by the DSB and relevant councils or committees, the panels and the AB seem to be well designed to resolve politically sensitive differences between states.

Thirdly, the interplay between the DSM and regional and bilateral free trade agreements (RTAs) is of importance when considering the peace-related functions of the WTO DSM. According to one study of the EU's RTAs, '[e]mpirical research has shown that trade flows per se have little effect on the likelihood of conflict between states that are not mutual RTA partners, but within RTAs there is a strong negative correlation between trade and political conflict.'[40] The study finds that there is 'essentially no' dispute settlement practice in the EU's RTAs. This finding seems confirmed by the practice under other RTAs, if we do not count economic integration agreements such as those establishing the European Union. Indeed, states under some RTAs prefer to bring cases to the WTO rather than to use the dispute settlement options under RTAs.[41] However, as pointed out in the study, we need to pay attention to the less formalized means of resolving disputes in the RTAs. Information on the activities of such mechanisms is generally hard to obtain.[42] Against this background, we may observe that RTAs do not

those cases in which rulings are issued, there is no apparent correlation between the involvement of third parties and the direction of a verdict' (p. 49). On the basis of this finding, we may question the extent to which third party participation has peace-related functions. However, such functions are not only related to the 'direction of a verdict', but also to the process preceding it, its exact content, and the legal and factual justification for it.

[37] The list is published as WTO Doc. WT/DSB/44/, which is established in accordance with Art. 8 of 'The Uruguay Round Understanding on Rules and Procedures Governing the Settlement of Disputes' (DSU).

[38] Art. 17.3 of the DSU. The emphasis on knowledge of general public international law does not seem to be as high on the agenda of WTO members as it was in the early years of the WTO.

[39] Arts. 11, 13, 15, and 17.6 of the DSU. See also Chris A. Thomas, 'Of Facts and Phantoms: Economics, Epistemic Legitimacy, and WTO Dispute Settlement', *Journal of International Economic Law* 14 (2011), 295–328.

[40] Broude, 'Between Pax Mercatoria and Pax Europea', 50.

[41] Examples include disputes in the WTO between the US, Canada, and Mexico, which could have been dealt with under the North American Free Trade Agreement (see Robert Howse and Susan Esserman, 'The Appellate Body, the WTO Dispute Settlement System, and the Politics of Multilateralism', in *The WTO at Ten: The Contribution of the Dispute Settlement System*, Giorgio Sacerdoti, Alan Yanovich, and Jan Bohanes (eds.) (Cambridge: Cambridge University Press, 2006), 65, as well as the lack of implementation of the decisions to establish a DSM in ASEAN. However, Broude, 'Between Pax Mercatoria and Pax Europea', 53, finds that 'the EC has never taken or been taken by any of its "regional" RTA partners to task in the WTO dispute settlement system'.

[42] Broude, 'Between Pax Mercatoria and Pax Europea', 53, found that there 'is virtually no record of EC RTA disputes, and those that have reached public attention have been settled discretely, diplomatically, such as the EC–Israel dispute over the produce of Israeli enterprises located in the Golan Heights, East Jerusalem, the West Bank and the Gaza Strip'.

necessarily eliminate the use of the WTO DSM among the parties to the RTAs, but that they are likely to lead to decreased use of the DSM. While the less transparent RTA mechanisms, which are essentially based on bilateral negotiations, are likely to favour powerful states, the WTO DSM may remain a safeguard for the less powerful states in RTAs. Such use of the WTO DSM may be particularly important in politically sensitive disputes between the parties to RTAs. On the other hand, RTAs provide a platform for powerful states to prevent or at least delay resort to the WTO DSM in such cases. The latter observation could be further explored by studying the design of dispute settlement provisions of RTAs and state practice; do the RTAs favour expedient resolution of disputes through adjudication or do they rather favour open-ended negotiations?[43] The increased opportunity of forum and rule shopping that the proliferation of RTAs represents is regarded as a fundamental challenge in international economic law.[44]

Turning to individual instances of dispute resolution, the focus is on the extent to which, and how, the DSM deals with cases that involve peace-related issues. We may distinguish between interstate and intrastate peace-related functions of disputes. As to the former, the question that arises is how we may determine that a particular dispute is peace-related in an interstate context. The basic starting point is the link between the dispute and political, economic, military, natural resource, or other conflicts and tensions between the states. There are several factors that may serve to identify relevant disputes, including but not limited to: (1) the general level of conflict or tensions between the states; (2) the relationship between the contested measures and essential interests of the states, for example the sectors involved and the extent of trade effects; (3) the character of the contested measure in terms of unilateralism (i.e. that it is not taken as part of bilateral or multilateral initiatives to deal with the relevant issue); (4) the extent to which the measure has extraterritorial effects; and (5) the impact of the WTO procedures and final decisions on the level of conflict or tension between the states, for example in terms of abstention from measures that might escalate tensions and compliance with recommendations of the panel or the AB.

The intrastate peace-related functions of the DSM concern the relationship between the government (as responsible for international trade relations) and private parties, in particular major interest groups, sectors of the economy that are easily affected by changes in international trade conditions, and individuals or groups that are economically and socially vulnerable. One group of cases consists of those where governments' decisions to initiate disputes in the WTO are the result of lobbying by major interest groups. The numerous disputes regarding

[43] In relation to EU RTAs, Broude, 'Between Pax Mercatoria and Pax Europea', 57, observes: 'They lack the effectiveness required to shorten the duration and reduce the intensity and salience of trade disputes, and to increase the durability of dispute settlement findings. By de-automaticizing the shift from consultations to arbitration, they suppress RTA or WTO judicialized dispute settlement between RTA parties, encouraging a diplomatic mechanism for resolving the dispute. Additionally, the option of resorting to WTO procedures is not regulated expressly, resulting in legal uncertainty that deters from taking such action, for political reasons.'

[44] Petersmann, 'Justice as Conflict Resolution', 278.

anti-dumping and countervailing duties generally belong to this category. Another group of cases consist of those where trade measures taken for significant domestic policy reasons are challenged in the WTO DSM. Cases where the defendant invokes security exceptions, balance of payment difficulties, or general exceptions may belong to this category. A third group of cases consist of those that are initiated as a result of disagreements between political parties or other political groups within a country. Such disputes may serve to diffuse domestic criticism against the government or provide evidence that the government is taking a political concern seriously, for example relocation of key industries to other countries. While such cases may serve to reduce internal political conflicts or tensions in the short term, their longer-term effects may be less predictable. A fourth group of cases covers those where the results of cases in the WTO are used as leverage for domestic policy reforms. The extent of domestic conflict regarding policy reforms may increase or decrease as a result of the link to the DSM, and the policy reform as such may subsequently aggravate or alleviate domestic conflicts or tensions. Hence, it may be difficult to determine whether the DSM has peace-related functions in this respect. The four main groups of cases display a mixed picture regarding the relationship between the DSM and internal conflicts and tensions. In addition, they indicate that the relationship in many instances is likely to change over time.

It has been argued that the DSM should not be involved in what has been referred to as 'high policy disputes'.[45] Such disputes would largely overlap with disputes in which the DSM could serve peace-related functions. Moreover, it has been claimed that the DSM is mainly faced with 'easy cases'. This claim is essentially based on the observation that close to 90 per cent of the cases conclude in favour of the claimant.[46] On the other hand, we have seen that the DSM may potentially have important peace-related functions and that it may be a critical factor for ensuring that trade liberalization and peace remain mutually supportive.

In the following, these views will be examined in light of the practice of the DSM and its potential peace-related functions. On the basis of the discussion of

[45] Petersmann, 'Justice as Conflict Resolution', 344–6, argues that such disputes should rather be settled through political negotiations than through the DSM. The discussion is based on three cases: the GATT case concerning Nicaragua's complaint against US import restrictions (panel report of 1984, see GATT Doc. L/5802 and C/M/188), the WTO dispute over the Helms-Burton legislation that extends US sanctions against Cuba to companies from the EU engaged in business transactions with Cuba (DS38 United States—The Cuban Liberty and Democratic Solidarity Act and DS176 United States—Section 211 Omnibus Appropriations Act of 1998), and the WTO dispute regarding the EU's conditions for granting tariff preferences to developing countries (DS246 European Communities—Conditions for the Granting of Tariff Preferences to Developing Countries). The concept 'high policy disputes' should not be confounded with the frequently used concept of 'high politics' disputes, which would generally be limited to the much narrower range of issues concerning survival of states and state sovereignty. On balance of payment and RTAs, see Frieder Roessler, 'Are the Judicial Organs of the World Trade Organization Overburdened?', in *Efficiency, Equity, and Legitimacy: The Multilateral Trading System at the Millennium*, Roger B. Porter, Pierre Sauvé, Arvind Subramanian, and Americo Beviglia Zampetti (eds.) (Washington, DC: Brookings Institution, 2001), 308–28.

[46] Matthew C. Turk, 'Why Does the Complainant Always Win at the WTO? A Reputation-Based Theory of Litigation at the World Trade Organization', *Northwestern Journal of International Law & Business* 31 (2011), 385.

interstate and intrastate peace-related functions of the DSM, these factors have been selected as a means of identifying cases of particular interest:

1. Characteristics of the states involved, in particular whether there is a history or situation of conflicts or tensions
2. Characteristics of the issues involved:
   (a) Is an essential sector of the state at stake (e.g. agriculture, raw materials, well-established export industries, infant industries)?
   (b) To what extent is the contested measure politically or economically sensitive in an intrastate context?
   (c) To what extent is the contested measure politically or economically sensitive in an interstate context (is it unilateral or are its effects mainly extraterritorial)?
3. Characteristics of the WTO rules invoked (e.g. security exceptions, balance of payment exceptions, and the Enabling Clause[47]).

In addition to these criteria, the extent of attention that disputes get in the DSM, in particular the number of states that join the dispute as complainants or third parties, has also been taken into account when assessing the relationship between disputes and peace.

4. The Peace-Related Functions of the DSM in Practice

This section will identify and analyse individual cases that are relevant to the peace-related function of the DSM. To some extent, it will also touch upon aggregate (jurisprudential) effects for trade issues that are relevant to peaceful coexistence of states and conflicts or tensions within states. The starting point for both topics is a qualitative assessment of all disputes registered with the WTO up to DS474[48] based on the criteria identified in Section 3. The qualitative assessment identified 25 cases or clusters of cases that qualified as peace-related.[49] The assessment is by necessity affected by the author's perspectives and preconceptions, and can be challenged on that basis. However, even if there is likely to be disagreement

[47] The Enabling Clause is the legal basis for the Generalized System of Preferences. See 'Differential and More Favourable Treatment, Reciprocity and Fuller Participation of Developing Countries', GATT 1947 decision of 28 November 1979, GATT Doc. L/4903.

[48] Due to space constraints, all references to WTO cases are limited to their DS number. The cases are listed in chronological order. Cases that are closely related (belonging to a 'cluster' of cases) are listed together. The cases can be accessed at http://wto.org/english/tratop_e/dispu_e/dispu_status_e.htm (accessed 18 June 2014).

[49] DS16, 27, 105, 158, 361, and 364; DS26, 39, 48, 320, and 321; DS38 and 176; DS46, 70, 71, 316, and 353; DS90, 91, 92, 93, 94, and 96; DS136, 162, 217, 234, and 322; DS146 and 175; DS149 and 279; DS152; DS154, 209, 242, and 246; DS190; DS207 and 220; DS248, 249, 251, 252, 253, 254, 258, and 259; DS265, 266, and 283; DS267; DS273; DS291, 292, and 293; DS333; DS363; DS394, 395, 398, 431, 432, and 433; DS447 and 448; DS455, 465, and 466; DS461; DS469; DS472.

regarding the classification of individual cases or clusters of cases, the assessment serves to identify issues and trends regarding the peace-related functions of the DSM. It also serves as a point of reference for further discussions of the legitimate roles of the DSM.

There were no cases that clearly qualified under the first criterion; existing or previous conflicts or tensions between the states. Only two cases in Latin America could possibly be alleged to involve states with a relatively recent history of tensions.[50] If we apply this criterion broadly to include significant interstate tensions in the field of international trade (sometimes referred to as 'trade wars' and characterized by retaliatory use of the DSM), a broad range of disputes could be included, such as a number of cases between the EU and the US, as well as between the US and China. However, none of these disputes were considered sufficiently serious to fulfil this criterion. Against this background, we can observe that the DSM has not so far played any important role in resolving existing serious conflicts or reducing significant tensions among states.

The second criterion (2(a)) focuses on whether the disputes concern essential *sectors* for the defendants or the complainants. Such disputes would be related to peace issues primarily where states are in economically vulnerable positions, for example due to dependence on a narrow range of industries or due to high levels of poverty or unemployment. This criterion was considered fulfilled in 17 cases. One group of cases is where *defendants* fear that surges in imports may lead to social problems or unrest, in particular as regards the agricultural sector,[51] established and vulnerable industries,[52] and infant industries.[53] Vulnerable defendants could typically be states whose economies are dependent on a limited range of sectors, and with high levels of unemployment. A second group of cases are those where *complainants* are concerned that restrictions on market access[54] or that the policies of other states to expand their market shares[55] will lead to a decline in the complainants' essential export industries. Vulnerable complainants could typically be states with balance of payment problems, or a high degree of economic dependence on a limited range of export industries. In addition, a third group of cases concerns import or export of products or technologies that are sensitive from a public policy (e.g. access to raw materials in situations of limited supply) or security perspective (e.g. products or technologies that are likely to be used for military purposes).[56] A closely related group of cases concerns measures that are linked to core issues of national sovereignty, such as control over natural resources, foreign policy, and national security.[57] These two groups of cases would

[50] See DS207 *Chile—Prince Band System*, 22 May 2007, and DS461 *Colombia—Textiles*, 18 June 2013.

[51] DS207 and 220; DS455, 465, and 466.

[52] DS248, 249, 251, 252, 253, 254, 258, and 259; DS273; DS461.

[53] DS146 and 175; DS472.

[54] DS16, 27, 105, 158, 361, and 364; DS267; DS447 and 448; DS469.

[55] DS265, 266, and 283; DS267.

[56] DS26, 39, 48, 320, and 321; DS46, 70, 71, 316, and 353; DS248, 249, 251, 252, 253, 254, 258, and 259; DS394, 395, and 398; DS431, 432, and 433.

[57] DS16, 27, 105, 158, 361, and 364; DS154, 209, 242, and 246; DS363; DS469.

be initiated by countries that are denied access to such products, technologies, raw materials, or markets.

The third criterion (2(b)) focuses on whether the contested *measure* is politically or economically sensitive in a *domestic* context. The relationship to peace would be particularly relevant for states that rely heavily on public intervention in order to safeguard essential interests. This criterion was considered to be fulfilled in nine cases. The essential interest in question may be within both the respondent (i.e. the state taking the measure) and the complainant (i.e. the state whose trade interests are being affected by the measure). One group of cases concerns measures taken to safeguard essential interests in the state taking the measure, in particular to protect vulnerable groups (e.g. poor farmers)[58] and core values or objectives (e.g. sustainable development).[59] Such measures could potentially be taken by a broad range of states, since most states have sectors that are vulnerable to international competition and ability to adopt measures to protect those sectors. Relevant measures could typically be safeguard measures.[60] According to the WTO's survey of safeguard measures, however, no least developed country and no Sub-Saharan country (except for South Africa) has notified such measures to the WTO so far. Otherwise, safeguard measures seem to be broadly distributed both geographically and in terms of level of development.[61] A somewhat related but still different group of cases consists of those that concern a broad range of policy measures.[62] Such cases may arise in relation to states that still are or recently were 'non-market economies'. Cases could be brought to the DSM where negotiations to resolve such trade issues fail. A third group of cases are those where defendants are asked to make significant changes to domestic policy measures.[63] Such cases could relate to peace if reforms of measures are associated with significant political conflicts or tensions.

The fourth criterion (2(c)) focuses on whether the contested *measure* is politically or economically sensitive in an *interstate* context. This criterion was considered to be fulfilled in seven cases.[64] We may place these measures along a continuum ranging from measures taken by one state to force another state to adopt a certain policy in accordance with the specific interests of the state taking the measure, to measures taken by one state in order to provide a mild incentive for other states to adjust their policy in accordance with existing duties under international law, for example human rights or environmental treaties.[65] The closer a measure is to

[58] DS190; DS207 and 220; DS455, 465, and 466.

[59] DS291, 292, and 293; DS394, 395, 398, 431, 432, and 433.

[60] See Art. XIX of GATT, the Safeguards Agreement and Art. X of GATS.

[61] The basis for these statements is the notifications received by the WTO until 31 March 2013, which include 255 safeguard measures in total. The two major users of safeguard measures were India (29) and Indonesia (23).

[62] DS149 and 279; DS472.

[63] DS136, 162, 217, 234, and 322; DS333.

[64] DS38 and 176; DS136, 162, 217, 234, and 322; DS152; DS154, 209, 242, and 246; DS291, 292, and 293; DS394, 395, 398, 431, 432, and 433; DS469.

[65] While DS469 can be seen as an example of a case close to the former end of the continuum, DS58 and 61 (the so-called shrimp–turtle case, which was not considered to qualify as a peace-related case) are close to the other end of the continuum.

the former end of the continuum, the more likely it is to qualify as a peace-related measure. A second factor that may affect the level of conflict or tension associated with such measures is the extent to which the measure is aimed at resolving issues or concerns within other states, global commons, or within the state taking the measure. Obviously, the further removed the measure is from dealing with internal concerns in the state taking the measure, the higher is its degree of extraterritoriality and the risk that it may lead to conflicts or tensions.[66] The cases that fall into this category will frequently generate significant interest among other members of the WTO and therefore involve a high number of third parties.[67]

Finally, the fifth criterion is the characteristics of the WTO rules invoked. Some provisions are clearly peace-related; in particular the security exceptions (see the discussion of these provisions in the introduction).[68] Other provisions are less clearly related to peace issues, in particular the provisions on safeguards,[69] the Enabling Clause,[70] and the general exceptions.[71] Only if other factors are present, including in particular those already discussed, would cases involving these provisions be considered peace-related. All these provisions concern justifications for trade measures that otherwise would have been prohibited.

On the basis of the above survey, we may ask to what extent and under what circumstances the DSM will contribute to reduce conflicts and tensions, or conversely aggravate conflicts and tensions. As to cases between states that have a history of conflicts or tensions, we may assume that the DSM would clearly be most likely to reduce such interstate conflicts and tensions. However, as has been demonstrated by the practice to date, such cases seem unlikely to be brought to the DSM. For the cases concerning *essential sectors* we may assume that cases brought to prevent the use of measures to protect such sectors are likely to increase internal conflicts and tensions, and that they may contribute to reduce interstate conflicts and tensions. However, the former seems to be the more dominant effect due to the importance of the measure for the defendant. The same reasoning applies in cases concerning *measures* that are politically or economically sensitive in a *domestic* context. Turning to cases concerning measures that are politically or economically sensitive in an *interstate* context, we may observe that the measures as such in general lead to or aggravate existing interstate conflicts or tensions, and thus that the DSM is most likely to reduce such tensions or conflicts. While these cases may indirectly increase intrastate tensions or conflicts, such effects may be assumed to be less significant. Finally, as to peace-related provisions of the WTO Agreement, the DSM is likely to clarify the rights and duties of states and thereby

[66] A case concerning a measure with a high degree of extraterritoriality is DS469, while DS136, 162, 217, 234, and 322 can be regarded as having a low degree of extraterritoriality.

[67] See DS152; DS154, 209, 242, and 246; and DS291, 292, and 293.

[68] Only one case of relevance was identified: DS149 and 279 where the claimant listed a broad range of measures, including some for which GATT Art. XXI had been invoked by the defendant.

[69] DS207 and 220; DS248, 249, 251, 252, 253, 254, 258, and 259.

[70] DS154, 209, 242, and 246. The Enabling Clause is the legal basis for the Generalized System of Preferences.

[71] DS149 and 279. Art. XX of GATT and Art. XIV of GATS are the most important exceptions for this purpose.

increase predictability and prevent potential conflicts or tensions associated with measures justified under these provisions. In sum, and as a general observation, the DSM is most likely to reduce interstate conflicts and tensions, and to aggravate intrastate conflicts and tensions. Hence, it may be particularly important when reforming the DSM to consider how its potential for generating intrastate conflicts and tensions can be reduced.

A second general question is which countries are more or less likely to benefit from the activities of the DSM. This question will initially be discussed under the assumption that countries have comparable real opportunities of making use of the DSM.[72] As to cases concerning existing or previous conflicts or tensions between the states, we may assume that the DSM could benefit weaker states and that powerful states may be less likely to use the DSM for such purposes due to their access to other means. Most of the cases concerning *essential sectors* are likely to be brought against states that are heavily dependent on such sectors, that is, developing and small countries. Such cases may be brought by any country having an interest in the sector. Cases involving sectors that are important for security reasons are harder to predict; they could be brought by and against any country. As to cases concerning measures that are politically or economically sensitive in a *domestic* context, the cited survey of the resort of states to safeguard measures indicates that small and economically weak states are unlikely to make use of such measures, and are thus not likely to be sued under the DSM. On the other hand, small and weak states may have recourse to the DSM in order to prevent other states from resorting to such measures. Measures that are politically or economically sensitive in an *interstate* context are most likely to be used by economically strong or dominant states, and the DSM is therefore likely to benefit weaker and smaller states. As to the *peace-related provisions* of the WTO Agreement, the DSM would be used typically by advanced states in some instances, for example balance of payment measures, while it might be more relevant to less advanced countries in other contexts, for example, application of the Enabling Clause. In sum, there is significant potential for the DSM to benefit small and weaker states, in particular in cases involving interstate conflicts and tensions. However, the DSM is unlikely to contribute significantly in this direction unless serious efforts are made to increase the availability of the DSM to such states.

In conclusion, we may in very general terms expect that in cases concerning interstate conflicts or tensions, the DSM is likely to reduce the conflicts and tensions and benefit smaller and weaker states. Conversely, where cases involve internal conflicts or tensions, the DSM is more likely to increase such conflicts and tensions and benefit bigger and more powerful states. These conclusions are based on general assumptions regarding the regulatory and institutional framework of the WTO, as well as regarding states' use of trade measures and the DSM. These assumptions, which to a significant extent are based on the case studies, need to be further explored in light of the practice of states and the WTO.

[72] This assumption is clearly not realistic, despite efforts to level the playing field between WTO member states in this area, as noted already.

5. Concluding Remarks

By the time of the adoption of the WTO Agreement in 1994, the focus just after World War II on trade's contribution to world peace in the Havana Charter had been replaced by the emphasis on standards of living, employment, sustainable development, environmental protection, developing countries' effective participation in world trade, and non-discrimination. One way of looking at this development is as a shift away from peace-related issues, and another way of looking at it is as a change in focus from 'negative peace' to 'positive peace'. Regardless of how we regard this move, the relationship between peace and trade is no less significant today than it has been previously.

There remains significant disagreement as to the extent to which the WTO DSM should be involved in 'high policy disputes'. Regardless of the position one may take on this issue, this chapter has shown that the DSM has been and will most likely continue to be used to resolve cases that are linked to peace. Moreover, it has shown that the DSM can be expected to both reduce and aggravate interstate and intrastate conflicts and tensions.

At least in theory, it should be easy to establish consensus in the WTO on initiatives to reduce the risk that the DSM will aggravate conflicts and tensions. Such initiatives would be aimed at preventing use of the DSM to attack measures taken to protect essential sectors and measures that are politically or economically sensitive in a domestic context. The focus of such initiatives should be on safeguarding the interests of least developed countries and Sub-Saharan states.

A second initiative that should be considered is to facilitate use of the DSM to reduce conflicts and tensions between states. While it may be controversial to argue that the DSM should increasingly be used for such purposes, it is less controversial to argue that states should have equal opportunities in this respect. Hence, additional initiatives to facilitate resort to the DSM for least developed countries and Sub-Saharan states are needed.

It has been indicated that bilateralism and regionalism which may lead to discrimination and may facilitate domination of less powerful states is likely to increase conflicts and tensions. The resilience of the WTO DSM to the current trend of bilateralism and regionalism is remarkable. The fact that states continue to use the DSM despite increasing availability of means of resolving disputes elsewhere indicates that states appreciate the functions of the WTO DSM, in particular the multilateral setting in which it operates, including aspects of participation and transparency. However, the trend of relying on the WTO DSM is not predetermined to remain. Initiatives may be needed to safeguard the DSM, in particular when considering bilateral and regional trade agreements in the WTO Committee on Regional Trade Agreements.

11

The Potential of the Arms Trade Treaty to Reduce Violations of International Humanitarian Law and Human Rights Law

Gro Nystuen[1] *and Kjølv Egeland*

1. Introduction

This chapter may stand out somewhat, given the purpose of this book. While the Arms Trade Treaty (ATT) might serve as an instrument to reduce violations of human rights and humanitarian principles, it does not address peace in the conventional sense. On the contrary, it is a trade agreement that allows for the continued transfer over national borders of lethal weapons intended for fighting wars and law enforcement. On the other hand, a more nuanced definition of peace (whether conceived of negatively as 'absence of violence' or positively as 'social justice') allows us to investigate the role of the ATT in promoting peace.[2]

The chapter is divided into six parts. First, we explore the theoretical underpinnings of the ATT, identifying it as a limited normative framework. Second, we narrow down the scope, exploring the background of the ATT, including its context and the consensus requirement governing the negotiations. Third, we analyse the negotiation process of the ATT before we look at the outcome and key provisions of the Treaty. Fifth, we examine some implications for the academic field, arguing that while there are important overlaps between peace studies and international law, there are also some fundamental differences. Lastly, we end with a short conclusion.

In the normative study of armed conflict, there are three broad positions, which can only be dealt with briefly in this chapter.[3] Firstly, *pacifists* hold that violence

[1] Nystuen took part in the negotiations on the Arms Trade Treaty from 2010 until the Treaty was adopted in April 2013, as an adviser to the Norwegian MFA delegation.

[2] See Johan Galtung, 'Violence, Peace, and Peace Research', *Journal of Peace Research* 6 (1969), 183.

[3] See the Introduction to this volume for an overview of normative approaches to peace and conflict, and a more nuanced (and inclusive) definition of pacifism. The form of pacifism we have in mind here could be identified as 'principled'.

and war are illegitimate and should be avoided at all costs.[4] According to Roger P. Alford, 'populist pacifists generally resisted laws that attempted to "humanize" war through international humanitarian law, because to enumerate how war was to be conducted was to concede that it was lawful to conduct'.[5] Secondly, *realists* hold that international politics is an amoral social sphere and that states will, and perhaps should, pursue their national interests regardless of any international ethics.[6] Thirdly, scholars subscribing to the *just war tradition* hold that war is legitimate, but only under specific conditions, and only when conducted in a specific manner.[7] The just war tradition combines parts of the normative impetus of pacifism with parts of the empirical insight of realism, sharing with pacifists the view that war has undesirable effects, and with realists the understanding that given the lack of a centralized enforcing mechanism, states are likely to pursue their national, or government's, interests. Henry Shue captures the issue with great precision:

> I think the fundamental attitude of the laws of war to the violations of the absolute prohibitions against attacks, assaults, wounding, and killings that are part of ordinary law and morality can be well captured with the contemporary pithy phrase 'shit happens'. We are dealing with war. In wars terrible actions are taken: assaults, attacks, wounding, and killings are carried out. That they happen in every war does nothing to make them less terrible, but to prevent them all we must prevent all wars. *The prevention of wars is a morally urgent task, but it is not the task of the laws of war.* The purpose of the laws of war is to constrain the 'shit' when the 'shit' happens: when armies are assaulting and attacking, the laws of war specify firm limits. This same purpose was stated more elegantly in the Preface to the Oxford Manual of 1880: 'to restrain the destructive force of war, while recognizing its inexorable necessities'.[8]

Like just war theorists, the creators and analysts of international humanitarian law (IHL) recognize that wars do in fact occur, and aim to mitigate superfluous injury to combatants and spare civilians as far as possible. By doing so, armed conflict is tacitly acknowledged as an existing political tool. Construed in this sense as dealing in part with ethics, the creators of international law, and most of its analysts, approach justice from a largely non-ideal position.[9]

[4] See Leo Tolstoy, *Government is Violence: Essays on Anarchism and Pacifism* (London: Phoenix, 1990); Bertha von Suttner, *Die Waffen nieder! Eine Lebensgeschichte* (Berlin: Verlag der Nation, 1990 [1889]).

[5] Roger P. Alford, 'The Nobel Effect: Nobel Peace Prize Laureates as International Norm Entrepreneurs', *Virginia Journal of International Law* 49 (2008), 61–153 at 68.

[6] See Hans Morgenthau, *Politics Among Nations: The Struggle for Power and Peace* (New York: McGraw Hill, 2006 [1948]); John J. Mearsheimer, *The Tragedy of Great Power Politics* (New York: W. W. Norton, 2001).

[7] See Michael Walzer, *Just and Unjust Wars: A Moral Argument with Historical Illustrations* (4th edn. New York: Basic Books, 2006); Augustine, *The City of God* (Peabody, Mass., Hendrickson, 2009 [426]).

[8] Henry Shue, 'Laws of War', in *Philosophy of International Law*, Samantha Besson and John Tasioulas (eds.) (Oxford: Oxford University Press, 2010), 516 (emphasis added).

[9] See Samantha Besson and John Tasioulas, 'Introduction', Allen Buchanan, 'Legitimacy of International Law', Andreas Paulus, 'International Adjudication', Liam Murphy, 'International Responsibility', all in *Philosophy of International Law*.

The distinction between ideal and non-ideal theory is a common one in political theory, and regards the rudimentary assumptions an analyst makes when investigating an issue. While theorists subscribing to ideal theory approach questions of construing perfect institutional arrangements and ultimate justice from a *tabula rasa*, the non-ideal position is to try to approximate justice in light of practical constraints.[10] The fundamental assumption made by theorists of ideal theory is that individuals will comply with and uphold institutional (re)arrangements and laws, often labelled 'strict compliance'. While ideal theory may be necessary to identify justice in its ideal form, critics argue that the assumption of strict compliance is an unrealistic one—and probably even more so in international affairs than in national politics—ultimately lending decision-makers poor advice.[11] For example, hypothetical prohibitions of the uses of force under any circumstances, or against any civilian casualties whatsoever under IHL, would be unacceptable to the states. Thus, such provisions would render themselves irrelevant, or, worse still, could lower respect for international law as a whole by setting impossible standards and normalizing unlawful acts.

2. Background

2.1. The ATT in context

Given the non-ideal nature of international affairs and, in many cases, the conflicting interests of states, the legal approach to peace and conflict is also non-ideal. IHL—understood in terms of its sources—has no specific political aim in itself, but its creators have sought to minimize the negative humanitarian impact of war, while at the same time protecting the states' interests both internally and externally. It is in this context the Arms Trade Treaty, adopted by the UN General Assembly, 2 April 2013, should be seen. Per December 2014, the ATT has been signed by 122 UN Member States, of which 54 have ratified.[12]

Humanitarian considerations are clearly important motivating factors behind the ATT, and mark their presence in the text of the Treaty. For example, in Article 1, the purpose of the Treaty is identified as:

> Contributing to international and regional peace, security and stability;
> Reducing human suffering;

[10] See John Rawls, *A Theory of Justice* (rev. edn. Cambridge, Mass., Harvard University Press, 1999 [1971]), 215–16.

[11] Colin Farrelly, 'Justice in Ideal Theory: A Refutation', *Political Studies* 55 (2007), 844–64. The distinction between ideal and non-ideal theory is not black and white, as analysts typically incorporate elements from both into their work. However, the distinction is helpful for heuristic purposes. See Zofia Stemplowska, 'What's Ideal About Ideal Theory?', *Social Theory and Practice* 34 (2008), 319–40.

[12] United Nations Office of Disarmament Affairs (UNODA), 'Arms Trade Treaty', http://disarmament.un.org/treaties/t/att/deposit/asc (accessed 10 Nov 2014).

> Promoting cooperation, transparency and responsible action by States Parties in the international trade in conventional arms, thereby building confidence among States Parties.[13]

In the sense that the ATT is indeed partly motivated by states' desire to facilitate adherence to human rights law and international humanitarian law, the regulations it provides are addressed to what Galtung labels 'negative peace' or 'absence of violence'.[14] Its creators seek to make arms transfers more transparent, and prevent transfers when the arms are likely to be used unlawfully. As negative peace is in a sense a precondition of positive peace and social justice, one may broadly say that the latter is also addressed. It is, however, very difficult, and perhaps not even desirable, to legislate for positive peace. In the words of Thomas Paine, there is an important distinction to make between society and government (the former pertaining to ethics and solidarity and the latter to law and governance): 'SOME writers have so confounded society with government, as to leave little or no distinction between them; whereas they are not only different, but have different origins. Society is produced by our wants, and government by our wickedness; the former promotes our happiness positively by uniting our affections, the latter negatively by restraining our vices.'[15]

The ATT is an international agreement and therefore the perspective offered is predominantly that of states. In many instances, states have conflicting interests and visions for the future, which may or may not be particularly peaceful. States do, however, all share one key interest: to ensure their own power and sovereignty. Thus, while the ATT does stress pacific and humanitarian considerations, it is still an agreement on regulations of international arms sales, and acknowledges the interests of states vis-à-vis other institutions. In this regard, the state parties recognize 'the legitimate political, security, economic and commercial interests of States in the international trade in conventional arms', and furthermore, '[t]he respect for the legitimate interests of States to acquire conventional arms to exercise their right to self-defence and for peacekeeping operations; and to produce export, import and transfer conventional arms.'[16] The common interest of states in protecting their sovereignty can easily be identified. States generally share the interest in monopolizing the use of force on their own territory, curbing the capabilities of enemies within. These, in turn, could be anything from common bandits and criminals to more legitimate liberation movements struggling against repressive dictatorships. Going back to Hegel, the repression of a people through autocracy undermines freedom and progress, a clear contradiction to Galtung's conception of a 'positive peace'.[17] In other words, it is not obvious, from the point of view of peace studies, that the ATT is entirely for the good.

[13] UNGA Res. 67/234 B, The Arms Trade Treaty (ATT) (2 April 2013) A/RES/67/234 B, Art. 1.

[14] Galtung, 'Violence, Peace, and Peace Research', 167–91 at 183.

[15] Thomas Paine, 'Common Sense', in *Common Sense, The Right of Man and Other Essential Writings of Thomas Paine* (London: Penguin, 1984 [1776]).

[16] ATT Art. 1.

[17] G. W. F. Hegel, *Elements of the Philosophy of Right*, ed. Allen Wood, trans. H. Nisbet (Cambridge: Cambridge University Press, 1991), §§261, 278, 355; Robert R. Williams, *Hegel's Ethics of Recognition* (Berkeley: University of California Press, 1997), 342–3.

When the core security interests of states are at stake, humanitarian considerations are often less prominent. The ATT would not have come into existence if it did not further the interests of its creators, notwithstanding that the interests of the negotiating states lay in short-term security interests as well as in humanitarian considerations, taking into account that in the long term, national security often depends on stability and peace in other states and regions.

2.2. Negotiation process of the ATT

The ATT has a complex and even somewhat confused origin and history, unlike other recent international humanitarian law instruments where the aim was to ban a specific type of weapon.[18] The conventions on anti-personnel landmines and cluster munitions for example, were developed on the basis of a recognized, and easily understandable, situation of human suffering because of specific weapons that would kill civilians long after the actual conflict was over. The military utility of the weapons in question also appeared questionable.[19] These weapons were easily defined, and the only 'sensible' answer to the particular problems arising from their use was to prohibit them. In other words, these were issues that were easy to communicate and understand (although the processes that resulted in the two conventions were long and cumbersome).

The ATT's evolution has been far more complex and obscure. The treaty was negotiated largely by disarmament diplomats, in a typically disarmament environment and under disarmament procedures, but it contains no disarmament elements. It is called a *trade* treaty, but it does not belong in the company of international trade agreements, which typically prohibit discrimination among its states parties in the agreed fields of trade. The ATT does the opposite: Not only does it specify the right to discriminate on certain grounds; it actually obligates states parties to discriminate against other states parties in certain situations. Many civil society organizations have seen the ATT as an instrument for *curbing international arms trade*, particularly in small arms and light weapons and ammunition, but the treaty does not prevent arms trade, it merely regulates it.

The ATT is mainly an international agreement on *export control.* Although there are regional treaties and arrangements on export control regarding arms and ammunition, there has not been, until now, a global instrument in this field. As such, the ATT does come closer to contributing to a goal of peace than many other instruments of international law predominantly occupied with conduct and means of warfare. These instruments take the earlier-mentioned axiom 'shit happens' as their point of departure and concern themselves with how war can be

[18] For example the conventions on, respectively, biological weapons (1972), chemical weapons (1993), anti-personnel mines (1997), and cluster munitions (2008).

[19] See 'Anti-personnel Mines: Friend or Foe? A Study of the Military Use and Effectiveness of Anti-personnel Mines', International Committee of the Red Cross (ICRC) (1994), http://www.icrc.org/eng/assets/files/other/icrc_002_0654.pdf, 73 (accessed 5 February 2013); Ove Dullum, 'Cluster Weapons; Military Utility and Alternatives', Norwegian Defence Research Establishment (FFI), report 02345 (2007), 143.

fought in less inhumane ways. The ATT, on the other hand, actually lays down an obligation to refrain from selling arms to states where they can be used to violate human rights or humanitarian law, thus potentially preventing armed conflict. Considering, however, that any state that authorizes arms export must reasonably accept the risk of the recipient actually using them, the restrictions on arms exports laid down in the ATT are not an obstacle for arms being used in general.

3. The ATT Negotiation History and Consensus Requirement

The General Assembly mandated negotiations of the ATT began in 2010 and were finalized in March 2013—almost a year after schedule—and without an outcome. The text that had been circulated by the chairman of the diplomatic conference could not be adopted because the rules of procedure required consensus, which could not be achieved (Syria, North Korea, and Iran blocked a consensus decision on the final night of the diplomatic conference). The text was therefore submitted by a handful of delegations to the General Assembly, which adopted the treaty text by a vote a few days later (2 April 2013).[20]

The consensus requirement in the Rules of Procedure made the ATT negotiations even more complex and difficult than they would otherwise have been—and the states that wanted a less restrictive approach to arms sale could comfortably rely on their right to prevent adoption if things didn't go their way—which influenced the level of legally binding obligations that the treaty could contain. A simple delegation count would have showed, with the whole of Africa, Latin America, and the Caribbean as well as most of Europe and several other states, that there would easily have been a two-thirds majority for stronger and clearer restrictions on arms trade than the current treaty contains. Having said that, it must be recognized that the chairman of the March diplomatic conference[21] presented a stronger treaty text than there was basis for in the conference, and thus he must have known that consensus would not be achieved with such a text. The plan appeared to be to ensure that the US would not block consensus (as it had in the diplomatic conference in July the year before) and preferably that Russia and China also would abstain from doing this. Given the restrictions stemming from the consensus rule, the ATT thus became a stronger text than one could have expected. Had the treaty been negotiated under the ordinary rules of the law on treaties,[22] it could have become significantly stronger and more efficient.

There were roughly four groups of states in the negotiations; first there were the 'progressive' states that wanted a strong arms trade treaty based on humanitarian considerations and that had also strongly opposed the consensus rule in the procedural debates; second, there were the states who wanted an ATT, but who didn't want it to complicate or restrict their arms exports too much; third, there was a

[20] UNGA Res. 67/234 B, The Arms Trade Treaty (2 April 2013), UN Doc. A/RES/67/234 B.

[21] Australian Ambassador Peter Woolcott.

[22] Vienna Convention on the Law of Treaties (VCLT) (22 May 1969) Art. 9.

group of states who were somewhat sceptical and apprehensive; and fourth, there was a relatively small group of states who did not want an ATT at all, and who did everything they could to prevent the negotiations from achieving success. The first group consisted of several African and Latin American states, as well as New Zealand, Norway, Iceland, and a few others. The second group consisted of the US, many of the EU states, and a few Asian countries. The third group comprised many Asian and Arab states as well as Russia and China. Finally, the relatively small fourth group consisted of the three states that explicitly broke consensus, along with a handful of others.

There was no real expectation of a consensus text throughout the negotiations, the issue was to get the 'right' states to block consensus. At the end of the first diplomatic conference (July 2012), the US delegation unexpectedly blocked consensus, and thus in the autumn it was decided that the negotiations would continue to yet another diplomatic conference the following spring. Finally, in March 2013, when it became clear that the United States and Russia could live with the text, the 'usual suspects' Iran, Syria, and North Korea played their part and blocked consensus on the last night of the diplomatic conference.

When the treaty text was voted on in the UN General Assembly a few days later, 154 states voted 'yes' to the final draft resolution and 23 abstained. Iran, North Korea, and Syria were the only states to vote 'no'. Particularly Iran and North Korea have a history of blocking consensus and opposing new treaties. Syria's rejection of the ATT was unsurprising considering the potential ramifications of the ATT on its then ongoing civil war. For North Korea's part, several issues stood in the way of endorsement: the failure to include provisions for nuclear disarmament, the failure to recognize the differences between developed and developing countries, an alleged lack of respect for the right to self-defence and to legitimate arms trade,[23] and, somewhat contradictory to the rest of the grievances, the inclusion of 'articles of a political nature'.[24] For one thing, North Korea found the United States 'hell bent on selling to South Korea . . . driving the already tense situation of the Korean peninsula to its worst level ever'.[25] In North Korea's view, the emerging ATT clearly did not create peace. Iran was similarly unassertive toward stronger regulation of the global arms trade, stressing that the rights of the importing countries had not been sufficiently addressed. This particular argument was repeated by a number of states throughout the negotiations and reflects the confusion regarding the subject matter of the treaty—had

[23] The latter two of these arguments are difficult to grasp, given the text of the ATT.

[24] Statement by HE Mr Ri Tong Il, Ambassador/Deputy Permanent Representative Permanent Mission of the Democratic People's Republic of Korea to the United Nations, Final United Nations Conference on the Arms Trade Treaty, New York, 18 March 2013, http://www.un.org/disarmament/ATT/statements/docs/20130318/20130318_dprk_E.pdf (accessed 10 Nov 2014); statement by HE Mr Sin So Ho, Ambassador/Permanent Representative of the Democratic People's Republic of Korea to the United Nations, United Nations Conference on the Arms Trade Treaty, New York, 2–27 July 2012, http://www.un.org/disarmament/ATT/statements/docs/20120709/20120709_DPRK_E.pdf (accessed 11 September 2014).

[25] Statement by HE Mr Sin So Ho, http://www.un.org/disarmament/ATT/statements/docs/20120709/20120709_DPRK_E.pdf, 2. (accessed 10 Nov 2014).

it been a *trade* treaty, it would have made sense that the importing states would have rights to buy what the exporters sold. But because giving states a right to buy arms would by implication mean that others would be under an obligation to sell arms, this was never seriously debated. No arms exporting state would ever agree to be denied its national sovereign decision-making power regarding to whom it may choose to sell arms. Iran, together with several other states, was also of the opinion that the ATT ought to have been limited to curbing illegal arms trade:

> In our view, the only purpose of a future Treaty shall be 'to prevent the diversion of conventional arms into the illicit market.' Accordingly, it shall ensure legal trade in conventional arms and respect and protect the right of each State to freely participate in the international transfer and trade of conventional arms, which is essential in ensuring the realization of the inherent right of States to security and self-defense.[26]

The sceptical stance of some of the states in the second and third categories is also understandable given their economic interests in the international arms trade. Between 2008 and 2012, US arms exports covered 30 per cent of the world's total demand, more than seven percentage points larger than the 22.7 per cent American share of the world's total GDP. The Russian export, second largest in absolute terms, was even larger in relative terms, with a GDP of less than 3 per cent of the world total, and 24 per cent of the world's total arms sales.[27] Germany, France, China, and the United Kingdom followed on the list of the world's top arms exporters, which may help explain their relative hesitancy towards strong export controls in the ATT. In addition to being one of the largest exporters, China followed India as the second largest importer of arms.[28]

In contrast, the states in the first, 'progressive', category wanted extensive regulation. Norway, for example, suggested that the ATT should include provisions to curb the, in legal terms ambiguous, category of 'armed violence': 'It is important that the Arms Trade Treaty contains strong and binding language that will bring about significant reductions of arms transfers that cause armed violence and human suffering.'[29] Iceland similarly wanted a treaty with extensive provisions for protecting humanitarian principles and human rights:

> It is vital that the treaty takes this into account and contains a specific gender-based violence criterion to prevent any such violence against women and girls. Accordingly the

[26] Statement by HE Ambassador Mohammad Khazaee, Permanent Representative of the Islamic Republic of Iran to the United Nations, United Nations Conference on the Arms Trade Treaty, New York, 10 July 2012, http://www.un.org/disarmament/ATT/statements/docs/20120710/20120710_Iran_E.pdf (accessed 10 Nov 2014).

[27] See The World Bank, '(GDP, current US$)', http://data.worldbank.org/indicator/NY.GDP.MKTP.CD (accessed 10 Nov 2014).

[28] See Paul Holtom et al., 'Trends in International Arms Transfers, 2012', Stockholm International Peace Research Institute (SIPRI), March 2013, http://books.sipri.org/product_info?c_product_id=455 (accessed 11 September 2014).

[29] Statement by Mr Heikki Holmås, Norwegian Minister of International Development, Final United Nations Conference on the Arms Trade Treaty, New York, 3 July 2013, http://www.un.org/disarmament/ATT/statements/docs/20120703/2012.07.03_Norway_E.pdf (accessed 10 Nov 2014).

treaty should require States to not allow an international transfer of conventional arms where there is a substantial risk that the arms under consideration are likely to be used to perpetrate or facilitate acts of gender-based violence, including rape and other forms of sexual violence.[30]

For the negotiations to result in something that could pass for diplomatic success, many states thought it vital that the United States, Russia, and China did not oppose the draft; and thus the Treaty was written with their interests in mind. As noted, there was disagreement during the negotiations over the aim of the treaty. While curbing already illegal trade (which many states wanted) would have little effect on the fiscal situation of states and governments, a more extensive regulation of the international trade in arms would have a significant impact on certain states' balance of trade. In addition to having economic interests in the arms trade, great powers typically take interest in armed conflicts around the globe, often having supplied parties to ongoing armed conflicts, including non-state actors, with weapons. To what extent the ATT regulates such arms transfers will be discussed in the following.

4. Outcome of the ATT Negotiations: Key Provisions of the Treaty

As mentioned above, the ATT is mainly an international agreement on export controls. There was considerable disagreement during the negotiations on whether the aim of the treaty should be to curb *illegal* arms trade, or if it should also comprise restrictions and prohibitions with regard to *irresponsible* trade in arms. Many states argued that there was no real merit in prohibiting illegal arms export as clearly it was already prohibited, either nationally or internationally. The aim of the treaty was finally linked to specific criteria that would also capture arms exports that were not necessarily illegal.

The material scope of the ATT, set out in the treaty's Articles 2, 3, and 4, was also subject to diverging views. Some of the powerful delegations (e.g. USA, Russia, China, India) were strongly opposed to including ammunition on the list of items to be covered by the treaty. Others (most African, Latin American, and many European states) were equally strongly against the exclusion of ammunition. This was the single most difficult topic concerning the material scope of the ATT, and it was solved by including ammunition on the list of items to be subject to authorization before export, but with less stringent reporting obligations. The materiel scope of the ATT is thus a list of conventional weapons, small arms, light weapons, their ammunition, and their parts and components.[31]

[30] Statement by HE Ambassador Gréta Gunnarsdóttir, Permanent Representative to the United Nations, Final United Nations Conference on the Arms Trade Treaty, New York, 9 July 2013, http://www.un.org/disarmament/ATT/statements/docs/20120709/20120709_Iceland_E.pdf (accessed 10 Nov 2014).

[31] ATT Arts. 2, 3, and 4.

The ATT sets out an implicit requirement that all states parties must have a national system for authorization of arms exports.[32] This authorization authority must assess all export applications against the provisions in ATT pertaining to prohibitions and export assessment.[33] From a humanitarian point of view, the rules aiming at preventing arms sales to where the arms may be used in contravention of international rules on human rights and international humanitarian law constitute the core of the treaty.

Article 6 (1) of the ATT sets out in which situations arms exports shall be prohibited. Such export is prohibited when the transfer would violate international obligations, for example UN Security Council arms embargoes. Why many states saw it as necessary to include a provision prohibiting what is already prohibited under international law is not clear, but one might speculate that the sanctions against Iran could have something to do with it.[34]

Article 6(2), continuing in the same vein, prohibits arms sales that would violate other obligations 'under international agreements to which it is a Party'. Here, however, there is a clear implication of the wording besides stating the obvious: it is prohibited to violate what would follow from international *treaty* obligations, in other words, it may not necessarily be prohibited to violate what would follow from international customary law.

Article 6(3) requires a state party not to authorize an arms sale when there is knowledge that the arms would be used to commit genocide, crimes against humanity, or specific war crimes. Obviously, the threshold for considering applying this provision is very high; there has to be *knowledge* on the part of the state authorizing export at the time of issuing permission to the arms exporter. The enumeration of crimes covered is also short and implies a high threshold: the arms sale must not be authorized when the arms 'would be used in the commission of genocide, crimes against humanity, grave breaches of the Geneva Conventions of 1949, attacks directed against civilian objects or civilians protected as such, or other war crimes defined by international agreements to which it is a party'.[35]

The main reason for not wanting simply to make a reference to war crimes in general, but rather insist on this quite strange and unique listing of war crimes, was a strong resistance among several delegations against having this assessment obligation apply in situations where the recipient state was in an non-international armed conflict. Many persistent attempts to include a reference to at a minimum Common Article 3 to the Four Geneva Conventions, and thus cover such situations, were struck back. Many delegations made statements, however, saying that they did understand the text, as it was adopted, to actually include non-international armed conflicts, because of the reference to 'war crimes defined by international agreements to which it is a party'—which reasonably must include the four Geneva Conventions (which have universal application), and therefore

[32] ATT Art. 5. [33] ATT Arts. 6 and 7.

[34] Apparently, this provision was a key reason why Iran chose to block consensus.

[35] ATT Art. 6(3).

also their Common Article 3 which deals with war crimes in non-international armed conflicts.[36]

If an arms transfer is not prohibited under Article 6, the exporting state must still assess a list of criteria before authorizing an arms transfer. This assessment obligation is laid down in Article 7.

Article 7 is designed as follows: Article 7(1) specifies this duty of assessment of information about the recipient state when considering authorizing an arms export. The exporting state shall assess 'the potential that the conventional arms or items: (a) would contribute to or undermine peace and security', and '(b) could be used to commit or facilitate a serious violation of' international humanitarian law or international human rights law, or an act constituting an offence under international conventions on terrorism or transnational organized crime. Article 7(3) then requires that each state party, if it 'determines that there is an overriding risk of any of the negative consequences in paragraph 1', 'shall not authorise the export'.

This somewhat odd compromise text was agreed after long and hard negotiations. It appears that to some states, the wording implies a certain flexibility because of the combination between the reference in litra (a) to both *contribution to* and *undermining of* peace and security through arms export, and the word '*overriding*' in Article 7(3). Some states interpreted the term 'overriding' in this context to allow a balancing of assumed positive and negative effects of arms exports. Other states have noted that the provision lays down the unequivocal '*shall not authorize*' in cases of serious violations of the criteria (negative consequences) in litra (a) and (b), and that the term 'overriding' does not have a specific legal content and therefore cannot reasonably imply such a balancing act. Many states made it clear in their statements at the closing session of the Diplomatic Conference as well as at the adoption session in the General Assembly a few days later, that their interpretation of Article 7 was that *if* any of the negative consequences in litra (a) or (b) were likely to happen, then there is an obligation not to authorize export of arms, notwithstanding the somewhat unclear term 'overriding'.[37]

Another controversial provision was Article 7(4) which lays down an obligation to take into account, while making the assessment described above, the risk of the arms export 'being used to commit or facilitate serious acts of gender-based violence or serious acts of violence against women and children'. The provision is not in the 'shall not authorize' category and its meaning and implications are therefore unclear. It was hugely controversial because of its reference to the term 'gender', something that the Vatican in particular had very

[36] The Norwegian Statement on 28 March 2013 said for example: 'Article 6(3) does not *explicitly* refer to situations of non-international armed conflict, but these are nevertheless covered under the treaty obligations undertaken by all states through the four Geneva Conventions and are therefore covered by this provision.'

[37] In the Norwegian translation of the ATT, preceding the ratification by Norway in February 2014, the term 'overriding risk' is translated 'overveiende sannsynlig' which simply means more likely than not.

serious problems with.[38] In the end, the provision made it into the operative part of the treaty instead of being tucked away in the preamble, and this appears to be the first time that this term has been used as treaty language.

These key provisions of the ATT; the scope of *objects* to be covered and the *criteria* for denying arms exports, together form the potential tools to ensure that conventional arms including their ammunition and parts and components are not exported to states where they might exacerbate situations of oppression, armed conflict, or violence in violation of international norms in the fields of human rights, humanitarian law, terrorism, transnational organized crime, and other areas of international law.

4.1. A practical example: US arms export to Syrian rebels

In January 2014 it was disclosed that the US Congress had sanctioned the transfer of small arms and light weapons to insurgent groups in Syria. Apparently, these were the 'good' rebels, out of the many factions fighting with and against the Assad regime.[39] The Syrian civil war began with peaceful protests against the regime in March 2011, but soon escalated, attracting foreign fighters and armed groups from other countries.[40]

The US has signed the ATT, but is unlikely to ratify it. Hence, a discussion of whether or not US arms exports to Syrian rebels would be a violation of ATT remains hypothetical. It is nevertheless an interesting hypothetical discussion, not least because the United States appear to take the norms of the ATT seriously, arguing not for the inapplicability of the ATT in their own case, but for the justifiability of their arms transfers in light of the ATT. Russia has also been highly present on the Syrian arms market, primarily selling to the Assad regime. Russia, however, has neither signed nor ratified the ATT, and does not appear to share the United States' view that the ATT—implicitly or explicitly—is nonetheless worth relating to.[41] Reports that Russia was transferring attack helicopters to the Syrian Government in 2011 led the then US Secretary of State Hillary Clinton to warn that the transfer would 'escalate the conflict quite dramatically', to which the Russian foreign minister Sergei Lavrov correctly replied that '[w]e are not violating any international law in performing these contracts.'[42]

[38] Discussions on the term 'gender' occur in many UN forums, and the Vatican has issues with it apparently because of its implications that there might be more categories than just 'men' and 'women'.

[39] Mark Hosenball, 'Congress Secretly Approves U.S. Weapons Flow to "Moderate" Syrian Rebels', Reuters, 27 January 2014, http://www.reuters.com/article/2014/01/27/us-usa-syria-rebels-idUSBREA0Q1S320140127 (accessed 10 Nov 2014).

[40] See Seth G. Jones, 'Syria's Growing Jihad', *Survival: Global Politics and Strategy* 55 (2013), 53–72.

[41] Jonathan Saul, 'Exclusive: Russia Steps Up Military Lifeline to Syria's Assad—Sources', Reuters, 17 January 2014, http://www.reuters.com/article/2014/01/17/us-syria-russia-arms-idUSBREA0G0MN20140117 (accessed 10 Nov 2014).

[42] Ian Black, 'Syria Crisis: Russia Denies Hillary Clinton Claim Over Helicopters', The Guardian, 13 June 2012, http://www.theguardian.com/world/2012/jun/13/syria-russia-denies-helicopters-clinton-claim (accessed 10 Nov 2014).

The US Congress allegedly sanctioned the transfer of small arms and light weapons to the opposition groups in the south of the country, drawing the line at anti-tank and anti-aircraft missile launchers. Small arms and light weapons are included in Article 2 of the ATT, and thus covered by Articles 6 and 7 specifying the criteria for the transfer of arms. As the Security Council has failed to put in place an arms embargo against the belligerents in Syria, or any other sanctions for that matter, the US arms transfers would not appear to conflict with the obligation in Article 6(1) to conform with measures adopted by the Security Council acting under Chapter VII of the UN Charter. In the context of the present chapter, the inability of the Security Council to mandate an embargo further underlines the limitations of international law in creating—or even facilitating—peace when the conflict lines run deep among the Council's five permanent members themselves.

Article 6(3) is also relevant in this discussion, as it requires a state party not to authorize an arms sale when there is knowledge that the arms would be used to commit genocide, crimes against humanity, or specific war crimes. As the US is exporting arms to rebel groups that they believe respect international law, the requirement of *knowledge* at the time of the authorization is probably not, according to the US, fulfilled here.

The transfer of light weapons to the Syrian insurgents is more problematic in the light of Article 7. To be in line with the ATT, the United States would have to assess the possibility of the transferred arms being used to *contribute* to or *undermine peace and security*, being used to commit *serious violations of IHL and HRL*, or being used to commit or facilitate acts of *terrorism* and *transnational organized crime*. If any of the negative consequences (which would be all of the above criteria except 'contribute to peace and security') were deemed to be overridingly likely, the transfer, according to Article 7(3), 'shall not be authorized'. In other words, such an authorization would be in violation of the treaty. The question one must ask is whether the term 'overriding' gives a state party the right to perform a balancing act between whether the arms transfer would *contribute* to or *undermine* peace and security, and hence, if it is deemed to contribute, whether the transfer would be allowed. The authors of this chapter would suggest that since the term 'shall not authorize' is linked to the *negative* consequences in Article 7(1), the term 'overriding' could not reasonably be understood as allowing the criteria laid down in Article 7(3) to be disregarded.

In practical terms, at least two observations make the transfer questionable:

First, there is strong evidence to suggest that groups on both sides of the conflict have committed some of the above transgressions on a large scale. Summary executions, indiscriminate attacks, torture, terrorism, and the infamous use of chemical weapons on 21 August 2013 are among the reported violations of international law.[43] Second, while

[43] According to Human Rights Watch, 'attacks against the civilian population appear to have been planned and executed as a matter of policy' by at least 20 different groups. See Human Rights Watch, 'You Can Still See Their Blood: Executions, Indiscriminate Shooting, and Hostage Taking by Opposition Forces in Latakia Countryside' (10 October 2013), 95. See also 'Conference Room

not all of the belligerent groups have necessarily committed such international crimes, the alliances and schisms appear to be highly confusing and contingent, making it difficult to limit support to a specific actor.[44] This is, of course, assuming that the receiving party itself has not committed any of the crimes listed in article 7 (1). The experiences of western donors testify to the difficulty of limiting aid to certain groups. The United States and Britain froze the transfer of so-called 'non-lethal aid' to groups in Northern Syria in December 2013, when it became known that Islamist rebels had seized the aid—and weapons—from the western backed groups.

The United States issued a presidential directive on arms transfer policy on 15 January 2013, using much of the language in the ATT.

The United States will not authorize any transfer if it has actual knowledge at the time of authorization that the transferred arms will be used to commit: genocide; crimes against humanity; grave breaches of the Geneva Conventions of 1949; serious violations of Common Article 3 of the Geneva Conventions of 1949; attacks directed against civilian objects or civilians who are legally protected from attack or other war crimes.[45]

Apart from the inclusion of the word 'actual' and the reference to Common Article 3,[46] the US policy mirrors Article 6(3) of the ATT almost to the letter. The introduction of the qualifying adjective 'actual', however, seems to imply a slightly lower threshold for authorization than the wording in the ATT. In the case of the Syrian Civil War, the wording '*actual knowledge* ... that the transferred arms *will*' appears strong, implying direct causality. The language in Article 7(3) contains a lower threshold for application, requiring Parties to determine whether 'there is an overriding risk', and if this is confirmed, not to authorize export. It would be reasonable to suggest that the US arms transfers to Syrian insurgents falls foul of this standard, considering the scale of the violations of IHL and HRL, and the confused battlefield situation. The term 'overriding' does appear in the presidential directive, but it symptomatically qualifies 'national interests', not risk of violations of IHL and HRL: '[T]he United States will exercise unilateral restraint in the export of arms in cases where such restraint will be effective or is necessitated by overriding national interests.'[47] One might suspect that this holds true also the other way around;

Paper: Assault on Medical Care in Syria', United Nations Independent International Commission of Inquiry on the Syrian Arab Republic, 13 September 2013, and '6th Report of Commission of Inquiry on Syria', 11 September 2013; 'Deprival of Food, Water, Shelter and Medical Care—a Method of War in Syria, and a Crime Against Humanity', United Nations Office of the High Commissioner of Human Rights, 6 February 2014, http://www.ohchr.org/EN/NewsEvents/Pages/DisplayNews.aspx?NewsID=14224& (accessed 11 September 2014).

[44] Seth G. Jones, 'Syria's Growing Jihad', *Survival: Global Politics and Strategy* 55 (2013), 53–72.

[45] The White House, 'Presidential Policy Directive: United States Conventional Arms Transfer Policy', 15 January 2013, http://www.whitehouse.gov/the-press-office/2014/01/15/presidential-policy-directive-united-states-conventional-arms-transfer-p (accessed 11 September 2014).

[46] The inclusion of Common Art. 3 was a hotly debated topic during the diplomatic conference, and was omitted in the very last version of the text, possibly after pressure from states with internal conflicts going on.

[47] The White House, 'Presidential Policy Directive', 15 January 2013.

the United States, and possibly other countries, will authorize transfer when necessitated by overriding national interests.

5. A Reflection on the Field: Peace Studies and International Law

The present volume theorizes the link between peace and peace studies on the one hand, and international law on the other. Historically, the association between international law and peace studies and philosophy is strong. Some commentators have even gone as far as to suggest that if these fields are not already two sides of the same coin, practitioners should take steps to push them closer together. Along these lines, Edward Gordon has argued that it is remarkable 'that peace studies and international law are regarded as separate academic disciplines'.[48] While we agree that there is great potential for cooperation and even convergence of the disciplines, we dissent from the notion that international law and peace studies should be conflated.

Peace studies or peace research is not, in the same sense as for example political science, law, anthropology, or economics, a singular academic field, although it is increasingly seen as a subject at many universities. While the latter four are all fairly old and established university disciplines with broad scopes, providing more or less distinct approaches and methodologies, peace studies has a much narrower thematic scope, and does not supply a unifying methodology (which is, however, not to say that it is any less reliable or valid than other social sciences). Peace studies is normally understood as a multidisciplinary field of inquiry in which practitioners from different scholarly backgrounds come together in a shared enterprise of 'research into the conditions—past present and future—of realizing peace'.[49] While the aim of creating peace may be less pronounced today than when Johan Galtung formulated his definition in 1969, the fundamental goal of achieving peace remains an implicit foundation stone of peace research (an open renunciation of the aim of creating peace would logically reduce it to a subgenre of its cousin International Relations (IR)). Thus, peace studies are at least in theory defined by their contributors' aim of realizing global security and creating social justice through academic inquiry.

While the discipline of peace studies is easily distinguished from the object its practitioners aim to investigate (peace and conflict), it is less easy to distinguish the object of international law from its vocation. International law is, on the one hand, the body of rules and customs applicable to states, organizations, and individuals on the international arena, and on the other, the *study* of these rules and customs. Often, international legal practitioners will have dual roles

[48] Edward Gordon, 'From Erasmus to Tolstoy: The Peace Literature of Four Centuries: Jacob Ter Meulen's Bibliographies of the Peace Movement Before 1899', *Harvard International Law Journal* 34 (1993), 641–44 at 641.

[49] Galtung, 'Violence, Peace, and Peace Research', 167–91 at 183.

as academics and civil servants responsible for negotiating treaty law, implying that when they practise the former role they may in fact be studying what they produce in the latter.

In contrast to domestic law, envisioned as being imposed and enforced top-down by a state (or 'leviathan'),[50] international law is commonly seen as a horizontal system of agreements between sovereign states. The interest of states as the origins of international law are translated into the sources of international law, identified by the Statute for the International Court of Justice as (a) international conventions, (b) international customs, (c) general principles of law as primary sources, and (d) 'judicial decisions and the teachings of the most highly qualified publicists' as subsidiary sources.[51] Once in existence, the law is separated from the contingent interests of states, taking on a dynamic of its own. The room for interpretation, however, is generally quite limited.

In the study of international law, legal positivism is the dominant methodology when venturing to determine *lex lata*, or 'the law as it is'. As an alternative to *lex lata*, analysts sometimes discuss *lex ferenda*, or 'how the law should be'. Although an interesting, and often politically important, exercise, courts and legal practitioners operate on the basis of *lex lata*. Legal positivism has its roots in the philosophy of Jeremy Bentham and John Austin, and received its most famous formulation by H. L. A. Hart, who asserted that both domestic and international law were clearly different from both morality and coercion, but refused to define law in terms of its content.[52] According to John Gardner, legal positivism can be summarized as the proposition: 'In any legal system, whether a given norm is legally valid, and hence whether it forms part of the law of that system, depends on its sources, not its merits.'[53] This is in sharp contrast to the definition of peace studies above, as 'research into the conditions of realizing peace', that is, research not only defined in terms of its content, but also in terms of its political goals. While peace studies are predicated on the—indeed admirable—goal of creating peace, international law is inherently tied to the interests of states. These form complex calculuses in which ethics and humanitarian considerations feature to varying degrees.

The link between peace and international law has long roots in the history of ideas. Indeed, *lex ferenda* is arguably an important part of pushing the evolution of norms forward, and has been practised by many of the most important figures of legal and political thought. Immanuel Kant famously propounded that perpetual peace be built on the values of democracy, international law, and universal hospitality.[54] This, however, presupposes that the creators of

[50] See Thomas Hobbes, *Leviathan* (Cambridge: Cambridge University Press, 2008 [1651]).

[51] Statute for the International Court of Justice (ICJ) (enacted 26 June 1945, in force 24 October 1945), Art. 38(1).

[52] H. L. A. Hart, *The Concept of Law* (Oxford: Oxford University Press, 1961), 14–15, 217–20.

[53] John Gardner, 'Legal Positivism: 5½ Myths', *American Journal of Jurisprudence* 46 (2001), 199–227 at 199.

[54] Immanuel Kant, *Perpetual Peace: A Philosophical Essay*, trans. M. C. Smith (London: Allen & Unwin, 1917), 120–37. In the modern peace studies and international relations literature, Kant's ideas have translated into research on the so-called democratic and liberal peace. See Håvard

the law seek peace. Having experienced the Napoleonic Wars first hand, G. F. W. Hegel was less positive to the potential of international law, as such agreement, 'whether based on moral, religious or other grounds and considerations, would always be dependent on particular sovereign wills, and therefore would continue to be tainted with contingency'.[55] For Hegel, ethics and peace were primarily matters of the nation-state, making the viability of a true international community difficult.[56]

As such, international law is no more than its creators want it to be; while a peace student by definition could not be a peace student and simultaneously research the conditions for realizing war, it is entirely possible to practise law in the service of war. Notwithstanding this point of departure, peace is generally seen to be in the interest of states, and many international laws are created for its promotion, the most prominent example being the UN Charter itself. The ATT negotiations demonstrate this point. While no states would themselves concede that they were opposed to a strong instrument promoting peace or humanitarian values or human rights, economic or political interests were clearly just as important for some states. The fact that the US used selected language from the ATT in their arguments *for* supplying arms to Syrian rebels, when such transfers arguably constitute exactly what the ATT reasonably should prohibit, demonstrates this point. A generous definition of peace could furthermore make nearly any policy one that appears to be promoting peace.

6. Conclusion

International law does not prohibit war, it restricts the manner in which one may conduct it. The ATT does not prevent arms transfers, it aims at ensuring that the transferred arms themselves are consistent with the requirements of international humanitarian law (capable of hitting military targets), and that they are used in accordance with the various regimes in international law mentioned in this chapter. States parties' national security interests in importing or exporting arms according to their own defence strategies, consistent with the perceived strategies of various allies or potential enemies, will hardly be affected by this Treaty. Arms are considered necessary, and most states have them.

Having said that, one might express the hope that if arms were used only in ways that are consistent with human rights and international humanitarian law

Hegre, Tanja Ellingsen, Scott Gates, and Nils Petter Gleditsch, 'Toward a Democratic Civil Peace? Democracy, Political Change, and Civil War, 1816-1992', *American Political Science Review* 95 (2001), 33–48; John R. Oneal and Bruce M. Russett, 'The Kantian Peace: The Pacific Benefits of Democracy, Interdependence, and International Organizations, 1885–1992', *World Politics* 52 (1999), 1–37.

[55] Hegel, *Elements of the Philosophy of Right*, §333.

[56] See Robert R. Williams, *Hegel's Ethics of Recognition* (Berkeley: University of California Press), 352.

requirements, then this in itself would contribute to peace. This particularly holds true if one views peace in line with Galtung, as absence of violence.[57] Positive peace or social justice is not directly addressed, but may be facilitated through the absence of violence. As such, the international rules regulating the use of armed force, be it under human rights law in law enforcement or in armed conflict during hostilities, aim at establishing conditions for maintaining or creating peace.

[57] Galtung, 'Violence, Peace, and Peace Research', 167–91 at 183.

PART III

CIVIL SOCIETY PARTICIPATION IN THE PROMOTION AND SAFEGUARDING OF PEACE

12

Non-Discrimination and Equality as the Foundations of Peace

Vibeke Blaker Strand

1. Introduction

Hierarchies have always existed and remain all over the world. Hierarchies cause discrimination and inequality, leaving people in a disadvantaged position because of, for instance, gender, ethnicity, disability, religion, age, nationality, or social status. Different characteristics may also intersect in a way that leaves a person in a particularly vulnerable situation. For instance, disabled immigrant women often face grave barriers when seeking employment. Inequality exists between countries, within countries, and across borders. In a world that is still going through a period of financial instability, where there are high unemployment rates in many countries, where the differences between rich and poor countries increase, where natural disasters strike hardest those who are already vulnerable, and where there is war, more people than before migrate. Immigrants and asylum seekers are often at the bottom of the societal hierarchy and are, thus, particularly vulnerable to discrimination and inequality. When looking at societies as a whole, research shows that violence, poor health, and other social problems are more common in societies with greater inequality.[1]

Equality as an ideal is a relatively modern notion. Throughout history there are several examples of how hierarchy has been argued and implemented as synonymous with justice. Aristotle, for instance, argued that nature contains a 'principle of rule and subordination' leaving free male citizens with particular power.[2]

[1] Richard Wilkinson and Kate Pickett, *The Spirit Level: Why Equality is Better for Everyone* (London: Penguin Books, 2010), 18. Erik Melander has 'shown that political gender equality in the form of female representation in parliament is associated with lower levels of personal integrity rights abuse by state agents', cf. Erik Melander, 'Political Gender Equality and State Human Rights Abuse', *Journal of Peace Research* 42 (2005), 149–66 at 163.

[2] Sandra Fredman, 'Combating Racism with Human Rights: The Right to Equality', in *Discrimination and Human Rights: The Case of Racism*, Sandra Fredman (ed.) (Oxford: Oxford University Press, 2001), 9–44 at 14.

Equality was slowly introduced as a central value[3], and both equality and freedom gained momentum in the theories put forward by the Enlightenment philosophers in the seventeenth and eighteenth centuries. Their notion of equality and freedom had, however, a paradoxically selective nature. The right to equality was reserved for those designated as rights-holders, and 'by deftly excluding women, slaves, and the unpropertied classes from the definition of "individuals" worthy to be rightsbearers, liberal thinkers were able to justify continued domination'.[4] The mere acceptance of freedom and equality for all individuals, however, provided 'feminists and other disadvantaged groups [with] the necessary vocabulary to argue for the emancipation of all'.[5] As articulated by Fredman: 'It was as a focus for political activism, rather than as a legal concept, that equality began to emerge as a real force for combating sex discrimination and racism.'[6] Civil society has played—and continues to play—a crucial role in advocating equality and non-discrimination. Political struggles have shaped the legal instruments at international, regional, and domestic levels on non-discrimination and equality, establishing close ties between the political and the legal spheres.

The formalization of human rights that started after the United Nations was founded in 1945 reflects the experiences that the world had gone through, with two world wars during a relatively short period of time, and the aspiration to take steps so as never to experience the same again.[7] World War II is considered a war 'made possible by the denial of the democratic principles of the dignity, equality and mutual respect of men, and by the propagation, in their place, through ignorance and prejudice, of the doctrine of the inequality of men and races'.[8] It was therefore no coincidence that the first international human rights convention to be adopted by the UN General Assembly was the 1965 International Convention on the Elimination of All Forms of Racial Discrimination (ICERD).[9] One decade after adopting ICERD, the UN General Assembly adopted the 1979 Convention on the Elimination of All Forms of Discrimination against Women (CEDAW). Through ICERD and CEDAW it was established that inequality and discrimination related to race and gender are major challenges that need to be addressed on a global level.

[3] According to Fredman ('Combating Racism with Human Rights'), it was 'not until the dissolution of feudalism and the advent of mercantile capitalism that notions of individual equality came to the fore'.

[4] Fredman, 'Combating Racism with Human Rights'.

[5] Fredman, 'Combating Racism with Human Rights'.

[6] Fredman, 'Combating Racism with Human Rights'.

[7] This is clearly reflected in the very first words of the preamble to the 1945 Charter of the United Nations, where it is stated that the peoples of the United Nations are determined 'to save succeeding generations from the scourge of war, which twice in our lifetime has brought untold sorrow to mankind'.

[8] Cf. the preamble to the Constitution of the United Nations Organization for Education, Science and Culture (UNESCO), which was founded on 16 November 1945.

[9] It should be noted, however, that the UN, before adopting ICERD, had already adopted the 1926 Slavery Convention and the 1948 Convention on the Prevention and Punishment of the Crime of Genocide. In 1973, the UN adopted the International Convention on the Suppression and Punishment of the Crime of Apartheid.

The principles of equality and non-discrimination are today considered 'fundamental components of international human rights law'.[10] They are formalized in nearly all the core international human rights instruments,[11] as well as in regional and domestic legal instruments. What equality and non-discrimination further entail is developed and shaped through the practice of supervisory organs on international, regional, and domestic levels. Thus, from a legal perspective, discrimination and inequality are targeted and combated through a multi-layered approach.

The principles of equality and non-discrimination put individuals at the centre, a starting point resting on a deep recognition that all human beings—all individuals—are entitled to the same rights and freedoms. Already the first sentence of the preamble to the 1948 Universal Declaration of Human Rights reflects this individualistic point of departure, in which the states recognize that the 'inherent dignity and the equal and inalienable rights of all members of the human family is the foundation of freedom, justice and peace in the world'.

Norms on non-discrimination and equality, and in particular the way in which they seek to achieve substantive equality, can be seen as mechanisms to protect and promote the inherent dignity of every human being. Through this, non-discrimination and equality can be considered parts of 'the foundation of freedom, justice and peace in the world'.

While other treaties and bodies established under international law play important roles in the processes of maintaining and restoring peace by settling interstate disputes or by prosecuting persons suspected of having committed mass atrocity crimes, particularly the International Court of Justice (ICJ) and the International Criminal Court (ICC), international human rights conventions in the field of non-discrimination and equality approach the issue of peace from another angle.[12] The primary goal of these instruments is to achieve substantive equality—equality in practice—for every human being. Substantive equality is a concept with close connections to the term 'positive peace', as it involves the redistribution of power, the equal right for all to participation in society and equal opportunities. However, substantive equality cannot be realized if there is incitement to, or existing, violence and discrimination.[13] Therefore, substantive

[10] 'General Comment No. 20 Non-Discrimination in Economic, Social and Cultural Rights (Art. 2, para. 2 of the ICESCR)', Committee on Economic, Social and Cultural Rights, 2009, UN Doc. E/C.12/GC/20 (2009), para. 2.

[11] An overview of the nine international human rights treaties that are considered core treaties can be found on www.ohchr.org/EN/ProfessionalInterest/Pages/CoreInstruments.aspx (accessed 11 Nov 2014).

[12] See Gentian Zyberi's chapter in this volume. The ICJ has addressed issues involving racial discrimination in several cases, see in particular *Barcelona Traction, Light and Power Company, Limited* (Merits) [1970] ICJ Rep 1970, 32; *Legal Consequences for States of the Continued Presence of South Africa in Namibia (South West Africa) notwithstanding Security Council Resolution 276 (1970)* (Advisory Opinion) [1971] ICJ Rep 1971, 57 para. 131, and *Application of the International Convention on the Elimination of all Forms of Racial Discrimination (Georgia* v. *Russian Federation)* (Provisional Measures) [2008] ICJ Rep 2008, 353.

[13] See para. 7 of the preamble to the CERD (entered into force 4 January 1969), where it is clearly established that 'discrimination between human beings on the grounds of race, colour or ethnic

equality requires the establishing of negative peace, understood as the absence of violence.[14]

In this chapter, particular emphasis will be put on ICERD and CEDAW, including interpretative practice from the two committees established to supervise the contracting states' implementation of the conventions, the CERD Committee and the CEDAW Committee. ICERD and CEDAW have been the driving forces under international law when it comes to setting out a global common ground in the combat against discrimination and inequality, and they are relevant to most UN member states.[15] Other UN human rights conventions, and interpretative practice connected to such instruments, will only to some extent be integrated.

The focus on the international legal sources must not be understood to insinuate that these legal instruments exist independently from regional and domestic legislation and interpretation in the field of non-discrimination and equality. The different legal instruments on the different levels have influenced each other with regard to the formulation of rights and freedoms,[16] and they continue to influence each other when rights and freedoms are being interpreted.[17]

The chapter proceeds in four sections. In Section 2, I give some examples on how civil society has played a crucial role in advocating equality and non-discrimination throughout history. In Section 3, I comment on the close relationship between substantive equality and peace, with particular emphasis on positive peace. In Section 4, I seek to paint a broad picture of the different ways in which non-discrimination and equality contribute to the founding of peace. Four approaches are identified as embedded in and developed under international law; acknowledging that peace starts in the home; addressing racial hate speech and violence; addressing direct and indirect discrimination, and the introduction of active steps targeted at transformation of society. Finally, in Section 5, I address the road ahead. Here it is emphasized that it is of grave importance that civil society and the legal sphere pull together as both are essential to the foundation of peace.

origin is an obstacle to friendly and peaceful relations among nations and is capable of disturbing peace and security among peoples and the harmony of persons living side by side even within one and the same State'.

[14] Further elaboration of negative and positive peace is found in the introductory chapter to this volume, written by Bailliet and Larsen.

[15] As of May 2014, there were 177 parties to the CERD and 188 parties to the CEDAW out of the 193 UN member states.

[16] Arts. 18 and 19 on freedom of religion and belief and on freedom of expression in the 1966 UN International Covenant on Civil and Political Rights (ICCPR) are for instance very similar to Arts. 9 and 11 in the European Convention on Human Rights (ECHR).

[17] It follows from the 1969 Vienna Convention on the Law of Treaties Art. 31 para. 3(c) that when interpreting a treaty 'any relevant rules of international law applicable in the relations between the parties ... shall be taken into account, together with the context'. This implies that international courts and supervisory organs have to look at each other's practice in order to avoid contradictory obligations being imposed in the States parties. Central on the regional level are the European Court of Human Rights, the Inter-American Court of Human Rights, and the African Court of Justice and Human Rights. In the domestic arena, international, regional, and domestic legislation will all have to be taken into consideration as states are obliged to follow all the instruments that they have ratified.

2. Struggles from Below: Some Examples

Before looking at the international legal tools in this field, a broader picture needs to be painted. Civil society has throughout history advocated, struggled, and made grave sacrifices in the fight for the removal of hierarchy, discrimination, and inequality. The human rights instruments do not exist in a vacuum, but are surrounded by historical and contemporary events that have influenced, and continue to influence, the legal tools.

While some of the struggles have been characterized by violence, such as in the struggle for social justice, equality, and the removal of hierarchy during the French Revolution in the years following 1789, there are several examples on the application of a different strategy: to fight discrimination and inequality through peaceful means.

The struggle against racial segregation fought by the US civil rights movement in the late 1950s and 1960s is a prominent example of the power that lies with civil society when seeking to eliminate discrimination. African-Americans in the US lived in a segregated society where different rights and obligations were imposed on people according to race. In the late 1950s the civil rights movement transformed their struggle against racial segregation into a non-violent crusade of civil rights.[18] Martin Luther King Jr. and other central figures in the movement were inspired by Gandhi's success using non-violent resistance in winning independence for India.[19] Gandhi rejected passivity and developed his method as an active form of struggle 'transcending the passivity of nonresistance while offering a strategy for fighting effectively to resist social evil'.[20] Examples of measures taken by the civil rights movement in the US were bus boycotts, boycotts against downtown stores, organized sit-ins at whites-only lunch counters, and peaceful marches and demonstrations. The measures taken generated bottom-up engagement in the African-American population as well as publicity. This resulted in public opinion turning against racial segregation. The Civil Rights Act of 1964 and the Voting Rights Act of 1965 ended racial discriminatory laws.

The Gandhian method of strategic non-violent action has, by many, been considered a 'force more powerful'.[21] The strategy has been applied and enlarged upon in a growing number of countries.[22]

While some battles have been successful, others are still being fought.[23] Under difficult circumstances in Zimbabwe, there are several NGOs working

[18] Peter Ackerman and Jack DuVall, *A Force More Powerful: A Century of Nonviolent Conflict* (New York: St Martin's Press, 2000), 312.

[19] David Cortright, *Peace: A History of Movements and Ideas* (Cambridge: Cambridge University Press, 2008), 211.

[20] Cortright, *Peace*, 19.

[21] Cortright, *Peace*, 213, referring to Ackerman and DuVall, *A Force More Powerful*.

[22] For further elaboration and examples, cf. Cortright, *Peace*, 212.

[23] For the stories of women and men living in Muslim majority countries, or in diaspora populations of Muslim heritage, and their struggle against fundamentalist oppression, see Karima Bennoune, *Your Fatwa Does Not Apply Here: Untold Stories from the Fight Against Muslim Fundamentalism* (New York: Norton, 2013).

to enhance human rights. One example is Women of Zimbabwe Arise (WOZA), which is a membership organization with approximately 70,000, mainly black, impoverished women from urban and rural areas.[24] WOZA arranges peaceful, non-violent demonstrations, based on civil disobedience, often resulting in arrests of its members. Through a combination of civic education and public demonstrations, WOZA has created spaces where women can address issues affecting their day-to-day lives and 'press for solutions to the current social and economic crisis'.[25] WOZA has experienced some success in the legal sphere, by bringing cases before the courts, but the ability to affect the police, the courts, and the military has thus far been limited.[26] On an individual level, however, WOZA functions as a tool for initiating processes of 'individual transformation', resulting in women no longer seeing the government as having absolute power over them; '[i]nstead they see themselves as having power to speak up and act against injustices and abuse of power.'[27]

The history of teenager Malala Yousafzai, who was shot by the Taliban in 2012 for her activism for education for girls in the Swat District in Pakistan, is a living reminder of how inequality remains and the price some individuals have to pay in the struggle for equality. Living under constant death threats from the Taliban, she was asked what she would do if a Taliban assassin came calling again. She answered: 'I'll tell him how important education is, and that I even want education for your children as well ... And I would tell him, "that's what I want to tell you, now do what you want?"'[28]

Peace, dialogue, and education are Malala's strategies for fighting the inequality and discrimination imposed on girls by the Taliban. Her peaceful approach embodied in such a young, innocent person has gained massive support and attention.

The crucial role played throughout history by civil society in advocating equality and non-discrimination has not only been played out domestically; the struggle has also been fought across borders. This has particularly been the case with regard to women's rights. Today women's organizations are often structured as NGOs, and they carry out a number of activities including 'the launching of social and development programmes, promoting social justice and human rights, monitoring governments and numerous other functions'.[29] The efforts made by women's organizations have been—and continue to be—essential in

[24] Anne Hellum, Bill Derman, Geoff Feltoe, Ellen Sithole, Julie Stewart, and Amy Tsanga, 'Rights Claiming and Rights Making in Zimbabwe: A Study of Three Human Rights NGOs', in *Human Rights, Power and Civic Action: Comparative Analyses of Struggles for Rights in Developing Societies*, Bård A. Andreassen and Gordon Crawford (eds.) (London: Routledge, 2013), 22–54 at 31.

[25] Hellum et al., 'Rights Claiming and Rights Making', 39.

[26] Hellum et al., 'Rights Claiming and Rights Making', 40, 48.

[27] Hellum et al., 'Rights Claiming and Rights Making', 45.

[28] David Simpson and Ben Brumfield, 'Malala Yousafzai turns the other cheek to the Taliban', CNN, 9 October 2013, www.edition.cnn.com/2013/10/07/world/asia/taliban-malala/ (accessed 11 Nov 2014).

[29] Hilda Rømer Christensen, Beatrice Halsaa, and Aino Saarinen (eds.), *Crossing Borders: Re-mapping Women's Movements at the Turn of the 21st Century* (Odense: Heraldisk Selskab, 2004), 15.

enforcing improvements to women's legal and factual situations in countries all over the world.[30] The importance of advocating women's rights across borders was emphasized in the Beijing Declaration and Platform for Action, the international declaration of women's rights set up at the UN's landmark Fourth World Conference on Women, held in Beijing in 1995. It recognized that 'women share common concerns that can be addressed only by working together and in partnership with men towards the common goal of gender equality around the world'.[31]

3. Substantive Equality and Peace

A society that is built on and reproduces inequality and discrimination is not a society where people live peacefully together. It is not a society in peace. Peace requires not just the absence of violence, 'negative peace'; respect for human rights and social justice are also components relevant to peace. The term 'positive peace' rests on an understanding of peace that includes this broader picture. Cortright sees positive peace as 'transcending the conditions that limit human potential and assuring opportunities for self-realization'.[32] Human rights norms on non-discrimination and equality are particularly relevant to the notion of positive peace, in that the aim of these norms is to achieve not only formal equality, but also equality in practice, often referred to as 'substantive equality'.

There is a close connection between positive and negative peace in the sense that positive peace—to which substantive equality is pulling—can be seen as a way of preventing violence—a breach of negative peace—from occurring. At the same time it is clear that absence of violence, negative peace, is necessary if substantive equality and positive peace are to be achieved. Therefore, substantive equality includes both negative and positive peace.

The Committee on Economic, Social and Cultural Rights (the ICESCR Committee), the committee monitoring the implementation by contracting states of the International Covenant on Economic, Social and Cultural Rights (ICESCR), has issued a General Comment on 'Non-discrimination in Economic, Social and Cultural Rights' that expresses the current understanding of how inequality and discrimination are to be approached under the international human rights instruments. The committee states that '[m]erely addressing formal discrimination will not ensure substantive equality', and that elimination

[30] For a presentation of a Nepalese NGO that has embarked on a legal education programme teaching law enforcement agencies and judges about Nepal's obligations under the CEDAW, see Kabita Pandey, 'Judicial Education on the Convention on Elimination of Discrimination against Women in Nepal', in *Women's Human Rights: CEDAW in International, Regional and National Law*, Anne Hellum and Henriette Sinding Aasen (eds.) (Cambridge: Cambridge University Press, 2013), 410–29. See also the other chapters in part III in the same volume.

[31] The Beijing Declaration and Platform for Action, adopted by the Fourth World Conference on Women on 15 September 1995, para. 3.

[32] Cortright, *Peace*, 7.

of discrimination in practice 'requires paying sufficient attention to groups of individuals which suffer historical or persistent prejudice instead of merely comparing the formal treatment of individuals in similar situations. States parties must therefore immediately adopt the necessary measures to prevent, diminish and eliminate the conditions and attitudes which cause or perpetuate substantive or de facto discrimination.'[33] We see that, in order to establish substantive equality, focus must be put on the conditions and attitudes that cause or perpetuate discrimination and inequality. Society needs to go through a transformation that enables the breakdown of hierarchies. What substantive equality contains on a concrete level is not always clear-cut, as substantive equality involves complex decisions as to the objectives to be achieved and the means to be taken.[34] The aim of this chapter is first and foremost to sketch out in a broad manner the different ways in which non-discrimination and equality contribute to the founding of peace. The legal norms and practice in the field of equality and non-discrimination, to which we will turn in Section 4, contain a multifaceted approach towards substantive equality.[35] The approach includes negatively defined prohibitions and positively defined obligations, as well as focus on individuals and on groups.

4. The Founding of Peace through Non-Discrimination and Equality

In this section, focus is put on the different ways in which human rights instruments on non-discrimination and equality are relevant to substantive equality and therefore to the foundation of peace. Of particular interest are interpretative practices issued by the CEDAW Committee and the CERD Committee, who, by applying dynamic interpretation, have contributed to the clarifying of the contents of CEDAW and ICERD and to the strengthening of the protection against discrimination and inequality. The presentation does not seek exhaustively to include all practices of the committees relevant to the topic, but seeks to include practices that shed light on how non-discrimination and equality contribute to the foundation of peace.[36] References will be made to some General

[33] General Comment No. 20, ICESCR Committee, para. 8(b).

[34] Sandra Fredman, *Human Rights Transformed* (Oxford: Oxford University Press, 2008), 178.

[35] This is e.g. underlined in 'General Recommendation No. 25 On Article 4, paragraph 1, of the Convention on the Elimination of All Forms of Discrimination against Women, on temporary special measures', CEDAW Committee, 2004, UN Doc. HRI/GEN/1/Rev.7 at 282 (2004), para. 7. See also Rikki Holtmaat, 'The CEDAW: A Holistic Approach to Women's Equality and Freedom', in *Women's Human Rights: CEDAW in International, Regional and National Law*, Anne Hellum and Henriette Sinding Aasen (eds.) (Cambridge: Cambridge University Press, 2013), 95–123 at 120.

[36] The conventions are subject to the general rules of interpretation embedded in the UN Vienna convention on the law of treaties adopted on 23 May 1969. Arts. 31 and 32 do not exhaustively list the relevant means of interpretation, cf. Morten Ruud and Geir Ulfstein, *Innføring i folkerett* (3rd edn. Oslo: Universitetsforlaget, 2011), 89. Practice from the supervising committees

Recommendations/Comments[37] and to some views given as part of the individual complaints procedures.[38]

In Subsections 4.1–4.4, four ways in which non-discrimination and equality contribute to the founding of peace are discussed; acknowledging that peace starts in the home; addressing racial hate speech and violence; addressing direct and indirect discrimination and the introduction of active steps targeted at transformation of society.

While the terms 'non-discrimination' and 'equality' are often applied interchangeably in everyday life, the legal use of the terms is usually to consider 'discrimination' to be relevant to individual cases where direct or indirect discrimination is on the agenda, while '(substantive) equality' is used in a broader sense, covering both negatively formulated prohibitions against direct and indirect discrimination and positive state duties. In the rest of the chapter, this understanding is applied.

4.1. Peace starts in the home

The CEDAW does not contain an explicit mention of violence against women. This issue was not high on the international agenda when CEDAW was drafted in the 1970s.[39] As time passed there was increased awareness of the prevalence of violence against women and its severe consequences.[40] In its 1992 General Recommendation on violence against women, the CEDAW Committee took steps to fill this gap in the scope of the convention by stating that the definition of discrimination against women in CEDAW Article 1 'includes gender-based violence'.[41] Today it is established under international law that the obligation put on states is not limited to discrimination caused directly or indirectly by states

is, under international law, considered 'authoritative interpretation' of the human rights conventions, cf. Manfred Nowak, *U.N. Covenant on Civil and Political Rights* (2nd edn. Kehl: N. P. Engel, 2005), p. xxvii.

[37] CERD and CEDAW refer to these official statements as 'General Recommendations' while the International Covenant on Civil and Political Rights (ICCPR), the International Covenant on Economic, Social and Cultural Rights (ICESCR), the Convention on the Rights of the Child (CRC), and Convention on the Rights of Persons with Disabilities (CRPD) refer to them as 'General Comments'.

[38] For an overview of the competence that is afforded to the different UN supervisory committees with regard to the monitoring of the conventions, visit the UN webpages for each committee. Links to all the committees are found on www.ohchr.org/EN/HRBodies/Pages/HumanRightsBodies.aspx (accessed 13 March 2014).

[39] Andrew Byrnes and Eleanor Bath, 'Violence against Women, the Obligation of Due Diligence, and the Optional Protocol to the Convention on the Elimination of All Forms of Discrimination against Women—Recent Developments', *Human Rights Law Review* 8 (2008), 517–533 at 518.

[40] For a presentation of how gender crimes became part of the institutionalized international law regime, including a presentation of how regional human rights instruments contributed as well as involvement from NGOs, see Catharine A. MacKinnon, 'Creating International Law: Gender as New Paradigm', in *Non-state Actors, Soft Law and Protective Regimes: From the Margins*, Cecilia Bailliet (ed.) (Cambridge: Cambridge University Press, 2012), 17–31.

[41] 'General Recommendation No. 19 Violence against Women', CEDAW Committee, 1992, UN Doc. A/47/38 at 1 (1993), para. 6.

parties themselves, but also includes a due diligence obligation to prevent discrimination by private actors. The CEDAW Committee has recognized that '[i]n some cases, a private actor's acts or omission of acts may be attributed to the State under international law. States parties are thus obliged to ensure that private actors do not engage in discrimination against women as defined in the Convention.'[42]

Since the adoption of the optional protocol to the CEDAW in 1999 that establishes an individual complaints procedure, the most substantive contribution of the Committee's practice is the due diligence standard in domestic violence cases. The Committee has found violations of the States' obligations in several cases.[43] Having analysed how the Committee has dealt with individual complaints in the field of domestic violence, Byrnes and Bath conclude that 'the Committee has insisted that States Parties provide not just an appropriate legal framework [. . .], but that this formal protection be real protection in practice once individual women have been identified as being at risk'.[44] The state obligation therefore applies not only on a formal level, imposing obligations on the states to adopt certain legal standards and structures, but also to individual women who are experiencing violence.

Violence in the home is a breach of negative peace. By establishing clear obligations for states parties to take active steps to protect women against violence in the home, a link between negative and positive peace comes to the fore. It is acknowledged that substantive equality requires striking down existing violence. Peace is not only relevant to the public sphere: through the application of international legal standards on non-discrimination and equality in the domestic arena, it is acknowledged that peace starts in the home.

4.2. Addressing racial hate speech and violence

If group-based hatred is allowed to flourish without restrictions, conflict will often be the result. Therefore, eradication of racial hate speech and violence is central in the struggle for non-discrimination and equality. Regulations that deal with racial hate speech can be understood to have a particularly close connection to the notion of negative peace, as they contribute to absence of violence.

Under ICERD Article 4 the contracting states:

> condemn all propaganda and all organizations which are based on ideas or theories of superiority of one race or group of persons of one colour or ethnic origin, or which attempt to justify or promote racial hatred and discrimination in any form, and undertake to

[42] 'General Recommendation No. 28 On the Core Obligations of States Parties under Article 2 of the Convention on the Elimination of All Forms of Discrimination against Women', CEDAW Committee, 2010, UN Doc. CEDAW/C/GC/28 (2010), para. 13.

[43] See *Şahide Goekce (deceased)* v. *Austria*, Communication 5/2005, 6 August 2007, CEDAW Committee, UN Doc. CEDAW/C/39/D/5/2005; *Fatma Yildirim (deceased)* v. *Austria*, Communication 6/2005, 6 August 2007, CEDAW Committee, UN Doc. CEDAW/C/39/D/6/2005, and *Karen Tayag Vertido* v. *Philippines*, Communication 18/2008, 1 September 2010, CEDAW Committee, UN Doc. CEDAW/C/46/D/18/2008.

[44] Byrnes and Bath, 'Violence against Women', 533.

adopt immediate and positive measures designed to eradicate all incitement to, or acts of, such discrimination.[45]

When the ICERD was adopted, this provision was considered important to avoid the revival of authoritarian ideologies.[46] ICERD Article 4(a) requires states parties to penalize four categories of misconduct:[47]

(i) dissemination of ideas based upon racial superiority or hatred;
(ii) incitement to racial hatred;
(iii) acts of violence against any race or group of persons of another colour or ethnic origin; and
(iv) incitement to such acts.

Article 4(a) also penalizes the financing of racist activities.[48] According to Article 4(b), racist organizations shall be declared illegal and shall therefore be prohibited. Participation in these organizations shall be recognized as an offence punishable by law.[49] Finally, according to Article 4(c), public authorities at all administrative levels are bound by this paragraph.[50] Apartheid is explicitly prohibited under ICERD Article 3 as an example of governmental policies that are based on racial superiority or hatred.[51]

In order to eliminate hate speech and racist organizations, there are a number of positive obligations embedded in the ICERD. These state obligations are imposed both in the public and in the private sphere. According to Articles 2(1)(a), 2(1)(b), and 2(1)(d), each State party 'undertakes to engage in no act or practice of racial discrimination against persons, groups of persons or institutions', the state party 'undertakes not to sponsor, defend or support racial discrimination by any persons or organizations', and the state party 'shall prohibit and bring to an end [. . .] racial discrimination by any persons, group or organization'. ICERD Article 6 concerns the obligations of the states parties to assure to everyone within their jurisdiction effective protection, and remedies if there has been a violation of the ICERD.

[45] This provision goes further than the 1966 International Convention on Civil and Political Rights (ICCPR) Art. 20 para. 2 where it is stated that: 'Any advocacy of national, racial or religious hatred that constitutes incitement to discrimination, hostility or violence shall be prohibited by law.' The Human Rights Committee has underlined that Art. 20 para. 2 applies whether the 'propaganda or advocacy has aims which are internal or external to the State concerned'. Cf. 'General Comment No. 11 Prohibition of propaganda for war and inciting national, racial or religious hatred (Article 20)', Human Rights Committee, 1983, UN Doc. HRI/GEN/1/Rev.6 at 133 (2003), para. 2.

[46] 'General Recommendation No. 15 Organized violence based on ethnic origin (Art. 4)', CERD Committee, 1993, UN Doc. A/48/18 at 114 (1994), para. 1.

[47] 'General Recommendation No. 15', para. 3.

[48] 'General Recommendation No. 15', para. 5.

[49] 'General Recommendation No. 15', para. 6.

[50] 'General Recommendation No. 15', para. 7.

[51] When the convention was drafted it was discussed whether also to include explicit condemnation of other racial evils, such as Nazism and anti-Semitism. The conclusion was, however, that only apartheid was explicitly mentioned. For a critique of this, see Natan Lerner, *The U.N. Convention on the Elimination of all Forms of Racial Discrimination* (Alphen aan den Rijn: Sijthoff & Noordhoff, 1980), 22–3.

With regard to racial hate speech it is—as was the case with domestic violence—acknowledged that the private sphere is not irrelevant to, but is considered at the heart of, the struggle for peace. This is the case not only when violence has occurred. The mere dissemination of discriminatory ideas and incitement to hatred by any person, group or organization is considered contrary to the founding of peace.

The CERD Committee may consider individual petitions alleging violations of the ICERD by states parties which have accepted this competence under ICERD's Article 14. There are several examples of the Committee finding violations of the ICERD where the state party has not dealt with the dissemination of ideas based upon racial superiority or hatred towards groups in a way that gives effective protection of the rights in the convention.[52] The CERD Committee has in its General Recommendations also focused on the positive obligations of states to protect particularly vulnerable groups. This includes the situation of Roma people, the situation of non-citizens, and the situation of people of African descent.[53] The Committee has underlined that the contracting states have positive obligations to protect these groups from experiencing hate speech and racial violence.[54]

4.3. Addressing direct and indirect discrimination

The legal concepts 'direct' and 'indirect' discrimination are well-known in the field of anti-discrimination law. They can frequently be found, explicitly or implicitly, in domestic law, in regional legal instruments that deal with discrimination (for instance in European Union law),[55] and in international human rights conventions. While 'direct' discrimination is defined as a situation where 'an individual

[52] See *TBB-Turkish Union in Berlin/Brandenburg* v. *Germany*, Communication No. 48/2010 (2010) CERD Committee. This case regarded offensive statements towards the Turkish immigrant group of Berlin. See also *The Jewish Community of Oslo* et. al. v. *Norway*, Communication 30/2003, CERD/C/67/D/30/2003 (2005), CERD Committee, that regarded offensive statements towards the Jewish community.

[53] 'General Recommendation No. 27 Discrimination against Roma', CERD Committee, 2000, UN Doc. A/55/18, annex V at 154 (2000); 'General Recommendation No. 30 Discrimination against Non-citizens', CERD Committee, 2004, UN Doc. CERD/C/64/Misc.11/rev.3 (2004); and 'General Recommendation No. 34 Racial discrimination against people of African descent', CERD Committee, 2011, UN Doc. CERD/C/GC/34 (2011).

[54] General Recommendation No. 34, CERD Committee, paras. 27–33; General Recommendation No. 30, CERD Committee, paras. 11–12; and General Recommendation No. 27, CERD Committee, paras. 12–16.

[55] From EU law, these Directives are of particular interest: Council Directive 2006/54/EC of 5 July 2006 on the implementation of the principle of equal opportunities and equal treatment of men and women in matters of employment and occupation (recast), [2006] L 204/23; Council Directive 2004/113/EC of 13 December 2004 implementing the principle of equal treatment between men and women in the access to and supply of goods and services, [2004] L 373/37; Council Directive 2000/78/EC of 27 November 2000 establishing a general framework for equal treatment in employment and occupation, [2000] L 303; and Council Directive 2000/43/EC of 29 June 2000 implementing the principle of equal treatment between persons irrespective of racial or ethnic origin, [2000] L 180.

is treated less favourably than another person in a similar situation for a reason related to a prohibited ground', 'indirect' discrimination is defined as 'laws, policies or practices which appear neutral at face value, but have a disproportionate impact on the exercise of [. . .] rights as distinguished by prohibited grounds of discrimination'.[56] Prohibitions against direct and indirect discrimination are essential when individuals claim to be victims of discrimination.

The terms 'direct' and 'indirect' discrimination are not explicitly mentioned in either CEDAW or ICERD.[57] Both aspects are, however, implicitly made part of the definitions of discrimination in ICERD Article 1 and CEDAW Article 1, two provisions that are very similar.[58] To use CEDAW Article 1 as an example, the term 'discrimination against women' is here defined as 'any distinction, exclusion or restriction made on the basis of sex which has the *effect* or *purpose* of impairing or nullifying the recognition, enjoyment or exercise by women, irrespective of their marital status, on a basis of equality of men and women, of human rights and fundamental freedoms in the political, economic, social, cultural, civil or any other field'.[59] The term 'purpose' refers to situations of direct discrimination, while the term 'effect' relates to situations of indirect discrimination.[60]

In individual cases, a claim of discrimination follows a strict structure. Generally speaking, three conditions need to be met before a national court or an international supervisory organ can establish that discrimination has occurred. First, it has to be established that a person has ended up in a disadvantaged situation. Next, it has to be established that the disadvantage experienced is connected to one of the discrimination grounds identified, such as sex, disability, religion, or ethnicity.[61] Thirdly, and finally, an assessment has to be made of the rationale that lies behind the practice or regulation that has resulted in the disadvantaged situation. Not all differential treatment is unlawful. Only unjust differential treatment is considered discriminatory under international human rights law. The ICESCR Committee has described this in the following terms:

> Differential treatment based on prohibited grounds will be viewed as discriminatory unless the justification for differentiation is reasonable and objective. This will include an assessment as to whether the aim and effects of the measures or omissions are legitimate [. . .]. In addition, there must be a clear and reasonable relationship of

[56] General Comment No. 20, ICESCR Committee, para. 10(a) and (b).

[57] Neither term is explicitly mentioned in any of the UN human rights conventions.

[58] Cf. also the UN Convention on the Rights of Persons with Disabilities (CRPD), Art. 2.

[59] My emphasis.

[60] The ICESCR Committee refers to these definitions and adopts the same understanding with regard to ICESCR, cf. General Comment No. 20, ICESCR Committee, para. 7.

[61] Several human rights conventions contain a list of discrimination grounds that ends with an open-ended 'or other status' criterion, cf. *inter alia* CRC Art. 2 No. 1; ICCPR Art. 2 No. 1; ICCPR Art. 26, and ICESCR Art. 2 No. 2. This has provided flexibility when it comes to incorporating grounds that are not included in the list, such as e.g. disability, age, nationality, sexual orientation, and gender identity, cf., General Comment No. 20, ICESCR Committee, paras. 27–35. Even though the list of discrimination grounds has been extended through interpretation, a link between the discrimination ground(s) in question and the disadvantage experienced still has to be established in individual cases.

proportionality between the aim sought to be realized and the measures or omissions and their effects.[62]

If the practice or regulation in question cannot be justified, the practice or regulation is to be considered 'discriminatory' and therefore unlawful.

The scope for justifying differential treatment will vary according to the facts of each case. In many instances there will be less room for justifying direct differential treatment than for justifying indirect differential treatment, and the discrimination ground involved will often influence the scrutiny to be applied.[63]

The concepts of direct and indirect discrimination offer mechanisms through which individual claims can be put forward, and these concepts are considered essential to the establishing of substantive equality, and therefore to the founding of peace. However, the structure of these norms carries challenges when making the protection against discrimination effective in practice. The supervisory committees are seeking to respond to these challenges in their practice.

4.3.1. Challenges connected to the requirement to fit into a discrimination ground

The way in which norms on non-discrimination and equality are constructed in categories—the requirement that a situation fits into a discrimination ground—can be seen as an obstacle to effective protection against discrimination and the realization of substantive equality. Crenshaw has emphasized that:

> Black women's experiences when it comes to facing discrimination are much broader than the general categories that discrimination discourse provides. Yet the continued insistence that Black women's demands and needs be filtered through categorical analyses that completely obscure their experiences guarantees that their needs will seldom be addressed.[64]

From the mid-1990s to date there has, however, been 'increased awareness of the complex structural social factors that intervene in the playing field that the law previously presumed was neutral and an increased awareness of how individual and group identities that create vulnerabilities to discrimination are multidimensional'.[65] The acknowledgement that human life, human identities, and experiences are more complex than what is captured in a list of discrimination grounds

[62] General Comment No. 20, ICESCR Committee, para. 13.

[63] This is the case in European anti-discrimination law, cf. Sarah Haverkort-Speekenbrink, *European Non-discrimination Law: A Comparison of EU Law and the ECHR in the Field of Non-discrimination and Freedom of Religion in Public Employment with an Emphasis on the Islamic Headscarf Issue* (Cambridge: Intersentia, 2012), 308.

[64] Kimberle Crenshaw, 'Demarginalizing the Intersection of Race and Sex: A Black Feminist Critique of Antidiscrimination Doctrine, Feminist Theory and Antiracist Politics', in *Anti-Discrimination Law*, Christopher McCrudden (ed.) (Aldershot: Ashgate, 2004), 479–507 at 489–90.

[65] Oddný Mjöll Arnardóttir, 'A Future of Multidimensional Disadvantage Equality?', in *The UN Convention on the Rights of Persons with Disabilities: European and Scandinavian Perspectives*, Oddný Mjöll Arnardóttir and Gerard Quinn (eds.) (Leiden: Martinus Nijhoff, 2009), 41–66 at 54.

has been responded to by the supervisory committees through increased focus on multiple discrimination,[66] on intersectionality,[67] and on vulnerability in general. This has led to more groups and more situations being included into the equality and non-discrimination framing. The focus on multiple forms of discrimination is explicitly reflected in the most recently adopted international human rights instrument, the Convention on the Rights of Persons with Disabilities (CRPD), adopted by the UN General Assembly in 2006. This is the only UN convention that contains a provision explicitly dealing with multiple discrimination, which is found in Article 6, in which: 'States parties recognize that women and girls with disabilities are subject to multiple discrimination, and in this regard shall take measures to ensure the full and equal enjoyment by them of all human rights and fundamental freedoms.'[68]

There are several examples on how the committees in their General Recommendations/Comments seek to identify combinations of characteristics that leave a person in a particularly vulnerable situation. One General Recommendation from the CEDAW Committee targets the situation of disabled women, while another targets the situation of older women.[69] Here the intersections between gender/disability and gender/high age are put to the fore. One General Recommendation takes up the situation of women migrant workers as a group facing violations of their human rights both in 'countries of origin, countries of transit and countries of destination'.[70] The targeting of vulnerability can also be found in General Recommendations issued by the CERD Committee that focus on the situation of Roma people, the situation of non-citizens, and the situation of people of African descent.[71] With regard to people of African descent, the committee states that it is 'aware that millions of people of African descent are living in societies in which racial discrimination places them in the lowest positions in social hierarchies'.[72] The Committee underlines that '[p]eople

[66] Multiple discrimination is defined as situations where: 'Some individuals or groups of individuals face discrimination on more than one of the prohibited grounds, for example women belonging to an ethnic or religious minority.' The ICESCR Committee emphasizes that '(s)uch cumulative discrimination has a unique and specific impact on individuals and merits particular consideration and remedying.' Cf. General Comment No. 20, ICESCR Committee, para. 17.

[67] An intersectional approach towards gender equality acknowledges that: 'discrimination of women based on sex and gender is inextricably linked with other factors that affect women, such as race, ethnicity, religion or belief, health, status, age, class, caste and sexual orientation and gender identity'. Cf. General Recommendation No. 28, CEDAW Committee, para. 18. The notions of multiple discrimination and intersectionality often overlap, but not always.

[68] CRPD Art. 7, which deals with disabled children, also reflects situations where several characteristics apply at the same time. Here, the term 'multiple discrimination' is, however, not mentioned explicitly.

[69] 'General Recommendation No. 18 Disabled women', CEDAW Committee, 1991, UN Doc. A/46/38 at 3 (1993); and 'General Recommendation No. 27 On older women and protection of their human rights', CEDAW Committee, 2010, UN Doc. CEDAW/C/GC/27 (2010).

[70] 'General Recommendation No. 26 On women migrant workers', CEDAW Committee, 2008, UN Doc. CEDAW/C/2009/WP.1/R (2008), para. 9.

[71] General Recommendation No. 27, CERD Committee; General Recommendation No. 30, CERD Committee; and General Recommendation No. 34, CERD Committee.

[72] General Recommendation No. 34, CERD Committee, para. 2.

of African descent shall enjoy all human rights and fundamental freedoms in accordance with international standards, in conditions of equality and without any discrimination.'[73]

One General Recommendation deals with gender-related dimensions of racial discrimination. Here the Committee stresses that:

> [R]acial discrimination does not always affect women and men equally or in the same way. There are circumstances in which racial discrimination only or primarily affects women, or affects women in a different way, or to a different degree than men. Such racial discrimination will often escape detection if there is no explicit recognition or acknowledgement of the different life experiences of women and men, in areas of both public and private life.[74]

As we have seen, focus on multiple forms of discrimination, intersectionality, and vulnerability has enabled a strategy that includes a broader spectrum of people's experiences and challenges than a formalistic approach primarily focusing on discrimination grounds one by one. This broadens the picture and puts pressure on states to establish strategies and policies to address the whole spectrum of reasons that result in inequality, discrimination, and absence of peace. In individual cases, however, the need to establish one or more links to discrimination grounds remains. However, the approach taken by the committees can be seen as the first step in pushing forward a possible change of focus also in individual cases, where the focus to some extent will move away from the discrimination ground(s) in question and towards the justification for upholding the practice or regulation that has resulted in the disadvantage experienced by an individual.[75] Such a development is likely to strengthen the impact of prohibitions against discrimination as tools for breaking down hierarchies, thereby contributing to the founding of peace.

4.3.2. Challenges connected to difficulties in establishing indirect discrimination

The existence of the two categories of direct and indirect discrimination can lead to difficulties when combating discriminatory laws and practices. McKinders has compared the former racial discriminatory laws in the US, often referred to as Jim Crow laws, that were racist on paper, with recently adopted anti-immigrant laws that are formally neutral, but have discriminatory effects towards groups of

[73] General Recommendation No. 34, CERD Committee, para. 3.

[74] 'General Recommendation No. 25 Gender Related Dimensions of Racial Discrimination', CERD Committee, 2000, UN Doc. A/55/18, annex V at 152 (2000), para. 1.

[75] Cf. Section 4.3 on the justification-criteria. With regard to the ECHR, O'Connell finds that the list of discrimination grounds embedded in Art. 14, which is open-ended, is often interpreted very widely in Strasbourg: '[I]t would seem like almost any distinction within the ambit of a Convention right can trigger an Art 14 inquiry.' Cf. Rory O'Connell, 'Cinderella Comes to the Ball: Art 14 and the Right to Non-discrimination in the ECHR', *Legal Studies* 29 (2009), 211–29 at 222. This suggests that it is the justification that is central rather than the discrimination ground(s) in question.

immigrants and, in particular, Latino immigrants.[76] When comparing the past with the racism that occurs today, McKinders finds:

> A common element between Jim Crow and anti-immigrant laws is the alleged reasoning for passing the laws. Jim Crow laws on their face overtly excluded African Americans from certain communities and asserted neutral reasons to justify the laws. Anti-immigrant laws, however, are neutral on their face but have an underlying discriminatory motive. Under current frameworks for addressing discriminatory laws, the ways in which the laws are crafted make it more difficult to address the underlying discriminatory motives articulated by the drafters but not included in the text of the laws.[77]

In McKinders' opinion the drafters of the anti-immigration laws are considered to be 'attuned to how to draft laws to withstand legal challenges'.[78] However, the reasoning behind the passing of the laws has similarities to the rationale behind the Jim Crow laws, resting on the assumption 'that Latino immigrants are a drain on fiscal resources, unwilling to assimilate to American culture, and largely responsible for rising crime rates'.[79] This results in 'the creation of a system where Latinos are second-class members of society'.[80] The anti-immigration laws are now 'being called "Juan Crow" laws because of their similar ability to exclude both citizens and non-citizens from the rights of membership as persons within the United States'.[81]

The example of US anti-immigration laws draws the attention to the challenges of establishing indirect discrimination in concrete cases. Even though the international human rights regime prohibits regulations and practices that indirectly have discriminatory effects, it is often harder to trace discriminatory effects than discriminatory purposes. It is also often easier to justify indirect differential treatment than direct differential treatment.[82] An effective protection against indirect discrimination in individual cases remains a challenge under international law, even though strategies are adopted in order to strengthen the protection against discrimination.[83] For instance, such strengthening takes place through the weakening of what is required in order to establish that indirect differential treatment connected to a discrimination ground has occurred, and through the fact that the burden of proof is put on the defendant in order to justify that such differential treatment rests on an objective and reasonable justification.[84]

[76] Karla Mari McKanders, 'Sustaining Tiered Personhood: Jim Crow and Anti-Immigrant Laws', *Harvard Journal on Racial and Ethnic Justice* 26 (2010), 163–210.
[77] McKanders, 'Sustaining Tiered Personhood', 189.
[78] McKanders, 'Sustaining Tiered Personhood', 188.
[79] McKanders, 'Sustaining Tiered Personhood', 166.
[80] McKanders, 'Sustaining Tiered Personhood', 171.
[81] McKanders, 'Sustaining Tiered Personhood', 172.
[82] Cf. Haverkort-Speekenbrink, *European Non-discrimination Law*, 308.
[83] Haverkort-Speekenbrink, *European Non-discrimination Law*, 153.
[84] See Nicholas Bamforth, Maleiha Malik, and Colm O'Cinneide, *Discrimination Law: Theory and Context* (London: Sweet & Maxwell, 2008), 313–30.

The approach applied by the UN supervisory committees that seek to address vulnerability with regard to discrimination and inequality in a broad manner, as explained in Section 4.3.1, will to some extent remedy the challenges that accompany the strict legal structure that prohibitions against direct and indirect discrimination rest upon. A broad approach to combating inequality and discrimination is essential in the struggle for substantive equality and peace.

4.4. The transformation of society

Substantive equality cannot be reached by merely addressing the status quo, but requires transformation of society so that old structures and hierarchies can be removed. The need for a transformation of society in order to achieve equality is fully recognized within CEDAW and ICERD, which contain in particular two sets of legal norms that seek to impose such transformation; provisions on the introduction of temporary special measures and provisions on the removal of stereotypes and prejudices.

CEDAW Article 4 No. 1 states that:

> Adoption by States Parties of temporary special measures aimed at accelerating de facto equality between men and women shall not be considered discrimination as defined in the present Convention, but shall in no way entail as a consequence the maintenance of unequal or separate standards; these measures shall be discontinued when the objectives of equality of opportunity and treatment have been achieved.

Similar provisions are found in ICERD Article 1 paragraph 4 and Article 2 paragraph 2.

Temporary special measures encompass, in the words of the CEDAW Committee, 'a wide variety of legislative, executive, administrative and other regulatory instruments, policies and practices, such as outreach or support programmes; allocation and/or reallocation of resources; preferential treatment; targeted recruitment, hiring and promotion; numerical goals connected with time frames; and quota systems'.[85] The Committee defines the purpose of temporary special measures:

> to accelerate the improvement of the position of women to achieve their de facto or substantive equality with men, and to effect the structural, social and cultural changes necessary to correct past and current forms and effects of discrimination against women, as well as to provide them with compensation. These measures are of a temporary nature.[86]

The CERD Committee builds on the same understanding and states that:

> The concept of special measures is based on the principle that laws, policies and practices adopted and implemented in order to fulfil obligations under the Convention require supplementing, when circumstances warrant, by the adoption of temporary special

[85] General Recommendation No. 25, CEDAW Committee, para. 22.
[86] General Recommendation No. 25, CEDAW Committee, para. 15.

measures designed to secure to disadvantaged groups the full and equal enjoyment of human rights and fundamental freedoms.[87]

When drawing attention to the particularly vulnerable situation of persons of African descent, and in particular the children, the CERD Committee recommends in one of its General Recommendations that the state parties '[a]dopt and implement special measures meant to eliminate all forms of racial discrimination against people of African descent' and 'adopt special measures to ensure equality in the exercise of their rights, in particular corresponding to the areas that most affect the lives of children'.[88] Here we see that the targeting of vulnerable groups includes special measures as a means of taking steps towards substantive equality and peace.

The CEDAW Committee and the CERD Committee are encouraging the active use of temporary special measures and have both expressed that temporary special measures shall not be considered an exception to the norm of non-discrimination, but rather part of a necessary strategy towards the achievement of substantive equality.[89]

ANorms that address the obligation of states to remove stereotypes and prejudices are likewise aiming for transformation of society. Cook and Cusack define a stereotype as 'a generalized view or preconception of attributes or characteristics possessed by, or the roles that are or should be performed by, members of a particular group ... [that] ... presumes that all members of a certain social group possess particular attributes or characteristics ... or perform specified roles'.[90] The problem with stereotypes is that individuality is 'filtered through the lens of a generalized view or preconception of the group with which the individual is identified.'[91]

According to CEDAW Article 2(f), states parties undertake '[t]o take all appropriate measures, including legislation, to modify or abolish existing laws, regulations, customs and practices which constitute discrimination against women.' CEDAW Article 5(a) sets out that states parties are required to take all appropriate measures '[t]o modify the social and cultural patterns of conduct of men and women, with a view to achieving the elimination of prejudices and customary and all other practices which are based on the idea of the inferiority or the superiority of either of the sexes or on stereotyped roles for men and women.'

These provisions oblige states to take active steps to change the structures that discrimination often rest upon. This includes the modification of religious and cultural practices that clash with the right to gender equality.[92] The obligation

[87] 'General Recommendation No. 32 The meaning and scope of special measures in the International Convention on the Elimination of All Forms Racial Discrimination', CERD Committee, 2009, UN Doc. CERD/C/GC/32 (2009), para. 11.

[88] General Recommendation No. 34, CERD Committee, paras. 18, 25.

[89] General Recommendation No. 25, CEDAW Committee, para. 18, and General Recommendation No. 32, CERD Committee, para. 20.

[90] Rebecca J. Cook and Simone Cusack, *Gender Stereotyping* (Philadelphia: University of Pennsylvania Press, 2009), 9.

[91] Cook and Cusack, *Gender Stereotyping*, 9.

[92] Frances Raday, 'Culture, Religion, and Gender', *International Journal of Constitutional Law* 4 (2003), 663–715 at 678.

to take steps to remove customs and practices that are based on stereotyped roles for men and women also includes an obligation to take steps to protect women against discrimination by private parties.[93]

Also the ICERD includes an obligation on states to take steps to change the social norms, structures, and customs that may lead to discrimination. According to ICERD Article 7 the contracting states 'undertake to adopt immediate and effective measures, particularly in the fields of teaching, education, culture and information, with a view to combating prejudices which lead to racial discrimination and to promoting understanding, tolerance and friendship among nations and racial or ethnical groups'.

The obligation of contracting states to address stereotypes and prejudices applies not only to state policies, but is also applicable in individual cases. In the communication *Karen Tayag Vertido* v. *Philippines*, the CEDAW Committee opined that the state party had violated, *inter alia*, CEDAW Article 2(f) and Article 5(a) because the legal procedures in a case involving rape was affected by stereotypical gender notions.[94]

It is recognized that structures in society cannot be seen as isolated from the situation experienced by individuals and groups; stereotypes and prejudices are often part of the rationale that lies behind discrimination on an individual level. Therefore, active steps to combat prejudices and stereotypes, as well as the introduction of temporary special measures seeking to accelerate the societal transformation, are essential if substantive equality and peace are to be achieved.

5. Integrating Civil Society While Moving Forward

The human rights instruments, including existing practice from the supervisory committees, approach issues of discrimination and inequality in a multifaceted and rather sophisticated way. Therefore, these legal instruments offer a broad approach to the foundation of peace. In addition to the legal norms and practice from the UN committees interpreting the norms, we have seen that civil society has played, and continues to play, a central role in the struggle for equality and removal of discrimination.

There is great potential for accelerating the creation of substantive equality and peace if we combine the legal approach with engagement from civil society. The importance of pulling civil society into the legal sphere is today acknowledged. The CEDAW Committee, the CERD Committee, as well as, for instance, the UN Committee on the Rights of the Child and the UN Committee on the Rights of Persons with Disabilities, are all facilitating the active participation by NGOs in their procedures of considering periodic state reports, as the NGOs are central

[93] General Recommendation No. 28, CEDAW Committee, para. 9.
[94] *Karen Tayag Vertido* v. *Philippines*, para. 8.4.

in providing the committees with country-specific information.[95] The NGOs contribute to keeping the committees as well informed as possible of the situation in the states parties. The importance of bringing civil society into the human rights sphere was underlined during the drafting of the newest international human rights instrument, the CRPD, as the drafting process was characterized by strong involvement of individuals with disabilities and civil society organizations representing them, as well as national human rights institutions, rather than only or mainly states. This process is considered to mark a new departure in international treaty-making.[96] The importance of including persons with disabilities and their representative organizations is also reflected in CRPD Article 33 that deals with the issue of national implementation and monitoring of the convention. Subparagraph 3 states that '[c]ivil society, in particular persons with disabilities and their representative organizations, shall be involved and participate fully in the monitoring process.'[97]

The text of the conventions, the interpretation of the conventions, and the increased focus on pulling civil society into the human rights sphere, all point in the direction of non-discrimination and equality-law as being powerful sources for the founding of peace. However, obstacles remain.

It is within the contracting states that rights become effective. Therefore, national implementation of international human rights standards is essential. Even though the human rights conventions in the field of non-discrimination and equality apply in a significant number of the 193 UN member states, not all countries have ratified the conventions or the adopted additional protocols that establish competence for the committees to handle individual complaints. The submission by states of declarations and reservations, often with reference to religion, also limits the implications of the conventions.[98] Even if a state is party to the conventions, the actual impact of the human rights instruments will depend on the weight afforded by the governments to the texts of the

[95] Information for NGOs and civil society on how they can participate in the monitoring processes is easily accessible, as it is available on the webpages of all the committees.

[96] Grainne De Burca, 'The European Union in the Negotiation of the UN Disability Convention', *European Law Review* 35 (2010), 174–96 at 175.

[97] Until the adoption of the CRPD, the CRC was the only international human rights treaty that expressly gave NGOs a role in monitoring its implementation; cf. CRC Art. 45(a) referring to 'other competent bodies'; cf. 'Guidelines for the participation of partners (NGOs and individual experts) in the pre-sessional working group of the Committee on the Rights of the Child' (1999) UN Doc. CRC/C/90, Annex VIII.

[98] The numbers of ratifications as well as submitted declarations/reservations are available at https://treaties.un.org/Pages/Treaties.aspx?id=4&subid=A&lang=en (accessed 11 Nov 2014). The number of ratifications is significantly lower when it comes to protocols establishing individual complaints procedures than when it comes to the main treaties. Note that with regard to CERD, the establishing of an individual complaints procedure is regulated in the convention itself, cf. Art. 14. With regard to the lower number of ratifications to the CRPD, it should be noted that the convention was adopted only in 2006 and has quickly become one of the most widely ratified human rights instruments in the UN system, cf. Gerard Quinn and Charles O'Mahony, 'Disability and Human Rights: A New Field in the United Nations', in *International Protection of Human Rights: A Textbook*, Catarina Krause and Martin Scheinin (eds.) (Turku: Åbo Akademi University Institute for Human Rights, 2012), 265–300 at 268.

conventions, as well as the interpretative practice issued by the UN committees: the General Comments/Recommendations, the Views given as part of the individual complaints procedures, and the Concluding Observations directed to the state.

There are also several other factors that may be obstacles to the effectiveness of the provisions on non-discrimination and equality. The formal possibility for individuals and groups to take legal steps is not enough to impose change, as very few will be able to put forward legal claims in practice. To claim that one has been the victim of a human rights violation requires knowledge of the rights, and the resources to come forward with a claim, first in the national legal order and thereafter on the international arena, after the exhaustion of national remedies. People who experience disadvantage and who are vulnerable to discrimination often have more pressing issues to handle in their everyday lives than taking action to enforce their legal rights.[99]

Therefore, substantive equality requires that somebody speaks up and gives voice to the ones who are marginalized and vulnerable, so that their claims can be heard and reflected both inside and outside the legal sphere. NGOs and independent supervisory mechanisms on a domestic level, as well as UN committees and other agents on the international level, all play crucial roles here. Also individuals can play an essential role in giving voice to the marginalized, as clearly shown us by Malala Yousafzai.

Giving voice to the vulnerable and marginalized involves an obligation to respond to claims for equality that are actually being put forward, and not to leave them unnoticed. Sadly, such response is not always given. On the International Women's Day, 8 March 2014, Saudi women activists petitioned the country's consultative council to back a demand to curb the 'absolute authority' of male guardians over women in the kingdom.[100] The women are clearly trying to make their voices heard. So why is it that the international community does not respond more strongly to their pleas, and really speak up on behalf of Saudi women?[101] The international community should engage with the voices of women in Saudi Arabia and help increase their volume so that they can be heard.

[99] The CEDAW Committee sees access to justice as an 'essential component of rule of law' and has started preparing a General Recommendation on access to justice, thereby contributing to 'enhance the visibility of the issue and to call States' attention to the measures required', cf. 'Access to Justice—Concept Note for Half Day General Discussion. Endorsed by the Committee on the Elimination of Discrimination against Women at its 53rd Session', available at http://www.ohchr.org/Documents/HRBodies/CEDAW/AccesstoJustice/ConceptNoteAccessToJustice.pdf (accessed 12 May 2014).

[100] 'Saudi women demand end of male control', 2 March 2014, Aljazeera, www.aljazeera.com/news/middleeast/2014/03/saudi-activists-demand-end-male-control-201432132928215484.html (accessed 11 Nov 2014).

[101] Sofie A. E. Høgestøl, 'Apartheid anno 2014', 8 March 2014, Dagbladet, www.dagbladet.no/2014/03/07/kultur/meninger/kronikk/saudi-arabia/kvinnedagen/32192939/ (accessed 14 March 2014).

In addition to giving heed to, and amplifying, the voices of the vulnerable, substantive equality and founding of peace requires perseverance, because it takes time to impose change.[102] It also requires the ability to integrate new problems into the human rights framework, as we experience that new groups of people become marginalized. The wrapping might be new, but the ways in which discrimination and inequality occur remain unchanged.

[102] Even though racial discriminatory laws are removed in the US, marginalization remains within the African-American population.

13

Refugees and Peace

Maja Janmyr

1. Introduction

Refugees and the notion of peace are intricately linked in a number of ways. The majority of today's refugees—estimated to be over 15 million throughout the world—exist as a consequence of armed conflict. They originate from some of the world's most fragile states. The continuously escalating armed conflict in Syria, for example, has caused the internal and external displacement of more than six million people.[1] As are many other refugees today, these people are found in some of the world's poorest and most unstable regions. Their condition often becomes protracted—the average duration of a refugee situation now exceeds seventeen years.[2] In exile, refugees may exacerbate conflict or frustrate efforts to find peace, but, and as shown in prominent examples such as those of Eritrea and South Sudan, refugee participation in peace-building efforts has proved to be crucial in many attempts to achieve peace in the country of origin. This chapter aims to shed light upon these linkages, and, more specifically, to explore how these are played out in international law.

While international law contains several different understandings of peace,[3] this chapter seeks to explore how refugeehood is—and always has been—intrinsically linked to the notions of both positive and negative peace. Negative peace refers to the absence of violence, while positive peace concerns the presence of social justice through equal opportunity, a fair distribution of power and resources, and the constructive resolution of conflict.[4] This chapter first examines how international refugee law relates notions of peace to grounds for asylum and refugee status. It does so by specifically exploring how refugees fleeing armed conflict and other

[1] For regularly updated figures on registration of Syrians, see Syria Regional Refugee Response Information Sharing Portal, http://data.unhcr.org/syrianrefugees (accessed 11 Nov 2014). See also 'Syria: Head of Independent UN Panel Appeals to Member States to End Relentless Carnage', 29 July 2013, UN News Service, http://www.refworld.org/docid/51f7786559.html (accessed 11 Nov 2014).

[2] 'Protracted Refugee Situations', Executive Committee of the High Commissioner's Programme, 10 June 2004, UN Doc. EC/54/SC/CRP.14.

[3] See Ch. 3 of this book.

[4] David Cortright, *Peace: A History of Movements and Ideas* (4th edn. Cambridge: Cambridge University Press, 2011).

violence do so in consequence of breaches of peace, how peace activism may be a specific ground for asylum, and how individuals engaged in crimes against peace and other atrocities are clearly excluded from refugee status. Second, it considers peace and threats against peace in exile. It shows how the international community has emphasized the peaceful and humanitarian nature of asylum ever since the very inception of the modern refugee regime, and explores one clear expression of this notion—the principle of the civilian and humanitarian character of asylum. Third, this chapter demonstrates how refugees in several important aspects can be seen as contributors to peace. By examining the direct participation of refugees in peace and political processes, it considers refugee participation in peace-building in exile. It specifically explores how skills training in exile allows refugees to make important contributions to peace-building in their countries of origin. Fourth, it shows how resolving displacement is intrinsically related to achieving peace, and considers the three durable solutions to refugee situations as laid out in international refugee law: repatriation, resettlement, and local integration. Finally, when concluding, this chapter points to the need for new approaches to ensure that refugees may live their lives in peace.

2. Grounds for Asylum and Refugee Status

2.1. Generally on the existence of refugees as a consequence of breaches of negative peace

Armed conflicts and other situations of violence have long been the major reasons for the involuntary displacement of people across borders. Such displacement has proved not only to be an indication of the intensity of the conflict, but on occasion also to be used as a direct military strategy, including 'ethnic cleansing' or genocide.[5] International refugee law developed in the early and mid-twentieth century against the backdrop of conflict-induced displacement, and the 1951 Convention Relating to the Status of Refugees, as amended by its 1967 Protocol, is the primary instrument for the protection of refugees.[6] Applying both in times of peace and in armed conflict, Article 1 defines a refugee as:

[5] See Sarah Kenyon Lischer, 'Causes and Consequences of Conflict-Induced Displacement', *Civil Wars* 9 (2007), 142; William Hayden, 'The Kosovo Conflict: The Strategic Use of Displacement and the Obstacles to International Protection', *Civil Wars* 2 (1999), 35; Klejda Mulaj, 'Forced Displacement in Darfur, Sudan: Dilemmas of Classifying the Crimes', *International Migration* 46 (2008), 27.

[6] Convention Relating to the Status of Refugees (adopted 28 July 1951, entered into force 22 April 1954), 189 UNTS 137 (1951 Refugee Convention). It was amended by the 1967 Protocol relating to the Status of Refugees, see Protocol Relating to the Status of Refugees (adopted 31 January 1967, entered into force 4 October 1967), 606 UNTS 267 (1967 Protocol). It should be mentioned that Palestine refugees receiving assistance from the United Nations Relief and Works Agency for Palestine Refugees in the Near East (UNRWA) are excluded from international protection under the 1951 Refugee Convention. See Lex Takkenberg, *The Status of Palestinian Refugees in International Law* (Oxford: Clarendon, 1998), in particular chs. 2–4, 7; Brenda Goddard, 'UNHCR and the International Protection of Palestinian Refugees', *RSQ* 28 (2009), 475.

> A person who owing to a well-founded fear of being persecuted for reasons of race, religion, nationality, membership of a particular social group or political opinion, is outside the country of his nationality and is unable or, owing to such fear, is unwilling to avail himself of the protection of that country; or who, not having a nationality and being outside the country of his former habitual residence as a result of such events, is unable or, owing to such fear, is unwilling to return to it.

As is clear from this definition, refugees fleeing armed conflict or other violence are—surprisingly—not explicitly covered by the Convention. Rather, and as Section 2.2 will show, it has long been a matter of controversy as to how one should interpret the 1951 Convention refugee definition in the context of situations of armed conflict in the country of origin. That said, several regional refugee instruments broaden the refugee definition explicitly to cover individuals fleeing internal conflicts, massive human rights violations, or situations of generalized violence or public disorder. The 1969 Organization of African Unity Convention Governing the Specific Aspects of Refugee Problems in Africa (1969 OAU Convention) has added to the definition that a refugee is '[a]ny person compelled to leave his/her country owing to external aggression, occupation, foreign domination or events seriously disturbing public order in either part or the whole of his country of origin or nationality,'[7] while the Latin American 1984 Cartagena Declaration on Refugees determines that a refugee furthermore includes '[p]ersons who flee their countries because their lives, safety or freedom have been threatened by generalised violence, foreign aggression, internal conflicts, massive violation of human rights or other circumstances which have seriously disturbed public order.'[8] These persons are also clearly encompassed within the scope of the European complementary/subsidiary protection instrument, the EU Qualifications Directive.[9]

2.2. Victims of armed conflicts and other situations of violence: applying the 1951 Refugee Convention

With regard to the 1951 Refugee Convention, victims of armed conflicts and other situations of violence are particular cases, and it remains a matter of controversy exactly how its refugee definition should be interpreted with regard to claims to refugee status arising out of situations of armed conflict in the country of origin.[10] Even though many states parties to the 1951 Convention explicitly

[7] Organization of African Unity Convention Governing the Specific Aspects of Refugee Problems in Africa (adopted 10 September 1969, entered into force 20 June 1974), 1001 UNTS 45 (1969 OAU Convention), Art. 1(2).

[8] Cartagena Declaration on Refugees (Colloquium on the International Protection of Refugees in Central America, Mexico and Panama, held at Cartagena, Colombia, 19–22 November 1984), Art. 3(3).

[9] Council Directive 2004/83/EC of 29 April 2004 on minimum standards for the qualification and status of third country nationals or stateless persons as refugees or as persons who otherwise need international protection and the content of the protection granted [2004] L 304/12, Art. 15.

[10] For discussions, see Vanessa Holzer, 'The 1951 Refugee Convention and the Protection of People Fleeing Armed Conflict and Other Situations of Violence', *UNHCR Legal and Protection Policy Research Series* PPLA/2012/05 (2012); UNHCR 'Expert Meeting on Complementarities between International Refugee Law, International Criminal Law and International Human

acknowledge that individuals who have fled from countries experiencing armed conflict are refugees if they fulfil the criteria set out in Article 1A(2),[11] a wide variation in refugee recognition rates for individuals fleeing situations of armed conflict suggests discrepancies in the application of the 1951 Refugee Convention.[12] Too frequently, a situation of armed conflict and violence in the country of origin is perceived by decision-makers as giving rise to situations of general insecurity that preclude the finding of a well-founded fear of being persecuted for any of the five 1951 Convention grounds.[13]

This diverging approach to the refugee definition may be explained, at least in part, by recourse to UNHCR's 1992 'Handbook on Refugee Status Determination'. This Handbook appears to suggest that individuals fleeing armed conflict are refugees only in exceptional circumstances: '[p]ersons compelled to leave their country of origin as a result of international or national armed conflicts are not normally considered refugees under the 1951 Convention.'[14] Importantly, however, this view has since been reconsidered, and today UNHCR promotes the idea that individuals displaced by armed conflict are eligible for 1951 Convention refugee status if they have a well-founded fear of persecution for reasons grounded in the 1951 Convention.[15] Most Syrians seeking international protection, for example, are considered by UNHCR probably to fulfil the requirements of the refugee definition, since they will have a well-founded fear of persecution linked to one of the Convention grounds.[16] UNHCR has specified in the case of Syria that conduct amounting to persecution may be more general and include shelling and bombardments, cutting of food supplies, militarization of hospitals and schools, but also conduct that is more indirect, such as food insecurity, poverty,

Rights Law: Summary Conclusions, Arusha 11–13 April 2011', July 2011; UNHCR 'Summary Conclusions on International Protection of Persons Fleeing Armed Conflict and Other Situations of Violence, 13–14 September 2012', 20 December 2012.

[11] For France, see Commission des recours des réfugiés, *Zein El Abiddine* [13 June 1985]; *Taha* [30 October 1989]; for the US, see *In re H-*, 21 I. & N. Dec. 337 (Interim Decision) 3276 [1996] WL 291910 (BIA). For further examples concerning the United Kingdom, New Zealand, Australia, Germany, Costa Rica, and Venezuela, see Holzer, 'The 1951 Refugee Convention and the Protection of People'.

[12] See UNHCR, 'Safe at Last? Law and Practice in Selected EU Member States with Respect to Asylum-Seekers Fleeing Indiscriminate Violence', Geneva, 27 July 2011; UNHCR, 'Summary Conclusions on International Protection'.

[13] See *Adan* v. *Secretary of State for the Home Department* [1998] 2 WLR 702, per Lord Slynn of Hadley.

[14] Emphasis added. UNHCR, 'Handbook on Procedures and Criteria for Determining Refugee Status under the 1951 Convention and the 1967 Protocol Relating to the Status of Refugees' (Geneva, 1992) UN Doc. HCR/IP/4/Eng/REV.1, para. 164. This approach was also reflected in the first wave of judicial decisions, such as *Salibian* v. *Canada (Minister of Employment and Immigration)* 3 FC 250 (1990), and *Adan* v. *SSHD* [1998] UKHL 15.

[15] See UNHCR, 'UNHCR Eligibility Guidelines for Assessing the International Protection Needs of Asylum-Seekers from Afghanistan' (Geneva, 2009), 12–13. See also Guy Goodwin-Gill and Jane McAdam, *The Refugee in International Law* (3rd edn. Oxford: Oxford University Press, 2007), 126ff.; Walter Kälin, 'Flight in Times of War', *International Review of the Red Cross* 83 (2001), 629.

[16] UNHCR, 'International Protection Considerations with regard to people fleeing the Syrian Arab Republic, Update II' (Geneva, 22 October 2013), para. 14. (Henceforth 'International Protection Considerations: Syria'.)

collapse of the political, healthcare, and education systems, or displacement.[17] It may also include conduct that is more individual in nature, including security checks, house or office raids, interrogation, personal and property searches, forced evictions, sexual violence, or restrictions on freedom of movement.[18] A more in-depth analysis of the armed conflict or violence in the country of origin will indeed often establish a link to the 1951 Convention grounds.[19]

2.3. Peace activism as grounds for asylum

One special case of the existence of refugees being consequential upon breaches of negative peace concerns that of the peace activist, or the conscientious objector. Conscientious objection can manifest as pacifism, an objection to fighting in all wars, or it can be a selective objection to a particular conflict.[20] The UN Office of the High Commissioner for Human Rights (UN OHCHR) has characterized conscientious objection as an objection to service based on 'principles and reasons of conscience, including profound convictions, arising from religious, moral, ethical, humanitarian or other motives'.[21] Even though no international legal instruments explicitly recognize the right to conscientious objection, there is an increasing trend to interpret the right to freedom of thought, conscience, and religion as encompassing the right to conscientious objection.[22]

Conscientious objection has also been addressed as a basis for refugee status.[23] The general rule is that because all states have an intrinsic right to call upon

[17] UNHCR, 'Summary Conclusions on International Protection', para. 11.

[18] UNHCR, 'Eligibility Guidelines: Afghanistan', para. 17; UNHCR, 'Summary Conclusions on International Protection', para. 11. See also UNHCR, 'Expert Meeting on Complementarities', paras. 13–21.

[19] See further Walter Kälin, 'Refugees and Civil Wars: Only a Matter of Interpretation?', *IJRL* 3 (1991), 435; Hugo Storey and Rebecca Wallace, 'War and Peace in Refugee Law Jurisprudence', *American Journal of International Law* 95 (2001), 353; Vanessa Holzer 'The Relevance of the 1951 Refugee Convention for the Protection of Individuals Forced to Flee Armed Conflicts', in *Global Risks: Constructing World Order through Law, Politics and Economics*, Jana Hertwig Sylvia Maus, Almut Meyer zu Schwabedissen, and Matthias Schuler (eds.) (Frankfurt: Peter Lang, 2010), 104–11.

[20] 'Conscientious Objection to Military Service' (1985), UN Doc. E/CN.4/Sub.2/1983/30/Rev.1; Karen Musalo, 'Conscientious Objection as a Basis for Refugee Status: Protection for the Fundamental Right of Freedom of Thought, Conscience and Religion', *RSQ* 26 (2007), 69.

[21] 'Report of the Office of the High Commissioner for Human Rights, Civil and Political Rights, Including the Question of Conscientious Objection to Military Service', 16 February 2004, ECOSOC, UN Doc. E/CN.4/2004/55, para. 38(c). See also 'Report of the Human Rights Council Advisory Committee on the Right of Peoples to Peace', 16 April 2012, UN Doc. A/HRC/20/31, Art. 5.

[22] Emily N. Marcus, 'Conscientious Objection as an Emerging Human Right', *VJIL* 38 (1998), 507; 'General Comment 22: The Right to Freedom of Thought, Conscience and Religion (Art. 18)', 30 July 1993, UN Doc. CCPR/C/21/Rev.1/Add.4; ECOSOC, UN Doc. E/CN.4/2004/55, para. 16; UNHCR, 'Guidelines on International Protection No. 10: Claims to Refugee Status Related to Military Service within the Context of Article 1A(2) of the 1951 Refugee Convention and/or the 1967 Protocol relating to the Status of Refugees' (Geneva, 3 December 2013), para. 3 (Henceforth 'Guidelines on Military Service'.)

[23] Noteworthy scholarly examples include Cecilia Bailliet, 'Assessing Jus ad Bellum and Jus in Bello within the Refugee Status Determination Process: Contemplations on Conscientious Objectors Seeking Asylum', *GILJ* 20 (2006), 337; Musalo, 'Conscientious Objection as a Basis for Refugee Status'.

their citizens to undertake military service, and the aversion to military service is thus not a legitimate reason for refusal to serve,[24] punishment for evasion or desertion is not usually considered to be persecution under the refugee definition. Nevertheless, there is one important exception; once an individual's refusal to serve can be grounded in any of the 1951 Convention grounds, he or she may have a legitimate claim to refugee status. In the words of UNHCR, this exception arises when 'performance of military service would have required . . . participation in military action contrary to . . . genuine political, religious, or moral convictions, or to valid reasons of conscience'.[25] This approach has also been adopted by the UN High Commissioner for Human Rights.[26]

Grants of asylum to conscientious objectors have most often been linked to political opinion claims.[27] The refusal to bear arms, for example, has been considered to reflect a political opinion regarding the permissible limits of state authority, and, as such, is a political act.[28] A specific wording in the UNHCR Handbook, where it is stated that the military service to which an individual objects on grounds of political opinion must be 'condemned by the international community as contrary to basic rules of human conduct'[29] has nevertheless caused much controversy as to which political justifications can serve as the basis for objection. Courts have notably recognized that a person who objects solely to participating in an internationally condemned conflict can claim that the risk of prosecution amounts to persecution. This means that an objection based on political opinion appears to require an external assessment regarding the international community's perspective on the military action.[30] This stands in contrast to situations where an objection to military service is based on religion or conscience, which require an internal assessment of the subjective beliefs of the applicant. In the UK case of *Sepet* v. *Secretary of State for the Home Department*, for example, the House of Lords denied refugee status to two Kurdish asylum seekers—on the basis of a failure to show international condemnation of Turkish military action against the Kurds. The asylum

[24] States are entitled to require citizens to perform military service, and this does not in itself violate an individual's rights. For military recruitment to be justified it nevertheless needs to fulfil certain criteria: prescribed by law, implemented in a way that is not arbitrary or discriminatory, the functions and discipline of the recruits must be based on military needs and plans, and be challengeable in a court of law. Explicit safeguards also exist to prevent the exposure of children to military service. See 'Fourth Report on the Situation of Human Rights in Guatemala', 1 June 1993, Inter-American Commission on Human Rights, OEA/Ser.L/V/II.83, Doc. 16 rev., ch. 5. See also UNHCR, 'Guidelines on Military Service', 2, 4.

[25] UNHCR, 'Handbook on Procedures and Criteria for Refugee Status' (Geneva, reissued December 2011), para. 170. See also UNHCR, 'Religion-Based Refugee Claims under Article 1A(2) of the 1951 Convention and/or the 1967 Protocol Relating to the Status of Refugees' (Geneva, 28 April 2004), UN Doc. HCR/GIP/04/06, para. 26.

[26] ECOSOC, UN Doc. E/CN.4/2004/55, para. 38(h).

[27] Bailliet, 'Assessing Jus ad Bellum and Jus in Bello', 345. For an overview of situations where other convention grounds may be triggered, see UNHCR, 'Guidelines on Military Service', 10–12.

[28] This approach was taken in *Zolfagharkani* v. *Minister for Employment and Immigration* [1993] 3 FC 540, para. 36.

[29] UNHCR, 'Handbook', para. 171. No such formulation is found in UNHCR, 'Guidelines on Military Service'.

[30] Bailliet, 'Assessing Jus ad Bellum and Jus in Bello', 346.

seekers objected to military service in Turkey where they believed they would be compelled to fight fellow Kurds and engage in acts contrary to international norms.[31] Several cases, notably in the US, have further interpreted the UNHCR Handbook as requiring an actual UN resolution condemning the military action.[32] In its 2013 Protection Guidelines relating to military service, however, UNHCR firmly establishes that:

> In determining the legality of the conflict in question condemnation by the international community is strong evidence, but not essential for finding that the use of force is in violation of international law. Such pronouncements are not always made, even where objectively an act of aggression has taken place. Thus, a determination of illegality with regard to the use of force needs to be made through the application of the governing rules under international law.[33]

More recent developments, the EU Qualification Directive being a case in point, have shifted the emphasis away from the requirement of an international condemnation to that of an evaluation of the military action within a humanitarian law and human rights framework. The Directive limits refugee status to extreme circumstances where the individual would be engaged in crimes against peace, war crimes, crimes against humanity, serious non-political crimes, or acts contrary to the purposes and principles of the United Nations.[34] These developments clearly go against the views of both leading scholars and the UNHCR.[35] The latter has recently responded to these developments in its 2013 Protection Guidelines relating to military service:

> Where an armed conflict is considered to be unlawful as a matter of international law [in violation of *jus ad bellum*], it is not necessary that the applicant be at risk of incurring individual criminal responsibility if he or she were to participate in the conflict in question, rather the applicant would need to establish that his or her objection is genuine, and that because of his or her objection, there is a risk of persecution.[36]

That said, refugee status may be accorded to an individual for a number of reasons in addition to the above, and several factors need to be taken into account. Indeed, as emphasized by the UNHCR Handbook, individuals who object for religious, moral, or valid reasons of conscience must demonstrate the sincerity of their beliefs, the fact that military service is obligatory, and that the state provides no

[31] [2003] UKHL 15 [2003] 1 WLR. 856 (appeal taken from Eng.) (UK).

[32] See *M.A.* v. *INS*, 899 F.2d 304, 313 (4th Cir. 1990).

[33] 'Guidelines on Military Service', para. 24.

[34] EU Qualifications Directive 2004/83/EC of 29 April 2009 on minimum standards for the qualification and status of third country nationals or stateless persons as refugees or as persons who otherwise need international protection and the content of the protection granted [2009] L 304/12, Art. 9(2)(e). See also UK case of *Krotov* v. *Secretary of State for the Home Department* [2004] EWCA (Civ) 69, [2004] 1 WLR 1825; and Canadian cases of *Hinzman* v. *Canada (Minister of Citizenship and Immigration)* (FC) [2006] FC 420 (CanLII) [2007] 1 FCR 561; *Hughey* v. *Canada (Minister of Citizenship and Immigration)* [2006] FC 421.

[35] Bailliet has even argued that the developments regarding conscientious objection within the European Union displays a type of 'schizophrenia'. See Bailliet, 'Assessing Jus ad Bellum and Jus in Bello', 367.

[36] 'Guidelines on Military Service', para. 23.

accommodation for these beliefs.[37] As such, the fundamental issues in determining an individual's refugee status on the basis of objection to military service appear to be 'the sincerity of the conviction which sets him or her in opposition to their government, and the risk of treatment amounting to persecution, by reason of such objection'.[38] Whether the treatment in question amounts to persecution within the meaning of the 1951 Convention will depend on a number of factors, including the object and purpose of the law, the precise motivation of the individual who breaches such law, the 'interest' that such individual asserts, and the nature and extent of the punishment.[39] As UNHCR exemplifies, disproportionate or arbitrary punishment for refusing to undertake state military service or engage in acts contrary to international law—such as excessive prison terms or corporal punishment—would be a form of persecution.[40] This also means that, contrary to the development that was highlighted earlier, it should not make any difference whether 'religion' or 'political opinion' form the basis of evasion of military service.[41]

2.4. Exclusion from refugee status: crimes against peace and other international crimes

While victims fleeing armed conflict or other violence are often granted refugee status, there are acts so grave that they render their perpetrators, otherwise considered refugees, undeserving of international protection as refugees. Indeed, such persons often contribute to the creation of refugees and to breaches of negative peace. The exclusion clauses embedded within the 1951 Refugee Convention and in regional instruments aim at depriving those guilty of heinous acts (such as crimes against peace or humanity) and serious common crimes, of international refugee protection.[42] In such cases, exclusion is meant to ensure that these individuals will not abuse the institution of asylum in order to avoid being held legally accountable for their acts. Article 1(f) of the 1951 Refugee Convention clearly links international refugee law to other fields of international law, and specifically provides that:

> The provisions of this Convention shall not apply to any person with respect to whom there are serious reasons for considering that:
> (a) He has committed a crime against peace, a war crime, or a crime against humanity, as defined in the international instruments drawn up to make provision in respect of such crimes;

[37] 'Handbook', paras. 170, 172–4; 'Guidelines on Military Service', paras. 17–20.

[38] Goodwin-Gill and McAdam, *The Refugee in International Law*, 104–5.

[39] Goodwin-Gill and McAdam, *The Refugee in International Law*, 114–15. See also 'Guidelines on Military Service', para. 13.

[40] 'Guidelines on Military Service', para. 14.

[41] Atle Grahl-Madsen, *The Status of Refugees in International Law* (Leiden: A. W. Sijthoff, 1966), 238.

[42] See generally Goodwin-Gill and McAdam, *The Refugee in International Law*, 162ff.; UNHCR, 'Guidelines on International Protection: Application of the Exclusion Clauses: Article 1F of the 1951 Convention Relating to the Status of Refugees' (Geneva 2003), UN Doc. HCR/GIP/03/05. (Henceforth 'Guidelines: Exclusion'.)

(b) He has committed a serious non-political crime outside the country of refuge prior to his admission to that country as a refugee;
(c) He has been guilty of acts contrary to the purposes and principles of the United Nations.

Similar provisions are contained in Article I(5) the OAU Convention. Several international instruments offer guidance on the scope of the international crimes mentioned in the exclusion clauses; a crime against peace, for instance, is explained in the 1945 Charter of the International Military Tribunal and involves the 'planning, preparation, initiation or waging of a war of aggression, or a war in violation of international treaties, agreements, or assurances, or participation in a common plan or conspiracy for the accomplishment of any of the foregoing'.[43] The category 'acts contrary to the purposes and principles of the United Nations' in 1(f)(c) may furthermore include crimes capable of affecting international peace, security, and peaceful relations between states, as well as serious and sustained violations of human rights.[44] The exclusion clauses are meant to be exhaustive, and, given the possible serious consequences of exclusion, should be interpreted in a restrictive manner.[45] Importantly, an excluded individual may still be protected against return to a country where he or she is at risk of ill treatment by virtue of other international instruments.[46]

Individual responsibility must also be established in relation to a crime covered by Article 1(f).[47] This essentially means that participation in armed conflict is not in itself a ground for exclusion, nor is mere membership in a group or organization.[48] This obviously makes the task of excluding an intricate one—only in Syria have at least 1,200 different armed groups been identified, and many of these have reportedly been engaged in human rights violations and serious violations of international humanitarian law.[49] An additional aggravating factor when it comes to exclusion is also the large-scale influx of refugees. In these cases, recourse is often made to group determination of refugee status, whereby each member of the population in question is regarded *prima facie* as a refugee.[50] This approach

[43] See the Charter of the International Military Tribunal, in Agreement for the Prosecution and Punishment of the Major War Criminals of the European Axis (8 August 1945) 58 Stat. 1544, EAS No. 472, 82 UNTS 280, Art. 6.

[44] 'Guidelines: Exclusion', para. 17. See also the Charter of the United Nations (adopted 26 June 1945, entered into force 24 October 1945) 1 UNTS XVI, Arts. 1 and 2.

[45] 'Guidelines: Exclusion', paras. 2–3.

[46] For example, the Convention against Torture absolutely prohibits the return of an individual to a country where there is a risk that he or she will be subjected to torture. Other international and regional human rights instruments contain similar provisions. See Convention against Torture and Other Cruel, Inhuman or Degrading Treatment or Punishment (adopted 10 December 1984, entered into force 26 June 1987) 1465 UNTS 85.

[47] 'Guidelines: Exclusion', paras. 18–20.

[48] 'International Protection Considerations: Syria', para. 17.

[49] See, in particular, the reports of the Independent International Commission of Inquiry on the Syrian Arab Republic, http://www.ohchr.org/EN/HRBodies/HRC/IICISyria/Pages/IndependentInternationalCommission.aspx (accessed 6 February 2014).

[50] Bonaventure Rutinwa, 'Prima Facie Status and Refugee Protection', *UNHCR New Issues in Refugee Research Working Paper* 69 (2002).

has a number of limitations; perhaps the greatest of these is precisely the difficulty of excluding criminal and other elements not deserving international protection. In certain situations, the presence of excludable elements among refugees as a result of group determination creates security problems in camps, as happened in the Rwandan refugee camps in Zaïre (today the Democratic Republic of the Congo) in the mid-1990s.[51] Today, in Turkey's Syrian refugee camps, the distinction between rebels and refugees has also become increasingly compromised.[52]

3. Peace and Threats against Peace in Exile

3.1. Asylum: peaceful and humanitarian

Ever since the very inception of the asylum regime, the international community has emphasized the provision of asylum as a peaceful and humanitarian act. In 1967, the UN General Assembly unanimously adopted the United Nations Declaration on Territorial Asylum, which provided that 'States granting asylum shall not permit persons who have received asylum to engage in activities contrary to the purposes and principles of the United Nations,' and, more importantly, recognized that the grant of asylum is 'a peaceful and humanitarian act and ... as such, cannot be regarded as unfriendly by another State'.[53] This notion is also reflected in important legal instruments such as the 1951 Refugee Convention, the Preamble of which expresses the wish that 'all States, recognizing the social and humanitarian nature of the problem of refugees, will do everything within their power to prevent this problem from becoming a cause of tension between States'.[54] The regional 1969 OAU Convention similarly recognizes that '[t]he grant of asylum to refugees is a peaceful and humanitarian act and shall not be regarded as an unfriendly act by any ... State' and stresses the need to make a 'distinction between a refugee who seeks a peaceful and normal life and a person fleeing his country for the sole purpose of fomenting subversion from outside'.[55] It specifically restricts participation of refugees in any subversive activities against an OAU member state and further prohibits refugees from engaging in activities likely to cause tension between these states.[56] Indeed, by emphasizing that the granting of asylum by a host state should not be taken as an act of aggression by the country of origin, Conventions such as these were concluded *inter alia* to tackle a difficult problem of interstate relations.[57]

[51] Rutinwa, 'Prima Facie Status and Refugee Protection'.

[52] Kristian Harpviken and Mark Naftalin, 'Conflating Spaces: Syrian Rebels and Refugees in South Turkey', *ISN Security Watch* (18 September 2012).

[53] UNGA Res. 2312 (XXII) (14 December 1967) UN Doc. A/RES/2312(XXII), Art. 4 and preamble.

[54] 1951 Refugee Convention, preamble.

[55] 1969 OAU Convention, Art. 2 and preamble.

[56] 1969 OAU Convention, Art. 3(2).

[57] Ralf Alleweldt, 'Preamble 1951 Convention', in *The 1951 Convention Relating to the Status of Refugees and its 1967 Protocol: A Commentary*, Andreas Zimmermann (ed.) (Oxford: Oxford University Press, 2011), 238 para. 61.

At first glance, the notion of asylum as a peaceful and humanitarian act—by aiming to create a peaceful coexistence between states—appears to signify an ambition to achieve peace both in its positive and negative understanding. As UNHCR has emphasized, '[a]s asylum is a humanitarian institution, military activities of any kind are incompatible with refugee status'.[58] This includes recruitment of, or volunteering by, refugees for participation in armed activities. Closer scrutiny nevertheless suggests that while the notion clearly purposes to achieve negative peace, evident for example in UNHCR's above statement and further discussed in Section 3.2, it may potentially threaten, or at least constrain, the achievement of peace in the positive sense. As was highlighted in this chapter's introduction, positive peace *inter alia* refers to the presence of social justice through a fair distribution of power and the constructive resolution of conflict. To achieve positive peace, refugees should arguably be included in political and peace-building efforts in the country of origin. As argued in Section 4, such inclusion is imperative for the resolution of displacement and for building sustainable (positive) peace in the country of origin. Indeed, refugee flows have tremendous political implications, and exiles are frequently under enormous pressure to organize politically.[59] Most refugees want to return to their countries of origin and many times the only truly secure way to return home is a change in the political status quo in the country of origin. Indeed, Syrian refugees have recently engaged in a wide range of activities directed towards Syria, ranging between non-violent and organized (yet deeply divided) political opposition groups, to local activist networks and non-organized demonstrators, to armed opposition groups.[60]

The notion of asylum as a peaceful and humanitarian act, however, implies that asylum is non-political—indeed, the Commentary to the 1951 Refugee Convention explains that the underlying idea is that receiving refugees is seen as a humanitarian act rather than a political measure.[61] It can therefore be argued that abstention from certain internationally significant political activities is a condition attached to the granting of asylum.[62] This means that while refugees may participate politically in certain types of activities in their countries of asylum, a restriction may seemingly be placed when it comes to other political activities directed against the country of origin. To what extent, and precisely which, political activities may be lawfully restricted is nevertheless not entirely clear, but the key question appears to be whether or not a certain political activity has the potential of threatening the relations between the country of origin and the

[58] UNHCR, 'Protection Guidelines Relating to Refugee Security' (Geneva, 1999), paras. 2, 5.

[59] Stephen Corliss, 'Asylum State Responsibility for the Hostile Acts of Foreign Exiles', *IJRL* 2 (1990), 181.

[60] Aron Lund, *Divided They Stand—An Overview of Syria's Political Opposition Factors* (Brussels: Foundation for European Progressive Studies, 2012); Hala Naufal, 'Syrian Refugees in Lebanon: The Humanitarian Approach under Political Divisions', *Migration Policy Centre Research Report 2012/13* (2012).

[61] Alleweldt, 'Preamble', 238.

[62] See generally Maja Janmyr, *Protecting Civilians in Refugee Camps: Unable and Unwilling States, UNHCR and International Responsibility* (Leiden: Martinus Nijhoff, 2014), 136ff.; Maja Janmyr, 'Revisiting the Civilian and Humanitarian Character of Refugee Camps', in *Refuge from Inhumanity*, David Cantor and Jean-François Durieux (eds.) (Leiden: Martinus Nijhoff, 2014).

country of asylum. An additional factor to take into account is that the right to express a political opinion and engage in political associations is a fundamental standard in international human rights law.[63]

3.2. The civilian and humanitarian character of refugee camps

The notion of refugees actively contributing to violent resistance predates the contemporary international refugee regime and has existed for as long as individuals have been forced into exile.[64] Rather than serving as safe havens, on a number of occasions, camps for refugees have become notorious for breaches of negative peace and serious problems of insecurity, including armed attacks, arbitrary killings, torture, exploitation, and military recruitment.[65] UNHCR has even argued that militarized camps pose the single biggest threat to refugee security, and that such camps, seen by host states as security concerns, may undermine public and political support for the principles of refugee protection and asylum.[66] Indeed, in these cases, refugees may exacerbate conflict or frustrate efforts to find peace. Examples of this are frequent in history—for example, Norwegian refugees, fleeing Germany's occupation of Norway, were trained and armed in so-called health camps in neighbouring Sweden during World War II.[67] During the 1950s, 1960s and 1970s, the majority of refugees also fled in the context of wars of liberation and independence, specifically from Apartheid in South Africa and the Portuguese colonies of Mozambique, Angola, and Guinea Bissau. Struggles for liberation in Latin America and South East Asia equally generated vast numbers of refugees.[68] Newly independent states generally maintained an open-door policy to those fleeing wars of national liberation, and many liberation movements were allowed by host states to pursue their armed struggles from bases in refugee camps on their territory.

[63] See International Covenant on Civil and Political Rights (adopted 16 December 1966, entered into force 23 March 1976) 999 UNTS 171 (ICCPR), Arts. 19–22.

[64] See generally Kristian B. Harpviken, 'From "Refugee Warriors" to "Returnee Warriors": Militant Homecoming in Afghanistan and Beyond', *Global Migration and Transnational Politics Working Paper* 5 (2008).

[65] Janmyr, 'Revisiting the Civilian and Humanitarian Character of Refugee Camps', 136ff.; UNHCR, 'The Security, Civilian and Humanitarian Character of Refugee Camps and Settlements: Operationalizing the "Ladder of Options"' (Geneva, 2000) UN Doc. EC/50/SC/INF.4, para. 1.

[66] UNHCR, 'The Security, Civilian and Humanitarian Character'. See also 'The Civilian and Humanitarian Character of Asylum', (2002), UNHCR EXCOM Conclusion No. 94 (LIII), preamble.

[67] See Anders Johansson, *Den Glömda Armén: Norge-Sverige 1939–1945* (Rimbo: Fischer, 2008).

[68] See Elly-Elikunda Mtango, 'Military and Armed Attacks on Refugee Camps', in *Refugees and International Relations*, Gil Loescher and Laila Monahan (eds.) (Oxford: Oxford University Press, 1989). See also Pierre Centlivres and Micheline Centlivres-Demont, 'The Afghan Refugee in Pakistan: A Nation in Exile', *Current Sociology* 36 (1988), 71; Rudiger Schöch, 'Afghan Refugees in Pakistan during the 1980s: Cold War Politics and Registration Practice', *UNHCR New Issues in Refugee Research* 157 (2008); Stephen Golub et al., *Seeking Shelter: Cambodians in Thailand* (New York: Lawyers Committee for Human Rights, 1987); Fiona Terry, *Condemned to Repeat?: The Paradox of Humanitarian Action* (New York: Cornell University Press, 2002).

During this period, the notion of asylum as a peaceful and humanitarian act was challenged by widespread ideologies of anti-colonialism.[69] Rather than promoting the peaceful and humanitarian character of asylum, several UN organs also explicitly supported refugee camp-based armed liberation groups.[70] UNHCR, for instance, was under pressure to 'turn a blind eye to freedom fighters among the civilian population', and in fact channelled much of its assistance through these very movements.[71] At the same time, heated deliberations took place within the Executive Committee, UNHCR's governing organ. The question of the civilian and humanitarian nature of refugee camps paralyzed the debate within the Committee for years, and a discussion raged about whether the primary onus was on the host states to ensure the civilian and humanitarian character of refugee camps, or on neighbouring states to abstain from attacking them.[72] Indeed, the issue at hand was firmly wedged between claims of, on the one hand, a 'just war' waged by the encamped refugees based on the principle of self-determination and to secure a return home, and, on the other, the right of states—seeing the camps as legitimate military targets—to respond in self-defence to external aggression.[73] The fact that African states are obliged under the African Charter on Human and Peoples' Rights to support armed struggles conducted by national liberation movements surely complicated this situation.[74] In 1987, after several strenuous years of discussion, UNHCR's Executive Committee finally coined the principle of the civilian and humanitarian character of refugee camps in its Conclusion No. 48 on military or armed attacks on refugee camps and settlements.[75]

Following the end of the Cold War, when refugees were only rarely fleeing wars of liberation, the civilian and humanitarian character of refugee camps gained focus anew. The Principle's importance has since been repeatedly emphasized, first under the auspices of the UNHCR, and later by the UN General Assembly.[76]

[69] Jeff Crisp, 'Africa's Refugees: Patterns, Problems and Policy Challenges', *JCAS* 18 (2000), 157; James Milner, 'Golden Age? What Golden Age? A Critical History of African Asylum Policy' (2004), paper presented to the Centre for Refugee Studies (York University, 28 January 2004), 2. See also Bonaventure Rutinwa, 'The End of Asylum? The Changing Nature of Refugee Policies in Africa', *UNHCR New Issues in Refugee Research Paper* 5 (1999), 4; Louise W. Holborn, *Refugees: A Problem of Our Time: The Work of the United Nations High Commissioner for Refugees 1951–1972* (Metuchen: Scarecrow, 1975), ii. 825.

[70] See UNGA Res. 41/123 (4 December 1986) UN Doc. A/RES/14/123(1986).

[71] See Guy Goodwin-Gill, 'Rwanda-Zaire: Refugee Camps and the Protection of Refugees', *IJRL* 8 (1996), 630. See also UNHCR, 'Confidential Status Report II: Projects of Assistance to National Liberation Movements' (1974), on file with author.

[72] Janmyr, 'Revisiting the Civilian and Humanitarian Character of Refugee Camps', 136ff.

[73] See 'Addendum to the Report of the United Nations High Commissioner for Refugees' (1982) UNHCR EXCOM, UN Doc. A/37/12/Add.1, para. 70(3)(c); 'Report by Ambassador Felix Schnyder on Military Attacks on Refugee Camps and Settlements in Southern Africa and Elsewhere' (1983), UNHCR EXCOM, UN Doc. EC/SCP/26.

[74] See African Charter on Human and Peoples' Rights (adopted 27 June 1981, entered into force 21 October 1986), Art. 20(2) and (3). Importantly, the clauses of the 1969 OAU Convention prohibiting subversive activities were not intended to contradict this commitment. See further Mtango, 'Military and Armed Attacks on Refugee Camps', 88.

[75] 'Military attacks on refugee camps and settlements in Southern Africa and elsewhere' (1987) UNHCR EXCOM Conclusion no. 48 (XXXVIII), preamble.

[76] Janmyr, 'Revisiting the Civilian and Humanitarian Character of Refugee Camps', 136ff.

The enormity of the militarization crisis taking place in Rwandan refugee camps in Zaïre during the mid-1990s also triggered the attention of the UN Security Council. Most important among a considerable number of Council Resolutions concerning refugee camp security are those recognizing that a breach of the refugee camps' civilian and humanitarian character may develop into threats against international peace and security. In Resolution 1296, for example, the Security Council invites the Secretary-General to bring to its attention situations where refugee and IDP camps are vulnerable to infiltration by armed elements and 'where such situations may constitute a threat to international peace and security.'[77] Security Council Resolution 1208 on refugees in Africa furthermore recognizes that provision of security to refugees and the maintenance of the civilian and humanitarian character of refugee camps and settlements is an 'integral part of the national, regional and international response to refugee situations and can contribute to the maintenance of international peace and security.'[78] Today, the Principle is arguably part of customary international law, grounded *inter alia* in early treaty and customary law, such as the UN Charter and the laws of neutrality.[79] That said, challenges still persist when it comes to implementation.[80]

4. Refugees as Contributors to Peace

4.1. Peace-building in exile

As recognized by the UN Security Council and other UN organs, refugees are imperative contributors to peace and should play a direct role in peace-building.[81] Peace-building intends to create positive peace and consists of a wide range of activities—capacity building, reconciliation, and societal transformation—focusing *inter alia* on the social conditions that foster violent conflict.[82] While peace-building thus encompasses a certain degree of political action, exactly how it relates to the notion of asylum as peaceful and humanitarian (discussed in Section 3.1), requiring that the political activities of refugees be kept within bounds, is not clear-cut.[83] As will be discussed in the following, however, refugees

[77] UNSC Res. 1296 (19 April 2000) UN Doc. S/RES/1296(2000), para. 14.

[78] UNSC Res. 1208 (19 November 1998) UN Doc. S/RES/1208(1998), preamble.

[79] Janmyr, 'Revisiting the Civilian and Humanitarian Character of Refugee Camps', 136ff. For an explicit discussion of the relation between international humanitarian law and refugee law when it comes to this principle, see Janmyr's complete chapter.

[80] For the case of Syria, see Lund, *Divided They Stand*. See also Harpviken and Naftalin, 'Conflating Spaces'.

[81] UNSC Res. 1325 (31 October 2000) UN Doc. S/RES/1325(2000), para. 8(a); UN Sub-Commission on the Prevention of Discrimination and Protection of Minorities, Res. 1998/26 (26 August 1998); 'Internally displaced persons', HRC Res. 2005/46, UN Doc. E/CN.4/RES/2005/46.

[82] Report of the Secretary-General, 'An Agenda for Peace: Preventative Diplomacy, Peacemaking and Peace-keeping', 17 June 1992, UN Doc. A/47/277-S/24111; John Paul Lederach, *The Moral Imagination: The Art and Soul of Building Peace* (Oxford: Oxford University Press, 2005).

[83] Indeed, some host states have restricted even peaceful protests of refugees against human rights violations in their country of origin. Vowing to prevent all anti-Chinese activity, Nepali

do participate in a wide range of peace-building activities, and predominantly so when these activities are sanctioned by the host state and/or the international community. While Section 4.2 will explore how refugee participation in peace-building is closely linked to the resolution of displacement, this section focuses on how refugees may make important contributions to peace-building in three notable ways: first, as contributors to the development of peace agreements; second, as participators in peace-building elections and referenda; and third, if they benefit from skills training and *self-reliance*.

4.1.1. Peace agreements

Throughout history, refugees—particularly women refugees—have only rarely been consulted or represented in peace processes.[84] Peace-building initiatives have often marginalized them and they have been viewed as passive recipients of outcomes that are negotiated in distant arenas of power.[85] Early peace agreements did not always consider forced displacement; one example of this is the 1992 peace agreement in El Salvador which, following El Salvadoran government opposition to the return of refugees to rebel-held areas, did not mention refugee return.[86] Today, there is a growing trend in which refugees are able to influence conflict and peace outcomes. Contemporary changes, not the least advances in communications technology, are giving refugees more prominent roles.[87] It is increasingly acknowledged that refugees may contribute to the development of peace agreements that more comprehensively address the causes and consequences of conflicts. Indeed, as this chapter highlights, where opportunities for political participation are not guaranteed, refugees in exile risk becoming politicized or militarized. Disregarding refugees' interests may be explicitly destructive to peace processes, and particularly so in protracted refugee situations or in cases where refugee populations become party to the conflict.[88] In these scenarios, their inclusion is absolutely necessary for conflict resolution.

authorities e.g. have cracked down on Tibetan refugees calling for a free Tibet. See '12 Free Tibet Activists in Police Net', *Himalayan Times*, 23 June 2011, www.thehimalayantimes.com/rssReference.php?headline=12+Free+Tibet+activists+in+police+net&NewsID=292941 (accessed 11 Nov 2014).

[84] Khalid Koser, 'Introduction: Integrating Displacement in Peace Processes and Peacebuilding', *RSQ* 28 (2009), 5.

[85] Karen Jacobsen, Helen Young, and Abdalmonim Osman, 'Refugees and IDPs in Peacemaking Processes', in *Contemporary Peacemaking: Conflict, Peace Processes and Post-war Reconstruction*, John Darby and Roger Mac Ginty (eds.) (New York: Palgrave MacMillan, 2008), 313.

[86] Refugee return was rather addressed in the regional Central American Conference on Refugees, Returnees and Internally Displaced Persons. See Declaration and Concerted Plan of Action in Favour of Central American Refugees, Returnees and Displaced Persons, 30 May 1989, CIREFCA, 89/13/Rev.1.

[87] Jacobsen, Young, and Osman, 'Refugees and IDPs', 315.

[88] Elements opposed to the peace process in Burundi, for example, remained active in western Tanzania for several years after the end of the conflict. See James Milner, 'Refugees and the Regional Dynamics of Peacebuilding', *RSQ* 28 (2009), 13, 17. See also Tammi Sharpe and Silvio Cordova, 'Peacebuilding in Displacement', *FMR* 33 (2009), 46; Gil Loescher, James Milner, Edward Newman, and Gary G. Troeller (eds.), *Protracted Refugee Situations: Political, Human Rights and Security Implications* (Tokyo: United Nations University Press, 2008).

Many major peace agreements in the last decades have included references to, and often more detailed provisions on, refugees or other displaced populations.[89] These agreements often incorporate legal protections for returning refugees with a view both to address past injustices and to prevent future rights violations. Burundian refugees, for example, participated in the Arusha Peace Process consultations where they promoted refugees' interests in the negotiations.[90] Issues put forward by refugees that were subsequently included in the peace agreement included the recovery of land and property, and procedures to guarantee the voluntary and safe return and reintegration of refugees into Burundian society. Along this same line, Liberian civil society, backed by refugees, formally participated in the 2003 peace negotiations.[91] Their participation *inter alia* contributed to the establishment of a Truth and Reconciliation Commission. Furthermore, individual refugee elites have played important roles as participants in peace-building commissions and other forms of peace-building activity. For example, Somali diaspora have drafted strategic documents that constitute a basis for peace dialogues between conflicting factions within Somalia, and the Eritrean constitution was in part drafted by Eritreans in exile.[92]

4.1.2. Peace-building elections and referenda

Refugees may also participate in peace-building elections and referenda without being forced physically to repatriate first.[93] Considering the fact that refugees are excluded—sometimes very deliberately—from the structures of political power in their country of origin, this opportunity is particularly pertinent.[94] Noteworthy examples include the Eritrean independence referendum (1993), and elections in Bosnia (1996 and 1997), Kosovo (1999), Afghanistan (2004), Iraq (2005 and 2010), and South Sudan (2010 and 2011).[95] The Eritrean referendum, in which 99.7 per cent voted for independence, can be considered a highly successful example of refugee participation in peace-building through out-of-country voting.

[89] For an overview, see Christine Bell, *Peace Agreements and Human Rights* (Oxford: Oxford University Press, 2000), 233ff. See also Koser, 'Introduction: Integrating Displacement'.

[90] Sharpe and Cordova, 'Peacebuilding in Displacement'.

[91] Priscilla Hayner, *Negotiating Peace in Liberia: Preserving the Possibility for Justice* (Geneva: Henry Dunant Centre for Humanitarian Dialogue, 2007).

[92] See 'Mobilising African Diaspora for the Promotion of Peace in Africa', May 2005, African Diaspora Policy Centre.

[93] See generally, Katy Long, 'Voting with their Feet: A Review of Refugee Participation and the Role of UNHCR in Country of Origin Elections and Other Political Processes', UNHCR Policy Development and Evaluation Service, UN Doc. PDES/2010/12 (2010), 17ff. See also Jeremy Grace and Erin Mooney, 'Peacebuilding through the Electoral Participation of Displaced Populations', *RSQ* 28 (2009), 95; Patrik Johansson 'Putting Peace to the Vote: Displaced Persons and a Future Referendum on Nagorno-Karabakh', *RSQ* 28 (2009), 122.

[94] Long, 'Voting with their Feet', 1.

[95] 'Case Studies on the Participation of Conflict Forced Migrants in Elections: Participatory Elections Project (PEP)', May 2003, International Organization for Migration (IOM). (Henceforth IOM, 'Case Studies'.)

Some 300,000 Eritreans in exile, out of approximately 1.2 million (including children), registered for out-of-country voting—which amounted to around a third of the total electorate.[96] The Dayton Agreement furthermore explicitly linked refugee participation to refugee repatriation in the Bosnian context, confirming that 'the exercise of a refugee's right to vote shall be interpreted as confirmation of his or her intention to return to Bosnia and Herzegovina'.[97] But again, experience suggests that refugee participation in out-of-country voting is not always straightforward. The difficulties associated with such participation have been highlighted, for example, in the 2010 election in Iraq, where the nature and form of refugee participation were subject to fierce disputes, not the least because of continued sectarian struggles for political power.[98]

4.1.3. Skills training: training in provision of basic services and peace education programmes

If refugees benefit from skills training and self-reliance while in exile, they can make an important contribution to peace-building in their country of origin. In a 2006 statement to the UN Security Council, the UN High Commissioner for Refugees noted that 'refugees return with schooling and new skills … Over and over, we see that their participation is necessary for the consolidation of both peace and post-conflict economic recovery.'[99] Such skills training may generally take two different forms. First, it may include being trained with a range of skills and qualifications that could address specific gaps in the provision of basic services in their country of origin. For example, such efforts may focus on health and education—notably, teacher-training programmes in the Kakuma refugee camp in Kenya have been found to help address the significant shortage of teachers in South Sudan.[100] Such training may also assist in the actual implementation of peace agreements, where one major reason for their lack of implementation has been suggested to be a lack of local capacity to do so.[101] Thus, in order to tackle the lack of educational opportunities for Syrian refugee youths, a group of exiled university professors recently launched the Free Syrian University in Turkey where they offer courses 'to prepare educated generations who seek to build a country of law and justice and institutions'.[102]

[96] IOM, 'Case Studies', 74.

[97] Dayton Peace Agreement (adopted 14 December 1995), Art. 4.

[98] Long, 'Voting with their Feet', 30.

[99] Statement by Mr António Guterres, United Nations High Commissioner for Refugees to the United Nations Security Council (New York, 24 January 2006), http://www.unhcr.org/43d643334.html, (accessed 11 Nov 2014).

[100] Milner, 'Refugees and the Regional Dynamics of Peacebuilding', 6.

[101] See Patricia Weiss Fagen, 'Peace Processes and IDP Solutions', *RSQ* 28 (2009), 31; Gry Tina Tinde, 'Top United Nations Peacebuilders and Advocacy for Women, Peace and Security', *RSQ* 28 (2009), 140.

[102] Daniel Seckman and Matt Trevithick, 'The Scholar-Rebels of the Free Syrian University', 17 January 2014, *The Atlantic*, http://www.theatlantic.com/international/archive/2014/01/the-scholar-rebels-of-the-free-syrian-university/283175/ (accessed 11 Nov 2014).

Second, peace education programmes for refugees in exile could enhance prospects of reconciliation and conflict resolution upon return. For example, returnees will be better equipped to reconcile with former community members and mediate conflicts during fragile post-conflict and reintegration processes. Indeed, on several occasions, UNHCR's Executive Committee has emphasized education for peace and the promotion of a culture of peace.[103] As UNHCR also has noted: 'While living in exile, long-term refugees also have an ideal opportunity to acquire valuable skills in areas such as leadership, advocacy, mediation and conflict resolution, which will again enable them to contribute to the rebuilding of their communities once return becomes possible.'[104] Refugee camps have been emphasized as particularly good sites for participatory political education, where refugees can be encouraged to act as decision-makers within camp settings.[105] In the late 1990s, the UNHCR and the Inter Agency Network for Education in Emergencies developed the Peace Education Programme (PEP), which fosters critical conflict mediation skills based on the idea that everyone is responsible for peace.[106] These efforts aim at developing skills that would help refugees build a more peaceful life while in the camp, and for later when they can return home, settle permanently in their host country, or resettle in a third country. The PEP has been implemented in refugee and returnee camps in the DRC, Eritrea, Ethiopia, Kenya, Uganda, Liberia, and Guinea, to name a few.

Incorporating refugees into peace-building activities would also provide support to refugee-hosting states, who might perceive the prolonged presence of refugees as a burden and a security concern.[107] In response to growing tensions in Côte d'Ivoire, the UNHCR and some refugees launched a campaign and aired twelve episodes of the soap opera Résidence Akwaba.[108] The soap opera, directed by a Rwandan refugee, depicted the realities of daily life in the interactions between refugees and the local population.

4.2. Durable solutions: rebuilding refugee lives in peace

As the previous section evidenced, resolving displacement is inextricably linked with achieving peace. International refugee law provides three options for the resolution of displacement—voluntary repatriation, local integration in the country

[103] See 'Comprehensive and Regional Approaches Within a Protection Framework' (1996), UNHCR EXCOM Conclusion No. 80 (XLVII), para. (e)(xi); 'Children at Risk' (2007) UNHCR EXCOM Conclusion No. 107 (LVIII), para. (h).

[104] UNHCR, 'Protracted Refugee Situations' (2008) PDES Background Document UN Doc. UNHCR/DPC/2008/Doc. 02. See also Jacobsen, Young, and Osman, 'Refugees and IDPs', 318–19.

[105] Long, 'Voting with their Feet', 40.

[106] 'UNHCR Peace Education Programme (PEP)', http://www.unhcr.org/3ee980d717.pdf (accessed 11 Nov 2014).

[107] Milner, 'Refugees and the Regional Dynamics of Peacebuilding', 4.

[108] UNHCR 'Rwandan refugee's soap opera promoting tolerance wins film festival award' (10 May 2006), UNHCR News Story.

of first asylum, or resettlement in a third country.[109] The restoration of citizenship and the remaking of state–citizen bonds lie at the heart of all of these solutions. In other words, the search for solutions to refugee situations is very much a struggle of the politically excluded for political inclusion.[110] The following sections will particularly explore how durable solutions all have the ultimate goal of allowing refugees to rebuild their lives in dignity and peace, and how they more specifically relate to broader aspects of peace.

4.2.1. Repatriation and reintegration

Refugee repatriation and peace-building are linked in a number of ways. First, considering that the existence of refugees is the very manifestation of the collapse of state protection, refugee repatriation can be seen as an indicator that national protection is re-established, and, consequently, of successful peace-building.[111] In addressing the UN Security Council in January 2009, the UN High Commissioner for Refugees explained how 'the scale of return and success of reintegration are two of the most tangible indicators of progress in any peace-building process'.[112] On the other hand, the fact that not all refugees are repatriated may demonstrate that problems still persist, and suggests that there can be no sustainable peace as long as a substantial number of citizens are excluded from the process and no durable solutions have been found. Second, the repatriation of refugees legitimizes and gives credibility to the new post-conflict regime. Indeed, it is a significant part of the peace process that can indicate change to the international community.[113] Third, refugee return can be a precondition for peace if these refugees are politically and/or militarily active in the conflict. Their inclusion is necessary for conflict resolution. It has also been argued that refugee participation in formal political negotiations will lead to a more sustainable return, and particularly so because refugees become more inclined to see themselves as stakeholders in the peace-building and reconstruction process.[114] With regard to peace agreements, Goal 5 of UNHCR's Agenda for Protection ('Redoubling the search for durable solutions') explicitly encourages states 'to facilitate the participation of refugees, including women, in peace and reconciliation processes to ensure that such agreements duly recognise the right to return and contemplate measures to encourage repatriation, reintegration, and reconciliation'.[115] Finally, and

[109] The search for durable solutions is a central part of UNHCR's mandate. See Statute of the Office of the United Nations High Commissioner for Refugees, 14 December 1950, UNGA Res. 428 (V), annex, 5 UN GAOR Supp. (No. 20) 46, UN Doc. A/177, ch. 1 para. 1.

[110] Long, 'Voting with their Feet', 1.

[111] UNHCR, *The State of the World's Refugees—a Humanitarian Agenda* (Oxford: Oxford University Press, 1997), 160–3.

[112] Statement by António Guterres to the UNSC, 2006.

[113] Jeff Crisp, 'Africa's Refugees: Patterns, Problems and Policy Challenges', *UNHCR New Issues in Refugee Research Working Paper* 28 (2000); Richard Black and Saskia Gent, 'Sustainable Return in Post-Conflict Contexts', *International Migration* 44 (2006), 15.

[114] Long, 'Voting with their Feet', 6.

[115] 'Agenda for Protection' (2002), UNHCR EXCOM, UN Doc. A/AC.96/965/Add.1.

as mentioned earlier, returnees may contribute to the implementation of peace agreements and to the economic recovery of the country. As High Commissioner Guterres remarked in 2006, speaking to the UN Security Council about South Sudanese peace-building: 'Over and over, we see that [refugees'] participation is necessary for the consolidation of both peace and post-conflict economic recovery. Sustainable peace and recovery are necessary to allow refugee returns. Yes. But refugee returns are every bit as essential to sustained peace and recovery.'[116] At the same time, return in the context of protracted conflict may be difficult, where physical infrastructure, homes, and social services have been damaged, and prolonged exile may complicate issues of access to land and reintegration into the local economy.[117] This is exemplified in the case of Burundi, where approximately two-thirds of the returnees in 2008 had limited or no access to land.[118] It is precisely issues such as these that are important to address in peace processes and agreements.

4.2.2. Resettlement or local integration

The second durable solution, resettlement of refugees to third countries, can also be used to further peace. Resettlement countries provide individual refugees with legal and physical protection, but, as UNHCR has pointed out, the planned or strategic use of resettlement can also maximize the benefit of resettlement, either directly or indirectly, other than to those being resettled.[119] For example, these benefits may accrue to other refugees, the host state, or other states, and might apply when a small group represents a stumbling block in the way of peace negotiations or a wider repatriation agreement. Indeed, the repatriation of all refugees to their country of origin may not always contribute to peace-building. A sudden and large influx of returnees may, for example, alter the ethnic balance in an area of that country, and create renewed tensions. This may have been the case in El Salvador, where it was argued that, rather than repatriation, the resettlement of refugees to third countries contributed to the successful implementation of the peace agreement.[120]

In a similar manner, the third durable solution—local integration of refugees in the country of asylum—also has the potential of contributing to peace-building in the country of origin.[121] In Tanzania, the Government's desire to further

[116] UNHCR, 'Guterres warns UN Security Council of possible "catastrophe" in Darfur' (24 January 2006), UNHCR Press Release.

[117] Koser, 'Introduction: Integrating Displacement', 6; Milner, 'Refugees and the Regional Dynamics of Peacebuilding', 7.

[118] Milner, 'Refugees and the Regional Dynamics of Peacebuilding', 8.

[119] UNHCR 'Convention Plus: Framework of Understandings on Resettlement' (2003), UN Doc. FORUM/CG/RES/04.

[120] Stephen J. Stedman, 'Implementing Peace Agreements in Civil Wars: Lessons and Recommendations for Policymakers', *IPA Policy Paper Series on Peace Implementation* 18 (2001). See also Bell, *Peace Agreements and Human Rights*, 256.

[121] Local integration means in essence that 'a refugee is granted some form of durable legal status that allows him or her to remain in the country of first asylum on an indefinite basis, and

peace-building in Burundi arguably contributed to its decision in 2007 to consider the naturalization of approximately 220,000 Burundians who had been in exile in Tanzania since 1972.[122] This move was also supported by peace-building actors in Burundi, and the UN Special Representative for Burundi even mobilized additional resources from the international community for the local integration of refugees in Tanzania.

5. Conclusions: New Approaches to Securing Refugee Peace?

This chapter has explored how refugees and peace are inextricably linked in a number of ways. Drawing upon international refugee law, it has argued that the existence of refugees fleeing armed conflict is the consequence—or even intended outcome—of breaches of peace. It continued with an exploration of peace and threats against peace in exile, and explored how the notion of asylum as a peaceful and humanitarian act aims at creating a peaceful coexistence between states but may also result in restricting refugee political space, and thus constrains the achievement of peace in the positive sense. In its final section, this chapter considered refugees as important contributors to (positive) peace, and explained how three options provided by international refugee law for the resolution of displacement—voluntary repatriation, local integration in the country of first asylum, or resettlement in a third country—can be used to further peace.

Contemporary displacement nevertheless exposes the many challenges associated with resolving displacement and achieving a durable peace. There are many examples of a failure on the part of the international community to secure a lasting peace for refugees and other displaced persons. The current Syrian refugee crisis is only the most recent illustration of this letdown. For these refugees, prospects of an imminent return are fading as the conflict drags on, and their presence in neighbouring countries has proved to aggravate the already severe political, security, sectarian, and economic repercussions of the Syria conflict. This, together with overburdened education, health, housing, and water systems in the host countries, has made local integration almost as difficult. Owing to reluctance on the part of the international community to resettle any meaningful number of refugees, the third durable solution has also been challenging to implement.[123]

to fully participate in the social, economic, and cultural life of the host community'. See James Hathaway, *The Rights of Refugees under International Law* (Cambridge: Cambridge University Press, 2005), 977.

[122] Milner, 'Refugees and the Regional Dynamics of Peacebuilding', 8. See also UN, 'Joint Communique of the 14th Meeting of the Tripartite Commission Concerning the Situation of Burundian Refugees Living in Tanzania' (Bujumbura, 21 August 2009).

[123] Rather, many states have implemented a wide range of practical and bureaucratic obstacles aimed at keeping Syrian refugees out of the EU. See Amnesty International, 'An International Failure: The Syrian Refugee Crisis', 13 December 2013, Index: ACT 34/001/2013.

Against this reality where the burdens and responsibilities of offering protection to refugees are today unfairly apportioned, it is clear that there is a need for new approaches towards enabling refugees to live their lives in peace. Burden-sharing and solidarity—two notions central to the entire refugee regime—are in desperate need to be concretized and formalized. Meaningful thoughts on burden-sharing have been put forward over the years, but a major, binding, and practically enforceable obligation is yet to materialize.[124] Only through such measures—where states become legally obligated to share the world's refugee burden—may tomorrow's refugees achieve true peace.

[124] See Alexander Betts, *Protection by Persuasion: International Cooperation in the Refugee Regime* (New York: Cornell University Press, 2009); Agnès Hurwitz, *The Collective Responsibility of States to Protect Refugees* (Oxford: Oxford University Press, 2009); James Hathaway 'Why Refugee Law Still Matters', *Melbourne Journal of International Law* 8 (2007).

14

Barely Begun

The Inclusion of Women as Peacemakers, Peacekeepers, and Peacebuilders in International Law and Practice

Cornelia Weiss

1. Introduction

This chapter addresses the inclusion of women as peacemakers, peacekeepers, and peacebuilders in international law and practice. This includes me. The editors extended their inclusion in the discussion of international peace law to an author who does not come from academia. Instead I have served almost a quarter of a century as a reserve military lawyer in the US military in Europe, the Pacific, and the Western Hemisphere. I therefore come with a different approach and perspective. The opinions and views expressed are my personal views and are not intended to represent in whole or in part the opinions of the US government or any of its components.

I start by defining inclusion, peacemakers, peacekeepers, and peacebuilders. I explore whether the data demonstrate the inclusion of women as peacemakers, peacekeepers, and peacebuilders. I analyse whether an international treaty regarding the elimination of discrimination against women requires inclusion as peacemakers, peacekeepers, and peacebuilders. I investigate whether treaty compliance measures exist and whether they have been used for inclusion. I then turn to UN Security Council resolutions and ask whether Security Council resolutions regarding the inclusion of women as peacemakers, peacekeepers, and peacebuilders require compliance or whether they are simply aspirational. I address the conjunction of international treaty and Security Council resolutions. I conclude by addressing options to influence practice when the law does not.

My methodology includes legal and historical research as well as interviews, correspondence, and advocacy. I do not confine myself to an ideological normative orientation. Instead I am rule-of-law, results-oriented. Whether the lack of inclusion of women is the causal consequence of negative influences of power interests is beyond the scope of this chapter; however, I do address correlative consequences. There are many gaps in knowledge in existing literature to fulfil the components and preconditions of peace articulated by the editors in Chapter 1.

I address some in this chapter. These gaps present opportunities for original and transformative research.

2. Inclusion, Peacemaking, Peacekeeping, and Peacebuilding Definitions

I define 'inclusion' as, at minimum, including 50 per cent women at every level and at every activity of peacemaking, peacekeeping, and peacebuilding.

For this chapter, I define 'peacemakers' as 'first line of key negotiators in the peace process'.[1] The UN defines 'peacemaking' as 'action to bring hostile parties to agreement essentially through such peaceful means as those foreseen in Chapter VI'.[2] Chapter VI of the UN Charter addresses 'Pacific Settlement of Disputes'.[3]

I define 'peacekeeper' to include, but not be limited to, those employed in UN peace operations. The UN defines 'peacekeeping' as 'the deployment of a United Nations presence in the field, hitherto with the consent of all the parties concerned, normally involving United Nations military and/or police personnel and frequently civilians as well', with peacekeeping as 'a technique that expands the possibilities for both the prevention of conflict and the making of peace'.[4]

I define 'peacebuilder' as a participant in building peace. I include peacemakers and peacekeepers in my definition of peacebuilders. The UN defines 'peacebuilding' as 'action to solidify peace and avoid relapse into conflict'[5] as well as, with certain modifications, the seven points of the 2010 UN Women's Participation in Peacebuilding.[6] Its seven points of participation are:

1. women are fully engaged in, and timely gender expertise is provided to, all peace talks;
2. in post-conflict planning processes, including donor conferences, women should play substantive roles and methods should be used to ensure that comprehensive attention is paid to gender equality;
3. adequate financing—both target and mainstream—is provided to address women's specific needs, advance gender equality and promote women's empowerment;

[1] Committee on the Elimination of Discrimination against Women (CEDAW Committee), 'Concluding Observations on the Combined Seventh and Eighth Periodic Reports of Colombia', CEDAW/C/COL/CO/7–8 (29 October 2013), para. 23.

[2] Report of the Secretary-General pursuant to the statement adopted by the Summit Meeting of the Security Council on 31 January 1992, 'An Agenda for Peace: Preventive Diplomacy, Peacemaking and Peacekeeping' (17 June 1992), UN Doc. A/47/277–S/24111, para. 20, http://www.un-documents.net/a47-277.htm (accessed 12 Nov 2014).

[3] Charter of the United Nations (signed 26 June 1945, entered into force 24 October 1945), ch. VI.

[4] Report of the Secretary-General, 'Agenda for Peace', para. 20.

[5] Report of the Secretary-General, 'Agenda for Peace', para. 21.

[6] UN General Assembly, UN Security Council, 'Women's Participation in Peacebuilding: Report of the Secretary-General', 7 September 2010, UN Doc. A/65/354–S/2010/466, http://www.un.org/ga/search/view_doc.asp?symbol=A/65/354 (accessed 12 Nov 2014).

4. deployed civilians possess the necessary specialized skills, including expertise in rebuilding States institutions to make them more accessible to women;
5. women can participate fully in post conflict governance, as civic actors, elected representatives or decision-makers in public institutions, including through temporary special measures such as quotas;
6. rule-of-law initiatives encourage women's participation in the process of seeking redress for injustices committed against them and in improving the capacity of security actors to prevent and respond to violations of women's rights; and
7. economic recovery prioritizes women's involvement in employment-creation schemes, community development programmes, and the delivery of front-line services.[7]

Point 4's definition should not restrict State institution accessibility for women to merely 'more accessible' but, instead, should require 'easily accessible'. Further, the requirement to possess expertise in building State institutions that are easily accessible to women should not be restricted to only deployed 'civilians'. Deployed military and police should also possess this expertise. Point 5's governance definition should be expanded from 'can participate' to 'participate' with the caveat that women not be limited by quotas of less than 50 per cent participation. Regarding point 6's rule of law efficacy, the UN definition appears to view women only as accessing the legal system as victims. Women should be able to use the legal system to solve all disputes. These include disputes that are the root of conflicts, such as land disputes. Rule of law exists to resolve disputes peacefully, without violence. Concerning point 6, the definition should require 'ensuring', not simply 'improving', the capacity of security forces to respond.

3. Data

The data illustrate that inclusion of women as peacemakers, peacekeepers, and peacebuilders is rare, despite evidence that inclusion enhances mission success. Mission success is defined by enabling peace.

In peacemaking, studies demonstrate that 'post-conflict agreements that are negotiated without women break down faster than those that do include women'.[8] Yet since the end of the Cold War, women have represented:

- only four per cent of signatories to peace agreements;
- less than three per cent of mediators of peace talks; and

[7] UNGA, UNSC, 'Women's Participation in Peacebuilding', para. 6.

[8] Valerie M. Hudson, 'What Sex Means for World Peace—The evidence is clear: The best predictor of a State's stability is how its women are treated', Foreign Policy, 24 April 2012, http://www.foreignpolicy.com/articles/2012/04/24/what_sex_means_for_world_peace?page=0,1 (accessed 16 June 2014).

- less than ten per cent of those sitting at the table to negotiate on behalf of a party to the conflict.[9]

In peacekeeping, the numbers are similar to peacemaking despite evidence, addressed in this chapter's section 8.2, that women peacekeepers enhance security. In 2013, focusing simply on police and military, women made up about 9.8 per cent of UN police and about 2 per cent of the UN military personnel.[10]

In the area of peacebuilding, research is still required to find the data concerning if, and to what extent, women are included.

4. The Convention on the Elimination of All Forms of Discrimination Against Women

International treaties are binding international law for ratifying States. The international treaty on the elimination of discrimination against women, including in the quest for peace, is the 1979 Convention on the Elimination of All Forms of Discrimination Against Women (CEDAW), also referred to in this chapter as the 'Convention'.[11] Only the US, Iran, Somalia, Sudan, South Sudan, Tonga, and Palau have not ratified CEDAW.[12] Discrimination against women affects approximately 50 per cent of the earth's population, more than any other categorical discrimination.

CEDAW's Preamble declares 'the cause of peace require(s) the maximum participation of women on equal terms with men in all fields'. Maximum participation of women on equal terms with men in all fields means that peacemaking, peacekeeping, and peacebuilding are not unequally the prerogative of men.[13]

[9] 'UN Women Executive Director stresses importance of women in leadership positions', UN Women, Statement of UN Women Executive Director Phumzile Mlambo-Ngcuka at the launch of Women Leading Africa Programme in Namibia on 24 October 2013', http://www.unwomen.org/en/news/stories/2013/10/ed-speech-at-women-leading-africa-programme (accessed 12 Nov 2014).

[10] Sahana Dharmapuri, 'Core Issues Stall Women's Participation in UN Missions', Global Observatory, 13 March 2013, http://www.theglobalobservatory.org/analysis/455-core-issues-stall-womens-participation-in-un-peacekeeping.html (accessed 12 Nov 2014).

[11] UNGA Res. 34/180, 34 UN GAOR Supp. (No. 46), p. 193, UN Doc. A/34/46; 1249 UNTS 13; 19 ILM 33 (1980).

[12] United Nations Treaty Collection, Convention on the Elimination of All Forms of Discrimination against Women, status 16 June 2014, https://treaties.un.org/Pages/ViewDetails.aspx?src=TREATY&mtdsg_no=IV-8&chapter=4&lang=en (accessed 16 June 2014). For those wishing to examine the failure of the US to ratify CEDAW, see Luisa Blanchfield, 'The U.N. Convention on the Elimination of All Forms of Discrimination Against Women (CEDAW): Issues in the U.S. Ratification Debate', Congressional Research Service (28 June 2011), http://www.fas.org/sgp/crs/row/R40750.pdf (accessed 16 June 2014).

[13] Defence is not a male business either. Women head three of the six largest defence companies in the US—BAE (USA), Lockheed-Martin, and General Dynamics—Linda Hudson, Marillyn Hewson, and Phebe Novakovic respectively. Carola Hoyas, 'The women piloting an industry', *Financial Times*, 3 January 2013, http://www.ft.com/intl/cms/s/0/2763537a-38a4-11e2-bd7d-00144feabdc0.html#axzz2lcdwsdMn (accessed 12 Nov 2014).

CEDAW requires States parties to condemn and eliminate discrimination,[14] to ensure full development and advancement of women,[15] to modify social and cultural patterns of conduct that result in discrimination,[16] to ensure women's 'equal representation in political and public life',[17] to take 'all appropriate measures to ensure women, on equal terms with men and without discrimination, the opportunity to represent their Governments at the international level',[18] and to take 'all appropriate measures to ensure women, on equal terms with men and without discrimination, the opportunity ... to participate in the work of international organizations'.[19]

In October 2013, 34 years after the emergence of CEDAW, its Committee issued general recommendation no. 30 on women in conflict prevention, conflict, and post-conflict situations (General Recommendation 30).[20] This recommendation defines legal obligations arising out of the Convention. Paragraph 2 mandates State responsibility for 'advancing substantive gender equality before, during and after conflict and ensuring that women's diverse experiences are fully integrated'. I address General Recommendation 30 more fully in Section 8 of this chapter.

5. CEDAW's Compliance Mechanisms

Compliance mechanisms under CEDAW include those arising out of the periodic scrutinization of States parties' compliance, complaints under the Optional Protocol to the Convention on the Elimination of All Forms of Discrimination Against Women (Protocol),[21] and cases brought to the International Court of Justice (ICJ).

The CEDAW Committee, per CEDAW's Article 18, periodically scrutinizes the de facto and de jure status of women in each ratifying State. For example, the CEDAW Committee, in its 29 October 2013 concluding observations on the combined seventh and eighth periodic reports of Colombia, criticized Colombia's 'exclusion [of women] in the first line of key negotiators in the peace process'.[22] Colombia had refused to acknowledge it had the legal obligation to include women at the peace table.[23] Colombia's first line of key negotiators included only

[14] CEDAW, Art. 2. [15] CEDAW, Art. 3. [16] CEDAW, Art. 5.
[17] CEDAW, Art. 7. [18] CEDAW, Art. 8. [19] CEDAW, Art. 8.

[20] 'General recommendation No. 30 on women in conflict prevention, conflict and post-conflict situations', Committee on the Elimination of Discrimination against Women (18 October 2013) UN Doc. CEDAW/C/GC/30, http://www.ohchr.org/Documents/HRBodies/CEDAW/GComments/CEDAW.C.CG.30.pdf (accessed 16 June 2014). General Recommendation 30 is not the first time the CEDAW Committee addressed State failure regarding the inclusion of women as peacemakers, peacekeepers, and peacebuilders. See CEDAW General Recommendations 23 (in 1997) and 8 (in 1988).

[21] UNGA Res. 54/4, annex, 54 UN GAOR Supp. (No. 49) at 5, UN Doc. A/54/49 (Vol. I); 2131 UNTS 83.

[22] 'Concluding observations on the combined seventh and eighth periodic reports of Colombia', CEDAW, 29 October 2013, UN Doc. CEDAW/C/COL/CO/7–8, para. 23, http://daccess-dds-ny.un.org/doc/UNDOC/GEN/N13/535/21/PDF/N1353521.pdf?OpenElement (accessed 16 June 2014).

[23] 'Aunado a lo anterior y teniendo en cuenta, que la finalidad del mencionado instrument jurídico no se agota con el nombramiento de una mujer en la Mesa de Conversaciones'. ('In addition to

men. The CEDAW Committee recommended Colombia 'ensure the effective and meaningful participation of women in the first line of negotiations within the peace process'.[24] About two weeks later, Colombia added the first woman to the peace talks and shortly thereafter a second woman.[25] The addition occurred after a year of male-only talks. During that year, the negotiators finalized agreements on land and political power;[26] issues that started the conflict five decades previously. Whether adding two women to a group of six men at that point in the negotiations is 'effective and meaningful participation' is doubtful. What is beyond doubt is that after the Committee issued its report, Colombia took action. Whether this correlation translated into causation is an area ripe for future research.[27]

A second compliance mechanism arises out of the Optional Protocol to the CEDAW (Protocol). The Protocol enables individuals claiming violation of the Convention to 'communicate' to the CEDAW Committee.[28] Exhaustion of remedies within the State is required first though.[29] The CEDAW Committee then has the power to 'urgently' request that the State party 'take steps to protect the alleged victim or victims from irreparable harm'.[30] The State party must 'provide a written response, including remedial steps taken'.[31] To date, no 'communication' has been used to address State failure to include women as peacemakers, peacekeepers, and peacebuilders.[32]

A third compliance mechanism is the CEDAW Committee's power to designate an 'inquiry'. It may designate an inquiry if it receives 'reliable information indicating ... systemic violations by a State Party'.[33] For example, the CEDAW

what has been stated and bearing in mind that the aim of the aforementioned legal instrument does not end with the appointment of a woman to the negotiation table'.) Sergio Jaramillo, Colombian High Commissioner for the Peace, letter to author, dated 24 June 2013.

[24] CEDAW/C/COL/CO/7–8, para. 24.

[25] Anastasia Moloney, 'Colombia appoints female peace negotiator', Thomson Reuters Foundation, 19 November 2013, http://www.trust.org/item/20131119171835-o0wuv/?source=hpeditorial (accessed 12 Nov 2014); Elespectador.com, 'Dos mujeres reforzarán equipo de Gobierno en La Habana El presidente Santos formalizó el ingreso de María Paulina Riveros y Nigeria Rentería', 26 November 2013, http://www.elespectador.com/noticias/paz/dos-mujeres-reforzaran-equipo-de-gobierno-habana-articulo-460571 (accessed 12 Nov 2014).

[26] Reuters, 'Colombia, FARC agree on rebels' future if peace signed', 6 November 2013, http://www.reuters.com/article/2013/11/06/us-colombia-rebels-idUSBRE9A50JM20131106 (accessed 12 Nov 2014).

[27] Only the future will tell if Afghanistan addresses the Committee's concerns about women's 'meaningful and effective participation in the peace and reconciliation process is being jeopardized by several factors' to include 'women's exclusion from the major decision-making processes'. 'Concluding observations of the combined initial and second periodic reports of Afghanistan', 30 July 2013, UN Doc. CEDAW/C/AF/CO/1–2, para. 9, http://tbinternet.ohchr.org/_layouts/treatybodyexternal/Download.aspx?symbolno=CEDAW%2fC%2fAFG%2fCO%2f1-2&Lang=en (accessed 16 June 2014).

[28] Protocol Arts. 1, 2.

[29] Protocol Art. 4.

[30] Protocol Art. 5.

[31] Protocol Art. 7.

[32] For 'communications' brought to date, see Optional Protocol to the Convention on the Elimination of Discrimination against Women, Jurisprudence, http://www2.ohchr.org/english/law/jurisprudence.htm (accessed 12 Nov 2014).

[33] Protocol Art. 8.

Committee used this tool in the 2005 Ciudad Juárez, Mexico femicide inquiry. It addressed 'the negligence and complicity of public authorities'.[34] The femicide inquiry language points to potential use in initiating inquiries regarding the failure of States parties to comply with their CEDAW obligations of inclusion.

A fourth compliance mechanism could have States suffering from their neighbour State's lack of peace bringing a case to the International Court of Justice (ICJ). The ICJ, under CEDAW's Article 29, exercises jurisdiction over claims arising out of CEDAW (except for those States that have made such a reservation). The ICJ has the power to judicially compel the peace-lacking State to comply with CEDAW.

Thus, compliance mechanisms exist. To date, most mechanisms have not been utilized. This is an area for expansion.

6. UN Security Council Resolutions Regarding Women Peacemakers, Peacekeepers, and Peacebuilders

When the CEDAW Committee issued General Recommendation 30, the UN Security Council already had a decade of creating a new set of legal tools. These were UN Security Council resolutions. The first one was UNSCR 1325[35] in October 2000. Subsequent resolutions include UNSCR 1888[36] in September 2009; UNSCR 1889[37] in October 2009; UNSCR 1960[38] in December 2010, and UNSCR 2122[39] in October 2013. We now turn to whether these UN Security Council resolutions have legal effect.

[34] 'Report on Mexico produced by the Committee on the Elimination of Discrimination against Women under article 8 of the Optional Protocol to the Convention, and reply from the Government of Mexico', CEDAW Committee, Thirty-second session (January 10–28, 2005) UN Doc. CEDAW/C/2005/OP.8/MEXICO, para. 274, http://www.un.org/womenwatch/daw/cedaw/cedaw32/CEDAW-C-2005-OP.8-MEXICO-E.pdf (accessed 12 Nov 2014).

[35] UNSC Res. 1325 (31 October 2000) UN Doc. S/RES/1325.

[36] UNSC Res. 1888 (30 September 2009) UN Doc. S/RES/1888.

[37] UNSC Res. 1889 (5 October 2009) UN Doc. S/RES/1889.

[38] UNSC Res. 1960 (16 December 2010) UN Doc. S/RES/1960.

[39] UNSC Res. 2122 (18 October 2013) UN Doc. S/RES/2122. The family of UNSCR 1325 resolutions is not limited to the above. This chapter does not concentrate on sexual crimes. To address such crimes adequately is beyond the scope of this chapter, although their impact on peacemaking is undeniable. As articulated by Bedouma Alain Yoda, Minister for Foreign Affairs of Burkina Faso, 'sexual crimes created long-lasting enmity between peoples, making it hard to bring about peace. Degrading the dignity of women reduced their crucial ability to contribute to peacemaking,' in 'Security Council Adopts Text Mandating Peacekeeping Missions to Protect Women, Girls from Sexual Violence in Armed Conflict', Security Council, Department of Public Information (30 September 2009), UN Doc. SC/9753, http://www.un.org/News/Press/docs/2009/sc9753.doc.htm (accessed 12 Nov 2014).

7. The Legal Effect of UN Security Council Resolutions Regarding Women as Peacemakers, Peacekeepers, and Peacebuilders

Legal scholars differ as to the legal status of UN Security Council resolutions addressing women peacemakers, peacekeepers, and peacebuilders. Some legal scholars maintain these Security Council resolutions are binding. Others contest that they are not.

Legal scholarly writings contending that the resolutions are binding range from in-depth legal analysis to declarative statements. Appiagyei-Atua, in 2011, in an article devoted to addressing the legal status of UNSCR 1325, concludes UNSCR 1325 is legally binding 'because it authorizes acts that are *intra vires* the UN Charter and other international laws'.[40] Haynes, Cahn, and Ní Aoláin, in 2012, claim 'U.N. Security Council ... resolutions [1325 et al.] are both determinative and binding as legal, political, and normative pronouncements.'[41]

Those contending the resolutions are not binding use UN Charter Chapter VI-based rationale. Bell and O'Rourke, in 2010, argue that 'Resolution 1325 is a "thematic" resolution best understood as a Chapter VI UN Charter (non-binding) resolution. Its legal authority has been accentuated by the fact it was passed unanimously and that the resolution uses the language of obligation.'[42] Chapter VI addresses 'Pacific Settlement Of Disputes'.[43] Otto, in 2009, maintains UNSCR 1325 is not binding, using the Chapter VII rationale.[44] Chapter VII addresses 'Action With Respect to Threats to the Peace, Breaches of the Peace, and Acts of Aggression'.[45]

While legal scholars differ, on point case law regarding interpretation of UN Security Council resolutions has existed since 1971.

The ICJ, in *Legal Consequences for States of the Continued Presence of South Africa in Namibia (South West Africa) notwithstanding Security Council Resolution* 276 (1970), Advisory Opinion of 21 June 1971,[46] hereinafter *Namibia*, addressed interpretation of UN Security Council resolutions.

[40] Kwadwo Appiagyei-Atua, 'United Security Council Resolution 1325 on Women, Peace, and Security—Is It Binding?', *Human Rights Brief* 18, Issue 3 (Spring 2011), 2–6 at 6, http://www.wcl.american.edu/hrbrief/18/3atua.pdf (accessed 16 June 2014).

[41] Dina Francesa Haynes, Naomi Cahn, and Fionnuala D. Ní Aoláin, 'Women in the Post-Conflict Process: Reviewing the Impact of Recent U.N. Actions in Achieving Gender Centrality', *Santa Clara Journal of International Law* 11 (2012), 217–50 at 226.

[42] Christine Bell and Catherine O'Rourke, 'Peace Agreements or Pieces of Paper? The Impact of UNSCR 1325 on Peace Processes and Their Agreements', *International & Comparative Law Quarterly* 59 (2010), 941–80 at 943.

[43] UN Charter, Chapter VI.

[44] Diane Otto, 'Exile of Inclusion', *Melbourne Journal of International Law* 10 (2009), 11–12.

[45] UN Charter, Chapter VII.

[46] *Legal Consequences for States of the Continued Presence of South Africa in Namibia (South West Africa) notwithstanding Security Council Resolution* 276 (Advisory Opinion), 1970, http://www.icj-cij.org/docket/files/53/5595.pdf (accessed 16 June 2016). (Hereafter ICJ, *Legal Consequences*.)

One argument the ICJ addressed in the *Namibia* case was whether Article 25 of the Charter applies only to enforcement measures adopted under Chapter VII of the Charter. Article 25 of the United Nations Charter states: 'The Members of the United Nations agree to accept and carry out the decisions of the Security Council in accordance with the present Charter'. In *Namibia*, the ICJ rejected the argument that the obligation of the Members of the UN to accept and carry out the decisions of the Charter was restricted to Article 25 enforcement measures adopted under Chapter VII. The ICJ found: 'It is not possible to find in the Charter any support for this view. Article 25 is not confined to decisions in regard to enforcement action but applies to "the decisions of the Security Council" adopted in accordance with the Charter.'[47] The ICJ continued: 'Moreover, that Article is placed, not in Chapter VII, but immediately after Article 24 in that part of the Charter which deals with the functions and powers of the Security Council.'[48] Article 24 gives the Security Council the 'primary responsibility for the maintenance of international peace and security'. The ICJ found: 'If Article 25 had reference solely to decisions of the Security Council concerning enforcement action under Articles 41 and 42 of the Charter ... if it were only such decisions which had binding effect, then Article 25 would be superfluous.'[49] Article 41 gives the Security Council the power to 'decide what measures not involving the use of armed force are to be employed to give effect to its decisions' on economic, diplomatic, and communication disruption. Article 42 gives the Security Council the power to take actions to include blockades and land force operations. The ICJ concluded such a determination would make Article 25 superfluous 'since this effect is secured by Articles 48 and 49 of the Charter'.[50] Article 48 requires that Members of the UN, as determined by the Security Council, carry out Security Council decisions. Article 49 mandates that the Members of the UN afford 'mutual assistance' in carrying out the Security Council decided measures. Within the Charter, Articles 41, 42, 48, and 49 fall under the Charter's Chapter VII. Within the Charter, Articles 24 and 25 fall under Chapter V.

Therefore, given the plain language of the ICJ's *Namibia* opinion that States can be obligated to accept and carry out non-Chapter VII resolutions, the continuing arguments that only Chapter VII resolutions are binding are puzzling unless the ICJ's *Namibia* case is invalid. Yet De Wet, in a revised version of her Habilitationsschrift,[51] found the *Namibia* case to signify UN Security Council 'decisions were binding on all member States'.[52] Former ICJ Chief Judge Higgins, in 1972, before she became a member of the ICJ, proclaimed 'a reading of the Charter, its travaux, and the limited subsequent practice, testify to the correctness of this conclusion [the ICJ *Namibia* decision]'.[53] To date, the *Namibia* case has

[47] ICJ, *Legal Consequences*, para. 113.
[48] ICJ, *Legal Consequences*, para. 113.
[49] ICJ, *Legal Consequences*, para. 113.
[50] ICJ, *Legal Consequences*, para. 113.
[51] Postdoctoral thesis required for qualification as a professor.
[52] Erika De Wet, *The Chapter VII Powers of the United Nations Security Council* (Oxford: Hart, 2004), 36, although she asserted it could be countered by 'several arguments', p. 38.
[53] Rosalyn Higgins, 'The Advisory Opinion on Namibia: Which UN Resolutions are Binding under Article 25 of the Charter?', *International & Comparative Law Quarterly* 21 (1972), 270–86 at 286. Interestingly, despite the language of the *Namibia* decision, Higgins contended 'it is agreed

not been overturned. Instead, as articulated by Murphy in 2013 regarding the ICJ Advisory Opinion on Kosovo interpreting UNSCR 1244, 'the Court listed with apparent approval the methodology it used in prior cases for interpreting and applying Security Council resolutions. In particular, the Court confirmed its view in the South West Africa [*Namibia*] advisory opinion.'[54]

Therefore, whether a UN Security Council resolution is binding or not depends on something other than whether or not it has a Chapter VII characterization. *Namibia* addresses whether the specific language of a resolution is the test of determining whether a resolution is binding or not. In discussing the contention that the language of a UN Security Council resolution can affect its applicability, the ICJ addressed the argument that the resolution in *Namibia* was non-binding given its language. The ICJ stated: 'It has also been contended that the relevant Security Council resolutions are couched in exhortatory rather than mandatory language and that, therefore, they do not purport to impose any legal duty on any State nor to affect legally any right of any State.'[55] The ICJ concurred: 'The language of a resolution of the Security Council should be carefully analysed before a conclusion can be made as to its binding effect.'[56]

The language of UNSCR 276, addressed by the ICJ in the *Namibia* case, contains 'strongly condemns', 'declares', 'considers', 'calls upon', and 'requests'.[57] The language of UNSCR 1325 contains 'urges', 'encourages', 'expresses', 'requests', 'calls on/calls upon', 'emphasizes', 'encourages', 'reaffirms', and 'invites'. The 'decides' paragraphs of both resolutions address Security Council, not state, action.[58]

The ICJ, in *Namibia*, found UNSCR 276's paragraph 2, which used the term 'declares' and paragraph 5, which used the term 'calls upon', as binding but did not reach its conclusion on a simplistic formula of term usage. Instead, the ICJ required a case-by-case, multifactoral analysis to determine whether a particular resolution was binding. As stated in *Namibia*, '[i]n view of the nature of the powers under Article 25, the question whether they have been in fact exercised is to

that generally speaking, resolutions under Chapter VI will be recommendatory, rather than decisions that bind the membership at large by reference to Article 25'. Rosalyn Higgins, 'Peace and Security: Achievements and Failures', *Themes and Theories: Selected Essays, Speeches, and Writings in International Law* (Oxford: Oxford University Press, 2009), 290–305 at 290.

[54] Sean D. Murphy, 'Reflections on the ICJ Advisory Opinion in Kosovo: Interpreting Security Council Resolution 1244 (1999)' (October 2013), 34, forthcoming in *The Law And Politics of the Kosovo Advisory Opinion*, Michael Wood and Marko Milanovic (eds.) (Oxford: Oxford University Press), http://scholarship.law.gwu.edu/cgi/viewcontent.cgi?article=2216&context=faculty_publications (accessed 16 June 2014).

[55] ICJ, *Legal Consequences*, para. 114.

[56] ICJ, *Legal Consequences*, para. 114.

[57] UNSCR 276, 'The Situation in Namibia', 30 January 1970.

[58] The 'decides' paragraphs of UNSCR 276 address establishing an ad hoc sub-committee to study how UN Security Council resolutions can be 'effectively implemented', para. 6, and 'to resume consideration of the question of Namibia as soon as the recommendations of the Sub-Committee have been made available', para. 9. The 'decides' paragraph of UNSCR 1325 addresses 'to remain actively seized of the matter', para. 18.

be determined in each case'.[59] The ICJ required, 'having regard to the terms of the resolutions to be interpreted', the factors to include:

- the discussions leading to [the resolution];
- the Charter provisions invoked; and
- in general, all circumstances that might assist in determining the legal consequences of the resolution of the Security Council.[60]

At this time there is no comparative study of the discussions leading to UNSCR 276 and UNSCR 1325. The passage of UNSCR 276 was unanimous with two abstentions.[61] The passage of UNSCR 1325 was unanimous with no abstentions. Neither UNSCR 276 nor UNSCR 1325 contains the term 'Chapter VII' or the term 'Article 25'. The preamble language of UNSCR 276 related resolution 269 (1969) does contain the term 'Article 25'. The ICJ, in *Namibia*, found UNSCR 276's paragraphs 2 and 5 as binding. Neither paragraph invoked the term 'decides'. Paragraph 2 used the term 'declares' and paragraph 5 used the term 'calls upon'. UNSCR 1325 does not invoke the term 'declares' but does use the terms 'calls on' and 'calls upon'. The ICJ, in arriving at its decision, used relational analysis—'paragraphs 2[62] and 5[63] of resolutions 276 (1970), as related to paragraph 3[64] of resolution 264 (1969) and paragraph 5[65] of resolution 269 (1969)'.[66] The ICJ found UNSCR 276's paragraphs 2 and 5 'were adopted in conformity with the purposes and principles of the Charter and in accordance with its Articles 24 and 25'.[67] As a result, the ICJ held: 'The decisions are consequently binding on all States Members of the United Nations, which are thus under obligation to accept and carry them out.'[68]

Yet determining whether a UN Security Council resolution is binding does not address whether it is enforceable. As Higgins asserts, 'it is incorrect to assume that non-binding resolutions are necessarily without legal effect'.[69] Ignoring UN Security Council resolutions can have consequences. The 1992 UN Legal Adviser's memo on resolutions is clear: 'NO SECURITY COUNCIL RESOLUTION CAN BE DESCRIBED AS UNENFORCEABLE.'[70]

[59] ICJ, *Legal Consequences*, para. 114.

[60] ICJ, *Legal Consequences*, para. 114.

[61] UNSCR 276, 'The Situation in Namibia'.

[62] 'Declares that the continued presence of the South African authorities in Namibia is illegal and that consequently all acts taken by the Government of South Africa on behalf of or concerning Namibia after the termination of the Mandate are illegal and invalid.'

[63] 'Calls upon all States, particularly those which have economic and other interests in Namibia, to refrain from any dealings with the Government of South Africa which are inconsistent with paragraph 2 of the present resolution'.

[64] 'Calls upon the Government of South Africa to withdraw immediately its administration from the Territory'.

[65] 'Calls upon the Government of South Africa to withdraw its administration from the Territory immediately and in any case before 4 October 1969'.

[66] ICJ, *Legal Consequences*, para. 115.

[67] ICJ, *Legal Consequences*, para. 115.

[68] ICJ, *Legal Consequences*, para. 115.

[69] Rosalyn Higgins, 'The Identity of International Law', in *Themes and Theories: Selected Essays, Speeches, and Writings in International Law* (Oxford: Oxford University Press, 2009), 91–107 at 95.

[70] Boutros Boutros-Ghali, *Unvanquished: A U.S.–U.N. Saga* (New York: Random House, 1999), 182.

8. CEDAW, the UN, and the UNSCR 1325 Family of Resolutions

As stated earlier, General Recommendation 30[71] mandates state responsibility for 'advancing substantive gender equality before, during and after conflict and ensuring that women's diverse experiences are fully integrated'.[72] In General Recommendation 30, the CEDAW Committee determined implementing CEDAW obligations 'in conjunction with' the [the family of] UNSCR 1325 obligations 'guarantee women's meaningful participation'.[73]

8.1. Paper and practice: peacemakers

General Recommendation 30 and UNSCR 1325, UNSCR 1888, UNSCR 1889, UNSCR 1960, and UNSCR 2122 address women in the role of peacemakers. This requires addressing potential reasons for, as well as the impact of, the lack of inclusion; the continued UN resolutions requiring inclusion; and the obligations and failures of third parties, the UN, and the UN Security Council to include women.

Since 2000, the UN Security Council has passed three resolutions regarding the failure of inclusion of women in peacemaking. It started with UNSCR 1325 in 2000 requiring 'increased representation of women';[74] it continued in 2009 under UNSCR 1888 which marvelled at the 'underrepresentation of women in formal peace processes'; and it escalated its resolutionary power in 2013 under UNSCR 2122 in that it '*calls on* all parties to such peace talks to facilitate the *equal and full* participation of women at decision-making levels' [emphasis mine].[75] The 'calls on' terminology in *Namibia* was in the paragraph the ICJ determined as 'binding'. Thus continuing with the example of Colombia, it is unknown if UNSCR 2122 was instrumental in Colombia's adding two women to the peace talks about a month after UNSCR 2122 emerged or whether other factors were the cause. This is an area for future research. But what is known is that adding two women to a team of more than two men fails today's post 'separate but equal' definition of 'equal and full'. General Recommendation 30 paragraph 44 requires 'measures, including temporary special measures' [to 'ensure women's equal representation'].[76] States parties have failed to create such measures in the peacemaking arena. Further analysis is needed to determine whether 'temporary special measures' should require the inverse of current representation until such time as historic equality is achieved and whether equality should be ever temporary or special.

[71] General Recommendation 30 is not the first time the Committee addressed the failure of States in their responsibilities to implement the Convention. See No. 23 in 1997 and No. 8 in 1988.

[72] General Recommendation 30, para. 2.

[73] General Recommendation 30, para. 45.

[74] UNSCR Res. 1325, para. 1.

[75] UNSCR Res. 2122, para. 7(c).

[76] CEDAW's Art. 4(1) addresses temporary special measures.

The question must be raised and addressed as to why there is continued failure of inclusion of women at the front line of peace negotiations. According to General Recommendation 30, the non-inclusion of women and the over-inclusion of men are often due to 'deeply entrenched stereotypes, reflected in the traditionally male leadership of State and non-State groups, which exclude women from all aspects of decision-making'.[77] In an October 2013 academic setting discussion with members of the security and defence community of the Western Hemisphere, a high-ranking military male's response to the author's concern about the absence of women at the Colombian peace negotiation table was 'women not important'. Further, a male presiding professor declared women do not need to be represented at the 'peace table' because 'male negotiators are able to fully represent women's interests'.

Such opinions lack factual support. When responding to such opinions, effective strategic communication requires addressing quantitative analysis as well as empirical evidence. Quantitatively we have learned that 'post-conflict agreements that are negotiated without women break down faster than those that do include women'.[78] Empirically the geographically separated cases of the Angola and Northern Ireland peace agreements may be of assistance when responding to such opinions.

- The 1994 Angola Peace Agreement peace negotiation team failed to include a single woman among its forty negotiators. According to the then US ambassador to Angola, because the negotiation team failed to include women, it failed to incorporate the needs of both sexes. Because it failed to incorporate the needs of both sexes, it fell apart within a few years.[79]
- The 1998 Belfast (Good Friday) Agreement negotiation team included two women, Williams and Fearon. According to Williams, had women not been at the table, the Agreement would not have contained victim issues, trauma healing, integrated education, housing, and health care.[80] Fearon maintains victim's rights and reconciliation issues 'became touchstone issues in the referendum campaign' and absent the issues the women put in the agreement,

[77] General Recommendation 30, para. 43, finds the exclusion also results from 'gender-based violence and other forms of discrimination against women'. The push to exclude women in Ireland included misogynistic and threatening attitudes such as graffiti outside Williams's office instructing her to 'get back to the kitchen' and penises painted on posters near her home. Avila Kilmurray and Monica McWilliams, 'Struggling for Peace: How Women in Northern Ireland Challenged the Status Quo', *Solutions* 2 (2011), http://www.thesolutionsjournal.com/node/893 (accessed 12 Nov 2014). Male negotiators 'mooed' the women. Author interview of Aisling Swaine, 2014.

[78] Hudson, 'What Sex Means for World Peace'.

[79] Steinberg's response to author's 17 May 2011 question at the 'US Agency for International Development and Conflict: Hard Lessons from the Field' presentation at the Center for American Progress.

[80] Precarious Progress: UN Resolutions on Women, Peace, and Security Final Report (September 29–1 October 2010), 1, http://catcher.sandiego.edu/items/peacestudies/2010_IPJ_Conference_Report.pdf (accessed 16 June 2014).

'many people could have voted against it and thus jeopardised the greatest opportunity for peace in 30 years'.[81]

Third parties to peace processes are also required to apply the Convention.[82] Therefore, for example, third parties to the Colombia peace process, such as Norway, are obliged to apply the Convention. The Norwegian 2011–13 Women, Peace and Security Strategic Plan mandates: 'There is to be an even gender balance among Norwegian participants in peace and reconciliation processes'.[83] Yet it appears even Norway excluded women. Norway sent no women in its role as a third party to the Colombia peace negotiations.[84]

Continuing the analysis into third party obligations, General Recommendation 30 acknowledges that outside actors, such as those providing money to support peace processes, affect women thereby potentially raising 'simultaneous and complementary sets of obligations under the Convention'.[85] UNSCR 2122 '[e]ncourages the development of dedicated funding mechanisms to support women's full participation in all levels of decision-making'.[86] Dedicated funding mechanisms would complement General Recommendation 30. Money talks. Actors can influence the inclusion of women by making their funding contingent on women's inclusion as peacemakers. It is unclear as to whether actors are ensuring that their funding involves women's inclusion in peace processes. The lack of transparency,[87] for example, makes it unclear as to whether the Norwegian-chaired Peace Donor Support Group invokes women's inclusion. The Peace Donor Support Group is a consortium of international donors that has provided millions of dollars of support.[88] Its key findings on priority interventions, while acknowledging the non-exhaustive nature of the findings, only acknowledge women once. The acknowledgement is in addressing the

[81] Kate Fearon, 'Northern Ireland Women's Coalition: institutionalising a political voice and ensuring representation', *Women Building Peace, Conciliation Resources* (2013), 33, http://www.c-r.org/sites/c-r.org/files/AccordInsight_WomenBuildingPeace_1.pdf (accessed 16 June 2014).

[82] General Recommendation 30, para. 9.

[83] Norwegian Ministry of Foreign Affairs, 'Women, Peace, and Security, Norway's Strategic Plan 2011-2013', 7, citing sect. 21 of the Norwegian Gender Equality Act, http://www.regjeringen.no/upload/UD/Vedlegg/FN/Kvinner_likestilling/sr1325_strategic_planE880E_web.pdf (accessed 16 June 2014).

[84] Reuters, 'Nylander of Norway and Benitez of Cuba read a joint declaration in Havana', 6 November 2013, http://www.trust.org/item/20131106200658-u3c4y/?source=search (accessed 12 Nov 2014); Joey O'Gorman, '4 Cuban and Norwegian guarantors accompany Colombia peace process: Report', Colombia Reports, 5 September 2012, http://colombiareports.co/4-cuban-and-norwegian-guarantors-accompany-colombia-peace-process-report/ (accessed 12 Nov 2014).

[85] General Recommendation 30, para. 13.

[86] UNSCR 2122, para. 7(b).

[87] In analysing the monetary figures, it appears Norway allocates 18% of its development assistance funding to gender equality in conflict and post-conflict countries. Yet Norway's contention that '[i]t is difficult to track all the funding that Norway allocates to this work, as much of it is a contribution to broader efforts' results in a lack of certainty. See 'Women, Peace and Security: Norway's Strategic Plan 2011–13: 2011 Progress Report', Norwegian Ministry of Foreign Affairs, 7, http://www.regjeringen.no/upload/UD/Vedlegg/Utvikling/Kvinner%20og%20likestilling/Rapport_2011_Gender_E894_web.pdf (accessed 12 Nov 2014).

[88] Hannah Hindstrom, 'Norway backed Burma peace initiative "probably" to end', 12 January 2014, https://www.dvb.no/analysis/norway-backed-peace-initiative-probably-to-end-burma-myanmar/35957 (accessed 12 Nov 2014).

widespread malnutrition among women,[89] not the lack of inclusion in peace processes. Tying aid to specific conditions 'such as ensuring effective representation of women (50%) in peace and security related processes, agencies, and commissions that are donor-funded'[90] is a yet unexplored practice which might serve two functions—yielding the highest return on investment while having the satisfaction of complying with the law.

Finally, looking within the UN, resolution after resolution[91] has addressed the failure of the UN to include women. Starting in 2000 with UNSCR 1325, the Security Council 'encouraged' the Secretary-General to 'implement his strategic plan of action (A/49/587) calling for an increase in the participation of women at decision-making levels in conflict resolution and peace processes'.[92] A/49/587, the 'Advancement of women human resources management: Other human resources questions: Improvement of the status of women in the Secretariat—Report of the Secretary-General', dated 1 November 1994, sought gender parity by 2000.[93] Gender parity did not happen by 2000. Gender parity did not happen by 2014. Despite the encouragement, it does not appear A/49/587 has been implemented. In 2009, UNSCR 1888 noted 'with concern' the 'lack of women as Chief or Lead peace mediators in United Nations-sponsored peace talks'. Yet the UN, even two years after the passage of UNSCR 1888, had still not appointed a woman to be the chief mediator of a peace process.[94] In 2013, the UN Security Council, via UNSCR 2122, yet again requested the Secretary-General to support the appointments of women at senior levels as United Nations mediators and within the composition of United Nations mediation teams.[95] The male UN Secretary-Generals have failed. Therefore the question must be asked whether the Secretary-General position needs to be: (1) a woman's position; or (2) co-shared by a woman and a man; or (3) rotated between women and men for a Secretary-General to finally support 'equal and full' participation of women in representing the UN. These are issues guaranteed to generate opinions. Yet the UN must foreclose the ability of a State to argue it need not comply with a UN Security Council resolution. Such

[89] 'Desktop Review of Needs and Gaps in Conflict-Affected Parts of Myanmar', Peace Donor Support Group (22 April 2013), 51, http://www.peacedonorsupportgroup.com/uploads/1/8/1/9/18194913/stocktake_mpc_20130701_final.pdf (accessed 16 June 2014).

[90] Sanam Naraghi Anderlini, 'What the Women Say: Participation and UNSCR 1325: A Case Study Assessment by the International Civil Society Action Network and the MIT Center for International Studies', ICAN and MIT (October 2010), 9, http://web.mit.edu/cis/pdf/WomenReport_10_2010.pdf (accessed 12 Nov 2014).

[91] UNSCR 1325, 1888, 1889, 1960, and 2122.

[92] UNSCR 1325, para. 2.

[93] 'Advancement of Women Human Resources Management: Other Human Resources Questions—Improvement of the Status of Women in the Secretariat', Report of the Secretary-General, 1 November 1994, UN Doc. A/49/587, para. 32, http://www.securitycouncilreport.org/atf/cf/%7B65BFCF9B-6D27-4E9C-8CD3-CF6E4FF96FF9%7D/WPS%20A%2049%20587.pdf (accessed 12 Nov 2014).

[94] OSCE, 'Gender Balance Report OSCE Parliamentary Assembly: The Effective Implementation of UN Security Council Resolution 1325 within the OSCE and in Participating States', July 2013, presented by Dr. Hedy Fry, Special Representative on Gender Issues of the OSCE PA, 23, http://www.oscepa.org/publications/reports/special-reports/gender-issues-reports/1879-2013-sr-on-gender-issues-report/file (accessed 12 Nov 2014).

[95] UNSCR 2122, para. 7(c).

an argument is strengthened when the UN Secretary-General, although not a State, fails to comply with the requirement of inclusion of women.

And while the UN Security Council, as articulated by its resolutions, is concerned about the non-inclusion of women, the UN Security Council itself has been guilty of non-inclusion. For example, it denied access to a Kosovo-based women's network despite UNSCR 1325's requirement that the Security Council consult with women's organizations during 'missions'.[96] The Security Council met with the women's network only after being shown the operative paragraph of UNSCR 1325, paragraph 15.[97] Whether this was an aberration or standard practice is an area for future study. What it does show is that resolutions can have an effect upon their makers.

8.2. Paper and practice: peacekeepers

Inclusion includes in the roles of military, police, and civilian peacekeepers. Inclusion requires analysing the de jure and de facto discriminatory exclusion of women peacekeepers as well as the impact of inclusion and exclusion. While this section's focus is police and military-centric, as stated earlier, even in the area of the female civilian peacekeepers, the UN has failed to meet its own 50 per cent goal. General Recommendation 30 and UNSCR 1325, 1820, 1888, 1960, 2106, and 2122 address women peacekeepers.

General Recommendation 30, UNSCR 1325's paragraph 4, 1820's paragraph 8, 1960's paragraph 15, 1888's paragraph 19, 2106's paragraph 4, and 2122's paragraph 9 all exhort increasing the number of female peacekeepers. Yet, despite CEDAW, and despite six UN Security Council resolutions, in 2013, ten years after the passage of UNSCR 1325, women made up less than 4 per cent of UN peacekeepers globally, about 9.8 per cent of UN police, and about 2 per cent of the UN military personnel.[98]

One answer as to the continued lack of women military peacekeepers in 2014 may be found in the failure of States to apply the Convention. The Convention requires the elimination of all forms of discrimination against women. General Recommendation 30 paragraph 9 states that state responsibility 'to apply the Convention' includes 'national contingents that form part of an international

[96] UNSCR 1325, para. 15.

[97] Aisling Swaine, 'Assessing The Potential of National Action Plans to Advance Implementation of United Nations Security Council Resolution 1325', *Yearbook of International Humanitarian Law* 12 (2010), 403–33 at 406 n. 13, citing Nobel Women's Initiative (2007), 'The Nobel Women's Initiative's First International Conference: Women Redefining Peace in the Middle East and Beyond Ireland'.

[98] Dharmapuri, 'Core Issues Stall Women's Participation in UN Missions', 10. Today's peace operations employ 3,557 uniformed women and 1,603 civilian women. Ethiopa leads with the most military women at 394 and Rwanda leads with the most female police at 183, 'Women in Peacekeeping', United Nations in Peacekeeping, http://www.un.org/en/peacekeeping/issues/women/womeninpk.shtml (accessed 12 Nov 2014) (click on the image when the link is accessed to view the corresponding infographic). Norway's Major General Kristin Lund, at the time of this writing, is the first and only military woman selected to head a UN peacekeeping operation (in 2014).

peacekeeping or peace-enforcement operation'. Yet all militaries of the world have de jure[99] sex-based discrimination with the exception of a few States such as New Zealand. And even in New Zealand, other forms of anti-woman discrimination exist. An example is the appointment of a male military officer, despite the New Zealand Human Rights Commission's finding against him of sexual harassing behavior,[100] to two of the highest-ranking positions in the New Zealand Defence Force (NZDF). Unlike the New Zealand Human Rights Commission, a military court-martial found his behaviour neither 'an act likely to prejudice service discipline' nor as 'behaving in a disgraceful and indecent manner'.[101] Not surprisingly, given his retention and promotion to high office, sexual harassment in the NZDF continues.[102] The discrimination against female military peacekeepers extends to UN Security Council resolutions. For example, UNSCR 1820 refuses to acknowledge that military members should also be free of sexual assault by their military siblings.

Whether the implementation of General Recommendation 30 and the UNSCR 1325 family of resolutions 'guarantee' women's 'meaningful participation' is unanswerable at present. They have not been implemented. General Recommendation 30 paragraph 42 claims 'the inclusion of a critical mass of women in peacekeeping activities' … 'can make a difference'. General Recommendation 30 paragraph 44 requires 'measures, to include, temporary special measures' to address 'gender discrimination and inequality in conflict-affected areas' and to ensure 'women's equality'. UNSCR 1888 contends that women peacekeeper presence 'may encourage local women to participate in the national armed and security forces, thereby helping to build a security sector that is accessible and responsive to all, especially women'. Evidence as to whether the presence of women peacekeepers effects the building of a security sector that is accessible and responsive to all can be found in the rare examples of women peacekeepers. One example is the 2008 Indian Formed Police Unit (FPU) in the UN Mission in Liberia (UNMIL), consisting of 105 women and 20 men with the men acting in support and logistics roles.[103] According to Rakhi Sahi, the 2008 commander, some of the impacts of the FPU include a decline in prostitution, sexual violence, and domestic and

[99] For this chapter, I define de jure discrimination to include, such as in the US, policy-based discrimination.

[100] He told a female crew member while on a seagoing vessel on a mission to enforce sanctions against Iraq, 'I didn't notice it was you who walked in, I only noticed your tits,' Tony Wall, 'Sexual harassment charges released', 30 June 2013, http://www.stuff.co.nz/national/crime/8859153/Sexual-harassment-charges-released (accessed 12 Nov 2014), and under whose command crew wore T-shirts stating "BITCHES—biggest inconvenience the crew has ever suffered', Tony Wall, 'Going down with the ship', 9 June 2013, http://www.stuff.co.nz/national/8772866/Going-down-with-the-ship (accessed 12 Nov 2014), and 'allowed a culture to develop on board his ship in which male sailors felt it was OK to make sexual demands, use degrading language and touch and grab at …. breasts, crotch and bottom'.

[101] Tony Wall, 30 June 2013, 'Sexual harassment charges released'.

[102] Cornelia Weiss, 'Respect for Human Rights and the Rule of Law: The New Zealand Defence Force', Ian Axford (New Zealand) Fellowship in Public Policy, 20, available at http://www.fulbright.org.nz/wp-content/uploads/2012/08/axford2012_weiss.pdf (accessed 15 September 2014).

[103] Precarious Progress, 11.

gender-based violence, and increased levels of confidence and motivation among Liberian women (due to seeing the FPU women in action).[104] Whether General Recommendation 30's 'critical mass' requires 105 front-line female peacekeepers for every 20 male support staff demands future exploration. Further, in addition to the 'critical mass' needed, examination into what 'temporary special measures' would entail to ensure 'women's equality' is rich in possibilities for research. 'Temporary special measurements' might be as simple as transforming militaries into institutions that evaluate people on the quality of their character rather than on the content of their chromosomes. 'Temporary special measures' could include defence white papers, professional military education, wargaming, dedicated funding, troop selection, and troop promotion that emphasize, and result in, building security sectors that do address 'gender discrimination and inequality in conflict-affected areas'. One metric for success could be 'women's equality'.

What is potentially more answerable is whether the failure to implement General Recommendation 30 in conjunction with the family of UNSCR 1325 resolutions impacts insecurity. According to Heidi Hudson, a major factor in insecurity is wrongful sexual conduct by males.[105] She provides the example in the Balkans of US military males 'routinely grop[ing] the breasts and buttocks of women during searches in town'.[106] General Recommendation 30 paragraph 13 claims '[w]omen's rights' are 'affected by various actors' including 'States ... contributing to international peacekeeping forces'. Yet militaries continue to employ individuals who engage in wrongful sexual conduct. Whether States employing and sending persons who engage in wrongful sexual conduct should enjoy de jure and de facto immunity, given State responsibility, is an issue the author anticipates will be heavily litigated in the future. State responsibility will have to be weighed against State immunity. Ultimately, the jurisprudence for such litigation will need to be supported by political will.

8.3. Paper and practice: peacebuilders

Peacebuilding inclusion requires inclusion along the entire continuum of peace. As acknowledged by UNSCR 1889's paragraph 1, '[m]ember States, international and regional organisations [are] to take further measures to improve women's participation during all stages of peace processes.' The same paragraph recommends further measures, including 'by enhancing their engagement in political and economic decision-making at early stages of recovery processes'. It advises, *inter alia*, further measures:

- promoting women's leadership and capacity to engage in aid management and planning;

[104] Precarious Progress, 11.

[105] Heidi Hudson, 'Peacekeeping Trends and Their Gender Implications', in *Gender, Conflict and Peacekeeping*, Dyan Mazurana, Angela Raven-Roberts, and Jane Parpart (eds.) (New York: Rowman & Littlefield, 2005), 111–33 at 153.

[106] Heidi Hudson, 'Peacekeeping Trends and Their Gender Implications', 153.

- supporting women's organizations; and
- countering negative societal attitudes about women's capacity to participate equally.

Whatever 'further measures' States, along with international and regional organizations, are taking to improve women's participation are not evident when they do not result in transformative results. Peacebuilding requires 'concrete strategies',[107] which appear lacking at present.

These 'concrete strategies' must address, as acknowledged by UNSCR 1889's paragraph 10, 'greater physical security and better socio-economic conditions' through 'education, economics, access to basic services and justice, gender-responsive law enforcement, and enhanced public decision-making engagement'. This section addresses money, gender-responsive law enforcement, and public decision-making.

Economic inclusion is a must. As UNSCR 2122 states, 'the economic empowerment of women greatly contributes to the stabilization of societies emerging from armed conflict'.[108] An area for States and organizations to examine closely is Afghan Parliamentarian Shinkai Korakhail's success in making the Afghanistan national budget contain line items of the percentage of funds allocated for women.[109] The line item allocation of funds deserves further study of other States, as well as international and regional organizations, to determine the international practice of economic empowerment of women needed for societies emerging from conflict.

Peacebuilding requires security sector inclusion. General Recommendation 30 paragraph 9 mandates state responsibility 'to apply the Convention' which includes 'bilateral or multilateral donor assistance for ... post-conflict reconstruction'. Yet, for example, the UNMIH (UN Mission in Haiti), mandated to create a new police force, made no specific efforts to recruit women[110] and made no evident efforts to stop exclusionary behaviour.[111] One explanation for such ignorance is that missions are populated by 'mostly male police officers, hailing from diverse countries that often have their own forms of institutionalized sexism'[112] despite research that shows women are more likely than male officers to defuse potentially violent situations.[113] For example, the average US male police officer costs approximately two and a half times more than the average female officer in compensation payments due to the use of excessive

[107] UNSCR 1889, para. 10.

[108] See 'Draft Declaration: Women's economic empowerment for peacebuilding', Peacebuilding Commission, 20 September 2013, UN Doc. PBC/7/OC/L.1, http://www.un.org/en/peacebuilding/pbso/pdf/women_economic_empowerement_draft_declaration.pdf (accessed 16 June 2014).

[109] Author interview of Shinkai Korakhail, November 2013.

[110] Tracy Fitzsimmons, 'The Postconflict Postscript: Gender and Policing in Peace Operations', in *Gender, Conflict and Peacekeeping*, Dyan Mazurana, Angela Raven-Roberts, and Jane Parpart (eds.) (New York: Rowman & Littlefield, 2005), 185–201 at 188.

[111] Fitzsimmons, 'The Postconflict Postscript', 190.

[112] Fitzsimmons, 'The Postconflict Postscript', 196.

[113] Fitzsimmons, 'The Postconflict Postscript', 199 n. 17.

force.[114] On the other side of security inclusion is the case of Nicaragua's National Police. The Director-General is a woman, Aminta Elena Granera Sacasa. The composition of the force is 40 per cent women.[115] It is a force in which 'the incorporation of female ex-guerrillas shaped gender issues in policing more than the international actors did; that is, the Nicaraguans managed to construct a system in which women officers and gender sensitivity are characteristics of the police force, not appendages of it'.[116] Thus it fulfils the requirement of UNSCR 1889's paragraph 10 that greater physical security and better socio-economic conditions must be addressed through 'gender-responsive law enforcement and access to justice'. Did having women and gender sensitivity make a difference? According to Granera, 'Nicaragua is the only country in Central America that has been able to consistently bring down its homicide rate over the last two years.'[117] Again, correlation is not causation, but the facts are suggestive.

General Recommendation 30 paragraph 13 acknowledges '[w]omen's rights in … post-conflict processes are affected by various actors, including States.' Just as outside actors can disempower women as articulated in the MINUSTAH police training example, outside actors can politically empower women through the drafting and influencing of legal documents. In Japan after World War II, 22-year-old Beate Sirota prepared the draft Japanese Constitution provision guaranteeing women's rights. When the Japanese objected, a US male military colonel told the Japanese: 'This article was written by Miss Sirota. She was brought up in Japan, knows the country well, and appreciates the point and feelings of Japanese women.'[118] He continued: 'There is no way in which the article can be faulted. She has her heart set on this issue. Why don't we just pass it?'[119] They did.

General Recommendation 30 paragraph 42 proclaims 'prerequisites for creating a society with lasting democracy, peace and gender equality' require at the national level:

- women's equal, meaningful and effective participation in the various branches of government;
- their appointment to leadership positions in government sectors; and
- their ability to participate as active members of civil society.

Defining 'equal, meaningful, and effective participation' may be helped by looking at Article 12 of the SADC (South African Development Community)

[114] Sahana Dharmapuri, 'Not Just a Numbers Game: Increasing Women's Participation in UN Peacekeeping', International Peace Institute (2013), 16, http://www.providingforpeacekeeping.org/wp-content/uploads/2013/08/IPI-EPub-Not-Just-a-Numbers-Game.pdf (accessed 12 Nov 2014).

[115] Larry Luxner, 'Nicaraguan Police Chief Aminta Granera Explains Success in Fighting Crime', *Dialogo Americas*, 7 February 2012, http://dialogo-americas.com/en_GB/articles/rmisa/features/regional_news/2012/07/02/nicaragua-granera (accessed 12 Nov 2014).

[116] Fitzsimmons, 'The Postconflict Postscript', 197.

[117] Luxner, 'Nicaraguan Police Chief … Explains Success'.

[118] Beate Sirota Gordon, *The Only Woman in the Room* (Tokyo: Kodansha, 1997), 123.

[119] Sirota Gordon, *The Only Woman*, 123.

Protocol on Gender and Development (2008) which requires that 'States Parties shall endeavor that, *by 2015, at least fifty percent* of decision-making positions in the public and private sectors are held by women including the use of affirmative action measures as provided for in Article 5' [emphasis mine].[120] Under this definition, at present the only State in which women are potentially equally represented in political life is Rwanda, with 64 per cent of members of Parliament being women.[121] The year 2015 will tell whether SADC has achieved what the UN Secretary-General has failed to do. Whether General Recommendation 30 paragraph 44's raising of 'specific and multiple barriers to women's equal participation that are linked to additional conflict-related restrictions on mobility, security, fundraising, campaigning and technical skills' resounds in peacebuilding States deserves further research especially in light of States such as Rwanda.

Despite the reality acknowledged by General Recommendation 30 paragraph 43 that the 'immediate aftermath of conflict can provide a strategic opportunity for States parties to adopt legislative and policy measures to eliminate discrimination against women in the political and public life of the country' as well as 'to ensure that women have equal opportunities to participate in the new, post-conflict structures of governance', General Recommendation 30 paragraph 43 acknowledges the alternative reality that frequently 'at the official cessation of hostilities, the promotion of gender equality and women's participation in decision-making processes is not seen as a priority and may even be side-lined as incompatible with stabilization goals'. In analysing the two approaches, research could be directed to comparative analysis such as comparing the factors that resulted in the sidelining of women during the drafting of Egypt's Constitution under Morsi versus the inclusion of women in Egypt's post-Morsi Constitution.

Ultimately, the inclusion and exclusion of women, whether through action or inaction, arise from negative societal attitudes about women participating equally. As acknowledged by UNSCR 1889, 'the persistent obstacles to women's full involvement' include:

- violence and intimidation;
- lack of security and lack of rule of law;
- cultural discrimination and stigmatization, including the rise of extremist or fanatical views on women; and
- socio-economic factors including the lack of access to education.

[120] 'Protocol on Gender and Development', SADC, 17 August 2008, http://www.sadc.int/files/8713/5292/8364/Protocol_on_Gender_and_Development_2008.pdf (accessed 12 Nov 2014).

[121] James Munyaneza, 'Rwanda: Women Take 64 Percent Seats in Parliament', *New Times*, 19 September 2013, http://allafrica.com/stories/201309190110.html?viewall=1 (accessed 12 Nov 2014). Whether this percentage of women in the Rwandan parliament translates into political decision-making power by women in Rwanda requires further study. At least one presenter at the 2014 American Society of International Law's 'Gender and Its Under-Scrutinized Role in International Law', 11 March 2014, argues it does not.

Examining what strategies and approaches have resulted in the inclusion of women in peacebuilding is needed scholarship.

9. Inclusion Beyond Words: Influencing Behaviour when the Law Does Not

When law fails in influencing behaviour,[122] money can make the difference. Funding despite non-compliance must be replaced with funding contingent on compliance. The deliverables are easy to define and easy to implement.

Money-contributing States should make their funding of UN peace activities contingent on the recipient's compliance with the law. For example, when the UN appoints more than 50 per cent men to peacemaking and peacekeeping missions, the money-contributing States should refuse funding until the UN complies with its own Security Council obligations. Whether refusing to fund non-compliance is the international law obligation of States is a question for exploration.

With regard to conflict States, for example Colombia, part of the funding of US aid to Colombia should have been contingent on Colombia's inclusion of women in peacemaking, peacekeeping, and peacebuilding. There should have been the requirement to repay funds plus fines for non-compliance. Since 2000, the birth of UNSCR 1325, the US has provided about $9.4 billion in aid to Colombia, of which about $6.8 billion has been in the form of military and police assistance.[123] Even so, Colombia failed to include women in peacemaking. Given that Colombia failed to include women in peacemaking, the prospects that Colombia will include women in peacebuilding are not encouraging. It is not even certain as to whether Colombia includes women in exterior peacekeeping missions. Colombia, despite being in a conflict, does send troops on peacekeeping missions such as to the Sinai Peninsula.

A further mechanism is for the UN to sanction a non-compliant State. Under Chapter VII of the Charter, the Security Council can take enforcement measures to maintain or restore international peace and security. Sanctions can be as simple as travel bans.[124] Mikulaschek's quantitative analysis finds compliance with UN Security Council resolutions is higher in the presence of UN sanctions.[125] Mikulaschek also advocates monitoring of sanctions by non-UN bodies.[126] He

[122] Simply addressing the issue through the tool of issuing more law may only result in the 'cosmetic changing of deck chairs on a ... passageway to failure'. Fionnuala D. Ní Aoláin, 'International Law, Gender Regimes and Fragmentation: 1325 and Beyond', in *Non-State Actors, Soft Law and Protective Regimes: From the Margins*, Cecilia M. Bailliet (ed.) (Cambridge: Cambridge University Press, 2012), 53–68 at 55.

[123] Chelsey Dyer, '50 years of US intervention in Colombia', Colombia Reports, 4 October 2013, http://colombiareports.co/50-years-us-intervention-colombia/ (accessed 12 Nov 2014).

[124] Travel bans impede shopping. Travel enables shopping—a foremost requested activity by military men when in a State not their own.

[125] Christoph Mikulaschek, 'From Paper to Peace? Compliance With UN Security Council Resolutions in Civil War', 7 April 2013, unpublished paper presented at the Annual Conference of the Midwest Political Science Association held in Chicago on 11–14 April 2013.

[126] Mikulascheck, 'From Paper to Peace?'.

finds that 'UN sanctions and monitoring by non-UN bodies reduce the probability of non-compliance from 74 to 17 percent, on average.'[127] Thus, to enhance compliance, the UN should sanction non-compliant States with monitoring by non-UN bodies.

10. Conclusion

Regardless of its status, law is just 'paper' unless it is complied with. The evidence does not demonstrate compliance. The quest for peace is illusory when half the population is excluded. As articulated by UNSCR 2122 paragraph 15, 'without a significant implementation shift, women and women's perspectives will continue to be underrepresented'. Achieving peace requires the inclusion of women as peacemakers, peacekeepers, and peacebuilders. To get there requires fresh and innovative thinking such as has been explored throughout this chapter.

[127] Mikulascheck 'From Paper to Peace?', 3.

PART IV

INSTITUTIONAL IMPLEMENTATION OF PEACE

15

United Nations Peace Operations and International Law

What Kind of Law Promotes What Kind of Peace?

Kjetil Mujezinović Larsen

1. The Purpose of this Chapter

The United Nations is the international organization with the primary responsibility to maintain or restore international peace and security, and the creation of international peace operations is one of the tools that the organization has at its disposal for this purpose. As such, international peace operations with a UN mandate[1] represent an important tool to maintain or restore peace in conflict-ridden areas. However, from their very inception more than six decades ago, peace operations have been subject to controversies and discussion on issues pertaining to practically every aspect of their existence. Two controversial issues are particularly relevant for this volume's general theme of 'promoting peace through international law', namely: (1) what is the relevant concept of 'peace' in the context of UN peace operations? and (2) how does international law contribute to the achievement of such peace?

The UN Secretary-General asserted in the 1992 report 'An Agenda for Peace' that the 'concept of peace is easy to grasp'.[2] With regard to peace operations, this assertion may (arguably) have been true at the time: until the end of the Cold War, peace operations were deployed to protect peace between states, that is, to prevent interstate war and armed violence. The concept of 'peace' in peace operations was primarily a negative concept, referring to the absence of war and armed conflict. But since the 1990s peace operations have undergone a significant

[1] In the following, the term 'peace operations' is used to include all peace operations with a UN mandate, regardless of their character of peacekeeping, peace-enforcement, peace-building, or other, and regardless of whether they are conducted under UN command and control. Conversely, in the present chapter 'peace operations' excludes international peace and security operations without a UN mandate, unless otherwise stated.

[2] 'An Agenda for Peace: Preventive Diplomacy, Peacemaking and Peace-keeping', Report of the Secretary-General, 17 June 1992, UN Doc. A/47/277-S/24111, para. 12.

normative transformation.[3] Now, operations are also being deployed to protect or strengthen peace *within* states, and contemporary mandates aim to promote a more complex concept of peace rather than only an 'easy to grasp' negative peace. This reconceptualization has been subject to considerable scholarly discussion, of which the present chapter will take stock (Section 3). Section 4 examines contemporary mandates in order to consider how the abstract concept of peace is translated into concrete functions.

With regard to the application of international law, equally controversial questions arise at several levels. In keeping with the overall approach of the present volume, the chapter will first address those rules under international law that pertain to the creation of peace operations (Section 2), but attention will also be devoted to the current confusion with regard to the applicability of important legal regimes to the conduct of the personnel during the execution of their mandate (Section 5). The overall purpose of this exercise is to discuss whether international law actually contributes to the promotion of 'peace' through the use of international peace operations.

2. Creation of Peace Operations: The Role of International Law

2.1. The UN Charter

UN peace operations are created by a resolution of the competent UN organ. As a rule this is the UN Security Council. A necessary initial inquiry concerns the legal basis upon which the Security Council acts in this regard. The UN Charter itself says nothing about the creation of peace operations.

It is undisputed that the Security Council has competence to create peace operations on the basis of Chapter VII of the UN Charter, which authorizes it to 'take such action ... as may be necessary to maintain or restore international peace and security'.[4] In recent years, it has become the norm rather than the exception that peace operations are based expressly in Chapter VII. But even though the Council's competence per se is not disputed, there has been some controversy with regard to the substantive requirements for the exercise of this competence. The starting point is that UN shall not be authorized 'to intervene in matters which are essentially within the domestic jurisdiction of any state', but this principle of non-intervention 'shall not prejudice the application of enforcement measures under Chapter VII'.[5] The UN Charter grants the Security Council competence to

[3] Alex J. Bellamy, Stuart Griffin, and Paul Williams, *Understanding Peacekeeping* (Cambridge: Polity, 2004), 75, referring to a 'triple transformation' of peace operations: In addition to the normative transformation, there has been a *quantitative* transformation (i.e. the number of peace operations has increased significantly) and a *qualitative* transformation (i.e. peace operations perform more complex functions than in the past).

[4] Charter of the United Nations (entered into force 24 October 1945), Art. 42.

[5] Art. 2.7.

act for the promotion of '*international* peace and security',[6] and this requirement applies for action under Chapter VII. These provisions suggest that the preoccupation of the founders of the UN was with preventing armed conflict between states, whereas *domestic* peace and security, that is, peace within a state, was the concern only of the state in question and accordingly fell outside the scope of the UN's responsibilities. However, the Council has developed a practice whereby this limitation has little effect as a restriction on the Council's authority. The Council has frequently intervened in situations that essentially concern domestic matters in a state, with the justification that an unstable situation within a state in itself constitutes a threat to international peace and security. The Council may describe how international peace and security is threatened, for example through the risk of destabilization of neighbouring countries, but it may also simply assert that the humanitarian situation within a state in itself constitutes a threat to international peace and security. A recent example concerns the authorization of the military intervention in Libya in 2011.[7] It is today indisputable that the Security Council considers humanitarian disasters or gross human rights violations within a state to be sufficient justification for characterizing a situation as a threat to international peace and security, so that the Council can exercise its competence under Chapter VII.[8]

It has been more uncertain whether the Security Council has the power to create peace operations also under Chapter VI of the UN Charter. This is, however, a question that has primarily theoretical interest. The Council's power to create peace operations under Chapter VI has never been challenged by any state. Further, one can argue that the Council's power in this regard now in any case constitutes international customary law. Finally, peace*keeping* operations—which are the operations that are normally based on Chapter VI—are traditionally grounded on three fundamental principles that have reduced the potential for conflicts relating to the uncertain legal basis. These principles are: (1) consent, that is, that an operation could only be deployed to an area if the host state consented to the deployment; (2) impartiality, that is, that the operation had to remain impartial and neutral at all times, and that it could not intervene in a conflict on the side of one party; and (3) minimum use of force.[9] Since operations that are not adopted under Chapter VII are always based (also) on consent from the host state, Chapter VI offers adequate legal basis in the UN Charter for the creation of peacekeeping operations. Non-consensual operations, on the other hand, cannot be based on Chapter VI.

While the Security Council undoubtedly has the competence to create peace operations, it must be underlined that nothing in the UN Charter can be construed as imposing a *duty* for the Council to do so in any given circumstance.

[6] In particular Arts. 24, 39, 42.

[7] UNSC Res. 1973 (17 March 2011) UN Doc. S/RES/1973(2011), preamble.

[8] For recent confirmations of this, see UNSC Res. 1894 (11 November 2009), UN Doc. S/RES/1894(2009), or UNSC Res. 1911 (28 January 2010), UN Doc. S/RES/1911(2010).

[9] For contemporary doctrine on the matter, see the 'Capstone Doctrine', 'United Nations Peacekeeping Operations: Principles and Guidelines' (UN: DPKO, 2008), para. 3.1.

When the requirements for Security Council action are met, the Council 'may' take measures, it is never under a legal obligation to do so.

2.2. Regional peace operations

There is now an increasing tendency for international peace operations to be carried out by regional organizations (such as the European Union or the African Union), or by permanent alliances (such as NATO). Such regional or delegated peacekeeping needs a legal basis beyond the organization itself, typically through consent from the host state or authorization from the UN Security Council. Without a legal basis, such peacekeeping will be unlawful under international law, regardless of whether the organization's own framework claims to offer a legal basis. The present chapter's focus on UN operations means that these issues are not pursued further here.[10]

3. The Concept of 'Peace' in Peace Operations

Assuming, then, that a peace operation has been created with an appropriate legal basis, the next inquiry concerns the general objective of these operations. What kind of 'peace' are they intended to promote?

The general reconceptualization of 'peace' in international relations, combined with the 'triple transformation' of peace operations,[11] has inspired a specific reconceptualization of 'peace' in the context of international peace operations since the end of the Cold War. An initial step in this process was taken by the UN Secretary-General in the report 'An Agenda for Peace' in 1992.[12] The report is primarily known for introducing the distinction between four categories of peace operations (preventive diplomacy, peacemaking, peacekeeping, and peace-building), but it also took important steps in clarifying the relevant concept of 'peace'. As already noted, the report asserts that the concept of peace is 'easy to grasp',[13] but the report also underlines that a range of factors must be present in order for peace to exist. The report pointed to the aim of 'rebuilding the institutions and infrastructures of nations torn by civil war and strife';[14] to the need to 'address the deepest causes of conflict: economic despair, social injustice and political oppression';[15] to the UN's responsibilities with regard to 'an integrated approach to human security';[16] and to the need to 'identify and support structures which will tend to consolidate peace and advance a sense of confidence and well-being among people';[17] all with the aim

[10] For the EU, see Frederik Naert, *International Law Aspects of the EU's Security and Defence Policy* (Antwerp: Intersentia, 2010), esp. 233–48.

[11] Bellamy, Griffin, and Williams, *Understanding Peacekeeping*.

[12] UN Secretary-General, 'An Agenda for Peace'.

[13] UN Secretary-General, 'An Agenda for Peace'. [14] Para. 15. [15] Para. 15.

[16] Para. 16. [17] Paras. 21, 55.

of 'securing peace in the spirit of the Charter'.[18] The purpose of peacebuilding operations is further proclaimed to be 'to deal with underlying economic, social, cultural and humanitarian problems' in order to 'place an achieved peace on a durable foundation'.[19] Seen as a whole, the report demonstrates that the focus of UN peace efforts would not (or no longer) be merely to secure the negative dimension of peace, i.e. the absence of violence, but to promote a positive concept of peace by addressing the underlying conditions and prerequisites for a stable and durable peace. The report also demonstrates that 'peace' would not be treated as a concept that is relevant only for the relationship between states, but as a concept which is also (and perhaps even *primarily*) relevant for the situation *within* a state. These views were accentuated even further in the Secretary-General's supplementary report in 1995, where he observed, *inter alia*, that the particular features of intrastate conflicts mean that 'international intervention must extend beyond military and humanitarian tasks and must include the promotion of national reconciliation and the re-establishment of effective government'.[20]

In 2000, the so-called Brahimi Report acknowledged and elaborated on this position. In an attempt to define the elements of peace operations, the report observed that '[l]ong-term conflict prevention addresses the structural sources of conflict in order to build a solid foundation for peace.'[21] With regard to peace-building, the report asserted that this

> includes but is not limited to reintegrating former combatants into civilian society, strengthening the rule of law (for example, through training and restructuring of local police, and judicial and penal reform); improving respect for human rights through the monitoring, education and investigation of past and existing abuses; providing technical assistance for democratic development (including electoral assistance and support for free media); and providing conflict resolution and reconciliation techniques.[22]

The Brahimi Report also emphasized that 'crisis-related efforts often prove either too little or too late', which speaks in favour of a focus on addressing the underlying causes of conflicts;[23] further, it criticized traditional peacekeeping for treating 'the symptoms rather than sources of conflict'.[24]

However, neither of these reports in any way suggests that peace operations should receive mandates to promote 'peace' as an abstract and general concept. Quite to the contrary: the Brahimi Report emphasized as one of its key recommendations that peace operations need to have 'clear, credible and achievable mandates'.[25] Although one can identify a general trend for peace operations to

[18] Para. 22. [19] Para. 57.

[20] 'Supplement to An Agenda for Peace: Position Paper of the Secretary-General on the Occasion of the Fiftieth Anniversary of the United Nations', Report of the Secretary-General, 25 January 1995, UN Doc. A/50/60-S/1995/1, para. 13.

[21] 'Report of the Panel on United Nations Peace Operations' ('the Brahimi Report'), 21 August 2000, UN Doc. A/55/305-S/2000/809, para. 10. [22] Brahimi Report, para. 13.

[23] Brahimi Report, para. 16. [24] Brahimi Report, para. 17.

[25] Brahimi Report, paras. 56–64.

promote a positive conception of peace, they always receive specific, ad hoc mandates adapted to the particular circumstances in each situation.

In 2004, the journal *International Peacekeeping* devoted a special issue to the theme 'Peace Operations and Global Order'. The editors wanted to challenge the apparent assumption in, *inter alia*, the Brahimi Report that 'a consensus exists on what constitutes a crisis, the elements of the solution, and the most appropriate strategies to achieve it', which in the editors' view represents a problem-solving approach that fails to address structural issues relating to peace operations.[26] What is needed, they argued, is a critical evaluation of the purposes of peace operations and a reflection of alternative visions of their function in global politics. They drew up two 'broad and competing images of the liberal democratic peace thesis that underpin ideas about what role peace operations should play', namely a 'Westphalian' image with an emphasis on the internal integrity and political independence of sovereign states, and a 'post-Westphalian' image focusing on the promotion of liberal democratic governance through active contributions to the construction of liberal polities, economies, and societies.[27] The dilemma they introduced was, in abbreviated terms, first that while many states (particularly Western states) favour the post-Westphalian approach, other states favour the Westphalian approach, and second that contemporary peace operations tend to take the post-Westphalian approach without a clear conceptual awareness of whether this is appropriate in a given situation.

Several authors have described how 'peace operations attempt to create a particular type of international order', and that this type of order is 'a distinctly liberal one'.[28] Pugh has claimed that 'modern versions of peacekeeping can be considered as forms of riot control directed against the unruly parts of the world to uphold the liberal peace',[29] and that the evolution of peace operations and 'the merger with humanitarianism has reflected and reinforced the structure of the world system, promoted the globalization of a particular ideology of good governance—the "liberal peace"'.[30] Richmond describes how 'the contemporary peace-building project … has been subsumed within a liberal state-building enterprise', which rests on a '"peacebuilding consensus" aimed at the construction of the liberal peace'.[31] Paris states that 'peacebuilding missions are not merely exercises in conflict management, but instances of a much larger phenomenon: the globalisation of a particular model of domestic governance—liberal market democracy'.[32]

[26] Alexander J. Bellamy and Paul Williams, 'Introduction: Thinking Anew about Peace Operations', *International Peacekeeping* 11 (2004), 1–15 at 2.

[27] Bellamy and Williams, 'Introduction: Thinking Anew about Peace Operations', 3–5.

[28] Bellamy and Williams, 'Introduction: Thinking Anew about Peace Operations', 8, with further references.

[29] Michael Pugh, 'Peacekeeping and Critical Theory', *International Peacekeeping* 11 (2004), 39–58 at 41.

[30] Pugh, 'Peacekeeping and Critical Theory', 53.

[31] Oliver P. Richmond, *Peace in International Relations* (London: Routledge, 2008), 105. By the same author, *The Transformation of Peace* (New York: Palgrave Macmillan, 2005), 159, and 'A Genealogy of Peacemaking: The Creation and Re-Creation of Order', *Alternatives* 26 (2001), 317–48.

[32] Roland Paris, 'International Peacebuilding and the "mission civilisatrice"', *Review of International Studies* 28 (2002), 637–56 at 638.

Buchan argues that 'peacebuilding missions can in no way be regarded as politically neutral. They exhibit a profound bias in favour of promoting respect for liberal democratic standards'.[33]

However, even if there now appears to be considerable agreement that peace operations in fact pursue a liberal peace, there is less agreement on the normative aspect, namely whether this is what peace operations *should* do. There is also considerable disagreement on how peace operations can be successful and effective in the pursuit of the liberal peace that they set out to promote. Bellamy argues that 'the frames that some use as a basis for evaluating when and how to intervene may be rejected by others as, for example, unwarranted intrusions on sovereignty or the imposition of "Western" techniques of conflict resolution on societies that have their own—very different—indigenous methods for resolving disputes'.[34] Referring to other studies, he also discusses the argument that 'the liberal bias of peacemaking ... and peacebuilding ... not only fails to alleviate human insecurity or promote emancipation but may even help create the conditions for further violence',[35] and that 'liberal peace operations may reinforce the social, political and economic structures that contribute to protracted violent conflict'.[36] Pugh is one of the authors who describe a 'liberal peace crisis', and he summarizes critiques of the liberal peace project as a project that 'merges security and development; "romanticises the local" as victims or illiberal; builds hollow institutions; designs economic life to reproduce assertive capitalism; equates peace with state-building; and assumes the interveners have privileged knowledge and that liberalization is the only system available'.[37] The concern is that the pursuit of a 'liberal peace' through international peace operations is, or can be perceived to be, a Western-led cultural imperialism that ignores local traditions and that promotes a 'peace' that lacks the prerequisites that would allow for a stable and durable peace in concrete circumstances.[38]

These concerns paved the way for a new special issue of *International Peacekeeping* in 2009, where the editors asked, basically, whether 'liberal peacebuilding [is] compatible with cultural and political pluralism'.[39] They called for a 'more politically hybridized form of peacebuilding' which engages with 'non-Western' views and which is 'better at representing, providing for and respecting the rights and needs of post-conflict societies and communities'.[40] This issue lies at the core of

[33] Russell Buchan, *International Law and the Construction of the Liberal Peace* (Oxford: Hart, 2013), 151.

[34] Alexander J. Bellamy, 'The "Next Stage" in Peace Operations Theory?', *International Peacekeeping* 11 (2004), 17–38 at 23.

[35] Bellamy, 'The "Next Stage"', 32.

[36] Bellamy, 'The "Next Stage"', 34.

[37] Michael Pugh, 'Reflections on Aggressive Peace', *International Peacekeeping* 19 (2012), 410–25 at 411.

[38] Kristoffer Lidén, 'Building Peace between Global and Local Politics: The Cosmopolitical Ethics of Liberal Peacebuilding', *International Peacekeeping* 16 (2009), 616–34 at 616, describes how 'peacebuilding has also been discarded as a fraud, and even cursed as the new face of diabolic imperialism'.

[39] Kristoffer Lidén, Roger MacGinty, and Oliver P. Richmond, 'Introduction: Beyond Northern Epistemologies of Peace: Peacebuilding Reconstructed?', *International Peacekeeping* 16 (2009), 587–98 at 587.

[40] Lidén, Mac Ginty, and Richmond, 'Introduction: Beyond Northern Epistemologies of Peace', 594.

a new generation of peace operations theory, focusing on reforms that will make international intervention more effective over time.[41]

This chapter accepts as a premise for the following discussion that contemporary peace operations in practice tend to pursue a 'liberal peace'. However, it is necessary for further inquiry also to consider how contemporary mandates of peace operations are drafted, in order to concretize the general and abstract concept of a 'liberal peace'.

4. Contemporary Mandates

At the time of completion of this chapter, there are 17 ongoing operations led by the UN Department of Peacekeeping Operations.[42] In terms of functions, these operations vary from the purely political mission in Afghanistan (UNAMA[43]) to the first ever UN-led 'intervention brigade' in the Democratic Republic of the Congo (MONUSCO). Despite the considerable variation, there are a number of common features to the mandates.

First, the operations tend to have functions pertaining to the traditional, negative definition of peace, as they are commonly called upon to monitor ceasefire agreements or peace agreements, to monitor and verify troop withdrawals, to maintain and protect buffer zones between the conflicting parties, and perform similar functions aimed at preventing violence between the conflicting parties. In a few ongoing operations these negative functions are predominant. The UN Military Observer Group in India and Pakistan (UNMOGIP) was established in 1948, and its current mandate dates back to 1971. UNMOGIP's mandate is limited to observing that the ceasefire agreement between India and Pakistan is respected by the parties.[44] Also in 1948, the UN Truce Supervision Organization (UNTSO, Middle East) was established, with a mandate that was limited to supervising the observance of the truce in Palestine.[45] The UN Disengagement Observer Force (UNDOF, Golan) was established in 1974 to maintain the ceasefire between Israel and Syria, to supervise the disengagement of Israeli and Syrian forces, and to supervise the areas of separation and limitation.[46] The mandate of the UN Peacekeeping Force in Cyprus (UNFICYP)

41 Lidén, 'Building Peace between Global and Local Politics', 620.

42 For updates, please visit http://www.un.org/en/peacekeeping/operations/current.shtml (accessed 12 Nov 2014). A tabular inventory of peacebuilding operations from the end of the Cold War until 2009 is provided in Volker C. Franke and Andrea Warnecke, 'Bulding Peace: An Inventory of UN Peace Missions since the End of the Cold War', *International Peacekeeping* 16 (2009), 407–36.

43 UNAMA was established by UNSC Res. 1401 (2002) at the request of the Afghan government to assist in laying the foundation for sustainable peace and development in Afghanistan. UNAMA will not be addressed further here.

44 UNSC Res. 39 (20 January 1948) UN Doc. S/654; UNSC Res. 47 (21 April 1948) UN Doc. S/726, and UNSC Res. 307 (21 December 1971) UN Doc. S/RES/307.

45 UNSC Res. 50 (29 May 1948) UN Doc. S/801.

46 UNSC Res. 350 (31 May 1974) UN Doc. S/RES/350.

is similar, but somewhat wider. UNFICYP was created in 1964 to 'prevent a recurrence of fighting' between the parties,[47] and since 1974 it has focused primarily on supervising a de facto ceasefire and maintaining a buffer zone. However, the original resolution also called on UNFICYP to 'contribute to the maintenance and restoration of law and order and a return to normal conditions', and the Security Council has later emphasized that UNFICYP's tasks include 'humanitarian functions'.[48] As such, the operation's mandate extends beyond the mere prevention of violence, even if this remains its primary function. Another example is the UN Interim Force in Lebanon (UNIFIL), which was established in 1978 to confirm Israeli withdrawal from Lebanon, restore international peace and security, and assist the Lebanese Government in restoring its effective authority in the area.[49] However, the mandate has been revised on three later occasions, most lately in 2006 when the mandate was expanded while remaining focused on aspects pertaining to the negative elements of peace.[50]

Also after the end of the Cold War there have been created operations whose functions predominantly pertain to negative elements of peace, that is, the prevention of violence. These more modern operations nevertheless have wider, more robust mandates. A clear shift in the practice of the Security Council occurred in the late 1990s, when the Council started taking a more proactive role towards the protection of civilians and of human rights. The protection of civilians has always been a fundamental purpose of the organization's peace efforts, but the functions of peacekeepers with regard to the protection of civilians have traditionally not been addressed directly in the mandates of peace operations. The end of the Cold War, and the following revitalization of UN-mandated peace operations, brought with it clearer functions for the protection of civilians. The protection of civilians in armed conflicts has been explicitly included as a regular topic on the Security Council's agenda only since 1999, and consequently this aspect has also been commonly included in the mandates of peace operations. In 2006, the Council made an effort to clarify the role of peace operations with regard to the protection of civilians:

> [The Security Council] [R]eaffirms its practice of ensuring that the mandates of United Nations peacekeeping, political and peacebuilding missions include, where appropriate and on a case-by-case basis, provisions regarding (i) the protection of civilians, particularly those under imminent threat of physical danger within their zones of operation, (ii) the facilitation of the provision of humanitarian assistance, and (iii) the creation of conditions conducive to the voluntary, safe, dignified and sustainable return of refugees and internally displaced persons, and expresses its intention of ensuring that (i) such mandates include clear guidelines as to what missions can and should do to achieve those goals, (ii) the protection of civilians is given priority in decisions about

[47] UNSC Res. 186 (4 March 1964) UN Doc. S/RES/186, op. clause 5.
[48] UNSC Res. 359 (15 August 1974) UN Doc. S/RES359.
[49] UNSC Res. 425 (19 March 1978) UN Doc. S/RES/425.
[50] UNSC Res. 1701 (11 August 2006) UN Doc. S/RES/1701.

the use of available capacity and resources, including information and intelligence resources, in the implementation of the mandates, and (iii) that protection mandates are implemented . . .[51]

Modern operations are generally mandated to take necessary action to protect civilians even if their mandate is predominantly focused on promoting a negative concept of peace.

The key function of the UN Interim Security Force for Abyei (UNISFA, Sudan) is to monitor the demilitarization of the Abyei area, and it is authorized to take the necessary measures to protect civilians under imminent threat of physical violence.[52] However, UNISFA offers a useful illustration that traditional peacekeeping operations are now uncommon, as operations are given wider mandates even if peacekeeping is their primary function. UNISFA is mandated to participate in relevant bodies in the Abyei area, to provide de-mining assistance and technical advice, to facilitate the delivery of humanitarian aid and the free movement of humanitarian personnel, and to strengthen the capacity of the local police. A similar situation exists for the UN Mission for the Referendum in Western Sahara (MINURSO), which was established in 1991 to monitor the ceasefire and perform certain functions relating to the organization of a referendum.[53] For political reasons, it has been impossible to organize the referendum, but MINURSO continues to monitor the ceasefire, to perform functions that aim at reducing the threat of mines and unexploded ordnances, and support confidence-building measures in the area. Again, the mandate is predominantly focused on the prevention of armed conflict, but there are also aspects in the mandate that aim instead to address the underlying causes of conflict.

This provides a useful segue to the second general element in contemporary mandates, namely that operations have functions that aim at promoting a positive concept of peace. Most contemporary operations can be characterized as peace-building operations, which perform functions pertaining to security and public order, to justice and reconciliation, to governance and participation, or to social and economic well-being. One classification of peace-building mandates was offered by Ulrich Schneckener, who distinguishes between (1) peacebuilding consultation, where small deployments offer advice and guidance to local actors; (2) specialized peacebuilding, where small deployments perform monitoring or implementing tasks relating to one single area; (3) multidimensional peace-building, where civil-military operations perform comprehensive tasks in several sectors while respecting local sovereignty; and (4) international transitional administrations, where the local government is temporarily replaced by external actors.[54]

[51] UNSC Res. 1674 (28 April 2006) UN Doc. S/RES/1674, op. clause 16.

[52] UNSC Res. 1990 (27 June 2011) UN Doc. S/RES/1990, op. clauses 2, 3.

[53] UNSC Res. 690 (29 April 1991), UN Doc. S/RES/690.

[54] Ulrich Schneckener, 'Frieden Machen: Peacebuilding und Peacebuilders', *Die Friedenswarte* 80 (2005), 17–39. Franke and Warnecke, 'Building Peace', use this classification for their inventory.

International transitional administrations were created in East Timor,[55] Cambodia,[56] and Kosovo.[57] From 1999 onwards, UNMIK represented the civilian administration in Kosovo, working alongside the NATO-led Kosovo Force (KFOR) which had responsibilities pertaining to security. UNMIK's original mandate included the performance of governmental functions far exceeding merely the prevention of violence. From 2008 onwards, Kosovo's independence has resulted in a much reduced scope of functions for UNMIK, which now focuses on the promotion of security, stability, and respect for human rights in Kosovo through engagement and cooperation with other actors.

UNMIL in Liberia was created in 2003 with a mandate that contained a range of functions pertaining to support for implementation of the ceasefire agreement, protection of UN staff and facilities and of civilians, and support for humanitarian and human rights assistance, security reform, and the implementation of the peace process.[58] The mandate was revised in 2012, giving UNMIL the tasks, *inter alia*, of supporting efforts to solidify peace and stability in Liberia and to protect civilians, to achieve a successful transition of complete security responsibility to the national police, to work for progress in the reform and restructuring of the justice sector, and to support national reconciliation, constitutional reform, and decentralization, while enhancing its support for security sector and rule of law reforms.[59]

UNOCI in the Ivory Coast represents another example of a multidimensional peacebuilding operation. Since 2013, UNOCI has had a mandate that contains tasks relating to (a) protection of civilians, (b) addressing remaining security threats and border-related challenges, (c) disarmament, demobilization and reintegration (DDR) and collection of weapons, (d) reconstitution and reform of security institutions, (e) monitoring of the arms embargo, (f) support for compliance with international humanitarian and human rights law, (g) support for humanitarian assistance, (h) public information, (i) redeployment of state administration and the extension of state authority throughout the country, and (j) protection of UN personnel.[60] A similar mandate applies to UNAMID in the Darfur region in Sudan, and also to UNMISS in South Sudan. Established in 2007, UNAMID has been given functions relating to support for the peace process and good offices, the security situation, rule of law, governance and human rights, and humanitarian assistance.[61] UNMISS was created in 2011 to support the Government in the consolidation of peace in the new country, thereby promoting long-term state-building and economic development. Its functions included

[55] UN Transitional Administration in East Timor (UNTAET), established by UNSC Res. 1272 (1999) and terminated in 2002.

[56] UN Transitional Authority in Cambodia (UNTAC), established by UNSC Res. 745 (1992) and terminated in 1993.

[57] UN Interim Administration Mission in Kosovo (UNMIK), established by UNSC Res. 1244 (1999).

[58] UNSC Res. 1509 (19 September 2003) UN Doc. S/RES/1509.

[59] UNSC Res. 2066 (17 September 2012) UN Doc. S/RES/2066.

[60] UNSC Res. 2112 (30 July 2013), UN Doc. S/RES/2112.

[61] UNSC Res. 1769 (31 July 2007), UN Doc. S/RES/1769.

assisting the authorities in developing capacity to provide security, establishing the rule of law, and strengthening the security and justice sectors in the country.[62] As a result of the tense situation in the country, the Security Council amended the mandate in May 2014, by emphasizing 'that protection of civilians ... must be given priority in decisions about the use of available capacity and resources within the mission', that is, that the focus should be on the protection of civilians rather than on peacebuilding activities, but it retains functions pertaining to monitoring and investigating human rights issues, and to creating the conditions for delivery of humanitarian assistance.[63] Another multidimensional peace-building operation is the MINUSCA operation in the Central African Republic. Created in 2014 to support the peace process in the country, MINUSCA was given functions pertaining to, *inter alia*, protection of civilians, support for the implementation of the transition process, facilitation of the delivery of humanitarian assistance, promotion and protection of human rights, and support for national and international justice and the rule of law.[64] Finally, MINUSMA in Mali has similar functions that place it in the category of multidimensional peace-building. It was created in 2013 to assist in the stabilization of key population centres and to support the re-establishment of state authority throughout the country, to support the implementation of the peace process, national political dialogue, and the electoral process, to protect civilians, to promote and protect human rights, to support humanitarian assistance, to support cultural preservation, and to support national and international justice.[65]

The mandate of MINUSTAH in Haiti has frequently been revised following political developments and natural events. It was originally set up in 2004 to support the transitional Haitian Government in ensuring a secure and stable environment,[66] but the earthquake in 2010 led to a significant change in the mandate towards supporting immediate recovery, reconstruction, and stability efforts, which still remains its primary focus.[67]

MONUSCO took over from its predecessor MONUC in 2010 as a response to the new phase in the peace process in the Democratic Republic of the Congo. It was given an extensive mandate relating to protection of civilians and to stabilization and peace consolidation, but its key function is to assist the Government in achieving a stable and secure situation.[68] However, the subsequent escalation of violence in the region led the Security Council to establish an unprecedented 'Intervention Brigade', with the responsibility 'of neutralizing armed groups ... and the objective of contributing to reducing the threat posed by armed groups

[62] UNSC Res. 1996 (8 July 2011), UN Doc. S/RES/1996.
[63] UNSC Res. 2155 (27 May 2014) UN Doc. S/RES/2155.
[64] UNSC Res. 2149 (10 May 2014) UN Doc. S/RES/2149.
[65] UNSC Res. 2100 (25 April 2013) UN Doc. S/RES/2100.
[66] UNSC Res. 1542 (30 April 2004), UN Doc. S/RES/1542.
[67] UNSC Res. 1908 (19 January 2010) UN Doc. S/RES/1908; 1927 (4 June 2010) UN Doc. S/RES/1927, and 2070 (12 October 2012) UN Doc. S/RES/2070.
[68] UNSC Res. 1925 (28 May 2010) UN Doc. S/RES/1925, and 2053 (27 June 2012) UN Doc. S/RES/2053.

to state authority and civilian security in eastern DRC and to make space for stabilization activities'.[69]

What this summary of contemporary mandates shows is that the abstract concept of a 'liberal peace' is pursued through the creation of multidimensional peace-building operations with concrete functions relating to capacity-building, rule of law reforms, security sector reforms, and the promotion and protection of human rights.

5. The Unclear 'Law of Peace Operations'

5.1. Context

So far, we have seen that international law is a relatively neutral factor with regard to the creation of peace operations: international law permits the creation of peace operations, but it does little to actively *promote* such creation. We have also seen that the concept of 'peace' in peace operations remains based on ad hoc considerations, but that the more general, overarching concept is one of liberal peace. Let us then proceed to the final stage of this chapter's inquiry, namely to what extent international law promotes or impedes the establishment of this 'liberal peace' once the operation has been created. As a prelude to this inquiry, however, one should note that in the same way as peace operations are not, then, objective or neutral, international law may not be neutral, either in interpretation or in application. International law is itself occasionally criticized for being a tool for strong states, often Western states, to legitimize actions that are in accordance with the political interests of those states. States comply with international law when it is in their self-interest to do so, some argue.[70] If one subscribes to this view, international law may simply be a tool which in itself legitimizes and reinforces the 'liberal peace imperialism' discussed earlier; the goals and values that underlie a liberal concept of peace simultaneously underlie international law, which is used to legitimize and promote that precise concept of peace.

The inquiry can be approached from several angles, but the approach chosen here is to inquire to what extent international law concerning the conduct of personnel during international peace operations has an impact on the effectiveness (or success) of the operation. However, this inquiry requires an initial consideration of what the highly ambiguous concept of 'effectiveness' actually means in the context of international peace operations: when is a peace operation effective in the pursuit of its mandate?[71]

[69] UNSC Res. 2098 (28 March 2013) UN Doc. S/RES/2098, and 2147 (28 March 2014) UN Doc. S/RES/2147.

[70] e.g. Jack L. Goldsmith and Eric A. Posner, *The Limits of International Law* (Oxford: Oxford University Press, 2005).

[71] Section 5.2 is a revised version of the corresponding section in the author's book *The Human Rights Treaty Obligations of Peacekeepers* (Cambridge: Cambridge University Press, 2012), 72–6.

5.2. The 'effectiveness' of a peace operation

In the context of peace operations, 'effectiveness' normally refers to *operational* effectiveness. This concept is often used as an important goal (or value) for international peace operations, but it is rarely specified what is meant by the concept. The Capstone Doctrine, for example, says that a 'multi-dimensional United Nations peacekeeping operation is likely to be far more effective when it is deployed as part of a United Nations system-wide response based on a clear and shared understanding of priorities, and on a willingness on the part of all United Nations actors to contribute to the achievement of common objectives',[72] and that an operation should have a strategy that reflects 'a shared understanding of the operating environment and agreement on how to maximize the effectiveness, efficiency, and impact of the United Nations overall response',[73] but nowhere does it say what this 'effectiveness' is or when an operation can be considered 'effective' in this regard. Even in the Brahimi Report, which was a response precisely to a call from the UN Secretary-General for recommendations on how to enhance the ability of the UN to conduct peace operations effectively, 'effectiveness' is not expressly defined other than in the particular context of the demand for a rapid and effective deployment.[74] However, the report stated that every recommendation therein was meant to ensure that three conditions 'for the success of future complex operations' are met.[75] Effectiveness is thus equated with operational *success*, which can be rephrased as a high level of mission accomplishment. An international peace operation is considered 'effective' if it accomplishes its mission, that is, if it accomplishes 'peace' in the concrete, ad hoc sense relevant to that particular operation. More complex approaches can be offered. Duane Bratt argued in 1996 that operational success in peace operations can be measured in four different ways: mandate performance, facilitation of conflict resolution, conflict containment, and limitation of casualties.[76] Sarah-Myriam Martin-Brûlé has recently argued that 'the success of peace missions is defined by two dimensions: a) accomplishment of the mandate; and b) establishment of order within and by the state', but further that 'these dimensions of success are not always compatible, succeeding in one dimension while failing in another'.[77]

'Effectiveness' can in certain contexts be defined as the degree to which the *actual* outputs of a system correspond to its *desired* (or *planned*) outputs, and the application of such a definition would support the assumption that operational effectiveness simply refers to the level of mission accomplishment—the *desired* objectives of the operation must be measured against the *actual* results. But 'effectiveness' can also, in other contexts, be defined in terms of 'output per unit of input' (although this is more commonly applied as a definition of *efficiency*, not

[72] Capstone Doctrine, 53. [73] Capstone Doctrine, 53–4.
[74] Brahimi Report, paras. 86–91. [75] Brahimi Report, para. 4.
[76] Duane Bratt, 'Assessing the Success of UN Peacekeeping Operations', *International Peacekeeping* 3 (1996), 64–81.
[77] Sarah-Myriam Martin-Brûlé, 'Assessing Peace Operations' Mitigated Outcomes', *International Peacekeeping* 19 (2012), 235–50 at 235.

effectiveness). It this definition is applied, effectiveness must be measured against one or more relevant parameters, such as applied personnel, actual costs, damage or casualties, duration of the operation, duration and stability of the achieved results, etc., but there exists no common agreement about the relevant parameters. One could argue that operational effectiveness should refer to the achievement of the mandate at the earliest possible moment with the minimum expenditure of life and resources.

In the *Behrami/Saramati* case, the European Court of Human Rights applied arguments relating to operational effectiveness as part of its justification to declare the case inadmissible. The Court held that operations under Chapter VII of the UN Charter 'rely for their effectiveness on support from member states', and that scrutiny of conduct that is covered by a UN Security Council resolution would be 'to interfere with the fulfilment of the UN's key mission in this field including ... the effective conduct of its operations'.[78] This was a response to a submission of the respondent states, who argued that the application of human rights law could deter participation in peace operations, thereby 'undermining the coherence and therefore effectiveness of, such peacekeeping missions'.[79] The written submissions to the Court focused partly on the difficulties of the UN in obtaining troops, and partly on the practical challenges that arise if Troop Contributing States have different human rights obligations. No state suggested that the application of the Convention would jeopardize the accomplishment of a mission once a proper force had been deployed, only that the mission accomplishment would be more difficult, that is, more costly, time-consuming, etc. There is also room for discussion about whether the argument is in fact appropriate. Some commentators promote the exact opposite view, namely that 'international human rights law is key to enhancing operational effectiveness'.[80] The underlying assumption is that compliance with human rights law is necessary for the credibility of an operation, and 'the maintenance of credibility is fundamental to the success of a mission'.[81] If an operation is perceived as violating internationally recognized human rights norms, operational success becomes exceedingly difficult. Why, then, would scrutiny by the Court endanger the 'effectiveness' of the operation? From this perspective, the only remaining valid part of this particular argument is that states would be more unwilling to contribute troops to UN-mandated peace operations if they were risking being held responsible for human rights violations, that is, that the 'effectiveness' of an operation is linked to the practical difficulties the UN faces with regard to assembling the required number of troops. This is

[78] *Behrami and Behrami* v. *France* and *Saramati* v. *France, Germany and Norway*, App. nos. 71412/01 and 78166/01 (ECtHR, 2 May 2007), para. 149(2).

[79] *Behrami/Saramati*, para. 94, joint (oral) submissions of France and Norway. The same point was made by several states as third parties: Denmark (para. 101), Germany (para. 108), Poland (para. 111), the United Kingdom (para. 115), and Portugal (para. 117, who adopted the observations of the United Kingdom).

[80] Todd Howland, 'Peacekeeping and Conformity with Human Rights Law: How MINUSTAH Falls Short in Haiti', *International Peacekeeping* 13 (2006), 462–76 at 462.

[81] Capstone Doctrine, 38.

clearly a too narrow approach to effectiveness, but precisely what the effectiveness of peace operations generally refers to remains uncertain. For the purposes of the following discussion, however, 'effectiveness' describes the level of mission accomplishment, that is, to what extent peace operations succeed in achieving the situation-specific concept of 'peace'. Let us then proceed to consider whether, and how, relevant international legal regimes contribute to or impede the effectiveness of peace operations in this context.

5.3. International humanitarian law and human rights law

The applicability of international humanitarian law (IHL) and human rights law to the conduct of personnel during peace operations raises challenging questions and has been a source of considerable controversy. Today it is widely acknowledged that IHL applies to military forces in peace operations if they are or become a party to an armed conflict. While this may sound a self-evident truth, the applicability of IHL during peace operations has traditionally been a contentious issue, and still today it is unclear what this assertion means in practice.

During the Cold War period, the official position of the UN was that the organization was bound only by 'the principles and spirit' of the conventions that regulate the conduct of military personnel, while the International Committee of the Red Cross (ICRC) called for a commitment to respect the full corpus of IHL.[82] After the end of the Cold War, the reference to the 'principles and spirit' of IHL was repeated in the regulatory framework of peace operations, but events during the 1990s demonstrated that this was insufficient as a regulation of the forces' rights and obligations during participation in armed conflicts. In 1999, the UN Secretary-General promulgated the 'Bulletin on observance by United Nations forces of international humanitarian law', which provides fundamental rules and principles of IHL that are applicable to UN forces.[83] This Bulletin is 'binding on members of UN forces in the same way as are all other instructions issued by the Secretary-General in his capacity as "commander in chief" of UN operations', but the basis 'of the legal obligation, however, lies in the international humanitarian law provisions incorporated in the respective national laws ... or in the customary international law provisions that are independently binding'.[84] Most actors accept that the UN, as a subject of international law, is bound by international customary law, including customary IHL. Consequently, there are two independent bases (with different status and legal effect) for claiming that the

[82] For a historical overview, see Finn Seyersted, *United Nations Forces in the Law of Peace and War* (Leiden: A. W. Sijthoff, 1966), 182–91.

[83] UN Secretary-General's Bulletin (6 August 1999) on observance by UN forces of international humanitarian law, UN doc. ST/SGB/1999/13, sect. 1.1.

[84] Daphna Shraga, 'UN Peacekeeping Operations: Applicability of International Humanitarian Law and Responsibility for Operations-Related Damage', *American Journal of International Law* 94 (2000), 406–12 at 409.

UN as an organization is bound by international humanitarian law, namely (1) international customary law, and (2) internal UN law as articulated in the Secretary-General's Bulletin.

For forces involved in peace operations, there is also a third legal basis for such obligations, namely the obligations of their Troop Contributing States. It is today commonly accepted that states remain bound by their IHL obligations when they contribute military personnel to peace operations. The primary legal basis for this position is Common Article 1 of the four Geneva Conventions, which places an obligation on the contracting states both to 'respect' and to 'ensure respect' for the Conventions in all circumstances.[85] This obligation applies to all states that contribute military personnel forces to peace operations, and it applies regardless of other actors' compliance with the Conventions.

Thus, the simple conclusion is that military personnel in peace operations have rights and obligations under IHL if they participate in an armed conflict. Two arguments may explain why this is relevant for the present chapter. First, neutrality is one of the fundamental principles of peacekeeping operations. If a peace operation is or becomes a party to an armed conflict, this neutrality is jeopardized. If a peace operation at any given time is perceived as having lost its neutrality and impartiality, this may never be regained. In certain situations, this (perceived) lack of impartiality may complicate the efforts of peace operations to achieve a stable and durable peace—a perceived lack of impartiality in the process may create a perceived lack of impartiality in the outcome. However, while peace operations should protect and maintain their impartiality with all possible diligence, it does not suggest that peace operations should not be bound (and protected) by IHL if they nevertheless—intentionally or unintentionally—become actively involved in an armed conflict. Quite to the contrary, if peace operations become involved in an armed conflict without the restrictions that apply to other parties to the conflict, this would in itself have a negative impact on subsequent peace-building efforts.

Second, one of the ambitions of IHL is to create a scenario where the conduct of hostilities is considered by everyone involved to be just and fair. If wars are fought with full respect for IHL, post-conflict reconciliation and peacebuilding could potentially be easier, whereas unfair fighting creates an atmosphere where subsequent reconciliation becomes much more difficult. Respect for IHL is, therefore, an important prerequisite for operational effectiveness and success in peace operations.

Turning to human rights law, some of the same concerns arise. If peace forces are seen as violators of human rights law, operational success and effectiveness will be jeopardized. But the applicability of human rights law during peace operations is a more complex question than that of the applicability of IHL, because of the legal requirements that must be satisfied in order for human rights obligations to apply as a matter of law.

[85] Geneva Conventions 12 August 1949, entered into force 21 October 1950.

Human rights law is, in principle, applicable at all times, in peacetime as well as during armed conflict. However, human rights law was primarily developed to regulate the exercise of a state's powers towards individuals within its own territory, and a number of complex legal issues arise when one inquires whether human rights law applies to the conduct of personnel in international peace operations. First, military personnel in international peace operations always operate outside the territories of their sending states. This gives rise to the question of the so-called extra-territorial applicability of human rights treaties, and of the relationship between the obligations of a Troop Contributing State and the operation's host state. Second, the personnel retain their position as members of the armed forces of their sending state, but they may be placed at the disposal of another entity, such as an international organization, for example the UN. This brings into play the question of the relationship between human rights obligations of Troop Contributing States and those of the organization. Third, personnel from different States will cooperate in the exercise of their mandate, and the sending states may be bound by different human rights obligations. This gives rise to questions relating to legal interoperability. Fourth, the personnel will operate under a mandate from the Security Council, and this mandate may be (or may be perceived to be) in conflict with human rights treaty obligations. Fifth, the personnel will operate in a difficult environment, where the local infrastructure may be damaged or have broken down, and where the unstable security situation may limit the potential of the personnel to comply with human rights standards.

On the other hand, several developments in the last few decades have contributed to an increased relevance of human rights norms in peace operations. In reality, the issue has only recently (i.e. post-Cold War) emerged as a relevant issue in peace operations. First, the 1990s brought with it a number of tragic events, such as in Rwanda and Bosnia-Herzegovina, where the UN demonstrated its inability to prevent or react to genocides and massive human rights violations. The UN's involvement in these conflicts led to extensive soul-searching within the UN, and one factor in the evaluation of the organization's response to international crises concerns the responsibility and capability of the organization to protect and to promote human rights in the area of deployment of UN personnel. As a result, the Council became more active and assertive with regard to the protection of human rights.[86] Second, in 1997 the UN Secretary-General called for a strengthening of human rights in the UN system, and for the integration of a human rights dimension across the full spectrum of the UN's activities. This is commonly referred to as the 'mainstreaming' of human rights, and this has an impact on the perception of the role and responsibilities of peace operations.[87] Third, on a more abstract level, there is today a clear tendency of 'juridification' of international relations,

[86] Katarina Månsson, 'UN Peace Operations and Security Council Resolutions: A Tool for Measuring the Status of International Human Rights Law?', *Netherlands Quarterly of Human Rights* 26 (2008), 79–107.

[87] Larsen, *Human Rights Treaty Obligations of Peacekeepers*, 48–9. See, generally, http://www.undg.org/index.cfm?P=1452 (accessed 22 June 2014).

by considering ever greater parts of international relations in terms of legal rules, procedures, and conflict resolution mechanisms.[88] In the context of human rights, the tendency is to focus ever more on the articulation of human rights as legal entitlements and on the possibility of pursuing human rights ambitions through legal mechanisms. Earlier, one spoke exclusively about the human rights *functions* of peace operations, but now it becomes ever more common to speak about human rights *obligations*. Fourth, there is a tendency towards stronger regional efforts in peace operations, which has given rise to increased attention on the possible role of regional human rights instruments in peace operations. However, fifth, there has also been a dramatic increase in the number of allegations of human rights violations committed by UN personnel. The realization that UN personnel are not only protectors of human rights, but also potential violators of human rights, results in heightened attention on the human rights norms that govern their conduct.

But the position that international military personnel should have obligations to respect (or even to protect and promote) human rights, is contested. This can be illustrated by one well-known dilemma: is the primary purpose of a peace operation to secure peace or to promote human rights? These two good intentions are not always compatible. To quote an anonymous commentator: 'What should one do if the quest for justice and retribution hampers the search for peace, thereby prolonging a war and increasing the number of deaths, the amount of destruction, and the extent of human suffering?'[89] A rapid establishment of peace may be the most effective means to improve the human rights situation, and it may potentially be counter-productive if too much is demanded in terms of compliance with human rights law. One relevant question concerns the possibility of security detention, that is, the possibility of peace operations to capture and detain individuals who represent a security threat. Preventive detention is generally prohibited by Article 5 of the European Convention on Human Rights but such security detention may be an important tool for peace operations to pursue mandates relating to the establishment of a secure and stable situation.

One element in this consideration is whether an authorization in a UN Security Council resolution would prevail over a conflicting obligation in a human rights treaty.[90] The legal basis for such a question is Article 103 of the UN Charter, which states that in case of conflict, the obligations under the Charter shall prevail over obligations under 'any other international agreement'. It is arguable that this provision also applies to obligations in Security Council resolutions, and that it also applies to authorizations and not merely to obligations. Under this interpretation, the Security Council would be able to authorize conduct that violates human rights treaties. Some limitations apply, however.

[88] As an introduction, see Kenneth W. Abbott, Robert O. Keohane, Andrew Moravcsik, Anne-Marie Slaughter, and Duncan Snidal, 'The Concept of Legalization', *International Organization* 54 (2000), 401–19.

[89] Anonymous, 'Human Rights in Peace Negotiations', *Human Rights Quarterly* 18 (1996), 249–58 at 250.

[90] Larsen, *Human Rights Treaty Obligations of Peacekeepers*, ch. 8.

First, the Council may not authorize conduct that violates peremptory norms of international law, nor may it authorize conduct that violates the purposes and principles of the UN Charter. Second, there is a presumption of human rights compliance, meaning that the Council will have to express itself unequivocally if it intends to authorize conduct that violates a Troop Contributing State's human rights obligations. In the previously mentioned *Behrami/Saramati* case, the European Court of Human Rights was reluctant to interfere with the Security Council's competence. The possible conflict of norms here concerned the authorization from the Security Council to detain individuals who represented a security threat, which is conduct that is prohibited under the ECHR. The Court expressed that 'the Convention cannot be interpreted in a manner which would subject the acts and omissions of Contracting Parties which are covered by UNSC Resolutions ... to the scrutiny of the Court'.[91] In the *Al-Jedda* case, however, which also concerned preventive detention of an individual who represented a security threat, by UK forces in Iraq, the Court was more assertive, and considered that it is only when a Security Council resolution contains an *obligation* to act in a manner which is inconsistent with a human rights treaty obligation, that a conflict of norms arises.[92] Since there was no such 'obligation' in that particular case, but merely an authorization, the Court applied the ECHR unqualified. The reality of the matter is, however, that the Security Council will never say that it requires a particular conduct, and in practice the question is what applies when the Council authorizes states to use 'all necessary means' to achieve a particular goal.

Let us also outline a third legal regime of relevance to the promotion of a positive peace by peace operations. In the case of territorial administration, the UN may exercise an authority which is similar to the de facto authority of a belligerent occupying force. This observation gives rise to a controversial question, namely whether an analogy can be drawn between UN transitional administrations and belligerent occupation with the result that the law of belligerent occupation is applicable.[93] If this body of law is applicable, the occupying force is under an obligation, *inter alia*, to respect the laws in force, and this may have an impact on the possibility of a peace operation to pursue the local reforms that its mandate requires. The legal basis for the dilemma is the 1907 Hague Regulations, which provide that an 'occupation' exists if a territory 'is actually placed under the authority of the hostile army',[94] and there is an underlying assumption here that the occupation is preceded by an invasion by a military (hostile) army. Article 2.2 GC IV took steps away from this assumption by stating that the Convention applies to all cases of occupation 'even if the said

[91] *Behrami/Saramati*, para. 149.

[92] *Al-Jedda* v. *the United Kingdom*, App. 27021/08 (ECtHR, 7 July 2011), paras. 100–10.

[93] For a thorough analysis of the doctrinal discussion, see Siobhán Wills, *Protecting Civilians: The Obligations of Peacekeepers* (Oxford: Oxford University Press, 2009), ch. 4, in particular pp. 212–39.

[94] Hague Convention IV respecting the Laws and Customs of War on Land and its annex: Regulations concerning the Laws and Customs of War on Land, 18 October 1907 (entered into force 26 January 1910), Art. 42 of the Annex.

occupation meets with no armed resistance'. This has led to a broad definition of occupation in the literature, for example by Benvenisti who defined occupation as 'the effective control of a power (be it one or more states or an international organization, *such as the United Nations*) over a territory to which that power has no sovereign title, without the volition of the sovereign of that territory'.[95] The prevailing view appears to be that while UN *enforcement* (combat) operations may result in a genuine belligerent occupation, this is not the case for UN transitional administrations where both the legal basis and the factual circumstances are fundamentally different from that of an occupation. Dinstein is a proponent of this view.[96] The analogy between territorial administrations and occupations has also been criticized for example by Shraga, who acknowledges that the UN 'have, on occasion, exercised effective control in their areas of operation in circumstances ostensibly analogous to those of military occupation', while nevertheless arguing that 'the laws of occupation have never been applicable to any of these operations *de jure* or by analogy'.[97] On the other hand, Fox uses the term 'humanitarian occupation' instead of territorial administration with the intention to capture more precisely (1) that the missions have a humanitarian purpose, by aiming to end human rights abuses, reform governmental institutions, and restore peaceful coexistence between groups, and (2) that the authority is similar to the de facto authority of a belligerent occupier. He argues that 'occupation law is thus an appropriate framework to analyze the missions'.[98] The issue remains unsettled, but it appears that territorial administration can be conducted without adherence to the limitations that follow from the law of belligerent occupation.

6. Conclusions

Little can be offered here by way of conclusions. It is clear that international law permits the creation of peace operations, but it does little either to actively promote such creation or to set out its framework. It is further apparent that peace operations in general pursue a concept of 'liberal' or 'positive' peace, which is concretized in each specific operation, but it is more contentious whether this is what peace operations *should* do, or how one decides whether the operation has been effective or successful in the pursuit of its goal. Finally, international

[95] Eyal Benvenisti, *The International Law of Occupation* (Princeton: Princeton University Press, 1993), 4 (emphasis added).

[96] Yoram Dinstein, *The International Law of Belligerent Occupation* (Cambridge: Cambridge University Press, 2009), 37. Similar views are expressed by Christopher Greenwood, 'International Humanitarian Law and United Nations Military Operations', *Yearbook of International Humanitarian Law* 1 (1998), 3–34 at 28.

[97] Daphna Shraga, 'Military Occupation and UN Transitional Administrations—the Analogy and Its Limitations', in *Promoting Justice, Human Rights and Conflict Resolution through International Law—Liber Amicorum Lucius Caflisch*, M. G. Kohen (ed.) (Leiden: Brill, 2007), 479–98, 481, 498.

[98] Gregory H. Fox, *Humanitarian Occupation* (Cambridge: Cambridge University Press, 2008), 3–4, 271.

law pertaining to the conduct of personnel in peace operations is not developed for that particular context. Rather than promoting effective mission accomplishment, international law tends to limit the means which are at the disposal of the personnel to pursue their mandate. In short, the promotion of 'peace' in international peace operations is in general not actively facilitated by international law, and much may be gained if international courts and tribunals and other actors continue their search for a coherent body of international law applicable to peace operations.

16

It's About Trust

Transitional Justice and Accountability in the Search for Peace

Jemima García-Godos

1. Introduction

Processes of transition from armed conflict and authoritarian rule present a number of challenges for the societies and states involved, not only concerning the present and the future of their nations, but also their troubled past. The various ways such societies deal with their past are commonly referred to as 'transitional justice', that is, the attempt to see justice done in relation to past sufferings and harm.[1] The quest for accountability, for justice to be done, can be fulfilled in various ways. Retribution through the prosecution and punishment of perpetrators is the realm of retributive justice. Learning the truth about what happened is the aim of truth-seeking processes. Also institutional reforms can be promoted to pursue accountability, in order to avoid repeating the mistakes of the past, a field that has been referred to as 'prospective justice'. The issue of reparations in transitional justice emerges as a way of addressing the needs and demands for redress of those who suffered some form of harm in a previous regime, that is, the victims. This is what is commonly referred to as 'restorative justice',[2] a dimension of transitional justice that focuses on the victims of human rights violations, acknowledging their suffering and needs, and attempting to restore the damage done.

The democratic transitions in Latin America, the end of the Cold War, and later the atrocities of the Balkan wars, Rwanda, and Sierra Leone, formed the background for the increased attention given to issues of transitional justice in the 1990s—from human rights organizations, public institutions, and academics alike. Faced with the challenge of how to combine democracy with justice in a

[1] Naomi Roht-Arriaza and Javier Mariezcurrena (eds.), *Transitional Justice in the Twenty-First Century: Beyond Truth versus Justice* (Cambridge: Cambridge University Press, 2006); Siri Gloppen, 'Roads to Reconciliation: A Conceptual Framework', in *Roads to Reconciliation*, Elin Skaar, Siri Gloppen, and Astri Suhrke (eds.) (Lanham, Md.: Lexington, 2005), 17–50.

[2] Martha Minow, *Between Vengeance and Forgiveness: Facing History after Genocide and Mass Violence* (Boston: Beacon, 1998).

context of transition,[3] the growing body of literature on transitional justice paid most attention to mechanisms such as truth-finding missions and where possible, criminal prosecutions of perpetrators.[4] Later on, more attention has been given to victim reparations and institutional reforms that might enhance the rule of law in democratizing societies.[5]

The international trend promoting accountability for past crimes in post-conflict societies and post-authoritarian regimes is present in many different arenas and at many levels, involving a variety of actors, from United Nations bodies to human rights organizations and academics.[6] The establishment of the ICC and the exercise of universal jurisdiction, the ad hoc international criminal tribunals for the former Yugoslavia and Rwanda and hybrid courts such as those in Sierra Leone and East Timor, as well as the legacy of the Pinochet case,[7] have posed a challenge to long-term impunity. It is now widely accepted that 'accountability must be recognized as an indispensable component of peace and eventual reconciliation'.[8]

Thus the point of departure for this chapter is that accountability plays an important role in the pursuit of long-term peace because it contributes to rebuild relations of trust in post-conflict societies. This normative argument will be based on a discussion of victims' rights because a context of accountability provides the best setting for the protection of these rights as well as the victimizers' right to

[3] Neil Kritz (ed.), *Transitional Justice: How Emerging Democracies Reckon with Former Regimes* (Washington, DC: United States Institute for Peace, 1995).

[4] See *inter alia*, Alexandra Barahona de Brito, Carmen González-Enríquez, and Paloma Aguilar (eds.), *The Politics of Memory: Transitional Justice in Democratizing Societies* (Oxford: Oxford University Press, 2001); Neil J. Kritz (ed.), *Transitional Justice: How Emerging Democracies Reckon With Former Regimes*, ii. *Country Studies* (Washington, DC: United States Institute of Peace, 1995); Minow, *Between Vengeance and Forgiveness*; Naomi Roht-Arriaza (ed.), *Impunity and Human Rights in International Law and Practice* (New York: Oxford University Press, 1995); Robert I. Rotberg and Dennis Thompson (eds.), *Truth v. Justice: The Morality of Truth Commissions* (Oxford: Oxford University Press, 2000); Priscilla Hayner, *Unspeakable Truths: Confronting State Terror and Atrocity* (New York: Routledge, 2001).

[5] See Naomi Roht-Arriaza, 'Reparations in the Aftermath of Repression and Mass Violence', in *My Neighbor, My Enemy: Justice and Community in the Aftermath of Mass Atrocity*, Eric Stover and Harvey M. Weinstein (eds.) (Cambridge: Cambridge University Press, 2004); Koen De Feyter, Stephan Parmentier, Marc Bossuyt, and Paul Lemmens (eds.), *Out of the Ashes: Reparation for Victims of Gross and Systematic Human Rights Violations* (Antwerp: Intersentia, 2005); Pablo De Greiff (ed.), *The Handbook of Reparations* (Oxford: Oxford University Press, 2006); Jon Elster, *Closing the Books: Transitional Justice in Historical Perspective* (Cambridge: Cambridge University Press, 2004); Jon Miller and Rahul Kumar (eds.), *Reparations: Interdisciplinary Inquiries* (Oxford: Oxford University Press, 2007); Ruth Rubio-Marín, *What Happened to the Women?: Gender and Reparations for Human Rights Violations* (New York: Social Science Research Council, 2006); John Torpey, *Making Whole What Has Been Smashed: On Reparations Politics* (Cambridge, Mass.: Harvard University Press, 2006); Max Du Plessis and Stephen Peté (eds.), *Repairing the Past? International Perspective on Reparations for Gross Human Rights Abuses* (Antwerp: Intersentia, 2007).

[6] Naomi Roht-Arriaza, 'The New Landscape of Transitional Justice', in *Transitional Justice in the Twenty-First Century: Beyond Truth Versus Justice*, Naomi Roht-Arriaza and Javier Mariezcurrena (eds.) (Cambridge: Cambridge University Press, 2006), 1–16.

[7] Naomi Roht-Arriaza, *The Pinochet Effect: Transnational Justice in the Age of Human Rights* (Philadelphia: University of Pennsylvania Press, 2005).

[8] M. Cherif Bassiouni, 'Accountability for Violations of International Humanitarian Law and Other Serious Violations of Human Rights', in *Post-Conflict Justice*, M. Cherif Bassiouni (ed.) (Ardsley: Transnational, 2002), 3–54.

due process. Furthermore, it is in a context of accountability that the reincorporation of ex-combatants into society can proceed without neglecting victims' rights. The chapter puts forward a simple but vital argument: to acknowledge the rights of victims, victimizers, and ex-combatants is essential for long-term peace. The chapter is structured thus: Section 2 provides a brief account of the justice versus peace debate, which was the context in which contemporary transitional justice emerged. Section 3 takes on developments in the field of victims' rights, a field that is now part and parcel of transitional justice practice. Section 4 provides a brief account of each of the three main mechanisms of transitional justice (TJ) applied (or at least claimed for) in most transitional societies: truth commissions, prosecutions, and victim reparations.[9] Examples from specific TJ experiences in Latin America will be used throughout the chapter.[10] In the Conclusions, the chapter wraps up the discussion with an argument for TJ as a constitutive element of positive peace.

2. The Justice and Peace Debate

As a field of intellectual inquiry and practice, transitional justice emerged from a very specific historical context: the processes of transition to democracy from authoritarian rule and armed conflict experienced in Latin America in the 1980s, and later in Eastern Europe in the 1980s and early 1990s with the end of the Cold War. The challenges were many, yet a common preoccupation rose among politicians and observers: How to combine peace and democracy with justice? An immediate problem in the transitions was 'how new leaderships in former totalitarian countries would treat previous governments. [. . .] democracy would not

[9] Other mechanisms such as lustration or vetting, institutional reform, and amnesties are not addressed in this chapter for reasons of space. For literature on lustration, see among others Roman Boed, 'An Evaluation of the Legality and Efficacy of Lustration as a Tool of Transitional Justice', in Bassiouni (ed.), *Post-Conflict Justice*, 345–82; Alexander Mayer-Rieckh and Pablo de Greiff (eds.), *Justice as Prevention: Vetting Public Employees in Transitional Societies* (New York: Social Science Research Council, 2007). For literature on amnesties, see in particular Louise Mallinder, *Amnesty, Human Rights and Political Transitions: Bridging the Peace and Justice Divide* (Oxford: Hart, 2008). The issue of institutional reform as part of a transitional justice agenda overlaps greatly with literature on democratization and rule of law, which is vast. Also at the United Nations we can see this interconnection. UN documents on rule of law and transitional justice can be found at http://www2.ohchr.org/english/issues/rule_of_law/transjustice.htm (accessed 12 Nov 2014).

[10] There are two reasons for this choice. The Latin American region can be considered the birthplace of contemporary transitional justice, and there are several ongoing cases of transitional justice implementation. A second reason is my professional area expertise. For literature on transitional justice in other regions, see *inter alia*: John Borneman, *Settling Accounts. Violence, Justice and Accountability in Postsocialist Europe* (Princeton, NJ: Princeton University Press, 2007); Beátrice Pouligny, Simon Chesterman and Albrecht Schnabel (eds.), *After Mass Crime: Rebuilding States and Communities* (Tokyo: United Nations University, 2007); Chandra Lekha Sriram and Sure Pillay (eds.), *Peace versus Justice? The Dilemmas of Transitional Justice in Africa* (Scottsville: University of KwaZulu Natal Press, 2009), and Rosalind Shaw and Lars Waldorf with Pierre Bazan (eds.), *Localizing Transitional Justice. Interventions and Priorities after Mass Violence* (Stanford, Calif.: Stanford University Press, 2010).

be safe over time without a thorough and careful application of normative rules to ensure that *justice* was achieved upon a foundation of the rule of law.'[11] Right from the outset, it was acknowledged that some level of accountability (Kritz's *justice*) for past wrongs would have to be in place in order to secure the stability of emergent democracies. The rule of law was considered the way forward, instrumental, in a way, to secure the consolidation of democratic rule. It is thus clear that it was the political processes and agendas in transitional societies that were at the base of any consideration regarding justice and accountability for past wrongs. In what Bassiouni calls the 'realpolitik' approach to post-conflict societies, justice was often bartered away to secure peace settlements.[12] Instead of accountability (in any form), impunity prevailed for the sake of peace and 'reconciliation'. Such was the case in several Latin American countries, where amnesty laws prevailed until fairly recent. In other cases, former rulers were kept in positions of power to ensure that the past would be left in peace. In Chile for example, General Augusto Pinochet appointed himself as Congress representative for life, thus benefiting from congressional immunity.[13] Taking into consideration the political balance of forces, justice and accountability were considered by many as the price to pay for peace and democracy.

It is in this context that the so-called justice versus peace dilemma emerged in the 1990s. Accordingly, the political needs of peace processes would be impeded by demands for accountability for past human rights violations, such that at transitional periods, in countries emerging from authoritarian regimes or conflict, a choice would have to be made between pursuing peace *or* seeking justice.[14] Demands for accountability were presumed to constitute obstacles to peace.[15] In the field of peace negotiations emphasis was often placed on incentives to combatants such as power-sharing,[16] while accountability for past crimes was kept off the agenda[17] or was to be resolved at a later stage. It is fair to say then that a

[11] Charles D. Smith, 'Introduction', in *Transitional Justice*, Kritz (ed.), pp. xv–xvii.

[12] Bassiouni, Accountability for Violations of International Humanitarian Law'.

[13] Roth-Arriaza, *The Pinochet Effect*; Cath Collins, *Post-transitional Justice: Human Rights Trials in Chile and El Salvador* (University Park: Pennsylvania State University Press, 2010).

[14] For an excellent discussion on the peace versus justice debate, see Chandra Lekha Sriram, *Confronting Past Human Rights Violations: Justice vs Peace in Times of Transition* (London: Frank Cass, 2004). See also Wendy Lambourne, 'Transitional Justice and Peacebuilding after Mass Violence', in *International Journal of Transitional Justice* 3 (2009), 28–48; Chandra Lekha Sriram, 'Transitional Justice and the Liberal Peace', in *New Perspectives on Liberal Peacebuilding*, Edward Newman, Roland Paris, and Oliver P. Richmond (eds.) (Tokyo: United Nations University Press, 2009), 112–30; Gerhard Thallinger, 'The UN Peacebuilding Commission and Transitional Justice', *German Law Journal* 8 (2007), 681–710.

[15] Michelle Parlevliet, 'Bridging the Divide. Exploring the Relationship between Human Rights and Conflict Management', *Track Two* 11 (2002), http://ccrweb.ccr.uct.ac.za/archive/two/11_1/bridging.html (accessed 23 June 2014); Ellen Lutz, Eileen F. Babbitt, and Hurst Hannum, 'Human Rights and Conflict Resolution from the Practitioners' Perspectives', *Fletcher Forum of World Affairs* 27 (2003), http://fletcher.tufts.edu/chrcr/pdf/Lutz4.pdf (accessed 23 June 2014).

[16] Chandra Sriram, *Peace as Governance: Power-Sharing, Armed Groups and Contemporary Peace Negotiations* (London: Palgrave Macmillan, 2008).

[17] Paul R. Williams, 'The Role of Justice in Peace Negotiations', in *Post-Conflict Justice*, Bassiouni (ed.), 115–33.

narrow understanding of peace as peace agreements focuses, almost by necessity, on the negotiating parties and their interests. Those not included in the negotiations, particularly victims, have no guarantee that their interests will be voiced and heard. Even if negotiations were to include accountability issues, the participation of perpetrators of gross human rights violations (or their representatives) would bias the process in the direction of potential privileges to perpetrators. However, the apparent dilemma between justice and peace is based on a narrow understanding of peace as a peace agreement or political settlement coming out of negotiations. Seeking accountability for past crimes could certainly overshadow incentives for parties struggling to arrive to an agreement. However, if we understand *peace as an ongoing process of political and social transformation based on the rule of law*, justice and accountability—in all its forms—are a premise for peace. In terms of this book, accountability is a major premise for positive peace. In other words, transitional justice is 'part of an effective transition to positive peace'.[18]

Against the background of the justice versus peace debate, towards the end of the 1990s and early 2000s practice started to show that while the justice versus peace dilemma was still present, an increasing number of peace processes included measures of TJ, if not always criminal accountability.[19] An international trend promoting accountability for past crimes became more visible in the field of political settlements.[20] Today, we are witnessing different ways in which TJ mechanisms contribute to peace implementation. The issue is no longer *whether* accountability is possible in processes of peacemaking and peace-building, but rather *how* and under what conditions accountability measures, that is, transitional justice, can support positive peace.[21] This will be discussed in the remainder of this chapter.

3. Victim's Rights: Are They Important for Positive Peace?

Over the past decades, developments in TJ have shown that justice and accountability are not only about criminal accountability, retribution, and perpetrators,

[18] Pamina Firchow and Roger MacGinty, 'Reparations and Peacebuilding: Issues and Controversies', *Human Rights Review* 14 (2013), 231–9 at 238.

[19] To give one example, the Peace Accords finalized in Guatemala in 1996 included the establishment of a truth commission, which was created shortly afterwards. The Commission for Historical Clarification (CEH) delivered its Final Report in 1999. For thorough discussions on the range of TJ measures that are often taken in the context of peace processes see Christine Bell, *Peace Agreements and Human Rights* (Oxford: Oxford University Press, 2000); Sriram, *Confronting Past Human Rights Violations*; and Leslie Vinjamuri and Aaron P. Boesenecker, *Accountability and Peace Agreements: Mapping Trends from 1980–2006* (Geneva: Centre for Humanitarian Dialogue, 2007).

[20] Luc Huyse, 'Amnesty, Truth or Prosecution', in *Peace-building: A Field Guide*, Luc Reychler and Thania Paffenholz (eds.) (Boulder, Colo.: Lynne Rienner, 2001); 'The Rule of Law and Transitional Justice in Conflict and Post-conflict Societies', Report of the Secretary-General, 23 August 2004, UN Doc. S/2004/616.

[21] Chandra Lekha Sriram, Jemima García-Godos, Johanna Herman, and Olga Martin-Ortega (eds.), *Transitional Justice and Peacebuilding on the Ground: Victims and Excombatants* (London: Routledge, 2013).

but also about truth, reparation, and victims. However, in spite of decades of applicable human rights law, the promotion of victims' rights is a relatively recent development.

Victims' rights have emerged as a body of norms within the fields of international human rights law, international criminal law, and international humanitarian law, determining the treatment and entitlements that victims of human rights violations ought to have with regard to remedy and reparations.[22] Two parallel processes or 'tracks' have directly contributed to this development and will be discussed in more detail: (i) the UN's work on the Basic Principles and Guidelines on the Right to Remedy and Reparation;[23] and (ii) the International Criminal Court's (ICC) focus on victims.[24]

The UN General Assembly approved the Basic Principles on the Right to Remedy and Reparation in December 2005, after about 16 years in the drafting process. According to Shelton, the principles refer to three categories of obligations and rights.[25] First, general obligations emanating from international human rights law (IHRL) and international humanitarian law (IHL) to ensure and protect victims' right to access to justice and to provide substantive remedies. Second, the obligation to investigate and prosecute violations to IHL and IHRL that constitute international crimes. And third, rights of access to justice, the right to substantive reparations, and the right to access to information (read 'truth') in the event of gross violations of IHL and IHRL. Common to all three categories is the right to access to justice, while the right to substantive remedies is common to the first and third categories.

In its Preamble, the Basic Principles document identifies not only the legal sources from which the principles derive, but also announces the international community's adoption of a 'victim-oriented perspective' based on human solidarity and respect for the international legal principles of accountability, justice, and the rule of law. On these legal and moral grounds, the Basic Principles bring together existing standards of IHRL and IHL regarding victims of human rights violations and violations of IHL to establish a more comprehensive and detailed set of rights to which all victims are entitled. The Basic Principles establish what is to be understood as victims' rights: access to justice, reparations, and truth. Each element is addressed by the Basic Principles, although the section on reparations is

[22] A broader discussion of victims' rights can be found in the García-Godos and Sriram, 'Introduction', in Sriram et al. (eds.), *Transitional Justice and Peacebuilding on the Ground* (London: Routledge, 2013).

[23] UNGA Res. 147 (16 December 2005) UN Doc. A/RES/60/147. (Henceforth *Basic Principles*.)

[24] For a more detailed discussion of each of these tracks, see Jemima García-Godos, 'Victim Reparations in Transitional Justice: What is at Stake and Why', *Nordic Journal of Human Rights* 26 (2008), 111–30. Developments in international law supporting this trend include also jurisprudence and court sentences, such as the influential *Velásquez-Rodríguez* v. *Honduras* decision by the Inter-American Court of Human Rights in 1988, which identified a 'right to truth'. See http://www.corteidh.or.cr/docs/casos/articulos/seriec_04_ing.pdf (accessed 12 Nov 2014).

[25] Dinah Shelton, 'The United Nations Draft Principles on Reparations for Human Rights Violations: Context and Content', in *Out of the Ashes: Reparations for Victims of Gross Human Rights Violations*, Koen De Feyter, Stephan Parmentier, Marc Bossuyt, and Paul Lemmens (eds.) (Antwerp: Intersentia, 2005), 20.

developed in most detail. They list specific forms of reparation, including compensation, restitution, rehabilitation, satisfaction, and guarantee of non-repetition. The latter two also include elements referring to the right to truth and access to information, as well as institutional and legal reform to guarantee non-repetition of abuses. The Principles establish that reparations to victims must be adequate, effective, and comprehensive.

The Basic Principles make explicit reference to the ICC Statute and the ICC's requirements concerning the treatment of victims of international core crimes, specifically the establishment of various forms of reparation, the creation in the ICC Statute of a trust fund for victims, and the protection and participation of victims during court proceedings. Indeed, the ICC's Statute and Rules of Procedure and Evidence both establish a series of rights for victims of crimes that fall under its jurisdiction.[26] One innovation in the Statute is the provision for the participation of victims during court proceedings and the chance to present their views and observations before the court. Regarding reparations, the court has the power to order individuals to pay reparation to other individuals, and it has the option of granting individual or collective reparation. Reparations may include restitution, indemnification, and rehabilitation, and the court may order these to be paid through the Victims' Fund. The ICC has two special units to ensure victims' participation. While the Victims' Participation and Reparation Section provides public information on reparation proceedings and applications, the Office of Public Counsel for Victims provides legal support and assistance to the legal representatives of victims and to victims.

The most recent development regarding victims' rights is the approval of General Comment No. 3 (2012) on the Implementation of Article 14 of the Convention against Torture and Other Cruel, Inhuman or Degrading Treatment or Punishment. This general comment explains and clarifies to states parties the content and scope of the obligations under CAT Article 14, by which states parties have both a procedural and a substantive obligation to provide redress to victims of torture and ill-treatment.[27]

What do victims' rights have to do with positive peace? First, addressing victims' needs is central to the promotion of peace because it supports ongoing processes of political transformation by enhancing the legitimacy of transitions in the eyes of victims. Various forms of remedy and reparations demonstrate to victims that the state and society at large recognize and address their needs, signalling social inclusion in a society where their rights have previously been violated.[28] Secondly, victims' rights have become a legitimate tool applied by victim organizations and human rights advocates to frame claims to often unwilling governments. The anchoring of contemporary transitional justice on victims' rights as it

[26] García-Godos, 'Victim Reparations in Transitional Justice', 116.

[27] General Comment No. 3 of the Committee Against Torture, 19 November 2012, UN Doc. CAT/C/GC/3.

[28] Pablo De Greiff, 'Justice and Reparations', in *The Handbook of Reparations*, Pablo De Greiff (ed.) (Oxford: Oxford University Press, 2006), 451–77.

has happened over the past decade—the rights to truth, justice, and reparations—opens up a new way to talk about justice and peace: transitional justice and victims' rights present the opportunity to discuss peace on a basis where impunity is no longer an option. On this basis, the next section focuses on the three most common mechanisms of transitional justice addressing victims' rights to truth, justice, and reparations.

4. Addressing Victims' Rights: Mechanisms of Transitional Justice and Their Contribution to Peace

4.1. The right to truth: does peace need truth?

In transitional justice, the right to truth refers to having access to information and a truthful account of past human rights violations. Apparently straightforward, this right has been the source of much expectation and fear on the part of victims, and repression on the part of authoritarian regimes. Although commonly associated to the work of truth commissions setting the record straight for entire societies, the right to truth encompasses also the individual and groups of people, for example, by having the right to know the whereabouts or the fate of a 'disappeared' relative or the events affecting a given community, such as a massacre or forced displacement. The act of truth-telling, setting the record straight, can have many sources, from comprehensive investigation and reporting by truth commissions, to local, collective initiatives of memory construction and recollection, such as 'Memoriales de Agravio' led by families of victims in Guatemala and local histories of the armed conflict in Peru.[29] Truth can also be obtained in judicial[30] or semi-judicial proceedings, as in Colombia's Justice and Peace proceedings.[31] Commissions of inquiry set up by national legislatives or governments can also produce truth. The discussion here focuses on official truth commissions, that is, commissions officially sanctioned and authorized by national states to investigate patterns of abuse committed in the past over a period of time; they are usually independent bodies limited in time to complete a given mandate.[32]

Truth commissions across the world have had mixed experiences, depending on their mandate and the context in which they operate.[33] Some commissions

[29] For Peru, see Carola Falconí, Edilberto Jiménez, and Giovanni Alfaro, *Lucanamarca: Memorias de nuestro pueblo* (Lima: COMISEDH, 2007). Other locally constructed histories of the armed conflict include Ayahuanco, Tambo, and Huancavelica.

[30] For a critical view on history construction by courts, see Richard Ashby Wilson, *Writing History in International Criminal Trials* (Cambridge: Cambridge University Press, 2011).

[31] Jemima García-Godos and Knut Andreas O. Lid, 'Transitional Justice and Victims' Rights before the End of a Conflict: The Unusual Case of Colombia', *Journal of Latin American Studies* 42 (2010), 487–516.

[32] These features are based on Priscilla Hayner's definition of truth commissions. See Priscilla B. Hayner, *Unspeakable Truths: Transitional Justice and the Challenge of Truth Commissions* (New York: Routledge, 2001).

[33] Hayner, *Unspeakable Truths*; Eric Wiebelhaus-Brahm, *Truth Commissions and Transitional Societies: The Impact on Human Rights and Democracy* (London: Routledge, 2010).

concentrate on writing an account of past events, some focus on reconciliation, while others can investigate and lead to trials of perpetrators of human rights violations. The power of a truth commission lies in particular in its potential capacity for producing an official account of events, an official history of a particular period and society.[34] Furthermore, if a truth commission has a mandate to address the needs of victims and those who suffered as a result of armed conflict and authoritarian rule, the categories employed to define victims and perpetrators have direct and practical consequences. The conceptual framework and terminology employed to construct such official versions of the events have the potential to define real people as victims or perpetrators, heroes or villains. In other words, they determine who deserves praise and who deserves condemnation, who deserves reparation and who deserves prison, who enters the history books and who remains forgotten.[35]

While truth commissions became internationally known through the South African experience,[36] this TJ mechanism had its origins in the Latin American experience. While not the first to be established, the Argentinian truth commission (*Comisión Nacional para la Desaparición de Personas*—CONADEP) was the first to produce a final report (*Nunca Más*, published in 1985) establishing a systematic pattern of human rights violations during the period of military dictatorship. Since then, 11 official and 5 alternative truth commissions have taken place in 13 different Latin American countries.[37]

There are many aspects that could be discussed concerning truth commissions, such as their mandates, composition, operational strategies and resources available, the political context in which they operate, and more. Yet one aspect that bears particular importance with regard to long-term peace is what I call the issue of ownership over the findings of a truth commission report. While it can expected that truth commission reports will be received with criticism and suspicion from sectors affiliated to former oppressive regimes, broader societal support of their findings is too often taken for granted. What might be obvious conclusions for human rights groups and advocates, as well as victim organizations, is not necessarily so for other sectors of society. Mobilization in support of the findings and recommendations of truth commission reports needs to be broad and persistent enough in order for recommendations to enter the political agenda. Creating a constituency that 'owns' the findings of truth commissions and has enough political leverage to influence political processes remains a challenge in various

[34] Richard A. Wilson and Jon P. Mitchell, 'Introduction: The Social Life of Rights', in *Human Rights in Global Perspective: Anthropological Studies of Rights, Claims and Entitlements*, Richard A. Wilson and Jon P. Mitchell (eds.) (London: Routledge, 2003).

[35] For an example of how truth-telling and history construction interconnect, see Jemima García-Godos, 'Victim Reparations in the Peruvian Truth Commission and the Challenge of Historical Interpretation', *International Journal of Transitional Justice* 2 (2008), 63–82.

[36] Much has been written on the South African Truth and Reconciliation Commission. For an excellent and critical account, see Richard Ashby Wilson, *The Politics of Truth and Reconciliation in South Africa: Legitimizing the Post-Apartheid State* (Cambridge: Cambridge University Press, 2001).

[37] These countries are Bolivia, Argentina, Uruguay, Chile, El Salvador, Haiti, Brazil, Ecuador, Guatemala, Peru, Paraguay, Honduras, Mexico.

post-truth commission settings. In the absence of such a broad constituency, truth commission reports, including their recommendations, will be challenged, giving scope for struggles over the memory of a violent past. Only with broad societal and political backing, can the truths revealed by the reports become the official histories of transitional societies. The most positive experience can be observed in Argentina, where the Nunca Más report became a national bestseller, supporting the continuous work of human rights organizations to reach the high levels of criminal accountability that can be observed in Argentina today. Experiences in Guatemala and Peru point in a different direction; these will be discussed briefly.

In Guatemala, the debate over the truth and causes, development and consequences of the internal armed conflict was stimulated first by the report 'Guatemala Never Again', developed by the Catholic Church's Interdiocesan Project for the Recovery of Historical Memory (REMHI). The second impetus to the debate was the report 'Guatemala: Memory of Silence', produced by the Commission for Historical Clarification, CEH, whose mandate comes from the Oslo agreement of June 1994. The first was presented on 24 April 1998 and the second on 25 February 1999. Despite methodological, operational, and budgetary differences as well as the availability of resources and time, both come to relatively similar conclusions about the tragedy. Briefly stated, the reports conclude that the internal armed conflict caused the death of 200,000 people, and close to 50,000 were detained or disappeared. The state was deemed responsible for over 90 per cent of human rights violations, massacres, and criminal acts against the mostly indigenous population committed during the internal armed conflict (IAC). The Commission's report highlights the existence of the genocide of people of Mayan descent; the REMHI report does not.

Today, debates over the memory of the armed conflict have intensified in Guatemala, and a process of polarization has become evident again, even acknowledged by the country's media. In May 2012, the civil association Forensic Anthropology Foundation of Guatemala (FAFG) unearthed at the military base in Cobán, Alta Verapaz, the largest mass grave found to date, with the remains of 250 people.[38] Almost simultaneously, opinion pieces and comments in letters from readers appeared in newspapers regarding military personnel pending criminal trial.[39] Several months later, in September, the recently formed Association of Relatives and Friends Acting in Solidarity with the Military ('Familia', family) held a demonstration in support of the officers and generals who face or have faced trial for crimes committed during the 1980s in the context of IAC. Some of the placards carried slogans such as 'there was no genocide in Guatemala', 'thanks to

[38] See the article by Gamazo Carolina, 'Ghosts of Coban', *El Diario*, 8 July 2012, and the comments of Juan Luis Font in the same newspaper a day later, 'The Appeared', in which he rightly concludes that the state should undertake and institutionalize the process of exhumation, pointing out that the country has stubbornly turned its back on what happened during the conflict, but that it is not possible to wait any longer.

[39] *Inter alia*, Marcela Gereda wrote an article entitled 'Efrain the Great', which opposes the opinion of a reader's letter praising the military exploits of Rios Montt 'for saving Guatemala from the guerrilla and for having done good for the country'. See *El Periódico*, 16 July 2012.

the soldiers and not the poets we can speak in public'. One of the keynote speakers, the daughter of Efrain Rios Montt, made the now renowned phrase: 'A soldier should not apologize.'[40]

The Peruvian Truth and Reconciliation Commission (Comisión de la Verdad y Reconciliación, CVR) was established in 2001 by the transition government of President Agustín Paniagua, and confirmed later by elected President Alejandro Toledo. The creation of the CVR was not by popular mass demand, but was the result of the strength gained by human rights NGOs in the negotiations surrounding the transition. NGOs were vocal concerning the demands of a few victims' organizations and strongly supported by the international community.[41]

The CVR received an ample mandate: to investigate the crimes and human rights violations committed in the context of subversion and counter-subversion; to produce an explanation of the factors leading to violence; to contribute to justice; and to make recommendations for reparations and for institutional reform. During its 26 months of operations, the CVR collected 17,000 testimonies of victims, investigated a number of cases trying to identify perpetrators, demonstrated that the armed actors had committed crimes against humanity, proposed a legal framework to try human rights violations, identified the existence of 2,600 mass graves, and made a total estimate of the number of dead and disappeared persons (70,000). It identified 24,000 full names of victims, made a list of 8,000 disappeared persons, and organized 12 public hearings with victims in different regions. On 28 August 2003 the CVR delivered its Final Report, which included an in-depth account of the events and a sound analysis of the armed conflict in Peru between 1980 and 2000, along with an elaborate set of recommendations.[42]

The conclusions of the CVR's Final Report spoke of a truth waiting to be told: 'The TRC has established that the tragedy suffered by the populations of rural Peru, the people of the Andes and the jungle, Quechua and Ashaninka Peru, the peasant, poor and poorly educated Peru, was neither felt nor taken as its own by the rest of the country; this reveals, in the CVR's view, the veiled racism and scornful attitudes persisting in Peruvian society almost two centuries after its birth as a Republic.'[43] The CVR estimated that the number of dead and disappeared reached 69,000 people—almost three times more than the official figure

[40] *El Periódico*, 10 September 2012. The following day, well-known communicator Gustavo Berganza commented on the march, remarking on the predominance of the Cold War language and prevailing impunity. *El Periódico*, 11 September 2012.

[41] The quest for truth, however, had existed from the earliest years of the conflict, when families of disappeared persons organized and established close networks with Peruvian human rights organizations in the search for their relatives. The first victim organization in Peru is probably ANFASEP (Asociación Nacional de Familiares de Secuestrados, Detenidos y Desaparecidos del Perú), founded in 1983 in Ayacucho, the area most affected by violence. Only two years later, in the midst of the armed conflict, the National Coordination Body for Human Rights (Coordinadora Nacional de Derechos Humanos, CNDDHH) was established, gathering over 50 smaller organizations of victims' families, peasant organizations, displaced peoples, religious groups, and human rights advocates. See Jemima García-Godos, 'Victims' Rights and Distributive Justice: In Search of Actors', *Human Rights Review* 14 (2013), 241–55.

[42] The 9-vol. Final Report can be found at http://cverdad.org.pe/ifinal/ (accessed 12 Nov 2014).

[43] CVR, Informe Final, Conclusiones Generales, paras. 8 and 9, p. 316.

of 25,000 that Peruvians used to refer to as the human cost of the armed conflict. How does one explain the enormous gap between the official figure and the CVR estimate? The answer is likely to be in the neglect of Peruvian state and society of citizens whose existence they simply ignored.[44]

Although the delivery of the Final Report caused some controversy and public debate,[45] the CVR's narrative was well received or at least passively accepted during the first years following its release. An aspect that received much attention in political circles, human rights organizations, and the media was the recommendations presented in the Final Report. The CVR made recommendations in the areas of justice (to create a specialized prosecutions system), on reparations (to create a comprehensive reparations plan), and on institutional reforms. These recommendations have been very insufficiently attended to. All in all, there have been some advances in the fields of justice and reparations, while institutional reforms have been completely neglected by the three Administrations that have been in place since 2003. In recent years, however, a more hostile trend towards the findings of the CVR has emerged. As in Guatemala, a 'struggle for memory' has gained momentum in the media and with the participation of different and aggressive 'stakeholders' such as organizations of retired army generals who produced as early as 1998 a 'counter-report' to challenge the Commission's version.[46] This emergence is at least partly explained by ongoing human rights trials in Peru, both against high level military officials and former President Fujimori. This hostility is against any decision of the state towards adopting the CVR's report as an element of its public policies. The opposition to bringing the TRC's lessons to the educational system is the most notorious aspect of this hostility.

As these two examples demonstrate, to unearth the truth and to publicly expose it is not enough to set the record straight, or cause the findings to become the the official history of a particular country. Ownership over truth commissions' findings by a broad constituency that goes beyond human rights organizations is necessary to be able to influence political processes in transitional societies.

4.2. The right to justice: how can trials and prosecutions promote peace?

The independence of powers in democratic systems is supposed to guarantee the protection of the rule of law and the rights of citizens in any given democratic country. In theory, this principle is supposed to prevail even in the event of internal armed conflict, states of emergency, or even in the cessation of democratic

[44] García-Godos, 'Victim Reparations in the Peruvian Truth Commission'.

[45] As expected, it was the armed forces and leaders from the political parties that were in government during the armed conflict that voiced most criticisms of the work of the CVR and Final Report.

[46] AVEMILGUA, *Testimonio de una agresión* (Guatemala, 1998). See also Berthold Molden, 'Remember the Past... But How and Why? Guatemala's Post War Debates over Narrative Authority as a Case of Renegotiating Historical Responsibility and Political Rights', in *Inquiries into Past and Present*, D. Gard, I. Main, M. Oliver, and J. Wood (eds.) (Vienna: IWM, 2005).

rule. In practice, judiciaries often become prey to authoritarian regimes, their functions being obstructed in various ways. In Latin America in the 1980s, for example, people whose basic human rights had been violated turned to courts for legal protection and justice, soon finding out that attorneys, judges, and prosecutors were impeded in their functions by political–military authorities. Cases could be opened and registered, only to get stuck for years, even decades in messy judicial proceedings. With the support of human rights organizations and international advocacy, some cases have been moved forward to regional human rights courts, such as the Inter-American Court of Human Rights. Unfortunately, for every one that reaches the regional system, hundreds are left behind.

Trials and prosecutions are the mechanism of transitional justice that receive most international and media attention. Proceedings in international courts are particularly highlighted, such as in the International Criminal Court, international ad-hoc tribunals like the ICTY and the ICTR, and also hybrid tribunals, such as the Special Court for Sierra Leone or the Extraordinary Chambers in the Courts of Cambodia. International courts are discussed in the chapter by Gentian Zyberi in this volume. Here, I want to focus the discussion on trials and prosecutions in domestic courts, that is, at the national level. Judicial processes in domestic courts seldom make international headlines, yet they have particular importance for national processes of accountability. Criminal accountability, retribution, and seeing justice done by national courts is an important element in the protection and fulfilment of victims' rights. For defendants, those charged with human rights violations, it is important that the right to due process be respected. It is in the interests of both victims and victimizers that criminal accountability and judicial processes are clear and transparent.

National prosecutions for human rights violations face many challenges in most transitional societies; obstructions to judicial independence, lack of resources and personnel, large backlogs of cases, inefficiency, and, often, corruption are among these problems. To move forward with their cases, victims, human rights organizations, and advocates across the Latin American region have deployed a number of strategies. 'Strategic litigation' (*persecución penal estratégica*—PPE)[47] in Guatemala is one of them. This strategy, which is endorsed by judicial authorities in Guatemala, takes account of the backlog of cases pending upon the national judicial system, and recognizes the difficult conditions surrounding justice administration and accountability. PPE implies a shift away from a case-by-case approach towards a focus on the identification and investigation of criminal phenomena, patterns, and connections between cases. The case against General Rios Montt on charges of genocide is a result of this new approach.

Indeed, former military dictator Efraín Ríos Montt was judged and sentenced for genocide and crimes against humanity in 2013. This case is illustrative of the fate that criminal accountability for past human rights violations has in Guatemala. In 2001, the Association for Justice and Reconciliation (AJR),

[47] Ministerio Público, 'Memoria de Labores Año 2011', 33.

a collective of victim communities affected by the internal armed conflict, put forward a claim to the Attorney-General against Rios Montt, his former Minister of Defence Oscar Humberto Mejía Víctores and former army general Héctor Mario López Fuentes for genocide and crimes against humanity. The Attorney-General's Office failed to open investigations, and it was not until 2007 that a lower court allowed the AJR's request for documentation from the Ministry of Defence regarding military operations in the early 1980s. The Ministry ignored the decision, and continued to do so in spite of a 2009 Constitutional Court's order to allow the search for documents.[48] That same year, army records for Operation Sofia (conducted in the 1980s) were found at the National Security Archives in the USA. This has been a vital piece of evidence for the claimants, whose legal advisers are from CALDH, one of the main human rights organizations in Guatemala. In June 2011, ten years after the case started, the Attorney-General formally completed the investigation and in 2012 Ríos Montt was formally indicted. The judicial process itself started in January 2013 at the Guatemalan High Risk Court, and on 10 May the court sentenced Ríos Montt to 80 years in prison for genocide and crimes against humanity. The relief and sense of justice for thousands of victims was short-lived, however, when on 20 May the Guatemalan Constitutional Court nullified the sentence reached by the High Risk Court, based on procedural failures of the right to due process. This decision brings the process back to the moment in time when the procedural failures occurred, 19 April 2013. This implies that all proceedings taking place from that date onwards will have to be repeated, including the sentencing. The decision was met with disbelief both nationally and internationally. There is speculation about changes in the composition of the courts, new legal obstacles, etc. At the moment of writing, it is still uncertain when the process will restart. In a sense, it is not Ríos Montt who stands on trial, but the struggle for truth, memory, and the acknowledgement that genocide did happen in Guatemala.

The Ríos Montt trial in Guatemala is considered emblematic on account of the charge, genocide. Another case considered emblematic, not only for the national quest for justice, but also for setting international precedent, is the Fujimori trial in Peru. In November 2000, former President Alberto Fujimori abandoned Peru amidst a corruption scandal, seeking refuge in Japan for three years. Attempts by the Peruvian government to get him extradited from Japan failed, in spite of serious charges.[49] In November 2005, Fujimori unexpectedly travelled to Chile, where he was arrested by the Chilean authorities at the request of Peru. After a lengthy extradition process, the Chilean Supreme Court voted in favour of Fujimori's extradition to Peru in September 2007. The former president would be sent to Peru to be tried for 7 out of 13 charges that the Peruvian authorities had

[48] 'Caso contra alto mando de Rios Montt', http://www.caldh.org/index.php?option=com_content&view=article&id=59&Itemid=76&lang=es (accessed 12 Nov 2014).

[49] Jo-Marie Burt, 'Guilty as Charged: The Trial of Former Peruvian President Alberto Fujimori for Human Rights Violations', *International Journal of Transitional Justice* 3 (2009), 384–405.

documented against him. It is worth noting the great reduction in the number of charges since the extradition negotiations with Japan started, which amounted to several dozens. The seven charges included two cases of human rights violations and five cases of corruption.

Fujimori was sentenced to 25 years in prison for two cases of human rights violations on 7 April 2009. The verdict marked the end of a 15-month-long judicial process about the events that took place in La Cantuta–Barrios Alto and *Sótanos SIE*. The first case concerned the disappearance or killings of 25 people, in November 1991 and July 1992, including an 8-year-old child, committed by the paramilitary Colina-group. The other case involved several incidents of illegal arrest, kidnapping, and torture at the headquarters of the Army's Intelligence Service. These cases were dealt with as one single process since they are both about human rights violations. According to the prosecuting authorities Fujimori was directly responsible for these atrocities. The charge refers to the national security policy that allowed the creation of paramilitary groups in order 'to eradicate' guerrilla group members. The argument was that Fujimori knew about the existence of the Colina-group, endorsed its methods, and showed little or no willingness to stop the group's activities in spite of having the powers to do so.

In the beginning there was no concrete evidence, documents, or testimonies that could confirm that Fujimori ordered the events in La Cantuta, Barrios Altos, and SIE HQ. This changed after January 2008, when several members of the Colina-group were interrogated by the court. Through these inquiries the prosecutors' claim was strengthened: the atrocities had been reported to Fujimori, counting on his approval, who therefore had full knowledge of them. Fujimori's defence argued that the Colina-group was created by the army in secret, and that the president neither knew about nor accepted their actions: the president could not stop something that he knew nothing about.

The trial and Fujimori's sentence had great legal significance as it was the first time in history that a former state leader had been extradited to his country of origin to be prosecuted for human rights violations. In the decision, the Court established that the crimes that Fujimori was sentenced for constituted crimes against humanity. The judges found sufficient evidence for the existence of a national security policy that allowed systematic violations of human rights. Fujimori was convicted as the man responsible for the crimes committed within the framework of this policy. Against a grim background of weak judicial independence, Fujimori's conviction has been considered a test for the Peruvian judicial system. In this particular test, the Court led by Judge César San Martín succeeded in every way.

In Peru, the Fujimori trials opened a window of opportunity for domestic human rights trials to advance. The momentum gained by Fujimori's conviction, however, has suffered several setbacks over the past two years, with several acquittals and few convictions in other human rights cases. The right to justice is a continuous struggle for the families of victims and human rights organizations that support them.

How can trials and prosecutions at domestic courts contribute to positive peace? Based on the two examples discussed here, it could be argued that trials at the domestic level polarize post-transitional societies rather than promote peace. Former dictators may enjoy various forms of protection or amnesty on the basis of former status, and they may even enjoy political support from various sectors of society, either in a latent or openly active manner. In Peru, Fujimori's daughter Keiko Fujimori ran for the presidency in 2011, obtaining 23 per cent of the votes in the first round of elections,[50] and 48 per cent in the second round.[51] Except for party members, few Peruvians would openly admit to being a *fujimorista*, that is, a Fujimori supporter, because of the association with authoritarian and clientelistic practices as well as with corruption. However, the 2011 election results testify to the contrary: a large number of Peruvians trusted candidate Fujimori with their votes. Seeing the former head of state in court has indeed been questioned time and again by his supporters, who emphasized the achievements of Fujimori's administration, particularly those regarding economic liberalization and the establishment of institutions. Yet, the message conveyed by domestic human rights trials and the conviction of those most responsible is that no one is above the law—not even presidents. There are several ways by which human rights trials in general, and the conviction of high-ranking officials in particular can contribute to peace. Kathryn Sikkink provides empirical evidence of the fact that countries where human rights trials for past violations take place show improved human rights records, although she explicitly states that there are no established truths about the mechanisms at work to explain this relation.[52] Accordingly, a deterrence effect upon potential perpetrators might be as valid an explanation as the effect of socialization and collective memory of a painful past brought to the fore by trials.[53] For the common citizen in post-conflict and post-authoritarian societies, the message conveyed through trials and convictions of those most responsible is that justice can, after all, be achieved for crimes of the past.

4.3. The right to reparations: mending the past as a basis for peace[54]

In the context of transitional justice, victims' right to reparations encompass a wide variety of measures aimed at restoring the harm done during armed conflict

[50] Resultados Elecciones Generales y de Parlamento Andino 2011, http://www.web.onpe.gob.pe/modElecciones/elecciones/elecciones2011/1ravuelta/ (accessed 12 Nov 2014).

[51] Resultados Elecciones Generales Segunda Eleccion Presidencial 2011, http://www.web.onpe.gob.pe/modElecciones/elecciones/elecciones2011/2davuelta/ (accessed 12 Nov 2014).

[52] Kathryn Sikkink, *The Justice Cascade: How Human Rights Prosecutions are Changing World Politics* (New York: W. W. Norton, 2011), 188.

[53] Hunjoon Kim and Kathryn Sikkink, 'Explaining the Deterrence Effect of Human Rights Prosecutions for Transitional Countries', *International Studies Quarterly* 54 (December 2010), 939–963; Sikkink, *The Justice Cascade.*

[54] This section is based on previous work where I address the issue in more detail. See García-Godos, 'Victim Reparations in Transitional Justice', 111–30.

or authoritarian regimes. In the media, reparations are often viewed as synonymous with monetary compensation, ignoring the fact that compensation is just one of many forms of victim reparations. In order to have a meaningful discussion of victim reparations in transitional justice and their contribution to peace, it is useful to distinguish, as De Greiff has suggested, between conceptualizations of reparations as used in international law and as used in reparation programmes. Although related to each other, these two contexts involve different choices and motivations.[55]

In international law, reparations refer to all sorts of reparatory measures implemented to address human rights violations, without necessarily targeting specific violations. A juridical definition of reparations differentiates between the categories of restitution, compensation, rehabilitation, satisfaction, and guarantees of non-recurrence. This is the type of definition enshrined in the Basic Principles discussed earlier. It is noteworthy that the latter two categories are related not only to other mechanisms of transitional justice (disclosure of truth, judicial and administrative sanctions), but also address processes of institutional reform, development projects, and symbolic acts, among others.

In the context of reparations programmes and implementation a narrower definition of reparations is needed, often referring to a specific target group (the victims) and a specific type of crime or human rights violation. Narrower definitions do not include truth-telling, criminal justice, or institutional reform. Instead, they are based on two fundamental elements: the types of reparation (material and symbolic) to be provided, and the forms of distribution (individual and collective) to be applied; this will be discussed in more detail in the next section. Narrower definitions of reparations are, in that way, operational, thus putting certain limits on the responsibilities of those in charge of designing reparation programmes.

The distinction between a juridical and an operational conceptualization of reparations might prove useful at the analytical and operational level, yet it should also be said that the operational definition is not only grounded on the broader juridical definition, but it becomes itself a legal category that determines many aspects of the reparation involved. For this reason, the debate between jurists active in international law and reparation officers and advocates seems to be more a matter of form and scope rather than content. In my view, there is no inherent contradiction between juridical and operational definitions, as they both focus on and acknowledge the victim's right to redress. As we shall see in the next section, most debates on reparations evolve around the applicability and implementation of juridical definitions to specific cases, particularly those involving massive human rights violations—which is usually the case in situations of transition from armed conflict and authoritarian regimes.

[55] Pablo De Greiff, 'Justice and Reparations', in *The Handbook of Reparations*, Pablo De Greiff (ed.) (Oxford: Oxford University Press, 2006), 451–77.

4.3.1. Implementing victim reparations

In spite of the apparent consensus over the right to remedy for victims of human rights violations, the design and implementation of reparation programmes (including their legal framework and categories) are highly contested issues involving a series of substantive, ultimately political decisions to be taken by new regimes.[56] These decisions are highly contextual, depending not only on the political conditions of the post-conflict or transitional period, but also on the historical legacy of the previous regime, power structures, and even practical matters (such as the feasibility of implementation and funding). Some of the most important decisions involved in the elaboration and implementation of reparation programmes will be discussed further.

While truth commissions may recommend the need for reparations as an integral part of a transitional justice process, there is no immediacy in governments' responses towards reparation. In order to opt for reparations, a political regime has first to acknowledge the existence of a situation that calls for reparations, as well as the existence of people who have been harmed and should be entitled to the attention of the state through a reparations programme. Whatever the legitimacy of the claims and actors involved, these are not light decisions to take.

Opting to provide reparations involves the initiation of a comprehensive and sensitive process usually accompanied by high expectations among victim groups and potential beneficiaries, and volatile political commitment and public budgets. On the other hand, political will to develop and implement a reparations programme might lend popular support and legitimacy to the new regime. Having said yes to victim reparations, regimes will then have to act effectively and quickly in order to prove their commitment and sustain credibility. An illustrative example is the development of the Peruvian Reparations Programme. While the legislation establishing the programme was in place in 2005, two years after the Truth Commission Report was published, the design and elaboration of the National Victims Registry was not completed until 2011. Individual reparations could not be awarded before the Registry was complete. While this may be technically reasonable, the lapse of time was understood by victims as a lack of commitment by incumbent governments.[57]

Human rights violations are often depicted in terms of victim and perpetrator, those who have been harmed and those who have inflicted harm upon others and/or bear responsibility for the violations. In the context of reparations, *the identification of the victim* is vital, as it is he or she who will be entitled to whatever form of remedy or benefit is to be provided. Through the use of legal categories, reparation programmes can identify the universe of victims to which the programme is addressed, often by reference to specific types of human rights violations. In

[56] Elster, *Closing the Books*.

[57] There is unfortunately an element of truth in the victims' interpretation of the situation, as budgets were often reduced or restrained, particularly during the administration of President Alan García, 2006–11.

that manner, victims tend to refer to all those who have suffered a specific type of violation. The most common types of violation in authoritarian regimes and armed conflict situations are, among others, murder, kidnappings, torture, forced disappearance, rape, sexual abuse, mutilation, forced draft, and displacement. In other words, the victim is identified on the basis of the type of violation inflicted upon him or her.

While the identification of victims is the cornerstone of any victim reparation programme, it is necessary to problematize the dichotomy of victim/perpetrator. The human rights discourse that informs most of the transitional justice literature tends to reduce complex realities into neat, clear-cut, legalized categories.[58] However, these two categories do not cover the universe of actors that take part in armed conflict or are involved in human rights violations. Neither are the boundaries of these categories always clearly delineated. It is not uncommon to find that a single individual can have been a victim and a perpetrator at different points in time, or that he or she might have had various degrees of involvement in activities leading to human rights violations.[59] These alternative roles are a challenge for transitional justice processes, where clear legal identifications are at the basis of the decisions that need to be taken.

A closely related issue to the identification of victims is the burden of proof, which is usually seen as the responsibility of the claimant. The main emphasis has usually been on the need to avoid paying compensation to those not entitled to it, rather than to avoid denying it to those who are entitled. The demand for rigorous proof of victimization may, for some victims, add to their burden.[60]

Elster's distinction among three types of suffering, that is, situations that are wider in scope than specific legally defined violations, are useful in understanding what may constitute the basis for different forms of reparation.[61] Material suffering involves the loss of real or personal property coming about either by destruction or confiscation; by personal property one refers to physical objects or financial assets. In some cases, the way the loss occurred may strengthen or delegitimize certain claims. Personal suffering refers to harm to life, body, or liberty, which can take place both during and outside combat situations. Intangible suffering refers to the loss or lack of opportunities.

The different types of suffering call for different approaches to the issue of reparations, each of them posing several challenges. Material suffering is most commonly addressed in terms of restitution, including the return of specific assets or objects, as well as land or property. Personal suffering is usually addressed through rehabilitation and various satisfaction measures. Intangible suffering is often addressed in terms of monetary compensation. It is particularly with regards to intangible suffering that the debate revolves around what

[58] Richard Ashby Wilson, 'Representing Human Rights Violations: Social Contexts and Subjectivities', in *Human Rights, Culture and Context: Anthropological Perspectives*, R. A. Wilson and J. P. Mitchel (eds.) (London: Routledge, 1997).

[59] This is what political scientist Ivan Orozco in Colombia refers to as 'complex victims'. See also Erika Bouris, *Complex Political Victims* (Bloomfield, Conn.: Kumarian, 2007).

[60] Elster, *Closing the Books*, 183.

[61] Elster, *Closing the Books*, 127.

is to be considered the optimal or legitimate grounds for compensation, past suffering or present/future needs. Will compensation be enough to ensure that a victim not only recovers from past suffering/violations, but also has her present and future needs met? This is at the heart of an ongoing debate in transitional justice: it is not enough to bring the victim back to her original social and economic status, often one of poverty and deprivation, but she should be given the opportunity to improve her situation. The Colombian Victims' Law and the reparations and restitution programmes that are being implemented since 2012 are partly guided by the principle of 'transformative reparations', incorporating various measures of satisfaction, rehabilitation, and compensation among their activities.

Thus a third element in the implementation of reparations programmes is *the choice of type of reparation* to be provided. There are two basic distinctions to be made concerning types of reparation, one regarding their form (symbolic or material), and the other concerning their distribution (individual and collective). Symbolic reparations include various forms of recognition and acknowledgement for the suffering of victims, such as commemorations, rituals in homage to the victims, changing the names of streets, creating places of memory, and apology in the name of the nation, either in public acts or in private letters. Material forms of reparation include all tangible assets that are provided to repair the harm done, such as money, goods, or services. These might in turn be provided as a single lump sum, or a series of payments (such as pensions), the return of lost property, or privileged access to educational and health programmes. There has been an expansion of the forms that material reparations may take, moving from what was previously the most dominant form of reparation (i.e. individual monetary compensation) towards services, such as mental health schemes, legal counselling, physical medical treatment, scholarships, priority in housing schemes, and more. Collective reparations, the most preferred option for governments facing redress for massive human rights violations, offer as well a variety of options, the most common being the provision of basic public infrastructure (water and sanitation, health posts, schools, bridges, and local roads). In that particular case, the distinction between development projects and reparations becomes blurred, and there are those who argue that the development responsibilities of governments can never stand as reparation for human rights violations.[62]

Regarding the form of distribution of reparation benefits, practice has demonstrated emphasis on the provision of individual benefits. While the ideal reparation programme should include both individual and collective forms of reparation, governments with limited resources tend to prefer collective

[62] This is an ongoing debate in countries where collective reparation programmes are being implemented, such as in Peru, where the author has conducted research on the reparations programme. It is worth noting that there is no clear position among victim groups/beneficiaries and human rights organizations on whether or not development projects can or should be consider as an appropriate form of reparation. Different positions can be found in all groups.

reparation schemes, while human rights activists and not a few victims' organizations prefer individual reparations. Arguments in favour of one or the other form of distribution are many, and include pragmatic as well as normative and philosophical reasons. Would an individual victim of torture receive the acknowledgement and redress he deserves through a collective reparation scheme providing, say, housing and public services? There are those who argue that he would, because the programme would address present needs, while others argue that the acknowledgement of individual personal suffering is lost in the collective character of the reparation. Individual and collective reparations need not be exclusive, nor do they have to limit the possibility of resorting to civil litigation. The Colombian Justice and Peace process is an example of the possibility of combining individual and collective judicial proceedings and reparations. Current prioritization and selection of cases by the Justice and Peace prosecutors are an effort to contextualize individual cases in a given historical and social context. This facilitates the effectiveness of proceedings, as well as giving access to truth regarding the socio-economic and political context in which violations took place.[63]

What is the contribution of victim reparations to positive peace? A first issue to consider is that of acknowledgement, that is, the first element discussed above. The implementation of victim reparations programmes in post-conflict and post-authoritarian societies rests on the acknowledgement that harm has been done. It cannot be taken for granted that victim reparations will automatically follow truth commission recommendations. Thus the significance of reparations in such societies lies in the public acknowledgement that states make regarding crimes of the past. A timely and proper implementation will reinforce public acknowledgement and commitment, strengthening relations of trust between victims and the state (usually the one granting reparations). Delays and foot-dragging on the part of the state will, unfortunately, produce the opposite effect: a sense of abandonment and mistrust, of being left behind or ignored by the state. The expectation created by victim reparations can thus be supportive of relations of trust between state and society, and it can also provide the basis for mobilization among victim's groups.[64] Such mobilization does not need to be a threat to positive peace, rather the contrary. Mobilizing for victims' rights involves holding the state accountable to its commitments to transitional justice and accountability. Mobilizing for victims' rights in general, and reparations in particular, can contribute to setting the issue on the public agenda. Such has been the case in Colombia, where victim organizations have become a legitimate interlocutor of state agencies in charge of implementing victim reparations and land restitution.[65]

[63] Jemima García-Godos, 'Colombia: Accountability and DDR in the Pursuit of Peace?', in Sriram et al. (eds.), *Transitional Justice and Peacebuilding on the Ground*, 219–37.

[64] García-Godos, 'Victims' Rights and Distributive Justice'.

[65] García-Godos, 'Victims' Rights and Distributive Justice'.

5. Conclusions: Building Trust through Accountability and Justice

In this brief introduction into transitional justice and its relation to peace, I have taken a leap of faith and put forward a normative argument for considering transitional justice as a constitutive element of positive peace. Yet, what empirical evidence do I have to support this argument? As the field of transitional justice has expanded, not only in terms of academic interest but also and mainly in terms of practice, much focus has been given to measuring the impact of transitional justice mechanisms, or at least establishing observable effects on long-term peace and reconciliation.[66] Several statistical and comparative studies have been made over the past decades, bearing different, often opposite results.[67]

The impact of transitional justice upon peace is indeed a difficult task to assess without taking into consideration socio-political and economic factors in which measures of accountability are embedded. It would be an exaggeration to argue that transitional justice mechanisms per se bring peace. Instead, and according to De Greiff regarding victim reparations, what transitional justice does is 'to contribute (modestly) to the reconstitution or the constitution of a new political community. In this sense also, they are best thought as part of a political project.'[68]

The (re)constitution of this new political community lies in a conceptualization of justice that includes three elements; recognition, civic trust, and solidarity. Recognition refers to the recognition of individuals as individuals (thus recognizing their agency), as citizens, and as victims (because individuals actually can become subject to harm effected by others). Civic trust refers to the expectation of a shared normative commitment, while social solidarity refers to the ability to empathize with the situation of others. Here, I believe, lies then the contribution of transitional justice and accountability measures to the construction of positive peace: in the constitution of a shared political project built on trust.

[66] See *inter alia*, Hugh van der Merwe, Victoria Baxter, and Audrey R. Chapman. (eds.), *Assessing the Impact of Transitional Justice: Challenges for Empirical Research* (Washington, DC: United States Institute of Peace, 2009); Tricia Olsen, Leigh Payne, and Andrew G. Reiter (eds.), *Transitional Justice in Balance: Comparing Processes, Weighing Efficacy* (Washington, DC: United States Institute of Peace, 2009); Sikkink, *The Justice Cascade.*

[67] For statistical studies, see *inter alia* Tove Grete Lie, Helga Malmin Binningsbø, and Scott Gates, 'Post-Conflict Justice and Sustainable Peace', *World Bank Policy Research Working Paper* 4191 (April 2007). http://econ.worldbank.org (accessed 12 Nov 2014); Kathryn Sikkink and Carrie Booth Walling, 'The Impact of Human Rights Trials in Latin America', *Journal of Peace Research* 44 (2009), 427; Hunjoon Kim and Kathryn Sikkink, 'Explaining the Deterrence Effect of Human Rights Prosecutions for Transitional Countries', *International Studies Quarterly* 54 (2009), 939–63. For cross-country studies see, *inter alia*, Eric Wiebelhaus-Brahm, 'Uncovering the Truth: Examining Truth Commission Success and Impact', *International Studies Perspectives* 8 (2007), 6–35, and Eric Wiebelhaus-Brahm, *Truth Commissions and Transitional Societies* (London: Routledge, 2010).

[68] De Greiff, *Handbook of Reparations*, 454.

Political projects are obviously highly contested processes and in transitional contexts even more so. Contested narratives of the past built on conflict and mistrust may be difficult to reconcile, and what might be seen as accountability by one group might be considered vengeance by the other. Visions of the future are equally contested, as different groups will have divergent interests in preserving or changing the status quo. The challenges to accountability are many and comprehensive, yet in most transitional societies the quest for justice to be done, for accountability to take place in any of its forms, most often prevails. This chapter has addressed three mechanisms of transitional justice to illustrate ways in which accountability can be achieved. Long-term positive peace necessitates civic trust. Accountability is about creating the conditions for civic trust to thrive.

17

The Role and Contribution of International Courts in Furthering Peace as an Essential Community Interest

Gentian Zyberi

1. Introduction

> The reign of law, represented by the incorporation of obligatory arbitration as a rule of positive international law, is not the only means for securing and preserving peace among nations. Nevertheless, it is an essential condition of peace.[1]

The maintenance or restoration of peace and the quest for sustainable peace have been part of international legal thought for a long time. Lauterpacht considered the idea of peace as an important aspect of the Grotian tradition, reflected in Grotius's ground-breaking work, *De Jure Belli ac Pacis*.[2] Constraining the effects of war and working towards sustainable peace have been important features of the activity of the international community for many decades, if not centuries. The result of these efforts is a complex normative and institutional framework for monitoring and enforcing human rights and for the peaceful resolution of disputes.[3] International courts and tribunals (ICs) are an important component of that ever-evolving system of global governance. In acknowledging the role of ICs with regard to peace, Hersch Lauterpacht has pointedly noted that, the primary purpose of the International Court (including both the Permanent Court of International Justice and the International Court of Justice) lies in its function as one of the instruments for *securing peace in so far as this aim can be achieved by*

[1] Hersch Lauterpacht, *The Function of Law in the International Community* (Oxford: Clarendon, 1933), 437.

[2] Hersch Lauterpacht, 'The Grotian Tradition in International Law', *BYIL* 23 (1946), 46.

[3] For the core international human rights instruments and their monitoring bodies see www.ohchr.org/EN/ProfessionalInterest/Pages/CoreInstruments.aspx (accessed 13 Nov 2014). For a better overview of the UN system see www.un.org/en/aboutun/structure/org_chart.shtml (accessed 13 Nov 2014). See also J. G. Merrills, *International Dispute Settlement* (Cambridge: Cambridge University Press, 2011).

law.[4] That statement underlines the enabling as well as the constraining effects of international law on the activity of ICs.

The last several decades have been marked by a conspicuous process of 'humanization of international law' in several aspects.[5] That *humanization* is expressed in the impressive development of several branches of international law as human rights, humanitarian law and international environmental law. Another related process is that of increased *judicialization* of international law and international relations, expressed in the qualitative and quantitative expansion of the international institutional framework entrusted with the monitoring and enforcement of international law, including a large number of international and regional judicial and quasi-judicial mechanisms.[6] International courts are an important component of the operating system of international law, and exercise an increasing influence on interpreting and developing the normative content of international law.[7] As mechanisms for the enforcement of international law, international and regional courts can play an important role in providing the necessary forums for ensuring the peaceful solutions of interstate disputes, for dealing with individual complaints concerning human rights violations, or for prosecuting individuals alleged to have committed internationally recognized crimes, such as genocide, war crimes, and crimes against humanity.

This chapter will first discuss the role and contribution of ICs with regard to promoting, maintaining, or restoring peace, as a community interest, within the larger legal and institutional framework of the international legal system. Simma has defined *community interest* as a consensus according to which respect for certain *fundamental values* is not to be left to the free disposition of states individually

[4] Hersch Lauterpacht, *The Development of International Law by the International Court* (London: Stevens & Sons, 1958, repr. 1982), 3 (emphasis added).

[5] Theodor Meron, *The Humanization of International Law* (Leiden: Martinus Nijhoff, 2006). For a historical perspective see Martti Koskenniemi, *The Gentle Civilizer of Nations: The Rise and Fall of International Law 1870–1960* (Cambridge: Cambridge University Press, 2001); Antônio Augusto Cançado Trindade, *International Law for Humankind: Towards a New Jus Gentium* (Leiden: Brill, 2010), esp. 635–45; Ruti G. Teitel, *Humanity's Law* (Oxford: Oxford University Press, 2011).

[6] See *inter alia* Martin Shapiro and Alec Stone Sweet, *On Law, Politics, and Judicialization* (Oxford: Oxford University Press, 2002); Karen J. Alter, 'The Multiplication of International Courts and Tribunals', in *The Oxford Handbook of International Adjudication*, Cesare Romano, Karen Alter, and Yuval Shany (eds.) (Oxford: Oxford University Press, 2014), 63–89.

[7] For a discussion of the relationship between the normative system and the operating system of international law see *inter alia* Paul F. Diehl and Charlotte Ku, *The Dynamics of International Law* (Cambridge: Cambridge University Press, 2010), 28–73. For the discussion of the contribution of different international courts to the development of international law see *inter alia* Lauterpacht, *The Development of International Law*; Gideon Boas and William A. Schabas (eds.), *International Criminal Law: Developments in the Case Law of the ICTY* (Leiden: Martinus Nijhoff, 2003); Larissa van den Herik, *The Contribution of the Rwanda Tribunal to the Development of International Law* (Leiden: Martinus Nijhoff, 2005); Gentian Zyberi, *The Humanitarian Face of the International Court of Justice: Its Contribution to Interpreting and Developing International Human Rights and Humanitarian Law Rules and Principles* (Antwerp: Intersentia, 2008); Shane Darcy and Joseph Powderly (eds.), *Judicial Creativity at the International Criminal Tribunals* (Oxford: Oxford University Press, 2010); Christian J. Tams and James Sloan (eds.), *The Development of International Law by the International Court of Justice* (Oxford: Oxford University Press, 2013); Nerina Boschiero, Cesare Pitea, Tullio Scovazzi, and Chiara Ragni (eds.), *International Courts and the Development of International Law: Essays in Honour of Tullio Treves* (The Hague: T.M.C. Asser, 2013).

or *inter se* but is recognized and sanctioned by international law as a *matter of concern to all states*.[8] Moreover, he has noted that international peace and security is the most prominent among such community interests.[9] International courts serve as guardians of community interests and values, which have come into being in a piecemeal fashion.[10] Those community interests, even if in an embryonic fashion, have been read into or have been embedded in relevant international human rights and humanitarian law treaties and customary international law. Nollkaemper has categorized courts themselves as an intermediate public good, which contributes towards the provision of 'final global public goods', as peace.[11] That shows the importance of ICs as important tools that can contribute to the interests of peace.

The second aim of this chapter is to analyse the contribution of these courts to clarifying different aspects of state responsibility, the responsibility of international organizations, as well as individual responsibility with regard to promoting, maintaining, or restoring peace. The issues selected for a more detailed discussion include the prohibition of the unlawful use of force and non-intervention, the duty to prevent mass atrocities, to investigate and punish perpetrators thereof, and to cooperate with international criminal courts and tribunals. By analysing relevant case law and referring to the legal findings of these ICs, this chapter tries to shed light on different components of required conduct for individual states, third states, international organizations, and non-state actors more generally. As Lauterpacht and Rosenne have noted,[12] while discussing the role and contribution of ICs with regard to furthering peace, it is necessary to be mindful of the institutional and other limitations imposed by their statutes, international law, and the actions and interests of important actors.

Kingsbury distinguishes ten major types of IC, namely intergovernmental claims commissions, ad hoc interstate arbitration, interstate arbitration, standing international courts, international criminal courts, international administrative

[8] Bruno Simma, 'From Bilateralism to Community Interest in International Law', in *Recueil des Cours (Collected Courses of the Hague Academy of International Law)* 250 (1994) (Leiden: Martinus Nijhoff, 1997), 233 (emphasis added)

[9] Simma, 'From Bilateralism to Community Interest', 236. In Simma's list of community interests are solidarity between developed and developing countries, protection of the environment, the 'common heritage' concept, and international concern with human rights.

[10] See *inter alia* Simma, 'From Bilateralism to Community Interest', 217–384; Santiago Villalpando, 'The Legal Dimension of the International Community: How Community Interests Are Protected in International Law', *European Journal of International Law* 21 (2010), 387–419; André Nollkaemper, 'International Adjudication of Global Public Goods: The Intersection of Substance and Procedure', *European Journal of International Law* 23 (2012), 769–91. See also Ulrich Fastenrath, Rudolf Geiger, Daniel-Erasmus Khan, Andreas Paulus, Sabine von Schorlemer, and Christoph Vedder (eds.), *From Bilateralism to Community Interest: Essays in Honour of Bruno Simma* (Oxford: Oxford University Press, 2011). On the issue of global values see *inter alia* Otto Spijkers, *The United Nations, the Evolution of Global Values and International Law* (Antwerp: Intersentia, 2011). Spijkers argues that a common desire to eradicate war, poverty, and inhuman treatment, and to halt the exploitation of peoples, has led to an affirmation of the values of peace and security, social progress and development, human dignity and the self-determination of all peoples.

[11] Nollkaemper, 'International Adjudication of Global Public Goods', 783.

[12] Lauterpacht, *The Development of International Law*, 4–5; Shabtai Rosenne, *The Law and Practice of the International Court 1920–2005* (4th edn. Leiden: Brill, 2006), 175–93, analysing the attitude of states towards judicial settlement by the ICJ.

tribunals, regional human rights courts, regional economic integration courts, the WTO dispute settlement system, and investment arbitration tribunals.[13] This chapter, however, will focus on the work of the International Court of Justice (ICJ) which is entrusted with settling interstate disputes and providing legal advice to the main UN organs and specialized agencies; the work of the International Criminal Court (ICC); and the work of the two ad hoc international criminal tribunals for the former Yugoslavia and for Rwanda (ICTY and ICTR), which are entrusted with investigating and prosecuting individuals for having committed mass atrocity crimes, namely genocide, war crimes, and crimes against humanity. These selected ICs have dealt extensively with specific issues and aspects of state responsibility and individual criminal responsibility for mass atrocity crimes that present a threat to international peace and security.

Albeit not dealt with in this chapter, the activity of regional human rights courts is relevant even if these courts are not particularly well suited for addressing widespread and systematic violations of human rights.[14] These judicial mechanisms provide an important remedy against violations of individual rights and freedoms and have had a significant impact on improving the domestic legal systems of the countries party to the regional human rights treaties. In that sense, regional human rights courts have contributed to the strengthening of the rule of law and human rights protection, which are important for a peaceful society. The choice to deal with some ICs, while excluding others, does not mean that these other ICs are not relevant to peace, since it can be claimed that by solving international disputes any of the existing ICs contributes in one way or another to promoting, maintaining, or restoring peace. Such contributions to peace extend not only to interstate relations, but also to relations between different groups within a society, making it relevant also at an intrastate level.

2. The Multifaceted Role of International Courts with Regard to Promoting, Maintaining, or Restoring Peace

First, it must be noted that peace treaties have been material to the formation of international law[15] as well as to the establishment of arbitration and adjudication

[13] Benedict Kingsbury, 'International Courts: Uneven Judicialisation in Global Order', in *The Cambridge Companion to International Law*, James Crawford and Martti Koskenniemi (eds.) (Cambridge: Cambridge University Press, 2012), 205–11. For a discussion of the WTO dispute settlement see Ole Christian Fauchald, Chapter 10 in this book.

[14] While their procedural law is not particularly well suited for dealing with mass claims, regional human rights courts have dealt with several issues that are relevant to interstate peace. Examples include cases by the IACtHR concerning the laws on amnesties in a number of Latin-American States. The ECtHR has been involved in a number of cases stemming from armed conflicts in Cyprus, the former Yugoslavia, Chechnya, and Georgia. Thus, the ECtHR was seized with a request for provisional measures concerning the August 2008 armed conflict between Russia and Georgia and concerning the conflict between Russia and Ukraine in March 2014.

[15] See *inter alia* Randall Lesaffer, 'Peace Treaties and the Formation of International Law', in *The Oxford Handbook of the History of International Law*, Bardo Fassbender and Anne Peters (eds.) (Oxford: Oxford University Press, 2012), 71–94.

mechanisms entrusted with the peaceful resolution of international disputes. As Roelofsen points out, institutions for the peaceful settlement of disputes developed considerably since the hesitant start at The Hague Peace Conferences of 1899 and 1907.[16] The Versailles Peace Treaty made the German Emperor liable to criminal prosecution under Article 227 for his 'supreme offence against international morality and the sanctity of treaties', while also providing for the prosecution of other individuals responsible for violations of the laws and customs of war.[17] The prosecution of war criminals continued with the August 1945 Charter of the International Military Tribunal for Nuremberg (IMTN) and the January 1946 International Military Tribunal for the Far East (IMTFE).[18] While not much happened with regard to international criminal justice during the Cold War period, the two ad hoc international criminal tribunals for the former Yugoslavia and Rwanda and the permanent International Criminal Court were established within a short period in the 1990s.[19] Their activity, together with that of a number of hybrid criminal tribunals established in the early 2000s, put considerable emphasis on individual criminal accountability for mass atrocity crimes.[20] Regional human rights protection mechanisms were established and further evolved in Europe, the Americas, and in Africa, with similar efforts undertaken also in Asia and the Arab world. Notably, the last few decades have seen the coming into being of several specialized international and regional courts.

The *general legal basis* for the role of ICs with regard to maintaining peace is laid down in Article 33 of the UN Charter, which requires the parties to a dispute the continuance of which is likely to endanger the maintenance of international peace and security to seek a solution by negotiation, enquiry, mediation, conciliation, arbitration, *judicial settlement*, resort to regional agencies or arrangements, or other peaceful means of their own choice.[21] While the UN Charter does not impose any preference or hierarchical order among the various means of international dispute

[16] Cornelis G. Roelofsen, 'International Arbitration and Courts', in *The Oxford Handbook of the History of International Law*, 168. For a general overview see Cesare Romano, Karen Alter, and Yuval Shany (eds.), *The Oxford Handbook of International Adjudication* (Oxford: Oxford University Press, 2014).

[17] See *inter alia* Mark Lewis, *The Birth of the New Justice: The Internationalization of Crime and Punishment, 1919–1950* (Oxford: Oxford University Press, 2014), 27–63.

[18] See *inter alia* Franz B. Schick, 'Crimes against Peace', *Journal of Criminal Law and Criminology* 38 (1947–8), 445–65; B Röling and C Rüter (eds.), *The Tokyo Judgment: The International Military Tribunal for the Far East (I.M.T.F.E), 29 April 1946–12 November 1948* (Amsterdam: APA-University Press, 1977).

[19] See respectively UNSC Res. 827 (25 May 1993) UN Doc. S/RES/827; UNSC Res. 955 (8 November 1994) UN Doc. S/RES/955; and, 'Statute of the International Criminal Court' (17 July 1998) UN Doc. A/CONF.183/9.

[20] See *inter alia* Cesare P. R. Romano, André Nollkaemper, and Jann K. Kleffner (eds.), *Internationalized Criminal Courts: Sierra Leone, East Timor, Kosovo, and Cambodia* (Oxford: Oxford University Press, 2004).

[21] For a commentary to this article see *inter alia* Christian Tomuschat, 'Article 33', in *The Charter of the United Nations: A Commentary*, Bruno Simma et al. (eds.) (2nd edn. Oxford: Oxford University Press, 2002), 583–94; Christian Tomuschat, 'Article 33', in *The Statute of the International Court of Justice: A Commentary*, Andreas Zimmermann, Christian Tomuschat, Karin Oellers-Frahm, and Christian J. Tams (eds.) (2nd edn. Oxford: Oxford University Press, 2012), 119–33.

settlement, it provides a clear link between judicial settlement and the protection of an important community interest embedded in the UN Charter, namely the maintenance or restoration of peace. A *specific legal basis* for the furtherance of peace is explicitly or implicitly included in the Statutes establishing a number of ICs, including the ICJ, the ICC, and the ICTY and the ICTR. Since its Statute is annexed to the UN Charter, and the ICJ is one of the UN's main organs and its principal judicial organ, the maintenance of international peace and security is part and parcel of the considerations for the establishment and for the activity of this court.[22] On its part, the UN has emphasized the obligation of states to settle their disputes by peaceful means, including, when appropriate, by the use of the ICJ.[23] Through its case law the ICJ has clarified a number of general principles intrinsically relevant to peace, including the prohibition of the threat or use of force, self-determination of peoples, the prohibition of racial discrimination, and the prohibition of genocide.[24] The third paragraph of the preamble of the ICC Statute recognizes that mass atrocity crimes threaten the peace, security, and well-being of the world.[25] Other paragraphs in the preamble of the ICC Statute are also related to the maintenance of peace in one way or another, since such interests are served by emphasizing the prohibition of the threat or use of force and the principle of non-intervention in an armed conflict or in the internal affairs of any state. Schabas has argued that, as a result of their inclusion in the preamble, the 'interests of peace' become germane to the Court's activities, and to policy

[22] The ICJ settles interstate disputes and advises the main UN organs and specialized agencies on different legal questions. For a discussion of the ICJ's contribution in this regard see *inter alia* Mohamed Sameh M. Amr, *The Role of the International Court of Justice as the Principal Judicial Organ of the United Nations* (The Hague: Kluwer Law International, 2003), 213–62.

[23] UNGA Res. 60/1, '2005 World Summit Outcome' (25 October 2005) UN Doc. A/RES/60/1, para. 73.

[24] See *inter alia Corfu Channel* (*United Kingdom of Great Britain and Northern Ireland* v. *Albania*) (Judgment) [1948] ICJ; *United States Diplomatic and Consular Staff in Tehran* (*United States of America* v. *Iran*) (Judgment) [1980] ICJ; *Military and Paramilitary Activities in and against Nicaragua* (*Nicaragua* v. *United States of America*) (Merits) [1986] ICJ; *Questions of Interpretation and Application of the 1971 Montreal Convention Arising from the Aerial Incident at Lockerbie* (*Libyan Arab Jamahiriya* v. *United States of America; Libyan Arab Jamahiriya* v. *United Kingdom*) (Judgment) [1998] ICJ; *Application of the Genocide Convention* (*Bosnia and Herzegovina* v. *Serbia and Montenegro*) (Judgment) [2007] ICJ; *Armed Activities on the Territory of the Congo* (*Democratic Republic of the Congo* v. *Uganda*) (Judgment) [2005] ICJ; *Arrest Warrant of 11 April 2000* (*Democratic Republic of the Congo* v. *Belgium*) (Judgment) [2002] ICJ; *Armed Activities on the Territory of the Congo (New Application: 2002)* (*Democratic Republic of the Congo* v. *Rwanda*) (Judgment, jurisdiction of the Court and admissibility of the application) [2006] ICJ; *Legal Consequences of the Construction of a Wall in the Occupied Palestinian Territory* (Advisory Opinion) [2004] ICJ; *Accordance with International Law of the Unilateral Declaration of Independence in Respect of Kosovo* (Advisory Opinion) [2010] ICJ; *Questions relating to the Obligation to Prosecute or Extradite* (*Belgium* v. *Senegal*) (Judgment) [2012] ICJ; and so on. See *inter alia* Amr, *The Role of the International Court of Justice*; Gentian Zyberi, 'Self-Determination through the Lens of the International Court of Justice', *Netherlands International Law Review* 56 (2009), 429–53; Bruno Simma, 'Human Rights Before the International Court of Justice: Community Interest Coming to Life', in Tams and Sloan (eds.), *The Development of International Law*, 301–25; Gentian Zyberi, 'The International Court of Justice and the Rights of Peoples and Minorities' in Tams and Sloan (eds.), *The Development of International Law*, 327–52.

[25] See *inter alia* William A Schabas, *The International Criminal Court: A Commentary on the Rome Statute* (Oxford: Oxford University Press, 2010), 31–53 at 42–3.

decisions, such as whom to prosecute.[26] He has also noted that both objectives are best promoted by an approach that seeks to deliver as much of each as possible in the circumstances of a particular conflict.[27] The Office of the Prosecutor of the ICC (OTP/ICC) has provided an explanation of its understanding of the interests of justice and their relationship to peace processes.[28] First, the 2007 policy paper of the OTP/ICC notes that the ICC was created on the premise that justice is an essential component of a stable peace. Subsequently, while recognizing the role of the Security Council under Article 16 of the ICC Statute, the OTP/ICC has taken the position that the broader matter of international peace and security is not the responsibility of the Prosecutor as it falls within the mandate of other institutions.

The ICTY and the ICTR were established by the UN Security Council respectively in 1993 and 1994 on the basis of its competences under Chapter VII of the UN Charter relating to action with respect to threats to the peace, breaches of the peace, and acts of aggression. Both resolutions establishing the ad hoc tribunals note that the prosecution of persons responsible for serious violations of international humanitarian law would *contribute to* the process of national reconciliation and to the *restoration and maintenance of peace*.[29] Despite the establishment of these tribunals, however, the situation in the former Yugoslavia and that in the Great Lakes region continued to be problematic and peace was established through subsequent political agreements. In the former Yugoslavia peace was achieved between the warring parties in a number of agreements which include the Dayton Accords in November 1995,[30] the Kumanovo agreement of June 1999,[31] and the Ohrid agreement of August 2001.[32] The conflict in Rwanda spilled over in the Democratic Republic of the Congo and the overall situation in the Great Lakes region has continued to be problematic, despite there being a number of peace agreements between the parties concerned.

The role and contribution of ICs with regard to peace can be discussed from different interrelated perspectives, namely from the scope of their jurisdictional reach, from the perspective of their judicial activity and from the perspective of how their users perceive and decide to employ them (or not) in relevant situations. Put differently, assessing their role is a matter of assessing what these courts are

[26] Schabas, *The International Criminal Court*, 42–3. See also Janine Natalya Clark, 'Peace, Justice and the International Criminal Court: Limitations and Possibilities', *Journal of International Criminal Justice* 9 (2011), 521–45, especially 538ff.; Nick Grono, *The Role of the International Criminal Court in African Peace Processes: Mutually Reinforcing or Mutually Exclusive?* (London: Institute for Public Policy Research, 2006).

[27] Schabas, *The International Criminal Court*, 43.

[28] See ICC/OTP, 'Interests of Justice' (Policy Paper), September 2007, available at www.icc-cpi.int (accessed 17 September 2014).

[29] See respectively UNSC Res. 827 (25 May 1993) UN Doc. S/RES/827 (1993), and UNSC Res. 955 (8 November 1994) UN Doc. S/RES/955 (1994) (emphasis added).

[30] General Framework Agreement for Peace in Bosnia and Herzegovina (Dayton Peace Accords) (21 November 1995) UN Doc. A/50/790, www.state.gov/p/eur/rls/or/dayton/52602.htm (accessed 13 Nov 2014).

[31] Military Technical Agreement between the International Security Force (KFOR) and the governments of the Federal Republic of Yugoslavia and the Republic of Serbia (Kumanovo agreement), 9 June 1999, in 38 ILM 1217, www.nato.int/kosovo/docu/a990609a.htm (accessed 13 Nov 2014).

[32] Ohrid Framework Agreement (Ohrid agreement), 13 August 2001.

meant to do, what they actually do, and the extent to which they are considered relevant and are used by important international actors when dealing with situations where peace is at stake. In terms of assessing their effectiveness, as Shany has pointed out, the goals of public organizations, such as courts, tend to be ambiguous, and the public goods that they generate, such as justice, *peace*, and legal certainty, are hard to quantify.[33] Discussing the role and contribution of ICs to peace is not easy, as peace is a concept that lends itself to many different understandings.[34] As any other concept, peace can be construed restrictively or expansively. *Positive peace*, as a broader understanding of peace, includes national peace and concerns a number of issues including social justice, human rights protection, and elimination of structural violence. For Galtung, positive peace addresses among other things respect for human rights, provision of social justice, and elimination of structural violence causing poverty and exclusion.[35] A restrictive understanding of the concept of peace is that of *negative peace*, closely related to the prohibition of unlawful use of force. The legal findings of the selected ICs provide some important insights on aspects of both *negative* and *positive* peace under contemporary international law.

Generally speaking, the purpose of the judicial function has two interrelated components: first, an IC provides legal services to those entities that have access to it, including states, international organizations, and individuals. Besides the parties directly concerned, the provision of these legal services benefits more broadly the international community as a whole. Second, through interpreting and developing applicable rules and standards of conduct under international law for states, international organizations, and individuals, the ICs strengthen the rule of law both at an international and at the domestic level.[36] The international legal system remains state-centred, although non-state actors are increasingly recognized as playing an important role and as being accountable under international law.[37]

[33] Yuval Shany, 'Assessing the Effectiveness of International Courts: A Goal-Based Approach', *American Journal of International Law* 106 (2012), 239.

[34] See Bailliet and Larsen, Chapter 1 in this volume. See also David P. Barash, *Approaches to Peace: A Reader in Peace Studies* (2nd edn. Oxford: Oxford University Press, 2010).

[35] See Johan Galtung, *A Theory of Peace: Building Direct Structural Cultural Peace* (Grenzach-Whylen: Transcend University Press, 2013), esp. 52–61. See also Johan Galtung, *Peace by Peaceful Means: Peace and Conflict, Development and Civilization* (London: Sage, 1996), esp. 31–3.

[36] See *inter alia* Gentian Zyberi, 'The Role of International Courts in Post-Conflict Societies', in *Human Rights and Conflict: Essays in Honour of Bas de Gaay Fortman*, Ineke Boerefijn, Laura Henderson, Ronald Janse, and Robert Weaver (eds.) (Cambridge: Intersentia, 2012), 367–85; Armin von Bogdandy and Ingo Venzke, 'On the Functions of International Courts: An Appraisal in Light of Their Burgeoning Public Authority', *Leiden Journal of International Law* 26 (2013), 49–72; Karen J. Alter, *The New Terrain of International Law: Courts, Politics and Rights* (Princeton, NJ: Princeton University Press, 2014), 161–331; Armin von Bogdandy and Ingo Venzke, *In Whose Name? A Public Law Theory of International Adjudication* (Oxford: Oxford University Press, 2014). Domestic courts are also quite important in terms of ensuring accountability and strengthening the rule of law. For a detailed discussion of their contribution see *inter alia* André Nollkaemper, *National Courts and the International Rule of Law* (Oxford: Oxford University Press, 2011).

[37] See *inter alia* Rosalyn Higgins, *Problems and Process: International Law and How We Use It* (Oxford: Oxford University Press, 1994), 39–55; Jean d'Aspremont (ed.), *Participants in the International Legal System: Multiple Perspectives on Non-State Actors in International Law* (New York: Routledge, 2011).

Besides its corrective effect in righting wrongs, the exercise of judicial function by ICs is also ascribed a potentially preventive effect, exercised either directly in the course of their judicial activity or through the indirect effect that the mere possibility of being subjected to judicial proceedings has on the behaviour of states or non-state actors. The preventive effect of the activity of ICs, relevant for purposes of ensuring peace or deterring atrocities, has been subject to considerable criticism.[38] In any event, provisional measures by the ICJ or by regional human rights courts,[39] and investigations and statements by the ICC Prosecutor carry the potential to change the behaviour and actions of states or non-state actors involved in activities that might be detrimental to peace. The UN Secretary-General has noted that threat of referrals to ICC can undoubtedly serve a preventive purpose.[40] Rosenne has pointed out that, as a time-honoured attribute of the judicial mission courts should, within the limits of the judicial function, do what they can to prevent the escalation of the conflict between the litigating parties.[41] Provisional measures, indicated by the ICJ in several armed conflict situations, are relevant to restoring peace, despite a marked failure on the part of concerned states to comply with them and a little-developed procedure and possibilities for the Court to monitor such compliance effectively.[42] Even non-compliance with judgments of the ICJ or most other courts rarely

[38] For a critical discussion see *inter alia* Janine Natalya Clark, 'The Impact Question: The ICTY and the Restoration and Maintenance of Peace', in *The Legacy of the International Criminal Tribunal for the Former Yugoslavia*, Bert Swart, Alexander Zahar, and Göran Sluiter (eds.) (Oxford: Oxford University Press, 2011), 56–81; Niki Frencken and Göran Sluiter, 'The United Nations Criminal Tribunals for Yugoslavia and Rwanda', in *An Institutional Approach to the Responsibility to Protect*, Gentian Zyberi (ed.) (Cambridge: Cambridge University Press, 2013), 386–410.

[39] On the issue of provisional measures see *inter alia* Lawrence Collins, 'Provisional and Protective Measures in International Litigation', 234 *Recueil des Cours de la Académie de Droit International de la Haye*, 1992/III (Leiden: Martinus Nijhoff, 1992); Rudolf Bernhardt (ed.), *Interim Measures Indicated by International Courts* (Heidelberg: Springer, 1994); Shabtai Rosenne, *Provisional Measures in International Law: The International Court of Justice and the International Tribunal for the Law of the Sea* (Oxford: Oxford University Press, 2005); Chester Brown, *A Common Law of International Adjudication* (New York: Oxford University Press, 2007), 119–51; Clara Burbano Herrera, *Provisional Measures in the Case Law of the Inter-American Court of Human Rights* (Cambridge: Intersentia, 2010); Eva Rieter, *Preventing Irreparable Harm: Provisional Measures in International Human Rights Adjudication* (Cambridge: Intersentia, 2010); Gentian Zyberi, 'Provisional Measures of the International Court of Justice in Armed Conflict Situations', *Leiden Journal of International Law* 23 (2010), 571–84.

[40] UNSG Report, 'Responsibility to Protect: Timely and Decisive Response' (July 2012) UN Doc. A/66/874-S/2012/578, 25 para. 29.

[41] Shabtai Rosenne, 'A Role for the International Court of Justice in Crisis Management', in *State, Sovereignty, and International Governance*, Gerard Kreijen, Marcel Brus, Jorris Duursma, Elizabeth de Vos, and John Dugard (eds.) (Oxford: Oxford University Press, 2002), 181.

[42] See *inter alia* the provisional measures in the *Application of the Convention on the Prevention and Punishment of the Crime of Genocide (Bosnia and Herzegovina* v. *Serbia and Montenegro)* (Provisional Measures) [1993] ICJ Reports 1993, 3; *Armed Activities on the Territory of the Congo* (*Democratic Republic of Congo* v. *Uganda*), (Provisional Measures) [2000] ICJ Reports 2000, 111; *Application of the International Convention on the Elimination of All Forms of Racial Discrimination* (*Georgia* v. *Russian Federation*) (Provisional Measures) [2008] ICJ Reports 2008, 353; *Certain Activities Carried Out by Nicaragua in the Border Area* (*Costa Rica* v. *Nicaragua*) (Provisional Measures) [2011] ICJ Reports 2011, 6; *Request for Interpretation of the Judgment of 15 June 1962 in the Case concerning the Temple of Preah Vihear (Cambodia* v. *Thailand)* (Provisional Measures) [2011] ICJ Reports 2011, 537.

draws measures of coercion in response.[43] Preliminary investigations by the ICC also might have a preventive effect on the occurrence of mass atrocities by dissuading potential perpetrators from engaging in such conduct for fear of prosecution.[44] That said, generally ICs would be seized in the aftermath of mass atrocities and would be part of a larger process of transitional justice aimed at restoring peace between states or between opposed groups within a given society.[45] The fact that many individuals indicted by the ICC remain at large demonstrates that ensuring accountability for mass atrocity crimes requires strong international cooperation and a considerable degree of commitment on the part of the international community.

From a *jurisdictional* perspective, the role and potential contribution of ICs to promoting, maintaining, or restoring peace generally depends on the subject-matter and geographical and temporal scope of their activity. The contribution of ICs to peace is first and foremost linked to the independent and impartial exercise of their judicial function. A traditional dispute-settlement mechanism, as the ICJ, settles interstate disputes which, if left unaddressed, could potentially disturb international peace and security. Such international disputes range from armed conflict situations to the delimitation of land or maritime boundaries.[46] The ICJ has also provided a number of important advisory opinions on South West Africa (Namibia), Western Sahara, the Occupied Palestinian Territory, and Kosovo. As rightly noted by a judge of the ICJ, following the court's findings in such politically loaded cases would make a great contribution to the cause of international peace and security and, more, to the cause of friendly relations amongst not only the nations but amongst all men.[47] Under Article 38(2) of the ICJ Statute the Court can settle a dispute *ex aequo et bono*, if the parties agree thereto.[48] No state has made use of this procedure so far.

[43] von Bogdandy and Venzke, 'On the Functions of International Courts', 55. More generally on the issue of compliance see Constanze Schulte, *Compliance with Decisions of the International Court of Justice* (Oxford: Oxford University Press, 2005); Alexandra Huneeus, 'Compliance with International Court Judgments and Decisions', in Alter, Romano, and Shany (eds.), *Oxford Handbook of International Adjudication*, 437–63.

[44] For a detailed discussion see *inter alia* David Bosco, The International Criminal Court and Crime Prevention: Byproduct or Conscious Goal, *Michigan State Journal of International Law* 19 (2011), 163–200; Hector Olasolo, *Essays on International Criminal Justice* (London: Hart, 2012), 1–19. See also Michael Contarino and Selena Lucent, 'Stopping the Killing: The International Criminal Court and the Responsibility to Protect', *Global Responsibility to Protect* 1 (2009), 560–83; Michael Contarino and Melinda Negrón-Gonzales, 'The International Criminal Court', in Zyberi (ed.), *An Institutional Approach*, 411–35.

[45] For a discussion of peace and transitional justice see Jemima García-Godos, Chapter 16 in this volume; see also Jessica Lincoln, *Transitional Justice, Peace and Accountability: Outreach and the Role of International Courts after Conflict* (New York: Routledge, 2011).

[46] See Shabtai Rosenne, 'Lessons of the Past and Needs of the Future', in Connie Peck and Roy S. Lee (eds.), *Increasing the Effectiveness of the International Court of Justice* (Leiden: Martinus Nijhoff, 1997), 472.

[47] ICJ, *Legal Consequences for States of the Continued Presence of South Africa in Namibia (South West Africa) notwithstanding Security Council Resolution 276 (1970)*, Oral Statements and Correspondence: Declaration of President Zafrullah Khan, ICJ Reports 1971, 65–6.

[48] See *inter alia* Allain Pellet, 'Article 38', in *The Statute of the International Court of Justice: A Commentary*, Andreas Zimmermann, Christian Tomuschat, Karin Oellers-Frahm, and Christian J.

That said, equity is a part of the law and the ICJ has established a methodology which it usually employs in seeking an equitable solution to cases of maritime delimitation.[49] The judicial function of international criminal justice mechanisms, as the ICTY, ICTR, and ICC involves the investigation and prosecution of alleged perpetrators of mass atrocity crimes. This work is important, primarily for the societies affected by mass violence, but also more generally for the international community in terms of upholding a community interest, namely ensuring accountability for mass atrocity crimes. Notably, the work of the selected ICs includes and permeates both national and international dimensions of peace.

An important contribution of ICs with regard to peace is closely related to their *institutional function* within a larger organizational system, part of which they are. These international organizations are governed by the 'principle of speciality', which means that they are invested by the states that create them with powers, the limits of which are a function of the common interests whose promotion those states entrust to them.[50] Mainly through its advisory opinions the ICJ has rendered general support to the work of the Security Council and the General Assembly in pursuing the interests of peace.[51] An important aspect of such support has taken place in the context of the process of decolonization. The ICJ has managed to play a constructive role within the institutional framework of the UN with regard to the maintenance of peace by first recognizing UN international legal personality;[52] secondly by laying the legal basis for peace-keeping and other quasi-military operations of the UN;[53] and thirdly by interpreting the concurrent functions of the General Assembly and the Security Council in matters related to the maintenance of international peace and security.[54] Under Article 1(1) of the UN Charter the maintenance of international peace and security is considered to be one of the main purposes of the UN. Under Article 24(1) of the UN Charter

Tams (eds.) (2nd edn. Oxford: Oxford University Press, 2012), 791–7. See also Markus Kotzur, 'Ex Aequo et Bono', in *Max Planck Encyclopedia of Public International Law*, http://opil.ouplaw.com/home/EPIL (accessed 17 September 2014).

[49] See the latest Court judgment on this issue, *Maritime Dispute* (*Peru* v. *Chile*) (Judgment) [2014] ICJ, para. 180. See also Elihu Lauterpacht, *Aspects of the Administration of International Justice* (Cambridge: Grotius, 1991), 117–52.

[50] *Legality of the Use by a State of Nuclear Weapons in Armed Conflict* (Advisory Opinion) [1996] ICJ Reports 1996, 78 para. 25.

[51] See *inter alia* Mahasen Mohammad Aljaghoub, *The Advisory Function of the International Court of Justice 1946–2005* (Heidelberg: Springer Law, 2006).

[52] *Reparation for Injuries Suffered in the Service of the United Nations* (Advisory Opinion) [1949] ICJ Reports 1949, 178.

[53] See *inter alia Certain Expenses of the United Nations (Article 17, paragraph 2, of the Charter)* (Advisory Opinion) [1962] ICJ Reports 1962, 151. For a more detailed discussion see *inter alia* Kjetil Mujezinović Larsen, Chapter 15 in this volume; Michael Bothe, 'Peace-Keeping', in *The Charter of the United Nations: A Commentary*, Bruno Simma et al. (eds.) (2nd edn. Oxford: Oxford University Press, 2002), 648–700.

[54] *Legal Consequences of the Construction of a Wall in the Occupied Palestinian Territory* (Advisory Opinion) [2004] ICJ Reports 2004, 148–52 paras. 26–35; *Accordance with International Law of the Unilateral Declaration of Independence in Respect of Kosovo* (Advisory Opinion) [2010] ICJ Reports 2010, 418–23 paras. 36–48. See *inter alia* Shabtai Rosenne, 'The Contribution of the International Court of Justice to the United Nations', *Indian Journal of International Law* 35 (1995), 67–76; Amr, *The Role of the International Court of Justice*, 137–41.

the Security Council has primary responsibility in this regard, with the General Assembly retaining a subsidiary responsibility,[55] as well as the possibility of taking action should the Security Council be deadlocked.[56] The ICJ has noted that there has been an increasing tendency over time for the General Assembly and the Security Council to deal in parallel with the same matter concerning the maintenance of international peace and security, adding that, while the Security Council has tended to focus on the aspects of such matters related to international peace and security, the General Assembly has taken a broader view, considering also their humanitarian, social, and economic aspects.[57] This interpretation highlights the complementary nature of activities undertaken by the Security Council and the General Assembly.

Although an independent, treaty-based international court outside the UN system, there is a close relationship between the ICC and the United Nations, established through the ICC Statute and a separate agreement adopted in 2004.[58] Two situations deemed to endanger international peace and security have been referred to this court by the Security Council so far, namely that in Darfur, Sudan, and that in Libya.[59] The institutional relationship between the ICC and the UN is quite complex.[60] That relationship seems to be based on a broader understanding

[55] See Art. 11(2) of the UN Charter investing the General Assembly with competence to discuss 'any questions relating to the maintenance of international peace and security brought before it by any Member of the United Nations', subject to the limitation included under Art. 12(1), stating that 'While the Security Council is exercising in respect of any dispute or situation the functions assigned to it in the present Charter, the General Assembly shall not make any recommendation with regard to that dispute or situation unless the Security Council so requests.'

[56] See UNGA Res. 337, 'Uniting for Peace' (3 November 1950) UN Doc. A/RES/337(V).

[57] *Accordance with International Law of the Unilateral Declaration of Independence in Respect of Kosovo* (Advisory Opinion) [2010] ICJ Reports 2010, 419 para. 41.

[58] See respectively Art. 2 of the ICC Statute which requires that the court be brought into a relationship with the United Nations; Art. 13(b) under which the Security Council acting under Chapter VII of the UN Charter can refer to the ICC a situation where crimes falling under the jurisdiction of the ICC seem to have been committed; Art. 16 which provides that the UN Security may, in a resolution adopted under Chapter VII of the Charter, request the Court to defer (not commence or proceed with) an investigation or prosecution for a renewable period of twelve months; Art. 115(b) on funds provided by the United Nations, in particular in relation to the expenses incurred due to referrals by the Security Council; Art. 121(1) on amendments to the Statute requiring that the text of any proposed amendment be submitted to the Secretary-General of the United Nations, who shall promptly circulate it to all states parties; Art. 125 whereby the Secretary-General of the United Nations is the depositary of instruments of ratification, acceptance, or approval by member Sstates to the ICC Statute. See also 'Negotiated Relationship Agreement between the International Criminal Court and the United Nations', 7 September 2004, ICC-ASP/3/Res.1.

[59] Respectively Sudan in 2005 through UNSC Res. 1593 (31 March 2005) UN Doc. S/RES/1593, and Libya in 2011 through UNSC Res. 1970 (26 February 2011) UN Doc. S/RES/1970.

[60] See *inter alia* 'The Relationship between the International Criminal Court and the United Nations', War Crimes Research Office, Washington College of Law, August 2009 www.wcl.american.edu/warcrimes/icc/documents/WCRO_Report_on_ICC_and_UN_August2009.pdf (accessed 17 September 2014); Hemi Mistri and Deborah Riuz Verduzco (rapporteurs), 'The UN Security Council and the International Criminal Court', International Law Meeting Summary, with Parliamentarians for Global Action, 16 March 2012, www.pgaction.org/pdf/activity/Chatham-ICC-SC.pdf (accessed 17 September 2014); Larry D Johnson, 'The Lubanga Case and Cooperation between the UN and the ICC: Disclosure Obligation v. Confidentiality Obligation', *Journal of International Criminal Justice* 10 (2012), 887–903.

of the role of the Security Council in the maintenance of peace, which concerns not only peace between states, but also peace within states. This understanding, and the fact that the primary responsibility for the maintenance of peace is vested with the Security Council, is reflected in the latter being able to exercise a certain degree of control over the activity of the ICC.[61] The complex relationship between the ICC and the Security Council brings to the fore the close link that exists between international law and international politics. At the same time, this relationship also highlights the potential tension that might arise between the interests of peace and justice. Schabas has noted that deference to the Security Council, acting under Article 16 of the ICC Statute, may be the way to resolve the difficulty, assuming the wisdom of staying international justice in the interests of peacemaking.[62]

2.1. Key obligations with regard to promoting and enforcing the right to peace

An important development for peace has been the adoption in 2005 of the overarching *responsibility to protect* doctrine by the UN General Assembly, as a clear expression of community interests of the highest importance.[63] According to this doctrine, well-established under both treaty and customary international law,[64] ICs in general and the ICC in particular, have an important role to play in efforts aimed at ensuring that populations are protected from mass atrocity crimes, namely genocide, war crimes, and crimes against humanity.[65] International and regional courts have played an important role in clarifying a number of key legal obligations relevant to the right to peace. It must also be noted that while the existence of these judicial mechanisms offers a possibility for settling disputes, access to them is not automatic due to practical and jurisdictional obstacles.[66] The so-called compulsory

[61] Schabas, *The International Criminal Court*, 325–34.

[62] Schabas, *The International Criminal Court*, 333.

[63] See UNGA Res. 60/1, World Summit Outcome (24 October 2005) UN Doc. A/Res/60/1, paras. 138–9. See also the related Secretary-General reports, namely 'Implementing the Responsibility to Protect', UN Doc. A/63/677 (12 January 2009); 'Early Warning, Assessment and the Responsibility to Protect', UN Doc. A/64/864 (14 July 2010); 'The Role of Regional and Sub-Regional Arrangements in Implementing the Responsibility to Protect', UN Doc. A/65/877–S/2011/393 (27 June 2011); 'Responsibility to Protect: Timely and Decisive Response', UN Doc. A/66/874-S/2012/578 (25 July 2012); 'Responsibility to Protect: State Responsibility and Prevention', UN Doc. A/67/929–S/2013/399 (9 July 2013). For a detailed discussion of RtoP and peace see Engdahl, Chapter 6 in this volume. See also Gentian Zyberi, 'The International Court of Justice', in Zyberi (ed.), *An Institutional Approach*, 365–85.

[64] Since the initial 2001 ICISS report, it has been pointed out that RtoP has a strong foundation on specific legal obligations under human rights and human protection declarations, covenants and treaties, international humanitarian law, and national law (ICISS, 'The Responsibility to Protect', p. XI). See also 'Implementing the Responsibility to Protect', para. 3; 'Timely and Decisive Response', paras. 9, 59; 'Prevention', paras. 6, 40.

[65] See respectively 'Implementing the Responsibility to Protect', paras. 17–19, 53–4; 'Regional and Sub-Regional Arrangements', paras. 19–20 and 37; 'Timely and Decisive Response', paras. 29, 40; 'Prevention', paras. 25, 40.

[66] Only six of the major international human rights treaties have a compromissory clause bestowing jurisdiction on the ICJ: they are Art. IX of the Convention on the Prevention and Punishment

jurisdiction of the ICJ under Article 36(2) of its statute has been accepted by a limited number of states.[67] Despite calls on the part of the UN and proposals to increase that number, the situation has not changed much.[68] Similarly, the ICC Statute has not been universally ratified.[69] On several occasions states bringing cases before the ICJ have not been able to receive a judgment on the merits for lack of jurisdiction.[70] Notably, that has been the case even when violations of *jus cogens* norms, as the prohibition of genocide and torture have been at stake. The ICJ has been adamant in emphasizing that its jurisdiction is based on the consent of states. Another obstacle to the adjudication of international disputes is the fact that sometimes there is more than one state involved in the violations. In these cases one can speak of shared or joint state responsibility.[71] However, the procedures before ICs are not particularly well suited for handling such situations.

Despite such obstacles, the ICJ and its predecessor, the Permanent Court of International Justice (PCIJ), have interpreted and developed a number of important aspects of rights of peoples and minorities,[72] as well as rules and principles

of the Crime of Genocide; Art. 22 of the International Convention on the Elimination of All Forms of Racial Discrimination (CERD); Art. 29 of the Convention on the Elimination of All Forms of Discrimination against Women (CEDAW); Art. 30 of the Convention against Torture and Other Cruel, Inhuman or Degrading Treatment or Punishment (CAT); Art. 92 of the International Convention on the Protection of the Rights of All Migrant Workers and Members of Their Families (CMW); Art. 42 of International Convention for the Protection of All Persons from Enforced Disappearance (CEED). The main instruments of international humanitarian law, namely the Geneva Conventions of 1949 and their two Additional Protocols of 1977 do not include compromissory clauses bestowing jurisdiction on the ICJ.

[67] So far 70 states have accepted the compulsory jurisdiction of the ICJ. For a list of the states see the official website of the Court, www.icj-cij.org/homepage/index.php (accessed 13 Nov 2014), under 'Jurisdiction'. See also Renata Szafarz, *The Compulsory Jurisdiction of the International Court of Justice* (Leiden: Brill, 1993).

[68] UNGA Res. 60/1, World Summit Outcome (24 October 2005) UN Doc. A/Res/60/1, para. 134(f). See also Andrew Strauss, 'Cutting the Gordian Knot: How and Why the United Nations Should Vest the International Court of Justice with Referral Jurisdiction', *Cornell International Law Journal* 44 (2011), 603–58.

[69] So far 122 states have become a member to the ICC Statute. Out of them 34 are African States, 18 are Asia-Pacific states, 18 are from Eastern Europe, 27 from Latin American and Caribbean states, and 25 from Western European and other states. For a list of the states visit the official website of the ICC, www.icc-cpi.int (accessed 13 Nov 2014).

[70] See *Legality of Use of Force* cases (*Serbia and Montenegro* v. *Netherlands* (Judgment) [2004] ICJ; *Serbia and Montenegro* v. *Belgium* (Judgment) [2004] ICJ; *Serbia and Montenegro* v. *Canada* (Judgment) [2004] ICJ; *Serbia and Montenegro* v. *France* (Judgment) [2004] ICJ; *Serbia and Montenegro* v. *Germany* (Judgment) [2004] ICJ; *Serbia and Montenegro* v. *Italy* (Judgment) [2004] ICJ; *Serbia and Montenegro* v. *Portugal* (Judgment) [2004] ICJ; *Yugoslavia* v. *Spain* (Provisional Measures) [1999] ICJ; *Serbia and Montenegro* v. *United Kingdom* (Provisional Measures) [1999] ICJ; *Yugoslavia* v. *United States of America* (Provisional Measures) [1999] ICJ; *Armed Activities on the Territory of the Congo (Democratic Republic of the Congo* v. *Rwanda)* (Judgment) [2005] ICJ Rep 2006, 6; *Application of the International Convention on the Elimination of All Forms of Racial Discrimination (Georgia* v. *Russian Federation)* (Preliminary Objections) [2011] ICJ Rep 2011, 70.

[71] See *inter alia* André Nollkaemper, 'Issues of Shared Responsibility before the International Court of Justice', in *Evolving Principles of International Law: Studies in Honour of Karel C. Wellens*, Eva Rieter and Henri de Waele (eds.) (Leiden: Martinus Nijhoff, 2012), 199–237.

[72] See *inter alia* Anne-Laure Vaurs-Chaumette, 'Peoples and Minorities', in *The Law of International Responsibility*, James Crawford, Alain Pellet, and Simon Olleson (eds.) (Oxford: Oxford University Press, 2010), 993–1003. For a more general discussion see Alfred de Zayas, 'The

of international human rights and humanitarian law that are relevant to ensuring peace.[73] Besides solving the disputes at hand, these findings of the ICJ provide some clarity on the legal obligations incumbent upon states and international organizations with regard to ensuring the right to peace, as well as the relevant entitlements under international law accruing to individuals and groups of individuals. At the same time, by investigating and prosecuting alleged perpetrators of mass atrocity crimes, the ICC renders a contribution to the protection of fundamental human rights and ultimately to ensuring peace.[74] The success of the activity of these ICs with regard to peace is dependent on state cooperation and their willingness to comply with the decisions rendered and other relevant international legal obligations.

The discussion in the following subsections focuses on a number of selected key legal obligations that are important for promoting, maintaining, and restoring peace, namely the duties to refrain from the unlawful use of force and military intervention, to prevent mass atrocities, to investigate and punish perpetrators of mass atrocities, and to cooperate with ICs. There might be tension at times between these duties, especially between the duty to refrain from the unlawful use of force and that of preventing mass atrocities, in the event that the Security Council does not authorize such intervention in the face of ongoing mass atrocities. Also, occasionally the duty to investigate and prosecute alleged perpetrators of mass atrocity crimes might compete with the duty to cooperate with ICs,

International Judicial Protection of Peoples and Minorities' in *Peoples and Minorities in International Law*, Catherine Brölman, René Lefeber, and Marjolein Zieck (eds.) (Dordrecht: Martinus Nijhoff, 1993), 253–87; Zyberi, 'The International Court of Justice and the Rights of Peoples', 327–52.

[73] See *inter alia* Raymond Goy, *La Cour Internationale de Justice et les Droits de l'Homme* (Brussels: Bruylant, 2002); Shiv R. S. Bedi, *The Development of Human Rights Law by the Judges of the International Court of Justice* (London: Hart, 2007); Rosalyn Higgins, 'Human Rights in the International Court of Justice', *Leiden Journal of International Law* 20 (2007), 745–51; Gentian Zyberi, *The Humanitarian Face of the International Court of Justice: Its Contribution to Interpreting and Developing International Human Rights and Humanitarian Law Rules and Principles* (Antwerp: Intersentia, 2008); Sandesh Sivakumaran, 'The International Court of Justice and Human Rights', in *Research Handbook on International Human Rights Law*, Sarah Joseph and Adam McBeth (eds.) (Cheltenham: Edward Elgar, 2010), 299–325; Gentian Zyberi, 'Human Rights in the International Court of Justice', in *International Human Rights Law: 60 Years after the UDHR*, Mashood Baderin and Manisuli Ssenyonjo (eds.) (Aldershot: Ashgate, 2010), 289–304; Simma, 'Human Rights Before the International Court of Justice', 301–25; Ralph Wilde, 'Human Rights Beyond Borders at the World Court: The Significance of the International Court of Justice's Jurisprudence on the Extraterritorial Application of International Human Rights Law Treaties', *Chinese Journal of International Law* 12 (2013), 639–77.

[74] See *inter alia* Dinah Shelton (ed.), *International Crimes, Peace, And Human Rights: The Role of the International Criminal Court* (New York: Transnational, 2000); Errol P. Mendes, *Peace and Justice at the International Criminal Court: A Court of Last Resort* (Cheltenham: Edward Elgar, 2010). See also 'Strengthening the International Criminal Court and the Assembly of States Parties', 27 November 2013, UN Doc. ICC-ASP/12/Res.8, noting '*Convinced that the International Criminal Court* ("the Court") *is an essential means of promoting respect for* international humanitarian law and human rights, thus contributing to freedom, security, justice and the rule of law, as well as to the prevention of armed conflicts, the *preservation of peace* and the strengthening of international security and the advancement of post-conflict peacebuilding and reconciliation with a view to *achieving sustainable peace*, in accordance with the purposes and principles of the Charter of the United Nations' (emphasis added).

as states might have different understandings of what complementarity between domestic criminal jurisdiction and international criminal jurisdiction entails.

2.1.1. *The duty to refrain from the unlawful use of force and (unauthorized) military intervention*

The duty of states to refrain from the unlawful use of force and military intervention in conducting their international affairs is an important foundation of international law and a precondition for peaceful relations among states. As such, this important prohibition is laid down in Article 2(4) of the UN Charter and has become part of customary international law.[75] The duty of states to refrain from the unlawful use of force is intrinsically related to the prohibition of aggression.[76] Acts of aggression would potentially trigger both state responsibility and individual criminal responsibility. The ICJ has made a number of relevant legal findings concerning state responsibility. Thus, in the *Nicaragua* case, the ICJ has found that 'Principles such as those of the non-use of force, non-intervention, respect for the independence and territorial integrity of States, and the freedom of navigation, continue to be binding as part of customary international law, despite the operation of provisions of conventional law in which they have been incorporated.'[77] In noting the customary law character of the principle of non-intervention, the Court stated that 'The principle of non-intervention involves the right of every sovereign State to conduct its affairs without outside interference; though examples of trespass against this principle are not infrequent, the Court considers that it is part and parcel of customary international law.'[78] Moreover, the ICJ has emphasized that 'The element of coercion, which defines, and indeed forms the very essence of, prohibited intervention, is particularly obvious in the case of an intervention which uses force, either in the direct form of military action, or in the indirect form of support for subversive or terrorist armed activities within another state.'[79] Through these findings the ICJ has emphasized resorting to peaceful means for the settlement of disputes and refraining from the threat or use of force as expected standards of state conduct. While that has not always prohibited powerful countries from resorting to the illegal use of force, through its case law the ICJ has laid down standards for assessing state conduct and for assigning international legal responsibility in case of violations.

Besides state responsibility, the illegal use of force can trigger individual criminal responsibility. The military tribunals for Nuremberg and the Far East tried

[75] See *inter alia* UNGA Res. 290(IV) (1 December 1949) UN Doc. A/RES/290(IV); UNGA Res. 2625 (XXV) (24 October 1970) UN Doc. A/RES/2625(XXV).

[76] See *inter alia* Russell Buchan, *International Law and the Construction of the Liberal Peace* (Oxford: Hart, 2013), 54–9, 60–4. See also UNGA Res. 3314 (XXIX) 'Definition of Aggression' (14 December 1974) UN Doc. S/RES/3314(XXIX).

[77] *Military and Paramilitary Activities in and against Nicaragua (Nicaragua* v. *United States of America)* (Preliminary Objections) [1984] ICJ Rep 1984, 424 para. 73.

[78] *Nicaragua* v. *United States of America* (Merits) [1986] ICJ Rep 1986, 106 para. 202.

[79] *Nicaragua* v. *United States of America* (Merits), 108 para. 205.

individual major war criminals for such crimes at the end of World War II. Both Statutes included crimes against peace.[80] The same crime was initially included in the ICC Statute and further laid down in the 2010 Review Conference in Kampala.[81] Under the ICC Statute, the crime of aggression can be committed by a person in a position effectively to exercise control over or to direct the political or military action of a state to perform an act of aggression which, by its character, gravity, and scale, constitutes a manifest violation of the UN Charter. In other words, the crime of aggression can only be committed by senior state officials. By allowing these ICs to adjudicate issues of state responsibility or individual criminal responsibility concerning acts or omissions that disturb international peace, states have vested them with significant powers and responsibilities.

2.1.2. The duty to prevent mass atrocity crimes

Basically, the duty to prevent mass atrocity crimes includes the duty to prevent genocide, war crimes, and crimes against humanity. This community interest is expressed clearly in the doctrine of responsibility to protect (RtoP), adopted by the UN in the 2005 World Summit Outcome Document.[82] Based on treaty and customary international law the ICJ has made a number of important findings with regard to certain aspects of state responsibility and ensuing legal consequences for violations of the duty to prevent mass atrocity crimes. States have a duty to respect and ensure respect for international humanitarian law (IHL).[83] While the scope of the obligation to ensure respect for IHL incumbent upon a state, or the organized community of states, it is not entirely clear, at least a state must respect IHL in any international or non-international armed conflict to which it is a party. This subsection will deal mainly with the findings of the ICJ concerning the duty to prevent genocide.

With regard to the duty to prevent genocide, the ICJ has held that:

> The obligation on each contracting State to prevent genocide is both normative and compelling. It is not merged in the duty to punish, nor can it be regarded as simply a component of that duty. It has its own scope, which extends beyond the particular case envisaged

[80] Respectively Art. 6(a) of the Statute of the International Military Tribunal of Nuremberg and Art. 5(a) of the Statute of the International Military Tribunal for the Far East. For more information visit http://avalon.law.yale.edu/subject_menus/imt.asp (accessed 13 Nov 2014). See *inter alia* Larry May, *Aggression and Crimes Against Peace* (Cambridge: Cambridge University Press, 2008).

[81] ICC Statute, Art. 8*bis* (RC/Res.6, annex I, of 11 June 2010).

[82] UNGA Res. 60/1, 'World Summit Outcome' (24 October 2005), UN Doc. A/Res/60/1, paras. 138–40. For more on RtoP see *inter alia* Gareth Evans, *The Responsibility to Protect: Ending Mass Atrocity Crimes Once and for All* (Washington, DC: Brookings Institution, 2008); Alex J. Bellamy, *Responsibility to Protect: The Global Effort to End Mass Atrocities* (Cambridge: Polity, 2009); Jared Genser and Irwin Cotler (eds.), *The Responsibility to Protect: The Promise of Stopping Mass Atrocities in Our Time* (Oxford: Oxford University Press, 2011); Julia Hoffmann and André Nollkaemper (eds.), *Responsibility to Protect: From Principle to Practice* (Amsterdam: Amsterdam University Press, 2012); Zyberi (ed.), *An Institutional Approach*.

[83] See Common Art. 1 to the Geneva Conventions of 1949. See also *Nicaragua* v. *United States of America*, 114 para. 220.

in Article VIII, namely reference to the competent organs of the United Nations, for them to take such action as they deem appropriate.[84]

Indeed, the duty to prevent genocide cannot be equated with the duty to punish the culprits in its aftermath. Nor can it be understood as simply limited to a formal reference to certain important international organs, such as the Security Council, the General Assembly, or the Human Rights Council.[85] As the Court has emphasized, the obligation on the part of states to prevent genocide has a continuous and distinct character, extending alongside that of the competent organs of the UN:

> Even if and when these organs have been called upon, this does not mean that the States parties to the Convention are relieved of the obligation to take such action as they can to prevent genocide from occurring, while respecting the United Nations Charter and any decisions that may have been taken by its competent organs.[86]

This finding of the ICJ highlights the shared responsibility of individual states and the international organizations entrusted with protecting populations from mass atrocity crimes, as well as the need for international solidarity and close cooperation in putting a stop to grave violations of international law. However, while urging states to take action, the ICJ limits the scope of such action by reference to the UN Charter and any decisions that may have been taken by its competent organs.

2.1.3. *The duty to investigate and to prosecute perpetrators of mass atrocity crimes*

The duty to investigate and to prosecute perpetrators of mass atrocity crimes is largely a post-conflict process. Many authors have noted that peace and justice seem to enjoy a complex relationship in a post-conflict environment.[87] There seems to be a division also across disciplinary lines, with lawyers putting more emphasis on judicial processes and accountability and political scientists and international relations' scholars leaning more towards other forms of dealing with the past, such as amnesties and truth and reconciliation commissions. A moral theory of international law takes the chief moral goals of the international legal system to be peace, not just among, but also within states, and justice.[88]

[84] *Application of the Convention on the Prevention and Punishment of the Crime of Genocide (Bosnia and Herzegovina* v. *Serbia and Montenegro)* (Judgment) [2007] ICJ Reports 2007, 220 para. 427.

[85] See respectively chs. 4 (Terry D. Gill), 5 (Cedric Ryngaert and Hanne Cuyckens), and 7 (Lyal S. Sunga) in Zyberi (ed.), *An Institutional Approach.*

[86] *Bosnia and Herzegovina* v. *Serbia and Montenegro*, para. 427.

[87] See *inter alia* Colm Campbell, 'Peace and the Laws of War: The Role of International Humanitarian Law in the Post-Conflict Environment', *International Review of the Red Cross* 82 (2000), 627–52; Olivier Ribbelink (ed.), *Beyond the UN Charter: Peace, Security and the Role of Justice* (The Hague: Hague Academic Press, 2008); Carsten Stahn, Jennifer S. Easterday, and Jens Iverson (eds.), *Jus Post Bellum: Mapping the Normative Foundations* (Oxford: Oxford University Press, 2014).

[88] See *inter alia* Allen Buchanan, *Justice, Legitimacy, and Self-Determination: Moral Foundations for International Law* (Oxford: Oxford University Press, 2007), 60; Grenville Clark and Louis B. Sohn, *World Peace through World Law* (2nd edn. Cambridge, Mass.: Harvard University Press, 1960); Teitel, *Humanity's Law.*

The duty to investigate and to prosecute perpetrators of mass atrocity crimes is well established under both treaty and customary international law.[89] The ICJ has addressed in considerable detail the *duty to punish* under Articles IV, V, and VI and the *duty to co-operate with international courts and tribunals* under Article VI of the Genocide Convention.[90] Based on the fact that the genocidal acts were not carried out in its territory, the Court concluded that Serbia could not be charged with not having tried before its own courts those accused of having participated in the Srebrenica genocide, either as principal perpetrators or as accomplices, or of having committed one of the other acts mentioned in Article III of the Convention.[91] The ICJ has laid emphasis on territorial jurisdiction by finding that Article VI of the Genocide Convention obliges the Contracting Parties only to institute and exercise territorial criminal jurisdiction.[92] In accordance also with the *Lotus* principle,[93] states are not prohibited, however, from conferring jurisdiction on their criminal courts based on criteria other than where the crime was committed which are compatible with international law, in particular the nationality of the accused.[94] The jurisdiction of the permanent ICC is based on the principle of complementarity, whereby every participating state has a primary responsibility to investigate and prosecute alleged perpetrators of the serious crimes falling under the ICC Statute which have been committed in its territory.[95] Accordingly, the ICC would only get involved when a state is unable or unwilling to carry out this obligation. With eight situations and a number of cases before it, the ICC is an important tool in the fight against impunity for serious crimes, with all the challenges involved.

While most of this international judicial activity takes place *ex post facto*, that is, in the aftermath of egregious human rights and humanitarian law violations, both the ICJ and the ICC can potentially play a preventive role in terms of maintaining or restoring peace. The ICJ can do so mainly through its ability to indicate provisional measures to the parties to a dispute.[96] In seven cases involving situations of

[89] See *inter alia* the Statutes and the case law of the IMTN and the IMTFE; the ILC's Nuremberg Principles (29 July 1950); the 1948 Genocide Convention; the 1949 Geneva Conventions; the 1984 Convention Against Torture; the Statutes and the case law of the ICTY, the ICTR, and the ICC; and the Statutes and the case law of a number of hybrid criminal courts.

[90] *Bosnia and Herzegovina* v. *Serbia and Montenegro*, paras. 439–50.

[91] *Bosnia and Herzegovina* v. *Serbia and Montenegro*, para. 442.

[92] *Bosnia and Herzegovina* v. *Serbia and Montenegro*, paras. 439–45.

[93] PCIJ, *The Case of the S.S. 'Lotus' (France* v. *Turkey)*, PCIJ Reports 1927, Ser. A, No. 10.

[94] *Bosnia and Herzegovina* v. *Serbia and Montenegro*, paras. 439–45.

[95] See *inter alia* Mohamed M. El Zeidy, *The Principle of Complementarity in International Criminal Law: Origin, Development and Practice* (Leiden: Martinus Nijhoff, 2008); Carsten Stahn and Mohamed M. El Zeidy (eds.), *The International Criminal Court and Complementarity: From Theory to Practice* (Cambridge: Cambridge University Press, 2011); Sarah Nouwen, *Complementarity in the Line of Fire: The Catalysing Effect of the International Criminal Court in Uganda and Sudan* (Cambridge: Cambridge University Press, 2013).

[96] Under Art. 41 of its Statute the ICJ has been given the power to indicate, if it considers that the circumstances so require, any provisional measures that ought to be taken to preserve the respective rights of either party. See *inter alia* Hugh Thirlway, 'The Indication of Provisional Measures by the International Court of Justice', in *Interim Measures Indicated by International Courts*, Rudolf Bernhardt (ed.) (Heidelberg: Springer, 1994), 1–36.

armed conflict there were 17 requests for provisional measures filed with the ICJ.[97] The ICC can do so through its ability to receive information on gross human rights violations, its preliminary investigations, and the statements of its Chief Prosecutor. An interesting development in terms of enforcing state obligations concerning the investigation and prosecution of alleged perpetrators of serious crimes are the legal proceedings in the case of *Belgium* v. *Senegal*, which can be considered as the first successful case of protection of an international community interest by a third party.[98] There the ICJ found that Belgium as a state party to the 1984 Convention against Torture (CAT) had standing to invoke the responsibility of Senegal for the alleged breaches of its obligations under Articles 6(2) and 7(1) of CAT to make an immediate preliminary inquiry into the facts and prosecute or extradite Mr Hissène Habré, former President of Chad, for large scale violations of human rights.[99] According to the ICJ, Belgium's standing was based on the entitlement of each State party to CAT to make a claim concerning the cessation of an alleged breach by another State party.[100] However, similar cases where a third State invokes the responsibility of another State to take active steps to ensure individual criminal accountability for serious human rights violations are most likely to remain an exception to the norm.

2.2. Certain aspects of the responsibility of international organizations in ensuring peace

Through the broad range of their rights and duties, international organizations play an important role in ensuring peace. The ICJ has made a number of relevant findings with regard to the rights and obligations of the UN in ensuring peace, mainly through its advisory opinions.[101] While there are differing views with regard to the value and legal basis for such recommendations of the ICJ,[102] the advisory role of the ICJ, as the principal legal organ of the UN, and the authority

[97] Zyberi, 'Provisional Measures of the ICJ', 572.

[98] Simma, 'Human Rights Before the International Court of Justice', 313–14.

[99] For a summary of the facts of the case, see *Questions Relating to the Obligation to Prosecute or Extradite (Belgium* v. *Senegal)* (Judgment) [2012] ICJ, 431–40 paras. 15–41.

[100] *Belgium* v. *Senegal*, paras. 67–70.

[101] See *inter alia Reparation for Injuries Suffered in the Service of the UN* (Advisory Opinion), 174; *Certain Expenses of the UN* (Advisory Opinion), 151; *Legal Consequences for States of the Continued Presence of South Africa in Namibia* (Advisory Opinion), 16; *Western Sahara* (Advisory Opinion) [1975] ICJ Rep 1975, 12; *Legality of the Threat or Use of Nuclear Weapons* (Advisory Opinion) [1996] ICJ Rep 1996, 226; *Legal Consequences of the Construction of a Wall* (Advisory Opinion), 136. See generally Nigel D White, *The Law of International Organisations* (Manchester: Manchester University Press, 2005); Jan Klabbers, *An Introduction to International Institutional Law* (2nd edn. Cambridge: Cambridge University Press, 2009); Henry G. Schermers and Niels M. Blokker, *International Institutional Law: Unity Within Diversity* (5th edn. Leiden: Martinus Nijhoff, 2011). See also 'Draft Articles on the Responsibility of International Organizations, with Commentaries', *Yearbook of the International Law Commission* (2011), ii. pt. 2.

[102] See respectively Jean d'Aspremont, 'The Recommendations Made by the International Court of Justice', *International and Comparative Law Quarterly* 56 (2007), 185–98; cf. Hugh Thirlway, 'The Recommendations Made by the ICJ: A Skeptical View', *International and Comparative Law Quarterly* 58 (2009), 151–62.

of its legal opinions, cannot be underestimated. First, the ICJ has acknowledged the legal personality of the UN and its capacity to carry out its functions. Secondly, the ICJ has recognized the right of the UN to bring a claim for reparations for injuries suffered by its staff in the performance of duties assigned to them by this organization.[103] At the same time this court has cautioned that all agents of the United Nations, in whatever official capacity they act, must take care not to exceed the scope of their functions, and should so comport themselves as to avoid claims against the United Nations.[104] The ICJ has stated that when the Security Council adopts a decision in the course of fulfilling its responsibility for the maintenance of international peace and security, it is for all member states to comply with that decision, since to hold otherwise would be to deprive this principal organ of its essential functions and powers under the Charter.[105] In assisting the Security Council and the General Assembly in their work in the framework of the process of decolonization, the ICJ has clarified the scope of rights of these main organs under the UN Charter vis-à-vis the state and the peoples concerned.[106] As part of its recommendations, in the *Wall* advisory opinion the ICJ considered it its duty to draw the attention of the General Assembly to the need for efforts at negotiation to be encouraged with a view to achieving as soon as possible, on the basis of international law, a negotiated solution to the outstanding problems and the establishment of a Palestinian state, existing side by side with Israel and its other neighbours, with peace and security for all in the region.[107] In the *dispositif* of this decision the Court only called on the General Assembly and the Security Council to consider what further action is required to bring to an end the illegal situation resulting from the construction of the wall and the associated regime.[108] Through these legal findings the ICJ has provided necessary guidance, while supporting the activity of the main organs of the UN in pursuing the interests of peace.

2.3. The contribution of the international criminal courts and tribunals with regard to peace

International criminal courts and tribunals have been instrumental in establishing and enforcing the principle of individual criminal responsibility for internationally recognized crimes.[109] The ICTY was established in 1993, in the midst

[103] See *Reparation for Injuries Suffered in the Service of the UN* (Advisory Opinion), 187–8.

[104] *Difference Relating to Immunity from Legal Process of a Special Rapporteur of the Commission on Human Rights* (Advisory Opinion) [1999] ICJ Rep 1999, 89 para. 66.

[105] *Legal Consequences for States of the Continued Presence of South Africa in Namibia* (Advisory Opinion), 54 para. 116.

[106] *Western Sahara* (Advisory Opinion), 31–3 paras. 54–9.

[107] See *Legal Consequences of the Construction of a Wall* (Advisory Opinion), 200–1 paras. 161–2.

[108] *Legal Consequences of the Construction of a Wall* (Advisory Opinion), 201 para. 162.

[109] See respectively Art. 6, Charter of the Nuremberg Military Tribunal; Art. 5, Charter of the Military Tribunal for the Far East; Art. 7, ICTY Statute; Art. 6, ICTR Statute; Art. 25, ICC Statute; also Principles of International Law Recognized in the Charter of the Nuremberg Tribunal and in the Judgment of the Tribunal, *Yearbook of the International Law Commission* (1950), ii. para. 97. See generally Elies van Sliedregt, *Individual Criminal Responsibility in International Law* (New York: Oxford University Press, 2012); Kirsten Sellars, *'Crimes against Peace' and International Law* (Cambridge: Cambridge University Press, 2013).

of the armed conflicts unfolding in the former Yugoslavia. However, neither its establishment, nor the indictments the tribunal issued in the course of its activity managed to restore peace in this region, with conflicts erupting in Kosovo in 1998–9 and briefly in Macedonia in summer 2001. Nor did the parties to the conflict heed the repeated calls by the Security Council to respect human rights and humanitarian law and to bring the conflict to an end. The impact of the ICTY in limiting the scope of the conflict in the former Yugoslavia and restoring peace has been questioned.[110] Empirical research is necessary to measure the preventive effect of the ICC on the conflicts taking place in different parts of the world and in furthering peace. The establishment of international criminal courts and tribunals and the ensuing strong emphasis on individual accountability for mass atrocity crimes has triggered a peace versus justice discussion.[111] On its part, the UN has distanced itself clearly from amnesties which provide immunity for gross violations of human rights and serious violations of international humanitarian law.

In acknowledging the importance of reparations for the victims of mass atrocity crimes, the international community included in the ICC system a Trust Fund and allowed victims to participate in the legal proceedings. The ICTY has recognized that reparations for victims are important for peace and that the investigation and prosecution of perpetrators alone is not sufficient. Thus, the ICTY has stated that, 'The Tribunal cannot, through the rendering of its judgements alone, bring peace and reconciliation to the region: other remedies should complement the criminal trials if lasting peace is to be achieved, and one such remedy should be adequate reparations to the victims for their suffering.'[112] From a general perspective, reparations for the victims seem not to have received the necessary attention and the willingness on the part of the international community to shoulder the financial burden for such compensation is lacking.

3. Concluding Remarks

This chapter has tried to provide a general perspective on the role and contribution of ICs in promoting and ensuring peace within the broader framework of international law, alongside other methods and mechanisms of dispute settlement, as provided under Article 33 of the UN Charter. The case law and activity

[110] See *inter alia* Clark, 'The Impact Question', 56–81.

[111] See *inter alia* Paul R. Williams and Michael P. Scharf, *Peace with Justice? War Crimes and Accountability in the Former Yugoslavia* (Lanham, Md.: Rowman & Littlefield, 2002); Margaret E. McGuinness, 'Peace v. Justice: The Universal Declaration of Human Rights and the Modern Origins of the Debate', *Diplomatic History* 35 (2011), 749–68; Richard Falk, *Seeking Peace and Justice in the 21st Century: Humanitarian Intervention, Responsibility to Protect, and Legitimacy Wars* (New York: Routledge, 2014).

[112] 'Letter dated 12 May 2011 from the President of the International Tribunal for the Prosecution of Persons Responsible for Serious Violations of International Humanitarian Law Committed in the Territory of the Former Yugoslavia since 1991, addressed to the President of the Security Council', 18 May 2011, UN Security Council, UN Doc. S/2011/316, para. 90.

of these ICs demonstrate their significant role and contribution in clarifying certain aspects of the relevant legal obligations incumbent upon states, international organizations, and individuals. That said, their role and contribution to peace should not be overestimated, as it is heavily dependent on the willingness of states and international organizations to make use of their procedures and subsequently to comply with their decisions. Indeed, as Rosenne has aptly put it, the real test for states is found in their willingness in general to allow the law to occupy a prominent and constructive part in their international relations.[113] The contribution of the selected ICs to peace would fall broadly under the concept of *negative peace*, in that they try to prevent, stop, and condemn the unlawful use of force, as well as assign state responsibility and individual criminal responsibility for serious human rights and humanitarian law violations.

By settling interstate disputes and rendering advisory opinions to the main organs of the UN and its specialized agencies the ICJ has contributed in maintaining or restoring international peace and security, alongside the main organs of the UN. This role is mainly relevant for instances of interstate conflicts on various grounds, which could endanger peace and security. The ICTY and the ICTR have played an important role in investigating and prosecuting perpetrators of genocide, war crimes, and crimes against humanity. That function is continued on a permanent basis and with broader coverage by the ICC. By emphasizing individual criminal accountability for mass atrocities these judicial mechanisms can play a retributive as well as a preventive and deterrent role, which is potentially important for purposes of maintaining or restoring peace. At the same time, by exposing the truth and creating a broad narrative, these international judicial organs can contribute to the restoration of peace between different ethnic or religious groups within a state.

The first aspect of the contribution of ICs to peace is related to their primary function, namely the settlement of international disputes or the investigation and prosecution of individuals for crimes that are of concern not only to an affected society but also to the international community as a whole. The second aspect of their contribution is broader and relates to their institutional role within the respective organization, namely rendering support and legitimacy to the actions of their sister organs. Thus, the ICJ has supported the General Assembly and the Security Council on different issues relating to the maintenance of international peace and security, through clarifying the scope of their powers as well as the nature of their interrelationship. The ICTY and the ICTR have assisted the Security Council in addressing mass atrocity crimes committed in the former Yugoslavia and Rwanda respectively. The third aspect of ICs' contribution, which follows from their judicial function, is their ability to hold states as well as individuals responsible for serious crimes that disturb international peace and security. As the ICJ has rightly observed, that duality of responsibility continues to be a constant feature of international law.[114] A related, fourth aspect of the

[113] Rosenne, *The Law and Practice of the International Court*, 176.
[114] *Bosnia and Herzegovina* v. *Serbia and Montenegro*, 116 para. 173.

contribution of ICs to promoting and ensuring peace is the development of relevant standards of behaviour for states, international organizations, individuals, and non-state actors more generally, lest they incur international responsibility.[115] To the extent the main ICs have been engaged in these complex processes of maintaining or restoring peace and ensuring accountability for serious crimes that endanger peace, these four aspects of their activity seem to have been used to serve the interests of peace.

[115] On the issue of judicial lawmaking see *inter alia* Lauterpacht, *The Development of International Law*, 155–223; Edward McWhinney, 'The International Court of Justice and International Law-Making: The Judicial Activism/Self-Restraint Antinomy', *Chinese Journal of International Law* 5 (2006), 3–13; Thomas Buergenthal, 'Lawmaking by the ICJ and Other International Courts, Proceedings of the Annual Meeting' *Am. Soc'y Int'l L. Proc.* 103 (2009), 403–6; Shane Darcy and Joseph Powderly (eds.), *Judicial Creativity at the International Criminal Tribunals* (Oxford: Oxford University Press, 2010); Armin von Bogdandy and Ingo Venzke, 'Beyond Dispute: International Judicial Institutions as Lawmakers', *German Law Journal* 12 (2011), 979–1004; Niels Petersen, 'Lawmaking by the International Court of Justice—Factors of Success', *German Law Journal* 12 (2011), 1295–316; Armin von Bogdandy and Ingo Venzke (eds.), *International Judicial Lawmaking* (London: Springer 2012); Tams and Sloan (eds.), *The Development of International Law*; Yuval Shany, *Assessing the Effectiveness of International Courts* (Oxford: Oxford University Press, 2014).

18

International Fact-Finding Mechanisms: Lighting Candles or Cursing Darkness?

Cecilie Hellestveit

1. Introduction

Over the past two decades international fact-finding mechanisms have gained unprecedented ground as tools by which the international community responds to man-made emergencies that may threaten peace. International fact-finding missions, commissions of inquiry, mapping exercises, and panels of experts are mandated to inquire into factual circumstances of a variety of situations that raise international concern. International fact-finding has for over a century aimed at preventing armed conflict. Increasingly, fact-finding is also assuming a critical role in efforts to bring perpetrators of international crimes to justice.[1]

This chapter presents various types of fact-finding instruments, and assesses their role in the international legal architecture of peace. The chapter relies on a stringent view of peace as a reflection of the absence of armed conflict.

International fact-finding instruments have been around for a century. Their steady proliferation in recent years may be ascribed to various developments. First, they respond to a desire to strengthen the international toolbox of conflict prevention. Secondly, fact-finding lends ears and eyes to victims of atrocities in efforts to replicate successes of domestic fact-finding as a reconciliatory measure in post-conflict settings.[2] Thirdly, fact-finding may serve as enforcement-mechanisms enhancing the authority of a specific treaty.[3] Lastly, the trend towards international accountability for international crimes relies on fact-finding to consolidate and extend its scope.[4]

[1] 'International crimes' refers to the categories enumerated in the ICC Statute Art. 5: crimes against humanity, war crimes, or genocide.

[2] See 'Republic of Liberia: Truth and Reconciliation Commission, Final Report', Volume II: Consolidated Final Report, TRC (2009), 268–91, with reconciliatory, non-repetitive, and pragmatic accountability mechanisms.

[3] '[A]n impartial investigation of reports of possible use of chemical and bacteriological weapons would further enhance the authority of the 1925 Geneva (Gas) Protocol', UNCS Res. 42/37 (30 November 1987) UN Doc. A/RES/42/37C, preamble para. 5.

[4] Antonio Cassese, 'Fostering Increased Conformity with International Standards: Monitoring and Institutional Fact-Finding', in *Realizing Utopia: The Future of International Law*, Antonio Cassese (ed.) (Oxford: Oxford University Press, 2012), 295.

Fact-finding Mechanisms at the international level resemble administrative measures under domestic law. They do not have adjudicative elements, but are intended to investigate and report on facts. Tasks typically include examining data, hearing testimony, and considering contextual circumstances. The results are presented in a report at the end of the inquiry, or in the case of permanent mechanisms, with agreed intervals or following specific incidents.

International intergovernmental organizations are often in shortage of decisive enforcement mechanisms. Alternatively, they are reluctant to invoke them. Instruments of fact-finding may offer a *via media*, implying that action may eventually become decisive. Put bluntly, international fact-finding signals concern without commitment.

Fact-finding may serve as basis for negotiation, settlement, or containment of a crisis, and thereby offer a *preventive* tool of conflict mitigation.[5] It may also serve to determine which judicial forum is best suited to address the relevant incidents, in which case fact-finding is rather an instrument of *accountability*.[6] Finally, a fact-finding mission may have a symbolic role as recognition of victims of international crimes, which essentially is a measure of *reconciliation*.[7] The multiple purposes of international fact-finding mechanisms make them highly flexible and useful semi-legal tools for responding to an unfolding crisis.

Fact-finding mechanisms are not instruments of adjudication. Their primary objective is to move issues at the international level, influencing political processes. Multi-purpose fact-finding in this respect offers useful flexibility. Seen from the perspective of international law, a fact-finding mandate incorporating multiple ambitions may nevertheless pose problems.[8] Mandate, methodology, selection of law and facts, and thereby also conclusions and recommendations of fact-finding often diverge depending on whether the purpose is prevention, accountability, or reconciliation. Multipurpose fact-finding

[5] After the outbreak of the Second Intifada in September 2000, the Israelis and the Palestinians reached an agreement to form a fact-finding body to examine the facts and causes of the violent outbreaks, and to propose ideas to prevent their recurrence. See 'Report of the Sharm el-Sheikh Fact-Finding Committee', 30 April 2001, SN3552/01(Or.fr), also known as the 'Mitchell Report'.

[6] Robb Grace and Claude Bruderlein, 'Building Effective Monitoring, Reporting and Fact-Finding Mechanisms', *Working Paper Program on Humanitarian Policy and Conflict Research at Harvard University* (2012), 1–17 at 13–14.

[7] See notably Christine Chinkin, 'U.N. Human Rights Council Fact-Finding Mission: Lessons From Gaza', in *Looking to the Future: Essays on International law in Honor of W. Michael Reisman*, Mahnoush H. Arsanjani, Jacob Katz Cogan, Robert D. Sloane, and Siegfried Wiessner (eds.) (Leiden: Martinus Nijhoff, 2011), 475–98 at 496; Thomas M. Franck and H. Scott Fairley, 'Procedural Due Process In Human Rights Fact-Finding By International Agencies', *American Journal of International Law* 74 (1980), 308.

[8] For an overview of fact-finding mandates in recent years, see Robb Grace, 'The Design and Planning of Monitoring, Reporting and Fact-finding Missions', *Harvard University—Program on Humanitarian Policy and Conflict Research* (9 December 2013), 1–47. See also Marina Aksenova and Morten Bergsmo, 'Non-Criminal Justice Fact-Work in the Age of Accountability', in *Quality Control in Fact-Finding*, Morten Bergsmo (ed.) (Torkel Opsahl Academic EPublisher, 2013), 1–34.

risks becoming *purposeless* fact-finding, weakening its potential impact, except for its symbolic value as an expression of concern by the international community.

Fact finding missions will always satisfy a strong urge to act, thereby showing responsiveness.[9] Yet, critics suggest that fact-finding mechanisms are less a development of international law than a 'reason for multiplication of reports'.[10] Do international fact-finding mechanisms serve to bemoan violations of international law while concealing inadequacies in international law's ability to respond to armed conflict and serious human rights abuse? Or is fact-finding an increasingly decisive component in the architecture of the international law of peace and its ability to contain, alleviate, and ease recovery from armed conflict, responding to the predicament of fact-finding as 'a significant weapon in the armoury of world order'?[11]

2. Different International Fact-Finding Mechanisms

The subject here is fact-finding that is *international* in character or scope. Domestic fact-finding may share objectives with international fact-finding, and may indeed feed into international fact-finding instruments.[12] However, domestic inquiries are often considerably tainted.[13] They may have distinct domestic political purposes or serve additional objectives such as improvement of military defence capabilities in the wake of a military confrontation.[14] A fact-finding inquiry commissioned by national authorities, but consisting of internationally acclaimed experts may fall into either category depending on the terms of reference. If the objective is to assess facts and compliance with

[9] Cherif Bassiouni, 'Appraising UN Justice-Related Fact-Finding Missions', *Journal of Law and Policy* 5 (2001), 45.

[10] Marco Milanovic, 'UN Panel of Experts Report on the Sri Lanka Conflict', *EJIL Talk* (26 April 2011), suggesting that more reports equals less responsibility.

[11] Franck and Fairley, 'Procedural Due Process In Human Rights Fact-Finding', 308.

[12] See *inter alia* 'The Public Commission to Examine the Maritime Incident of 31 May 2010: The Turkel Commission', Report January 2010, http://www.turkel-committee.gov.il/files/wordocs/8808report-eng.pdf (accessed 13 Nov 2014). See also 'Report on the Israeli Attack on the Humanitarian Aid Convoy to Gaza on May 31, 2010', Turkish National Commission of Inquiry (Ankara, February 2011), http://www.mfa.gov.tr/data/Turkish%20Report%20Final%20-%20UN%20Copy.pdf (accessed 18 September 2014), both of which appeared in the 'Report of the Secretary-General's Panel of Inquiry on the 31 May 2010 Flotilla Incident', September 2011 (Palmer Report), http://www.un.org/News/dh/infocus/middle_east/Gaza_Flotilla_Panel_Report.pdf (accessed 13 Nov 2014).

[13] A UN fact-finding commission into events in Guinea in 2009 established that crimes against humanity were likely to have been committed and recommended referral to the ICC. The national fact-finding commission reached the exact opposite conclusion, see 'Report of the International Commission of Inquiry of the Events of 28. September 2009 in Guinea', UN Security Council (18 December 2009) UN Doc. S/2009/693, para. 278.

[14] Notably the Chilcot Inquiry by a committee of Privy Counsellors into the UK's role in the Iraq War for the former, and the Israeli Winograd Commission into the 2006 Lebanon War for the latter.

international legal norms by relevant actors, the mission may be deemed international.[15] This chapter is restricted to fact-finding mechanisms originating in mandates by international or regional intergovernmental institutions. Only fact-finding that is relevant to mitigation of armed conflict or accountability for international crimes is included.

No authoritative classification of international fact-finding mechanisms exists. Some differentiate between 'classical' and 'non-traditional' fact-finding and monitoring, where the purpose of the former is to provide information to the mandator, while the latter seeks to contribute to a political process.[16] Others classify according to the mandating body.[17] In the following a distinction is made between non-partisan establishment of facts by multilateral organizations with an emphasis on prevention (Section 2.1), fact-finding stipulated in individual treaties outside the UN where the objective is to secure performance of treaty obligations (Section 2.2), and finally fact-finding with the objective of establishing responsibility for international crimes (Section 2.3).

2.1. Multilateral conflict prevention

Fact-finding mandated by intergovernmental organizations aims at establishing an impartial recollection of certain events that may threaten peace. A non-partisan establishment of facts may serve as basis for a negotiated settlement of the dispute. It may alternatively create the basis for further measures by international institutions. The main objective is preventive. It seeks to prevent a tense situation from escalating or contain an unfolding crisis. It has been suggested that preventive fact-finding will be employed when the key issues involve fact, rather than policy or law, and when all parties are 'willing to accept that their version of events may be proven wrong'.[18]

Fact-finding mechanisms for preventive purposes were suggested as early as 1899. Pursuant to the Convention on the Pacific Settlement of International Disputes of 1899 an entity may be set up with the limited objective of 'elucidating the facts by means of an impartial and conscientious investigation'.[19] Only disputes involving neither honour nor essential interests are subject to such a

[15] Examples include the Independent International Commission of Inquiry into the events in southern Kyrgyzstan established following a joint initiative by the Nordic countries, the OSCE, the Kyrgyz President, and the UN; the Bahrain Independent Commission of Inquiry, established by Bahrain authorities, Bahrain Royal Orders nos. 28 and 29 (2011).

[16] For suggested definitions, see Grace and Brudelein, 'Building Effective Monitoring, Reporting and Fact-Finding Mechanisms', 15; see also Arthur Lenk, 'Fact-Finding as a Peace Negotiation Tool—The Mitchell Report and the Israel–Palestinian Peace Process', *Loyola Los Angeles International & Comparative Law Review* 24 (2002), 289–325.

[17] Marina Aksenova and Morten Bergsmo, 'Non-Criminal Justice Fact-Work in the Age of Accountability', in Bergsmo (ed.), *Quality Control in Fact-Finding*, 1–34 at 5ff.

[18] J. G. Merrills, *International Dispute Settlement* (3rd edn. Cambridge: Cambridge University Press, 1998), 61.

[19] 1899 Convention on the Peaceful Settlement of Disputes, part III on International Commissions of Inquiry Art. 9. Expanded in the 1907 Convention with a detailed series of procedures for inquiry commissions.

mechanism, a limitation intended to ease concerns by smaller states that commissions might serve as a vehicle for foreign intervention.[20] The idea of fact-finding as an important *safety valve* had evolved with the destruction of the US battleship *Maine* in 1898, precipitating the American–Spanish War.[21] Rival national inquiries had come to opposing conclusions. It was expected that fact-finding at the international level would represent a more impartial recollection of events.[22] Fact-finding in this perspective is an alternative to arbitration. The intention is to 'facilitate solution' of a crisis.[23]

Successful use of the measure to prevent escalation in 1904–5 in the war between Russia and Japan gave the mechanism a wave of support in 1907.[24] Although numerous bilateral treaties negotiated the early twentieth century contained provisions calling for permanent inquiry commissions, no pattern of inquiries was established.[25] Similarly, only very few incidents were subject to fact-finding under the Hague Convention.[26]

International ad hoc commissions were occasionally set up by international institutions in response to an unfolding crisis.[27] Yet, it was only following World War II that fact-finding mechanisms developed from essentially bilateral to multilateral instruments of conflict prevention.[28]

[20] Lenk, 'Fact-Finding as a Peace Negotiation Tool', 292.

[21] Nissim Bar-Yaacov, *The Handling of International Disputes by Means of Inquiry* (Oxford: Oxford University Press, 1974), 33–4.

[22] Bar-Yaacov, *The Handling of International Disputes*. See also Malcolm Shaw, *International Law* (4th edn. Cambridge: Cambridge University Press, 1997), 725.

[23] The Hague Convention proclaims that states involved in disputes arising from a difference of opinion on factual points should agree to establish a commission of inquiry whose task is to facilitate a solution to the dispute by an impartial and conscientious investigation. It must be distinguished from *conciliation*, a related method of conflict resolution, see 'Regulation on the Procedure of International Conciliation', International Institute of International Law (Salzburg, 11 September 1961), Art 1.

[24] Commissions of inquiry were established to elucidate an incident in the North Sea in the Russo-Japanese war (1904–5) between a Russian and a British fleet, known as the Dogger Bank incident: 'Finding of the International Commission of Inquiry Organized Under Art. 9 of the Convention for the Pacific Settlement of International Disputes of July 29, 1899', *American Journal of International Law* 2 (1905), 929; and the 'International Commission of Inquiry—Red Crusader Incident' (date of inquiry agreement 15 November 1961, date of report 23 March 1962), http://legal.un.org/riaa/cases/vol_XXIX/521-539.pdf (accessed 22 June 2014).

[25] Shaw, *International Law*, 1019–20; Lenk, 'Fact-Finding as a Peace Negotiation Tool', 292.

[26] Most notably it was relied on in an incident in the Italo-Turkish war (1911–12) where an Italian ship seized a French postal ship, known as the *Tavignano* incident, and an incident during World War I where Germany sank a Dutch steamer, known as the *Tubantia*, see *American Journal of International Law* 16 (1922), 485–92.

[27] The Lytton Commission established by the League of Nations was instructed to study the circumstance that threatened to disturb the peace between China and Japan, and report to the Council. See Arthur Kuhn, 'The Lytton Report on the Manchurian Crisis', *American Journal of International Law* 27 (1933), 96.

[28] The Hague Convention mechanism was relied on one single occasion after 1945, in 1962. A British trawler and Danish fisheries protection vessel exchanged fire, an incident known as the *Red Crusader*.

2.1.1. *United Nations*

The most important engine for fact-finding mechanisms is the United Nations (UN). For nearly 70 years the UN has dispatched fact-finding missions to trouble spots. Attempts to establish a permanent fact-finding instrument at the UN have not been successful.[29] A recurrent controversy has been whether to opt for a pure fact-finding mechanism, or a combination of fact-finding and conciliation.[30] The resulting lack of a centralized mandating body has caused fact-finding mechanisms to develop in an ad hoc manner, emerging from different institutional sources within the UN.[31] The mandating body may influence the scope, authority, and potential impact of fact-finding, causing a plethora of fact-finding mechanisms within the UN. Fact-finding instruments are mandated by a range of different UN bodies; the Security Council, the Secretary-General, the General Assembly, and subsequent to 2006, the Human Rights Council.[32] In 2001, the UN Security Council endorsed fact-finding as one of four key recommendations for the prevention of armed conflict, increasing the use of UN interdisciplinary fact-finding missions to volatile regions.[33]

The UN Security Council (SC) is the only organ with explicit investigative competence under the UN Charter. Article 34 authorizes the Council to 'investigate any situation or dispute that may endanger international peace and security'.[34] The Council is reluctant to use this provision explicitly, relying instead on its implied powers of investigation.[35] Fact-finding dispatched by the SC are different from SC *missions*, when representatives from the Council visit a country or a region to form an impression of the situation on the ground.[36]

[29] A proposal to establish a permanent commission of inquiry in the UN was rejected in 1967. Instead, a list of experts was suggested. See UNGA Res. 2329(XXII) (18 December 1967) UN Doc. A/RES/2329(XXII).

[30] Lenk, 'Fact-Finding as a Peace Negotiation Tool', 295.

[31] Philip Alston, 'Commissions of Inquiry as Human Rights Fact-Finding Tools', *American Society of International Law Proceedings* 105 (2011), 84.

[32] In addition, the UN Human Rights Treaty Bodies and their monitoring systems provide a large number of fact-finding mechanisms. They are not treated here. For a comprehensive overview, see Bertrand Ramcharan (ed.), *International Law and Fact-Finding in the Field of Human Rights* (Leiden: Martinus Nijhoff, 1982). For an updated view, see Alston, 'Commissions of Inquiry', and Grace and Brudelein, 'Building Effective Monitoring, Reporting and Fact-Finding Mechanisms'. See generally Richard Lillich, Hurst Hannum, S. James Anaya, and Dinah L. Shelton (eds.), *International Human Rights: Problems of Law, Policy and Practice* (New York: Aspen, 2006), 981.

[33] UNSC Res. 1366 (30 August 2001) UN Doc. S/RES/1633(2001), para. 18, see also Secretary-General's Report on 'Prevention of Armed Conflict' (7 June 2001) UN Doc. A/55/985-S/2001/574.

[34] 'The Security Council may investigate any dispute, or any situation which might lead to international friction or give rise to a dispute, in order to determine whether the continuance of the dispute or situation is likely to endanger the maintenance of international peace and security', 1945 United Nations Charter, Art. 34.

[35] Bruno Simma (ed.), *The Charter of the United Nations: A Commentary* (2nd edn. Oxford: Oxford University Press, 2002), 596, 606.

[36] Such missions are quite common. For example, UNSC 2994 (1971) special mission of members of the Council to Guinea-Senegal. In 2010–11 the SC undertook four such missions. See 'Repertoire of the Practice of the Security Council, 17th Supplement 2010–2011', Department of Political Affairs—Security Council Affairs Division, http://www.un.org/en/sc/repertoire/structure.shtml (accessed 13 Nov 2014).

The UNSC, in its early years, sent commissions of inquiry to numerous looming conflicts.[37] Mandate and scope of each mission was pragmatic and based on a case-by-case approach.[38] At the end of the Cold War, human rights perspectives were increasingly integrated into fact-finding mandates, a development influenced by the rise of fact-finding by the UN human rights treaty bodies.[39] It was also in line with the strong impetus seeking an end to impunity for international crimes during the 1990s. However, missions with distinct preventive aims continue to be dispatched by the SC.[40]

In 2001, the UNSC endorsed a report expressing the idea that fact-finding missions mandated by other UN or regional bodies could be referred to the SC for follow-up.[41] Over the next decade, the SC has been increasingly reliant on fact-finding reports mandated by other UN organs.[42]

The UN Secretary-General (SG) may 'bring to the attention of the Security Council any matter which in his opinion may threaten the maintenance of international peace and security'.[43] The SG has implied powers under the UN Charter to seek advice from anyone he chooses in carrying out his responsibilities under the Charter.[44] This extends to the creation of fact-finding missions.[45] Instead of waiting for the Security Council to act, the SG may rely on his residual powers under Article 99 to establish fact-finding commissions that will assist the SG in presenting to the Security Council a situation that may warrant action.

During the 1990s, the UN Secretary-General increased reliance on fact-finding missions to areas of tensions, a practice endorsed by the Brahimi Report in 2000, stressing member states' obligations under Article 2(5) of the UN Charter to give

[37] UNSC Res. 15 (19 December 1946) UN Doc. S/RES/15(1946); and UNSC Res. 23 (10 February 1947) UN Doc. S/RES/23(1947); UNSC Res. 39 (20 January 1948) UN Doc. S/RES/39(1948); UNSC Res. 48 (23 April 1948) UN Doc. S/RES/48(1948); UNSC Res. 67 (28 January 1949) UN Doc. S/RES/67(1949).

[38] Only two were subject to an Art. 34 decision; Greece in 1947: the Greek Frontier Incident Case (19 December 1946) UN Doc. S/RES/15(1946) and the India–Pakistan Question UNSC Res. 39 (20 January 1948) UN Doc. S/RES/39(1948).

[39] UNSC Res. 693 (20 May 1991) UN Doc. S/RES/693 (1991), para. 2 (on Guatemala) introduced human rights into the mandate language of the UNSC. See generally Katarina Månsson, 'The Forgotten Agenda: Human Rights Protection and Promotion in Cold War Peacekeeping', *Journal of Conflict & Security Law* 10 (2005), 379–403; see also Frans Viljoen, 'Fact-Finding by UN Human Rights Complaints Bodies—Analysis and Suggested Reforms', *Max Planck UNYB* 8 (2004), 49–100.

[40] UNSC Res. 885 (16 November 1993) UN Doc. S/RES/885(1993); UNSC Res. 1012 (28 August 1995) UN Doc. S/RES/1012(1995), para. 1(b); UNSC Res. 1306 (5 July 2000) UN Doc. S/RES/1306(2000), para. 19; UNSC Res. 1171 (5 June 1998) UN Doc. S/RES/1171(1998).

[41] Report of the Secretary-General, 'Prevention of Armed Conflict' (7 June 2001) UN Doc. A/55/985-S/2001/574; S/RES/1366 (30 August 2001) UN Doc. S/RES/1633(2001), para. 18.

[42] See *inter alia* Report of the Secretary-General, 'Progress Report on the Prevention of Armed Conflict' (18 July 2006), UN Doc.A/60/891, para. 77; Repertoires of the Security Council Supplement 2004–7, 19ff.; 2008–9, 45ff.; 2010-11, 14ff.

[43] UN Charter Art. 99.

[44] Nabil Elaraby, 'The Office of the Secretary General and the Maintenance of International Peace and Security', *The United Nations and Maintenance of International Peace and Security* (Leiden: Martinus Nijhoff, 1987), 177 at 190–6.

[45] See 'Declaration on Fact-Finding by the United Nations in the Field of the Maintenance of International Peace and Security' (9 December 1991) UN Doc. A/RES/46/59, para. 15.

assistance to such activities of the UN.[46] The Security Council expressly endorsed the role of the SG in conflict prevention in 2001.[47] In the following years, the number of SG mandated fact-finding missions have increased steadily.[48] Some missions are requested directly by the Security Council.[49] The Security Council will rely on these reports as a basis for further action. A fact-finding report on Sudan led to a subsequent referral by the Security Council to the ICC, whereas in the case of Guinea, the Security Council remained 'seized of the matter' whilst striving to solve the tensions by diplomatic means.[50]

The UN General Assembly (GA) possesses implied powers to request the appointment of a fact-finding mission.[51] A more common role is to endorse the results of reports mandated by other UN organs. In 1991 the GA adopted a Declaration on Fact-Finding by the UN in the Field of the Maintenance of International Peace and Security. The declaration outlines the relevance of fact-finding activities to the functions of the United Nations and the role of competent UN organs to undertake fact-finding missions. It affirms the central role of fact-finding in appropriate circumstances, consolidating an important role for the UN Secretary-General in exercising a degree of discretion, and setting out principles for acquisition of factual circumstances of any dispute or situation that might threaten the maintenance of international peace and security.[52]

The *Human Rights Council* (HRC) was established in 2006. Prior to its establishment other UN bodies concerned with human rights obligations undertook fact-finding missions at the request of the Secretary-General.[53] In recent years an increasing number of fact-finding missions originate with the HRC.[54] Commissions dispatched by the HRC have investigated allegations of serious human rights violations in a variety of geopolitical contexts. It has a distinct focus

[46] 'Report of the Panel on United Nations Peace Operations' (21 August 2000), UN General Assembly and Security Council, UN Doc. A/55/305-S/2000/809, also known as the Brahimi Report on UN Peace Operations, (b) A/55/305.

[47] S/RES/1366 (30 August 2001) UN Doc. S/RES/1633(2001), para. 18.

[48] UNSC Res. 1564 (18 September 2004) UN Doc. S/RES/1564 (2004) (Sudan); the Independent Special Commission of Inquiry for Timor-Leste, UNSC, 13 June 2006; International Commission of Inquiry for Guinea, UNSC informed 29 October 2009; the Secretary-General's Panel of Inquiry on 31 May 2010 Flotilla Incident, 2 August 2010.

[49] See UNSR Res. 1564(2004), para. 12; 'Report of the United Nations Fact-Finding Mission on the Djibouti-Eritrea Crisis' (28 July–6 August 2008) UN Doc. S/2008/602. Other fact-finding missions by the GS at the direct request of the SC include UNSR Res. 1744 (21 February 2008) UN Doc. S/RES/1744(2007), para. 9.

[50] UNSC Res. 1593 (31 March 2005) UN Doc. S/RES/1593(2005).

[51] Simma, *The Charter of the United Nations*, 595.

[52] See 'Declaration on Fact-Finding by the United Nations in the Field of the Maintenance of International Peace and Security' (9 December 1991) UN Doc. Annex to GA Res. 46/59, paras. 12–13; see also UNSC Res. 1405 (19 April 2002) UN Doc. S/RES/1405(2002), para. (2).

[53] One example is the Report of the United Nations Independent Special Commission of Inquiry for Timor-Leste (13 June 2006) UN Doc. S/PV.5457, endorsed by the Security Council in UNSC Res. 1690 (20 June 2006) UN Doc. S/RES/1690(2006). The Inquiry into the Occupied Arab Territories, including Palestine, of 2001 was carried out by the Commission, while the 2004 Inquiry in relation to Ivory Coast was established by the High Commissioner for Human Rights at the request of the UN Secretary-General.

[54] Within five years, the Council had established twelve international commissions of inquiry.

on questions of accountability. The HRC has also erected more lasting procedures for follow-up. One example is the Independent International Commission of Inquiry on the Syrian Arab Republic established by the HRC on 22 August 2011 in response to a fact-finding report by the UNCHR.[55] By February 2014 the permanent commission had delivered seven reports on Syria.[56]

In 2011 the Security Council for the first time explicitly recognized fact-finding mandated by the HRC as part of the Security Council's investigative functions.[57]

The Security Council has the power to act decisively based on information brought forward by fact-finding bodies. Increased reliance by the Security Council on fact-finding mandated by other UN bodies may increase institutional integration within the UN. It also provides the Security Council with more flexibility to refrain from acting where intervention may in fact cause a situation to escalate rather than be contained.

2.1.2. Regional intergovernmental organizations

Regional interstate organizations are becoming increasingly important in responding to threats of escalating violence. There are occasional historical examples of fact-finding by regional organizations, such as the Organization of American States dispatching fact-finding missions to inquire into Nicaraguan involvement in the Civil War in Costa Rica (1948), and tensions between Haiti and the Dominican Republic (1963).[58] However, following UNSC Resolution 1366 (2001) emphasizing the role of regional organizations in preventive measures, there has been a steady growth of reliance on fact-finding instruments of a regional character.[59] Notably the African Commission on Human and Peoples Rights and the African Security Council have relied on such instruments.[60] Regional

[55] HRC Res. 17/1, 23 August 2011, UN Doc. A/HRC/RES/S-17/1, providing a mandate to investigate all alleged violations of international human rights law since March 2011 in the Syrian Arab Republic. The Commission's mandate was extended in September 2012 and further on 17 September 2013, expanding the mandate to investigation of all massacres.

[56] See 'Reports of the Independent International Commission of Inquiry on the Syrian Arab Republic' (23 November 2011) UN Doc. A/HRC/S-17/2/Add.1; (22 February 2012) UN Doc. A/HRC/19/69; (15 August 2012) UN Doc. A/HRC/21/50; (5 February 2013) UN Doc. A/HRC/22/59; (4 June 2013) UN Doc. A/HRC/23/58 and (11 September 2013) UN Doc. A/HRC/24/46; (12 February 2014) UN Doc. A/HRC/25/65.

[57] See UNSC Res. 1970 (26 February 2011) UN Doc. S/RES/1970 (2011), 5th preambular paragraph (Libya). See also UNSC Res. 1975 (30 March 2011) UN Doc. S/RES/1975(2011), 10th preambular para. (Côte d'Ivoire); UNSC Res. 2000 (27 July 2011) UN Doc. S/RES/2000(2011), 16th preambular para. (Côte d'Ivoire).

[58] The Organization of American States (OAS) Council resolution of 14 December 1948 (Costa Rica), and OAS Council resolution of April 28 1963.

[59] Examples include the African Commission of Human and Peoples Rights decision to deploy a fact-finding mission to Sudan, ACHPR/Res.68. (XXXV) 2004; Decision, 'Solemn Declaration on the situation in Mali', Assembly of Heads of State and Government of the AU 19th Ordinary Session July, 2012; Council of Europe dispatching an independent international fact-finding mission to the conflict in Georgia, Council Decision 2008/901/CFSP, 2 December 2008.

[60] See African Charter Art. 47. Fact-finding missions have been dispatched to Sudan (2004), Botswana (2008), and Mali (2012).

fact-finding mechanisms often have very strong preventive focus. Such missions may be dispatched to inquire about less serious incidents, including issues that may in the future have the potential to become a concern for international peace and security.[61]

2.2. Treaty enforcement instruments

A different type of fact-finding instrument is aimed at *securing compliance with specific treaty-regimes*. Such fact-finding mechanisms seek to secure the performance of international obligations in treaties concerning subjects relevant to the maintenance of peace.[62] Numerous treaties outside the UN system are relevant to prevention or containment of armed conflict. While they may serve as enforcement mechanisms in terms of disclosing *violations* of treaties and unleashing punitive measures, their added function is to *confirm* compliance in an atmosphere of suspicion and mutual accusation, thereby serving as a confidence-building measure. Such mechanisms may increase faith in compliance of potential adversaries, improving mutual trust between parties to a treaty. They may offer procedures through which single incidents may be solved without escalation, and moreover strengthen the perception of a system reminiscent of the rule of law—a perception likely to influence incentives for compliance. In this respect, fact-finding instruments may be preventive and have confidence-building functions. Several of these fact-finding instruments are permanent.

Two types of treaty obligation are relevant here: disarmament treaties and humanitarian law treaties.

2.2.1. Disarmament treaties

Treaties dealing with subjects of sensitivity to national security are not easily included in fact-finding. This is typically the case with disarmament treaties where technology of banned weapons is relied on for dual purposes. Disarmament treaties instead tend to rely on *self-reporting*. One example is the Biological Weapons Convention (BWC) from 1972. With the objective of reducing the occurrence

[61] In 2013 the European Commission sent a 'technical fact finding mission' to Gibraltar to investigate border checks imposed on the Spanish side in an attempt to defuse the escalating diplomatic crisis between Britain and Spain, 24 September 2013, European Commission MEMO/13/810; See also the 'Report of the Fact-Finding Mission on Migrations of Mbororo Nomadic Pastoralists in the Congo and Central Africa Republic' [PSC/PR/2 (CXIX)] and the subsequent treatment by the Peace and Security Council of the African Union, 119th meeting, April 2008, doc. PSC/PR/Comm (CXIX). A High-Level Panel for Egypt was commissioned by the AU presidency on 8 July 2013 subsequent to a meeting by the AU Peace and Security Council on 5 July 2013; the Fact Finding Mission to Fiji was dispatched by the Bureau of the African, Caribbean, and Pacific States and the European Union Joint Parliamentary Assembly, 27 May 2012, to assess the progress made by the authorities to return the country to constitutional order and parliamentary democracy, see 'Report of the Fact-Finding Mission of the ACP-EU JPA Bureau to Fiji', 22–24 July 2012', CR\913035EN.doc, AP101.253/BUR.

[62] Karl Josef Partsch, 'Fact-Finding and Inquiry', in *Encyclopedia of Public International Law*, Rudolf Bernhardt (ed.) (Amsterdam: North-Holland, 1981), i. 61.

of ambiguities, doubts, and suspicions and improving international cooperation, the Review Conferences in 1986 and 1991 obliged states parties to provide annual reports on specific activities related to the BWC.[63] A similar duty of self-regulation is the review stipulated in Additional Protocol Article 36 to the Geneva Conventions relating to the development or acquisition of new conventional weapons.[64]

Compared to self-reporting, international fact-finding clearly offers a higher level of credibility. The Chemical Weapons Convention (CWC) relies on fact-finding mechanisms to determine facts about the possible non-compliance by member states.[65] The permanent organization of the CWC, the Organization for the Prohibition of Chemical Weapons (OPCW), is in general responsible for such inquiries.[66] A different example is the Non-Proliferation Treaty (NPT), subjecting non-nuclear states parties to the verification system of a separate entity, the International Atomic Energy Agency.[67] Ad hoc instruments also exist—such as the Nuclear Weapon Free Zone for South-East Asia (Bangkok Treaty), providing for a fact-finding mechanism to 'clarify and resolve a situation which may be considered ambiguous or which may give rise to doubts about compliance' with the treaty.[68]

2.2.2. Humanitarian law treaties

Humanitarian law treaties address excesses associated with hostilities and ongoing conflict. A fact-finding mechanism for breaches of humanitarian law was provided for in the Geneva Conventions. It is activated upon request by a party to the conflict and designed according to an agreement between the parties.[69] The International Committee of the Red Cross considers these provisions to be binding upon states parties.[70] However, the mechanism has never been relied upon, which is explained by reference to the fact that reaching agreements between belligerent states in times of armed conflict is very difficult.[71] The accused state may escape simply by refusing to cooperate.[72]

[63] An implementation support unit was established in order to assist states parties.

[64] Additional Protocol I to the Geneva Conventions, Art. 36.

[65] 1993 Convention on the Prohibition of the Development, Production, Stockpiling and Use of Chemical Weapons and on Their Destruction 1974 UNTS 45, S. Treaty Doc. Nos.103–21 entered into force 29 April 1997 (CWC) Art. IX.

[66] CWC Arts. VIII and XI (4) e.

[67] Treaty on the Non-Proliferation of Nuclear Weapons, 1 July 1968, entered into force 5 March 1970, 729 UNTS 161, Art. III.

[68] Treaty on the South East Asia Nuclear Weapon Free Zone, entered into force 27 March 1997, 35 ILM 635 (1995), Art. 13. See also the annex, containing the procedures for fact-finding missions.

[69] See Geneva Convention I Art. 52, Geneva Convention II Art. 53, Geneva Convention III Art. 132 and Geneva Convention IV Art. 149.

[70] See also Jean Pictet (ed.), *Commentary: III Geneva Convention Relative to the Treatment of Prisoners of War* (Geneva: ICRC, 1960), 632.

[71] Yves Sandoz, Christoph Swinarski, and Bruno Zimmermann (eds.), *Commentary on the Additional Protocols of 8 June 1977 to the Geneva Conventions of 12 August 1949* (Geneva; ICRC 1987), 632.

[72] See Rüdiger Wolfrum and Dieter Fleck, 'Enforcement of International Humanitarian Law', in *Handbook of International Humanitarian Law,* (ed.) Fleck (2nd edn. Oxford: Oxford University Press, 2008), para. 1420.

A more robust fact-finding mechanism was introduced by Additional Protocol I Article 90 in 1977.[73] Subject to additional adherence by states parties, a permanent commission is empowered to inquire into facts alleged to be grave breaches or serious violations of the Geneva Conventions and its Protocols. It also has competence to 'facilitate, through its good offices, the restoration of an attitude of respect for the Conventions'.[74] This permanent International Humanitarian Fact-Finding Commission (IHFFC) was established in 1991, and 72 states have deposited declarations of recognition to date.[75]

Unlike most UN mechanisms, IHFFC may provide reports confidentially to the parties. It has been suggested that confidentiality may increase incentives to rely on the Commission rather than other fact-finding mechanisms.[76] The IHFFC could serve as a confidence-building measure between the parties. Non-public reports may confirm compliance or even inform a party about excesses in its own ranks that may be politically unintended and undesirable—practices that may have corrosive effects on the discipline in the armed forces, morals, and the idea of a common cause. While public scrutiny may occasion confrontational responses, confidential reports may allow for alternative ways of action, easing tensions rather than exacerbating them, and addressing the cause of breaches of the Geneva Conventions. In this sense, the permanent fact-finding mechanism of the Geneva Conventions may also serve to address the causes for violations. The Commission has not yet been used. The UN Security Council recently renewed its commitment to rely on the IHFFC.[77]

These fact-finding mechanisms serve as enforcement agencies of treaty regimes in areas relevant to maintenance of peace. Particularly in fields such as disarmament and humanitarian law where independent enforcement mechanisms do not exist, fact-finding may indeed serve as a tool to promote compliance and build confidence between hostile neighbours. The emphasis of such fact-finding is compliance rather than accountability.

2.3. Accountability mechanisms

Other fact-finding mechanisms are more exclusively intended to establish indications of responsibility for international crimes. They are accountability

[73] For information on the negotiating history, see Michael Bothe, Karl Josef Partsch, and Waldemar A. Solf (eds.), *New Rules for Victims of Armed Conflicts: Commentary on the Two 1977 Protocols Additional to the Geneva Conventions of 1949* (The Hague: Martinus Nijhoff, 1982), 537ff.; Sandoz et al., *Commentary on the Additional Protocols*, 1037–52. See also Erich Kussbach, 'Commission internationale d'établissement des faits en droit international humanitaire', *Revue de droit pénal militaire et de droit de la guerre* 20 (1981), 89–116.

[74] See Additional Protocol I (2(c) (i) and (ii)).

[75] See IHFFC list of states parties, http://www.ihffc.org/index.asp?page=statesparties_list&listfilter=off (accessed 13 Nov 2014).

[76] Charles Garraway, 'Fact-Finding and the International Humanitarian Fact-Finding Commission', in Bergsmo (ed.), *Quality Control in Fact-Finding*, 427–46.

[77] UNSC Res. 1894 (11 November 2009) UN Doc. S/RES/1894(2009), para. 9, concerning protection of civilians, underlining the importance in this regard of receiving information that is

instruments that may assist in filling the gaps in an imperfect international legal architecture in order to bring an end to impunity for atrocities.

United Nations fact-finding during the Cold War was in general limited to establishment of facts. Allegations of the use of chemical and bacteriological weapons in the Iran–Iraq war were to be promptly investigated 'in order to ascertain the facts of the matter and to report the results'.[78] Over the past three decades, fact-finding mechanisms at the heart of the issues of international peace and security have reflected an increased expectation of international accountability.[79] The UN Security Council is explicit in recognizing 'international commissions of inquiry and fact-finding missions as valuable mechanisms to verify and investigate allegations of serious violations of international human rights and humanitarian law, and in accordance with their respective mandates to make recommendations to advance accountability and justice and protection for victims'.[80] Hence, fact-finding mechanisms increasingly serve to indicate violations of international law of such a severe nature that countermeasures or international criminal responsibility may be relevant or indeed required reactions. The Security Council has dispatched numerous fact-finding missions with the primary objective of ascertaining accountability.[81] So has the UN Secretary General.[82]

Establishment of the Commission of Experts for the Former Yugoslavia by the Security Council is deemed to be the point of departure for the development of this branch of fact-finding mechanisms in the last two decades.[83] The interim report of the fact-finding mission prompted the establishment of the International Criminal Tribunal for the Former Yugoslavia.[84] In the words of Antonio Cassese this signalled the beginning of an era where fact-finding is used as a mechanism for securing better compliance with international standards through a structure divorced from the will of particular states.[85]

timely, objective, accurate, and reliable. This was reiterated in 'Statement by the President of the Security Council' (12 February 2013) UN Doc. S/PRST/2013/2, 2.

[78] UNSC Res. 620, 26 August 1988, UN Doc. S/RES/620(1988), para. 2.

[79] See Report of the UN Secretary-General, 'Strengthening and Coordinating United Nations Rule of Law Activities' (10 August 2012) UN Doc. A/67/290, para. 19; Report of workshop of UNOCHA, 'Accountability and Fact-Finding Mechanisms, for Violations of International Humanitarian Law and Human Rights Law: the Role of the Security Council—Past and Future', 1 November 2011, https://docs.unocha.org/sites/dms/Documents/Accountability%20Workshop%201%20Nov%202011%20Highlights.pdf (accessed 23 June 2014); Cassese, 'Fostering Increased Conformity with International Standards', 295.

[80] See UNSC Res. 1894 (11 November 2009) UN Doc. S/RES/1894(2009), para. 9; 'Statement by the President of the Security Council', S/PRST/2013/2, 2.

[81] UNSC Res. 780 (6 October 1992) UN Doc. S/RES/680(1992); UNSC Res. 935 (1 July 1994) UN Doc. S/RES/935(1994); UNSC Res. 1595 (7 April 2005) UN Doc. S/RES/1595(2005), paras. 1, 4.

[82] The Secretary-General's Panel of Experts on Accountability in Sri Lanka, established in June 2010.

[83] UNSC Res. 780 (6 October 1992) UN Doc. S/RES/680(1992).

[84] UNSC Res. 827 (25 May 1993) UN Doc. S/RES/827(1993).

[85] Cassese, 'Fostering Increased Conformity with International Standards', 303.

While its predecessor the Human Right Commission appointed ad hoc committees to carry out inquiries with the consent of the state concerned, the Human Rights Council is not so restricted.[86] According to the 1991 GA Declaration, states should give fact-finding missions the full and prompt assistance necessary for the fulfilment of their mandates, and they should be accorded all immunities and facilities needed for discharging their mandate.[87] However, only the Security Council has the authority to *demand* cooperation. Therefore, a fact-finding instrument such as the HRC's permanent Inquiry on Syria has so far not been allowed by the Syrian Government to undertake investigations inside the country. Hence, while fact-finding mechanisms for accountability may be increasingly divorced from the will of particular states, the quality and integrity of the result of fact-finding mechanisms is still to a large extent dependent on the cooperation of implicated states.

A qualitative change took place with the fact-finding mission in Darfur in 2004. This fact-finding mission was explicitly mandated to make a formal determination about whether genocide had taken place and identify perpetrators of major violations. The report was characterized by General Secretary Kofi Annan as 'one of the most important documents in the recent history of the United Nations'.[88] Neither China nor the US vetoed the subsequent SC referral of the situation in the Sudan to the ICC in 2005. The response was in line with the December 2004 recommendation of the High-level Panel on Threats, Challenges, and Change calling on the permanent members 'in their individual capacities, to pledge themselves to refrain from the use of the veto in cases of genocide and large-scale human rights abuses'.

This development clearly put fact-finding for the purpose of accountability by the UN Security Council and Secretary-General into a different qualitative category, with increasing resemblance to investigations as preparations for criminal prosecutions. Fact-finding by UN bodies indicating that international crimes are being committed consequently raise expectations of decisive action by the Security Council.

These fact-finding mechanisms are therefore initial tools for securing subsequent accountability under international law. Their preventive or containing ambition is indirect. The objective is to secure repercussions when there are indications of international crimes. They are commonly established in response to convincing allegations of such crimes. However, like other fact-finding mechanisms, they are subject to political considerations, a fact that does not always resonate well with the objective of ending impunity for atrocities.

[86] For the former, see ECOSOC Res. 1503(XLVIII) (27 May 1970); for the latter, see Res. 5/21 paras. 85–109.

[87] UNGA, 'Declaration on Fact-Finding', paras. 22, 23.

[88] 'Secretary-General, High Commissioner for Human Rights call for urgent action by Security Council to halt violence in Sudan', 16 February 2005, UN Press Release SC/8313.

3. The Role of Fact-Finding in Strengthening the International Architecture of Peace

There is no legal duty under international law to inquire into massive violent events corresponding to the duty of state authorities under domestic law. Nevertheless, incidents that threaten to erode the peaceful coexistence within or between nations are increasingly perceived to be of concern to intergovernmental organizations. Likewise, allegations of crimes against humanity, war crimes, or genocidal acts are increasingly subject to some kind of reaction by the international community, occasionally framed under the rising norm of responsibility to protect.[89]

When the international community chooses to act, fact-finding mechanisms are increasingly relied on as a first semi-legal step, paving the way for robust legal responses. They are vested with an increasingly important role as the glue connecting different institutions and regimes. Three major roles for fact-finding mechanisms in strengthening the international legal response to crimes and crises may be identified.

3.1. To provide trustworthy and adequate information as a basis for action

Fact-finding missions provide *authoritative* and *impartial* accounts of events, making sure that international institutions are provided with impartial and correct information.[90] As expressed by one scholar, fact-finders help the mandator determine the most appropriate method of corrective action.[91] A non-partisan and authoritative presentation of events may serve as a factual basis for further handling of an unfolding crisis. It may deliver a narrative upon which mediation efforts may rely. It may also include a certain element of 'truth-seeking', which might serve as an important element of reconciliatory efforts, of justice and reparation, and the future prevention of similar incidents.[92] Finally, reliable and impartial reporting may also promote an element of transparency and accountability to the work of the Security Council.[93]

[89] See 'A More Secure World: Our Shared Responsibility', Report of the High-level Panel on Threats, Challenges and Change' (2 December 2004) UN Doc. A/59/565, paras. 138, 139, 203, reaffirmed in UNSC Res. 1674 (28 April 2006) UN Doc. S/RES/1674(2006).

[90] 'Strengthening and Coordinating United Nations Rule of Law Activities', 29 July 2013, UNHRC Report. UN Doc. A/68/213, para. 23.

[91] Grace and Brudelein, 'Building Effective Monitoring, Reporting and Fact-Finding Mechanisms', 13–14.

[92] See 'Report of the Special Rapporteur on the Promotion of Truth, Justice, Reparation and Guarantees of Non-Recurrence' (28 August 2013), UN Human Rights Council, UN Doc. A/HRC/24/42, para. 21.

[93] Philip Alston, 'The Darfur Commission as a Model for Future Responses to Crisis Situations,' *Journal of International Criminal Justice* 3 (2005), argues that it is much more difficult to ignore a carefully documented and powerfully argued analytical report.

3.2. To increase institutional integration

The imperfect structure of the international legal architecture has made it a major challenge to devise linkages ensuring that institutions function in a coherent and integrated manner.[94] Fact-finding mechanisms offer an instrument to improve international institutional integration.

Fact-finding may serve as glue between different institutions within the UN. Fact-finding links facts on the ground to institutional procedures that might result in robust international responses, such as the establishment of the ICTY in 1993.[95] When the HRC came into being in 2006 a certain division of labour was envisaged between the HRC and the SC.[96] The HRC has established numerous fact-finding missions, while the number of missions mandated directly by the Security Council has steadily decreased. The unanimous SC referral of Libya to the ICC in 2011 was accompanied by an endorsement of the fact-finding mission dispatched by the HRC to investigate human rights law violations in Libya, marking the first explicit recognition of the HRC fact-finding mechanisms as part of the Security Council's investigative functions.[97] This has been followed up by subsequent endorsements.[98] The UN Security Council may veil on a situation subsequent to a fact-finding mission, thereby serving as an implicit enforcer if the situation develops in the wrong direction. This conveys an image about UN fact-finding being bestowed with supreme authority that may resort to decisive action.[99] Increased reliance by the UNSC on different fact-finding mechanisms within the UN system has strengthened this tendency in recent years.

Fact-finding may also increase institutional cooperation between the UN and non-UN bodies. In 2004, the Darfur commission was the basis for the referral by the UN Security Council of the situation in the Sudan to the ICC.[100] The report succeeded in persuading sceptical members of the Security Council to permit a referral, thereby strengthening institutional integration between the SC and the ICC. Similarly, in response to allegations by UN member states, the UN Secretary-General in 2013 announced a UN fact-finding inquiry into the

[94] Alston, 'The Darfur Commission', suggests that fact-finding has great potential to complement other steps.

[95] UNSC Res. 827 (25 May 1993) UN Doc. S/RES/827(1993).

[96] Another body recently established is the UN Peace Building Commission (2005) with responsibility for transitional justice and reconciliatory measures. It has an advisory role to the SC and GA, see UNGA Res. 60/180 (30 December 2005) UN Doc. A/RES/60/180; UNCS Res. 1645 (20 December 2005) UN Doc. S/RES/1645(2005).

[97] UNSC Res. 1970 (26 February 2011) UN Doc. S/RES/1970 (2011), preambular para. 5.

[98] See S/RES/1975(2011), 10th preambular para. (Côte d'Ivoire); UNSC Res. 2000 (27 July 2011) UN Doc. S/RES/2000(2011), 16th preambular para. (Côte d'Ivoire).

[99] One example is the National Commission for an Independent Investigation established by the Guinean authorities into the allegations of human rights abuses committed by the military junta during incidents at Conakry, 28 September 2009. This Commission cooperated with a committee established by the UN Secretary-General to look into those same abuses. The UN Security Council 'follows the situation closely'. See 'Statement by the President of the Security Council' (28 October 2009) UN Doc. S/PRST/2009/27, paras. 4, 8.

[100] UNSC Res. 1564 (18 September 2004) UN Doc. S/RES/1564 (2004); 'Report of the International Commission of Inquiry on Darfur to the Secretary-General' (1 February 2005) UN Doc. S/2005/60; UNSC Res. 1593 (31 March 2005) UN Doc. S/RES/1593(2005).

possible use of chemical weapons in Syria.[101] The OPCW placed its resources at the disposal of the Secretary-General to conduct an investigation into alleged use of chemical weapons in a state not party to the CWC.[102] A fact-finding mission consisting of OPCW and WHO personnel were invited into Syria, and concluded that chemical weapons had been used.[103] In a parallel development, the Syrian government signed the CWC, a process promoted conjointly by the US and Russia.[104] Syria requested assistance by the OPCW to rid it of its chemical stockpiles in accordance with the CWC, a plan subsequently endorsed by the Security Council.[105] This process illustrated a mix of treaty mechanisms, UN (-initiated) fact-finding, and diplomatic measures to ensure a result that would respond to the increased danger stemming from chemical weapons in Syria in an appropriate way short of resorting to the use of force.

Finally, fact-finding reports are also relied on as supplementary documentation by international judicial organs as a basis of facts, understanding of parties, and qualification of situations for the purpose of application of international law.[106] In this respect, fact-finding may perform a complementary function.[107]

3.3. To extend the scope of international institutions

The lack of integration of international institutions gives fact-finding mechanisms an important role in extending the scope of international criminal law into situations of violence not subject to the jurisdiction of the ICC. Non-ratifying states to the Rome Statute are subject to the jurisdiction of the Court only pursuant to a declaration or a referral from the Security Council under the UN Charter Chapter VII.[108]

The process of establishing a commission of inquiry to evaluate whether or not a situation warrants a referral by the Security Council provides an appropriate filtering mechanism before the Council takes a decision.[109] A fact-finding commission ensures a thorough and systematic preliminary review of facts, it provides a fully reasoned legal analysis, and it gives Council members the opportunity to consider alternative approaches that might be better suited to the situation at hand.

[101] With a mandate pursuant to UNGA Res. 42/37C, 30 November 1987, reaffirmed by UNSC Res. 620, 26 August 1988, UN Doc. S/RES/620(1988).

[102] In accordance with the verification annex of the CWC, para. 27 of Part XI.

[103] 'United Nations Mission to Investigate Allegations of the Use of Chemical Weapons in the Syrian Arab Republic: Final Report', 13 December 2013.

[104] See 'Framework for Elimination of Syrian Chemical Weapons' (24 September 2013) UN Doc. A/68/398-S/2013/565.

[105] UNSC Res. 2118 (27 September 2013) UN Doc. S/RES/2118(2013), paras. 7, 8.

[106] *Armed Activities on the Territory of Congo (Democratic Republic of Congo* v. *Uganda)* (Judgment) [2005] ICJ. The fact-finding report on Darfur has also been relied on by the ICC, see *The Prosecutor* v. *Abdallah Banda Abakaer Nourain and Saleh*, ICC-02/05-03/09-362-Anx 4.

[107] Chinkin, 'U.N. Human Rights Council Fact-Finding Mission', 494.

[108] See Rome Statute Art. 13(b). The cases of Sudan and Libya are taken as evidence that such referrals are politically feasible under the right conditions.

[109] Alston, 'The Darfur Commission'.

Referrals have been successfully achieved in the cases of the Sudan and Libya. Persistent efforts have been made in recent years in the cases of Gaza, Syria, and North Korea.[110] It has been suggested that the process is made more legitimate if not all fact-finding leads to referral.[111] However, not expanding the scope of the ICC in spite of fact-finding repeatedly and persuasively arguing that horrendous international crimes are being committed is certainly more likely to expose the weaknesses of the current structure, with detrimental effects to its legitimacy. Although extensions are contingent on political constellations, a basic idea of an end to impunity is precisely that certain acts go *beyond* such considerations.[112]

In sum, fact-finding is becoming an increasingly important tool for institutional integration. However, there is a persisting tension between the flexibility required by fact-finding for prevention and the consistency expected from fact-finding with an emphasis on accountability.

4. A Range of Dilemmas Facing Fact-Finding Mechanisms

The proliferation of fact-finding instruments to ascertain disputed facts or provide a basis for robust international responses has triggered serious controversy about the impartial, independent, and even fair nature of fact-finding. It has also raised a host of questions linked to the scope of mandates, method, and quality control of fact-finding mechanisms.[113]

4.1. No authoritative guidelines or template for fact-finding

A persisting challenge of fact-finding missions has been the lack of standardization. There are currently no specific templates for how fact-finding missions interpret their mandate or what form the final report takes. It remains ad hoc and flexible in nature, or alternatively unpredictable and ambiguous. As expressed by Cherif Bassiouni, '[i]t strains one's belief that in fifty years the most elementary aspects of standardized organization, planning, documentation, and reporting [of fact-finding] have not been developed.'[114]

The Convention on the Pacific Settlement of International Disputes (1907) stipulates that facts should be elucidated by means of an 'impartial and conscientious investigation'.[115] Repeated attempts have been made within the UN system

[110] HRC Res. 22/13 (9 April 2013) UN Doc. A/HRC/RES/22/13, para. 5; 'Report of the Commission of Inquiry on Human Rights in the Democratic People's Republic of Korea' (7 February 2014) UN Doc. A/HRC/25/63.

[111] Alston, 'The Darfur Commission'.

[112] UNSC Res. 1674 (28 April 2006) UN Doc. S/RES/1674(2006).

[113] See Grace, 'The Design and Planning of... Missions'; Aksenova and Bergsmo, 'Non-Criminal Justice Fact-Work'.

[114] Bassiouni, 'Appraising UN Justice-Related Fact-Finding Missions', 40. Similar thoughts were expressed recently by another experienced fact-finder, Philip Alston, see 'The Challenges of Responding to Extrajudicial Executions: Interview with Philip Alston', *Journal of Human Rights Practice* 2 (2010), 357.

[115] Art. 9. Arts. 10–36 contain rules of procedure for such inquiry.

to suggest model rules of procedure for fact-finding.[116] The 1991 GA Declaration on Fact-Finding by the UN in the Field of the Maintenance of International Peace and Security Declaration provides a basic framework. For the purpose of the Declaration fact-finding is defined as 'any activity designed to obtain detailed knowledge of the relevant facts of any dispute or situation which the competent United Nations organs need in order to exercise effectively their functions in relation to the maintenance of international peace and security'.[117] The Declaration notes that fact-finding should be 'comprehensive, objective, impartial and timely'.[118] Fact-finding missions have an obligation to act in strict conformity with their mandate and perform their task in an impartial way.[119] The Declaration also underlines the lack of prejudice of a fact-finding mission towards other procedures of fact-finding and towards the Charter.

A 2012 Report by the UN Special Rapporteur on torture examining the scope and role of Commissions of Inquiry in the international context suggests that the primary objective of such mechanisms is to 'discover, clarify and formally acknowledge the causes and consequences of past violations in order to establish accountability'.[120] They aim to establish an accurate record of the past, contribute to accountability of perpetrators, respond to the needs of victims, and identify institutional responsibility and propose institutional, legal, and personnel reform, in addition to promoting reconciliation. The report notes the need for fact-finding mandates not to be excessively broad, to set clearly the scope of the inquiry, citing with precision the events and issues to be addressed.[121] It has also been suggested that increased reliance on the ICJ Statute Article 34(2) might increase legitimacy of the various UN fact-finding mechanisms.[122]

[116] See Report of Secretary-General, 'Methods of Fact-Finding', UN GAOR, 20th Sess., Annexes, Agenda Items 90 and 94, UN Doc. A/5694/Annexes (1965) and UN GAOR, 21st Sess., Annexes, Agenda Item 87, UN Doc. A/6228/Annexes (1966); Draft Model Rules of Procedure suggested by the UN SG for ad hoc bodies of the UN entrusted with Studies of Particular Situations Alleged to Reveal a Consistent Pattern of Violations of Human Rights, UN Doc. E/CN.4/1021/Rev.1 (1970); Model Rules of Procedure for UN Bodies dealing with Violations of Human Rights Working Group of the Commission on Human Rights (1 February 1974) UN Doc. E7CN.4/1134. None of these have been widely used, see Chinkin, 'U.N. Human Rights Council Fact-Finding Mission', 487. More recent attempts include the Manual on the Effective Investigation and Documentation of Torture and Other Cruel, Inhuman or Degrading Treatment or Punishment (Istanbul Protocol), submitted to the UN High Commissioner for Human Rights in 1999; Updated Set of principles for the protection and promotion of human rights through action to combat impunity by the Commission on Human Rights (8 February 2005) UN Doc. E/CN.4/2005/102.Add1.

[117] GA, Declaration on Fact-finding, UN Doc. A/RES/46/59, para. 2.

[118] GA, Declaration on Fact-finding, para. 3. See similarly Manual of Operations of the Special Procedures of the Human Rights Council', para. 24. Additionally, UNGA Res. 60/251 (3 April 2006) UN Doc. A/RES/60/251, which mandated the UNHRC, articulates impartiality as a guiding principle of the UNHRC, para. 4.

[119] GA, Declaration on Fact-finding, para. 25.

[120] Juan E. Méndez, 'Report of the Special Rapporteur on Torture and other Cruel, Inhuman or Degrading Treatment or Punishment' (18 January 2012) Human Rights Council, UN Doc. A/HRC/19/61(2012), para. 25.

[121] Méndez, 'Report of the Special Rapporteur on Torture', para. 64.

[122] 'The Court ... may request of public international organizations information relevant to cases before it, and shall receive such information presented by such organizations on their own initiative.' ICJ Statute Art. 34(2). See *inter alia* James Devaney, 'Killing Two Birds with One Stone: Can Increased Use of Article 34(2) of the ICJ Statute Improve the Legitimacy of UN Commissions of Inquiry and the Court's Fact-finding Procedure?', *STALS Research Paper* N 2/2013 (2013), 5.

Attempts have been made to erect minimal procedures to protect the integrity of human rights fact-finding outside the UN. The International Law Association in 1980 approved by consensus a set of minimal procedures for fact-finding by NGOs, proposing (1) *open* resolution authorizing a mission without prejudging findings, (2) *objective* terms of reference that do not prejudge the issues to be investigated, and (3) *specific* terms of reference so as to indicate the nature of the subject to be investigated.[123]

Academic scrutiny into different mandates has increased in recent years. So have suggestions concerning how to strengthen their procedures, predictability, and trustworthiness.[124] Ultimately, however, methodologies must be tailored to the task of the individual mission. While international inquiries into assassinations resemble domestic commissions save for the lack of investigative powers or the ability to determine civil or criminal liability, international fact-finding intended to clarify the facts of an event or crisis are much less specific. Mandates vary, and so will their level of detail and clarity.

4.2. Ambiguities in mandate

Lack of standardized methods increases the importance of the terms of reference of each fact-finding mandate. A mission should have 'a clear mandate' and 'precise requirements to be met by its report'.[125] However, the context of fact-finding mandates is highly politicized. The mandate may therefore be biased in various ways or intended to serve multiple objectives.[126] Temporal and geographic scopes of the mission, in addition to which parties are to be examined, are important elements that may create tensions within a mandating body. The UNHRC mandate to the Lebanon Commission in 2006 authorized investigation of violations committed by only one party to the conflict (Israel).[127] The report respected but explicitly criticized this restrictive mandate.[128] A similarly biased mandate by the UNHRC into events at Beit Hanoun (2006) was interpreted broadly by the commissioners in order to produce a balanced report.[129] A more far-reaching approach was

[123] Thomas M. Franck, 'The Belgrade Minimal Rules of Procedure for International Human Rights Fact-Finding Missions', 59th Conference of the ILA in Belgrade, reprinted in *American Journal of International Law* 75 (1981), 163.

[124] For a critical appraisal of different mandates, see Grace, 'The Design and Planning of ... Missions'. See also various contributions in Bergsmo (ed.), *Quality Control in Fact-Finding.*

[125] GA, Declaration on Fact-Finding, para. 17.

[126] One example is the Georgia Report. Although perceived by Western academics to make a significant contribution to the establishment of the causes of the conflict(s), and violations of *ius ad bellum* and *in bello* (see e.g. Tarcisio Gazzini, 'Criteria for Statehood as Applied by the EUs Independent Fact-Finding Mission on the Conflict in Georgia', *EJIL Talk*, 8 December 2009), the report resonated the contentions by NATO, and was not perceived as unbiased by academics pertaining to the Eastern sphere.

[127] UNHRC, Special Session Res. (11 August 2006) UN Doc. S-2/1, para. 7(a).

[128] 'Report of the Commission of Inquiry on Lebanon pursuant to Human Rights Council Resolution S-2/1' (23 November 2006) UN Doc. A/HRC/3/2, para. 7.

[129] 'Report of the High-level Fact-finding Mission to Beit Hanoun established under Council Resolution S-3/1' (1 September 2008) UN Doc. A/HRC/9/26, para. 6, see also para. 55.

adopted by commissioner Justice Richard Goldstone in response to the UNHRC one-sided mandate into Operation Cast Lead conducted by Israel in Gaza.[130] Following an agreement with the President of the UNHRC, Goldstone crafted a more 'even-handed' mandate himself.[131] This report illustrated well how divisive a fact-finding mission can be, politically and academically.[132]

If left unanswered by the terms of reference by the mandating body, these issues will force fact-finding missions to make choices that are likely to challenge the authority of their findings.

Expectations vested in the mechanisms may tilt interpretation of the mandate towards a result that responds to public expectations so as to avoid de-legitimization. It is clearly not desirable to have 'run-away fact-finding missions' in highly politicized settings. The Goldstone report, in spite of its mandate, recommended that the UN Security Council order Israel to investigate allegations of war crimes.[133] It also suggested that a copy be sent to the ICC and that the signatories of the GC rely on universal jurisdiction, prompting heavy criticism over its interpretation of the mandate. Similarly, the UNHRC fact-finding mission in Libya adjusted its mandate on human rights violations to fit developments on the ground as the crisis descended into an armed conflict.[134] The tensions between loyalty to an inadequate mandate on the one hand, and responding to expectations and developments on the ground on the other, subject fact-finders to difficult choices, where either alternative could undermine the integrity of the mission.

4.3. Selection of law and facts

Although the mandates of fact-finding mechanisms and their expectations increasingly resemble domestic fact-finding, international fact-finding are not adjudication mechanisms. They do not have investigative powers similar to those of domestic inquiries. An increasing gap between mandate and expectations on

[130] HRC Res. S-9/1 (12 January 2009), UN Doc. A/HRC/RES/S-9/1, para. 14.

[131] 'Report of the United Nations Fact Finding Mission on the Gaza Conflict' (25 September 2009) UN Doc. A/HRC/12/48, paras. 131, 134, 135.

[132] For critical scholars see *inter alia* Peter Berkowitz, 'The Goldstone Report and International Law: The March of Politics under the Banner of Law', *Policy Review* 162 (2010), 13; Tom Farer et al., 'The Goldstone Report on the Gaza Conflict: An Agora', *Global Governance* 16 (2010), 139. For a set of sympathetic scholars see Adam Horowitz, Lizzy Ratner, and Philip Weiss (eds.), *The Goldstone Report: The Legacy of the Landmark Investigation of the Gaza Conflict* (New York: Nation Books, 2010). Goldstone later retracted one of the main conclusions in the report, see Richard Goldstone, 'Reconsidering the Goldstone Report on Israel and War Crimes', *Washington Post*, 2 April 2011.

[133] Mandate 'To investigate all violations of international human rights law and international humanitarian law that might have been committed at any time in the context of the military operations that were conducted in Gaza during the period from 27 December 2008 and 18 January 2009, whether before, during or after.'

[134] 'Report on the International Commission of Inquiry to investigate all alleged violations of international human rights law in the Libyan Arab Jamahiriya' (7 June 2011) UN Doc. A/HRC/17/44, para. 4. See also interviews with the fact-finders, quoted in Grace 'The Design and Planning of … Missions'.

the one hand and access, resources, and what level of truth may actually be found on the other is putting international fact-finding under much strain.

Fact-finding is inherently subjective. The facts found depend on a multitude of elements relevant to the construction of the factual context. It is not possible to identify 'real facts' or 'the truth', either as a matter of pragmatism or as a matter of epistemology.[135] The idea that there is an objective truth, and that outside actors may in fact establish this truth in a matter of weeks—or even days—may be criticized from various perspectives.[136] Yet, there are also more pressing concerns with the facts that are actually selected. Fact-finding missions often encounter challenges with potentially very large amounts of information, conflicting information and considerable time pressure. Added to that, they often have less than adequate resources. The composition of the mission will influence the assessments of coherence, trustworthiness and plausibility of the sources they select. In addition, the individual background of fact-finders will inevitably determine their evaluations of probabilistic relations and the relative strength of different hypotheses. A discussion is therefore materializing on the selection and composition of fact-finding mechanisms.[137]

While fact-finding intended to serve as enforcement mechanisms of treaty regimes may have a dual focus of law (interpretation of the correct treaty obligations) and facts (establishment of facts that support compliance or breach of obligations), fact-finding for preventive purposes may primarily emphasize factual circumstances. At the other end are the more stringent requirements of law relative to accountability. Questions of scope of applicability are important for a thorough treatment of law. Yet, this is not the main objective of the fact-finding mission, occasionally causing a somewhat cursory presentation of the law.

A related challenge is the temptation to use such reports to profess a progressive interpretation of international law.[138] Some fact-finding missions have been heavily criticized because of their progressive or biased interpretation of the law.[139] If a fact-finding mission intends to ease tensions or suggest violations of a treaty, the

[135] For discussions on this issue, see Viljoen, 'Fact-Finding by UN Human Rights Complaints Bodies', 49–100; Simon De Smet, 'Justified Belief in the Unbelievable', in Bergsmo (ed.), *Quality Control in Fact-Finding*, 73–137, reviewing the main epistemic aspects of fact-finding.

[136] See *inter alia* Bergsmo, 'Non-Criminal Justice Fact-Work'; Chinkin, 'U.N. Human Rights Council Fact-Finding Mission'; Grace and Brudelein, 'Building Effective Monitoring, Reporting and Fact-Finding Mechanisms'; Grace, 'The Design and Planning of... Missions'.

[137] See notably Wu Xiaodan, 'Quality Control and the Selection of Members of International Fact-Finding Mandates', in Bergsmo (ed.), *Quality Control in Fact-Finding*, 193–210; Ted Piccone, *Catalysts for Change: How the UN's Independent Experts Promote Human Rights* (Washington, DC: Brookings Institution, 2012), underlining the importance of individual personalities and the multiple abilities required to get the job done.

[138] Notably the Darfur Report (2004), headed by Antonio Cassese, professed a progressive interpretation of the law of non-international armed conflict.

[139] See notably criticism against the interpretation of humanitarian law in the Goldstone Report (see n. 132). See also Zoran Oklopcic, 'Reflections on Determination, and the Status of Kosovo in Light of the Report of the Independent International Fact-Finding Mission on the Conflict in Georgia', *EJIL Talk*, 31 December 2009, criticizing the understanding of self-determination expressed in in the report; André De Hoogh, 'Georgia's Short-Lived Military Excursion into South Ossetia; The Use of Armed Force and Self-Defense', *EJIL Talk*, 9 December 2009.

wisdom of such approaches may be questioned. A core objective of a fact-finding mission ought to be the establishment of facts and law that at least the international community at large may agree upon. The lack of other appropriate forums to develop the law in a progressive direction may not warrant use of fact-finding missions for such purposes.[140]

4.4. Admission of on-site visits

While fact-finding for dispute resolution is dependent on consent by the target state, no such consent is necessary for mandates by the Human Rights Council.[141] However, only the Security Council acting under Chapter VII may demand admission.[142] Although states 'should endeavour to follow a policy of admitting UN fact-finding missions to their territory', HRC fact-finding missions will often be denied such access.[143] Hence, a large amount of human rights fact-finding by INGOs and IGOs is accomplished without on-site visits. This subjects fact-finders to a range of dilemmas.[144]

It also has the intriguing effect that different fact-finding missions into the same situation may have different levels of access. The UN fact-finding mission to Syria concerning chemical weapons confirmed use but did not question accountability.[145] It had access to Syria pursuant to an invitation by the Syrian regime. The UNHRC permanent commission of inquiry was mandated to look into the question of responsibility of the use of chemical weapons. However, the commission's evidentiary threshold with regard to perpetrators was not met in any incident due to lack of appropriate information.[146] This latter UN fact-finding mission did *not* have access to Syria. On-site admission, essential to the authority and trustworthiness of fact-finding, is in most cases subject to the will of the state in question. State authorities are hence mostly in a position to privilege the fact-finding mechanism that may best serve their interests.

4.5. Political pressures

International fact-finding mandates are often corroborated or tainted by political realities.

[140] It does not necessarily remove controversies in the fact-finding report. The Goldstone Report relied on a progressive interpretation of law, while the fact-finding mission to Sri Lanka (2010) adopted a more conformist interpretation. Both reports were controversial. However, in the latter case controversies relating to the fact-finding report concerned facts rather than law.

[141] Resolution 5/21 paras. 85–109.

[142] Chinkin, 'U.N. Human Rights Council Fact-Finding Mission', 487.

[143] 'Declaration on Fact-Finding by the United Nations', A/RES/46/59, para. 21.

[144] For a comprehensive illustration see Chinkin, 'U.N. Human Rights Council Fact-Finding Mission', 488ff. See also David Weissbrodt and James McCarthy, 'Fact-finding by International Non-governmental Organizations', *Va. J. Int'l L.* 22 (1981–2), 59.

[145] UN Mission to Investigate Allegations of the Use of Chemical Weapons: Final Report.

[146] 'Report of the Independent International Commission of Inquiry on the Syrian Arab Republic' (12 February 2014) UN Doc. A/HRC/25/65A/HRC/25/65, para. 129.

Political sensitivities involved with formulation of the mandate persist when the fact-finding missions' reports are ready, and may severely affect their potential impact. The UNSC mandated International Commission of Inquiry on Burundi (1995) set out to 'establish the facts relating to the assassination of the President of Burundi on 21 October 1993, the massacres and other related serious acts of violence which followed'. After the mission found both Tutsis and Hutus guilty of genocide, Burundi's Tutsi-led government opposed the release of the Commission's final report. In response, the commission 'made a political decision that the government of Burundi had to approve the report' and omitted any mention of Tutsis killing Hutus.[147] The report by the fact-finding panel appointed by the UN Secretary-General to investigate the circumstances of the final phases of the Sri Lankan war was dismissed by the Sri Lankan government as incorrect and biased.[148] Similarly, the inquiry into the assassination of Benazir Bhutto was rejected by the same Pakistani authorities that ordered the inquiry.

Exaggeration or under-reporting will weaken the authority of fact-finding. However, the impartiality and authority sought by fact-finding missions will almost invariably be at odds with the persisting narratives of parties involved. Ultimately, fact-finding mechanisms continuously risk becoming tools in the struggle between the parties to define history.

4.6. Proliferation of reports

The proliferation of institutions with international fact-finding competence and no settled hierarchy between them risk producing an *industry* of fact-finding. Disputed incidents or a controversial mandate may lead numerous fact-finding missions to investigate the same incident. The Arab League mandated a separate international fact-finding commission to investigate the Cast Lead operation, headed by renowned international scholars.[149] This fact-finding report was entirely independent of the UNHRC mandated report. Proliferation of fact-finding mechanisms within the UN may also cause certain tensions. The Israeli boarding of a Turkish flotilla destined to break the Israeli blockade of Gaza resulting in nine dead activists occasioned a fact-finding mission by the UNHRC, and a separate panel of experts by the UNSG with slightly diverging conclusions.[150] On

[147] Grace and Brudelein, 'Building Effective Monitoring, Reporting and Fact-Finding Mechanisms', 16–17.

[148] The Panel did not have a mandate to find facts, but gathered the many allegations related to the final stages of the war and suggested what legal duties arose in connection with the credible allegations, concluding that Sri Lanka had failed to carry out certain of its duties.

[149] See Arab League Decisions XXX, and the 'No Safe Place—Report of the Arab League's Independent Fact Finding Committee Following 'Operation Cast Lead', http://www.arableague-online.org/las/picture_gallery/reportfullFINAL.pdf (accessed 23 June 2014).

[150] See the Palmer Report and 'Report of the international fact-finding mission to investigate violations of international law, including international humanitarian and human rights law, resulting from the Israeli attacks on the flotilla of ships carrying humanitarian Assistance' (27 September 2010) UN Doc. A/HRC/15/21.

top of this, non-governmental organizations also perform fact-finding missions intended to influence governmental organizations. A vast array of reports at the level of international law is clearly detrimental to the objective of creating one authoritative narrative. This development may fatigue actors involved and produce conflicting narratives competing for supremacy.

Different fact-finding mechanisms may have complementary tasks. The HRC-mandated commission of inquiry on Libya was established in March 2011.[151] While the Security Council endorsed this fact-finding mission, the Council established a Committee for the surveillance of sanctions imposed by the SC, and subsequently a Panel of Experts to follow up and provide facts and recommendations to the Committee.[152] While the primary task of the UNSC Panel of Experts was to enable the Committee to follow up sanctions imposed by the SC, the HRC Commission of Inquiry followed the human rights situation.

When fact-finding does result in firm action by international institutions, proliferation of reports may be explained as a diligent preparatory step. However, when extensive fact-finding by international institutions fails to materialize in reaction despite the compelling content of countless reports, fact-finding may be seen precisely as a 'reason for multiplication of reports'. It risks dealing a substantial blow to the authority and integrity of the very international institutions that mandate fact-finding.

4.7. Risk of escalation

Occasionally there is a risk that fact-finding may not reduce tension, but instead cause a conflict to escalate. The publication on 1 September 2011 of the Palmer Report concerning the Flotilla incident exacerbated the diplomatic crisis between Israel and Turkey. The report was interpreted by some to cause a risk of regional conflagration.[153] Similarly, the Security Council has at times avoided action under Article 34, and instead requested the Secretary-General to dispatch an observer mission in order to prevent a situation that could lead to increased international friction.[154]

[151] The decision was taken on 25 February 2011, UN Doc. A/HRC/S-15/1. The commission was appointed 15 March 2011. The commission delivered two reports, see 'Report of the International Commission of Inquiry to investigate all alleged violations of international human rights law in the Libyan Arab Jamahiriya' (1 June 2011) UN Doc. A/HRC/17/44; 'Report of the International Commission of Inquiry on Libya' (2 March 2012), UN Doc. A/HRC/19/68.

[152] UNSC Res. 1970 (26 February 2011) UN Doc. S/RES/1970(2011), para. 24, UNSC Res. 1973 (17 March 2011) UN Doc. S/RES/1973(2011), para. 24. For the most recent extension of the mandate of the Panel of Experts, see UNSC Res. 2144 (14 March 2014) UN Doc. S/RES/2144(2014), para. 13.

[153] Tamar Feldman, 'A Tale of Two Closures: Comments on the Palmer Report Concerning the May 2010 Flotilla Incident', *EJIL Talk*, 20 September 2011.

[154] On example cited by Simma is the observer mission sent to Tajikistan in 1993, see Simma, *The Charter of the United Nations*, 607.

4.8. Core objectives difficult to reconcile

Fact-finding mechanisms may be swift and provide transparency. However, they do add a layer of institutional restraint, risking prolonging a circuit of responses, rather than facilitating preparation for swift and decisive action. Chinkin, a member of the fact-finding commission in Gaza, observed that while the process was a victory for the HRC, 'the primary objectives of fact-finding—international dispute resolution, contribution to peace and security, change in behaviour and human rights compliance by all relevant parties—have not been accomplished'.[155] This dilemma is part of a broader discussion about how international instruments for conflict prevention fit with the rising regime of international criminal law.

As a measure of *prevention*, identification of issues of fact and international law may alert the international community to an evolving situation threatening international peace and security. It is a tool to signal concern over a potentially explosive situation.[156] Fact-finding may buy time and opportunity for negotiations.[157] It would ideally emphasize the interrelationship between the parties, the dynamic of action–reaction in order to establish a narrative different from the opposed and conflict-fuelling narratives that often prevail with the adversary parties, providing an explanatory and analytical recollection of events. It may be submitted that the objective of fact-finding mechanisms for prevention is to offer a window of opportunity to reach a negotiated or forced settlement intended to prevent further escalation.

Fact-finding that is intended as a basis for *accountability*, would, on the contrary, ideally rely on a more descriptive approach. The main objective of fact-finding for accountability is punitive reactions and countermeasures by the international community, or at the very least lending eyes and ears to the stories of victims of international crimes. Explanatory and analytical presentation of such events will commonly have an unpleasant exculpatory dimension. It may indeed undermine the objective of lending eyes and ears to victims. A recollection of events intended to serve as a basis for prosecution or countermeasures will commonly decontextualize events and focus on excesses to an extent that the fact-finding loses its relevance as a basis for negotiated settlement between the parties. If anything, it will provide moral support and boost the political cause of the party getting recognition for their suffering. In addition, the prevailing notion that there can be no negotiation with war criminals further limits the choice of action.

Hence, the purpose of fact-finding will often influence its form and content. While mandating bodies may want all facts and possibilities on the table, multi-purpose fact-finding may turn out to be counterproductive. While fact-finding mechanisms may indeed alleviate some of the shortcomings of international law in managing the risks of armed conflict and responding to serious

155 Chinkin, 'U.N. Human Rights Council Fact-Finding Mission', 493.

156 See GA Declaration on Fact-Finding by the United Nations', A/RES/46/59.

157 In Guinea in 2009 the Security Council threw a veil over the process, but took no action, as the negotiation attempts succeeded in bringing in a transitional government of unity. See 'Statement by the President of the Security Council' (28 October 2009) UN Doc. S/PRST/2009/27, para. 8.

human rights abuses, the joint objective of preventing armed conflict and the aim to ensure accountability for violations of international law are difficult to reconcile within one fact-finding mechanism. Vesting more into fact-finding than it can carry might in the end be counter-productive to its potential in strengthening the responses of international law to man-made emergencies.

5. The Future Role of Fact-Finding in the International Architecture of Peace

Fact-finding mandated by intergovernmental organizations has proliferated over the past two decades. These mechanisms are useful tools for international institutions in various ways. They offer an important contribution to institutional integration in an imperfect international system. In addition, they represent the eyes and ears of the international community. However, fact-finding mechanisms are caught in a certain tension rising from international law's ambition of peace on the one hand and justice on the other. While fact-finding for the purpose of prevention and treaty enforcement is dependent on flexibility in modes of operation for its success, consistency is key to the credibility of fact-finding for the purpose of accountability for international crimes. The future success of international fact-finding mechanisms is likely to depend on the ability of international institutions to handle and adequately balance the various concerns and practical challenges deriving from this tension.

19

The Constitutional Dimension of Peace

Azin Tadjdini

1. Introduction: Linking Constitutions and Peace

What is the role of domestic constitutions in the preservation and promotion of peace?[1]

The promotion of positive and negative peace, policies that place peace at risk, and direct acts of violence, whether internal or external, are all political decisions. As the most political legal document of a country, establishing the foundations upon which policies must take place, constitutions will play a significant role in setting the framework for whether and how such decisions are made, and their legitimacy. Through its distribution of power and material rights, its prohibitions and guarantees, as well as its institutional and procedural provisions, the constitution brings together various elements affecting peace. The way in which a constitution regulates these elements informs us about the extent of peace potential that *formally* exists within a jurisdiction, including the existence of formal boundaries and obstacles for peace.[2]

As an analytical tool, the concept of 'peace' presents some difficulties. There is no unanimity as to its content, neither as a philosophical nor a legal concept.[3] It is understood differently by different people, in different situations, in and between

[1] I use 'peace' in a wide sense. See Cecilia Bailliet and Kjetil M. Larsen, Chapter 1 in this volume. For practical purposes, my reference to 'constitution' is, on the other hand, narrow, referring to the formal constitution enjoying some form of legal superiority. In this sense, the constitution is different from 'constitutionalism', since not every state that has a document called 'constitution' will qualify as a constitutional state.

[2] This chapter deals with the *formal* conditions and obstacles for peace. Practice may very well not meet the standards set by the formalities. Insisting on the presence of these formalities is nevertheless important, and constitutes a necessary first step towards the achievement of peace.

[3] See Kristoffer Lidén and Henrik Syse, Chapter 2 in this volume, for an overview of various perceptions of 'peace' in philosophy and law. More generally, the *Oxford English Dictionary* lists fifteen definitions of peace. Within the UN system, 'peace' remains an unclear concept. Absent a formal and unified legal definition of peace, a number of UN resolutions make an attempt to define 'the culture of peace'. See the 1998 UN Resolution on the culture of peace. In his remarks during the Security Council debate on post-conflict situations, UN Secretary-General Ban Ki-moon stressed the broadness of the term 'peace' and the task of peace-building: 'Building peace is about much more than ending war. It is about putting in place the institutions and trust that will carry people forward into a peaceful future.' 22 July 2009, SG/SM/12376, SC/9713.

jurisdictions, and over time.[4] Even within one subcategory of peace, such as, for example, 'internal peace', the concept has a wide range of meanings. A mere constitutional reference to 'peace' will therefore at best be vague and at worst risk counter-effective abuse.

In addition, and related to its ambiguity, 'peace' can play multiple roles in a constitution. Peace can be stated as an explicit constitutional right, either justiciable or not; it can have a normative, symbolic, or institutional role;[5] it can be a policy goal;[6] or it can play a more comprehensive role in denoting the *result* of a constitutional design that facilitates peace.[7] Put differently, the absence of peace in a country need not be due to a lack of an explicit constitutional reference to peace, but due to a constitutional design that creates weak conditions for peace to be achieved. When discussing the constitutional dimension of peace, we therefore need to look beyond the explicit constitutional references to peace—if such do exist in a constitution—and instead identify the constitutional structures and provisions that either in whole or in part do or do not facilitate peace. While this chapter falls short of providing a comprehensive analysis of the constitutional dimension of peace, it will highlight some of the factors that are relevant in such an analysis.

The chapter proceeds in four sections. Section 2 begins from a theoretical angle with an overview of the Kantian theory on the connection between constitutions and peace. Section 3 presents and discusses different forms of constitutional approaches to peace, beginning with the traditional constitutional approach to peace in Section 3.1. Section 3.2 moves on to present different forms of what has come to be known as 'peace constitutions'. Section 3.3 examines the issue of enforcement of peace provisions, and section 3.4 discusses the ways in which constitution-making has become recognized as one of the central elements of peace-building. Section 4 moves beyond explicit constitutional references to 'peace', and approaches the issue of the constitutional dimension of peace by asking what the *aim* of peace is. The section then seeks to identify constitutional conditions, structures, and institutional factors that undermine that aim and hence undermine peace.

[4] See Cecilia Bailliet, Chapter 3 in this volume, on the evolution of the law of peace.

[5] e.g. the Bolivian Constitution of 2009 is one among many constitutions that state peace as a goal in their preamble: 'We take on the historical challenge of collectively constructing a Unified Social State of Pluri-National Communitarian Law, which includes and articulates the goal of advancing toward a democratic, productive, peace-loving and peaceful Bolivia, committed to the full development and free determination of the peoples.'

[6] The Constitution of Nepal of 2006 contains several references to peace, amongst others as a foreign policy goal: 'The state shall pursue the foreign policy of Nepal based on the Charter of the United Nations, non-alignment, the principles of Panschsheel, international law and the norms of world peace,' Art. 35 (21).

[7] The idea of peace as a *result* of constitutional design rests partly on the idea that peace is not a right in itself but something that can be realized through the enforcement of existing identifiable and distinguishable human rights. Some of the delegations in the working group of the UN Declaration on the right to peace held this view. See 'Open-ended Inter-Governmental Working Group on the Draft United Nations Declaration on the Right to Peace', prepared by the Chairperson-Rapporteur, Christian Guillermet-Fernàndez, Doc. A/HRC/WG.13/1/2, 21 February 2013, para. 21.

2. The Kantian Theory on Constitutions as a Prerequisite for Peace

In politico-legal thought, the question of the relationship between constitutions and peace can be traced back to before the enactment of the first modern constitutions.[8] In *Towards Perpetual Peace,* Kant describes how real and permanent peace might be instituted, and he does so by determining reforms for a civil, international, and cosmopolitan constitution.[9] For Kant, therefore, the achievement of peace is the essential reason for creating and reforming constitutions.[10] Kant's theory is premised on the idea that human beings in a state of nature are in a state of war. Peace, therefore, is a constructive project—it is something that must be 'formally instituted'.[11] To that end, Kant proposes the adoption of a legal constitution in three stages:

(1) A constitution based on the *civil right* of individuals within a nation (*jus civitatis*);

(2) A constitution based on the *international right* of states in their relationship with one another (*ius gentium*);

(3) A constitution based on a *cosmopolitan right,* in so far as individuals and state, co-existing in an external relationship of mutual influences, may be regarded as citizens of a universal federation of mankind (*ius cosmopoliticium*).[12]

Through this theory, Kant tells us not only that constitutions are a prerequisite for peace. Equally important, he tells us that peace consists of external and internal as well as negative and positive elements. As a prerequisite for peace, a constitution must therefore reflect all these elements, and a condition for peace must be established at all three levels. At the same time, Kant acknowledges that perpetual peace is an ideal that may never be attained.[13] His theory is nevertheless intended as a guide to reach perpetual peace through constant reform of legal and political structures.[14]

[8] See Lidén and Syse, Chapter 2 in this volume.

[9] Immanuel Kant, 'Perpetual Peace: A Philosophical Sketch', in *Kant's Political Writings*, Hans Reiss (ed.) (Cambridge: Cambridge University Press, 1970), 93–130. See also Immanuel Kant, 'Towards Perpetual Peace (1795)', in *The Cambridge Edition of the Works of Immanuel Kant: Practical Philosophy*, Mary J. Gregor (ed.) (Cambridge: Cambridge University Press, 1996).

[10] The idea of peace is, for Kant, tied to the idea of freedom, central in his social and political philosophy. For a general overview I refer to the entry on Kant in *Stanford Encyclopedia of Philosophy*, http://plato.stanford.edu/entries/kant/ (accessed 15 Nov 2014).

[11] Kant, 'Perpetual Peace. A Philosophical Sketch', 98.

[12] Kant, 'Perpetual Peace. A Philosophical Sketch'.

[13] Truly perpetual peace is, according to Kant, a 'moral task', and arises from the recognition of duty. See Pauline Kleinsgeld, 'Approaching Perpetual Peace. Kant's Defence of a League of States and his Ideal of a World Federation', *European Journal of Philosophy* 12 (2004), 304–25 at 316.

[14] Here I follow Alyssa R. Bernstein, *Kant, Rawls and Cosmopolitanism: Toward Perpetual Peace and The Law of Peoples, Jahrbuch für Recht and Ethik/Annual Review of Law and Ethics* 17 (Berlin: Duncker & Humblot, 2009), 3–52.

In the first section of *Towards Perpetual Peace*, Kant lists six 'prohibitive laws' that must be enacted in order to obtain 'perpetual peace'. First, treaties that end hostilities must be permanent. In order to be effective, the agreement must 'nullify all existing reasons for a future war'.[15] Second, states, which are 'societies of men', and therefore not to be 'used and misused as objects to be manipulated at will', cannot be acquired by other states.[16] Third, standing armies should be phased out over time because their very existence can create a war of hostilities by engendering an arms race. Fourth, national debts should be paid because they are too often used to finance armies. Furthermore, debt can lead to national bankruptcy which Kant fears creates potential for war. Fifth, state interference in the constitutional or governmental affairs of other states is prohibited because this would be a 'violation of the rights of an independent people', as well as making the autonomy of all other states insecure. Sixth, Kant outlaws 'dishonourable' wartime practices that would 'make mutual confidence impossible during a future time of peace'.[17]

In addition to these six preliminary articles, the second section of *Towards Perpetual Peace* elaborates on three 'definitive articles'. The first is that the civil constitution of every state shall be republican.[18] Kant argues for the merits of 'republican' constitution, by which he refers to a constitution where all citizens are *free,* dependent upon common legislation and legally *equal.* Freedom and equality for Kant stand at the core of peace. His political philosophy is one that emphasizes laws to be enacted by the consent of the governed and which apply to all citizens equally, according to the concept of civil rights.[19] Kant believes that 'republics' would never declare war because the citizens of such states who bear the costs of war would never declare war. Despots, on the other hand, would not have a similar disincentive to conflict. In the second definitive article, Kant argues that the states should join into a common constitution that would preserve each member's right in a federation of states with the intention to 'preserve and secure the freedom of each state in itself'.[20] In the third and final definitive article, we find the cosmopolitan right 'limited to conditions of universal hospitality'. A constitution of cosmopolitan right would result as 'peaceful mutual relations … eventually become regulated by public laws'.[21]

[15] Kant, 'Perpetual Peace. A Philosophical Sketch', 93.

[16] Kant, 'Perpetual Peace. A Philosophical Sketch', 93.

[17] Kant, 'Perpetual Peace. A Philosophical Sketch', 96.

[18] Kant, 'Perpetual Peace. A Philosophical Sketch', 103. Kant's use of 'republican' can perhaps best be translated into 'democratic' in today's parlance.

[19] A prominent Kantian philosopher of the twentieth century, John Rawls, complements Kant's theory by specifying a list of human rights that must be respected by every political society as a condition of its being entitled to the rights of sovereignty, political autonomy, and freedom from international intervention. Moreover, Rawls argues that international peace can be justly attained only if a public political conception of justice applicable to international law and practice can be endorsed and adopted by all non-expansionist societies that meet at least certain minimal criteria for domestic social justice, which he refers to as the criteria of decency. See John Rawls, *The Law of Peoples* (Cambridge, Mass.: Harvard University Press, 1999).

[20] Kant, 'Perpetual Peace. A Philosophical Sketch', 104.

[21] Kant, 'Perpetual Peace. A Philosophical Sketch', 106.

Kant's overarching aim is thus to bring about perpetual peace worldwide by means of law that secures the basic rights of individual persons. The problem he addresses in his philosophy of international law is that of how to establish law among states, given that international law can have force only if states cooperatively establish and maintain it, and given that some states may not share Kant's aim or be interested in cooperating with other states on fair terms. The solution Kant develops is the following. The first step is for states to agree among themselves to abide by the preliminary articles in their mutual relations. These states will also aim to realize all three definitive articles. According to Kant, then, external and internal peace go hand in hand. Peace is both an interstate matter and a matter of domestic social justice.

3. Contemporary Constitutional Approaches to Peace

While Kant's theories offer a formula for the achievement of peace, they remain ideal theories. In this section we move on to consider some ways in which constitutions approach peace in practice, and the extent to which these approaches implement the normative ideals set by theory. We start with what we, for these purposes, can call the 'traditional' constitutional approach, by which I refer to the way in which the first constitutions of the eighteenth and nineteenth centuries approached peace. This constitutional model is, however, not limited to the past, as some of those constitutions are still in force and as a number of later constitutions were built on that model. The section continues with the post-World War II constitutional model, often referred to as 'peace constitution'. Next, the section considers the enforcement of peace provisions, before ending with considering the contemporary framework for constitution-making as peace-building.

3.1. The traditional constitutional approach

When looking at the first modern constitutions adopted in the late eighteenth and nineteenth centuries, war or the threat of war was often a powerful motivating force for adopting a constitution that could be a unifying instrument. In these constitutions, peace is often stated as one of the aims of the constitution, reflecting the Kantian idea of constitutions as tools to achieve peace.

The 1787 constitution of the United States, a source of inspiration for constitution-making elsewhere,[22] states this in its preamble:

> We the people of the United States, in order to form a more perfect Union, establish Justice, insure domestic Tranquility, provide for the common defense, promote the general Welfare, and secure the Blessings of liberty to ourselves and our Posterity, do ordain and establish this Constitution for the United States of America.

[22] See George Athan Billias, *American Constitutionalism Heard Around the World 1789–1989: A Global Perspective* (New York: New York University Press, 2009).

Domestic peace or 'tranquillity' as a stated constitutional goal inspired a number of other constitutions. The 1853 constitution of Argentina has the almost word-for-word copy of the US preamble in its own preamble: 'We, the representatives of the people of the Argentine Nation ... for the purpose of framing a Constitution for the National Union, to establish justice, insure domestic peace, provide for the common defense.'[23] While the US and Argentine constitutions are examples of constitutions primarily concerned with internal peace and the creation of a stable and viable state, the Weimar constitution of 1919 extended the ambitions of peace to include external peace. The preamble reads: 'The German people, united in all their racial elements, and inspired by the will to renew and strengthen their Reich in liberty and justice, to preserve peace at home and abroad and to foster social progress, have established the following constitution.'[24]

The goal of domestic peace was supported by a significant move represented by the introduction of a number of individual rights. This second feature whereby state power over the individual became constitutionalized, reflects elements of positive peace in the constitutions. In other words, the constitution limited the power of public authorities to impose on the people within their jurisdiction, and enhanced the legal protection of both positive and internal peace. This aspect of positive peace through constitutional acknowledgement of certain liberties, as well as the acknowledgement of the principle of equality in the enjoyment of those liberties, reflects the Kantian liberal peace idea in the first definitive article for perpetual peace:

> The civil constitution in every state shall be republican. A constitution established, first on principles of the freedom of the members of a society (as individuals), second on principles of the dependence of all upon a single common legislation (as citizens), and third on law of their equality (as citizens of a state) is a republican constitution.[25]

The introduction of representative government, typically through the establishment of parliament, and the separation of powers represents a third feature of the traditional constitutional approach to peace. As with the second feature, the third feature of the traditional constitutional approach is a breach with the arbitrary exercise of power, but this time the breach is achieved through institutional means, reflecting the Kantian idea about legitimate coercion through consent.

The fourth feature that characterizes the traditional approach is the constitutional regulation of war powers. Unlike the three first features, which can be linked directly to the Kantian liberal peace ideal, this fourth feature seems to be more linked with the practical concerns of the state. While the goal of peace is normally listed in the constitutional preamble, the regulation of the opposite of peace—namely war powers—is found in the operational parts of the constitution. Most early constitutions have provisions on war powers, on the organization

[23] Almost exact wording migrated across the Atlantic to the preamble of the 1847 constitution of Liberia.

[24] The 1919 Weimar Constitution, Art. 48, allowed for broad emergency powers, which ultimately led to the overriding of the peace goal as well as the rest of the constitution under the Third Reich. See Sect. 4.

[25] Kant, 'Towards Perpetual Peace (1795)', 322.

of the military, and on the duty to serve. For example, the Meiji Constitution of Japan of 1889 dedicates a number of provisions to the regulation of the armed forces and war powers. Article 13 states: 'The Emperor declares war, makes peace, and concludes treaties.'[26] Similar provisions are found in most other early constitutions, such as for example the 1931 constitution of Ethiopia,[27] and the US constitution.[28] In connection to the US constitution it is interesting to note that the war provisions are not merely directed to the *state,* but also to individuals through the second amendment which regulates 'the right of the people to keep and bear arms'.[29]

Although such provisions reflect the issue of balance of power within the state, they express at the same time an underlying presumption that recourse to war on some occasions is required, regardless of the peace ambitions stated in the constitutional preamble. Read in this way, the traditional constitution legitimizes a breach of peace under certain conditions. More often than not, the *material* conditions for recourse to war would not be stated in the constitution itself but would follow from the laws of war, whatever they were at the time and however they were chosen to be interpreted. Instead, the constitution regulated the *procedural* conditions for going to war. What we can note at this stage is that the constitutionalization of procedural conditions for the breach of peace in itself is significant. A number of early constitutions require the consent of parliament—that is, the representatives of the people—before the country can enter into a war.[30]

Recalling Kant's theory, the idea is that this element would reduce the recourse to war compared to a system where the executive is the sole decision-maker.[31] Consent by the people through their representatives in Parliament would establish a higher threshold for war as the people, upon whom the ultimate human and financial costs for war would rest, would be less willing than a sole executive to consent to war. The constitution thus establishes certain limits for how to breach peace. At the time of the adoption of the early constitutions, the legal and constitutional regulation of war therefore constituted an important step forward in limiting the ways in which peace could be breached. Instead of thinking of constitutional war provisions as a ground for recourse to war, the same provisions can therefore be read as a limitation of war precisely because of the conditions that the constitution established.

While this kind of constitutionalization of war powers can be viewed as initially constituting a step towards establishing peace, one could ask whether this function is retained today or whether the same conditions now have the

[26] See Arts. 12, 13, 20.

[27] The 1931 Constitution of Ethiopia, Arts. 12, 13.

[28] The 1787 Constitution of the US, Arts. 8, 10.

[29] The 1787 Constitution of the US, 2nd Amendment. The interpretation of the provision has been subject to vast disagreement. The purpose here is not to interpret the provision, but merely highlight the wording of it.

[30] See the 1787 Constitution of the US, Art. 1(8); the 1791 Constitution of France, ch. 3 sect. 12(2).

[31] A number of early constitutions also granted the executive the power to declare war, without the involvement of people's representatives. See the 1906 Constitution of Russia, Art. 13; and the 1931 Constitution of Ethiopia, Art. 12.

opposite function in that they contribute to the stagnation of the Kantian idea of reform of imperfect legal orders towards peace, and instead legitimize recourse to war. In the next section we shall see that this concern was addressed in part by the constitutional development in a number of countries following World War II.

3.2. 'Peace constitutions'

A new constitutional phenomenon emerged following World War II, through the adoption of what has come to be known as 'peace constitutions'.[32]

The experiences of the war together with international law's prohibition on the use of force, the general expansion and relevance of international law, and the emergence of non-domestic actors directly participating in constitution-making, created an environment that can help explain the rise of a certain type of constitution where two of the defining features of the traditional constitutions, regulation of war powers and the military, are omitted.

At first glance, therefore, 'peace constitutions' appear as a breach with the traditional constitutional approach to peace. However, one can also regard them as a continuance of the development towards peace. If we accept that the traditional approach can be viewed as a step towards peace through constitutionalizing the conditions for war, then the prohibition of war altogether can be viewed as a development along that line. Moreover, 'peace constitutions' in some respects fill the gap between two developments. One is the development of the international law regime that moves towards a limitation of war. The second is the development of constitutional design. During the first half of the twentieth century, domestic constitutional developments did not mirror but rather lagged behind international law's development towards peace expansion and war limitation. Following World War II and the adoption of peace constitutions in a number of countries, these two developments—domestic and international legal—to some extent began to converge in some areas.[33]

What characterizes the 'peace constitutions'? Fukase identifies three types of peace clauses: (1) constitutional clauses that renounce the waging of wars of aggression and conquest; (2) constitutions that resolve that the state maintains permanent neutrality; (3) constitutions that explicitly renounce war or war potential for security.[34]

[32] While the notion of 'peace constitutions' is normally used to describe some of the post-World War II constitutions, some scholars see France's 1791 Constitution as laying the foundation for current ideas about peace constitutions because it marked the first legalization of the use of force by the state. See Tadakazu Fukase, *Le Constitutionnalisme et ses problèmes au Japon: une approche comparative* (Paris: Presses universitaires de France, 1984).

[33] For a general overview of the interaction between international law and domestic law, including specific country analysis, see Dinah Shelton (ed.), *International Law and Domestic Legal Systems: Incorporation, Transformation, and Persuasion* (New York: Oxford University Press, 2011).

[34] Tadakazu Fukase, referenced in Jay Gilliam, 'Work Towards a (New) Definition of Peace Constitutions', *The Journal of Social Sciences* 72 (2011), 145–66 at 148.

It is worth noting that these three types of peace clause are concerned only with *external* and *negative* peace, they do not address internal and positive peace. This definition of 'peace constitution' can therefore be said to be more state-centred or sovereignty-centred. Assuming also that the internal and positive dimensions of peace are maintained, constitutions that include one or several of Fukase's peace clauses will nevertheless represent a significant step in the development of a constitutional design that facilitates peace. As such, they can be regarded as working to fulfil the second stage of Kant's three-stage process towards peace.

The most well known of the 'peace constitutions' is the Constitution of Japan. Its chapter 2, entitled 'Renunciation of War' contains the famous Article 9 which reads:

> Aspiring sincerely to an international peace based on justice and order, the Japanese people forever renounce war as a sovereign right of the nation and the threat or use of force as means of settling international disputes. In order to accomplish the aim of the preceding paragraph, land, sea, and air forces, as well as other war potential, will never be maintained. The right to belligerency of the state will not be recognized.[35]

Article 9 thus contains two elements of peace: the renunciation of war and the abolition of a state military.[36] The last sentence of the provision succinctly makes the connection between no military and a culture of peace.

While the constitution of Japan renounces war altogether, there are other constitutions that limit the prohibition on war to wars of *aggression*. Entering into force a year after the constitution of Japan, the constitution of Italy holds that:

> Italy rejects war as an instrument of aggression against the freedoms of other peoples and as a means for settling international controversies; it agrees, on conditions of equality with other states, to the limitations of sovereignty necessary for an order that ensures peace and justice among Nations, it promotes and encourages international organizations having such ends in view.[37]

Similarly, the Constitution of the Republic of Korea states in Article 5(1) that 'The Republic of Korea endeavors to maintain international peace and renounces all aggressive wars'.

Another constitution that makes an interesting case for the study of peace constitutions is that of Cambodia of 1993. In addition to guaranteeing rights

[35] Promulgated in 1946 and entering into effect on 3 May 1947, when the country was under occupation by the Allied Powers, the legitimacy of the constitution has been subject to debate. It has not, however, been revised by subsequent Japanese governments. For a discussion of the background of the Japanese constitution, see Shigenori Matsui, *The Constitution of Japan: A Contextual Analysis* (Oxford: Hart, 2011). The Liberal Democratic Party (LDP) has several times proposed amendments to the constitution. As of now, the latest is from 2012, where a modification of Art. 9 is one of a number of proposed changes, most of which go in a nationalist-protectionist direction, including a weakening of human rights. The draft is available at https://www.jimin.jp/english/news/117099.html (accessed on 15 Nov 2014).

[36] It should be pointed out that as the Constitution currently stands, Art. 9 has not been an obstacle for Japanese contributions to UN peacekeeping missions.

[37] The 1948 Constitution of Italy, Art. 11.

and otherwise regulating positive peace, the constitution in its Article 53 lays out principles of policy to be followed in foreign relations, and includes *inter alia* the adoption of a policy of permanent neutrality and non-alignment, and the prohibition against the invasion of any country. The provision furthermore limits the establishment of foreign military bases to only the ones that are mandated by the United Nations.

Ecuador's Constitution contains a similar policy goal:

> The state shall guarantee human safety by means of integrated policies and actions to ensure the peaceful coexistence of persons, to promote a culture of peace and to prevent forms of violence and discrimination and the perpetration of offenses and crimes. The planning and application of these policies shall be entrusted to specialized bodies at the different levels of government.[38]

Similarly, Bolivia's Constitution in Article 10(1) establishes that 'Bolivia is a pacifist State, which promotes the culture of peace and the right to peace.'

Related to constitutional provisions on the absence of a military are provisions that restrict the kinds of weapons that the military can use or that the state can introduce into its national territory. For example, the Constitution of East Timor aims for 'general, simultaneous and controlled disarmament' as a means to ensure peace and justice.[39] The Constitution of Cambodia goes further to say that: 'The manufacturing, use, storage of nuclear, chemical or biological weapons shall be absolutely prohibited.'[40] Similarly, the Constitution of Lithuania prohibits weapons of mass destruction on its territory.[41]

While Fukase's categories of peace constitutions were limited to categories reflecting external and negative peace, Jay Gilliam considers the state's commitment to respecting and protecting human rights as a fundamental element of a 'peace constitution', thus presenting a more human-centred definition of 'peace constitutions'.[42] Some constitutions in fact state this link expressly, such as for example the Constitution of Finland which holds that the state commits to participate in 'international cooperation for the protection of peace and human rights and for the development of society'.[43]

Related to such clauses are constitutional provisions that include a 'right to peace' or 'guarantee a culture of peace'. For example, Colombia's Constitution states that 'Peace is a right and duty whose compliance is mandatory'.[44] Ecuador's Constitution imposes on the state the duty to '[guarantee] for its inhabitants the right to a culture of peace, comprehensive security and [to] live in a free and democratic society without corruption.'[45] Japan's constitution takes this commitment

[38] The 2008 Constitution of Ecuador, Art. 249.
[39] The 2002 Constitution of East Timor, Art. 2.
[40] The 1993 Constitution of Cambodia (as revised in 1999), Art. 54.
[41] The 1992 Constitution of Lithuania (as revised in 2006), Art. 137.
[42] See Gilliam, *Work Towards a (New) Definition of Peace Constitutions.*
[43] The 2000 Constitution of Finland, Art. 1.
[44] The 1991 Constitution of Colombia (as revised 2005), Art. 22.
[45] The 2008 Constitution of Ecuador, Art. 3(8).

further and does not limit the right to peace to its own inhabitants but to all people of the world: '*We recognize that all peoples of the world have the right to live in peace, free from fear and want.*'[46]

Gilliam's definition of a peace constitution is based on four fundamental elements that he identifies. He explains peace constitutions as state constitutions that explicitly make commitment for the state and its people to work towards creating a global culture of peace either by (1) showing reluctance to go to war or use the state's monopoly on force and violence and, instead earnestly promoting peaceful conflict resolution; (2) by renouncing or severely restricting the role of its national military or foreign military hosted within its territory or the introduction and use of weapons of mass destruction; (3) by acknowledging universal human rights and creating a society where those rights can be realized; (4) by recognizing or subordinating national sovereignty to international law or promoting regional and international consolidation in order to create a global culture of peace; or (5) by any other constitutional means to create a global culture of peace.[47]

3.3. Enforcement

While constitutionalizing the elements of peace symbolizes a strong commitment to peace, the legal force of some of the peace provisions remains in question. To what extent are these provisions further institutionalized or justiciable? To what extent does the constitution treat peace, or the elements that constitute peace, as an enforceable legal right?

Starting with one of the elements of peace—the constitutional entrenchment of rights—one of the tests is whether such rights are acknowledged by the state and whether infringement of the rights can be brought before an independent court. This implies that the achievement of peace requires a constitutional acknowledgement of the principle of separation of powers as well as the principle of equality under law. A legal system where such features are absent does little to lift the references to peace above mere symbolism.

Several domestic courts have recognized the 'right to peace' as a right in itself, independent from the justiciability of other human rights. The jurisprudence of the Japanese High Courts has for example recognized that the right to live in peace is a legal right. In a decision from 1973, the Sapporo District Court acknowledged for the first time that the right to live in peace was a justiciable right. The background for the case was a decision by the Minister for Agriculture, Forestry, and Fishery to cancel the designation of a national forest in order to build a military base for air Self-Defence Forces. Residents of the area brought a lawsuit against the government arguing the unconstitutionality of the decision. In its decision, the Sapporo District Court held that the Self-Defence Forces missile

[46] The 1946 Constitution of Japan, preamble.

[47] Gilliam, *Work Towards a (New) Definition of Peace Constitutions*, 153–9.

site would be a 'first target' of attack from a foreign country in times of emergency, violating the plaintiff's right to live in peace.[48]

In *Mori* v. *Japan*, the plaintiffs (consisting of more than 5,700 citizens across Japan) challenged the constitutionality of Japan's deployment of its Self-Defence Forces to Iraq. The plaintiffs argued that the deployment violated their 'right to live in peace' under the preamble of the Japanese constitution, as well as violating Article 9. The main question before the court was whether the right to live in peace was justiciable—whether it was a 'concrete right'. The government argued that the right to live in peace was merely an abstract concept and not an enforceable right. While the Nagoya District Court dismissed the case due to lack of standing, it did *in dicta* state that the right to live in peace is 'a concrete right'. It reasoned that because peace is the foundation of all human rights, making their enjoyment possible, the right to live in peace is enforceable when combined with other rights provisions. The court stated that the integration of the Japanese Self Defence Force's air transport activities with the use of force by coalition forces in Iraq during military conflict constituted the use of force by the Self-Defence Force in violation of Article 9 of the constitution.[49]

Other domestic courts have also issued decisions that acknowledge the right to peace as a legal and justiciable right. Unlike Japan's Constitution which contains an explicit peace provision, the Constitution of Costa Rica does not mention peace explicitly. Costa Rican courts have, however, interpreted the constitution's commitment to international law, including human rights, as including a justiciable right to live a peaceful life. In 2003, a law student filed suit against the President and Minister of Foreign Affairs for including Costa Rica in the Iraq War's Coalition of the Willing. The Constitutional Court unanimously ruled that Costa Rica's inclusion in this coalition ran 'against the constitution, Costa Rica's neutrality declaration, international law and the UN system'.[50] Following the decision, Costa Rica asked to be removed from the Iraq Coalition of the Willing.

Three years later, the same law student filed a new suit against the government of Costa Rica. This time the issue concerned The Arms Decree, which regulated the import and manufacture of weapons. The decree was challenged because it granted permits for the manufacture of nuclear material. Again, the Constitutional Court unanimously judged in favour of the plaintiff, and annulled three sections of the decree.[51] In its reasoning, the court stated that these sections

[48] *Ito* v. *Minister of Agriculture and Forestry* (Sapporo Dist.Ct., 7 September 1973). I have relied on the English translation of the case by Lawrence W. Beer and Hiroshi Itoh, *The Constitutional Case Law of Japan, 1970 through 1990* (Seattle: University of Washington Press, 1996).

[49] *Mori* v. *Japan* (Nagoya High Ct., 27 April 2008). I have relied on the English translation of the case, see Hudson Hamilton, 'Mori v. Japan: The Nagoya High Court Recognizes the Right to Live in Peace', *Pacific Rim Law & Policy Journal Association* (2010), https://digital.lib.washington.edu/dspace-law/bitstream/handle/1773.1/514/19PacRimL&PolyJ549%282010%29.pdf?sequence=3 (accessed 15 Nov 2014). As the case was dismissed, the decision was not binding against the government.

[50] *Luis Roberto Zamora Bolaños* v. *Ministerio de Relaciones Exteriores y Otro*, Sala Constitucional de la Corte Suprema de Justicia, No. 2004-9992.

[51] *Luis Roberto Zamora Bolaños* v. *Ministerio de Salud*, Sala Constitucional de la Corte Suprema de Justicia, No. 2008-14193.

threatened Costa Rica's right to peace and the UN Declaration on the Right of Peoples to Peace (in addition to violating the right of the people to a healthy environment and ecological system and breaching international law and the Treaty on the Non-Proliferation of Nuclear Weapons). According to the court:

> A state that seeks to promote peace both domestically and internationally must take special care on authorizing the manufacture and/or import of weapons and chemical substances in its territory by rejecting categorically those that, because of their nature, were conceived and designed to encourage the negative value of war. (. . .) A State that takes peace as a constitutional fundamental value cannot conform itself with the limited notion that Peace is just the absence of war, it must go beyond that, preventing and rejecting continuously all decision and act which might derive and end in such a circumstance.[52]

While the constitutional courts of Japan and Costa Rica decided that participation in the Iraq war would be in breach of the Constitution, the constitutional court of the Republic of Korea on the same matter ended with a different result, confirming the injusticiability of the constitutional peace clauses. The case before the court was filed by a Korean national who sought to confirm the unconstitutionality of a decision by the President to dispatch the Korean national Armed Forces to Iraq, upon consulting the national Security Council.[53] The grounds for the suits were *inter alia* that this decision was in violation of Article 5 of the Constitution that renounces all aggressive wars. The constitutional court, in a unanimous opinion, dismissed the complaint due to lack of legal prerequisites for a constitutional complaint. In its reasoning for dismissing the case, the constitutional court stated that the decision regarding the constitutionality of dispatching the Armed Forces, including whether the war was aggressive in nature, was a decision that should be rendered by the President and the National Assembly, and not by the court.[54]

In addition to courts on the national level, the various regional human rights courts contribute to the institutionalization of peace, particularly elements of positive and internal peace. Therefore, countries that are parties to regional and international human rights treaties, and which have accepted the jurisdiction of these courts, offer an additional guarantee for peace, which we will return to in Section 4.

3.4. Constitution-making as peace-building

If the rationale behind the constitutional idea in the first place was the creation of peace as we have seen earlier in this chapter, then in principle, constitution-making as part of peace-building should be no different from any

[52] *Luis Roberto Zamora Bolaños* v. *Ministerio de Salud.*

[53] Case concerning the Presidential Decision to Dispatch Korean National Armed Forces to Iraq, 16-1 KCCR 601, 2003Hun-Ma814, 29 April, 2004. I have relied on the English translation of the case, available at http://www.ccourt.go.kr/home/att_file/library/decision_2004.pdf (accessed 15 Nov 2014), 1–11.

[54] Presidential Decision to Dispatch Korean National Armed Forces to Iraq, 8.

other form of constitution-making. As such we can say that all constitutions bear the characteristics of peace-building projects. It is important to bear this in mind as we move our focus to peace-building, understood as the word that has been used since the 1970s, referring to the involvement of the international community and the use of international law for building sustainable peace in countries emerging from conflict.

Within the UN system, Secretary-General Boutros Boutros-Ghali's report, *An Agenda for Peace*, defined peace-building as 'action to identify and support structures which will tend to strengthen and solidify peace and avoid relapse into conflict'.[55] The Brahimi Report defined peace-building as 'activities undertaken on the far side of conflict to reassemble the foundations of peace and provide tools for the building on those foundations [of] something that is more than just the absence of war'.[56]

Yet, the acknowledgement of constitutions as an integral part of peace-building processes under international law has not been constant. This has begun to change, as the centrality of constitutions for the achievement of peace has gained increased attention. What makes the dynamic relationship between constitutions and peace-building interesting from a legal point of view is the centrality of international law and international law standards for the content of constitutions and for the process of constitution-making. Put differently, peace-building internationalizes constitution-making.[57]

The 2009 Guidance note of the UN Secretary-General, which sets out a policy framework for peace-building, affirms the centrality of constitution: 'Constitution-making processes are a central aspect of democratic transitions, peacebuilding and state-building.'[58] Of the six guiding principles that this Note sets out, it is particularly the first and second principles that are important for our purposes since they recognize that constitution-making provides a 'key opportunity for peacebuilding in conflict and post-conflict countries', and that the UN should 'promote compliance of constitutions with international human rights and other norms and standards'.[59]

Efforts to standardize constitution-making are also found regionally. Created in 1990, after the fall of the Berlin Wall, the European Commission for Democracy through Law (the Venice Commission) operating under the Council of Europe, has had the role of helping its members to bring their legal and institutional

[55] Report of the Secretary-General, 'An Agenda for Peace: Preventive Diplomacy, Peacemaking and Peace-Keeping', A/47/277-S/24111, 17 June 1992, sect. 21.

[56] Report of the Panel on United Nations Peace Operations (Brahimi Report), A/55/305-S/2000-809, sect. 13.

[57] The involvement by the international community and international law since the mid-1990s in processes of state-building has reached such a level that we can speak of 'internationalized constitution-making'. See C. Grewe and M. Riegner, 'International Constitutionalism in Ethnically Divided Societies: Bosnia-Herzegovina and Kosovo Compared', in *Max Planck Yearbook of United Nations Law*, Armin Von Bogdandy and Rüdiger Wolfrum (eds.) (2011), xv. 1–64.

[58] UN, Guidance Note of the Secretary-General, United Nations Assistance to Constitution-making processes, April 2009, 3.

[59] UN, Guidance Note of the Secretary-General, 3.

structures into line with European standards. It aims to 'ensure the dissemination and consolidation of a common constitutional heritage', and provides constitutional assistance to countries in transition.[60]

Peace agreements are another feature of peace-building that bridges constitution-making and international law. Catherine Bell makes the observation that peace agreements are 'at once political and legal documents, treaties and constitutions, international and domestic legal documents'.[61] She argues that peace agreement solutions must be understood as a distinctive form of constitutionalism, containing classic constitutional features as well as new modes of solving some classical dilemmas of constitutional law.[62]

4. Constitutional Obstacles to Peace

So far, we have discussed the constitutional dimension of peace by asking how constitutions can promote peace and we have looked at different constitutional responses to this question.

No constitution will confess a direct opposition to peace, yet a number of constitutions have a problematically weak commitment to peace or severe obstacles for promoting it. Since a mere constitutional reference to peace or lack of such a reference says very little about the peace-promoting potential of a constitution, how do we identify elements that push either for or against peace? One way of approaching this issue is to ask the question: what is the *aim* of peace, and what kind of constitutional design will bring us closer towards that aim or create obstacles for its achievement? That is not to say that peace is not an aim in itself, but stopping at this point without asking *why* peace is an aim or what reason there is for us to value peace, we risk limiting the discussion to a surface discussion of 'peace' without further substantive content, thereby distracting the attention from more effective ways of promoting peace through domestic constitutions. Through identifying the *aim* of peace, this section looks at how constitutional law is used as a tool for pursuing policies that are either detrimental to peace or not ambitious enough to achieve peace.

4.1. Identifying the aim of peace

While the understandings of 'peace' take various forms, they converge at one point which we can identify as the core and the aim of peace: respect for each and every human being, sometimes aligned with the concept of dignity. Negative peace and the absence of violence aim to protect the life and dignity of the human being. Similarly, positive peace which includes social justice and human rights,

[60] Resolution 90(6), 'On a Partial Agreement Establishing the European Commission for Democracy through Law', adopted by the Committee of Ministers, 10 May 1990.

[61] Catherine Bell, *On the Law of Peace: Peace Agreements and the Lex Pacificatoria* (New York: Oxford University Press, 2008), 199.

[62] Bell, *On the Law of Peace*, 200.

endeavour to create an environment in which every person's autonomy and dignity is respected. Peace, in short, exists for the human being.[63]

The link between human dignity and peace is recognized in the preamble to the 1948 Universal Declaration of Human Rights, which states that 'the inherent dignity and ... the equal and inalienable rights of all members of the human family is the foundation of freedom, justice and peace in the world'.[64] If we agree on this aim, it becomes easier to identify constitutions and constitutional provisions that are in conflict with it, typically where human dignity is not an end in itself but where the human being operates as means to other ends, as a means to benefit other, more privileged groups, or where people's autonomy is severely restricted. In this respect, we can divide constitutions into two groups. One consists of constitutions where the human being is regarded as an end in itself. The other consists of constitutions where the human being is seen as instrumental in the achievement of other purposes. In the following section we will briefly consider three features of constitutional design that place a constitution in the latter group.

4.2. Three constitutional features that undermine the status of each and every human being

The presence of formal constitutional features that undermine the human being and hence undermine the aim of peace is significant because it implies legal obstacles for achieving peace. We shall consider three main categories of such formal features:

1. Comprehensive doctrines;
2. Constitutional inequality and restrictions on human rights;
3. Lack of control mechanisms for impositions by public authorities.

In Rawlsian terms, a comprehensive doctrine is a doctrine of moral, religious, or philosophical nature that is more or less comprehensive in so far as it establishes a view on a wide spectrum of values.[65] Since no comprehensive doctrine can be accepted by every person in a society, therefore no such doctrine can serve as the basis for the legitimate use of coercive political power, and thus cannot be a basis for the constitution. Yet, both in history and at present we find several examples of comprehensive doctrine constitutions. These can be secular such as, for example, constitutions based on Marxist ideology, or religious, such as for example constitutions based on 'Islamic', 'Buddhist', or 'Christian' ideology.

[63] This is also reflected in Kant's philosophy. His 'republican constitution' is centred around each and every human being. See Sect. 2.

[64] For an overview of the use of 'human dignity' in the context of human rights, see David Kretzmer and Eckhart Klein (eds.), *The Concept of Human Dignity in Human Rights Discourse* (The Hague: Kluwer Law International, 2002). For an overview of traces of human dignity in history, theology, philosophy, and law, see Christopher McCrudden (ed.), *Understanding Human Dignity* (Oxford: Oxford University Press, 2013).

[65] John Rawls, *Political Liberalism* (New York: Columbia University Press 1996), 13, see also 175.

In both cases, the constitution contains a system of moral belief imposed not only on political institutions but also on people within their jurisdiction. This often includes a system of belief on how best to lead one's life, what sort of virtues to aspire to, the respective role of women and men, etc. By this means constitutions limit the pluralism within the state and the autonomy of each individual within that pluralism.

Consider for example, the constitution of the Islamic Republic of Iran, which in its Article 2 defines the comprehensive doctrine:

The Islamic Republic is a system based on belief in:

1. The One God (as stated in the phrase 'There is no god except Allah'), His exclusive sovereignty and the right to legislate, and the necessity of submission to His commands;
2. Divine revelation and its fundamental role in setting forth the laws;
3. The return to God in the Hereafter, and the constructive role of this belief in the course of man's ascent towards God;
4. The justice of God in creation and legislation;
5. Continuous leadership (imamah) and perpetual guidance, and its fundamental role in ensuring the uninterrupted process of the revolution of Islam;
6. The exalted dignity and value of man, and his freedom coupled with responsibility before God; in which equity, justice, political, economic, social, and cultural independence, and national solidarity are secured by recourse to [. . .][66]

The article does mention 'dignity',[67] but it subjects this dignity to the comprehensive doctrine.[68] The same is the case with rights, which in a comprehensive doctrine constitution are not serving the individual human being but are instead subject to the doctrine. Therefore, comprehensive doctrine constitutions arguably preclude the enjoyment of human rights even if such rights are constitutionally enshrined, merely because they are not independent, but subject to the comprehensive doctrine. To take again the constitution of the Islamic Republic of Iran as an example, Article 20 states, 'All citizens of the country, both men and women, equally enjoy the protection of the law and enjoy all human, political, economic, social, and cultural rights, in conformity with Islamic criteria.'

The latter part of the provision, 'in conformity with Islamic criteria' subsumes the 'rights' under the comprehensive doctrine. A secular version of this is found in the Cuban Constitution, which limits freedom of speech and of the press to 'objectives of socialist society'.[69] These conditions could be interpreted in accordance with international human rights standards, but in that case it would not have been necessary to include the comprehensive doctrine conditions in the provision. In practice, such limitation clauses provide a way to diverge from international standards. Through conditioning the interpretation of rights, the comprehensive

[66] The 1979 Constitution of the Islamic Republic of Iran, Art. 2. The ideological basis for the constitution is expressly stated in Arts. 1–14, and Arts. 2 and 3 specify the comprehensive doctrine. This constitution is furthermore among the very few that expressly justify 'holy war' in their preambles.

[67] Constitution of the Islamic Republic of Iran, Art. 2(6).

[68] Interestingly, the 1982 Constitution of the People's Republic of China, embracing socialism and the people's democratic dictatorship as the comprehensive doctrine, speaks of the 'dignity of the socialist system'. See Arts. 1, 5.

[69] The 1976 Constitution of Cuba, Art. 53.

doctrine achieves superiority over the dignity of each rights holder. Therefore, while a number of rights are normally found in comprehensive doctrine constitutions, such constitutions ultimately place the individual human being not at the centre but in the margins, as a means to achieve a different aim or to further what is perceived as the interest of the state. Another example is the 1977 Soviet Constitution. This constitution contained a long list of rights[70] as well as a peace-friendly provision on 'the internationalist duty of citizens of the USSR to promote friendship and co-operation with peoples of other lands and help maintain and strengthen world peace'.[71]However, read in context of the comprehensive doctrine of achieving a socialist society, the rights and peace provisions were marginalized, aided by the lack of a separation of powers and independent courts. The domination of the comprehensive doctrine over the rights, and thereby over the dignity of each human being within its jurisdiction, becomes clear in the last section of Article 39: 'Enjoyment by citizens of their rights and freedoms must not be to the detriment of the interests of society or the state, or infringe the rights of other citizens.' The interest of the state, classed as something other than the rights of other citizens, can in other words override the rights of each individual, thereby allowing individuals to be used as instruments for the achievement of what the state defines as its own interest.

Because comprehensive doctrine constitutions preclude an independent protection of rights, they are arguably in conflict with international human rights law which requires rights to be interpreted on their own terms. Although a weak commitment to rights and thereby to the dignity of each individual person forms part of comprehensive doctrine constitutions, it is not limited to such constitutions. A number of constitutions that do not embrace a comprehensive doctrine do contain provisions that weaken rights, for example through justifying inequality based on religion, ethnicity, gender, sexual orientation, and political conviction. For example, in the years 1814–51 the Constitution of Norway prohibited Jews from entering the country.[72] Closer to our own time, the South African apartheid Constitution of 1983 operated with 'population groups', dividing the population into three groups: white, coloured, and Indians—with unequal rights.[73] A somewhat similar arrangement is found in the Iranian Constitution, which recognizes only three religious groups: Islam, Christianity, and Judaism, each with different status.[74] In the US, the de jure segregation of blacks was upheld by the Supreme Court in its decision in *Plessy* v. *Ferguson* in 1896.[75] In a number of countries, the highest political post is reserved to individuals of a particular religion or gender.[76]

[70] The 1977 Constitution of the USSR, Arts. 39–69 list the 'basic rights, freedoms and duties' of the people.

[71] Constitution of the USSR, Art. 69.

[72] The 1814 Constitution of Norway, Art. 2.

[73] The 1983 Constitution of South Africa, Art. 100.

[74] The 1979 Constitution of the Islamic Republic of Iran, Art. 13.

[75] *Plessy* v. *Ferguson*, 163 US 537 (1896).

[76] In a number of countries with official state religions, the head of state is required to profess to the official religion, even in places where the official religion is non-comprehensive, for example under the 1953 Constitution of Denmark, Art. 6, the monarch has to be member of the Evangelical Lutheran Church. The same is the case under the 1814 Constitution of Norway, Art. 4.

In addition to comprehensive doctrines and unequal regulation of rights, a third impediment for the promotion of peace is the lack of control mechanisms for impositions by public authorities. Without such mechanisms there is no way to ensure that the state in its legislation and actions does not infringe upon the rights of the persons within its jurisdiction or impose unreasonable burdens on them in pursuit of certain policy goals. In the following we shall mention two ways in which a constitution can weaken such control. One is through the absence of judicial review by independent courts. The other is through broad emergency powers.

Judicial review presumes a separation of powers, a competent court, and the potential for an individual who believes her rights to have been infringed to bring her claim to the court. Lack of judicial review does not mean that public authorities or the majority will necessarily infringe upon the rights of one or many of the individuals within their jurisdiction, but it leaves these persons powerless if it does occur.[77] Without a right to judicial review, constitutional rights exist only on paper, realized only at the mercy of the state.[78]

In addition to the lack of judicial review, broad emergency powers can nullify constitutional provisions, including rights provisions, and undermine the aim of peace.[79] No matter how thoroughly a constitution regulates internal and external peace, such provisions will have little significance if the constitution at the same time allows for broad emergency powers under which constitutional provisions can be derogated. In this regard an interesting duality arises. On the one hand, the reason behind state of emergency provisions is to 'keep peace' but it is also a tool which in some circumstances can do the opposite. In Germany, Hitler declared a state of emergency under Article 48 of the Weimar Constitution which subsequently became suspended for the whole duration of the Third Reich. Under this state of emergency, the government was enabled to enact laws without the participation of the legislative branch and thus implemented the *Gleichschaltung* allowing for the establishment of Nazi totalitarianism. In Egypt, a state of emergency ruled from 1967 to 2012 with an 18-month break in 1980. Under the Emergency Law No. 162 of 1958 several constitutional rights were suspended, censorship was legalized, and due process was overridden.[80] Following the ousting of President Mubarak, a state of emergency was again declared on two occasions

[77] Jacob Weinrib offers a convincing theory for the need for judicial review in order to protect the dignity and fundamental rights of each person. Weinrib argues that modern constitutionalism in this sense is not majoritarian but nonetheless is democratic because public power is accountable to each and every person. See Jacob Weinrib, 'Authority, Justice, and Public Law: A Unified Theory', *University of Toronto Law Journal* (forthcoming), 5 (2014), 703–735.

[78] The main argument against judicial review is based on its countermajoritarian nature. For a comprehensive account by one of its most prominent critics, see Jeremy Waldron, 'The Core of the Case Against Judicial Review', *Yale Law Journal* 115 (2006), 1346–406.

[79] For a general overview, see Oren Gross and Fionnuala Ní Aoláin (eds.), *Law in Times of Crisis: Emergency Powers in Theory and Practice* (New York: Cambridge University Press, 2006).

[80] See Sadiq Reza, 'Endless Emergency: The Case of Egypt', *New Criminal Law Review* 10 (2007), 532–53.

under President Morsi.[81] Israel has been in a state of emergency since the creation of the state in 1948.[82] The US is currently in a limited state of emergency, declared on different occasions and regarding different reasons, the most significant being the state of emergency declared following 9/11.[83] Although the countries mentioned share the fact of having been or being in a state of emergency, it has played out very differently in each context. It is not primarily the state of emergency itself that is the problem, but the type of derogations that the constitution allows for. What distinguishes state of emergency regulations that are peace threatening from those that are not? Leaving aside that both can be subject to abuse in practice, the question is whether some types of constitutional regulations are more prone to undermine peace. Derogations can concern both the separation and function of government powers (horizontal) and the relationship between the state and the people (vertical) through the limitations or abrogation from constitutionally guaranteed rights. Two main issues should be considered in this regard. One concerns the procedural element that regulates the type of situations in which a state of emergency can be declared and the procedure for declaring a state of emergency. Can it be declared solely by the executive power or does the constitution require the involvement of the legislative and/or the judicial power?[84] What are the conditions for renewing a state of emergency? The more participatory the process is, the more difficult will abuse of state of emergency declarations be. The second issue is material. Once the state of emergency is lawfully declared, what does the emergency power consist of and which constitutional provisions can be derogated? For example, under the German Constitution, the procedural element is broad, but the material part is strictly circumscribed.[85] The French model, by contrast, is broad both procedurally and materially, authorizing the president both to decide whether the conditions for state of emergency are present and to 'take the measures required by these circumstances'.[86]

Seeking to reduce violation of rights in time of emergency, international law operates with a distinction between derogable and non-derogable rights.[87] Under the International Covenant for Civil and Political Rights (ICCPR) Article 4, states can under certain conditions derogate from some of the rights guaranteed by the

[81] In November 2013, a court ruled to end the emergency rule: http://www.reuters.com/article/2013/11/12/us-egypt-curfew-end-idUSBRE9AB0R120131112 (accessed 15 Nov 2014).

[82] For an account of the state of emergency in Israel, see Suzie Navot, *The Constitutional Law of Israel* (The Netherlands: Wolters Kluwer, 2007), 293–300.

[83] e.g. the International Economic Emergency Powers Act of 1977 is still in force, authorizing the president to regulate commerce with respect to countries that pose 'unusual or extraordinary threat' to the US, Pub.L. 95-223, 91. Stat. 1626. The post-9/11 US state of emergency has been widely discussed in legal scholarship. Bruce Ackerman presents an overview and argues for a different constitutional paradigm in dealing with contemporary terrorism, see B. Ackerman, 'The Emergency Constitution', *Yale University Law Journal* 113 (2004), 1029–91.

[84] Although judicial review contributes to control emergency powers, the result is not necessarily in favour of civil rights. The US Supreme court decision in *Korematsu* v. *United States* provides an example of the limits of a court-centred approach: 323 US 214 (1944).

[85] The 1949 German Constitution, Arts. 115a–115l.

[86] The 1958 Constitution of France, Art. 16.

[87] ICCPR, 1966, 999 UNTS 171, Art. 4.

ICCPR but not from others. In a regional context, the European Convention on Human Rights and the American Convention on Human Rights have similar provisions.[88] The African Charter on the other hand does not contain a derogation clause, in principle making it possible to derogate from all its provisions. The emergency regime of a constitution will therefore be guided both by its own provisions and by any international or regional treaty regime that it is part of. With respect to both the procedural and the material aspect of an emergency regime, continuous checks and balances through the legislative or the judicial branch form the ultimate control against the abuse of it, thereby reducing its peace-threatening potential.

5. Conclusion

More than three hundred years have passed since Kant proposed the implementation of constitutions and their continuous reform as a prerequisite for achieving peace. Although his ideal is yet to be achieved, his emphasis on the need for constitutions to ensure domestic social justice and respect for the freedom of each and every human being continues to guide modern constitutionalism, particularly after World War II and the growth of the international legal system. This has given rise to a growing interdependency of domestic constitutional law and international law. The ultimate legitimacy and strength of both systems depends on their willingness to see every human being as an end. To do so requires a conscious understanding of peace as a human-promoting concept to be reflected and protected in the domestic constitutions.

[88] ECHR, 1950, 213 UNTS 221, Art. 15; and American Convention on Human Rights 1969, 114 UNTS 123, Art. 27.

20

Education for Peace

Epilogue

Maria D. Sommardahl

> Every opportunity must be seized to educate people about the horrors of war and blessings of peace.
>
> Daisaku Ikeda[1]

1. Introduction

This chapter advocates education for peace, characterized by UN Secretary General as the road to peace[2] and builds on the idea, outlined in the introductory chapter of this book, that education on the components of peace constitutes a pivotal part of the institutional implementation of peace.[3] The chapter explores and suggests a tangible approach to education for peace and explains its importance for promoting peace. The chapter will concentrate largely on different sources from the United Nations and international law that refer to the promotion of peace with regard to the institutional mechanisms that will foster peace.

Although there are a variety of peace research institutions, practitioners, and activists in the world today, little attention is being given to the process and design of acquiring the values and the knowledge and developing the attitudes and practical peace-making skills conducive to creating a culture of peace. Often there has also been a lack of theory or philosophy of peace education itself—it has been assumed rather than articulated. Johan Galtung suggested in 1975 that no theory for peace education existed and that there was clearly an urgent need for such theory. More recently there have been attempts to establish such a theory, or, rather

[1] Daisaku Ikeda in Johan Galtung and Daisaku Ikeda, *Choose Peace* (London: Pluto, 1995), 68.

[2] http://www.un.org/en/events/peaceday/2013/sgmessage.shtml (accessed 15 Nov 2014).

[3] See 'Education on the Components of Peace', Chapter 1 Sect. 4 in this volume,: 'All individuals should receive education on human rights, fundamental freedoms, non-violent dispute resolution, and protection of the environment as components and preconditions of peace.'

theories. Still, peace education faces continual elaboration, a theory–practice gap, and is indeed a frequent challenge to its own validity.

There is an obvious call for bridging the aforementioned gaps. Numerous United Nations declarations on the importance of peace education have been put forward. Peace education as a right is something that is now increasingly emphasized by peace researchers and there has recently been an enmeshing of peace and human rights education.

This chapter strives to suggest a tangible approach to these issues as well as to raise and respond to some of the critiques that the different streams of peace education have received. The epilogue will not suggest a peace education theory or a philosophy, however; this warrants a different approach than that of an advocacy effort.

1.1. Background

Early thoughts on education for peace can be traced back to Erasmus and Socrates, and are also found philosophically in the work of authors such as Tolstoy and Thoreau, social thinkers such as Foucault, and activists such as Gandhi, King, and Suu Kyi.[4] The growing literature on peace education reflects a dynamic field—a field that in many ways advocates the idea of promoting peace through international law. Ian Harris, for example, divides peace education into five categories: international education, development education, environmental education, human rights education, and conflict resolution education.[5] This division correlates well with the idea of the components of peace addressed in this book. Moreover, educators and activists have been working to promote a culture of peace for several decades. The United Nations, as facilitator, has strongly endorsed these efforts and continues to do so; in 1995 the UN General Assembly (UNGA) passed the *Declaration and Integrated Framework of Education for Peace, Human Rights and Democracy*, and the *Declaration on a Culture of Peace* (1998), and declared the year 2000 as the 'International Year for a Culture of Peace'. UNGA further declared 2001–10 as the 'UN International Decade on Education for Peace and Non-Violence for the Children of the World'. The 1995 and 1998 resolutions articulate necessary components of education for peace and again support the idea of international law as a mechanism for peace that is presented in this book. The aforementioned resolutions recall the international standards set forth in the Charter of the United Nations, the Constitution of the United Nations Educational, Scientific, and Cultural Organization, and the Universal Declaration of Human Rights. Article 3 in the 1998 resolution particularly stipulates that a culture for peace includes the compliance with international obligations under the UN Charter and international law, the promotion of democracy and development, including economic and social development, the respect for

[4] Kevin Kester, 'Education for Peace: Content, Form and Structure: Mobilizing Youth for Civic Engagement', *The Peace and Conflict Review* 4 (2010), 2.

[5] Ian Haris, 'Peace Education Theory', *Journal of Peace Education* 1 (2004), 5–20.

and observance of all human rights and fundamental freedoms, the eradication of poverty and inequalities, and the elimination of discrimination and racism. Article 4 particularly stipulates that '*education* at all levels is one of the principal means to build a culture of peace'. And further, that within this context, human rights education is of particular importance.[6]

The UN has, moreover, implemented peace education into its educational bodies (UNESCO, UNITAR, UNU, and UPEACE) to serve as a model for mainstreaming peace education into organizations, institutions, and agencies that support the idea of institutionalizing peace and peace education.[7]

2. The Right to Education

Although this chapter is not about the right to education as such, there are strong linkages between international law, the right to education, and to peace education, and hence it is constructive to lay the foundation for the international standards of the right to education before moving on to the idea of education for peace as part of promoting peace through education.

In accordance with their founding instruments, the UN and UNESCO have been responsible for initiating most of the international instruments concerning education adopted since the end of World War II. Normative instruments of the UN and UNESCO lay down international legal obligations for the right to education. These documents promote and develop the right of every individual to enjoy access to quality education without discrimination or exclusion.

2.1. The United Nations

The UN has developed a number of standard-setting instruments relating to the right to education, ranging from the Universal Declaration of Human Rights (notably Article 26) to various conventions, declarations, recommendations, frameworks, and programmes of actions, aimed at ensuring the implementation of this right or particular aspects of it. The specific dimensions of the right to education are principally covered by the International Covenant on Economic, Social, and Cultural Rights, the Convention on the Rights of the Child (notably Articles 28, 29, and 40), and the Convention on the Elimination of All Forms of Discrimination against Women (notably Article 5). In addition to the UN instruments, the American Declaration on the Rights and Duties of Man covers the right to education in Article 12. In Europe, Article 2 of the first Protocol (1952) to the European Convention on Human Rights (ECHR) states that the right to education is recognized as a human right and can be understood to establish an entitlement to education. Certain instruments or texts, particularly

[6] A/RES/53/243 A: http://www3.unesco.org/iycp/kits/uk_res_243.pdf (last accessed 15 Nov 2014).
[7] Kester, 'Education for Peace', 7.

Articles 13 and 14 of the International Covenant of the Economic, Social and Cultural Rights (ICESCR), are clearly more comprehensive than others. Article 13 of ICESCR can be interpreted as being the most comprehensive on the right to education.

2.2. UNESCO

The right to education is at the core of the mission of UNESCO. To fulfil this mission, UNESCO has also drawn up a number of standard setting instruments—conventions, declarations, recommendations, charters, programmes of action—relating to the right to education. These standard-setting instruments fall into two categories: those having binding force, as they are adopted and ratified by the member states, and those which, if they do not have binding force, represent a great political and moral authority. These instruments often constitute a step towards the formulation of binding instruments and to the creation of customary law. In December 1960, the UNESCO General Conference adopted the Convention against Discrimination in Education (CADE),[8] which entered into force in 1962. CADE is the only legally binding international instrument that *exclusively* focuses on the right to education. This Convention constitutes a milestone in providing international legal bases of the right to education. The Constitution of UNESCO further establishes certain fundamental principles such as the principles of non-discrimination, equality of opportunity and treatment, universal access to education, and solidarity. The principle of universal access to education is the cornerstone of the right to education. This principle can be found in most of the instruments elaborated by UNESCO in the field of education.[9]

2.3. Responsibility of states and legal foundations in national systems

It is categorically through normative action, with implementation mechanisms, that the right to education in its various dimensions—'from initial or basic education to lifelong learning'—can be realized.[10] Its beneficiaries[11] can only avail themselves of the right to education when state obligations are incorporated into the national legal system and their implementation is effectively ensured. Therefore it is crucial that the right to education in all its dimensions is incorporated into the

[8] CADE: http://portal.unesco.org/en/ev.php-URL_ID=12949&URL_DO=DO_TOPIC&URL_SECTION=201.html (accessed 15 Nov 2014).

[9] UNESCO Legal Instruments: http://www.unesco.org/new/en/education/themes/leading-the-international-agenda/right-to-education/ (accessed 15 Nov 2014).

[10] World Education Report 2000: 'The Right to Education—Towards Education for All Throughout Life', foreword.

[11] International law does not protect the right to pre-primary education, and international documents generally omit references to education at this level. The Universal Declaration of Human Rights states that everyone has the right to education; hence the right applies to all individuals, although children are understood as the main beneficiaries.

constitutions and legislation of all member States. UNESCO has begun analysing constitutional provisions and national legislation relating to the right to education in various countries and providing technical assistance to members states in developing and modernizing national legislation. As regards monitoring the implementation of the UN conventions on human rights, the UN Committee on Economic, Social, and Cultural Rights (CESCR), as a treaty body, monitors the implementation of the right to education as provided for in Articles 13 and 14 of ICESCR. Every five years each state party to ICESCR is obliged to submit a report to CESCR. These reports cover all rights in the Covenant and explain what the state in question is doing to achieve and implement the right to education. Other UN treaty bodies whose work relates to monitoring the implementation of the right to education in states are the Committee on the Rights of the Child and the Committee on the Elimination of All Forms of Discrimination against Women. In addition, the UN has a special rapporteur on the right to education who undertakes country visits; responds to information received on allegations concerning violations of the right to education in particular countries; develops constructive dialogue with Governments, civil society, and other relevant actors with a view to identifying solutions for the implementation of the right to education; and submits annual reports to the Human Rights Council and to the UN General Assembly covering the activities relating to the mandate of the special rapporteur.

3. Education for Peace and Main Challenges

While education as such is a well-established right for all individuals and also rather clearly defined by international standards, peace education is as multifaceted a concept as peace, and alike lacks a clear definition and boundaries. Peace education has been defined by prominent scholars as a 'series of teaching encounters' that draw from people and their desire for peace, non-violent alternatives for managing conflict, and skills for critical analysis of structural activities that produce and legitimize injustice and inequality.[12] Others have suggested that peace education should be thought of as 'encouraging a commitment to peace as a settled disposition and enhancing the confidence of the individual as an individual agent of peace; as informing the student on the consequences of war and social injustice; as informing the student on the value of peaceful and just structures and working to uphold or develop such social structures; as encouraging the student to love the world and to imagine a peaceful future; and as caring for the student and encouraging the student to care for others'.[13]

[12] Ian Harris and John Synott, 'Peace Education for a New Century', *Social Alternatives* 21 (2002), 3–6.

[13] James Page, *Peace Education: Exploring Ethical and Philosophical Foundations* (Charlotte, NC: Information Age, 2008), 8.

One reason for the scattered views and unclear boundaries might be the fact that peace education is profoundly influenced by non-formal education. This is not automatically to be seen as something negative; instead, this approach continuously challenges the formal education systems. Non-formal peace education introduces new contents, methods, and techniques of learning and teaching *about* and *for* human rights, peace and non-violence, civic participation, intercultural understanding, development, global perspective, and so forth and is indeed also endorsed by the UN as a facilitator for such an approach. A great number of important peace education initiatives have come from NGOs associated with peace, such as from the International Committee of the Red Cross (ICRC), Amnesty International, Save the Children, Greenpeace, Médecins sans frontières, Rapporteurs sans frontières, and Human Rights Watch, to mention a few.[14] Prominent NGOs have a strong impact on the development of peace education modules and curricula and are able to meet the needs of beneficiaries more swiftly. From this perspective it can also be noted that schools as institutions can represent violence in themselves and therefore offer little to the promotion of peace[15]—hence keeping peace education outside schools might be more advantageous for promoting peace. As outlined in Section 4.1, schools and school systems can find themselves in volatile situations due to conflicts and emergencies and here the international community, often through NGOs, are best suited to conduct the training and teaching of children and other beneficiaries.

The main challenge with an NGO/non-formal model is, however, what the lack of coordination, communication, and cooperation between the non-formal and the formal education systems, including peace researchers and scholars, do, or rather do not do, to build and form a holistic approach to peace education.

Since the beginning of the twentieth century, peace education has undergone several evolutions, focusing on pressing topics that have changed over time. For example, peace educators have focused at various times on opposing nuclear power, increasing environmental responsibility, fostering communications skills, encouraging non-violence, advocating democracy as a form of government, raising awareness of universal human rights, and breaking down racial and gender barriers.[16] The most popular topics covered in peace education in the early twenty-first century include conflict resolution training, human rights education, and democracy education. One thing is clear, however: peace education extends to include more than the notion of negative peace—although it might vary depending on the context in which peace education is conducted—but as a whole, it

[14] Other prominent NGOs are more directly involved in peace promotion and protection while others concern themselves more with the promotion of peace education than directly with initiating and developing peace education curricula.

[15] For more on these thought-provoking ideas, see Clive Harber, *Schooling as Violence: How Schools Harm Pupils and Societies* (London: Routledge, 2004).

[16] Most of the approaches build on the many UN resolutions, declarations, and SG's letters concerning the promotion of peace education. For more on this topic, see Werner Wintersteiner, Vedrana Spajić-Vrkaš, and Rüdiger Teutsch, *Peace Education in Europe: Visions and Experiences* (Münster: Waxmann, 2003).

certainly encompasses the notion of positive peace and beyond. Perhaps this is for the good of all, but there is also an obvious risk of peace education becoming too vague and hence becoming a challenge to itself.

Another risk is that peace education will be considered only as 'political correctness', which again can be considered as fashionable morality and lose its edge and importance. On the other side of the scale, some peace educators maintain that peace education is neutral, and should not be entangled with any political agenda; it should not be considered as 'political correctness' or as political in itself. However, by the very fact that education has objectives and social purposes it intends to foster among beneficiaries, education is political: the questions asked point learning and teaching in a particular direction, and the materials teachers use direct the classroom discussions towards a specific sphere.[17]

Since human rights have been included in, or combined with, peace education it is also appropriate to mention at least one very relevant challenge that is connected to the coming paragraphs addressing the importance of peace education in conflict and emergency settings: that is, the challenge inherent in human rights—the issue of enforcement. Teaching students about issues of justice and international principles, particularly if they live in communities where such rights are not guaranteed by the state, can create frustration and disillusionment rather than the transformative landscape that peace educators seek to cultivate. A critical yet optimistic approach would introduce beneficiaries to issues of asymmetrical power relations, structural violence, and how principles of human rights can inform action amid such a context.

4. The Relevance of Peace Education

For the sake of clarity, it might be beneficial to make a distinction between education *about* peace and education *for* peace. Education *about* peace broadly includes modules of war and peace and leaders of peace such as Gandhi and King. Education *for* peace, on the other hand, broadly includes nurturing knowledge, values, behavioiurs, and capacities to confront violence.[18] This adds to the clarity when speaking about peace education as a term, which in this chapter is used simultaneously with the terms 'education for peace' and 'educating for peace' in order to include both aspects.

Although peace education remains a contested term—ranging from its content, realization, and practice and to the theory and methodology of the same—it is clear that education for and about peace is of relevance in any setting, in peaceful environments and in conflict or emergency situations alike. However, the gravity of the importance of education as such, the *access* to education, and the *content* of the education become particularly evident in situations of conflict and emergencies.

[17] Kester, 'Education for Peace', 3.

[18] Kester, 'Education for Peace', 2.

4.1. Peace education in conflict and emergency settings

In 1996, Graça Macel documented the impact of violent conflict on children: 'More and more of the world is being sucked into a desolate moral vacuum. This is a space devoid of the most basic human values; a space in which children are slaughtered, raped and maimed; a space in which children are starved and exposed to extreme brutality.'[19] Young girls are subject to the threat of widespread, systematic rape and other forms of sexual violence. Despite a succession of United Nations Security Council resolutions,[20] sexual terror remains a weapon of war, a weapon that is inflicting indescribable suffering, fear, and insecurity on young girls and women and has a hidden damaging effect on their education. Children are abducted and forced into military service. Resources that could be used to finance productive investment in education are squandered. It is probably no coincidence that conflict-affected states have some of the world's worst indicators for education. Over 40 per cent of out-of-school children live in conflict-affected countries. The same countries have some of the largest gender inequalities and lowest literacy levels in the world.[21] Indeed, one of the most damaging yet least reported consequences of armed conflict is its impact on education. Although it will soon be 20 years since Macel's report, perhaps more than at any time in history, schoolchildren, teachers, and schools are in the frontline and crossfire of violence. Classrooms are destroyed and students are attacked, not just because they are caught in the crossfire, but because they are intentionally targeted.

The starting point is to recognize the scale of the damage caused by the fatal interaction between armed conflict and education. Development assistance is skewed towards a small number of states seen as strategic priorities. Furthermore, there are growing tensions between two types of aid: to advance national security goals or international development goals. The education sector is at the core of these tensions. Education accounts for a small fraction of humanitarian aid requests and an even smaller fraction of aid received in conflict-affected countries.[22]

Conflict has devastating consequences for education systems, but education can also contribute to the attitudes, beliefs, and grievances that fuel violent conflict. United Nations Educational, Scientific, and Cultural Organization was founded in 1945 as a direct response to World War II. UNESCO's Constitution explicitly acknowledges the power of ideas as a force for peace and as a source of war. The first line of the Constitution eloquently states that 'since wars begin in the minds of men [and women], it is in the minds of men [and women] that the defenses of peace must be constructed'. The UNESCO Constitution maintains its resonance. It recognizes that, whatever the underlying political causes,

[19] Report of Graça Macel, Impact of Armed Conflict on Children, UNICEF (1996), http://www.unicef.org/graca/ (accessed 15 Nov 2014).

[20] Mainly S/RES/1325; S/RES/1820; S/RES/1888, and S/RES/1960.

[21] EFA Global Monitoring Report (2011), i.

[22] The education sector currently receives 2% of humanitarian aid and 21 developing countries are currently spending more on arms than on primary schools. If these countries were to cut military spending by 10%, an additional 9.5 million children could receive primary education.

the war from which it emerged was 'made possible ... through ignorance and prejudice', and it affirms a belief in full and equal opportunities for education for all. It identifies knowledge as a key to 'mutual understanding and a truer and more perfect knowledge of each other's lives'.[23] Education systems are still used to transfer the ignorance, prejudice, and social injustice that make societies less cohesive, more divided, and more likely to descend into armed conflict. Schools are often, unfortunately, a part of the cycle of violence. But schools combined with good education systems have the potential to break and reverse that cycle. This kind of change requires practical policies at the national and international levels, backed by political leadership.[24]

Whether they are in conflict zones, displaced within their own countries, or refugees, parents, teachers, and children affected by conflict have at least one thing in common: the extraordinary level of ambition, innovation, and courage they demonstrate in trying to maintain access to education. Parents understand that education can provide children with a sense of normality and that it is an asset that they can carry with them if they are displaced.[25]

4.2. Recalling the international standards

The Convention on the Rights of the Child from 1989 emphasizes that governments and national agencies cannot claim that education of refugees or internally displaced children should wait until they return home, since there is no way to be certain whether the wait will be for weeks, months, years, or even decades. The Convention obliges governments to promote or facilitate access to education for children within their territory, regardless of their status—also children who are asylum-seekers must have access to education. At the World Education Forum held in Dakar in 2000,[26] the world's education ministers endorsed these principles, and pledged themselves to 'meet the needs of education systems affected by conflict, natural calamities, and instability and conduct educational programs in ways that promote mutual understanding, peace and tolerance, and that help to prevent violence and conflict'.

A follow-up technical consultation in November 2000 led to the establishment of the Inter-agency Network for Education in Emergencies (INEE).[27] INEE serves to ensure the right to education for all regardless of crisis or conflict, along a spectrum of preparedness, prevention, response, and recovery. The governing body comprises the Office of the United Nations High Commissioner for Refugees (UNHCR), the United Nations Children's Fund (UNICEF), UNESCO, the World Bank, and leading NGOs. This prominent network organizes regional and global consultations and has published the widely endorsed *Minimum Standards for Education in Emergencies, Chronic Crises and Early Reconstruction*. These

[23] UNESCO 1945, preamble. [24] EFA Global Monitoring Report (2011), 125.
[25] EFA Global Monitoring Report (2011), 175.
[26] http://www.unesco.org/education/wef/en-conf/index.shtm (accessed 15 Nov 2014).
[27] http://www.ineesite.org/en/ (accessed 15 Nov 2014).

standards are disseminated through regional and subsequently national and local training of trainers. The INEE *Minimum Standards Handbook* is the only global tool that articulates the minimum level of educational quality and access in emergencies through to recovery.[28] The standards are generic in order to be applicable to a broad range of contexts and are meant to serve as guidelines to practitioners and policy-makers.

The responsibility for promoting children's access to quality education rests principally with national governments,[29] as states party to the Convention on the Rights of the Child. However, in many countries affected by conflict, UN agencies and NGOs are well placed to get assistance quickly to stricken areas. In practice, the education of refugees is often organized by NGOs, since camps are largely located in remote rural areas where local schools do not have the space to accommodate additional students, even if the language of instruction is a shared one. In other crisis situations and early reconstruction, the international community typically assists the national government in restoring access to education.[30]

Although the Convention on the Rights of the Child is mentioned here as the primary international legal instrument to set out the standards, it is equally important to make reference to the other international instruments outlined in Section 2.

4.3. Unlocking the potential for education

Immediately after a conflict there is a window of opportunity in which to provide basic security, deliver peace dividends, build confidence in the political process, and lay the foundations for a sustainable peace. Perhaps more than any other sector, that of education offers opportunities to provide a key peace dividend. The development of an inclusive system that provides good-quality education for all can help build the foundations for more inclusive societies that are less prone to conflict. Yet aid donors are often slow to respond to opportunities for peace. When they do respond, they provide not the long-term development assistance that countries need, but instead highly unpredictable short-term aid. At the core of the problem is a division between humanitarian aid and development aid.[31] The main constraint on access, after insecurity, is usually poverty. If the aim is *education for all*, further resources are needed to reach the most marginalized groups.

[28] The INEE, *Minimum Standards Handbook* was first published in 2004 and revised in 2010.

[29] A special study commissioned as part of the EFA 2000 Assessment demonstrated the nature of this responsibility. This study documented the extent to which displaced populations and others suffering from chronic insecurity lack educational services. In some situations an entire generation of children may miss out on basic schooling. The study stressed the responsibility of the international community to affirm the fundamental human right to education, even under conditions of emergency, and to provide resources. A key recommendation was that education in emergency situations should be built into a country's development process from the outset, not seen as a 'relief' effort. Final Report, World Education Forum, Dakar, Senegal (26–8 April 2000), UNESCO (2000), 24.

[30] Margaret Sinclair, *Education in Emergencies*, Commonwealth Education Partnerships (Cambridge: Nexus Strategic Partnerships, 2007), 52–3.

[31] EFA Global Monitoring Report (2011), 134.

The reconstruction of education systems is not just about rebuilding schools, hiring teachers, and providing books. It is also about laying the foundations for peace. The right type of education is one of the best conflict prevention strategies available to any society. The wrong type can reinforce social division and hence lead to renewed conflicts.[32] It is indeed equally important to fill the educational institutions with well-trained teachers and other human support as with the right material and physical space. The school curriculum is critical. How and what history is taught, approaches to religious education, and representation of national identity in textbooks have an influential bearing on the attitudes children will carry into adulthood. The aim should be to continue with the applicable national or local curriculum and if necessary, omitting any controversial elements arising in social studies or other lessons, provide for a longer-term process of national curriculum renewal. Language is another critical policy area in many conflict or crisis-affected societies. In order to meet the goals of education in emergency or conflict settings, the national curriculum needs to be enriched with elements relating to the crisis, such as health measures, landmine awareness, and environmental awareness. The peace education teachers should focus on student-centred participative learning methods, which are especially needed for attitudinal and behavioural objectives—educating *for* peace. Unlocking education's potential to build peace requires policies and practices, and also research, that address underlying social tensions.

Maintaining the access to education of populations affected by conflict or disaster helps affected children and adolescents to see a positive future rather than experience incapacitating depression or seek destructive outlets for their feelings. Often these populations have already suffered from lesser educational and economic opportunities, which may have contributed to conflict or to vulnerability to disasters in the first place. Such fractures in society could lay the foundations for future violence. If the education itself promotes skills for peace, the chances for a better future might be further improved. With this is mind, it is in place to recall that education can also function as a preventive mechanism for a culture of peace—that is, a reminder of the fact that peace education is relevant in any setting, not only in conflict or emergency situations.

4.4. The international standards in practice, policy, and research

As the lead agency within the UN system for education, UNESCO is responsible for coordinating and directly implementing activities that promote a culture of peace[33] through education, the sciences, culture, communication, and

[32] EFA Global Monitoring Report (2011), 125–6.

[33] The culture of peace is defined as a set of values, attitudes, modes of behaviour, and ways of life that reject violence and aim to prevent conflicts by tackling their root causes through dialogue and negotiation between individuals, groups, and nations. See http://www.peace.ca/unesco.htm (accessed 15 Nov 2014).

information. The promotion of peace through education is at the core of UNESCO's mission. UNESCO's approach to educating for peace is multidimensional—it links education with a range of activities that address the root causes of violence, from human security to sustainable development. The objective of UNESCO's education programmes is the development of comprehensive systems of education that embrace the values of human rights, intercultural understanding, and tolerance.[34]

According to UNESCO, education for peace includes training, skills, and information directed towards cultivating a culture of peace based on human rights principles. UNESCO's educational approach not only provides knowledge and information about a culture of peace, but also includes the skills and attitudes necessary to recognize potential conflicts, and the people and institutions needed actively to promote and establish a culture of peace and non-violence.[35]

The dimensions of UNESCO's work on peace education include (1) cooperation with members states at the international, regional, and national levels, (2) networking, advocacy, and research, (3) policy and information exchange, and (4) textbooks, learning materials, and curricula development.[36]

UNESCO's work on education for peace encompasses a practical and policy approach that is a very necessary combination when tackling the enormous challenges described in the sections above with regard to the importance of educating for peace. UNESCO's approach, endorsed and implemented both by a number of members states and by a vast network of NGOs, also seems, at a first glance, to draw the criticisms mentioned in Section 3, that too little attention is being given to the process and design of acquiring the values and knowledge and developing the attitudes and practical peace-making skills conducive to creating peace. It should however be recognized, that a 'one size fits all' model is not sufficient; conflicts and emergencies break out in an increasingly rapid way and these settings all have their unique background, evolution, and outcome. In the present age of globalized economic and political structures that are increasing disparities and simultaneously dismantling avenues for citizens to hold governments and the international community accountable, it appears that renewed attention to larger structural realities, empirical, engaged, and systematic research would prove beneficial in understanding the possibilities and limitations of peace education.

Acknowledging the need for a critical approach to peace education that supports and encourages diversity and a multiplicity of perspectives, it is important to outline the components of peace. While human rights principles often guide peace education research and initiatives, the debates about these universal principles in addition to the promise they hold for sustainable peace are essential to a critical peace education approach.

[34] *UNESCO's Work on Education for Peace and Non-Violence* (2008), 2–3.

[35] *UNESCO's Work on Education*, 2–3.

[36] *UNESCO's Work on Education*, 2–3.

5. Concluding Remarks

The institutional status of peace education is somewhat more complex than the international status. It seems reasonable to describe peace education as a field rather than a discipline. Peace research suffers from the same disciplinary problem as peace education, or at least it is perceived to suffer from a lack of established theoretical and methodological foundation, much the same criticisms as those levelled at human rights research. Interestingly, UNESCO links the avenues of peace research and training, which might serve the purpose in practice when educating for peace. A simple and tangible working definition of peace research that supports UNESCO's approach is offered by James Page: 'research into the conditions and components of peace'. [37] In this way peace education can be regarded as applied peace research.

Educating for peace is important in any setting, in peaceful environments as a preventive peace mechanism and as part of understanding the international world order, and in conflict and emergency settings as a peacemaking and peace-building mechanism, whilst strengthening resilience and preventing relapse into conflict. This chapter has put more emphasis on the importance of education in general and peace education specifically in conflict and emergency settings in order to show the volatility of beneficiaries in these kinds of situation and because the universal access to quality education is the cornerstone of the right to education.

Peace studies have been marked by an absence of legal literature; the majority of texts are from the social sciences. This book presents international institutional and normative components of peace within international law by examining the different regimes, such as human rights, international criminal law, environmental protection, development, and fair trade—all components relevant to peace education. International law impinges on the life of all individuals several times daily and countries depend on international law for the daily function of most of its institutions. This is not often seen, as international law is consigned to the category of a complex discipline that operates at high levels of diplomacy and statesmanship, separate from the ordinary individual. However, international standards comprehensively influence labour protection, health, criminal justice, children's rights, trade, and environmental protection and education, and hence international law is highly relevant to peace studies.

The *right to education* is governed as a distinct right of all individuals in a number of international legal instruments in addition to universal principles and soft law documents. *Peace education* as a right is something which is now increasingly emphasized by peace researchers such as Betty Reardon[38] and

[37] Page, *Peace Education*, 9.

[38] Betty Reardon is the founder and director of the Peace Education Center and Peace Education Graduate Degree Concentration at Teachers College, Columbia University, and is internationally acknowledged as a founder of peace education. Columbia University's programme established a model for university-based peace education programmes replicated around the world. She founded the International Institute on Peace Education (IIPE). The significance of the IIPE was cited by UNESCO in a special honorary mention at the Peace Education Prize ceremony in 2002.

Douglas Roche.[39] This idea might however have to undergo further elaboration, as even the concept of peace, let alone the notion of 'the right to peace' remain contested.

A move towards greater empiricism in peace education research would respond to the critique that there is confusion at the conceptual level as to what peace education is and what it should contain, and this is underlined by a lack of scholarly research on the *impact* of peace education. The field would benefit from greater emphasis on research for the sake of greater knowledge about local meanings and experiences, as well as research as a form of evaluation of peace education programmes. This would also respond to the gap between practice, policy, and research of peace education.

[39] 'The peoples of the Earth have a sacred right to peace', is the conviction and the theme in Douglas J. Roche, *The Human Right to Peace* (Ottawa: Novalis, 2003).

Index